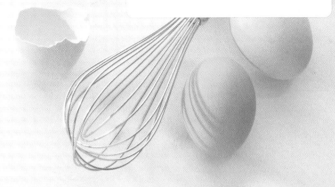

your
cooking questions
answered

your
cooking

First published in Australia in 1999 by Reader's Digest (Australia) Pty Limited
26–32 Waterloo Street, Surry Hills, NSW 2010

National Library of Australia Cataloguing-in-Publication data

Your cooking questions answered.

Includes index.
ISBN 0 86449 375 4.

I. Reader's Digest (Australia).

641.5

reader's digest

questions answered

SYDNEY · AUCKLAND

CONTRIBUTORS

The publishers would like to thank the following people
for their contributions to this book

AUSTRALIAN CONSULTANT
Anne Marshall

WRITERS
Pat Alburey · Val Barrett · Arabella Boxer · Jackie Burrow · Maxine Clark
Shirley Gill · Patricia Lousada · Caroline Marsh · Sonya Mills
Jenni Muir · Laraine Newberry · Ann Nicol · Janey Orr · Louise Pickford
Brenda Ratcliffe · Anne Sheasby · Rosemary Stark · Terry Tan
Jane Thomas · Caroline Waldegrave · Hilaire Walden · Jeni Wright

PHOTOGRAPHERS
Karl Adamson · Gus Filgate · John Hollingshead · Vernon Morgan

EDITOR
Laraine Newberry

HOME ECONOMISTS
Pat Alburey · Maxine Clark · Louise Pickford · Bridget Sargeson

STYLISTS
Suzanne Gibbs · Penny Markham · Fanny Ward

ILLUSTRATOR
Christine Pilsworth

DESIGNERS
Barbara Beckett · Stephanie Cannon · Kate Harris · Megan Huston
Keith Miller · Claire Sadler

PRODUCTION CONTROLLER
Bruce Holden

READER'S DIGEST GENERAL BOOKS

EDITORIAL DIRECTOR
Carol Natsis

ART DIRECTOR
Phillip Bush

MANAGING EDITOR
Averil Moffat

CONTENTS

SPECIAL FEATURES

TABLE OF RECIPES

Pineapple and rice salad 271

HOW TO USE THE RECIPES

All cup measures are level, based on a 250 ml cup. All spoon measures given, for both wet and dry ingredients, are for a level spoon. If you are using a set of cook's measuring spoons, the 5 ml spoon equals 1 level teaspoon, the 20 ml spoon equals 1 level tablespoon.

All the microwave recipes in this book were tested in an 800 Watt microwave oven. If you are using a less powerful one, increase the cooking time by 10 seconds for every minute given in the recipe and then check. If you are using a more powerful model, reduce the cooking time by 10 seconds for every minute given in the recipe and then check. If a dish appears to need further cooking, cook it in bursts of 10 seconds or so only, and keep checking for when it is ready.

$\mathscr{M}$EAT

$\mathscr{P}$OULTRY AND GAME

$\mathscr{S}$EAFOOD

$\mathscr{V}$EGETARIAN

Pheasant casserole with apple and walnuts 268

Celery stir-fry 74

VEGETABLES AND ACCOMPANIMENTS

DESSERTS

Choc-hazelnut and lime puddings 338

Slices 321, 322

Abalone

SINGULAR SHELLFISH

I have eaten abalone in Chinese restaurants but never seen it on sale. What is it?

Sometimes known as paua, this is a large shellfish that is found mainly in the South Pacific and on both coasts of North and South America. Blacklip and greenlip abalone are found around Tasmania and along the south coast of Australia.

The edible part of the shellfish is the muscle with which it clings to the rocks, concealed beneath its single pearly shell. It must be beaten to tenderise it, yet has a delicate flavour that is much prized in Asian cooking. Once tenderised, it can then be eaten raw or very quickly seared in butter or oil.

Fresh abalone may be difficult to find, but you can buy canned abalone in Asian shops. The abalone should be sliced thinly and then poached briefly in chicken stock, stir-fried or simply served with a squeeze of lemon. In many Chinese recipes calling for abalone, scallops are an acceptable substitute.

Fresh abalone needs to be tenderised before it can be eaten.

Additives

THE CONTENTS LIST

I find the names of additives and the numbers listed on foods very confusing. Can you explain them?

A wide variety of substances are added to foods during processing, including preservatives, antioxidants, emulsifiers and stabilisers, colourings and sweeteners. While some enhance the taste of food, others improve its keeping quality or increase the nutritional value. Both natural and synthetic substances have been approved as safe for use in food by the Australian National Health and Medical Research Council. The Australian number system is based on one that operates throughout the world.

The list of approved additives includes naturally occurring substances, such as pectin (440a), obtained from apples and used as a gelling agent, and lecithin (322), obtained primarily from soya beans and widely used as an emulsifier or stabiliser. Other permitted additives are manufactured copies of natural substances, such as ascorbic acid (300), the chemical name for vitamin C and identical to naturally occurring vitamin C.

In addition to these natural or nature-identical compounds, there are a substantial number of synthetic additives listed. All of these additives – natural, nature-identical and synthetic – have been recognised as safe additions to food.

COCHINEAL COPIES

Is red cochineal still available? If not, what alternative could I use for a strong red colouring?

Although genuine cochineal (120) is still available, it is rarely used because of its high cost: this colouring is extracted from the female cochineal insect, and it takes more than 70 000 insects to produce just 500 g of red colouring. However, true cochineal does provide a

strong colour that is hard to match. Another group of red food colourings, anthocyanins (163), derived from vegetables, fruit and berries, tends to have a bluish tinge.

Artificial cochineal is usually coloured with azorubine (122), which is a synthetic azo dye. People who suffer from asthma and eczema may be sensitive to azo dyes, and react – by wheezing or with a rash – to this and other red colourings based on them, such as amaranth (123) and ponceau 4R (124).

Such dyes are listed as safe because they are safe for most people, and it is believed that the benefits for the many outweigh the risks for the few. There is no absolute guarantee of safety in foods: some people are allergic to particular additives, just as some people are allergic to shellfish or berries.

ORGANIC STANDARDS

Does buying food labelled organic always mean the product will be free of additives and pesticides, or does it mean different things in different shops?

People who buy organic vegetables and fruit expect them to have been grown using only organic fertilisers (compost or animal manure) without the use of chemical pesticides and herbicides. They also expect that no synthetic additives have been used in their preservation after harvesting. If an additive has been used, such as pectin in an organic jam, it will have derived from an organic source.

Organic meat is taken to mean that the animal has been raised without any antibiotics or growth-hormone substances, and that it has been allowed space to roam in free-range or pasture conditions free from chemical fertilisers, eating natural food, not concentrates. The slaughter of organically reared animals must be carried out in an abattoir or butcher's facility that is organic-certified.

However, in some cases food advertised as organic has not lived up to customers' expectations. The higher prices that people are willing to pay for organic foods may tempt some unscrupulous traders to pass off non-organic produce as the real thing.

Consumers should look for foods with a 'certified organic' label, which identifies the food as grown to a specific standard that is regularly inspected. Farmers who want their produce labelled as organic must subscribe to one of the following organisations: the National Association for Sustainable Agriculture Australia (NASAA); Biological Farmers of Australia (BFA); the Demeter-Biodynamic Research Institute; Organic Herb Growers of Australia; Organic Retailers and Growers Association of Australia (ORGAA); Organic Vignerons Association of Australia.

Each of these organisations has its own logo, which can be used in labelling, and these labels guarantee that the produce is organic. Look out particularly for food that carries the approval of NASAA, as it is accredited by the International Federation of Organic Agriculture Movements (IFOAM) Accreditation Programme Board.

SPREADS OR BUTTER?

Low-fat spreads seem to list many chemicals in their ingredients. Are these spreads really healthier than butter or margarine?

There is general agreement among health experts that in Western countries we tend to eat too much fat, particularly saturated fat, and that reducing the overall amount of fat in their diet can help people to be healthier. Food manufacturers now produce a wide range of low-fat products, including low-fat and reduced-fat spreads based on butter or margarine. These spreads contain considerably more water than is permitted in margarine or butter and, as a result, a number of emulsifying agents are added to them to prevent the fats and water from separating. Labelling regulations require that these additives are declared. However, remember

that all foodstuffs are ultimately made of chemicals: there is just no legal requirement to declare the chemical composition of butter.

On balance, if using a low-fat spread helps to reduce someone's intake of fat, it is generally a healthier choice than butter or ordinary margarine. (See also **Nutrition**.)

Almonds

BITTER AND SWEET

How many different types of almond are there?

There are two types, bitter and sweet. Bitter almonds are in fact the kernel of the apricot, used in Chinese medicine. Sweet almonds are creamy white, smooth nuts with a brown skin, encased in a shell. They are mainly cultivated in California, as well as in Australia.

If possible, buy whole almonds with their skins on and blanch them yourself (see **Nuts**) for recipes such as the one overleaf, as they have more flavour than ready-skinned ones and are not so dry. Nuts lose their flavour quickly, so buy them in small quantities.

EXPENSIVE EXTRACTS

What is the difference between almond extract and essence?

Almond extract is a pure, natural product made from oil of bitter almonds and has a good flavour, but the quality is reflected in the high price. Almond essence is made using artificial flavourings and is therefore much cheaper.

It is worth the effort of seeking out almond extract in good delicatessens, health food shops and the larger branches of supermarkets. Whichever you use, for the best results always add cautiously.

PRALINE CRUNCH

What is praline and what would you use it for?

Almond praline is a mixture of caramelised sugar and almonds, ground up by hand or in a food processor after cooking. It is used as a crunchy flavouring for ice cream, creamy desserts, pastry and cakes, or sprinkled over puddings and gâteaux. Mixed with cream, chocolate and rum, praline makes wonderful truffles. Once made, praline will keep in an airtight container for one to two weeks.

MAKING PRALINE FLAVOURING

Sweet, nutty praline is made by caramelising almonds in sugar and then crushing the mixture to make a delicious, crispy flavouring for desserts.

1 Put 125 g (½ cup) caster sugar and 125 g (¾ cup) unskinned almonds into a heavy saucepan. Stir continuously over a moderate heat until the sugar dissolves completely and turns golden caramel. Pour onto a baking tray lined with nonstick baking paper and leave to set.

2 Peel the baking paper off the back of the set praline. Put the praline into a strong plastic bag and crush it with a rolling pin, coarsely or finely, as the recipe dictates. The praline may also be ground in a food processor, but process it for only a few seconds at a time, or it will turn to dust.

Almond and pear flan

Serves: 8
*Preparation time: 2 hours plus
3-4 hours or overnight chilling*
Cooking time: 40 minutes

For the filling
300 ml milk
150 ml fresh cream
1 vanilla pod, halved lengthways
100 g (⅔ cup) almonds, blanched
2 large eggs
2 large egg yolks
125 g (½ cup) caster sugar
90 g (¾ cup) plain flour
*75 g unsalted butter, diced
and chilled*
*90 ml amaretto, kirsch
or brandy*

For the pears
250 g (1 cup) white sugar
*Finely pared zest and strained
juice of 1 lemon*
1 kg small firm, ripe pears

For the flan case
125 g (1 cup) plain flour
30 g (2 tablespoons) icing sugar
50 g (½ cup) ground almonds
75 g unsalted butter
2 large egg yolks
6 tablespoons apricot jam

This glistening fruit and nut flan uses ground almonds in the pastry and in the filling to add both delicate flavour and a crunchy texture.

1 To make the flan filling, pour the milk and cream into a saucepan; add the vanilla pod and bring to the boil. Remove the mixture at once from the heat, cover and leave to infuse for 30 minutes.
2 Toast the almonds under a grill until they are pale golden all over. Grind finely and set aside.
3 Put the eggs, egg yolks and caster sugar into a bowl and whisk until thick and creamy. Fold in the flour.
4 Remove the vanilla pod from the milk, rinse and set aside. Gradually whisk the milk and cream into the egg and flour. Sieve into a saucepan and cook over a low heat, stirring, until the custard is extremely thick.
5 Remove from the heat, turn the mixture into a bowl and gradually beat in the butter, then the ground almonds and alcohol. Cover with plastic wrap to stop a skin forming and chill for 3-4 hours or overnight.

6 To cook the pears, pour 500 ml water into a stainless steel, enamel or nonstick saucepan, add the reserved vanilla pod, sugar, lemon zest and lemon juice. Bring to the boil, stirring, until the sugar has dissolved, then reduce the heat.
7 Peel, halve and core the pears. Add the pear halves to the sugar syrup, cover and cook gently for 10-15 minutes until only just tender. Let the pears cool in the syrup, then chill until needed.
8 To make the flan case, sift the flour and icing sugar into a mixing bowl, then mix in the ground almonds. Rub in the butter with your fingertips until the mixture resembles fine breadcrumbs. Add the egg yolks and mix with a fork to form a soft, but not sticky, dough.
9 Turn out onto a lightly floured surface and knead for a few seconds until smooth. Roll out the dough to a circle, large enough to line a 25 cm

fluted flan tin. Place the dough in the tin, pressing it well into the flutes using a little ball of dough to avoid tearing a hole in it. Trim the edge. Prick the base and sides with a fork. Chill for 30 minutes. Preheat the oven to 220°C.
10 Line the flan case with greaseproof paper and a layer of dried beans. Bake in the centre of the oven for 15-20 minutes, until crisp and golden. Remove from the oven and allow to cool in the tin.
11 To assemble the flan, first drain the pears on paper towels. Heat the apricot jam, sieve it, return it to the pan and bring to the boil.
12 Turn out the flan case onto a flat serving plate and brush the inside with some hot jam. Spoon in the filling, spread it evenly, then arrange the pears on top.
13 Boil up the remaining jam. Brush it evenly over the pears and chill the flan until ready to serve.

NUTTY THICKENER

Is it true that ground almonds can be used as a thickener in soups or stews?

Yes, they can: almonds were often used to add texture and flavour to a 'white' soup and are still used for this purpose in some traditional Spanish dishes. The delicate flavour of almonds blends particularly well with fish and chicken.

But ground almonds do not thicken soups in the same way as starchy ingredients such as flour, which blend into the liquid to make a thick, smooth sauce. Instead, ground almonds add body, texture, flavour and richness.

Rough guidelines on amounts to use are as follows: to a thin broth, add 50 g (½ cup) ground almonds to each 500 ml of liquid. To thicken about 1.25 litres of puréed fish or vegetable soup, add 25 g (¼ cup) ground almonds; or add 25 g (2 tablespoons) whole blanched almonds when you are puréeing the soup. It is best to start off with a small amount of almonds; you can always add more, a little at a time, if necessary.

Anchovies

MILKY SOLUTION

I love the flavour of anchovies, but they can be extremely salty. How can I reduce the saltiness?

Rinse them in cold water then pat them dry. Alternatively, if you have the time, soak them in milk for 20 minutes or so, then rinse and dry. Jars of anchovies in olive oil are less salty than canned brands, but they do cost more. Some specialty shops and delicatessens sell anchovy fillets marinated in olive oil loose by weight. These are sweet and delicious, and can be used in any recipe calling for anchovy fillets.

If you have visited Portugal or Spain, you may have seen pressed salted anchovies for sale loose, and these can now sometimes be found in Fremantle. They are very salty and bony and should be rinsed, scaled, boned, and then soaked in milk before use.

This Italian recipe (below) mixes milk-soaked anchovies with other simple yet flavour-intensive Mediterranean ingredients to make crisp Anchovy Crostini, ideal for handing round with pre-dinner drinks when a hint of salt whets the appetite.

Anchovy crostini

SERVES: 4-6
PREPARATION TIME: 30 minutes
COOKING TIME: 5 minutes

100 g canned anchovies in olive oil
125 ml milk
12 black olives
250 g mozzarella cheese
1 French baguette or Italian ciabatta bread
2 cloves garlic, halved
3 tablespoons virgin olive oil
125 ml sun-dried tomato paste or pesto
2 teaspoons dried mixed herbs
Black pepper

1 Drain the anchovies and soak them in the milk for 20 minutes. Meanwhile, cut the olives in half and stone them, and slice the mozzarella cheese into 24 thin portions.
2 Rinse and pat dry the anchovies, then cut each one in half.
3 Cut 24 slices of baguette, each about 1 cm thick. If using ciabatta bread, cut 12 slices, then cut each slice in half.
4 Toast the bread lightly, then immediately rub one side of each slice with the cut side of the garlic and brush with olive oil.
5 Spread each crostini with tomato paste or pesto and cover with a slice of mozzarella. Sprinkle with herbs, and top each with two pieces of anchovy, crisscrossed.
6 Put the crostini under a hot grill for 2-3 minutes until the mozzarella melts. Put half a black olive in the centre of each crostini, sprinkle on some pepper and serve hot, or at warm room temperature as party finger food or as a tasty snack.

Aniseed

SMALL BUT STRONG

What is aniseed?

Aniseed is the seed of the Mediterranean anise. This annual plant, a member of the parsley family, grows to a height of about 45 cm, and has sharply indented leaves and tiny, star-like white flowers. It resembles both dill and fennel in appearance although its flavour is quite distinct. Despite its name, it is not related to the star anise tree, which is an Asian flavouring.

The liquorice flavour is found in the seed, which looks much like a caraway seed: small, oval, grey and ribbed. It is best bought already ground as it should be finely and evenly ground before use and it is difficult to grind evenly at home. You will find it in most supermarkets. Because aniseed soon loses its flavour, it is best to buy a small amount and replace it often.

VERSATILE FLAVOURING

How is aniseed used?

Aniseed can be substituted for caraway seeds in seed cake, added to rye or wholemeal bread, used in plain or spiced biscuits and included in a Mediterranean fish soup. Or, as is done in the Middle East, it can be used to make an infusion, with or without tea leaves.

Aniseed was much used in medieval times, both as a medicament and as a flavouring, but its taste fell out of fashion and today aniseed balls are almost the only reminder of its past popularity.

It remains popular, however, in central Europe, where it is widely used for flavouring sweet dishes, cakes and biscuits. In many Mediterranean countries it is used to flavour absinthe-related drinks, called variously anisette, arak, ouzo, Pernod and raki. In India and Southeast Asia the seeds are used in curries, and are also chewed whole, after a meal, as a digestive.

Apples

WHICH TYPE TO USE?

Why do some recipes specify using dessert apples and others cooking apples - does it matter which ones are used?

Cooking and dessert apples react differently when cooked. If you want the apples to be soft and fluffy when they are cooked, a Granny Smith or similar cooking apple works best. If it is important for the apples to retain their shape - on top of a flan or cake, for instance - a dessert apple such as Cox or Golden Delicious is ideal.

MICROWAVE BAKING

Can I cook baked apples in the microwave? I have heard that they could explode.

Apples will not explode in the microwave as long as you score through the skin so that the steam can escape as they cook.

Cut deeply into the skin around the centre of some medium cooking apples, then core and place in a deep, microwave-safe dish, in batches of up to four. Fill the centres with sugar or fruit filling then add a few tablespoons of water or apple juice to the dish.

Cover with microwave-safe plastic wrap, ensuring it does not touch the apples, and pull back one edge to vent. Cook the apples on High for 4–6 minutes or until they are tender but retain their shape. Stand for 2–3 minutes before serving.

Keep the colour

To prevent apples discolouring after they have been peeled, put them, either whole or in slices, in water containing the juice of one or two lemons. Plain effervescent vitamin C tablets can be used instead of lemon juice and will not affect the apples' flavour.

PLUGGING THE LEAK

How can I stop the juices leaking out of my apple pies as they cook?

Many fruits, not just apples, make too much juice as they cook in a pie, which can make pastry soggy or make it stick to the tin on cooling. The answer is to toss the fruit in a little cornflour: this will soak up the juices and help to thicken them as they cook. Flavour the cornflour with spices if you like.

Toss apples for a pie in cornflour so it will absorb the juices. Mix with your hands to avoid damaging the fruit.

PERFECT PIE

Is one way of making apple pie better than all the others?

Most cooks develop their own method; personal preference dictates whether to use shortcrust pastry, flaky pastry or puff pastry, and whether the pie is filled with uncooked apple slices for a firm texture or precooked apples for a softer, fluffier filling.

The recipe for Perfect Apple Pie (right) is made with buttery pastry and a spicy apple filling which retains the shape and texture of the apples. If you choose the smaller amount of sugar specified in the ingredients list, it has a refreshing tangy flavour, but if you have a sweet tooth, use the larger amount.

Bake the pie in an enamel pie plate on a preheated baking tray. This ensures that the pastry at the bottom of the pie will be brown and cooked, and not soggy. And use a baking tray with a small edge to catch any juices that might overflow as the pie cooks.

Perfect apple pie

SERVES: 6
PREPARATION TIME: 45 minutes
COOKING TIME: 1 hour

FOR THE PASTRY
250 g (2 cups) plain flour
60 g (½ cup) self-raising flour
20 g (1 tablespoon) caster sugar
175 g chilled unsalted butter, diced
1 large egg, beaten with 2 tablespoons cold water
Caster sugar for dredging

FOR THE FILLING
30 g (¼ cup) cornflour
185-250 g (¾-1 cup) caster sugar
1 teaspoon ground mixed spice
Finely grated rind of 1 lemon
1 kg Granny Smith apples
25 g (¼ cup) ground almonds
25 g unsalted butter, diced
6-8 cloves
1 tablespoon lemon juice

1 To make the pastry, sift the flours and caster sugar into a large mixing bowl then rub in the butter until the mixture resembles fine breadcrumbs. Make a well in the centre, pour in the beaten egg and water and mix with a rounded knife to form a soft, but not sticky, dough.
2 Knead the dough on a lightly floured surface for a few seconds until smooth, then wrap and chill while preparing the filling. Put an ungreased baking tray on the centre shelf of the oven and preheat the oven to 220°C.
3 For the filling, put the cornflour, sugar, mixed spice and lemon rind into a mixing bowl and stir together.
4 Core, peel and slice the apples, add them to the bowl and mix.
5 To assemble the pie, roll out half the chilled dough into a neat round, about 28 cm in diameter. Line a 25 cm enamel pie plate with the dough. Roll out the remaining dough into a neat round just a little larger than the first.
6 Sprinkle the ground almonds over the dough on the dish and spread half the spiced apple mix on top. Dot half the butter over the apples and add half the cloves. Cover with

Granny Smith apples are flavoured with tangy lemon, warm spice and ground almonds to give a refreshing twist to every family's all-time favourite pie.

Apricots

MAKING JAM

Can I make a successful jam using fresh apricots?

Yes, this is a good way to use up imperfect or slightly unripe fruit. Apricots contain only a moderate amount of pectin, so the best way to ensure a good set, good flavour and attractive colour is to use sugar with added pectin and follow the manufacturer's instructions.

If you do not have any pectin, it might be necessary to add some lemon juice and to give the apricots a fairly lengthy boil in order to obtain a good set. However, this can darken the colour of the jam and also affect the flavour.

CHOOSING CAREFULLY

Which apricots are best for eating and which should I cook?

The apricots sold in local fresh produce shops are sweet dessert apricots, meant for eating. In some parts of Europe, cooking varieties known in French as *abricots à confiture* (jam apricots) are available. Their sharp flavour makes them more suitable for cooking.

For eating fresh, choose apricots that have a healthy blush to them, with no brown markings, or broken or dented skin. Avoid any that have a greenish tinge as these are unlikely to ripen once bought. Most dessert apricots can be poached for an elegant dessert, but avoid the larger, more exotic varieties as these disintegrate when cooked.

For any other cooking purposes, choose less perfect, firmer fruit and poach them in syrup to serve with cream, to purée into a sauce or to use in pies, tarts and flans – or the Apricot Pudding with Angostura Cream (see page 16). For this hot, light and spicy soufflé pudding, the apricots can be cooked a few hours ahead, or even the day before.

See also: ***Dried Fruit***

the rest of the apple slices and add the remaining cloves. Dot with the remaining butter and sprinkle over the lemon juice. Add any juices left in the apple bowl.

7 Brush the edge of the dough on the plate with cold water then cover the pie with the second round of dough. Squeeze the edges firmly together to seal then trim off the excess dough with a knife, holding the knife angled outwards to help to prevent the edge shrinking inwards as the pie bakes.

8 Using the back of the knife blade, tap all round the edge of the dough to give it a flaky appearance. With the tip of the knife, make shallow indents around the edge of the pie at 2 cm intervals to make an attractive fluted pattern.

9 Roll out the dough trimmings and use them to make apple shapes and leaves to decorate the pie. Brush the shapes with cold water and arrange them on top of the pie. With a small, sharp knife, make a small hole in the top of the pastry lid to allow the steam to escape during cooking.

10 Put the pie on the heated baking tray and bake on the centre shelf of the oven for 30 minutes.

11 Lower the temperature to 190°C, cover the pie loosely with foil to prevent it over-browning, and continue cooking for another 25-30 minutes, or until the apples are tender. Check that the filling is fully cooked by pushing a skewer through the hole in the top: it should meet no resistance.

12 When cooked, remove the pie from the oven and dredge it with caster sugar while it is hot so the sugar melts slightly and sticks to the pie. For the best flavour, allow the pie to cool for an hour or so to room temperature before serving.

13 Serve with vanilla-flavoured whipped cream, or with ice cream.

Apricot pudding with Angostura cream

SERVES: 4
PREPARATION TIME: 30 minutes
COOKING TIME: 50 minutes

FOR THE PUDDING
125 g (½ cup) white sugar
Finely pared zest and strained juice
     of 1 lemon
7.5 cm cinnamon stick
4 cloves
8 allspice berries
1 kg fresh apricots, halved and
     stoned

FOR THE TOPPING
3 large egg yolks
Finely grated zest and strained
     juice of 1 lemon
30 g (¼ cup) plain flour
4 large egg whites
60 g (¼ cup) caster sugar
1 tablespoon icing sugar for sifting

FOR THE ANGOSTURA CREAM
250 ml fresh or thickened cream
1 teaspoon ground cinnamon
1 tablespoon Angostura bitters
1 tablespoon caster sugar

1 To make the pudding, first pour 250 ml water into a wide flameproof casserole, or a stainless-steel, enamel or nonstick saucepan. Add the sugar, lemon zest and juice and all the spices and bring to the boil, stirring often until the sugar dissolves. Add the apricots, cover and cook gently for 5 minutes.

2 Using a slotted spoon, remove the apricots and place them in a buttered, shallow 1.25 litre ovenproof dish. Strain the syrup then boil it until reduced by about half. Pour the hot syrup over the apricots and set aside. Preheat the oven to 190°C.

3 To make the topping, whisk the egg yolks and lemon zest together in a large bowl until the mixture is pale and slightly thickened. Whisk in the lemon juice, then gently fold in the flour. If necessary, whisk briefly until smooth.

4 Whisk the egg whites until stiff but not dry, then gradually add the caster sugar, whisking each addition in well, until the meringue is stiff

and shiny. Fold a quarter of the meringue into the egg yolk, lemon and flour mixture until it is smoothly blended, and then fold in the rest of the meringue.

5 Spoon this soufflé mixture in mounds over the apricots and bake on the centre shelf of the oven for 25-30 minutes, or until it is set and golden. If the pudding appears to be browning too much as it cooks, cover it loosely with a sheet of foil.

6 To make the Angostura cream, whisk the cream with the other ingredients until thickened, pour into a serving bowl and chill.

7 Remove the apricot pudding from the oven and, while it is hot, sift the icing sugar over the top. Serve with the Angostura cream.

Arrowroot

CLEAREST OF ALL

What is the advantage of using arrowroot rather than cornflour to thicken dishes?

Arrowroot is a pure starch and has tiny grains, which makes it more easily digested than other thickening agents, and particularly good for invalid diets.

Arrowroot is also valuable for thickening liquids, such as fruit and vegetable juices, and to use in a glaze, as it makes a clear glaze with a gelatinous texture, whereas cornflour glazes go cloudy.

Arrowroot and cornflour are used in the same quantities to thicken liquids and in the same way: in order to thicken 300 ml of sauce, such as a gravy or a custard, mix 2 tablespoons arrowroot with the same quantity of cold liquid.

Heat the rest of the liquid to boiling point, then pour it into the blended mix and stir well. Return the sauce to the heat and bring to the boil, stirring continuously until it is thickened and smooth, then simmer gently for 1 minute.

If you are making a glaze, use only 1 tablespoon arrowroot for each 300 ml of liquid.

Artichokes

DISPOSABLE FEAST

Globe artichokes look rather spiky and daunting. Is there an easy way to deal with them?

Globe artichokes, also known as French artichokes, are members of the thistle family, as their hairy central 'choke' suggests. They are usually eaten as a starter.

The easiest way to cook artichokes is to boil them until soft and serve them whole. At the table, you pull off each leaf, dip the plump base end in sauce and then pull the flesh off with your teeth, discarding the rest of the leaf.

When you get to the papery purple leaves at the centre, pull them off and discard them, then cut away the choke and eat the delicious heart with a knife and fork.

Another way to prepare them is to trim the top third off each raw artichoke, then quarter them and cut out the chokes. To prevent discoloration, drop each piece as it is ready into a bowl of water acidulated with lemon juice. Then cook them as they are or add them to vegetable stews or other dishes.

MINIATURE DELIGHTS

While travelling in Italy I saw tiny artichokes in the shops. How are they prepared?

In recent years, 'baby' artichokes have become available in Italy in early spring. These have a delicate flavour and require almost no preparation, as the leaves are young and tender, and the choke is unformed. They cook in minutes: cut them in half or into quarters and fry in olive oil with some sliced garlic for 3-4 minutes. Serve with a sprinkling of sea salt, a squeeze of lemon juice and fresh crusty bread.

Alternatively, braise them gently with other vegetables such as eggplant, zucchini and tomatoes, with a generous amount of onion and garlic and some mixed herbs. In

Italy, they are sometimes cut in half, dipped in a lightly spiced coating batter and deep-fried to make an unusual fritter.

ARTICHOKES AND WINE

I have read that artichokes are incompatible with any wine. Is this true, and if so why?

Not exactly. Globe artichokes contain an acid named cynarin that affects our tastebuds, so that food and wine consumed with them, or soon after, taste sweeter than they normally would. Some baby-food manufacturers have used this to advantage, mashing soft artichoke bases into vegetable purées to appeal to the sweet palate of the infant. Adults have found that a young white riesling or a light red wine, such as a pinot noir, are good with an artichoke dish.

See also: ***Jerusalem Artichoke***

During summer, fresh artichokes, served hot or cold with a good French dressing, are an easy and elegant way to start a meal.

COOKING AND SERVING ARTICHOKES

An artichoke is usually boiled or steamed whole until it is tender, and then the leaves are pulled off and eaten one by one.

1 Wash the artichokes and remove discoloured leaves from the base.

2 Break off the stalks close to the base, pulling away any strings. Pack the artichokes in one layer in a stainless-steel or enamel saucepan. Sprinkle on some salt and lemon juice, then add enough water to come halfway up the artichokes.

3 Bring to the boil, cover tightly and simmer for 40–45 minutes until a leaf from the middle of an artichoke pulls out easily. Tip the artichokes into a colander and leave upside-down to drain for 5 minutes.

4 For a dinner party presentation, peel back the outer leaves, pull out the purple central cluster of leaves and scoop out the inedible choke beneath with a spoon.

Asparagus

A TASTE OF SPRING

Asparagus seems to be available all year round in some shops. Is there an optimum time to eat it?

The asparagus season in Australia starts in August and peaks for three months. This is the time to serve asparagus at its best, as a course in its own right, with French dressing for dipping. Asparagus is also fine for salads, soups, garnishes and in crispy stir-fries throughout the year.

HEADS ABOVE WATER

What is the best way to cook asparagus without spoiling the shape of the tips?

The trick is to keep the delicate heads above the cooking water (see box, right). The stems should be cut off to a level that leaves them all the same size. Perfectionists also peel the lower stems with a small sharp knife or vegetable peeler, and this is certainly necessary with older asparagus, especially white asparagus, which usually has a thick woody skin. Before cooking, wash the tips gently in cold water to rid them of any grit.

ECONOMICAL SPRUE

I have occasionally seen asparagus referred to as 'sprue'. What does this mean?

Sprue is the name for the thinnings or first pickings of the asparagus bed. The flavour is good, and they should be cheaper than asparagus proper. There is no need to scrape them before cooking.

Cook them fully immersed in water in a saucepan, and eat them hot or cold, on their own or as an accompanying vegetable. Use them in stir-fries or tarts, or with potatoes and peas or broad beans in an early summer vegetable stew. They can also be processed with some onion and potato to make a cream soup, as in the following recipe.

Sprue soup

SERVES: 4–6
PREPARATION TIME: 15 minutes
COOKING TIME: 15–20 minutes

50 g butter
1 medium onion, finely chopped
500 g sprue
150 g potato, diced
Salt and black pepper
100 ml thickened cream

1 Heat the butter in a large pan, add the onion and fry gently until soft but still white, for about 7 minutes.
2 Add the sprue, potato and 750 ml water, bring to the boil and cook for 5 minutes.
3 Remove 12 stems of sprue, cut off and reserve the top 5 cm of each one, then return the stems to the water and continue to cook the vegetables for a further 5–8 minutes, until they are all very soft.
4 Drain the vegetables but retain the cooking liquid. Then liquidise the vegetables in a blender or processor, and push the purée through a sieve, loosening it with a tablespoon or so of the cooking liquid if necessary.
5 Return the cooking liquid and the vegetable purée to the pan, stir well and bring to the boil. Turn off the heat, season to taste and add half the cream. Ladle the soup into four soup plates, then trickle in the remaining cream and arrange three sprue tips in the centre of each plate.

FINGER FOOD

How should I serve asparagus?

Asparagus is traditionally served hot with butter or a butter sauce, such as hollandaise, or cold with a vinaigrette dressing or mayonnaise. With your fingers, pick up the stem by its base, dip it in the sauce and eat from the tip downwards.

For a substantial starter or a light supper dish, serve it with a softly boiled or fried egg: dip the tips into the yolk, then eat with white bread or toast. Egg and butter can be incorporated in a dressing that provides contrasting crispness. In the recipe opposite, warm asparagus is topped with a crispy egg crumble.

COOKING ASPARAGUS

Asparagus takes 10–15 minutes to cook, depending on how thick the stalks are. These need longer cooking than the tips, and determining cooking time can be tricky. Here are three solutions to the problem:

IN AN ASPARAGUS STEAMER

To cook in a specially designed asparagus steamer, stand the stems upright in the wire basket and add water to about halfway up their length. Simmer until tender when pierced just above the water level with the tip of a knife.

IN A WOK

Shorter stems of asparagus can be cooked in a wok. Arrange them like the spokes of a wheel, so that only their bases are immersed in the cooking water. Cover with the lid and simmer until tender.

IN A SAUCEPAN

Tied bundles of asparagus can be cooked in a deep saucepan, held up by new potatoes. Cover with a dome of foil tucked in tightly around the outer rim of the pan and cook until tender. The asparagus-flavoured potatoes can be eaten hot or cold.

Warm asparagus with egg crumble

SERVES: 6
PREPARATION TIME: 15 minutes
COOKING TIME: 10–15 minutes

1 kg asparagus, prepared
6 slices soft white bread, with the
  crusts removed
150 g butter
2 eggs, hard-boiled
Salt and black pepper

A simple topping of fried breadcrumbs and hard-boiled egg adds crunch to tender green stems of fresh asparagus.

1 Cook the asparagus until tender, in an asparagus steamer, a wok, or a deep saucepan (see box, page 18).
2 Meanwhile, put some plates to warm. Make the breadcrumbs in a food processor or with a grater.
3 Heat the butter in a heavy-based pan, add the breadcrumbs and fry them until golden brown. Mash the eggs with a fork, mix them into the crumbs and season to taste.
4 When the asparagus is cooked, drain the stems well and arrange them on the warmed plates. Scatter the egg crumble mixture over each helping and serve immediately.

Avocado

TENDER FLESH

Is there a way of speeding up the ripening of an avocado?

It is sensible to buy avocados still on the firm side, since once ripe the flesh bruises very easily.

Avocados will ripen in a few days at room temperature in the fruit bowl, but the process can be speeded up by putting them in a roomy paper bag with a banana and leaving them in a warm place. They are ripe when they 'give' all over to slight pressure and feel especially yielding at the stem end. If you want to keep ripe avocados for a few days, store them in the salad drawer of the refrigerator.

KEEPING UP APPEARANCES

I have heard that brushing the cut surface of an avocado with lemon juice prevents it from discolouring. Is that true?

Brushing the cut surfaces of avocados with citrus juice or vinegar is the only way of conserving the pale green of avocado flesh (replacing the stone to keep the colour does not work). But the effect is not long-term: you cannot expect it to last for much more than a few hours, after which the flesh will darken. Guacamole, the spicy avocado dip, can be kept fresh-looking for about a day by placing plastic wrap directly onto its surface.

SIMPLE PLEASURES

I am tired of plain avocado vinaigrette. Can you suggest other ways of serving avocado?

Avocados are best eaten very ripe and uncooked, and are delicious halved and stoned, served with an olive oil vinaigrette dressing. They can also be puréed raw, with chicken stock and cream, into a chilled summer soup. Their buttery richness works well as a spread on toast and sandwiches (avocados were once called 'poor man's butter'), and in partnership with sharp fruits, such as tamarillo.

Three simple, fruity treatments for avocados:

• For a rich yet healthy starter, try a dressing thickened with lightly sweetened rhubarb. For four people, cook four thick stalks of rhubarb, purée and mix it with 2 tablespoons walnut oil and a splash of lemon juice. Season and spoon the dressing into the halved avocados.

• Avocado makes a good side salad, sliced and combined with chunks of pineapple (excellent with cold ham or prosciutto) or mixed with segments of sweet pink grapefruit and garnished with coriander leaves to serve with roast chicken.

• You can also fill the cavity of two halved avocados with a homemade Waldorf-salad mix: stir together a diced apple, two celery stalks and a little chopped walnut in a dressing made with 3 tablespoons walnut oil and 1 tablespoon lemon juice.

Fruity accompaniments such as a rhubarb dressing (top) or chunks of pineapple (bottom), suit rich avocado.

Babies' Diets

SPECIAL NEEDS

Should babies and toddlers be kept on a low-fat diet like adults?

The short answer is, no. A baby or toddler needs to get about 50 per cent of its kilojoules from fat. This concentrated source of energy is essential because of the small size of an infant's stomach and the enormous need for energy for growth.

Breast, formula or 'follow-on' milk should be used up to the age of one year. Even full-fat cow's milk does not provide enough vitamins and minerals, and should be used as the main milk drink only after the age of one. Light milk is not suitable before the age of two, and skim milk not before five, and then only if the child is eating a varied diet and growing well.

Fatty foods should be part of a varied diet, with plenty of fruit and vegetables, starchy foods, and protein. Dairy foods are important for calcium as well as protein.

A MENU FOR BABIES

How can I start my baby off on a truly varied and balanced diet?

Try a variety of foods, starting with baby rice or a rice-based cereal mixed with breast milk or formula, followed by puréed unsweetened fruit, unsalted vegetables and meat.

At four months, give 1 teaspoon of different single, smooth foods at one meal and gradually increase to 2 teaspoons. At five months increase the amount and variety of foods offered, and at six to eight months offer mashed foods and finger foods too. By one year, the child can be offered chopped-up family meals, plus 600 ml of milk a day.

PUT IT ON ICE

I want to make all my baby's food but am going back to work. How can I cope?

Freeze your own baby food. At first, freeze the purée in ice-cube trays, transfer the cubes to freezer bags and thaw one or two at a time. As your baby's appetite increases, freeze the food in larger containers. The following baby meals can be prepared alongside family meals and will each make four servings.

Fish in cheese sauce

75 g white fish, cooked,
* boned and skinned*
75 g potato, boiled
25 g cheese, grated
200 ml hot water

Mash the ingredients together with a fork, or purée in a food processor, then divide into portions and freeze.

Cauliflower and lentils

3 tablespoons red lentils
3-4 cauliflower sprigs

Cook the lentils and the cauliflower together in 300 ml of water for 15 minutes or until soft. Mash with a fork, then divide and freeze.

Chicken dinner

75 g chicken, cooked
50 g potato, boiled, or
* sweet potato, cooked*
50 g carrots, cooked
200 ml hot water

Purée all the ingredients in a food processor, then divide and freeze.

Fruity rice

2 tablespoons rice pudding
2 tablespoons fruit purée, or two
* pieces canned fruit in natural*
* juice, or half a banana*

Mash the ingredients together with a fork, then divide and freeze.

Bacon

TOO SALTY

How can I reduce the saltiness in a joint of bacon?

Soak the joint in cold water overnight. To test if this has removed enough salt, cut off a small piece and eat it as it is, or fry it gently first. If it is still very salty, put the joint into a saucepan, cover with cold water and bring to the boil. Drain off the water; the joint is now ready for cooking.

However, modern curing techniques mean that bacon is not as salty as it used to be, and it often does not need to be soaked at all.

TENDER AND MOIST

I recently boiled a bacon joint but the meat was tough and dry. What went wrong?

Toughness and dryness are the result of cooking at too high a temperature for a long time. If you cook a joint in water, adjust the heat so the water bubbles gently throughout. Simmer for 20 minutes per 500 g, plus 20 minutes. Calculate cooking time from when the water reaches simmering point.

'USE BY' DATES

How long can bacon be kept, and can it be frozen?

Bacon should not be kept for more than one to two weeks. The 'use by' date on prepacked bacon may state a longer period, but once the packet has been opened, use the meat quickly. Put loose bacon in a plastic bag in the refrigerator.

Vacuum-packed joints can be frozen for three months; vacuum-packed rashers for four to six weeks; home-packed rashers for four weeks (interleave rashers with freezer wrap to separate them easily, then store in a freezer bag). Rashers can be grilled or fried from frozen, but joints should be thawed overnight in the refrigerator.

Baking

DRY HEAT

What is the difference between baking and the other methods of cooking in the oven?

The chief difference between them is that baked foods, such as bread, biscuits, cakes, pastries, baked potatoes and soufflés, are cooked by dry heat. There is no surrounding bath of fat or liquid as there is with roasted or casseroled dishes.

Baking is one of the very oldest cooking techniques. Early ovens made of stone or brick were filled with wood, which was set alight. After burning, the ashes were raked out and bread or other dishes put in to cook in the residual heat. Today's baked dishes are cooked on the same principle, with heat coming from every side.

ACCURATE HEAT

Is it absolutely essential to have the right temperature for baking?

Because baked dishes do not have the protection of fat or liquid, they can burn easily and need to have fairly precise cooking temperatures. Unfortunately, the thermostats on many domestic ovens are not all that accurate. For best results, it is worth buying an oven thermometer and using it with your baking over a few weeks (see **Ovens**). This will give you the chance to adjust the oven settings.

PAPER PREFERENCES

What is the difference between greaseproof paper and nonstick baking paper?

Greaseproof paper is a type of non-absorbent paper that can be used for various purposes in the kitchen: layering fragile foods such as pancakes, wrapping food for storage and lining cake tins. Nonstick baking paper (which is sometimes also called parchment paper) has a nonstick coating that eliminates the need to grease the paper. Although it costs more than greaseproof paper, it is especially good for lining baking trays when you make meringues and other dishes with a high sugar content. These foods are liable to stick to greaseproof paper.

BAKING IN PARCELS

How can I tell when food being baked in individual paper or foil parcels has been fully cooked?

The whole point of cooking in a parcel, or *en papillote*, is for the diner to open it at the table and experience the sudden escape of aromas. Therefore, you should not open a parcel to check whether the food has been cooked. Choose food that cooks quickly at a high heat, such as filleted fish and finely chopped vegetables and fruit, and stay faithful to the times that are suggested in the recipe.

A small amount of liquid in the parcel creates a steamy atmosphere that helps to cook the food more quickly. The puffed parcels release an explosion of appetising smells as they are opened on the plate.

Bananas

GREEN OR YELLOW

Is it better to buy bananas while they are still green or when they have turned yellow?

That depends on what you intend doing with them. Bananas are fully ripe when they turn deep yellow and brown speckles appear on the skin. The flesh becomes sweeter and fuller in flavour as they mature, so buy ripe ones if you want to eat them the same day. If you are buying bananas to eat later in the week, choose those that are still green or just beginning to turn yellow as they will ripen quite quickly once you get them home.

For cooking purposes, especially for savoury dishes, use fruit that is not completely ripe and still has partly green or pale yellow skin, as

they are much easier to slice and the flavour is not so dominating. However, for the moist, high-fibre Banana Tea Bread recipe (right), it is best to use fruit that is ripe.

KEEPING A DISTANCE

Is it true that bananas should not be kept in a bowl alongside other sorts of fruit?

Bananas give off a gas called ethylene, which makes any surrounding fruit ripen faster and possibly spoil. Keeping bananas separate from other fruit lets them all ripen naturally. However, if you want to ripen fruit quickly, such as peaches that are hard, put a ripe banana in with them. Bananas dislike the cold, and it is best to store them at room temperature, not in the refrigerator.

STOP THE BROWNING

When I include sliced bananas in desserts they tend to turn brown very quickly. Is there any way I can prevent this from happening?

The riper the banana, the more quickly it seems to turn brown. If you need attractive slices, choose bananas that are not too ripe and use a stainless-steel knife to cut them. To decorate a gâteau or a dessert, just brush the slices with freshly squeezed lemon juice. Do not turn them in a bowl of lemon juice as this can make them slimy.

When mashing bananas, however, turning the slices in a bowl of lemon juice first not only keeps the flesh white but also encourages the slices to soften into a creamy paste.

Banana tea bread

MAKES: *12 slices*
PREPARATION TIME: *40 minutes*
COOKING TIME: *1¼–1½ hours*

500 g ripe bananas
Finely grated zest of 1 lemon, and
*   2 tablespoons lemon juice*
125 g unsalted butter
125 g (⅔ cup) light brown sugar
1 teaspoon vanilla essence
1 large egg
125 g (1 cup) self-raising flour
125 g (1 cup) plain wholemeal
*   flour*
1 teaspoon baking powder
1 teaspoon ground cinnamon
125 g (¾ cup) seedless
*   raisins*
175 g (1 cup) fresh dates, stoned
*   and roughly chopped*
30 g (¼ cup) slivered or flaked
*   almonds*
1 tablespoon icing sugar

1 Preheat the oven to 180°C. Line a 21.5 × 11.5 × 6 cm loaf tin with nonstick baking paper, allowing the paper to stand a full 2 cm above the edges of the tin.
2 Peel the bananas, cut them into slices and put them into a bowl. Add the lemon juice and mash well with a fork or potato masher.
3 Put the butter, sugar and lemon zest into a large bowl and beat well together with a wooden spoon or an electric hand-held mixer until light and fluffy, then beat in the vanilla.
4 Add the egg and beat well, then work in the mashed bananas.
5 Sift the flours, baking powder and cinnamon into the banana mixture, tipping the bran left in the sieve into the bowl. Then gently mix together with a large spoon and stir in the raisins and dates.
6 Spoon the mixture into the tin, level the surface and sprinkle on the almonds. Bake for 1¼–1½ hours, or until the loaf is well risen and golden brown. The tea bread is ready when a skewer or knife inserted in the centre comes out clean.
7 Let the loaf rest for 30 minutes before removing it from the tin, then put it on a wire rack to cool. When it is completely cold, gently remove the baking paper. Store the loaf in an airtight tin for up to three days.
8 When you are ready to serve the tea bread, sift the icing sugar over the top. Slice the loaf and eat either plain or spread with butter.

STRONG INGREDIENT

Are bananas a good addition to a mixed fruit salad?

Bananas have a strong flavour and are probably best left out of any fruit salads containing delicately flavoured fruits such as melons, peaches or grapes. They can work well in a highly spiced sugar syrup, perhaps with rum and one or two other fruits that are also strong in flavour, like orange or pineapple. Some red fruits, such as raspberries and plums, will turn bananas pink.

Almond flakes add a crisp decorative touch to this moist Banana Tea Bread, made with added dates and raisins.

Barbecues

CHOOSING EQUIPMENT

I am planning to buy a barbecue but am unsure about which type to choose. Can you advise me?

There are many types of barbecue available. The most basic is one you make yourself from bricks and an iron grill. Although this can be an attractive feature in the garden, it is permanently installed, and the grill is usually fixed so it is difficult to control the temperature.

Portable barbecues, which fold up, are easy to carry around and ideal for picnics and holidays. The most popular model, known as hibachi or firebowl in Japanese, has a grate to hold the charcoal, adjustable grills and vents to control the air flow. As portable barbecues are usually quite small, the amount you can cook at one time is limited.

Standard barbecues are usually about 60 cm across and have a built-in windbreak. They generally have a grill and a hotplate, which makes it easier to cook different types of food at the same time: for example, sausages that need quick cooking and chicken joints that need much slower cooking.

Covered, kettle barbecues are the most efficient. Charcoal burns in baskets on either side and the food is put on a rack in the centre so that it cooks using the indirect heat reflected off the lid.

The most expensive barbecues are covered models where blocks of lava rocks are heated by gas or electricity. This takes less time and is less messy than using charcoal, but the food is cooked in the same manner as in a conventional covered barbecue. It will have the smoky flavour, but this is from fat and juices spitting onto the lava rocks, not from the charcoal.

COOKING GUIDELINES

What are the cooking times for different foods on the barbecue?

Timings depend very much on the individual barbecue being used. As you gain more experience, you will be able to judge the cooking times very accurately. The key point to remember is that the coals ought to be ash-grey and radiating heat, but no flames, before you begin to cook. This can take anything from 40 minutes to as much as an hour, so you must plan ahead. Follow the guidelines shown below and you will avoid having meat or fish that becomes charcoal on the outside but stays raw in the centre.

Some foods can be precooked in the oven or on the stovetop to help ensure that they are well cooked. Thick chicken joints, large sausages and pork chops can all be cooked for half of their total time and then completed on the barbecue.

Below are some rough guidelines on the times to allow. The figures are total cooking times and you should turn the meat or fish over halfway through.

- CHICKEN: joints 40 minutes; drumsticks 20–30 minutes; wings 10–12 minutes
- HAMBURGERS: 10–15 minutes.
- LAMB CHOPS: 10–20 minutes, depending on thickness.
- LEG OF LAMB: (on the bone) allow 30 minutes per kilogram for well done meat.
- PORK CHOPS: 30–40 minutes, depending on size.
- RIB OF BEEF: 25 minutes per kilogram for rare.
- SAUSAGES: 10–16 minutes.
- STEAK: 6–10 minutes for rare, 10–16 minutes for medium and 16–20 minutes for well done.
- WHOLE SMALL FISH: 12–16 minutes.
- WHOLE LARGE FISH: 20–30 minutes.

CHOOSING CONVENIENT FISH RACKS

Barbecuing fish is easier if you use a special fish rack. To prevent the fish sticking to the metal, brush the rack inside and out with oil – but do not preheat it. Before starting, you can stuff a whole fish with fresh herbs or wrap it in vine leaves. Oil the fish or fish steaks, place in the rack, close it tightly and place the rack on the barbecue grill. Turn the rack over once during cooking and baste the fish often through the metal bars, so that the flesh will stay moist.

A large, fish-shaped rack is the ideal container for a good-sized whole fish such as snapper or barrumundi. These are otherwise hard to turn on the grill.

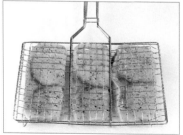

A square or rectangular fish rack allows you to line up wide and narrow fish fillets, steaks or cutlets side-by-side so that they all cook evenly.

Small whole fish such as sardines are best cooked in a rack with individual compartments. These will hold the fish firmly and stop them slipping around.

Vine leaves make a good protective coat for a snapper cooked on the barbecue, but peel them away before eating the fish.

EXPERIMENT WITH FISH

I would like to try cooking fish on the barbecue. As I am a complete novice, can you suggest the best fish to choose?

Fish is excellent to barbecue: the intense heat and quick cooking sear the outside while keeping the flesh moist and full of flavour. Oily fish cooked whole in their skins are ideal. The skins release their oils into the flesh while providing a protection against the heat, so the firm flesh does not fall apart.

The very best fish to cook whole are jewfish, kingfish, sea bream, mullet, salmon, sardines and trout. The recipe, right, for snapper is easy and a good one for beginners. Barramundi are more expensive, but can also be cooked in this way. For easy handling and turning, use a special fish rack to barbecue fish (see box, page 24).

Snapper in vine leaves

SERVES: 4
PREPARATION TIME: 20 minutes plus 1 hour marinating
COOKING TIME: 20-30 minutes

---

1 packet vine leaves preserved in brine
1 snapper, weighing about 1.5 kg, gutted with head and tail left on
Salt and black pepper
4 cloves garlic, sliced lengthways
1 large bunch fresh herbs such as chervil, dill or parsley, according to taste
2 tablespoons virgin olive oil
2 tablespoons dry white wine
2 tablespoons balsamic vinegar
To serve: lemon or lime wedges

---

1 Drain the vine leaves and place them in a bowl. Pour on enough boiling water to cover, soak them for about 5 minutes and drain again in a large colander.

2 Slash the skin of the fish quite deeply in several places on each side. Sprinkle the cavities with salt and pepper, and then push the garlic and fresh herbs very deep inside.

3 Put the fish in a nonmetallic dish. Whisk together the oil, wine and vinegar with salt and pepper to taste, then pour over the fish.

4 Cover and marinate the fish in the refrigerator for at least an hour. Meanwhile, preheat the barbecue.

5 Brush a fish rack liberally inside and out with vegetable oil, but do not preheat the metal bars. Wrap the fish in the vine leaves, then place the parcel carefully in the rack.

6 Close the metal rack and put it on the oiled barbecue grid. If you do not have a fish rack, you can also just secure the leaves with string.

7 Cook the fish for 20 minutes, turning once. Unwrap and serve the snapper immediately, garnished with lemon or lime wedges.

BARBECUING LARGE CUTS

How can I barbecue a large piece of meat, such as a leg of lamb?

It is possible to cook a large piece of meat successfully on a barbecue, and the Christmas turkey can also be cooked in this way. The technique works best with a covered barbecue, which gives an indirect, reflected heat and much greater temperature control.

Put the joint on the grill, with a drip pan underneath to catch the juices, and adjust the air vents to ensure very slow, even cooking. Check the coals from time to time and add more charcoal gradually if it seems necessary. The cooking times are approximately the same as when you are using an oven, although they can be quicker. This is because temperatures fluctuate in a barbecue and may become a good deal higher than they would be in an oven. If you are in any doubt, especially with poultry, use a meat thermometer to check the joint's inner temperature.

An excellent method of cooking a whole leg of lamb is to butterfly bone it. The joint is opened out like a book and the meat takes less time to cook (see *Boning*).

TENDERISING MARINADES

Why are meat and fish so often marinated before barbecuing?

Marinades are helpful to tenderise meat and enhance the flavour – and they are particularly useful for barbecuing, where the intense heat can result in dry food. Barbecue marinades are usually based on tomato, onion and garlic, which suit the smoky flavours particularly well. Tomato is often included for its tenderising effect, but any other acid ingredients, such as vinegar or lemon juice, can be used.

A marinade may include garlic, fresh ginger, lemon juice, olive oil, sherry and brown sugar, as well as soy sauce to provide a tangy flavour. The following recipe for Barbecued Lamb offers another suggestion (see also *Marinade*).

Barbecued lamb

SERVES 4
PREPARATION TIME: *5–15 minutes, plus 2–4 hours marinating*
COOKING TIME: *8–10 minutes*

FOR THE MEAT
750 g Trim lamb leg steak, cut into 2–3 cm cubes

FOR THE MARINADE
4 tablespoons olive oil
2 tablespoons lemon juice
1 tablespoon each chopped fresh flat-leaf parsley and chopped fresh thyme
A pinch of dried oregano
Black pepper and salt
To serve: lemon wedges

1 If the butcher has not prepared the lamb steak, trim it and cut it into cubes. Put these chunks of meat in a shallow, nonmetallic dish.
2 Mix together the olive oil, lemon juice, herbs and pepper. Pour the marinade over the lamb, turn the meat in it and leave in the refrigerator for 2–4 hours, turning the cubes occasionally.
3 Take meat from the refrigerator 30 minutes before cooking.
4 Meanwhile, preheat the barbecue until the coals are white hot. Oil the metal rack and put it 7.5–10 cm above the glowing coals.
5 Lift the lamb from the dish and reserve the marinade. Lightly oil four skewers and thread the cubed lamb onto them, keeping the meat towards the pointed skewer ends.
6 Put the kebabs on the grill rack and cook for 8–10 minutes, turning the skewers frequently and basting with the reserved marinade.
7 Sprinkle the cooked lamb cubes with salt, and serve them with lemon wedges and a mixed salad.

Turning sausages

If you are cooking lots of sausages over the barbecue, thread them onto skewers first to make turning them easier. The sausages will then brown more evenly as they grill.

PLAN TO DEFROST

Could I barbecue meat and fish directly from frozen?

Cooking frozen food on a barbecue is not recommended. Poultry, large cuts of meat and large whole fish that are frozen would be cooked, and even charred, on the outside by the fierce heat well before the centre had become sufficiently hot.

Small cuts of meat such as thin steaks and small fish could be cooked from frozen if you add extra time, but the texture of the rapidly defrosted meat will be impaired.

PREPARING KEBABS

What is the best way to cut up meat for a barbecued kebab?

Trim the fat and connective tissue from the meat, then cut across the grain into fairly even-sized cubes that are no larger than 5 cm thick. You should skewer the cubes closely together if you prefer rarer meat with pink centres. Make a point of separating the cubes more if you want to cook the meat so that it is much better done.

Any lean cut of meat can be used to make kebabs. For example, you can try using cubes of pork fillet, or the fillet end of leg of pork. Other good choices for making skewered kebabs are lamb fillet or fillet end of leg of lamb, fillet of beef and chunks of either turkey breast or chicken breast.

PROTECTING FISH

Does fish need to be wrapped in foil before going on the barbecue?

Fish cutlets, steaks or whole fish do not need to be wrapped in foil to be barbecued, but it is generally better to choose a firm-fleshed fish such as snapper, swordfish or tuna rather than a soft-fleshed fish, which may fall apart.

The fish can be wrapped up in bacon to provide protection, or it can be marinated to lubricate the flesh – but if the marinade has lime or lemon juice, do not leave it too long (see box, page 27).

Care with fish marinades

Do not marinate fish for longer than an hour in any mixture that contains either lime or lemon juice, as the acid in the citrus fruit will start to 'cook' the fish.

BARBECUING VEGETABLES

Should vegetables be marinated before they are barbecued?

Vegetables cannot be made tender by marinating, but using marinades does enhance the flavour of food. The results on vegetables can be surprising and delicious.

For instance, try marinating thick slices of eggplant, zucchini, and red and yellow peppers, plus halved egg tomatoes, in olive oil with some crushed garlic, sprigs of thyme and a squeeze of lemon.

Cook the vegetables on a grid placed directly over the hot coals, starting with the eggplant, which needs 6 minutes on each side; add the zucchini for 4–5 minutes on each side; followed by the peppers for about 2–3 minutes on each side; and then the tomatoes, skin side down only, for 2–3 minutes.

Grilled asparagus is wonderful with a mixture of hazelnut oil and red wine vinegar. Use three parts of oil to one part of vinegar, whisk the two together and pour the marinade over the asparagus .

You can cook the spears straight-away, or leave them soaking in the marinade for about an hour. Put the asparagus spears on a grill which is directly over the hot coals, and rotate them to allow quick cooking for 2–3 minutes on each side.

A popular choice to barbecue is corn-on-the-cob. Pull the corn husk back, without taking it off the stalk, and then remove the silky threads. Coat the corn cob with a barbecue sauce and cover it again with the husk. Wrap each cob in foil and leave to marinate for 30 minutes. Cook the prepared corn parcels on the cooler part of the grill for about 15–20 minutes, turning frequently.

BARBECUED FRUIT

Do you have any suggestions for barbecued desserts?

Your guests may have had enough of barbecued food after eating the main course, and a fresh fruit salad or some homemade ice cream to follow is often the most refreshing choice. However, fruit does lend itself to being barbecued and the soft flesh of bananas is especially delicious when grilled.

Split the whole banana length-ways through the skin, without removing the flesh, and sprinkle orange juice, rum, brown sugar and cinnamon down the middle.

Dot the banana flesh with butter, sandwich the fruit back together and wrap it in foil. Grill the banana slowly for about 5–10 minutes, turning the parcel over carefully about halfway through cooking. A variety of other fleshy fruits, such as nectarines and peaches, can be cooked in the same way, but they will need to have their hard stones removed beforehand.

Fruit kebabs are very attractive and cook quickly. Cut a mixture of firm-fleshed fruit into chunks and thread them onto a kebab skewer. Choose fruits that have a harmonious mix of colours and flavours. Sprinkle with caster sugar and a liqueur, or the juice and zest of one orange, and leave them to soak for at least 2 hours. Then drain the kebabs, save the marinade, and grill the fruit for 5–10 minutes. Turn them often while they cook, basting with a little marinade.

To serve, arrange the mixed fruit kebabs decoratively onto a platter and pour over the remaining juice.

Barbecued peaches and bananas sprinkled with sugar, cinnamon and rum are wonderful. Serve in their warm juices with the aromas wafting from the parcel.

Barley

LOW-GLUTEN FLOUR

What is barley flour, and how does it differ from other flours?

This is flour produced by milling the whole grain. Barley is notably low in gluten, the protein that gives bread dough its elasticity. For this reason, it needs to be used with other, higher-gluten flours to make successful yeasted bread.

While barley flour or meal does not make good leavened bread when used on its own, it adds considerable flavour to tea breads and scones and can be used to thicken soups and milk-based sauces.

As one of the earliest cereals farmed, barley grains were used for making bread before wheat. While much barley is now used for animal feed, it is still malted for brewing and remains an important grain for human food in the Middle East.

REFINED GRAINS

What is the difference between whole grains and pearl barley?

Whole grains are the grains as they are harvested, while pearl barley has had the outer layer removed to reveal a polished white kernel. Whole grains must be softened before being cooked in order to be edible. Soak them in plenty of cold water for at least 2 hours or even overnight. The whole grains are then often combined with meat, and lamb in particular, as in the classic recipe for Scotch broth. The barley thickens this wholesome soup as well as adding flavour and a pleasing nutty texture.

As pearl barley has been well polished to remove the outer husk, the grain cooks more quickly and no prior soaking is necessary. Pearl barley is also used to thicken and enhance the flavour and texture of soups and is the key ingredient in Lemon Barley Water (see the step-by-step instructions below).

MAKING LEMON BARLEY WATER

This traditional summer drink is extremely easy to make. Allow plenty of time for cooling, as it is most appealing served chilled with ice and lemon slices.

1 Wash three large lemons, dry them and pare the zest using a potato peeler. Place the pieces of peel in a bowl and add 60–125 g (¼–½ cup) caster sugar, according to taste.

Put 3 tablespoons pearl barley in a large saucepan, pour in 1.25 litres of water and bring to the boil. Cover and leave the grains to simmer for 10 minutes, until they are soft.

2 Pour the water and barley over the sugar and peel and leave to cool.

3 Squeeze the lemons and strain the juice into a jug to discard the pips. Strain the barley liquid into the juice.

Batter

RESTING BATTER

Should I let pancake batter stand for an hour or two before using?

While it is not strictly necessary, taking the time to cover and rest a pancake batter in a cool place for 15–30 minutes allows the starch in the flour to swell, giving a lighter result. If the batter is cooked just after being made, the pancakes will have a bubbly surface rather than appearing flat. But do not leave the batter to stand for more than 1 hour at room temperature or it may begin to ferment.

Batter left to stand for an hour or more may separate out. If so, just stir to remix. If it thickens slightly, thin it with some extra liquid.

VARYING THE MIX

Can I use the same batter for different dishes, such as waffles, fritters and pancakes?

The batters that are used to make pancakes, waffles and such dishes are much the same. It is the exact proportions of all the ingredients that vary slightly.

Pancakes, crêpes, baked batter puddings, Yorkshire pudding and toad-in-the-hole are all made with a basic pouring batter (see box, page 29). To make crêpes, which are slightly lighter than pancakes, the batter is thinned with a few tablespoons of extra liquid.

Fritters and battered foods such as fish, shellfish and vegetables are made with coating batter. This uses the same amount of flour, salt and egg as pouring batter, but only half of the liquid. Whisked egg whites may be folded into a coating batter, and sugar added for sweet fritters.

The type of liquid used in batters (whether milk, a mix of milk and water, or beer) will influence the result. Water makes a light batter, milk helps to make it smoother and causes it to brown faster, while beer adds lightness and flavour.

EASY ON WHISKING

How long should you beat batter to achieve a good texture?

Basic batter needs only fairly brief beating or whisking in order to combine the ingredients. If you beat the mixture too much, this tends to develop the gluten in the flour and results in the batter becoming tough when it is cooked. The exception is any yeast-raised batter, which does need to be beaten heartily to develop gluten.

MAKING BASIC BATTER

This basic batter will make 8–10 pancakes. Include 3 tablespoons of extra milk if making lighter crêpes, and halve the liquid for making a thicker, coating batter.

1 Sift 125 g (1 cup) plain flour and a pinch of salt into a bowl and make a well in the centre, then break in 1 egg and beat with a balloon whisk or wooden spoon. (You can also use a food processor for a few seconds or a hand-held electric mixer for slightly longer.)

2 Beat in 300 ml milk, little by little, incorporating the surrounding flour gradually so the batter becomes very smooth.

3 The batter may be used at once, but it is much better if it is left in a cool place for some 30 minutes, allowing the starch grains to soften.

SUCCESSFUL PIKELETS

My pikelets tend to be stodgy, although I leave the batter to rise. What am I doing wrong?

Pikelets, like waffles, need a raising agent to help make them light and bubbly – which is why self-raising flour is used for them. One disadvantage, however, is that self-raising flour starts into action as soon as it becomes wet, so the batter must be used straightaway.

If self-raising flour batter is left to stand, the bubbles escape and the results will be heavier instead of lighter pancakes. Try this speedy idea for making light-as-air Pikelets (below). The secret is that batter for this delicious recipe must be made just before you make the pikelets.

Pikelets

MAKES: 12-15 pikelets
PREPARATION TIME: 15 minutes
COOKING TIME: 10-15 minutes

---

125 g (1 cup) self-raising flour
1-2 tablespoons caster sugar
1 large egg, beaten
150 ml milk

---

1 Sift the flour and sugar into a bowl; make a well in the centre. Stir in the egg and add enough milk to make a thick batter, stirring gently.
2 Lightly grease a heavy frying pan or large griddle with vegetable oil and preheat it. Gently drop individual tablespoons of the mixture onto the pan or griddle and cook them over a moderate heat until bubbles show.
3 Flip the pikelets over with a palette knife, and cook them for a further 2–3 minutes, until golden. Repeat with the remaining batter.
4 Keep the cooked pikelets warm by wrapping them in a folded tea towel. Serve either warm or cold with jam, butter, cream or honey.
VARIATION
Add 50–75 g (¼–⅓ cup) raisins, sultanas, or chopped dried apricots, a teaspoon of ground mixed spice or the finely grated zest of an orange to the batter before cooking. Reduce the kilojoules and fat by using skim milk instead of whole milk.

Staying unstuck

For a richer flavour in pancakes and crêpes, and to help prevent their sticking to the pan, stir 1–2 tablespoons melted butter or oil into the batter before cooking.

YEASTY FISH BATTER

What sort of batter do I use for coating fish before deep-frying?

Batter helps to protect delicate foods such as fish from the intense heat of deep oil. A crisp coating forms which stops oil penetrating the food, so it stays soft and tender inside. The batter used for fish is usually a savoury coating batter, using beer instead of milk to add flavour as well as air, or a more robust yeast-raised batter.

Yeast batter is preferred for the coating of fish because although it is strong enough to protect the fish, it has a particularly light texture. To make a yeast batter that will coat 350 g fish, you need 1 teaspoon dried yeast, 150 ml milk or water, 125 g (1 cup) plain flour and a pinch of salt. The yeast is dissolved in the liquid and then added to the flour and salt.

Unlike an ordinary batter, yeast-raised batter is beaten vigorously to develop gluten in the flour. Leave it to stand in a cool place for up to an hour, until risen and bubbly.

Save it!

Cooked pancakes may be refrigerated for up to two days. They also freeze well for up to three months, if separated with pieces of greaseproof paper. Thaw the pancakes overnight in the refrigerator. To reheat, warm them in the oven or heat gently on both sides in melted butter in a frying pan.

Bavarois

ADDED EGG

What is the difference between a blancmange and a bavarois?

Blancmange is made from milk set with either cornflour or gelatine. Bavarois is a milk and egg custard, enriched with whipped cream and often egg whites, and set with gelatine. Also known as Bavarian cream or crème bavaroise, bavarois is lighter than blancmange and has generally replaced it as a popular dessert. Both are usually flavoured and sometimes coloured, poured into a mould to set and then chilled.

RICH OR LIGHT

Can I use cream instead of milk to make a richer bavarois?

Yes, and if you prefer to go the other way and reduce the kilojoule and fat content, you can choose instead to use reduced-fat or skim milk and fat-reduced cream. The following recipe for creamy Raspberry Bavarois lets you choose.

Raspberry bavarois

SERVES: 6
PREPARATION TIME: 1 hour, plus
3–4 hours chilling time
COOKING TIME: none

250 g raspberries, fresh or
    frozen, defrosted
500 ml fresh cream
3 large eggs, separated
125 g (½ cup) caster sugar
15 g (4½ teaspoons) powdered
    gelatine
150 ml thickened cream
Sunflower or vegetable oil,
    for greasing
To decorate: icing sugar, fresh
    raspberries and mint sprigs

1 Purée the raspberries in a blender or food processor then set aside.
2 Put the 500 ml fresh cream in a pan and bring it to the boil.
3 In a bowl, whisk together the egg yolks and sugar until pale and fluffy.

This luscious, creamy bavarois is flavoured and decorated with fresh raspberries, topped with icing sugar and mint. It can be low-fat if you choose the variation.

Pour the hot cream onto the whisked egg mixture, then strain the custard into a heavy-based saucepan. Cook over a gentle heat, stirring until it is thick enough to coat the back of a spoon. Do not boil.
4 Sprinkle the gelatine powder over 3 tablespoons water in a small bowl and leave to soak for about 2 minutes until spongy.
5 Place the bowl over a small pan of simmering water and stir until the gelatine has dissolved.
6 Stir the gelatine and the raspberry purée into the custard. Then stand the mixture in a bowl filled with ice and stir gently until thickened.
7 Lightly whip the 150 ml thickened cream and fold it into the fruity custard. Whisk the egg whites until stiff and fold them in carefully.
8 Lightly oil a mould, pour in the bavarois and chill 3–4 hours to set.
9 When the bavarois has become firm, dip the mould in hot water for a few seconds. This will make the dessert much easier to unmould.

Turn it out onto a serving dish, dust with icing sugar and decorate with fresh raspberries and sprigs of mint.
VARIATION
For a healthier version, use reduced fat or skim milk instead of cream in the custard, and light thickened cream for step 7, after the fruit and gelatine have been incorporated.

OCCASIONALLY SAVOURY

I saw bavarois included on a savoury menu. Does a bavarois not have to be a sweet dish?

Bavarois usually refers to a sweet dessert. However, you can make savoury bavarois using a custard base without sugar, combined with savoury ingredients. These may be asparagus, smoked fish or cheese and onion, usually in the form of a purée, which are then set with gelatine. Use either just cream, or a mixture of cream and yoghurt, and fold this into the cooled custard before it becomes fully set.

Beans

A QUESTION OF SEASON

Green beans seem to be available all year, but when is the best time for broad and runner beans?

Early summer is the time for home-grown broad beans, which are traditionally dressed with butter and summer savory. Dill also goes particularly well with these. When the pods become very large, the beans inside are best blanched and skinned. This treatment works all year round for frozen broad beans, and the bright green kernels add freshness to mixed-bean salads.

Runner beans come into season in the late summer. String and slice them, then cook quickly in boiling salted water. You can serve them hot, dressed with butter or olive oil, or in a sauce. Green beans are also delicious eaten cold as a salad. Try mixing the beans with omelette strips, as in the following recipe. Serve as a starter with warm bread.

Green beans are threaded with omelette ribbons for this piquant salad. The strips of egg and sun-dried tomatoes add good contrasts in colour and texture.

Green bean and omelette ribbon salad

SERVES: **4**
PREPARATION TIME: **15 minutes**
COOKING TIME: **8-9 minutes**

2 eggs
Salt and black pepper
350 g green beans
1 large clove garlic, thinly sliced
3 tablespoons olive oil
1 teaspoon red wine vinegar
1 teaspoon chilli vinegar
2 sun-dried tomatoes in oil, chopped
2 teaspoons capers

1 Beat the eggs lightly with a fork; add salt and pepper; then make two thin omelettes and turn onto plates.
2 Top and tail the beans and cook for 3–4 minutes in boiling, salted water. Drain and transfer to a dish.
3 Fry the garlic for 30 seconds in a tablespoon of oil; remove from the heat. Add the remaining oil, vinegars and sun-dried tomatoes, mix together and toss with the beans.
4 Roll each omelette and slice into thin ribbons. Curl the slices loosely over the salad; scatter with capers.

STRINGING BEANS

Many green beans are sold when they are small and do not need to have their strings removed. Older green beans and runner beans (pictured below) need stringing.

1 With a small, sharp knife, cut each bean from the outer side across the stalk end towards the deeply grooved inner side. Stop just short of the edge and pull the string along the length of each bean.

2 If a string breaks short, cut away a thin strip along the edge to remove it. Nick the top of the outer edge. If a string has been formed there, pull it out as well.

SLICING BEANS

Slicing larger green beans thinly and not too long ensures that they cook through more quickly and also retain their best flavour.

Making long diagonal cuts, slice across and down the pod right through the beans inside. Aim to produce slices measuring about 5 mm wide and 7.5–10 cm long.

Warm salad of tangled runner beans

SERVES: *4*
PREPARATION TIME: *15 minutes*
COOKING TIME: *4–5 minutes*

500 g runner beans
½ red onion
Salt and black pepper
3 tablespoons olive oil
1 tablespoon red wine vinegar
150 g cherry tomatoes, some halved
50 g small black olives
To garnish: basil leaves

1 String and thinly slice the beans diagonally. Peel the onion, cut it in half and then slice downwards into thin crescents. Put these slices into an attractive serving bowl.
2 Cook the beans in boiling salted water until they are just tender; this should take about 4 minutes after the water returns to the boil. Drain and put the beans immediately over the onion slices so that the heat slightly wilts the onions.
3 In a small bowl, stir the oil and vinegar briskly together and toss with the beans, along with the cherry tomatoes, olives and pepper.
4 Tear leaves of basil over the salad just before serving. The dish is best still warm or at room temperature.

Bean Sprouts

SPROUTING SEEDS

Can I sprout any dried bean?

Beans, peas and lentils are all seeds that can be used for sprouting. As long as they are not too old or have not been damaged or deliberately split in processing, they should sprout. You can also use grains such as barley, whole oats, wheat and millet. These can then be used singly or in mixtures in salads and sandwiches, very lightly cooked in stir-fries, or as a crunchy garnish for cooked food. Bean sprouts that are surplus to your immediate needs can be loosely wrapped in plastic wrap and stored in the salad drawer of the refrigerator.

GROWING BEAN SPROUTS

Sprouting beans is very easy and is a good way to have a fresh, crunchy, high-protein salad filling on hand. The sprouts can also be added to stir-fries as well as sandwiches.

Soak a handful of beans (mung beans are shown here) overnight in cold water and they will double their bulk. Rinse in a sieve under the cold tap and transfer to a jar. They should fill the jar about one-quarter full.

1 Cover the jar with a square of loose-woven cloth held in place with an elastic band. Leave the jar on its side.

2 Place in a warm, well-ventilated place out of direct sunlight. Twice each day, uncover the jar. Fill it with cold water, swirl, replace the cover and drain water through the cloth.

3 The seeds should start to sprout on the second day. After a few days, the sprouts will have grown to about 1–2 cm long, which is when they are at their most nutritious.

Beef

BREAKING DOWN FIBRES

Why should you beat steak?

Steak is beaten to break down the fibres a little, making the meat more tender. Nowadays, cattle are killed while still young and tender so beating steaks is less necessary, but you can do so if you want to shorten their cooking time. Place the uncooked meat between two sheets of plastic wrap or grease-proof paper, then pound it firmly with a meat mallet, the flat of a heavy knife, or a rolling pin. A gentler technique for tenderising steak is to marinate it for a few hours.

TOUGH STEAKS

Sometimes when I cook steak, it is very chewy. Is the problem with the meat I buy or the method I use for cooking?

The tenderness is affected by the choice of meat. Look for flesh with a little fine marbling of fat as this dissolves in cooking and helps to tenderise the steak. Meat from animals that have been carefully reared (see **Meat**) and cuts from muscles that do not move, such as eye fillet and scotch fillet, are apt to be most tender. It is also important that the meat should have been well hung in a cool place for about 14 days. During hanging, flavour develops and the natural enzymes in the meat break down the tough tissues, making it firmer, drier and more tender. The meat will also look much darker in colour. Bright red steak is more likely to be tough.

If you buy from a good butcher, these points will be covered. But how you cook steak, and for how long, also affects its tenderness. Good-quality raw steak is already tender and over-cooking it makes it tough. The following recipe for Perfect Steak (page 33) gives the optimum cooking times. Always bring the steak to room temperature before you start cooking.

KNOW YOUR STEAK

Steaks come in many forms, from dainty tournedos to chateaubriand that will feed two or more hungry people.

Choose fillet and sirloin steaks for real tenderness, but more robust cuts such as rump for their succulent flavour.

1 FILLET STEAK is cut from the thick centre section of the fillet, just below the sirloin. It is small in diameter, weighs about 175 g, is tender and very lean. Fillet steaks, also called eye fillet, are extremely good, but expensive.

2 SIRLOIN STEAK (with the bone in) can serve two people. It is usually a double thickness of sirloin steak with two separate 'eyes' of meat. (Called porterhouse steak in the United States.)

3 T-BONE STEAK is a thick cut that includes the rib bone with the sirloin on one side of the 'T' and the fillet on the other. It serves one person generously.

4 SIRLOIN STEAK (boneless) is cut from the top part of the sirloin, above the ribs. It is not as fine-textured or tender as fillet, but is less coarse than rump. It is also called New York Cut.

5 RUMP STEAK is cut across the grain of the rump. It is marbled with a little fat, has a border of fat and is coarser and tougher than fillet or sirloin. It has a good flavour and many people consider it the best for grilling and frying.

6 CHATEAUBRIAND is a joint cut from the thickest end of the fillet and can serve two to four people. After an initial grilling, the steak is usually put in the oven to finish cooking.

7 MINUTE STEAK is cut thinly from round, rump or blade steak and is beaten so that it cooks quickly to be tender.

8 TOURNEDOS are small round steaks cut from the centre or thin end of the fillet, each weighing about 125 g. These steaks are wrapped in pork fat or bacon and tied into shape before cooking.

Perfect steak

SERVES: 4
PREPARATION TIME: 5 minutes
COOKING TIME: 3-10 minutes

---

1 tablespoon light olive oil
4 rump, sirloin or fillet steaks
Salt and black pepper

TO FRY

1 Brush a large, heavy, nonstick frying pan with oil and place it over a high heat until very hot.

2 Sprinkle the steaks with black pepper, add them to the pan and brown for 1-1½ minutes each side then cook for these times, turning the meat over halfway through:

- BLUE: 2 minutes (the meat offers little resistance when pressed).
- RARE: 3 minutes (the meat feels spongy when pressed).
- MEDIUM: 4½ minutes (the meat resists when pressed).
- WELL DONE: 5-7 minutes (the meat feels firm when pressed).

3 For blue or rare steak, keep the heat high. For longer cooking, lower the heat after the initial browning.

TO GRILL

1 Preheat the grill for 10 minutes until it is very hot. Make vertical cuts through any fat around the edge of the steak at 2-3 cm intervals.

2 Brush both sides with oil. Season with black pepper, put on the grill rack and cook 7.5 cm from the grill for a minute each side.

3 Reduce the heat to medium and grill for these times, turning the meat over halfway through:

- BLUE: 2½ minutes.
- RARE: 3½ minutes.
- MEDIUM: 5½ minutes.
- WELL DONE: 6-8 minutes.

4 Transfer the steaks to warm plates, sprinkle with salt and serve with mustard or béarnaise sauce.

DRAMATIC RIB ROAST

I usually cook rolled topside or sirloin, but would like to try a standing rib. How is it cooked?

Because a standing rib roast is cooked on the bone, it has more flavour than rolled joints and looks more dramatic. It is not difficult to prepare, as the following recipe for Roast Rib of Beef shows.

Roast rib of beef

SERVES: *6–8; allow about 375 g per person*
PREPARATION TIME: *5 minutes*
COOKING TIME: *1¼–2 hours*

Standing rib roast weighing about 2.5 kg
Salt and black pepper
Plain flour, optional
Powdered mustard, optional

1 Preheat the oven to 230°C. Weigh the beef and calculate the cooking time. For rare beef, cook for 30 minutes per kilogram; for medium, cook for 45 minutes per kilogram; for well done beef, cook for 55 minutes per kilogram.
2 Sprinkle black pepper over the beef. If you would like a dry crust on the surface, rub a little seasoned flour, perhaps also flavoured with dry mustard, over the fat.
3 Place the beef with the rib bones pointing upwards, or balanced on the two ends of the bones with the fat uppermost, in a baking dish that will hold it comfortably. (If the tin is too small, the joint will steam, and if it is too large, the juices will burn.)
4 Roast for about 15 minutes, or until the joint is well browned on the outside. Then lower the temperature to 180°C and continue roasting for the time calculated. Baste frequently with the meat juices so it does not become too dry. Meanwhile, put a carving dish to warm.
5 Transfer the beef to the warmed carving dish, cover loosely with a dome of foil and leave to rest in a warm place for at least 15 minutes.
6 Carve the meat (see *Carving*) and serve with gravy, Yorkshire pudding and horseradish or béarnaise sauce.

Perfect roast beef is rosy in the centre and splendid served with béarnaise sauce. Offer horseradish as well, along with roast potatoes and Yorkshire pudding.

RAISED WITH KINDNESS

How can I tell if the meat I buy comes from an animal that has been raised kindly?

All animals should be reared and slaughtered according to basic legal welfare standards. However, some people believe that happier animals produce more tender meat.

If you are concerned that even greater care has been taken, find an organic producer who is accredited by Biological Farmers of Australia (BFA), the National Association for Sustainable Agriculture Australia (NASAA) or Demeter-Biodynamics: this means he farms to their standards. And find a butcher close to the producer who will butcher the meat for you. You could also look out for shrink-wrapped or vacuum-packed meat that has special accredited labels, such as one guaranteeing organic rearing.

DISEASE-FREE

I am going to Britain on holiday soon. How can I be sure that the beef I eat there is free from the disease BSE?

All British beef on sale should be clear of BSE (bovine spongiform encephalopathy). Parts of dead animals that could carry disease (the head, brain, intestines, spinal cord and offal from cattle aged over six months old, and the intestines and thymus gland from calves) may not be sold. Cattle over 30 months old may not be sold for beef, and the carcasses of younger cattle must be boned in licensed plants and the possibly infected trimmings destroyed. If an animal is thought to be infected with BSE, the whole body is destroyed. Precautions are being taken, but no guarantee is total.

BSE has never occurred in Australia or New Zealand.

Beer

COOKING WITH BEER

Which beer is best for cooking?

Any type of beer can be used for cooking. Strong, full-bodied ales and stout are the best for braising, stewing, casseroling or marinating dark meats and game; dark beer, particularly stout, will add a rich colour. The slight bitterness of dark ales and some stouts is used to counteract the richness of strongly flavoured meats such as venison, and also the sweetness imparted by some vegetables, such as carrots, onions and parsnips. Dark ale or stout can also be used to enrich fruit puddings, such as Christmas pudding. The very slight bitterness is the perfect foil for the sweetness of the fruit.

Light ales and lager go well with chicken, fish, pork or rabbit. They can also be used in desserts, for poaching fruits and for making cakes and puddings.

BEER FOR CARBONADE

Which beer should be used to cook the Flemish version of beef carbonade? When I made the dish recently it tasted very bitter. Was the beer responsible and, if so, how could I have corrected it?

The traditional Flemish version uses a light beer, but a darker beer such as stout will give carbonade a richer colour and flavour. The degree of bitterness varies from one brand of stout to another, and will be reflected in the dish. The bitterness in your carbonade could have been due to burning the onions slightly when frying, but it is more likely that you chose a beer that was too bitter. Next time, try using a Belgian-style beer such as a light lager.

Adding a bit more brown sugar, which is traditionally part of the recipe anyway, would have helped to counteract the bitterness. You could also have added some more gently fried onions for sweetness.

CRISPY BATTER

I have heard that beer can be used to make a tasty batter. How is such a coating made?

Light ale or lager can be mixed into a crisp batter for coating meat and fish as well as fruit and vegetables. Guinness can also be used to make a batter for oysters. The following recipe uses a light ale batter to coat a mixture of ready-prepared seafood. You can also use whatever other combination of seafood you prefer, such as prawns, squid and strips of white fish fillets.

Seafood in light ale batter

SERVES: 4
PREPARATION TIME: 20 minutes plus 1 hour standing time
COOKING TIME: about 25 minutes

FOR THE BATTER
150 g (1¼ cups) plain flour
A pinch of salt
250 ml light ale or lager
25 g butter, melted

FOR THE SEAFOOD
800 g mixed seafood (an equal mixture of mussels, green tiger prawns, scallops and calamari rings)
60 g (½ cup) plain flour
Salt and black pepper
3 tablespoons chopped fresh dill
2 tablespoons chopped fresh parsley
About 1.5 litres vegetable oil for deep-frying
1 large egg white
To garnish: 3 tablespoons chopped fresh dill or parsley, and some lemon wedges

1 To make the batter, sift the flour and salt into a large mixing bowl and make a well in the centre. Pour in the beer and whisk to a thick batter.
2 Whisk in the melted butter then cover and leave to stand for an hour.
3 Drain the seafood and dry it well with paper towels. Divide the various types of seafood into separate groups.
4 Put the remaining flour into a large bowl and season it well with salt and pepper, then add the herbs and mix well together so that all of the flavours are blended together.
5 Half fill a deep-frying pan with oil and heat it until it reaches 190°C on a frying thermometer. If you do not have a thermometer, drop a cube of dry bread into the oil; it should brown in about 30 seconds.
6 Meanwhile, preheat the oven to 150°C, and line two large baking trays with paper towels. These are used to drain the cooked fish while the remaining pieces are fried.
7 To complete the batter, whisk the egg white until stiff but not dry, and gently fold it into the batter mixture.
8 Add the mussels to the seasoned flour and toss them until lightly coated. Remove them from the flour, shaking off the excess, and put them into the batter. With your fingers, gently turn the mussels in the batter until evenly coated. Lift them out carefully one at a time, allowing the excess batter to run into the bowl.
9 Carefully drop the coated mussels into the hot oil and then cook for about 2–3 minutes until the batter is crisp and golden brown, turning to ensure an even browning. Remove the mussels with a slotted spoon and drain them well on one of the baking trays, then transfer to the second tray and keep warm in the oven.
10 Flour and batter the prawns as you did the mussels, then cook them in two batches. Coat and cook the scallops, in two batches, and repeat with the calamari.
11 Arrange the seafood pieces on a heated serving dish and garnish with chopped dill or parsley.
12 Serve with lemon wedges, crusty bread and add a bit of colour with a tossed mixed-leaf salad.

Deep-frying in batches

Do not be tempted to deep-fry too many pieces of food at any one time, as this causes the oil temperature to drop and the food then becomes soggy. Cook only six to eight pieces at a time, and give the oil an opportunity to come back to temperature in between.

Beetroot

HOT AND COLD

Why is beetroot almost always served straight from the can? How can I prepare beetroot at home?

You can grate raw beetroot into a salad or add it to the Russian soup borscht, but you will miss out on the soft, voluptuous sweetness that is a main feature of this tasty vegetable when it is freshly cooked.

While the cooking process is very simple, it can be quite lengthy and must be done while the beetroot is unpeeled. Any break in the skin will allow the colour to run, leaving a vegetable that is pale and less flavoursome.

Remove the leaves from whole beetroot, leaving about 3 cm of stem. Either boil in lightly salted water for about 1½ hours, steam for about 1 hour, or bake in a 180°C oven for 1–1½ hours. When cooked, a fine skewer should pass through easily. Rub off the skins under running water.

Cooked and peeled beetroot can be pickled, reheated in a sauce, or dressed cold as a salad – for example, sliced onto a bed of radicchio and garnished with rings of red onion, or served with alternating slices of orange, garnished with chives, coriander leaves or parsley.

Freshly cooked beetroot also makes a wonderful purée, blended with cream. Or try this unusual mixture of beetroot and apple (above right). The timbales are an excellent partner to roast lamb, duck breast, venison or kangaroo. Bake them on the bottom shelf, below the meat.

Stylish dressing

A simple dressing for sliced hot beetroot is a spoonful of good marmalade thinned lightly with fresh orange juice. Garnish with coriander leaves or ground seeds.

Beetroot and apple timbales

SERVES: 4
PREPARATION TIME: 20 minutes
COOKING TIME: 45 minutes

200 g Granny Smith apples, peeled, cored and sliced
4 tablespoons ruby port
75 ml light sour cream
175 g beetroot, cooked, peeled and sliced
½ teaspoon ground cumin
2 large eggs
Salt and black pepper
Cayenne pepper
2 teaspoons lemon juice
To garnish: sprigs of fresh dill

1 Preheat the oven to 200°C. Generously butter and base-line four custard cups or small ramekins.

2 Put the apple and the port into a pan, cover and cook for 10 minutes or until the apple collapses.

3 Put all but a tablespoon of the sour cream into a food processor. Add the beetroot and the cumin, break in the eggs and process.

4 Add the cooked apple to the mixture and process briefly again to a chunky purée. Season with salt, black pepper, a pinch or two of cayenne to taste, and lemon juice.

5 Spoon into cups, tapping them down to settle. Stand the cups in a baking dish and pour in boiling water to halfway up the sides of the cups. Bake for 45 minutes.

6 Remove the cups from the water and allow to cool before turning out.

7 Add a swirl of the reserved sour cream to each timbale if you like, along with a sprig of dill.

Timbales of beetroot and apple, enriched with sour cream, are a superb accompaniment to strong-tasting meats such as duck breast. Use dill to garnish.

Berries

DELICATE WASH

Should berries be washed before you eat them?

It depends on the type of fruit and where it came from. Wild blackberries should always be washed, but those sold by supermarkets and greengrocers are cultivated varieties and should not need washing.

Do not wash raspberries, boysenberries or loganberries as this will spoil their juicy texture. Strawberries, too, should not be washed, unless they are particularly dusty.

Blackcurrants, gooseberries, redcurrants and whitecurrants should be put into a colander and rinsed under a gently running tap.

ADDING FLAVOUR

What can I do if I find I have bought strawberries that turn out to be virtually tasteless?

If serving such strawberries with cream or ice cream, you can develop their flavour by dusting them with sugar and leaving them to stand for about an hour. Slice any large ones first. Sprinkling them with a little kirsch, Cointreau or Grand Marnier will also improve the flavour. If the strawberries are to be put into a flan, or on top of a cake, they can be mixed with some hot, sieved strawberry jam, or glazed. This will compensate for their disappointing flavour.

STOP IT COLLAPSING

Why does my summer pudding always collapse?

There are several reasons why this might happen. The bread may not have been dry enough or the syrup not heavy enough; there may have been gaps in the bread lining the basin; or perhaps the pudding was not weighted down properly or thoroughly chilled. The secrets to making a good summer pudding are relatively simple, and you can

apply them to the party-sized Summer Pudding recipe below.

Use good-quality uncut bread, and buy it two to three days beforehand so it can dry out. Dry bread will absorb the juice from the fruit better and will swell, rather than just become soggy and disintegrate. Cook the fruit just long enough for it to soften yet remain whole. This will ensure you have a lusciously heavy, syrupy juice. Most importantly, make sure that the pudding is really well-weighted down.

Summer pudding

SERVES: 12
PREPARATION TIME: 30-40 minutes, plus 24 hours chilling
COOKING TIME: 15-20 minutes

250g redcurrants, removed from stalks, rinsed and drained
250g blackcurrants, removed from stalks, rinsed and drained
375-500g (1½-2 cups) sugar
Finely grated rind and juice of 1 large orange
250g raspberries
250g loganberries or boysenberries
500g blueberries, rinsed and drained
500g strawberries, halved if large
14-16 thin slices stale white bread, crusts removed

FOR SERVING
500ml fresh or thickened cream
1 tablespoon caster sugar
2-3 tablespoons rosewater
1-2 tablespoons orange flower water

1 Put the red and blackcurrants, the sugar (adding to taste), orange rind and juice into a large stainless-steel saucepan. Stir well, then cover the pan and cook over a moderate heat, stirring frequently, until the sugar has dissolved and the juice begins to flow, about 10-15 minutes.
2 Add the remaining fruits to the pan, stir to mix, then cover and stew for 10-15 minutes until all the fruits are softened, but not broken up. Remove from the heat.

HULLING STRAWBERRIES

Soft fruits such as blackberries, loganberries, boysenberries, raspberries and strawberries are each hulled in the same way.

Gently but firmly, pull the circle of green leaves away from the berry; the white central core, or the hull, of the fruit will come away at the same time. In some varieties, or if the fruit is not very ripe, it may be necessary to remove the core of the berry with the tip of a knife.

3 Cut a round from one of the slices of bread, making it large enough to fit the bottom of a 2 litre pudding basin, and put it in the base of the basin. Then cut the remaining bread slices in half lengthways and line the sides, overlapping the slices and not leaving any gaps. Reserve the rest of the bread for the top.
4 Carefully spoon all the fruit and most of the fruit juice into the lined basin, reserving any leftover juice. Completely cover the surface with the remaining sliced bread, cutting extra slices if necessary.
5 Stand the bowl in a deep dish to catch any juice that may overflow. Cover the top closely with plastic wrap and place a small flat plate on top with some heavy weights. Chill the pudding in the refrigerator for at least 24 hours. Pour any remaining juice into a bowl, cover and chill until needed.
6 Just before serving the pudding, whip the cream lightly with the sugar, rosewater and orange flower water and pour into a serving bowl. Remove the weights and plastic wrap from the pudding. Gently run a palette knife around the side of the pudding to loosen it from the basin, then turn out onto a serving dish.

7 Spoon some of the reserved juice over the pudding to make it glisten and also to colour any pale patches. Pour any remaining juice into a jug and serve with the pudding. Once it has been turned out, serve the pudding immediately, accompanied by the flavoured cream.

VARIATIONS

Substitute some of the berries in this recipe with cherries, sliced peaches or sliced lychees. To make a winter pudding, use tree fruits such as dessert apples, pears and plums flavoured with a little ground cinnamon or allspice, and use slices of wholemeal bread instead of white. Or, use reconstituted dried fruits flavoured with cinnamon to fill a wholemeal bread case.

SUPERIOR GLAZE

Fresh fruit tarts in patisseries look impressive - how do they make the fruit look so shiny?

By glazing the fruit. The easiest glaze is made from jam, ideally the same flavour as the fruit in the tart. This should be heated with a little water, sieved to remove any seeds, stones and skin, then brought to

---

STRINGING CURRANTS

Red, white and blackcurrants can be quickly and easily removed from their stalks using this method.

Taking a few small sprigs at a time, gently comb the prongs of a fork through the stems to push off the currants. The individual fruits will remain intact and unblemished. Alternatively, if you have the time, freeze the currants in a plastic box while still on their stalks; when frozen, shake the box. The currants then separate easily from the stalks.

---

the boil and brushed or spooned over the fruit.

Redcurrant jelly or apricot jam can be used as general-purpose glazes. Alternatively, fruit juice can be thickened with arrowroot to make a clear glaze (see also *Tarts*).

CURRANT AFFAIRS

Fresh currants have a very short season. Can I use anything else?

Red, black and white currants are available for only four weeks, over Christmas. They are also available frozen – use for fruit salad, coulis or the classic summer pudding. Raspberries and blueberries can replace them when they are used fresh.

WILD HARVEST

There are so many mulberries around in the autumn, can you suggest some interesting ways to use them?

Fresh mulberries have a wonderful affinity with other berries, autumn apples, sweet grapes and pears. They are often cooked with these fruits in crumbles, puddings, pies and compotes.

TRUE BLUE

What is the difference between a bilberry and a blueberry?

Bilberries and blueberries are from the same heather family. The bilberry, also known as the blaeberry or whortleberry, is slightly smaller but more flavoursome. It grows in Britain and Scandinavia.

The blueberry is a native of North America. Wild blueberries are usually smaller than cultivated varieties. In Australia, cultivated blueberries are available all year. In recipes, blueberries can be substituted for bilberries.

SAVOURY SOLUTION

Are there any ways to use blackberries in savoury dishes?

Blackberries go well with game birds and in Britain are in season at the same time. The following

---

recipe is for a farmed bird with a similar flavour to game, but if you cannot find guinea fowl, use poussins. The blackberry stuffing makes them succulent.

Guinea fowl with blackberry stuffing and piquant blackberry sauce

SERVES: *4*
PREPARATION TIME: *50-55 minutes*
COOKING TIME: *65-70 minutes*

60 g wild rice
Salt
85 g butter, softened
1 medium onion, finely chopped
2 dessert apples, peeled, cored and
 roughly chopped
2 guinea fowl, each about 1 kg
125 g blackberries, hulled
4 tablespoons chopped fresh parsley
Salt and black pepper
To garnish: washed blackberries
 and blackberry leaves, optional

FOR THE SAUCE
250 g blackberries, hulled
100 ml red wine
1 tablespoon plain flour
250 ml chicken stock
1 tablespoon dark brown sugar
2 tablespoons blackberry or
 raspberry vinegar
Salt and black pepper

1 Cook the wild rice in some gently boiling salted water for about 45-50 minutes, or until it is cooked.
2 Meanwhile, heat 25 g of the softened butter in a frying pan; add the chopped onion and cook over a gentle heat for 5 minutes, until it is softened but not browned.
3 Stir the apples into the onion and continue cooking for 5-10 minutes until the apples are just softened. Remove the pan from the heat and allow the mixture to cool.
4 Preheat the oven to 200°C. Rinse inside the cavities of the guinea fowl and pat them dry with paper towels.
5 When the rice is cooked, tip it into a sieve, rinse under a cold tap and drain well. Add the rice, the blackberries and the parsley to the onion and apple mixture, season with salt and pepper and mix well.

A colourful stuffing of wild rice, blackberries and parsley matches perfectly the gamy flavour of guinea fowl.

6 Fill the cavity of each guinea fowl with the blackberry stuffing. Fold the front neck skin over the opening; secure by folding the wings behind the birds; tie the legs together with kitchen string and put them in a baking dish. Spread the remaining butter evenly over each bird, season with salt and pepper and roast in the centre of the oven for 60 minutes, basting every 15 minutes or so until cooked; they are done when the juices run clear from a skewer piercing the thickest part of the thigh.

7 While the guinea fowl are in the oven roasting, put the blackberries for the sauce into a stainless-steel or enamel saucepan with half the wine. Cover and cook for 10–15 minutes or until they are very soft, then pass them through a nylon sieve to make a purée and set aside until needed.

8 Lift the cooked guinea fowl from the baking dish and put them onto a heated serving plate. Cover loosely with foil and leave to rest.

9 To make the fruit sauce, skim all but 2 tablespoons of the fat from the surface of the juices in the baking dish. Stir the flour into the juices, then add the remaining red wine and chicken stock. Bring to the boil, stirring and scraping any browned residue from the bottom of the tin.

10 Strain the gravy mixture into a saucepan then stir in the blackberry purée, the brown sugar, and the blackberry or raspberry vinegar. Season it well and simmer gently, stirring frequently, for 10 minutes. Taste the sauce and add more sugar if necessary. Pour the finished sauce into a heated serving jug.

11 Remove the trussing string from the guinea fowl, then garnish with blackberry leaves and blackberries. Serve with the sauce. Baby carrots, green beans, broccoli and new potatoes are good accompaniments.

SWEET CROSSES

Which are the sweeter fruits, boysenberries or loganberries?

Both of these berries are crosses between a blackberry and a raspberry, but usually boysenberries can be a little sweeter than loganberries. However, as with any fruit, the sweetness will vary.

AMERICAN NATIVE

I have a recipe for cranberry muffins that I would like to try, but I haven't been able to buy fresh cranberries. Are they available in Australia?

Unfortunately, no. The cranberry is a tart berry native to North America, and as yet, it is not available in Australia. However, frozen cranberries are available, and they can be used after thawing, and draining well on paper towels.

Biscuits

AVOIDING BURNT EDGES

Why do my biscuits always burn?

Oven temperatures do vary. If you think your oven may be slightly too hot, check the heat by using an oven thermometer (see *Ovens*). An extra minute or two can be crucial when you are baking thin biscuits, and you may find you need to use a slightly lower setting than the one indicated. Avoid the temptation to overcook. Cooked biscuits may seem soft when they have just come out of the oven, but they will be firm and crisp when cool. These popular biscuits (below) are less likely to burn than more fragile recipes, and they make good healthy treats for lunch boxes.

Anzac biscuits

MAKES: *about 48*
PREPARATION TIME: *20 minutes*
COOKING TIME: *15-20 minutes per batch (or 1-1 hour 20 minutes for the four batches)*

---

125 g unsalted butter, plus extra for greasing the baking trays
1 tablespoon golden syrup
125 g (1 cup) plain flour
100 g (1 cup) rolled oats
90 g (1 cup) desiccated coconut
185 g (³⁄₄ cup) caster sugar
1 teaspoon bicarbonate of soda
2 tablespoons boiling water

---

1 Preheat the oven to 180°C, and use the extra butter to grease four baking trays.
2 Melt the rest of the butter and the golden syrup gently in a pan. Remove it from the heat.
3 Sift the flour into a large mixing bowl, and then stir in the oats, coconut and sugar.
4 Blend the bicarbonate of soda with the boiling water and add it to the butter mixture.
5 Pour the melted butter mixture into the flour mixture and stir well until evenly combined.

6 Using a metal teaspoon, place heaped spoonsful of mixture on the baking trays, 5 cm apart.
7 Bake for 15-20 minutes or until golden brown. Cool for 2 minutes on the tray, then use a palette knife to transfer the biscuits to a wire rack until cold. Store in an airtight tin.

DIFFICULT DECISION

What biscuits should I use for a crumb crust for a cheesecake?

Plain sweet wholemeal biscuits are the best choice for making crumb crusts. Look for the granita variety, as their texture combines well with melted butter to give a firm base.

If a recipe calls for a chocolate crumb, use chocolate-flavoured biscuits, not chocolate coated.

KEEPING IN SHAPE

Why do my biscuits spread all over the tray, even though I am careful to spoon out only very small quantities of the mixture?

While some types of biscuits, such as brandy snaps, are meant to spread, others should hold their shape during cooking. Be sure to measure the ingredients accurately. Fat and sugar melt during cooking, and using too much of either will cause the biscuits to spread and merge into one another. Leave a space between each portion, about 7.5 cm, to allow room for some widening. This allows each biscuit to keep its shape.

Check that you are using the type of fat that is recommended. If a recipe uses butter and you want to use margarine, choose a type that is suitable for cooking. Firm packet or block margarine is better for biscuit mixtures than a softer tub margarine meant for spreading.

The recipe given for Refrigerator Biscuits (right) avoids the problem of spreading by including a large amount of flour to fat. This helps the biscuits to retain their shape well. The dough will keep in the refrigerator for up to a week (so you can slice and cook fresh biscuits when needed), or it can be

frozen for up to two months. Defrost it at room temperature for 15 minutes, then slice and bake.

Sugar and spice refrigerator biscuits

MAKES: *about 24*
PREPARATION TIME: *20 minutes plus 2 hours chilling*
COOKING TIME: *8-10 minutes per batch (or 16-20 minutes for the full three batches)*

---

125 g unsalted butter, chilled and diced, plus extra for greasing the baking trays
250 g (2 cups) plain flour
1 teaspoon baking powder
3 teaspoons ground mixed spice
185 g (1 cup) dark brown sugar
1 large egg, lightly beaten
2 tablespoons coffee crystal sugar

---

1 Grease two baking trays with butter. Sift together the flour, baking powder and mixed spice onto a sheet of greaseproof paper. Tip into the bowl of a food processor.
2 Add the butter and mix for 1 minute, or until the mixture resembles fine breadcrumbs.
3 Add the sugar and egg, and mix for 30 seconds, or until a soft pliable dough has formed.
4 Roll the mixture on a lightly floured surface to a 30 cm long, smooth sausage shape.
5 Divide the roll in half. Wrap each roll in plastic wrap or foil and chill in the refrigerator for 2 hours.
6 Preheat the oven to 190°C.
7 Cut each roll into about 12 rounds and place on the baking trays, spaced well apart. Sprinkle coffee sugar over each biscuit.
8 Bake for 8-10 minutes, or until light brown. Leave to cool slightly, then transfer to a wire rack and leave until cold.
9 Store in an airtight tin.

Sweet solution

Putting a few sugar cubes in your biscuit tins helps to keep biscuits crisp and fresh for much longer.

Blanching

RETAINING THE COLOUR

What is the point of going to the trouble of blanching vegetables?

Blanching and refreshing is a method of cooking vegetables for 1–2 minutes in boiling water and then cooling them rapidly in iced water. It is chiefly done to set the colour before they are added to another dish, such as a terrine or salad. This method is particularly suitable for green vegetables, such as green beans, as their colour survives and becomes very intense.

Blanching is also used to precook a large quantity of vegetables, as they can be boiled in advance until nearly tender, refreshed and chilled, and swiftly reheated when wanted.

The term comes from the French word for whiten and the technique was originally used to remove traces of blood from sweetbreads or brains, leaving them pale, or to boil off the brown skin of almonds.

VITAMIN LOSS

Do you lose many vitamins by blanching vegetables and then reheating them?

If you blanch and refresh the vegetables rapidly, and also reheat them very quickly, the vitamin loss will only be slight. However, certain vitamins, such as vitamin C, are water-soluble and will leach out during any water-based cooking process, so it is wise to eat raw vegetables on a regular basis, as well as cooked ones.

Boiling

SLOW TO FAST BOIL

What is the difference between boiling, poaching and simmering?

The three words all refer to cooking in liquid on top of the stove, but the temperatures are different.

Many dishes described as boiled are in fact poached or simmered.

When water is heated up just enough to 'shiver' at about 82°C, it is perfect for poaching fish and other delicate foods that would otherwise break up.

A gentle simmer at 85–93°C produces liquid that hardly moves except for occasional bubbles in the same place (ideal for cooking joints of meat and whole birds).

A true boil is used for the quick cooking of vegetables, rice and pasta, and some cereals. A gentle boil is used to reduce liquids when making jams and sauces.

BOILING MEAT OR FISH

Are boiled beef and other similar dishes really boiled?

When a recipe refers to boiled beef, fish or chicken, it really means it should be simmered: any meat or fish subjected to fast boiling would become tough and flavourless.

Unlike braising and stewing, the cooking liquid used in boiled meats is not generally part of the finished dish, but it is often used to make the sauce (with chicken) or used as a stock (corned beef or ham). Bacon stock can be used as the basis for a delicious pea soup.

PRESERVING NUTRIENTS

I have read that boiling is not the best way to cook vegetables. If this is true, what are the alternatives?

Boiling often results in a considerable loss of nutritional value, as many vitamins are lost if the cooking water is discarded. Vegetables cooked for only a few minutes will retain more vitamins than vegetables boiled for longer. It takes no more time to steam vegetables, and this method retains more of their nutritional goodness and flavour.

The best equipment for steaming is a bamboo or metal steamer, or a collapsible steamer that can be put inside a saucepan. Bring the water to a rolling boil (with bubbles all over), and then add the vegetables, spread out in a single layer. The

> ### Skimming the surface
>
> When simmering meat, add a spoonful of cold water to the pan every now and then to encourage the impurities to rise. When the liquid comes to a boil again, take the pan off the heat and skim off any scum with a metal spoon.

rack should be about 2.5 cm above the boiling water and the steamer should be covered with a tightly fitting lid to retain the heat.

COOKING ROOTS

Should root vegetables be boiled more fiercely than leaf vegetables?

Root vegetables such as potatoes should be covered with cold unsalted water and boiled to cook them through. Green leaf vegetables should be plunged into a large quantity of salted boiling water and cooked quickly to keep their colour, taste and nutrients.

PARBOILING METHOD

What is parboiling and what are the advantages of this?

Parboiling means partly boiling vegetables so that further cooking produces the right finished result. It is similar to blanching, but the vegetables are cooked longer (for 10 minutes rather than one or two).

For example, vegetables that will be roasted are often parboiled first to ensure they are fully cooked inside when golden outside.

ADDING SALT

When boiling vegetables, should salt be added before or after the water comes to the boil?

Salt water boils at a lower temperature than plain water so the water will come to the boil faster if you add the salt at the start. But you do not have to add salt at all. Try reducing the amount you use, or leaving it out altogether, to get a taste for healthier vegetables.

Boning

ADVANTAGES OF BONING

I sometimes see recipes that call for boned poultry or joints. As it seems to take a great deal of time and effort, is it really worth it?

The great advantage of boned meat or poultry is first that it is much easier to carve and second that it goes much farther. For example, a 1.5 kg chicken with stuffing will serve six to eight people. When you are catering for large numbers, boned poultry is especially useful.

Although boning poultry for the first time can be daunting, it becomes much easier with practice (see box, page 43). And you don't have to do it all at once: if you like, do the boning in stages – just cover the bird loosely with plastic wrap and refrigerate it each time you have a break. People with little experience of boning will probably find it easier and quicker to deal with a leg of lamb, as there are only three large bones to remove (see box, below).

Boning meat or poultry enables you to use delicious stuffing, which keeps the meat moist during cooking. For chicken, try a stuffing of ricotta and Parmesan cheeses, with black olives, basil and pine nuts – all bound together with egg. Or mix pistachio nuts and chopped dried apricots with chicken livers and fresh white breadcrumbs, also bound together with egg.

Turkey takes particularly well to a sausage-meat stuffing. For a traditional stuffing, add chopped mint, parsley, sage and thyme to the sausage meat. For a spicier version, add caramelised onion, sultanas, a pinch of cayenne pepper and some ground cumin. Duck and goose harmonise well with fruit, and citrus fruit in particular cuts through the fattiness. A small grain, such as burghul or couscous, makes a good stuffing base to which you can add a little orange juice, a few sliced kumquats and ginger, along with some chopped red onion.

A boned leg of lamb can be enriched by an Arabian stuffing of apricots, burghul, nuts and oranges (see *Lamb*).

BUTCHERS' SERVICE

Can I ask a butcher to do the boning for me?

Yes. Boneless roasts such as Easy Carve leg and Trim lamb roasts and boneless Lean beef roasts are readily available. If you are a regular customer and give a few days' notice, your butcher may bone a chicken for you too.

BONING A LEG OF LAMB

Boning a leg of lamb enables you to add a stuffing, which will give the meat extra flavour and succulence, and makes it very easy to carve. Or you can lay it flat under the grill or on a barbecue, skin side nearest the heat, where it will cook in just 15 minutes, being turned once. To ensure a neat, easy job, use a narrow, rigid boning knife.

1 There are three bones to remove: the shank bone, which juts out of the meat at the narrow end; the middle bone, which is attached to the shank bone by a ball and socket joint; and the V-shaped pelvic bone, which turns across the thick end of the joint.

2 Lay the leg fleshy side down. Start at the shank end and, holding the knife like a dagger, cut through the flesh down to the shank bone beneath. Change your grip to the normal one and cut along the bone, keeping the knife as close to the bone as possible, so as not to waste any of the meat.

3 Scrape round the ball and socket joint then cut along the middle and pelvic bones. Use your fingers to locate each bone in turn and work from both ends of the leg if you find it easier. Gradually ease the bones out, one by one. The boned meat is now ready to be stuffed, rolled and tied up for roasting.

4 To open the boned meat out flat for grilling (known as butterfly boning), make two further parallel cuts through the thick pieces of meat on either side of the space left by the middle bone. Beat the meat once or twice with a wooden mallet to even out the thickness, then grill or barbecue.

BONING CHICKEN

You can bone all poultry by the same method, bearing in mind that the carcass of a turkey is very much larger than that of a chicken. Essential tools for the job are a sharp kitchen knife and kitchen scissors.

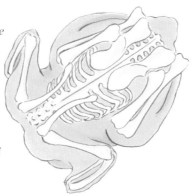

1 Put the chicken breast side down and cut through to the backbone. Feel for the fleshy 'oyster' at the top of each thigh and cut round it to remove it from its pocket, then gently scrape the flesh away from the carcass.

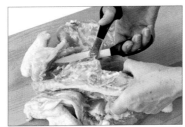

2 Continue cutting away from the backbone until the whole rib cage is exposed. Where the thigh meets the pelvis, cut through the sockets so that the legs stay attached to the body flesh and skin, not to the carcass.

3 Keep working right round the bird, then use scissors to cut off most of the rib cage, leaving only the breastbone in the centre. With a heavy knife, cut through the foot joints to remove the knuckle end of the legs.

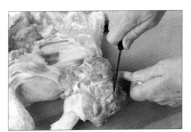

4 Working from inside the top of the thigh, scrape the leg bone clean, pushing the flesh down until you can free the bone. Remove the tendons, then bone the other leg.

5 Now for the wings. Cut off the pinions (the last small bone on the wing which has no real meat) with a heavy knife and scrape the wing bones clean as you did the leg bones.

6 Carefully lift up and scrape the breastbone free, working from the middle of the bird towards the tail. Take care not to puncture the skin, as there is no flesh under it at this point.

7 Keep the neck flap of skin intact, and fold it over once the chicken has been stuffed. Seal as much of the stuffing as possible, then sew up the bird or wrap it in a roasting net.

TRUSSING AND TYING

How do I tie up a boned bird?

There are two ways. In the first, you sew up a stuffed and rolled bird using a trussing needle and string, sewing across one end first, down the length of the roll and then across the other end.

Alternatively, you can fold the bird into shape around the stuffing then wrap it in a piece of muslin or a roasting net. First dip the cloth in melted butter or oil and wring out lightly. Put the stuffed bird in the centre of the cloth, flap side uppermost, then wrap the cloth around it tightly, securing it at both ends with string like a Christmas cracker.

The cooking time should be calculated according to the bird's weight after it has been stuffed, using the table in **Roasting**. Be sure it is fully cooked through, particularly if you have used a sausage-meat stuffing. Check by inserting a skewer into the centre of the joint – the juices should run clear.

If you have wrapped the bird in muslin there is no need to baste it during cooking – but remove the cloth before the bird is completely cold or it will stick.

Braising

GENTLE COOKING

What is the difference between braising and stewing?

Braising is a method of slowly cooking meat, game birds and poultry in a heavy-based covered pan or covered casserole, using a bed of chopped vegetables, which can also include some diced ham or bacon added for flavour. Water or stock should be added to come halfway up the joint.

Braising tends to use a slightly better cut of meat than stewing and a whole cut is generally chosen. The meat is usually fried briefly to brown it first, then placed in a pan or casserole with a tight-fitting lid and cooked either on the stove or in the oven. It cooks gently in its own juices and the steam from the vegetables, which impart flavour.

The term 'braising' is also used sometimes to mean cooking vegetables in the oven in a covered dish with a little liquid. For example, heads of celery are braised in vegetable or chicken stock.

Stewing is a method in which the added liquid (beer, cider, stock, water or wine) covers the meat and is heated to just under boiling point. This technique is reserved for the toughest cuts of meat which need long, slow cooking, and the meat is generally cut into chunks to aid the tenderising process.

Leftovers

When braising meat, chop any leftover bones, such as those from a chicken carcass, and add them to the bed of chopped vegetables. The bones and vegetables are discarded after cooking, but they add extra flavour to the braising liquid and to the meat.

RICH STOCK

Does braising meat create its own stock, or should I add some stock or alcohol for richness?

Braising meat produces a delicious, full-flavoured stock whether you use just water or add stock or alcohol. For a simple family meal, water flavoured with vegetables, herbs and black peppercorns produces a sufficiently well-flavoured dish. However, the addition of stock and/or wine enriches the taste and gives added flavour.

For a really elegant braised dish, set aside the cooked meat and keep it warm, then strain the stock, discarding the vegetables, and reduce it by rapid boiling to a syrupy consistency. Glaze the meat with the reduced sauce and serve with other freshly cooked vegetables.

BEST FOR BRAISING

Which are the best ingredients to use for braising?

Tougher cuts of meat, such as beef flank and older game birds, are ideal candidates for braising. They are often marinated in the braising liquid first to start the tenderising process and then cooked in a slow oven at 140°C with vegetables and herbs to add flavour. The traditional vegetables are leek or onion, carrot and celery.

Some other wonderful combinations are shin of beef with Spanish onions and thyme, or with onions, paprika and tomato purée. Venison is a very low-fat meat and is often braised to keep it moist. It is very tasty marinated and braised in red wine flavoured with garlic, juniper berries and orange peel. Pheasant is excellent braised in a mixture of chicken stock and white wine, with apples and celery.

Braising is also useful for vegetables with tough membranes which are then broken down by slow, moist cooking. Celery, for instance, is transformed into a mild aromatic dish when braised in stock and butter. Other vegetables that benefit from braising are fennel (delicious with olive oil and vermouth); artichoke hearts in beef stock with butter, thyme and a splash of red wine; leeks with butter and lemon juice; and chicory with chicken stock, butter and lemon juice.

Bran

RICH IN FIBRE

What exactly is bran?

Bran is the husk, or outer layer, of all cereals, although wheat bran is the most common bran sold commercially. Bran is usually separated from the grain during the milling process of flour production. It is a valuable source of fibre and is an added ingredient in many breakfast cereals. It is also sold simply as bran, which can be used to enrich

breads, muffins and tea breads, or it can be toasted and used in muesli. In the recipe below, bran and seeds are toasted and mixed with dried fruits and oats to produce a muesli that is less sweet than most commercial brands.

Homemade muesli

MAKES: *8–10 breakfast portions*
PREPARATION TIME: *5 minutes*
COOKING TIME: *10–12 minutes*

---

50 g (½ cup) wheat bran
50 g (2 tablespoons) sunflower
  seeds
25 g (1 tablespoon) poppy seeds
125 g (1 cup) hazelnuts, finely
  chopped
250 g (1⅓ cups) mixed dried fruits,
  such as apricots, cherries, figs,
  raisins and sultanas
125 g (1¾ cups) dried banana chips
250 g (2½ cups) rolled oats
125 g (1¼ cups) barley flakes
2 teaspoons ground cinnamon
To serve: milk, fresh fruits and
  brown sugar, optional

---

1 Dry-fry the bran, sunflower seeds and poppy seeds together in a large nonstick frying pan for 3–4 minutes or until they become golden and start to release their aroma. Transfer them to a large bowl.
2 Dry-fry the chopped hazelnuts for 5–6 minutes until browned. Add to the bran and leave to cool.
3 Cut the larger of the dried fruits into small chunks and stir them into the toasted mixture along with the oats, barley flakes and cinnamon. Transfer to an airtight container.
4 Serve the muesli as you wish with milk, chopped fresh fruits and a sprinkling of brown sugar.

OFF THE SHELF

Where can I buy bran?

Nowadays, many of the large supermarkets sell packets of bran, and they are normally found near the breakfast cereals. You can also buy bran in most good health food shops. It keeps well in its sealed packet or an airtight container, in a cool place, for up to three months.

A dash of cinnamon, a scattering of seeds and nuts, and fresh and dried fruit add life to a homemade muesli.

Brandy Butter

COUNTING KILOJOULES

Which is more fattening with my Christmas pudding, brandy butter or thick cream?

It is hard to say which is the more fattening of the two, since a typical recipe for brandy butter contains less fat than thick cream, but more kilojoules, because it has quite a high sugar content.

In a recipe such as the one to the right, 1 tablespoon brandy butter contains 6.1 g of fat and 381 kilojoules, whereas 1 tablespoon thick cream (48% fat) contains margin-ally more fat but only 280 kilojoules. You could always substitute a reduced-fat margarine spread for butter when you are preparing brandy butter, but that would be defeating the purpose of this rich indulgence. If you enjoy such luxuries in small amounts, and only on special occasions, it is probably best to let your tastebuds decide which is preferable.

Brandy butter

SERVES: 6–8 (makes about 10 tablespoons)
PREPARATION TIME: 20 minutes
COOKING TIME: none

125 g unsalted butter, softened
125 g (½ cup) caster sugar
2–3 tablespoons brandy

1 Using a wooden spoon, beat the butter until it is white and creamy.

2 Add the sugar a little at a time, beating well after each addition, until it has all been incorporated.
3 Gradually beat in the brandy, adding a few drops at a time only and being careful not to allow the mixture to curdle.
4 Put the brandy butter in a suitable dish, cover with plastic wrap and chill for 2–3 hours before serving.
VARIATIONS
If you prefer a smoother texture, use sifted icing sugar. For a darker brandy butter, use dark brown sugar instead of caster sugar.

For a change of flavour, add 50 g (⅓ cup) ground almonds to the brandy butter before chilling, or 1 tablespoon very finely chopped preserved stem ginger.

Or use a different alcohol, such as rum (perhaps with a dash of lemon juice) or whisky, with dark brown sugar instead of caster sugar.

Brandy Snaps

BE PREPARED

I love brandy snaps but they look very complicated and I have never summoned up the courage to make them. Is it difficult?

You don't need to be brave, but you do need to concentrate and be well prepared. Measure the ingredients accurately and, when melting the mixture, take care that it does not become too hot.

Line the metal baking trays with nonstick baking paper and leave plenty of space around each spoonful of the mixture on the sheet to allow for spreading. The biscuits should be about 7.5 cm apart.

Cook no more than two trays at a time, or some biscuits may become too firm before you are ready to roll them into shape. If this should happen, simply return the tray to the oven for a few seconds to let them soften, then roll up.

Be sure to have several wooden spoons and a few wire racks to hand so that you can cope very quickly with rolling and cooling.

The recipe (right) makes crisp and delicate biscuits which go well with creamy desserts like syllabub or ice cream. Alternatively, simply fill them with cream or fruit.

Brandy snaps

MAKES: about 30
PREPARATION TIME: 35-40 minutes
COOKING TIME: 8-10 minutes for each batch

---

60 g unsalted butter, plus extra for greasing
60 g (½ cup) plain flour, sifted
1 teaspoon ground ginger
60 g (¼ cup) caster sugar
3 tablespoons golden syrup
1 tablespoon brandy or lemon juice
150 ml fresh or thickened cream, whipped, optional

---

1 Lightly grease two baking trays and line with nonstick baking paper.
2 Preheat the oven to 180°C and be sure you have at least four wooden spoons to hand for rolling the biscuits round later.
3 Sift the flour and ground ginger into a small bowl.
4 Gently warm the butter, sugar and syrup in a small pan until the butter has melted. Remove from the heat and add the spiced flour and brandy or lemon juice. Stir until smooth.
5 Spoon level metal teaspoonsful of mixture onto the baking trays, spaced well apart as the mixture will spread. (Try about 4 teaspoons per baking tray for the first batch and see how much room is needed.)
6 Bake for 8-10 minutes until the brandy snaps have spread and are golden brown. Remove the trays

from the oven. Leave the biscuits to cool for a minute or two, then gently loosen them with a palette knife. They should be firm but pliable.
7 Using both hands, roll the biscuits neatly but not too tightly around the handles of the wooden spoons. Place them on a wire rack and leave them to set for 1-2 minutes.
8 As soon as one has set, slide it off the spoon and leave it until cold and crisp. Store the brandy snaps in an airtight tin, layered between sheets of baking paper, for up to four days.
9 Before serving, put whipped cream into a piping bag fitted with a 1 cm star nozzle. Pipe whirls of soft cream into the ends.

Bread

FRESH OR NOT?

Why should bread a few days old be used for summer pudding and bread-and-butter pudding?

Fresh bread loses both shape and texture when it is moistened by a sauce, while bread that is a day or two old will absorb moisture and still retain its shape. Stale bread is also preferable for french toast, since its firm shape makes it easier to crisp the outside when it is fried.

USE YOUR FIST

What does the term 'knocking back' bread dough mean?

It is the term used for punching the dough with the fist when it has risen to twice its original size. The punch helps to disperse the bubbles that are produced by the yeast throughout the dough.

PROVING IN A MICROWAVE

When making bread, is it possible to speed up the proving/rising by using a microwave oven?

Yes, dough can be risen in a microwave oven. Once the dough is kneaded, place it in an ungreased bowl and cover it with lightly oiled plastic wrap. Put the bowl in the

---

ROLLING BRANDY SNAPS

Use a palette knife to separate the baked brandy snaps from the metal trays. With careful handling, the biscuits should shape easily around the handles of wooden spoons. Gently slide them off the handles when they are formed.

1 Loosen the brandy snaps from the baking tray and roll them around the wooden spoon handles.

2 Remove the handles after a few minutes, when the biscuits are firm. Put the biscuits on a wire rack.

oven and heat on High for 10 seconds, then leave the bowl to stand for 20 minutes in the microwave or in a warm place, by which time the dough should have doubled in size. If it has not risen sufficiently, heat it on High for another 10 seconds, then stand for a further 10 minutes.

For the second rise, remember you cannot use a metal loaf tin in the microwave. If you have a nonmetallic tin, place the dough in it, microwave on High for 10 seconds, then let it stand for just 5 minutes. Continue with the recipe as usual after proving.

A CHOICE OF YEASTS

Does it make any difference whether you use fresh yeast or dried yeast in breadmaking?

There is little difference between the results achieved by using dried or fresh yeast. However, dried yeast is almost twice as concentrated as fresh, so in a recipe calling for 30 g fresh yeast, use no more than 15 g dried yeast. Instant rapid-rise yeast is even more concentrated (see box, page 48).

You will find that using a bit less yeast and leaving dough to prove longer produces a better-tasting and longer-lasting loaf. Any yeast can be used for the following recipe.

Freshly baked bread smells and tastes wonderful, and it need not take too much time or forward planning. You can use any type of yeast to make this white loaf.

Classic white loaf

MAKES: 2 small loaves
PREPARATION TIME: 25 minutes, plus 2–4 hours rising time
COOKING TIME: 40 minutes

---

15 g fresh yeast, or
   2 teaspoons dried yeast plus
   1 teaspoon sugar, or 1 sachet
   instant rapid-rise yeast
300 ml lukewarm water
500 g (4 cups) strong plain flour
2 teaspoons salt
15 g butter or lard
To glaze: a pinch of salt mixed with
   a little water

---

1 Blend the fresh yeast in the warm water. If using dried yeast, dissolve the sugar in the warm water first, then sprinkle in the dried yeast and set aside for 15 minutes until it is frothy. If using instant rapid-rise yeast, add it directly to the flour.
2 Sieve the flour and salt into a large mixing bowl and rub in the butter. Pour the yeast mixture, or the lukewarm water if using instant rapid-rise yeast, into the centre. Stir to form a dough, then knead with your hands until the dough gathers and leaves the side of the bowl.
3 Turn it out onto a floured surface and knead for 10 minutes or until the dough is firm, not sticky.
4 Put the dough back into the bowl, cover with oiled plastic wrap and leave in a warm place for 1–2 hours until doubled in volume.
5 Punch the raised dough down and knead well again. Grease two 500 g loaf tins. Divide the dough in two and roll each portion lightly into a loaf shape to fit in the tin.
6 Place the dough, seam side down, in the prepared tins. Cover the tins loosely with plastic wrap and leave for about 40 minutes at room temperature for the bread to rise.
7 Preheat the oven to 230°C. When the bread has risen, brush the top with some salted water, then bake for 35 minutes.
8 The loaves should have shrunk from the sides of the tins and if you remove them carefully, they should sound hollow when tapped on the base. If they do not sound hollow, return them to the tins and cook for just a few minutes more.
9 When the loaves are done, take them out of their tins and place on a wire rack to cool completely.

USING YEAST

Bread needs yeast to make it rise. While fresh yeast is both quick and easy to use, it may be difficult to find (try either health food shops or bakers' supplies stores).

Plain dried yeast and instant rapid-rise yeast can be bought in most supermarkets, and these can be used instead of the fresh variety. The quantities given below raise 500 g (4 cups) flour, which is enough to make two small loaves.

FRESH YEAST

To cream fresh yeast, combine 15 g of the yeast with the recipe's tepid (not hot) water in a bowl. Mash well with a fork until a very smooth paste is formed.

DRIED YEAST

To reactivate dried yeast, dissolve a teaspoon of sugar in the recipe's lukewarm water, then sprinkle over 2 teaspoons of the yeast and let it stand for 10-15 minutes until it is frothy. Stir the mixture well so it becomes a smooth paste.

INSTANT RAPID-RISE YEAST

Instant rapid-rise dried yeast is quick to use because it is added straight into the flour, and there is no need to mix it first with water. The instant rapid-rise variety comes in small sachets of 10 g and one is equivalent to 15-25 g fresh yeast or 2 teaspoons dried yeast. Check the instructions before you mix.

STORING YEAST

How long does yeast keep?

Fresh yeast will keep for up to two weeks in a plastic storage box in the refrigerator. The box should have a tight lid in which you have made a few small air holes. There should be enough holes to prevent any condensation, but not so many as to overexpose the yeast to air.

The yeast should be a creamy beige, smooth and in one piece. Yeast that is dry, crumbled and grey is stale and will not work.

Dried and instant rapid-rise yeast should be stored in a cool, dry place. They will keep almost indefinitely, but try to observe the 'use-by' date on the packet. If you use it after the expiry date, check that the yeast foams after it has dissolved. If it does not, the bread will not rise properly.

EASY MIXING

Is there a labour-saving way of making bread if you do not have a mixer with a dough hook?

A food processor will mix the bread ingredients together and will also form them into a ball so that considerably less kneading will be required. Bread that is made with wholemeal flour is much less work to produce because it has a low gluten content. It needs only a little kneading and then just one rising in the tin before being baked.

A computer-controlled electric bread-making machine is the ultimate labour-saving choice.

FRENCH COPY

Could I make French bread?

It is very difficult to make a good homemade baguette as it needs a special steam oven.

KEEPING MELBA TOAST

How long can I keep Melba toast in a tin before it goes soft?

If the tin is airtight, crispy Melba toast can be kept for a few weeks before it will taste stale. If it goes

soft, it can be made crisp again by heating it briefly in a hot oven.

You can make Melba toast using ordinary sliced white bread. Toast the slices, cut off the crusts, and use a very sharp thin knife to cut each slice open and separate it into two thinner slices. Toast the inner slices under a grill, and leave the bread to cool. Store in an airtight tin.

REACTIVE BUTTERMILK

Why is buttermilk an essential ingredient of soda bread?

Buttermilk is high in lactic acid, and when mixed with bicarbonate of soda, which is an alkali, the chemical reaction that results produces the gas carbon dioxide. This has the effect of aerating the dough and making it much lighter. Sour cream can be substituted for buttermilk, as it is also acidic.

SOURDOUGH STARTER

What is fermented dough starter?

It is a thick mixture of 15 g dried yeast, 600 ml water and 250 g flour which is covered tightly and left at room temperature for about three days to develop sourdough flavour. Half the blend is used to leaven bread.

The remaining half of the initial dough starter can be replenished by adding equal parts of flour and water, and half of it is used again after 24 hours when it has risen and become bubbly. Using dough starter gives bread more flavour.

CRISPY SNACKS

What is the difference between bruschetta and crostini?

Bruschetta is the Italian version of garlic bread. Slices are grilled, then rubbed with garlic, dribbled with olive oil and sprinkled with salt. These slices are often topped with roasted peppers, cheese or cold meats (see page 243).

Crostini are simply small rounds of grilled bread, used as a base for spreads made with chicken livers or other ingredients (see page 13).

USING BREADCRUMBS

When should you use different types of breadcrumbs?

Dried white breadcrumbs are used for coating foods such as rissoles, veal or fish before frying. Use day-old bread from a country-style loaf, remove the crusts and place slices in one layer on a baking tray. Bake at 120°C for 15–20 minutes until the bread is dry, but do not allow it to colour.

Alternatively, you can leave the slices in a warm place for one to two days, covered with paper towels, until they are dry. Crush the dried crumbs with a rolling pin, or in a food processor.

Browned, dried breadcrumbs are used for covering ham and for gratins. It is best to use crusts from country-style bread and dry them at 120°C for about 30 minutes until they just begin to take on colour, then crush with a rolling pin or in a food processor.

Fresh white breadcrumbs are preferred for thickening sauces, for stuffings and bread sauce – and for adding to desserts such as treacle tart. Use day-old, rather than just-baked bread, and cut the crusts off. Either rub the pieces through a sieve with your palm, or make crumbs in a food processor.

Fresh breadcrumbs can be stored in the freezer; thaw before use.

TASTY WHOLEMEAL

I find that the wholemeal bread I make is often rather dry and unappetising. Is there a way of giving it a more interesting taste?

Wholemeal flour tends to make heavier bread than white, so if you mix a little white flour into a wholemeal recipe, the bread will be lighter. Ground nuts also lighten the texture and add moisture.

The recipe for Walnut Bread (right) uses plenty of water and honey, which produces a very rich, moist, appetising loaf that makes a great partner for cheese. For the maximum flavour, use the freshest walnuts that you can find.

Roughly chopped fresh walnuts add a crunchier texture to a simple wholemeal loaf, while a tablespoon of honey keeps the consistency light and moist.

Walnut bread

MAKES: *2 small loaves*
PREPARATION TIME: *20-30 minutes, plus 2-3 hours rising time*
COOKING TIME: *45 minutes*

---

15 g fresh yeast, or
  2 teaspoons dried yeast plus
  1 teaspoon sugar, or 1 sachet
  instant rapid-rise dried yeast
500 ml lukewarm water
1 tablespoon honey
375 g (3 cups) wholemeal flour
185 g (1½ cups) strong white flour
2 teaspoons salt
Butter for greasing
125 g (1 cup) walnuts, finely
  chopped
To glaze: 1 egg, beaten with
  ½ teaspoon salt

---

1 Dissolve the fresh or dried yeast in water and honey. Add instant rapid-rise dried yeast directly to the flour.
2 Sieve the flours and salt into a bowl. Make a well in the centre and add the yeasty water or plain water if using instant rapid-rise yeast.
3 Stir with a wooden spoon to form a dough, adding a little more flour if the dough seems too moist, but keep it all as loose as you can possibly handle. This will make the final loaf that much lighter.
4 Turn out onto a floured board and knead for 10 minutes, flouring your hands if necessary, until the dough is smooth and elastic.
5 Lightly grease a bowl, put in the dough and cover with lightly oiled plastic wrap. Leave to rise in a warm place for about 1½-2 hours.
6 Grease two 18 cm round cake tins. Punch the dough down and knead in the walnuts. Divide the dough in two and place each portion in a tin. Cover with plastic wrap, allowing space for the bread to rise, and leave for about an hour until the dough has doubled in size.
7 Preheat the oven to 220°C.
8 Slash the top of each loaf a few times with a sharp knife and brush with the egg glaze.
9 Bake the loaves for 15 minutes, then lower the heat to 190°C and bake for a further 30 minutes. Turn out onto a rack to cool.

HOMEMADE FOCACCIA

My family like the Italian breads ciabatta and focaccia. I would like to be able to bake them myself. Are they easy to make?

Ciabatta is hard to reproduce at home as the dough has to be very soft, and it requires a special steam oven to achieve its airy texture. Focaccia bread, which is also made with olive oil, has a denser texture and is easier to bake at home – try the following recipe.

Virgin olive oil gives focaccia its rich flavour. The taste is sharpened and enhanced by the aroma of fresh sage.

Focaccia

MAKES: *1 loaf*
PREPARATION TIME: *25–35 minutes, plus 2–2½ hours proving time*
COOKING TIME: *35 minutes*

15 g fresh yeast, or
    2 teaspoons dried yeast plus
    1 teaspoon sugar, or 1 sachet
    instant rapid-rise dried yeast
300 ml lukewarm water
500 g (4 cups) plain or strong
    flour, or half of each
2 teaspoons salt
75 ml virgin olive oil
12 fresh sage leaves, chopped

1 Dissolve the yeast in the warm water, adding the sugar if using dried yeast. If using rapid-rise dried yeast, add it directly to flour.
2 Sift the flour and salt into a bowl, make a well and add the yeast water, or the plain water if using rapid-rise dried yeast, and 4 tablespoons of the olive oil. Stir from the centre, gathering up some flour as you stir, until you have a rough dough.

3 Turn the dough out onto a floured surface and knead for 10 minutes until it is smooth and elastic.
4 Place the dough in a lightly oiled bowl, cover with oiled plastic wrap and leave it to rise in a warm place for 1½–2 hours until doubled.
5 Place a heavy baking tray in the centre of the oven to heat, and preheat the oven to 200°C.
6 Punch the dough down and knead it again, this time sprinkling the sage on top and folding it in evenly.
7 On a lightly floured surface, roll the dough out into a circle 30 cm in diameter. Allow the dough to rise slightly for about 30 minutes. Make dimples in the surface and dribble over the remaining oil.
8 Either slide a floured board under the bread and then quickly slide it off onto the hot baking tray, or pick up the dough with your hands and toss it onto the baking tray. Do not worry if the shape is irregular.
9 Bake for about 35 minutes or until the bread has become a deep golden colour, then cool on a rack.

Broccoli

CRISP AND COLOURFUL

How can I cook broccoli so that the florets have not become soggy by the time the stem is tender?

Divide a fresh head of broccoli into biggish florets, and cut each stem into a short, tapering wedge. Thinly slice the centre stalk. Cook all the parts by either steaming or boiling briefly. You can also keep broccoli florets firm and crisp by putting them into a stir-fry.

VARIATIONS ON A THEME

What is the difference between purple and green broccoli?

There are two sorts of broccoli, sprouting broccoli with purple or white heads, and calabrese which has blue-green heads.

Sprouting broccoli is leafier than calabrese and can be served as a starter vegetable in its own right, with mayonnaise. Green broccoli, called calabrese, reflects the vegetable's Italian origins. The cooks of Calabria chop the florets into a pasta mix (see below) made salty-sweet with anchovy sauce or paste and some sultanas. This is topped with crisply fried breadcrumbs.

Calabrian pasta

SERVES: 5-6 as a starter,
3-4 as a main course
PREPARATION TIME: 15 minutes
COOKING TIME: 12-15 minutes

---

50 g (⅓ cup) sultanas
250 g green broccoli
350 g dried tagliatelle or
spaghetti
100 ml olive oil
75 g (1¼ cups) fresh white
breadcrumbs
2 cloves garlic, finely chopped
25 g (2 tablespoons) pine nuts
2 teaspoons anchovy sauce or
anchovy paste
Black pepper
3 tablespoons fresh parsley, chopped
Cayenne pepper

---

1 Leave the sultanas to soak in a cup of boiling water.
2 Slice the thick stem bases of the broccoli diagonally and divide the heads into small florets, each with a wedge of stem attached. Then blanch them in boiling water, cooking for just 30 seconds after the water has come back to the boil. Drain, refresh under the cold tap and leave to drain.
3 Cook the pasta in a large pan of boiling, salted water until al dente (cooked but firm), for about 12–15 minutes. While it is cooking, put a serving bowl in a low oven to warm.
4 Heat the oil in a frying pan and fry the breadcrumbs on medium heat for about 5 minutes until they start to become crispy, then add the garlic and pine nuts. After a minute or two, when the pine nuts begin to colour, add the broccoli and stir over the heat until everything is hot.
5 Drain the pasta, and then set the colander quickly back on top of the saucepan. This will catch the last of the water and help to keep the pasta warm and moist.

Dark-green calabrese makes a fine contrast to pale spaghetti, and goes well with other Italian ingredients such as anchovies, garlic, pine nuts and sultanas.

6 Return the pasta to the pan, stir in the anchovy sauce or paste and mix in the drained sultanas.
7 Add black pepper to taste and half of the chopped parsley, then tip the pasta into the heated serving bowl.
8 Mix the remaining parsley into the fried breadcrumb and broccoli mixture and scatter over the pasta.
9 Sprinkle with cayenne pepper and toss the mixture at the dining table.
VARIATION
Vegetarians can omit the anchovy sauce or paste and use chopped black olives to make a salty contrast.

NO WASTAGE

Is there anything I can do with large broccoli stalks? It seems wasteful to throw them away.

Cutting chunky stalks into diagonal slices produces attractive shapes, which can be cooked separately. They can also be added to the florets, or chilled and used later in a stir-fry or a soup, curry or casserole. Even thick stems can be used if they are first sliced into very thin discs. Cook these for the same time as the rest of the broccoli.

Brussels Sprouts

IN THE RAW

I try to eat lots of raw vegetables – but what can I do to make raw Brussels sprouts more appetising?

Raw Brussels sprouts are surprisingly good finely shredded in a slaw-type winter salad with carrots, celery and spring onion plus plenty of chopped parsley, watercress or snow pea sprouts. The salad below is good with baked potatoes and cold meat or hot sausages for a family meal; it is also appropriate for a winter buffet as it will stand for an hour or two without wilting and is easy to multiply for larger numbers.

Winter salad of shredded Brussels sprouts

SERVES: 4
PREPARATION TIME: 20 minutes
COOKING TIME: 10 minutes

8-10 fresh chestnuts or pecans
250 g Brussels sprouts
2 medium carrots, cut into ribbons
*   with a potato peeler*
2 medium leeks, thinly sliced
1 bunch watercress, trimmed
A small bunch of parsley, finely
*   chopped*
Salt and black pepper
2 teaspoons Dijon mustard
1 teaspoon runny honey
1 tablespoon cider vinegar
2 tablespoons olive oil
1 tablespoon walnut oil

1 Roast the chestnuts on a baking tray for 5-10 minutes until the skins crack. Peel them while they are still warm then break them into rough pieces. If using pecans, simply break them into pieces.
2 Trim the sprouts and shred thinly across. Mix the prepared vegetables, watercress, parsley and the broken chestnuts in a wide salad bowl. Add salt and black pepper to taste.
3 In a small bowl, mix together the mustard, honey and cider vinegar then beat in both of the oils. Toss the dressing into the salad and serve.

Chestnuts and Brussels sprouts are a traditional combination used here in a new way. This crunchy salad has a delicious honey and mustard dressing.

CROSS CUT

Why do some recipes tell you to make a crisscross in the stalk of a Brussels sprout?

The only time you need to cut a cross in the bottom of a sprout's stem is when you are cooking a batch of various sizes. On these occasions, cut a cross in the larger sprouts. This allows heat to penetrate more easily to the middle so that the larger sprouts cook in the same time as the smaller ones.

Brussels sprouts are at their best when they are very tight, small buds and, since most supermarkets now sell them in a fairly regular and quite small size, crosscutting the stalks is rarely necessary.

WIDE APPEAL

My children declare they hate Brussels sprouts. Is there any way of converting them?

Most children enjoy stir-fries, so try sprouts quartered into wedges and stir-fried. Use 2 tablespoons of peanut oil in a hot wok or frying pan and firstly stir-fry one onion, cut into 12 wedges, for a minute, to develop some flavour. Then add 250 g quartered Brussels sprouts and two carrots, obliquely sliced, and stir-fry for about three minutes, or until al dente, or tender-crisp. Stir in 2 tablespoons each of salt-reduced soy sauce and tomato sauce and ¼ cup vegetable stock; heat through and serve.

Buns

ROLL WITH IT

What is the difference between a bun and a roll?

Buns are made from sweetened, yeast dough enriched with butter, whereas rolls are less sweet, or unsweetened, and are not enriched. Buns often have raisins or spices added, and are glazed or decorated before baking. Chelsea and hot cross buns are popular examples.

DON'T RUSH BUNS

I recently made hot cross buns but they were leaden. Do you have any foolproof advice?

The most common mistake is not allowing enough time for the dough to rise. It can take longer than some recipes indicate because of variations in room temperature, yeasts and flour. The flavour and the texture of any yeast product improve with slow rising, so do not rush the process. The recipe below produces a batch of lovely, moist buns.

Hot cross buns

MAKES: *18 buns*
PREPARATION TIME: *25–40 minutes, plus 2–3 hours rising time*
COOKING TIME: *15–20 minutes*

500 g (4 cups) strong white flour
60 g (⅓ cup) light brown sugar
2 teaspoons mixed spice
½ teaspoon salt
25 g fresh yeast, or
*   15 g dried yeast plus*
*   1 teaspoon sugar, or 1 sachet*
*   instant rapid-rise yeast*
300 ml lukewarm milk
2 large eggs, lightly beaten
50 g unsalted butter, softened, plus
*   extra for greasing*
125 g (¾ cup) currants
30 g (2 tablespoons) mixed peel
To glaze: 4 tablespoons milk
*   mixed with 2 tablespoons sugar*

1 Put the flour, sugar, mixed spice and salt in a bowl and mix well.

2 Dissolve the fresh or dried yeast in 4 tablespoons of the milk, adding the sugar if using dried yeast. Blend the yeast mixture into the remaining milk. If using instant rapid-rise yeast, add it directly to the flour.
3 Make a well in the spiced flour and add the milk, eggs and butter. Stir until a soft dough is formed.
4 Turn out onto a floured board and knead for 5–10 minutes until the dough is smooth and elastic. Knead in the currants and mixed peel.
5 Place the dough in a greased bowl, then cover and leave it for 1½–2 hours until doubled in size.
6 Grease a baking tray. Knock the dough back, and then divide it into 18 small buns. Mark each one with a cross. Arrange them on the baking tray and leave to prove until doubled in size, about 30–45 minutes. Preheat the oven to 190°C .
7 Brush the tops with sweetened milk and bake for 15–20 minutes or until risen and browned.

Burghul

CRACKED GRAIN

What is burghul, and why does it cook so quickly?

Burghul, which is also known as bulgur wheat, or cracked wheat, is wheat that has been steamed, dried and cracked, which enables it to readily absorb moisture. Burghul is therefore ready to use in recipes far more quickly than the whole grain.

If burghul is to be served in a salad, such as the Middle Eastern

For chicken kibbeh balls, burghul is used both in the mixture and as a coating before cooking.

salad tabbouleh, it is usual to soak the grains for 30 minutes and then use them without further cooking. In the following recipe, however, the burghul is first soaked then fried in the chicken balls.

Chicken kibbeh balls

MAKES: *24 balls*
PREPARATION TIME: *30 minutes plus 30 minutes soaking*
COOKING TIME: *10–12 minutes*

40 g (¼ cup) burghul
500 g finely minced lean
*   chicken*
2 spring onions, thinly sliced
1 tablespoon chopped fresh
*   parsley*
Grated rind of 1 lemon
60 g Cheddar cheese, grated
1 egg, beaten
¼ teaspoon white pepper
Sesame seeds and extra burghul, to
*   coat*
Olive oil, for frying

1 Place the burghul in a bowl and cover with 1 cup cold water. Leave to soak for 30 minutes, then strain well. Squeeze the burghul dry with the fingertips.
2 Place the burghul in a mixing bowl. Add the chicken mince, spring onions, parsley, lemon rind, cheese, egg and pepper, and, using a fork, stir until well mixed.
3 Level the mixture and divide it into 12 equal wedges. Scoop out each wedge and divide into two equal pieces. Roll each piece, with clean hands, into a neat ball.
4 Place an equal quantity of sesame seeds and extra burghul on a sheet of greaseproof paper. Roll the balls in the sesame seed mixture until coated. Chill for 30 minutes.
5 Heat 5 mm oil in a large, heavy-based frying pan over a medium-high heat. Add the chicken balls and fry each for 1–2 minutes, turning after 1 minute, or until sealed. Reduce the heat to medium-low and continue frying for 8–10 minutes, turning occasionally, or until golden and cooked through. Drain on paper towels. Serve hot with Greek yoghurt and a Greek-style salad.

Butter

SALTY DISTINCTION

What is the difference between salted and unsalted butter?

Salted butter is cooled pasteurised cream that has been churned to form large globules of butter. After the remaining liquid from the cream (buttermilk) is drained off, a maximum of 3 per cent salt is added. Unsalted butter is produced in the same way, but no salt is added. In some countries, unsalted butter is known as sweet butter.

Cultured butter is also unsalted. Before churning, a selected culture is added to the cream, which is held at a controlled temperature overnight to allow the development of an acidic flavour.

FRYING WITH BUTTER

Why do recipes tell you to add oil to butter for frying?

Butter is not easy to use for frying. In addition to butterfat, it contains water, milk solids and other impurities that make it burn at lower temperatures than most vegetable oils. By putting a little oil in the pan, then adding the butter and cooking the food over a low heat, you can help to prevent the butter burning and spoiling the dish.

You can also minimise the problem by using clarified butter (see box, page 55).

BEST BUTTER

Which is the best or most versatile butter to use for cooking?

A lightly salted butter is fine for general cooking purposes except where the recipe specifically calls for unsalted butter. Using butter in cooking adds flavour and a certain richness to foods, as well as improving the taste and appearance. Unsalted butter is ideal for many cakes, sweet pastries and biscuits, such as the Butter Whirl Biscuits (above right).

Butter whirl biscuits

MAKES: 14–16
PREPARATION TIME: 25 minutes
COOKING TIME: 15–20 minutes

175 g salted butter, softened,
    plus extra for greasing
60 g (⅓ cup) icing sugar, sifted
A few drops of vanilla essence
185 g (1½ cups) plain flour, sifted
7–8 glacé cherries, halved

1 Preheat the oven to 180°C and lightly grease two baking trays.
2 Cream the butter and icing sugar together until light and fluffy. Add the vanilla essence, then stir in the flour and mix well.
3 Spoon the mixture into a piping bag fitted with a 1 cm star nozzle. Pipe 14–16 flat whirls onto the baking trays and place a cherry half in the centre of each one.
4 Bake for 15–20 minutes until pale golden. Cool on the trays for a few minutes, then transfer to a wire rack to cool completely. Store them in an airtight container for up to a week.
VARIATIONS
To make chocolate butter whirls, melt 25–50 g plain chocolate and beat into the creamed butter and sugar before adding the flour. For lemon or orange butter whirls, add the finely grated zest of a lemon or small orange to the creamed butter and sugar mixture.

BUTTER CLARIFIED

When and why would you need clarified butter?

Clarified butter is melted butter from which the salt, water, milk solids and other impurities have been removed, leaving pure butterfat (see box, page 55). It will not burn when heated and so is good for sautéing and shallow-frying.

STRONG, SWEET GHEE

Are ghee and clarified butter the same thing?

No, they are not. Ghee is an Indian version of clarified butter which is made by simmering butter until all the moisture has evaporated and the butter caramelises. This results in a stronger, sweeter and rather nutty flavour. Ghee is often made from buffalo's milk or cow's milk, although ghee made from vegetable oils is also widely available.

NOT EVEN A PINCH

If a recipe calls for unsalted butter, can I use salted butter instead if I do not have any, or will it spoil the finished recipe?

If a recipe states unsalted butter it is always best to use it. Unsalted butter is often specified for delicate pastries for fruit tarts and tartlets, and for Danish pastries and croissants. It is also used for icings, cakes, tea breads, sweet biscuits, baked desserts such as crumbles, confectionery such as butterscotch, and other sweet foods, where even a pinch of salt would be obvious and would change the flavour of the dish. It is also better to use unsalted butter for delicate sauces such as hollandaise, and then to add salt to taste to the sauce.

Sometimes, however, salted butter is a crucial part of the dish because the salt highlights the flavours of the other ingredients.

HOW TO MAKE BUTTER GARNISHES

Individual portions of butter can be presented as attractive curls, to spread on bread or cheese biscuits.

TO MAKE CURLS

First dip the butter curler into warm water to heat it a little, then draw it over the surface of a chilled block of butter, pressing gently. Put the curls in a bowl of iced water until they are needed, to preserve their shape.

HOW TO CLARIFY BUTTER

By melting and straining (or 'clarifying') butter, you separate the butterfat from the water, milk proteins, salt and carbohydrates which make it splutter and burn when used for cooking. Clarified butter will keep for up to two months in the refrigerator or up to three months in the freezer.

IN THE MICROWAVE

1 To make about 100 g clarified butter you will need to start with 175 g ordinary butter. Cube the butter and place it in a 500 ml microwave-safe jug. Heat it on High for 1–2 minutes, or until the butter is melted and foaming.

2 Using a metal spoon, skim off and discard the foam from the surface of the melted butter.

3 Carefully pour off and reserve the clear yellow liquid, which is the clarified butter, leaving any milky residue behind in the jug.

ON THE STOVETOP

1 Gently heat 175 g butter in a small, heavy-based saucepan over a low heat until the butter has melted and started to foam.

2 Remove from the heat and stand a few minutes, until the sediment has settled on the base of the pan.

3 Line a sieve with some fine muslin then pour the butter through into a clean bowl. Discard any milky sediment that is left in the pan.

ADDING VALUE

What can I do with herb and garlic butters besides use them to top steaks? And can you suggest some other flavourings for butter?

Herb and other savoury flavoured butters are excellent tossed with pasta, spread on hot breads, added to soups and sauces or used as a topping for jacket potatoes. Grilled chicken or fish and steamed vegetables are also good matches.

Anchovies, curry powder, lemon zest, mustard, onion, paprika and tomato paste can all add an interesting savoury flavour to butter.

Sweet butters for pancakes can be made with sugar plus ground almonds or hazelnuts, lemon or orange zest, mixed spices, brandy, rum or liqueur.

SAFE STORAGE

Will homemade herb butter keep as long as ordinary butter?

No, it will not. Unsalted butter may be kept in a refrigerator for up to two weeks; salted butter for three weeks. Herb butter will keep for two days only as the oil in the herbs will turn the butter rancid. It can be frozen for up to a month.

THEME AND VARIATIONS

Can you tell me the difference between beurre blanc, beurre monté and beurre noir?

They are all sauces based on butter but quite different in flavour.

- BEURRE BLANC is a pale, creamy sauce similar to hollandaise. To make beurre blanc, dice 75 g cold unsalted butter. Simmer 3 tablespoons white wine vinegar with 75 ml white wine or water in a small saucepan with a finely chopped shallot until the mixture has reduced to about 2 tablespoons of liquid. Add 1 tablespoon fresh cream if you like and bring to the boil. Reduce the heat and whisk in the butter pieces, one by one, until the sauce is thick, pale and creamy. The sauce may be served as it is or strained to remove the shallots. Beurre blanc marries well with chicken, egg, fish and vegetables.
- BEURRE MONTE is similar to beurre blanc but the base may be any slightly thickened liquid such as a sauce made by reduction, a sauce thickened with flour, or reduced stock. Cold butter is whisked into the sauce in the same way as when making beurre blanc.
- BEURRE NOIR or 'black butter', is a sauce made by cooking butter until it turns dark brown. A little vinegar or lemon juice is added to the butter, then flavourings such as capers or parsley. Beurre noir is best served with grilled or fried fish, eggs and vegetable dishes. Beurre noisette is similar to beurre noir, but the butter is cooked only until it is medium-brown, then the seasonings are added.

Cabbage

A QUESTION OF TIMING

I enjoy eating cabbage, but find the smell that is produced during cooking unpleasant. Is there any way of avoiding it?

There are dozens of varieties of cabbage – including red, green, white, savoy, pointed and drumhead, as well as closely related curly kale and spring greens – but they all release smelly hydrogen sulphide gas in cooking.

The amount of gas they produce doubles between the fifth and seventh minutes of boiling, so to cut down on the smell, you must either keep the cooking time to under 5 minutes, which suits the looser-headed varieties best, or opt for much longer cooking in a closed oven to cook off this effect and achieve a mellowness of flavour.

Green and savoy cabbages are best cooked fast by adding the leaves to boiling water. Red and white cabbage, having greatest resilience in the leaves, respond better to slow cooking.

Alternatively, all cabbages can be sliced into thin shreds and quickly stir-fried, perhaps with the addition of caraway seeds, lemon juice, soy sauce or chopped chilli, and eaten while still a little crisp.

Ruffled leaves and deep colour make savoy the distinctive aristocrat of the winter cabbage patch. Cooked fast with juniper berries and gin, as in the following recipe, it is a fitting partner for rich beef casseroles and roast pork, and will not cause smells in your kitchen.

Savoy cabbage in gin

SERVES: 4 as an accompaniment
PREPARATION TIME: 15 minutes
COOKING TIME: 5 minutes

1 savoy cabbage weighing
   500-700 g
6 juniper berries
2 cloves garlic
Salt
50 g butter, softened
3 tablespoons gin
Black pepper

1 Trim away any tired or damaged leaves from the cabbage, cut it into wedges and shred it finely, cutting out and discarding the stem. Wash thoroughly and drain well.
2 With a pestle and mortar, crush the juniper berries, garlic and salt together to produce a rough paste. Alternatively, if you have no pestle and mortar, chop the berries and garlic finely, sprinkle on the salt and mix thoroughly. Mix the paste into the softened butter.
3 Cook this flavoured butter in a large saucepan over a low heat until it starts to sizzle, but do not let it begin to brown. In the meantime, put a serving dish to warm.
4 Toss the drained cabbage in the flavoured butter, turn up the heat to medium and stir the cabbage well to coat it in the butter. Stir in the gin, cover the pan tightly and cook on a medium heat for 4 minutes, shaking the pan vigorously once or twice.
5 Remove from the heat, grind on black pepper to taste, stir and serve immediately in the warmed dish.
VARIATION
Baby cabbages can now be found in some shops, and they can be used in this dish instead of larger specimens. Cut them into wedges and blanch in boiling water for a minute. Drain well and add to the flavoured butter then continue with the recipe above.

A splash of gin and some chopped juniper berries and garlic turn baby savoy cabbage into an aromatic dish that goes well with strong-flavoured meat.

RETAINING COLOUR

How can I prevent red cabbage losing its colour during cooking?

Red cabbage is inclined to turn a dingy purple in the long cooking required to soften it. You can avoid this by cooking it in a microwave oven. Shred the cabbage finely, and cook it on High for 6 minutes.

If using a conventional oven, a good splash of red wine or red wine vinegar in the latter stages of cooking, as in the recipe below, goes some way to restoring its vibrant ruby colour. Because of the long cooking time of this dish, it makes sense to make it in a large quantity; the red cabbage keeps well in the refrigerator and some say it is even better reheated. Bake some potatoes or a potato gratin while it is cooking to utilise the oven heat, and serve with pork chops or good-quality sausages.

Baked red cabbage with apple and spice

SERVES: 6-8 as an accompaniment
PREPARATION TIME: 35 minutes
COOKING TIME: 2 hours

1 kg red cabbage
2-3 bay leaves
1 medium onion
4 cloves
Salt
3 Granny Smith apples
75 g butter or lard
1 tablespoon light brown sugar
2 tablespoons red wine vinegar
300 ml beef stock
100 ml red wine
Black pepper

1 Preheat the oven to 160°C. Cut the cabbage into quarters and chop it into shreds, cutting out the stalk from the centre. Put the bay leaves into a large, heavy casserole and pack the cabbage on top.
2 Peel the onion, stud it with the cloves and bury it in the middle of the cabbage. Sprinkle on some salt.
3 Peel the apples, cut them into quarters and discard the cores. Cut the apples into slices. Heat the butter in a large frying pan and fry the apple slices, tossing until they begin to turn golden, then tip them with the butter over the cabbage, spreading the apple in a layer.
4 Dissolve the sugar in the vinegar and add the stock. Pour it over the apples and cabbage, then cover the casserole and bake for 1½ hours.
5 Uncover, pour in the red wine, stir and return to the oven for a further 30 minutes.
6 Remove and discard the studded onion, sprinkle on some salt and a good dash of pepper, and serve.

VARIATION
Vegetarians can replace the butter or lard with 4 tablespoons cooking oil, and use good-quality vegetable stock instead of beef stock.

EXOTIC CABBAGE

I have heard of a cabbage called pak choi. Where can I get it, and how is it prepared?

Pak choi is a cabbage without a heart, with deep green and fleshy leaves clustered on thick, juicy, white stems. A native of China and Hong Kong, pak choi used to be available only in Chinese food shops, but it is now grown in Australia and is widely available in fresh produce shops.

Brief steaming or stir-frying is recommended to retain flavour and juiciness. It takes happily to the garlic, ginger and soy treatment of Chinese cooking, but also adapts well to being served as an accompanying vegetable without any herbs or spices, Western-style.

TENDER SLAW

I know that coleslaw is supposed to be good for you, but I find it boringly chewy to eat and rather indigestible. How can I make it more appealing?

It does seem perverse that slaws are usually made with white cabbage, whose raw leaves are almost as tough as those of red cabbage. Choose a Chinese cabbage – a much more tender member of the cabbage family – as in the following recipe. Heads can weigh up to 700 g, so one head will make enough for a small buffet party. Indeed, because the cabbages in slaws remain crisp and sit well in their dressing even if made some hours before, they are always a practical choice for a buffet table. However, because they require so little time to prepare, they are also good as part of an informal family lunch or barbecue.

Chinese cabbage slaw

SERVES: 4
PREPARATION TIME: 15 minutes
COOKING TIME: none

250 g Chinese cabbage
2 medium carrots
3 tablespoons mayonnaise
1 teaspoon Dijon mustard
3 tablespoons olive oil
2 teaspoons cider vinegar
Celery salt and black pepper
1 tablespoon coarsely chopped walnut kernels, optional

1 Rinse the Chinese cabbage leaves, shake dry and shred, cutting across the head and discarding the stem.
2 Peel and coarsely grate the carrots and mix them with the shredded leaves in a salad bowl.
3 Mix the mayonnaise and mustard together then stir in the olive oil and vinegar. Season with celery salt and plenty of black pepper and toss into the salad. Scatter it, if you like, with chopped walnuts.
4 Serve the salad immediately, or cover it and store in the refrigerator for up to 6 hours before serving.

Save it!

If you have some Chinese cabbage left over after making the Chinese Cabbage Slaw above, keep it in the salad drawer of the refrigerator and use it as part of a stir-fry later in the week. Try it cooked with garlic, ginger, and a Chinese black bean sauce.

Cakes

STEPS TO SUCCESS

Why do my cakes sometimes have airholes, or crack and peak?

Holes can be caused by overmixing, or unevenly or insufficiently folding in the flour. The mixture should be soft and dropping at this stage, and if it is too dry, pockets of air can get trapped. This also happens if the flour and raising agent are not sifted together thoroughly.

To prevent cracking, make sure you use the right sized tin and that the oven is not too hot. Place cakes in the centre of the oven, not too high up where it will be hotter and the cake will peak and crack.

AVOIDING CURDLING

How do you prevent a cake mixture from curdling, and can you save it if it does?

Curdling occurs when the butter and sugar have not been creamed sufficiently – until light and fluffy – to form a strong emulsion to absorb the eggs. Also if cold eggs are added to the mixture too quickly, separation occurs. A curdled mixture holds far less air, so the cake will be flat. Eggs should be at room temperature and added gradually. Adding a teaspoon of flour with each addition of egg can also help to prevent curdling.

If the mixture starts to curdle, dip the base of the bowl into warm water briefly, and whisk to restore the light consistency.

THAT SINKING FEELING

Why does my cake come out of the oven looking perfect and then sink dramatically?

Cakes will sink if they have not been baked for long enough, so follow the time stated in the recipe, use a timer, and don't be tempted to open the oven door during cooking. Using too cool an oven, or opening and shutting the oven door during baking will cause sinking, as will too much raising agent in the cake mixture.

Cakes are ready when they are firm in the centre and have slightly shrunken away from the sides of the tin; sponges should spring back when touched with your finger.

RESCUE REMEDIES

Is there any way to save a cake that has turned out badly?

If things go wrong during baking, disguise the damage as follows.
• For a burnt cake, slice off the top and shave the sides with a potato peeler. Paint the surface with some warmed sieved jam and cover with a thin layer of bought marzipan or icing.
• If a cake breaks, stick the pieces back together with jam, then cover with frosting or jam sprinkled with desiccated coconut.
• If the middle sinks, cut it out and turn the cake into a ring cake. Spread whipped cream over the cake, and fill the cavity with fresh fruit, such as raspberries.
• If a sponge comes out flat, cut it into fancy shapes, sandwich them together with cream and jam and dust them with icing sugar.

LIGHT AS A FEATHER

How can I make a really feather-light cake?

To produce light cakes, it is vital to measure out the ingredients accurately and stick to the recipe. If you add too much egg, butter, flour or baking powder, this will make the cake heavy and doughy.

It is air that makes cakes light, so beat the sugar and butter until the mixture is pale, soft and fluffy, and fold in the flour gradually, being careful not to knock out any air. And be sure to use an appropriate fat – if you use soft tub margarine instead of butter in a creamed recipe, the mixture will be too wet and the cake will be flat.

The following recipes will produce light, airy cakes by the creaming method.

Classic Victoria sandwich

SERVES: 8
PREPARATION TIME: 20 minutes
COOKING TIME: 30 minutes

---

185 g unsalted butter or block margarine, softened
185 g (¾ cup) caster sugar
3 large eggs, beaten
185 g (1½ cups) self-raising flour, sifted
A few drops vanilla essence
75 ml raspberry jam
150 ml fresh or thickened cream, whipped
2 tablespoons icing sugar

---

1 Preheat the oven to 180°C. Grease two 20 cm round sandwich tins, and line the base of each one with greaseproof paper.
2 Beat the butter or margarine until very soft, using a mixer if possible. Add the sugar and cream them together until the mixture is light, pale and fluffy.
3 Beat in the egg gradually, adding a teaspoon of flour with each addition to prevent curdling. Fold in the rest of the flour then add the vanilla essence and a teaspoon of water.
4 Divide the mixture between the tins and smooth the surfaces level. Bake for 30 minutes or until risen and light golden. The cakes should spring back when lightly pressed in the centre with your fingers.
5 Leave to cool in the cake tins for a couple of minutes, then turn out onto wire racks to cool thoroughly.
6 Sandwich the two layers together with the jam and whipped cream, and lightly dust over the icing sugar.

Basic buttercake

You will need 185 g unsalted butter, 250 g (1 cup) caster sugar, 3 large eggs, 250 g (2 cups) self-raising flour and 60 ml milk. Follow the creaming method described above, and fold the milk in with the flour. Bake in a deep 21 cm round cake tin for 50–60 minutes, or until a warm skewer inserted in the centre comes out clean.

FAT-FREE SPONGE

Is it possible to make a sponge cake without using fat?

The lightest cakes – and the classic sponge – are made without any fat at all, and by the whisking method. To replace the bulk of the missing fat, the sugar and eggs are whisked together until the mixture becomes so thick that a trail is left when the beaters are lifted away.

Alternatively, you can replace some of the flour with lighter cornflour, as in the following recipe for Angel Food Cake. This is usually served as a cake, perhaps accompanied by some whipped cream, but you can also serve it as a dessert, each slice accompanied by fresh fruit and a raspberry coulis.

Whisked egg whites give a melt-in-the-mouth lift to a delicate Angel Food Cake, a classic fat-free sponge.

Angel food cake

SERVES: 12
PREPARATION TIME: 30 minutes
COOKING TIME: 35 minutes

60 g (½ cup) plain flour
30 g (¼ cup) cornflour
90 g (½ cup) icing sugar
1 teaspoon cream of tartar
A few drops vanilla essence
A few drops almond essence
6 large egg whites
A pinch of salt
185 g (¾ cup) caster sugar
To decorate: whipped cream and a selection of fresh fruit such as raspberries and whitecurrants

1 Preheat the oven to 190°C. Have ready to hand an ungreased 23 cm ring-shaped or tubular cake tin. If you do not have one of these, you can use a round cake tin and put an empty can upside-down in the centre to make the hole.

2 Sift the flour, cornflour and icing sugar together in a small bowl.
3 Put the cream of tartar, essences, egg whites and salt in a large bowl. Whisk until the egg whites form soft peaks, then gradually whisk in the caster sugar and continue whisking until the mixture forms stiff peaks.
4 Fold in the flour mixture a little at a time, being very careful not to overmix so you don't lose the air, then spoon it into the tin.
5 Bake for 35 minutes or until the cake springs back when touched with a finger and a skewer inserted into the mixture comes out clean.
6 To cool, invert the cake upside-down in the tin on a wire rack: the steam from the cake will help to release it from the tin.
7 When cool, gently run a palette knife round the sides of the tin, then turn out. Decorate the top and fill the hole with fresh fruit, and serve with whipped cream.

BUTTER OR OIL?

Can cakes be made with oil instead of butter or margarine? If so, would they be healthier?

Cakes made with lightly flavoured oils, such as corn, sunflower or macadamia nut oil, are very easy to mix (though they do need extra raising agent to stop them becoming heavy), and they stay moist longer. But it is debatable whether they are healthier: although some oils contain less saturated fat than butter or margarine, they have just as many kilojoules.

This Carrot Cake is made using oil, is easy to make and will keep for up to three days in a cake tin. The cream cheese icing also adds some extra protein to the cake.

Carrot cake

SERVES: 8
PREPARATION TIME: 30 minutes
COOKING TIME: 50 minutes

FOR THE CAKE
1 large ripe banana
90 ml macadamia nut or
    sunflower oil
90 g (½ cup) dark brown sugar
2 large eggs, beaten
50 g carrots, finely grated
90 g (½ cup) sultanas
30 g (¼ cup) walnuts, chopped
Finely grated zest of 1 orange
½ teaspoon ground cinnamon
185 g (1½ cups) plain flour
1 teaspoon baking powder
1 teaspoon bicarbonate of soda

FOR THE ICING
75 g soft cream cheese
60 g (⅓ cup) icing sugar
Finely grated zest of 1 lemon
1 tablespoon lemon juice

1 Preheat the oven to 180°C. Grease a 1 kg loaf tin and line it with nonstick baking paper.
2 With a fork, mash the banana in a large mixing bowl, then mix in all the remaining ingredients briefly, sifting in the flour, baking powder and bicarbonate of soda last.
3 Beat until smooth, then pour into the tin and bake for 30 minutes.

4 Turn the heat down to 160°C and bake for a further 20 minutes until the cake is firm to the touch and a warmed skewer inserted in the middle comes out cleanly.
5 When cooked, leave the cake to cool in the tin for 5 minutes until it is firm enough to handle, then turn it out and peel away the paper. Leave to cool completely on a wire rack.
6 When the cake is thoroughly cool, beat all the ingredients for the icing together with a wooden spoon, then swirl the mixture over the cake.

Is it done?

To test if a cake is cooked, warm a skewer or knitting needle and insert it into the centre; it should come out cleanly, with no cake mixture sticking to it.

RIGHT-SIZED TINS

Does it matter if a cake mixture is baked in a slightly different tin to the one specified in the recipe?

Yes, very much. If the tin is too large, the cake will be flat and shrunken. If it is too small, the cake will bubble or bulge up and over the sides of the tin.

However, the mixture for a round tin will fit a square tin that is about 2 cm smaller; for instance, a mixture that is designed to fill a 20 cm round tin can be used to fill a 18 cm square tin.

To adapt a recipe to fill a shaped tin, for example the number '9' for a birthday cake, fill your usual tin with water to the level the mixture normally reaches. Then pour the water into the new tin to the level required and estimate the quantity of mixture needed, doubling or halving the recipe as required.

TURNING OUT

Should I turn cakes out of the tin as soon as they are cooked?

Most light cakes, such as a Victoria sandwich, should be turned out of their tins while they are still warm,

or else the underside may go soggy with condensation or form a thick, dark outer crust. However, they will break up if they are turned out immediately they are out of the oven, so leave them in the tin for 3–5 minutes to firm up.

Heavy cakes, such as fruit cakes, are best left in the tin until they are completely cold to allow them to solidify, especially if they are going to be stored and matured.

RAISING AGENTS

What exactly is baking powder?

Baking powder is a mixture of bicarbonate of soda, which is an alkali, and cream of tartar, which is an acid. When liquid is added, the two react to produce carbon dioxide, and the heat of the oven expands these gas bubbles to raise the mixture. Baking powder also contains a filler in the form of a food starch, usually rice flour, which prevents the premature release of carbon dioxide during storage. You can make your own baking powder from one part bicarbonate of soda to two parts cream of tartar. Bicarbonate of soda can be used as a raising agent on its own, but it has an unpleasant aftertaste, so it is best used for strongly flavoured, spicy cakes.

GIVING FLOUR A LIFT

Why do some recipes use plain flour and baking powder, and others self-raising flour?

Self-raising flour has more lifting power than a blend of plain flour and baking powder, so this is the best flour to use for heavy mixtures. Plain flours can raise a light mixture with the aid of baking powder, especially if the recipe also contains eggs or egg whites which will help to aerate the mix.

If you want to make your own self-raising flour, sift 500 g (4 cups) plain flour with 4 level teaspoons baking powder.

The following recipe uses the easy all-in-one method and relies on self-raising flour to lift the cake.

Rich and creamy frosting turns a crunchy triple-decker walnut cake into a luscious teatime treat.

Frosted walnut cake

SERVES: 12
PREPARATION TIME: 40 minutes
COOKING TIME: 30 minutes

FOR THE CAKE
250 g (2 cups) self-raising flour
½ teaspoon ground cinnamon
250 g soft margarine
250 g (1½ cups) light brown sugar
4 large eggs, beaten
60 g (½ cup) walnuts, chopped
1 tablespoon treacle

FOR THE FROSTING
1 large egg white
185 g (¾ cup) caster sugar
A pinch of salt
A pinch of cream of tartar
To decorate: walnut halves and
    demerara sugar

1 To make the cake, preheat the oven to 160°C. Have ready to hand three 20 cm sandwich tins, greased and with their bases lined with a layer of nonstick baking paper.
2 Sift the flour and cinnamon together into a large bowl. Add the remaining cake ingredients and beat well for 1-2 minutes, until the mixture has a soft dropping consistency.
3 Spoon the mixture equally into the tins, level the surface and bake them for about 30 minutes or until springy to the touch in the centre.
4 Leave in the tins for 5 minutes then turn out to cool on wire racks.
5 To make the frosting, place all the frosting ingredients in a large, clean, heatproof bowl, add 2 tablespoons water and whisk, with an electric whisk if possible, until foaming.
6 Set the bowl over a pan of boiling water and whisk until the mixture forms soft peaks – about 7 minutes with an electric whisk.
7 Working quickly, as the frosting will set as it cools, sandwich the cakes together with one-third of the frosting to form a triple-layered cake, then swirl the remainder over the top and sides. Decorate with a few walnut halves scattered on top of the cake and sprinkle with demerara sugar if you like.

STORING CAKES

What is the best way to store cakes, and how do I keep a cake moist once it has been cut?

Store in airtight tins, not plastic boxes, as plastic encourages mould and taints cakes with lingering smells. Do not store cakes and biscuits together, as moisture from the cake will make the biscuits soggy.

Once a cake has been cut, you can keep it moist for a few days by wrapping it in foil before storing it, or by inverting a mixing bowl over it and storing in the refrigerator.

See also: *Slices*

All-in-one Cake

MAKES: 1 × 20 cm round cake, to serve 10
PREPARATION TIME:
15 minutes
COOKING TIME:
50–60 minutes

250 g soft margarine
250 g (1 cup) caster sugar
4 large eggs
250 g (2 cups) self-raising
  flour
1 teaspoon baking powder
A few drops vanilla essence

1 Preheat the oven to 180°C. Grease a 20 cm round cake tin and line the base of it with greaseproof paper.
2 Put the margarine, sugar and eggs in a mixing bowl, then sift in the flour, baking powder and vanilla essence. Beat the mixture lightly until it is thoroughly blended but be careful not to overmix.
3 Spoon the mixture into the tin and spread it level. Bake for 50–60 minutes or until the cake is golden and firm to the touch in the centre.
4 Leave the cake to cool in the tin for 3 minutes then turn it out onto a wire rack and leave to cool further; peel away the greaseproof paper while the cake is still slightly warm. It will keep for three days in an airtight tin.

CELEBRATION CAKES

◆

Even if you rarely bake cakes, there is no problem with this easy method – simply beat all the ingredients together and you have the base for the splendid cakes shown here. Icing is simple too: use ready-made sugarpaste icing to cover the cakes, and royal icing for all the pretty decorations.

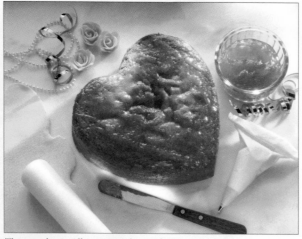

The easy basic All-in-one Cake, cooked in a heart shape, just needs to be iced and decorated to make the elegant cake below.

Golden Wedding Cake

PREPARATION TIME: 4 hours, plus 24 hours drying time, plus time to make the All-in-one Cake

1 heart-shaped All-in-one
  Cake (see below)
4 tablespoons apricot jam,
  sieved
750 g ready-made
  sugarpaste icing
Edible yellow food colouring
Royal icing to decorate
Roses, dried gypsophila
  and gift-wrapping ribbon

1 You will need a 20 cm heart-shaped cake tin for this cake. You might be able to borrow one from your local cake shop. Otherwise you can make the cake in a square tin and then cut it into a heart shape: trim away the sides to a slope and trim the offcuts to make the round shapes to put at the top. Stick them to the cake with a little jam.
2 Brush the cake all over with apricot jam. Add yellow colouring to 500 g of the ready-made icing and mix well. Roll out the icing and drape it over the cake. Smooth it down over the top and sides of the cake, then trim the edges. Smooth down with your palms to make a completely flat surface.

GOLDEN WEDDING CAKE

3 To give a quilted effect to the top of the cake, use the edge of a ruler to mark on crisscross lines.
4 With the royal icing, pipe small dots round the top edge and base of the cake.
5 To make the roses, divide up the remaining ready-made icing into two or three parts. Before rolling them out, add different amounts of colour to each to make two or three shades of yellow.
6 Roll each portion of icing into a number of pea-sized balls. Make a teardrop-shaped petal from one of these balls then make five or six more and roll each petal round the first one, overlapping. Pull away the bulky base part and open out the petals.
7 Place the rose in an egg carton or patty-cake tin lined with crumpled foil. Make the rest of the roses, harmonising the various shades of petal. Leave to dry for 24 hours.
8 To serve the cake, decorate it with the roses, gypsophila and strips of gift-wrapping ribbon pulled into curls.
VARIATION
If you are short of time, use bought silk flowers instead of making icing roses.

TEDDY BEAR
CAKE

Teddy Bear Cake

PREPARATION TIME: 2 hours, plus time to make the All-in-one Cake

1 round chocolate All-in-one Cake, flavoured with 2 tablespoons cocoa dissolved in 3 tablespoons boiling water added to the basic recipe with the vanilla
1 chocolate Swiss roll
6 tablespoons sieved marmalade
625 g ready-made sugarpaste icing
Edible brown, red and black food colouring
Thin liquorice straps and liquorice allsorts

1 Start by making the ears. Cut out two crescent-shaped indents from either side of the cake where the ears will be. Cut two pieces from the Swiss roll, each of the same height as the cake, and place one in each indent: these are the bear's ears.
2 Brush the top and sides of the cake with marmalade. Place the two cut-out pieces of cake in the centre of the face to form the snout.
3 Colour 300 g of the icing dark brown and roll it out thinly to a circle large enough to cover the cake.
4 Drape the icing over the top and sides, smooth down and trim the edges, setting the trimmings aside.
5 Roll out two circles from the reserved white icing to make up the eyes and place a liquorice allsort on each.
6 Colour all but a teaspoon of the remaining icing a lighter brown and divide it into three balls. Flatten one ball into an oval to cover the raised snout, place it over the top and smooth down. Roll out the remaining balls, cut them into two semicircular shapes and stick them on top of the ears. Prick them and the snout all over with a fork.
7 With the remaining icing, make a black nose and red tongue and stick them on.
8 Cut thin strips of liquorice for the eyelashes and mouth shape and press into place.

DAISY
CHRISTENING
CAKE

Daisy Christening Cake

PREPARATION TIME: 1 hour 20 minutes, plus 2–3 hours drying time, plus time to make the All-in-one Cake

1 round All-in-one Cake
6 tablespoons seedless raspberry jam
4 tablespoons apricot jam
750 g ready-made sugarpaste icing
Royal icing to decorate
Edible pink, yellow and blue food colouring
Narrow pink or blue ribbon

1 Divide the cake in two horizontally, spread raspberry jam on the bottom layer, then press the cake back together.
2 Brush the top and sides of the cake with sieved apricot jam. Roll out three-quarters of the sugarpaste icing to a circle large enough to cover the top and sides. Place it on the cake, trim the edges and smooth flat using your palms.
3 To make the daisies, roll half the remaining sugarpaste icing into 18 pea-sized balls, then shape each ball into a teardrop. Pinch the thin end to make a stalk, then flatten out the rounded end so it looks like a large thumb tack.
4 Using small scissors, snip tiny 'petals' all around the edge, then use the tips of the scissors to prick small dots over the centre.
5 Leave to dry out for a few hours on foil, crumpled to stop the icing sticking to it.
6 With an artist's small paint-brush, colour the outer tips pink and the centre yellow using food colouring.
7 Roll out the remaining sugarpaste icing thinly and cut it into six 1 cm wide strips. Dab the end of each strip with a little royal icing, then twist them and hang them in a garland round the top of the cake.
8 Using a dab of royal icing, stick on two or three daisies where the loops join.
9 Colour the remaining royal icing pink or blue. Pipe the child's name on the top of the cake, then pipe a simple border round the base.
10 When the icing is dry, tie pink or blue ribbon round the side of the cake.

Canapés

TASTY NIBBLES

I have eaten delicious canapés at parties, but never tried to make them at home. Can you suggest some quick and colourful ideas?

It is very easy to make your own canapés by simply using triangles of rye bread, shapes of toasted bread or tiny pikelets as the bases. Or try making attractive little croustade cases (see box, right).

The toppings and fillings used for canapés can be simple as well. Spread triangles of rye bread or toast with slivers of smoked salmon sprinkled with black pepper and lemon juice, or spread them with dill mayonnaise and top with some gravlax. Try also Provençal Tapenade (see page 66) with slices of soft mozzarella cheese and some halved cherry tomatoes, seasoned with olive oil, salt, pepper and basil.

For a tasty tuna pâté filling for croustades, blend 180 g canned tuna, 1 hard-boiled egg and the juice of a lemon with 3 tablespoons mayonnaise. This will make enough to fill about ten croustade cases. Even simpler, fill the bases with either whipped mascarpone cheese or some sour cream before adding a topping.

Choosing an attractive garnish with the right complementary taste is extremely important when you are making canapés. The garnish must be both delicate and small. Any of the following would make a good finishing touch: a slice of olive, a half teaspoon of caviar or salmon roe, a sprig of some fresh herb, a dusting of paprika or a tiny rosette of piped cream or mayonnaise. See below for more ideas.

Pink gin tastes great with filled croustade canapés. Try sour cream topped with smoked salmon; quail's eggs, salmon roe and dill; tapenade with mozzarella, cherry tomatoes and basil; or lumpfish roe and chives on sour cream.

MAKING CROUSTADE BASES FOR CANAPES

These baked bread shapes are easy and quick to make. Fill them with savoury mixtures and serve with drinks either before a meal or as part of a buffet dinner.

1 Preheat the oven to 180°C. Gently melt some butter – you will need 150 g for every 12 croustades you are making.

2 Use a fluted pastry cutter with a diameter of about 6–7.5 cm. Cut rounds of thinly sliced white bread and dip these in melted butter. Press the rounds firmly into the wells of patty-cake tins.

3 Place the tin in the oven, with a second patty-cake tin nested on top of the first to keep the bread in shape. Bake for 15–20 minutes, until the croustades are firm.

4 Lift the croustades from the tin with a palette knife and place them on a wire rack to cool. Fill imaginatively and serve.

WORKING AHEAD

Do canapés have to be made immediately before serving?

No, the various spreads for fillings can be made in advance and kept refrigerated (although the colour of some foods, such as avocado, might spoil). The croustade or toast bases can also be made 24 hours ahead if they are kept stored in an airtight container. However, it is best to assemble the canapés as near to the serving time as possible so the toast or croustade bases stay crisp.

HOW MUCH IS ENOUGH?

Are there any guidelines about how many canapés I should make for a drinks party?

The amount of food guests will consume depends on the occasion, as well as on their appetites. Here are some very rough guidelines for the number of canapés you should produce for various get-togethers:
- COCKTAIL PARTY: Allow around ten canapés for each person.
- DRINKS PARTY: Allow up to 15 canapés per person if guests are unlikely to go on to a meal.
- PRE-LUNCH OR PRE-DINNER DRINKS: Allow four to five canapés for each person before the meal.
- HOT OR COLD WEATHER: Allow half the canapés to be hot in cold weather, but only a quarter should be served warm in hot weather.

See also: **Cheese Biscuits**

Cannelloni

CHEESY FILLING

I am tired of cannelloni stuffed with spinach. Could you suggest a more interesting filling?

Spinach or meat are the most usual stuffings for the rolled pancakes of pasta called cannelloni, but this tasty recipe for Ricotta Cannelloni (right) shows a clever alternative. Three different cheeses are combined with a fresh vegetable sauce.

Ricotta cannelloni

SERVES: *4–6*
PREPARATION TIME: *30 minutes*
COOKING TIME: *50 minutes*

FOR THE SAUCE
2 tablespoons light olive oil
1 medium onion, chopped
1 carrot, finely chopped
1 stalk celery, chopped
400 g canned chopped
*   tomatoes*
A pinch of dried thyme
A pinch of sugar
Salt and black pepper
40 g Parmesan cheese,
*   freshly grated*

FOR THE CANNELLONI
250 g mozzarella cheese,
*   chopped*
175 g cooked ham, chopped
250 g ricotta cheese
2 tablespoons chopped parsley
2 large eggs
Several gratings of fresh nutmeg
Salt and black pepper
12 cannelloni tubes or 12 sheets
*   of fresh or dried lasagne pasta,*
*   measuring 10 × 8 cm*
Butter for baking

1 To make the sauce, gently heat the oil and sauté the onion, carrot and celery until they soften. Add the chopped tomatoes, thyme and sugar and season to taste. Simmer, partially covered, for at least 30 minutes.
2 Prepare the filling by mixing the mozzarella, ham, ricotta, parsley and eggs together very well. Season the mixture generously with gratings of nutmeg, salt and pepper.
3 Preheat the oven to 190°C.
4 Bring a large pan of water to the boil. Add 2 tablespoons salt and a little oil and poach the pasta, three tubes or sheets at a time. Dried pasta needs 4 minutes; fresh, 1–2 minutes.
5 Dip the cooked pasta in a bowl of cold water, then place on tea towels to dry. Butter an ovenproof dish.
6 When the pasta is cool enough to handle, spoon the ricotta filling equally into the tubes or among the lasagne sheets, placing the mixture on the shorter end of each sheet. Roll up and enclose.

7 Put a little sauce in the bottom of the dish, arrange the pasta (seam side down) in it and spread the rest of the sauce on top. Dot with butter and sprinkle with the Parmesan cheese.
8 Bake for 20 minutes, then serve.

Controlling your pasta

Lasagne sheets, cannelloni tubes and other pasta will not boil over if you rub oil inside the pan. And pour a little oil in the water to stop the pasta sticking together.

Capers

FLAVOURSOME BUDS

What are capers?

They are the small, unopened buds of a thorny plant that grows wild all around the Mediterranean. Capers are picked and then pickled in salty vinegar. They should be kept swimming in this liquid after the jar has been opened.

SAUCES AND SPREADS

How are capers used?

Some sauces, such as tartare, use capers – and the buds are also good served with sautéed chicken, veal schnitzel and char-grilled salmon.

In southern Europe, the caper is more likely to be included in salty spreads, such as the recipe for Provençal Tapenade (see page 66). This tasty purée is often served with raw vegetables or pasta.

You can also spread tapenade on thin slices of French bread and eat it as a savoury with drinks – perhaps while waiting for meat to cook on the barbecue.

Tapenade can be a tasty addition to sandwiches or party finger food. Try mixing 2 tablespoons tapenade with 250 g cottage cheese and ¼ cup sour cream. Use for a sandwich filling or spoon onto tiny pikelets or 5 mm thick slices of cucumber for a party savoury.

Capers have been used since Roman times and are essential to the tangy flavour of tapenade. This versatile spread tastes best on French bread, topped with olives.

Provençal tapenade

MAKES: 350 g, or about 30 smallish canapés
PREPARATION TIME: 30 minutes
COOKING TIME: none

35 g canned anchovy fillets, drained
2 tablespoons milk
85 g capers, drained
175 g black olives, drained and stoned
100 g canned tuna, drained and flaked
1 tablespoon mustard powder
150 ml olive oil
1-2 tablespoons brandy
½ teaspoon mixed spice, or a mix of black pepper, ground cloves and grated nutmeg

1 Put the drained anchovy fillets in a shallow dish, cover with milk and leave to soak for 10 minutes.
2 Put the capers and stoned olives in a processor and blend to a purée. · Drain the anchovies and add them to the caper and olive mixture, along with the tuna and mustard powder. Process until smooth.
3 Add the olive oil a little at a time, processing all the while. When it is properly amalgamated, stir in the brandy and spices.
4 This is best served immediately, spread on thin slices of French bread which have been dried in the oven.

Carrots

ADDING HERBS

Are there any herbs that would add a bit of excitement to a plain vegetable like carrots?

Carrots are simple and marry well with almost any herb. In winter, dried thyme, rosemary or even lavender bring a fragrance to the sweet, maincrop vegetable. Dill is the gentle, classic herb used with all types of carrots, while mint is a spring and early summer favourite. Parsley is a good addition any time, as is coriander, particularly if you like your carrots cooked in a blend of orange juice and butter.

CUTTING MATTERS

Does the way I cut carrots affect how the vegetable cooks?

The way a carrot is chopped does affect its finished texture (see box, page 67). Carrots that are sliced into discs cook soft and are ideal for simple boiled carrots or to be made into purées. Batons, which are cut lengthways, can be cooked fast and stay crisp for stir-fries or to toss into pasta. You can also 'roll-cut' a carrot for maximum surface and angles so that it will caramelise, as in the recipe below.

Roll-cut carrots in butter and Marsala

SERVES: 4
PREPARATION TIME: 10 minutes
COOKING TIME: 15–18 minutes

500 g medium carrots
Salt
25 g butter
4 tablespoons Marsala
Black pepper

1 Peel and roll-cut the carrots, then spread them in a wide, heavy-based pan. Sprinkle with salt, dot with the butter and add the Marsala. Cover and cook over a medium heat for about 15 minutes until they are soft.
2 Leave a serving dish to warm. Uncover the carrots and continue cooking, shaking the pan constantly over the heat until the carrots begin to look roasted around the edges and the liquor is reduced to a glaze.
3 Transfer the carrots to the warmed serving dish, grind black pepper over them and serve immediately.
VARIATION
To make a refreshing cooked carrot salad, substitute 2 tablespoons olive oil for the butter, and use water with the juice of a lime added in place of the Marsala. Allow the carrots to cool, then sprinkle shredded mint leaves over them.

CUTTING CARROTS

You can choose different styles of cutting carrots and these will suit varied occasions and dishes. Note that the variation in appearance also leads to some differences in how the carrots will cook. Here are some of the most common shapes and how to make them:

TO SLICE

Hold the peeled carrot firmly and cut in either diagonal or straight slices which are as thick as a 50-cent coin. These coin-sized slices will soften well during cooking.

TO MAKE BATONS

Halve the peeled carrot lengthways, and across if it is very long. You can then slice the carrot pieces into short batons which are about the thickness of a thin pencil.

TO 'ROLL-CUT'

Cut a wedge at an angle across the thick end of a peeled carrot, then continue making diagonal cuts, turning the carrot about one-third around between each cut.

Carving

BOARDS OR PLATES

Is it better to carve meat on a board or on a plate?

You can use either a board or a plate as long as it is large enough and sits firmly on a surface that is nonslip. The platter or board used should be almost flat, as carving in a deep dish is virtually impossible.

If the table is slippery and the serving plate is china, put a cloth mat or folded napkin underneath to keep the dish from moving. And while it may look attractive to put the potatoes and other vegetables around the joint, this can make carving awkward and messy.

Another essential requirement for carving is a razor-sharp knife and a carving fork with a guard to prevent the knife slipping.

RULES FOR CARVING

Are there some general rules for effective carving?

For regular, attractive slices, make sure that the cuts go across the grain of the meat. Cutting with the grain tends to result in slices that are shredded and stringy. However, when carving undersides of joints like sirloin of beef or leg of lamb, it is easier to cut more thickly and with the grain of the meat.

Cold meat is generally sliced thinner than hot meat. If you are going to serve the meat cold, wait until the joint cools before carving or the slices will lose their juices, colour and texture. It is also much easier to carve a cold joint.

NO WISHBONE

What is the best technique for carving poultry?

When carving small poultry, use a short, flexible carving knife and a table fork or small carving fork (see box, page 69). It is much easier to carve chicken at the table if the wishbone is removed before the bird has been cooked. The method is quite simple: pull back the skin at the neck end to expose the breastbone, then cut and scrape with a short, sharp knife to extract the wishbone. Do not cut too deeply into the meat as you work. After the bone has been removed, tuck the skin back under the bird.

RELAXED MEAT

I often read that you should let meat rest before carving. Why is this so important?

Whatever meat you have roasted, you should always take it out of the oven and leave it to stand for about 15–30 minutes, depending on size, before it is carved.

Cover the joint with aluminium foil and put it in a warm place. Resting allows the juices to sink back from the surface and they can then be reabsorbed to tenderise the meat. It also makes meat easier to carve, as juices will not spurt out.

POWER CARVING

Are electric carving knives worthwhile buying?

Electric carving knives are labour-saving if you have large amounts of meat to carve. However, they can be unwieldy and noisy and are not very suitable for use at the table.

Also, it can be difficult to achieve very thin slices with an electric knife, especially when carving hot meat. Great care must be taken as electric knives are very sharp and can be dangerous to use.

To the rescue!

If you want to avoid unattractive holes in your poultry when carving, turn the fork over. With practice, you will find that you can hold the bird securely with the back of the prongs without making marks in the meat.

SPECIAL TIPS

Are there different methods of carving various kinds of joints?

If the meat has been boned first, carving is easy, whatever the joint. You can simply cut the slices in the thickness you prefer, moving across the grain of the meat.

If the meat is on the bone, you will need to adjust your carving techniques accordingly. Always use a carving fork with a thumbguard, for safety. Here are a variety of common carving tasks with details about how best to proceed.

CARVING LOINS

Loins of lamb, pork and veal are all roasted on the bone to prevent shrinkage and preserve the flavour. But when you are ready to carve, it is easier to remove the meat from the rib cage and then slice it to the desired thickness. Pork is shown below.

1 Cut down between the chine bone and the meat and then angle the knife between the meat and the ribs, cutting the meat free of the bones. Remove the crackling from the joint in one piece.

2 The meat can now be sliced, and the crackling can be cut with scissors into the same number of pieces as there are slices of meat.

CARVING LEGS

Legs of lamb, pork and veal should all be carved in the same manner. The pictures below show the method used on a leg of lamb.

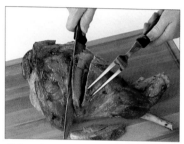

1 Put the leg meaty side up and cut a shallow 'V' from the middle. Carve slices downwards from both sides of the 'V', then turn the leg over and slice the rest of the meat horizontally.

2 Legs can also be cut in diagonal slices starting from the knuckle end. While this is most common with hams, the technique is an alternative you can try with all legs of meat.

CARVING A LARGE RIB OF BEEF

Cooking a rib of beef on the bone helps to conduct heat to the centre of a joint and gives a rich flavour. You can remove all the meat from the bone in one chunk and then carve it, but this rather spoils the effect. Try this way instead.

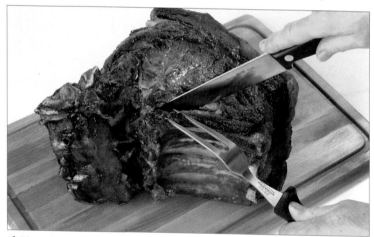

1 Place the rib of beef on its side and start by making a 5 cm deep cut along the ribs. Be sure to go the full length of the ribs with your cutting.

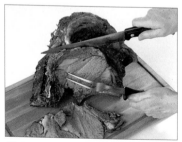

2 Stand the meat up, rib side down. Carve several slices, lift these off and place them on a warm dish.

3 Turn the rib back on its side and make a second 5 cm cut. Then stand the joint up and carve more.

CARVING POULTRY

A chicken, duck, goose and small turkey are all carved in the same manner. As it can be quite tricky to carve slices from the breast of a small bird, it is sometimes easier to remove the breast in one piece. See the pictures below and right for illustrations of this technique on a small chicken.

1 Place the bird on its side and cut under the thigh, lifting the whole leg up with a fork. To halve the leg and make two portions, cut through the joint at the top of the drumstick.

2 Cut down the breast, halfway across and through the shoulder, then cut all around to remove the shoulder, wing and a long strip of breast all in one piece. Lift this piece with the fork, holding the body down with the knife, and cut away.

3 If the chicken is only a small one, simply cut away the remaining breast in one piece. Alternatively, if the chicken is large enough, you can carve the breast into slices by starting at the wing end. Work your way systematically towards the back.

CARVING TURKEY

A small turkey can be carved like a chicken (see above) – but one that weighs more than 4.5 kg is not easy to move from side to side. For a bigger turkey, it can be much better to put it on a board and carve it while it is firmly in place, as shown in the pictures below and right.

1 Remove the trussing string then cut between the body and the thigh all around. When these cuts are made, cut through the connecting sinews.

2 Pull the leg away from the body and you can then carve the flesh into very small slices that are slanted parallel to the bone.

3 Cut down through the shoulder joint, removing a small piece of breast meat attached to the shoulder and wing. Turn the bird and cut away the shoulder and wing on the other side in the same manner. This now clears the way for slicing the breast.

4 A turkey breast is large enough to carve into thin slices on the bone. Turn the fork over so that the prongs do not puncture the meat and stay out of the way of the knife. Alternatively, you can remove the whole breast, lay it flat and carve it across the grain.

SHOULDER OF LAMB

A shoulder can be quite tricky to carve because of the arched bone that runs through it. The secret is to carve it with the bone away from you, so you can get at the meat.

Put the shoulder skin side up and cut a long slice from the centre, on the side opposite the bone. Carve out more thick slices on either side, then horizontal slices from the top over the central bone. Turn the joint over and carve horizontally.

SADDLE OF LAMB

You can carve saddle of lamb by removing the loins from either side of the backbone and cutting across the grain. Alternatively, carve it on the bone as shown here.

1 The chump end of the saddle should be carved into thin slices across the grain of the meat, and at right angles to the backbone.

2 The main part of the saddle, lying each side of the backbone, is cut into thin strips or narrow slices down its full length.

Casseroles

HEARTY MIXTURES

What is the difference between a casserole, stew and daube?

All use long, slow, moist cooking in a covered container to tenderise tough meats and vegetables, but they differ in the ingredients and type of pot used.

A casserole uses small pieces of meat and vegetables and is usually cooked in the oven. A stew is made on the top of the stove (and originally would have been cooked slowly over an open fire). A daube makes use of a large cut of meat, often beef, braised in wine. Traditionally, it was cooked over a fire in a tall casserole with an indented lid full of hot charcoal, so it had heat from both the top and bottom.

FLOURING AND FRYING

Why do recipes tell you to flour and fry the meat first when it is going to be casseroled for hours?

The meat is fried partly to seal in the juices, and also to give it a rich brown colour. Flour protects meat, and helps to thicken the gravy.

Fry the meat in small batches, for only a minute or two each batch. It is not necessary to move the meat around in the pan. Simply turn each piece so it browns all over.

To flour meat, place the cubes into a clean paper or plastic bag and add the flour and seasoning. Hold the bag closed and shake until all the meat has been coated.

Using a plastic bag to toss meat in flour helps to ensure an even coating.

MAKING AND USING BEURRE MANIÉ

If your finished casserole is too thin, you can thicken the sauce by adding beurre manié – a simple paste made with equal quantities of flour and butter.

1 Soften the butter and place it in a small bowl along with the flour. Stir and mash with a fork until a thick paste has been formed.

2 Gradually add small pieces of the beurre manié paste to the sauce of the cooked casserole. Stir in the paste until the sauce thickens and is smooth.

LENGTHY COOKING

Recipes often suggest cooking casseroles for 2 hours to make them tender, but I find that it can take about 3 hours. Am I doing something wrong?

The cooking time for a casserole depends largely on the cut of meat that is used. Nowadays, relatively tender cuts of meat are included, and these can be cooked successfully in as little as 1–2 hours.

In previous times, traditional casseroles were made with the tougher cuts from the leg, neck and shoulder of older animals. The well-developed muscle fibre and connective tissue could be broken down only by slow, moist cooking. Casserole meat is usually cut into pieces to accelerate this process.

These tough cuts of meat usually have an excellent flavour, with the connective tissue dissolving to a gelatine during slow cooking. This gives a very soft texture and an excellent rich, velvety sauce, but the process may take 3 hours.

To make a casserole that cooks in a shorter amount of time but still has plenty of flavour, try marinating the meat from a leg of kangaroo. It is too dry to roast, but it is tender when used in a fruity recipe, such as Kangaroo Casserole with Cherries and Orange (right).

Kangaroo casserole with cherries and orange

SERVES: 4-6
PREPARATION TIME: 25 minutes plus marinating time
COOKING TIME: 1¾ hours

FOR THE MARINADE
250 ml red wine
2 tablespoons olive oil
A sprig of fresh thyme
2 bay leaves
2 strips of orange rind

FOR THE CASSEROLE
1 kg kangaroo stewing
*   steak, diced*
2 tablespoons oil
150 g streaky bacon,
*   rind off and chopped*
250 g onions, peeled, sliced
1 stalk celery, sliced
60 g (½ cup) plain flour
250 ml stock or water
Juice of 1 orange
Salt and pepper
150 g cherries, stoned

---

1 Mix the marinade in a large bowl and add the kangaroo. Cover and leave for 2-3 hours, or overnight, in the refrigerator.
2 Preheat the oven to 160°C.
3 Drain the kangaroo meat, reserving the marinade to add to the casserole, but discarding the orange peel, and pat dry with paper towels.

Red cherries add a bright touch to the rich, dark colour of this kangaroo casserole. Using a marinade adds flavour and helps to speed the cooking time.

WHITE CASSEROLES

Are a fricassée and a blanquette the same dish?

No, although both are white stews. A fricassée is made from poultry and other white meat, and the meat is just turned in fat but not browned before cooking in a white sauce.

For a blanquette, the meat or seafood is poached in stock and a sauce is made with the liquor after cooking, to pour over the meat.

Fricassée really should be made with fresh meat but the modified Turkey Fricassée below is an excellent way to use leftovers.

Turkey fricassée

SERVES: 4
PREPARATION TIME: 20 minutes
COOKING TIME: 20 minutes

50 g butter
1 medium onion, chopped
1 stalk celery, sliced
500 g cooked turkey, boned, skinned and in pieces
60 g (½ cup) plain flour
500 ml turkey, chicken or ham stock
150 ml cream or milk
A pinch of ground nutmeg
1 tablespoon lemon juice
Salt and black pepper
150 g mushrooms, sliced
1 tablespoon chopped parsley, tarragon or thyme

4 Heat the oil in a large saucepan or flameproof casserole dish and fry the kangaroo until slightly browned, then remove from the pan. Add the bacon, onion and celery and sauté for 5 minutes. Stir in the flour and cook gently for a further minute.
5 Add the stock, reserved marinade and orange juice and bring to the boil, stirring until thickened. Add the kangaroo, salt and pepper and return to the boil. Then simmer for just 2 minutes, stirring occasionally.
6 Transfer the casserole to the oven and cook, covered, for 1¼ hours.
7 Add the cherries and return to the oven, covered, for 15 minutes until the cherries are cooked.
8 Remove the herbs from the liquid and garnish with fresh thyme. Serve with mashed potatoes or pasta.

STOCK QUESTION

Why do recipes require the use of stock for casseroles – don't the ingredients give enough flavour?

A well-flavoured stock will give a better taste than plain water. However, it is quite acceptable to use plain water with the tougher cuts of meat. These are anyway best left to cook for a long time along with other flavourings such as herbs, vegetables, spices and wine.

Adding some bones is another way in which you can help to improve the taste of a casserole. Shank bones have a hollow centre that contains a soft material called marrow. Putting these bones in enhances the stock flavour as well as providing good nutrients.

1 Heat the butter in a medium or large saucepan or flameproof casserole, then add the chopped onion and celery and sauté them over a medium heat for 5 minutes.
2 Add the turkey pieces and sauté for 5 minutes. Stir in the flour and cook gently for a minute, stirring constantly. Gradually add the stock and stir until the sauce boils and is thickened and smooth.
3 Add the cream, nutmeg and lemon juice, add salt and pepper to taste and bring to the boil slowly, stirring.
4 Add the mushrooms, cover and simmer gently for 10–15 minutes, stirring occasionally until heated.
5 Stir in the parsley, tarragon or thyme. Serve hot with rice and a green vegetable or salad.

Cauliflower

PICK AND CHOOSE

How should I go about selecting a cauliflower? Some have been very disappointing when cooked.

Look for firm, creamy-white florets that are tight and without brown speckles. Check also the condition of the base of the stem. If it is dry and discoloured, the cauliflower is certainly past its best.

The outer leaves of a cauliflower are usually cut away before they are sold. This helps you to see the head but removes what would be a clue to a limp, older cauliflower that is definitely best avoided.

SOAKING UP FLAVOURS

Why is cauliflower so often served with a sauce?

Cauliflower is a particularly bland vegetable served on its own. The absorbent heads are much better soaking up a cheese sauce to make a tasty lunch or family dinner dish, as in the recipe shown on the right.

The ability to soak up flavours also makes cauliflower an excellent ingredient to add to soup, or to include in vegetable curries.

Cauliflower cheese and bacon gratin

SERVES: 4
PREPARATION TIME: 20 minutes
COOKING TIME: 35 minutes

---

500 g cauliflower
250 ml milk
25 g butter, plus extra for greasing dish
1 clove garlic, finely chopped
75 g rindless bacon, diced
30 g (¼ cup) plain flour
100 ml fresh cream
50 g Gruyère cheese, grated
Salt and white pepper
Grated nutmeg
4 tablespoons finely grated Parmesan cheese

---

1 Break up the cauliflower into florets and cut the stalk diagonally into 5 mm slices.
2 Bring a large pan of salted water to the boil and cook both the florets and sliced stalk for 7–8 minutes. Take 4 tablespoons of the cooking liquid and mix it with the milk and then drain the cauliflower pieces thoroughly.
3 Preheat the oven to 200°C. Butter a gratin dish and scatter chopped garlic over the base.
4 Melt the butter in a frying pan and fry the bacon for 5 minutes or until it releases its fat. While it is cooking, heat the milk mixture.
5 Sprinkle the flour into the bacon pan and stir over a gentle heat for about 2–3 minutes without letting it brown. Remove the pan from the heat and gradually stir in enough milk mixture to make a thick sauce.
6 Add more milk mixture and as the sauce thins, return it to the heat and add the rest of the milk mixture; stir constantly until the sauce begins to bubble. Reduce the heat and simmer for about 2 minutes. Stir in the cream slowly and return to boiling point.
7 Remove from the heat and add half the Gruyère cheese. Stir until the cheese has melted, then season with salt, pepper and grated nutmeg.
8 Spread the cauliflower florets in the prepared gratin dish and slowly pour the sauce over, allowing it to permeate the florets.
9 Mix the remaining Gruyère cheese and the Parmesan and scatter over the sauce. Bake for about 20 minutes, until the top is bubbling nicely and has become well browned.

Bacon adds a scrumptious extra flavour to the traditional combination of cauliflower in a cheese sauce. Let the dish brown handsomely for best appeal.

Caviar

TYPES OF CAVIAR

What is the difference between the various types of caviar and why are some so expensive?

Caviar is the roe (or eggs) of the sturgeon. These are very lightly salted, which helps to preserve and flavour them. The three main types of caviar – beluga, oscietra and sevruga – come from different varieties of sturgeon. These originate mainly from fish in the Caspian Sea that are over 15 years old.

The most expensive caviar is from the beluga, as only about a hundred fish are caught each year.

The eggs are fragile and vary in colour from light to dark grey with a white spot. Sevruga is small and dark grey, with a light, sweet taste.

Nutty-flavoured eggs from the oscietra are small and black when the fish are young – but become larger and golden as the fish ages.

CAVIAR SUBSTITUTES

Are there any inexpensive versions of caviar available?

Pressed caviar, a favourite with the Russians, is a mixture of damaged or fragile eggs pressed through muslin after salting and costs less than whole caviar. Other less dear varieties include salmon caviar, also known as red caviar or keta, which is shiny and orange-red in colour, and lumpfish caviar, which is very small and black. Although these are not really 'true' caviars, they have a similar, highly salted taste.

SERVING SUGGESTIONS

If I were lucky enough to be given caviar, how should I serve it?

Set the can in a bowl filled with ice. Open the chilled can just before serving, as air causes caviar to oxidise, affecting the flavour. Serve it simply, with triangles of hot toast and unsalted butter.

Blini (buckwheat pancakes) and sour cream are also good with caviar, as are smoked salmon and new potatoes with crème fraîche. Avoid accompaniments such as egg, lemon, onion and parsley which only detract from the flavour. Serve champagne and iced vodka as the traditional drinks.

Celeriac

RICH MASH

How is celeriac prepared and then cooked?

Celeriac is one of the knobblier root vegetables; it needs to be thickly peeled and cut straight into water acidulated with lemon juice

to prevent discoloration. It cooks to a good purée, which is often mixed with mashed potato to soften its flavour and make the texture drier, as in the recipe below. Chopped celery adds a crunchy contrast. The purée goes well with chicken, and is very good with fish, particularly as the topping to a fish pie.

Celeriac and potato purée with celery

SERVES: 4
PREPARATION TIME: 10 minutes
COOKING TIME: 30 minutes

400 g celeriac
Juice of 1 lemon
400 g even-sized floury potatoes, suitable for mashing
50 g butter
2 tablespoons milk
Salt and black pepper
Grated nutmeg
1 large stalk celery, destrung and finely diced

1 Peel the celeriac thickly and cut it into even chunks. Drop the pieces straight into a bowl of water mixed with half of the lemon juice.
2 Drain the celeriac and put it into a pan of boiling water containing the rest of the lemon juice.
3 Bring the water back to the boil, then reduce the heat to simmering point and cook the celeriac until soft. Cooking time varies, but should be about the same as for potatoes.
4 Drain the celeriac well, returning it to the pan and shaking over the heat to dry the pieces thoroughly. Then purée the celeriac in a food processor or by thorough mashing.
5 Scrub the potatoes and cook them whole for 15–25 minutes until soft. Drain and skin when cool enough to handle, then mash with a potato masher. (Never use an electric tool on potatoes as it turns them gluey.)
6 Mix the two purées together. Warm the butter in the milk until it melts, swirl in salt and pepper and a good grating of nutmeg, and then beat it into the mash.
7 Mix in the celery, spread in an oven dish and keep warm until ready to eat, or reheat in the oven.

SALAD DAYS

Can celeriac be used in salads?

Yes. In France, celeriac is popular either sliced or grated as a crunchy first course – celeriac rémoulade, served tossed in mayonnaise spiked with capers (see recipe, page 218).

BLANCHING CELERIAC

Celeriac is blanched before being used in a salad both to set the colour and to soften the flavour.

1 Cut away the knobbly base using a strong, sharp knife. Peel the celeriac thickly and cut into slices. (If you were going to mash it, you could cut it into chunks.)

2 Cut the slices by hand into thin strips, or shred on the julienne-cutting disc of a food processor, and put them into cold water acidulated with the juice of half a lemon.

3 Boil water with juice from the other half lemon. Drain the celeriac and drop it in. When the water returns to the boil, take out the vegetable and run under a cold tap. Drain it and dress the salad.

Celery

KEEPING IT CRISP

Celery seems to wilt and go soft quite quickly, even when I keep it in the refrigerator. Is there a way to keep it crisp?

A whole head of celery will keep fresh for up to a week when placed in a vegetable crisper, or in a long-life green storage bag, in the refrigerator. However, it may need to be cut in half to fit in the crisper drawer. You can break off individual stalks for use and the remainder will keep well, especially if it is still attached to its root base.

To prepare celery, cut the strings from coarser outer stalks, trim the stalks and wash all the celery carefully to remove trapped earth. The celery stalks can then be sliced, diced, chopped or cut into strips to be cooked in soups and stews, braised or steamed as a vegetable, or used in stir-fries. Serve it raw as a crisp partner to cheese.

For best effect when serving as a raw accompaniment, especially on a cheese board, you can leave some of the leaves attached.

STRINGLESS STALKS

I find it time-consuming and fiddly to remove all the strings from celery sticks. Is there an easy way to do this?

Pull the strings from the long stalks before cutting them up into sticks. Better still, buy stringless celery, which is easy to prepare, particularly when using a large quantity of stalks in a recipe such as the following stir-fry.

Celery stir-fry

SERVES: 4
PREPARATION TIME: 15 minutes
COOKING TIME: 8 minutes

1 tablespoon sesame seeds
2 tablespoons peanut oil
1 teaspoon finely chopped green ginger
2 cloves garlic, crushed
300 g celery, sliced diagonally 5 mm thick
175 g bunch asparagus, trimmed and cut into 3 cm lengths
75 g snow peas, trimmed
4 spring onions, sliced diagonally into 3 cm lengths
1 tablespoon salt-reduced soy sauce
1 tablespoon lime juice
1 tablespoon sweet chilli sauce

1 Place the sesame seeds in a small frying pan and dry-fry over a medium heat for 1–2 minutes, stirring occasionally, or until golden. Do not let them get brown. Transfer the seeds to a small bowl. Or toast the sesame seeds on a baking tray under a medium-hot grill until they are golden.
2 Heat the peanut oil in a wok over a medium heat, or in an electric wok heated to 150°C, and stir-fry the ginger for 30 seconds.
3 Add the garlic and celery and stir-fry for 3 minutes.
4 Add the asparagus and stir-fry for a further 3 minutes.
5 Add the snow peas and spring onions and stir-fry for 2 minutes.
6 Stir in the soy sauce, lime juice, sweet chilli sauce and sesame seeds; toss until the vegetables are evenly coated. Serve immediately.

Some of the favourite flavourings of Southeast Asia combine in this crisp blend of celery, snow peas and asparagus, topped with toasted sesame seeds.

Cereals

SEEDS OF CIVILISATION

What's the difference between cereals and breakfast cereals?

Cereals are the edible grains, or seeds, of grasses. The name comes from Ceres, the Roman goddess of tillage and corn. The cultivation of wild grasses marked the transition of hunter gatherers to agriculturalists. The cultivation of grains developed according to geography and climate. The main cereal grains are wheat and barley, which spread from Egypt and the Middle East to Europe, India and parts of Asia. Rice became the staple cereal of Asia; millet developed in Africa and Asia; corn and maize became the staple cereals of North and South America.

Some of these cereal crops are processed to produce the large range of breakfast cereals available on supermarket shelves worldwide. Cereal grains have also given rise to other processed foods in several food cultures, such as noodles, pasta, tortillas, couscous, polenta, as well as several flours and breads.

Cheese

LOCAL FLAVOUR

What is farm and farmhouse cheese? Do these names mean the cheese is of better quality than cheese which is not labelled 'farm' or 'farmhouse'?

The terms 'farm' and 'farmhouse' are not legally regulated, so their use is no guarantee that the cheese has been made, as one might expect, on a small scale using traditional equipment. However, the terms usually indicate high quality, specialty cheeses. Generally, the cheese has been made on a farm, using the milk of that farm and, frequently, its neighbours. However, this can include a wide area and a large number of animals. Similarly, cheese producers not based on farms may have very large or quite small specialised operations.

Farm or farmhouse cheese makers in Australia tend to focus on European-style cheeses, such as chèvre or goat's cheeses, ewe's milk cheeses, washed rind and vine ash cheeses, Brie, Camembert, Feta, Haloumy and Swiss cheese styles. These fine or specialist cheeses are most often made on a small scale, by cheesemakers who use traditional methods and provide this country with a huge diversity of cheese.

NAME SHARING

Surely Cheddar cheese originated in the English town of Cheddar? So why is the name Cheddar still used for Australian and New Zealand cheeses?

Yes, Cheddar cheese was originally made in a town called Cheddar, in Somerset, England. In fact, the craft of cheese-making originated in Europe many centuries ago.

The Cheddar cheese variety is now manufactured widely all over the English-speaking world. It is a semi-hard cheese, with many variations, and has become the most popular and versatile cheese in Australia and New Zealand today.

Natural Cheddar is a firm close-textured cheese, light yellow in colour with a delicate to full, rich flavour, depending on its age. Mild Cheddar is three months old; semi-matured Cheddar is three to six months old; matured (tasty) is six to twelve months old. All are good for grating and slicing, for cooking and for sandwiches. Vintage Cheddar is 12 to 15 months old and is excellent for a cheese board.

Cheddar cheese is processed to a softer texture, sometimes in slices, to use conveniently in sandwiches. It is also processed into a cheese spread, which is handy for dips and sauces as well as sandwiches.

Cheshire, Leicester and Red Leicester cheeses are all Cheddar-type cheeses, originally from English cities, which are now also made in Australia. Colby cheese, which originated in the USA, is a milder, moister version of Cheddar cheese, and is also made in Australia. These variations can be used for cooking, melting, sandwiches and cheese boards.

VEGETARIAN CHOICE

Can I serve cheese to a vegetarian?

Yes and no! It depends if the vegetarian is a lacto-vegetarian or a vegan. Lacto-vegetarians do eat dairy products, which include cheese as well as milk, cream, butter, yoghurt, buttermilk and ice cream. A vegan does not eat dairy products or eggs, fish, meat, poultry or game. However, you can serve soycheese to a vegan. This is made from soy beans, available in various flavours such as black pepper, chives and garlic, and is suitable for cheese boards. It is available in health food shops.

A suitable main course to serve to a lacto-vegetarian is the Triple-layered Vegetable Crepe Cake (page 123) which includes cheese in the filling, while you will find Tofu Balls (page 360) are more appropriate to serve to a vegan.

SHEEP AND GOATS

How do goat's milk and other animals' cheeses differ from cheeses made with cow's milk?

When they are young, mild and creamy, fresh goat's milk cheeses taste quite similar to cheeses made from cow's milk. Their characteristic tang develops with age and very mature goat's milk cheeses have a strong 'farmyard' flavour though they should always taste clean. Unlike most cow's milk cheeses, the paste is usually bright white in colour, except for hard goat's milk cheese, which is pale yellow.

Goat's milk cheeses are just as high in fat as cow's milk cheeses, but both goat's and ewe's milk cheeses are easier to digest than cow's milk cheeses because their fat particles are smaller; some people who are intolerant of cow's milk can tolerate goat's milk.

With their high flavour, goat's cheeses cannot easily be substituted for cow's milk cheeses in cooking, but they are good in soufflés, or grilled, served with salads.

Ewe's milk is very high in fat and therefore is made into hard cheese such as Pecorino in Italy. However, some soft ewe's cheeses are made in Australia; though sharp, they are milder than goat's cheeses and have a pleasing mellow nuttiness and a firm, creamy texture.

Buffalo milk, used for Mozzarella in southern Italy and now in Victoria, has a distinctive high aroma and stronger flavour.

Save it!

If you have an abundance of cheese, freeze some for use in cooking. Blue vein cheese freezes well, as do semi-hard cheeses and ricotta. But fresh cheeses can go off while defrosting, or be bitter if frozen near the end of their use-by date.

FRESH UNRIPENED CHEESES AND STRETCHED CURD CHEESES

Fresh cheeses, such as cream and curd cheeses, are less than three weeks old and mild in flavour. They have a soft, moist texture, bright white colour and no rinds. Stretched | *curd cheeses, where the curd is soaked in whey to give a putty-like texture, are shaped by hand and have no rinds. They include Bocconcini, Mozzarella and Provolone.*

1 RICOTTA, a fresh Italian-style cheese, is low in fat, has a milky flavour, and is good for cooking.

2 BOCCONCINI is a fresh Mozzarella sold as moist, mild-flavoured white balls, in water or brine. Baby Bocconcini (shown in blue bowl) is also available.

3 MASCARPONE has a whipped cream consistency and a clean acidic flavour.

4 PROVOLONE is light golden, firm to soft, with a robust flavour.

5 GOAT'S CHEESE, when unripened, is a young, fresh cheese. It is available plain or, as shown here, coated with ash.

6 FETA tastes very salty, and is white with a soft to firm crumbly texture.

7 MOZZARELLA is pale yellow, smooth, mild and pear-shaped, good for melting.

• CREAM CHEESE (not shown) is made from cream and has a velvety texture.

• COTTAGE CHEESE (not shown) is mild in flavour and low in fat.

• QUARK (not shown) is white, soft and spoonable with a creamy sweet flavour.

• HALOUMY (not shown), originally from Cyprus, is white with a firm texture and is marinated in brine.

KEEPING CHEESE FRESH

Where is the best place to store cheese and how should I wrap it?

Ideally, cheese should be stored in the refrigerator, at a temperature of 4–6°C, because this provides a low temperature and low humidity.

To avoid cheese being tainted by the aromas from other foods, keep it in its own plastic box or separate compartment in the refrigerator, and store it in its original wrapper, where possible. Or else wrap individual pieces of cheese in waxed paper or foil. Greaseproof paper draws the fat from the cheese and encourages mould; plastic wrap can induce sweating, although it may be used to cover just the cut surfaces of hard and blue cheeses. Whatever the material used, do not wrap cheese tightly; allow it to breathe. The harder the cheese, the longer it will keep. Cheddar, Cheshire, Leicester, Colby, Emmental, Gouda, Gruyère, Parmesan and Romano can be kept for months if properly wrapped and stored. A little mould or cut surfaces which have become slightly dried and cracked can simply be trimmed away.

Ideally, buy only a quantity of cheese that you can consume within one to two weeks.

SURFACE RIPENED AND BLUE VEIN CHEESES

Ripened, unpressed cheeses are over three weeks old and have a bloomy white rind, as in Camembert or Brie, or boast the natural blue-grey surface mould of goat's cheeses.

Most blue vein cheeses are also unpressed: it is the spaces between the curds that create the environment in which the distinctive blue veining can develop.

1 BRIE, with its mushroomy aroma and flavour, should be golden and creamy. It comes in rounds and square blocks.

2 BLUE VEIN CHEESE, made from both cow's and ewe's milk, has veins of mould through a smooth, creamy-white cheese. Most blue cheeses are strong and pungent, but regional styles vary in flavour and texture. Natural rind blues have a crusty surface and soft interior. Foil-wrapped blues have a scraped rind and a stronger flavour.

3 WASHED RIND CHEESE is so-named because of the weekly washing of the pressed curd in brine. This develops a rich, strong-smelling rind, but the interior is sweet, mild and creamy. They are made from cow's and ewe's milk.

4 CAMEMBERT should be golden, creamy and have a flecked white rind; usually made in smaller rounds than Brie.

• GOAT'S CHEESE (not shown), when ripened, should have a clean white paste and a flavour that becomes more distinctive with age. Like the younger, unripened variety, ripened goat's cheese is also available plain and ash-covered.

COOK'S CHOICE

Which cheeses are best to have on hand in the kitchen for cooking?

Strong, mature cheeses are generally better for cooking than mild cheeses. Cheddar is the most widely used cheese for cooking in Australia, but other firm-textured cheeses are equally versatile and delicious. Gruyère is very popular for cooking because of its excellent flavour and good melting qualities. Gouda cheese is a good alternative.

Emmental and stretched curd cheeses, such as Mozzarella and Provolone, make excellent melting cheeses and are popular because, although they become stringy, they maintain their creamy qualities during cooking longer than other cheeses. Emmental is classically used with Gruyère in fondues, and Mozzarella and Provolone are good for topping pizzas. Haloumy, which is another stretched curd cheese, can be dry-fried like steak.

Blue cheeses melt well and retain their piquancy, making them useful for sauces, pasta, grilled dishes, soufflés, soups, salad dressings, dips and for topping red meats.

Very hard, grainy cheeses such as Parmesan and Romano are useful sprinkled over foods, but they also melt well in sauces, soufflés

CHEDDAR-TYPE, EYE AND HARD GRATING CHEESES

Cheddar and Cheddar-type cheeses are pressed during maturation to expel the whey from the curds. The result is a firm, close-textured cheese. Very hard pressed cheeses such as Parmesan develop a grainy texture with maturity and are very good for grating. Eye cheeses have eyes, or hollows, caused by the expansion of gases in them during ripening.

1 HAVARTI has a light, mild flavour, many holes and good melting qualities.
2 PARMESAN is hard and strong, and is excellent for grating.
3 EMMENTAL has a nutty flavour, and is similar to, but stronger than, Havarti.
4 PEPATO is light yellow, hard and quite grainy, with black peppercorns scattered throughout.

5 COLBY is similar to Cheddar, and also available with a rich orange colour.
6 CHEDDAR has a close texture and ranges in flavour from mild to mature. It is usually golden in colour.
7 AGED CHEDDAR has a nutty bite. It is made from cow's and ewe's milk.
8 GRUYERE is ivory coloured, firm, with small holes and a strong nutty taste.

9 EDAM has a red wax skin, is smooth and mild in flavour. Gouda (not shown), with a yellow rind, is similar.
• CHESHIRE (not shown) is firm yet flaky, with a pleasant acid flavour.
• LEICESTER AND RED LEICESTER (not shown) are firm, slightly crumbly, and sharp.
• PECORINO (not shown) is tangy, straw-coloured, soft and somewhat grainy.

and risottos. They are often combined with other cheeses such as Swiss Gruyère, but even a small quantity will add a lot of flavour.

Smooth, fresh cheeses such as curd cheese, cream cheese and ricotta have a mild, milky flavour that is excellent in desserts, and can also be used in savoury fillings for pastries or pasta. Soft, fresh, flavoured cheeses, such as those with garlic and herbs, can be melted to make sauces or used in savoury fillings. Keep the cooking time for these cheeses brief, otherwise they will separate.

Goat's milk cheeses are slightly less versatile than most but can be used for pizzas and crostini. They combine particularly well with nuts. Rinded goat's cheeses are best when peeled before being cooked in case the rind imparts too much of a farmyard flavour.

MELTING CHEESE TOPPING

When I grill or bake cheese on top of a dish, it looks unpleasant. What am I doing wrong?

Providing that you have chosen a cheese appropriate for grilling or baking, it is most likely that the cheese has been overcooked. In fact, cheese needs only to be melted. Do not put it too close to a fierce grill. Once cheese reaches temperatures above 75°C it is likely to become hard, stringy or chewy, because the heat encourages the proteins, fat and water in the cheese to separate.

For a successful result, try adding an equal quantity of fresh bread-crumbs to the grated cheese.

WHEN TO SERVE

At a dinner party, should I serve the cheese before or after dessert?

The French and other Continental Europeans offer the cheese board before dessert to accompany the last of the red wine that has been served with the main course. This completes the savoury part of the meal before guests move on to the sweet course, a logical progression for the palate and the one generally preferred by cheese enthusiasts.

In Britain, there was a tradition of ending a formal dinner with a savoury to accompany the port, and cheese was served after dessert. With today's lighter, more casual meals, cheese may be offered as an alternative to dessert. Do whichever you prefer.

ITALIAN STYLE

What are 'pasta filata' cheeses?

Australian Mozzarella, Bocconcini, Provolone and Haloumy belong to the family of 'pasta filata' cheeses originally produced in Italy. These cheeses are characterised by work-ing the curd to a plastic state in hot water, so that it may be drawn out to a rope. It is then cut into varying lengths for moulding into individual shapes. Pasta filata cheeses are also called stretched curd cheeses.

EYE TO EYE

What are 'eye' cheeses?

Eye cheeses are those that contain holes or eyes, such as the Swiss-style Emmental, Gruyère and Raclette, the Dutch-style Edam and Gouda, and Havarti and Tilsit.

The cheese is usually smooth and satiny and the eyes are formed by the production of carbon di-

oxide during ripening. The eyes can be large and quite distinct as in Emmental, or small in close-textured cheeses, such as Gouda.

The flavour of these eye cheeses is mild, slightly sweet and nutty, so they are enjoyed by most children. They are usually cut from a wheel so look attractive on a cheese board. They are also suitable for cooking. Raclette, in particular, is good for melting and serving Swiss-style over new potatoes.

CREAMY TREAT

How do you serve mascarpone?

Mascarpone is a fresh unripened cheese with a thick creamy texture. It should be used within two to three days of purchase. It is a versatile cheese and can be used in savoury or sweet recipes. Try using it in place of sour cream in your favourite dip, or add it to a cheese-cake. It is a perfect accompaniment to poached fruit or fruit salad when mixed with a little brandy or liqueur and icing sugar.

The following Italian recipe is delightful served alongside some fresh raspberries.

Cream of mascarpone

SERVES: 6–8
PREPARATION TIME: 20 minutes, plus chilling
COOKING TIME: none

---

3 eggs, separated
125 g (½ cup) caster sugar
250 g mascarpone
2 tablespoons amaretto liqueur

---

1 Put the egg yolks and caster sugar into a mixing bowl. Beat with an electric mixer until pale and creamy.
2 Add the mascarpone and amaretto and fold in gently, using a plastic spatula, until evenly combined.
3 In a cleanly polished mixing bowl, whisk the egg whites with an electric mixer until stiff peaks form.
4 Gently fold the egg whites into the mascarpone mixture.
5 Serve the cream of mascarpone at once with sugared raspberries, or cover and chill until ready to serve.

HOW TO CUT CHEESE

When serving a variety of cheeses on a board, provide a separate long-bladed sharp knife for each cheese so that the moulds and flavours do not mix.

BRIE AND OTHER LARGE, FLAT WEDGES

1 Do not cut across the centre of the cheese. Cut a triangle down one side, narrow at the outside edge and wider at the centre.

2 Repeat, cutting from alternate sides of the wedge. Do not cut too close to the outside rind towards the end – this ensures that the last piece contains a generous portion of the creamy paste.

CHEDDAR AND OTHER HARD WEDGES

Place the wedge of Cheddar on its side and cut thin, triangular slices across the wedge moving from top to bottom, so that each piece of cheese forms an equal-sized portion.

Save it!

Hard cheese seems to go further when grated finely. This is particularly useful for topping baked dishes, grilling, and for people who are watching their weight. Dried-up pieces of cheese can be grated and frozen for adding to cooked dishes.

IDEAL SELECTION

How do I put together a good, interesting cheese board?

The key is to maintain balance by choosing both mild and strong cheeses, so that even a fussy dinner guest can find something to enjoy. Choose cheeses of contrasting textures and flavours, for example one hard cheese (vintage Cheddar), one soft, milder cheese (Brie), and a piquant blue (blue vein).

Using this basic format, it is possible to substitute a number of cheeses to create variety and interest. For instance, the hard cheese could be an eye cheese, the softer cheese flavoured with pepper and herbs, and the piquant blue switched for an ash-covered goat's cheese. Do not overload the cheese board with too many cheeses.

For a dinner party of up to eight people, three or four cheeses is enough. Even buffet parties require no more than five. Each guest is likely to eat only 30–60 g of cheese in total, so it is best to opt for large, inviting pieces of a limited number of cheeses rather than meagre portions of several. Alternatively, try offering one cheese only, particularly at a small dinner party. A whole perfect cheese looks inviting and keeps cost and wastage low. Serve at room temperature.

Irrespective of which style of cheese board you offer your guests, try to keep the accompaniments to a minimum. Cheese connoisseurs will appreciate eating the cheese on its own, perhaps with a good sour-dough, fruit or nut bread or water biscuits. Celery and radishes are complementary accompaniments, and apples, pears, dried apricots, figs, grapes and walnuts match many cheeses. However, it is not necessary to offer all of these, or any accompaniments at all.

See also: *Low-fat Cheeses*

Cheese Biscuits

STRONG AND HARD

What is the best cheese to use when making cheese biscuits?

Choose a firm, hard cheese which will grate finely; ordinary Cheddar may be too soft and could produce a sticky dough that is difficult to roll. For a good strong flavour use a mature Cheddar or Gruyère, perhaps combined with some freshly grated Parmesan. To achieve a crisp, short texture, the pastry should be bound with a little egg, as in the following recipe for rich Cheese Biscuits and Straws.

Cheese biscuits and straws

MAKES: 20 biscuits or 40-60 straws
PREPARATION TIME: 25 minutes for biscuits; 40 minutes for straws, plus 30 minutes chilling time for both
COOKING TIME: 10-15 minutes for biscuits; 5-8 minutes for straws, per batch

---

125 g (1 cup) plain flour
A pinch each of salt, dry mustard powder and cayenne pepper
75 g butter, diced
25 g mature Cheddar, finely grated
25 g Parmesan, finely grated
1 large egg, beaten
For the biscuits: 20 flaked almonds or walnut pieces, or poppy or sesame seeds
For the straws: mild paprika

---

1 Sift the flour, salt, dry mustard powder and cayenne pepper into a bowl. Add the butter and rub it in with your fingers until the mixture resembles fine breadcrumbs. Using a fork, stir in the grated cheeses and gradually add half the beaten egg until the mixture clings together.

2 Draw the flour, cheese and egg mixture together with the tips of your fingers, then remove from the bowl and knead the dough gently for a few minutes on a lightly floured board until it is smooth.

3 Wrap the dough in greaseproof paper and chill in the refrigerator for about 30 minutes until the dough is firm enough to roll out.

4 When ready to bake the pastry, preheat the oven to 200°C and line two baking trays with nonstick baking paper.

TO MAKE BISCUITS

1 Roll out the prepared cheese pastry to 5 mm thick. Using plain or fluted cutters, cut out some rounds about 5 cm in diameter.

2 Place the cut rounds of pastry on the baking trays, then brush them lightly with the rest of the beaten egg. Place a piece of almond or walnut on each biscuit, or sprinkle each of them lightly with a pinch of poppy seeds or sesame seeds.

3 Bake the biscuits for 8-10 minutes or until golden. Remove from the oven and leave on the baking tray for 1-2 minutes, then place on a wire rack to cool. Repeat with the trimmings to make more biscuits.

TO MAKE STRAWS

1 Roll out the prepared pastry into a strip 5 mm thick and 20 cm wide. Using a sharp knife, trim the sides neatly then cut the pastry in half lengthways. Cut each strip across into straws 5 mm wide.

2 Arrange them in neat lines, but not touching, on baking trays (they do not need to be glazed). Bake for 5-8 minutes until pale in colour. Remove from the oven and leave on the tray for 1-2 minutes, then place them on a wire rack to cool.

3 To decorate, dip the ends of each cheese straw into mild paprika.

4 Reroll the pastry trimmings, cut out more cheese straws and bake.

Both these types of biscuit will keep well for a week providing they are stored in an airtight tin and kept in a cool place.

Cheesecake

SUITABLE CHOICE

Many cheesecake recipes specify the use of cream cheese. What would happen if I were to use reduced-fat, light cream cheese in them instead?

Many soft, fresh low-fat cheeses are suitable for making uncooked, chilled cheesecakes. You can substitute or combine reduced-fat cream cheese, neufchatel, ricotta, mascarpone, quark or, as in the recipe for the lemon cheesecake (right), you can use reduced-fat cottage cheese.

However, for a richer cooked cheesecake it is safer to use the cheese that is recommended in the recipe, or one very similar. Reduced-fat cheeses curdle more easily when heated and may separate in a cooked cheesecake.

Fresh lemon and muesli cheesecake

SERVES: *6–8*
PREPARATION TIME: *45 minutes, plus 4 hours chilling time*
COOKING TIME: *5 minutes*

75 g unsalted butter or margarine
185 g (1²⁄₃ cups) muesli with no added sugar
1 tablespoon powdered gelatine
300 g reduced-fat cottage cheese, sieved
60 g (¼ cup) caster sugar
150 ml reduced-fat cream
2 large eggs, separated
Finely grated rind and juice of 1 lemon
To decorate: fresh fruit such as cherries or strawberries

1 Melt the butter or margarine in a small saucepan then stir in the muesli. Press the muesli mixture over the base of a 20 cm flan tin or loose-bottomed cake tin to make a crust.

Chill the crust in the refrigerator for around 30 minutes while you are preparing the filling.
2 Put 3 tablespoons of cold water in a bowl and sprinkle the gelatine over it. Leave to soak for 2 minutes until it turns spongy. Place the bowl over a pan of simmering water and heat until the gelatine has dissolved to a liquid. Set aside to cool slightly.
3 Place the cottage cheese, sugar, cream, egg yolks, lemon rind and juice in a large bowl and stir well. Add the gelatine and mix again.
4 In a separate bowl, whisk the egg whites until stiff, then carefully fold them into the cheese mixture.
5 Pour the mixture into the tin and chill for 4 hours or until firm.
6 Carefully remove the cheesecake from the tin and place it on a serving plate. Decorate it with cherries or strawberries just before serving.

Sumptuous but low in fat, this tangy cheesecake is made with muesli, fresh lemon and reduced-fat cream.

Cherries

RAPID STONE REMOVAL

What is the quickest way to remove stones from cherries?

Use a cherry stoner, available from most kitchen shops. First, remove the stems from the cherries. Place them one at a time and with the stalk end uppermost on the base of the cherry stoner, then close the plunger to push out the cherry stone. Alternatively, you can use the point of a knife to split the fruit and carefully prise out the stones.

Stoning cherries inside a clean, plastic bag prevents the cherry juice splashing over the work surface or your clothes.

KNOW YOUR CHERRIES

Which are the best cherries to eat fresh and which should I choose for use in cooking?

There are three basic types of cherry: sweet, semi-sweet and sour. The cherries that you generally find in shops are sweet or semi-sweet dessert cherries and they can be red, black or pale-skinned (sometimes referred to as white cherries). Some are plump and tender, others have a firmer flesh.

Sour cherries are red and the best known is the morello cherry, which has a strong acidic flavour. Morello cherries are suitable only for cooking and can be poached, used for sweet and savoury pies, added to desserts, savoury dishes, or made into preserves. Dessert cherries can also be used for cooking but will not have the same deep cherry flavour as morello cherries.

Chestnuts

SOFT OPTIONS

How do you cook fresh chestnuts once they have been peeled?

For stuffings or to serve with vegetables, gently boil fresh chestnuts in salted water or stock for about 30 minutes until just tender – they should feel soft when pierced with a fine skewer but not break up.

For purées, fresh chestnuts need to be cooked a little longer so that the nuts will be soft enough to pass easily through a sieve or mouli mill, or be processed in a blender or food processor.

For soups and casseroles, add the chestnuts raw and allow to soften in the cooking liquid along with the recipe's other ingredients.

When using chestnuts in cakes and desserts, cook them barely covered with some sugar syrup or sweetened milk in a lidded, heavy-based saucepan, stirring often.

CHESTNUT CHOICES

When are fresh chestnuts in season, and is there an alternative to use in recipes?

There are several chestnut growers in Victoria and the fresh nuts are in season in autumn. They should be stored in the refrigerator.

Dried chestnuts are available from health food shops and when reconstituted, by soaking in water, they can be cooked and used in the same way as fresh chestnuts.

Home-frozen peeled chestnuts taste identical to the fresh variety and are well worth storing in the freezer.

Canned whole and puréed chestnuts have been processed so do not have as good a flavour as fresh. And when using canned chestnut purée in savoury recipes, always make sure that you have not purchased the sweetened version.

Fresh, dried or frozen chestnuts can be used for soups and stuffings, salads and vegetarian nut loaves and patties. Canned chestnuts are more suitable for sauces, cake fillings, desserts and ice cream recipes.

FIRE DRILL

Can I roast fresh chestnuts on an open fire at home?

Yes, but split the skins first to prevent them exploding. Shake the chestnuts over the fire in a long-handled frying pan, turning them occasionally, until the skins are blackened. The chestnuts will peel easily when cooled slightly.

PEELING CHESTNUTS

It is easier to peel off the thick outer skin and thin brown inner skin of fresh chestnuts after you have gently boiled them for around 5 minutes. Do this while they are still warm and have cooled only just enough to be handled.

1 Cut a deep cross through the tough skin on the rounded side of each chestnut. Cover with cold water in a large saucepan and boil for 5 minutes.

2 Remove the nuts from the water with a slotted spoon and peel. If they become harder to peel as they cool, bring them to the boil again.

Chicken

FREEDOM SHOWS

To buy humanely produced, delicious chicken, what do I look for when shopping?

Look for fresh chickens labelled free-range or certified organic.

SUCCULENT MEAT

What is the best way to keep a skinless breast succulent?

If you are on a low-fat diet, you can poach the breast in stock, or cook it in a foil parcel with some sliced vegetables and seasonings. If you do not mind using a little oil, marinate the chicken in a mixture of olive oil, orange juice, honey and mustard, then grill. Baste with the marinade during cooking.

FROZEN FLAVOUR

Can frozen chicken taste as good as the fresh variety?

While frozen chicken is inferior in taste to fresh, free-range frozen birds have more flavour than fresh battery chickens. Remember that frozen poultry has water which drains out when the bird is defrosted, so weigh the bird after it has thawed to calculate the cooking time. Defrost the chicken in the refrigerator, allowing 2 hours per 500 g. When buying packs of frozen poultry, avoid any with pink ice crystals as these show signs of thawing and refreezing.

PERFECT ROASTING

When roasting a bird, how do I achieve moist flesh as well as a crisp, brown skin?

Pat the skin dry with kitchen paper towels. Smear it with butter, season with salt and pepper and squeeze some lemon juice all over.

For even cooking, place the bird in the baking dish on its side for the first third of the time, turn on the other side for the next third and

JOINTING A CHICKEN INTO EIGHT PIECES

When cooking a dish that requires joints of chicken, such as a casserole, it is considerably cheaper to buy a whole chicken and joint it yourself than to buy the ready-prepared smaller cuts. Follow the simple process below:

1 Place the chicken breast side up on a board. Pull a leg gently away from the body and use a heavy cook's knife to cut through the skin between the body and leg. Bend the leg outwards until the ball pops out of the socket joint, then cut through the flesh under the joint. Repeat with the other leg.

2 To separate the thigh from the drumstick, stand one leg on the board so that it forms a natural 'V' shape. Hold the end of the drumstick in one hand and cut firmly through the joint where the two bones meet at the centre of the 'V'. Repeat the process with the other leg.

3 To separate the wings from the body of the chicken, make a deep cut into the breast meat near to the inside of each wing, angling the knife diagonally towards the neck end of the bird so that the uncut breast forms a diamond shape. Cut down into the meat far enough to expose the bones.

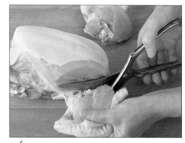

4 To free the wings completely from the rest of the body, use a pair of poultry shears or ordinary kitchen scissors to cut carefully between the ball and socket joints and through the remaining flesh and bone. Make sure there are no sharp splinters of bone embedded in the cut portions.

5 To remove the breast meat, place the carcass of the bird on its side, and, using poultry shears or kitchen scissors, cut through the thin rib cage on either side of the backbone. Do not throw the backbone away as it can be frozen and used for stock.

6 Divide the breast into two, cutting crossways or lengthways through the bird's flesh using a knife and then through the bones and cartilage with the shears or scissors. On large birds, each portion can be further divided into two to give four pieces of breast.

finish with the breast uppermost. This ensures the bird is evenly cooked and less likely to scorch. Roast at 200°C for 35–45 minutes per kg, plus 15–20 minutes. Baste often to keep moist and to colour the skin golden brown.

When the bird is cooked, turn off the heat and rest it for 15 minutes with the oven door ajar, then carve.

SELF-BASTING POTS

What is the reason for cooking chicken in a clay pot?

Cooking chicken in a clay pot is healthy, because you don't need to baste or use fat.

The pot is a hollow, unglazed container that is put into a cold oven. As the oven heats, steam from the food condenses on the lid and bastes the food. The bird will be tender, flavoursome and moist – lightly browned and sitting in its delicious juices.

Chicken in a brick

SERVES: 4-6
PREPARATION TIME: 15 minutes
COOKING TIME: about 1¾ hours

1.5 kg fresh roasting chicken
1 lemon
Salt and black pepper
1 onion, sliced
2 carrots, diced
2 stalks celery, sliced
Sprigs of fresh herbs
10 large cloves garlic, unpeeled

---

1 Soak the clay pot in cold water for 10-30 minutes before use. Halve the lemon and place one half inside the cavity of the bird.
2 Season the bird inside and out with the salt and pepper. Slice the remaining half of the lemon and place it in the bottom of the brick.
3 Put the vegetables on the sliced lemon. Place the chicken on the vegetables, add the herbs and scatter the garlic cloves over the bird.
4 Cover the pot and place it in a cold oven. Set the oven to 230°C and cook for 55 minutes per kg, plus an extra 25 minutes. Serve the bird with the vegetables and garlic.

Chickpeas

VERSATILE PULSE

Are there other uses for chickpeas besides hummous?

Chickpeas are versatile, nourishing and useful in soups and stews, cooked with or without meat. You can also incorporate them in bean salads and vegetable dishes and use them to make a type of Middle Eastern patty called felafel.

Dried chickpeas need overnight soaking and long cooking to make them tender. For this reason, it is much easier to buy canned chickpeas, which are already cooked, to make hummous. Traditionally, a fluid, oily paste of sesame seeds called tahina is added to the chickpea mixture, as in the recipe for Hummous below.

Hummous

SERVES: 2 as starter, 4 with other salads and dips
PREPARATION TIME: 5 minutes
COOKING TIME: none

---

400 g canned chickpeas
1-2 cloves garlic, crushed
Juice of ½ lemon
4 tablespoons olive oil
1 tablespoon tahina
Salt and black pepper
A pinch of cayenne pepper
To garnish: black olives
To serve: hot pita bread

---

1 Drain and thoroughly rinse the chickpeas, then purée them in a food processor with the garlic and lemon juice until smooth, or mash them vigorously with a potato masher in a large bowl.
2 Add 3 tablespoons of the olive oil, the tahina, salt and pepper to taste and process or mash again.
3 Spread the hummous in a shallow dish and trickle the remaining olive oil in a zigzag over the top.
4 Sprinkle the hummous lightly with cayenne pepper and garnish with the black olives. Serve at room temperature with hot pita bread.

Chilli

SHAPELY CUES

Is the colour of a fresh chilli any indication of how hot the flavour will be?

No. Most chillies are green when they are unripe and then ripen to yellow, orange, reddish-brown and purple or near-black. The fruity flavour increases with maturity but not the intrinsic heat. As a rough guide, smaller and slimmer chillies are the hottest, but there are exceptions. The only safe course is to become familiar with the common varieties (see chart, page 85).

CAYENNE SUBSTITUTES

If a recipe calls for cayenne and I have only chilli powder or hot sauce, could I use that instead?

Yes, chilli powder is very similar to cayenne pepper. Both are made from dried capsicums that have been finely ground, but cayenne is a little bit hotter. Hot pepper sauce (Tabasco) may be used as a substitute in liquid dishes, but it should not be used in dry mixtures.

THE CHILLI FAMILY

I am confused by the wide variety of chillies. How should all these different types be used?

Chilli is one of the world's favourite seasonings and there are hundreds of types. The capsicum family of pepper-producing plants was introduced to Europe in the 16th century from South America. Chillies were then taken to India and Asia where they became popular.

Some chillies are used fresh and the type of fresh chilli you choose for cooking will have a considerable effect on how hot the finished dish will be (see chart, page 85). Others are dried and ground and used to make such ingredients as chilli powder, cayenne pepper and red pepper flakes. Chillies are also used in fiery sauces like Tabasco.

IDENTIFYING FRESH CHILLIES

These are the most common fresh chillies, with their heat indicated on a scale of 1—10 (10 being the hottest). Removing the internal pith and seeds reduces the heat, but remember not to touch your face while cutting chillies and always wash your hands afterwards. Wear rubber gloves if you have any cuts.

TYPE	DESCRIPTION AND USES	HOTNESS
Anaheim	Red or green, up to 15 cm long, tapering and with thickish flesh. Stuff and roast them, or shred into sauces and salads.	2–3
Dutch	Bright green or red and shiny, 10 cm long, sweet, hot and intense. Use them in salsas or add to any other dish that needs a heat boost.	5–6
Fresco	Red or green, 5 cm long and quite stubby, smooth and waxy skin, thick flesh. These are good used raw in sauces and ceviches, or they can be roasted and then chopped into a sauce.	6–7
Thai	Skinny and curving, red or green, about 4 cm long, thin-fleshed and packed with red-hot seeds. These chillies add considerable fire to the cooking of Southeast Asia.	7–8
Habanero, Jamaican hot bonnet and Scotch bonnet	Habaneros can be red, yellow, green or brown in colour. Jamaican hot bonnets are red while Scotch bonnets are yellow. All are recognisable by their squat shape, 4–5 cm long. Use them in curries, tropical fruit sauces and chutneys, Caribbean dishes and marinades.	9–10

Chinese Cooking

GETTING STARTED

Can you suggest a starter pack of ingredients that I could use to make most Chinese dishes?

The following ingredients are the foundation of common dishes:
• SAUCES: Have on hand a bottle each of chilli sauce, hoisin sauce, oyster sauce, dark soy sauce, light soy sauce, yellow or black bean sauce and some sesame oil.
• CANNED VEGETABLES: Plan to stock a can each of bamboo shoots, black beans, straw mushrooms and some water chestnuts.
• SEASONINGS: Keep a jar of five-spice powder, garlic (fresh or puréed), green ginger (fresh or puréed) and some sesame seeds.

• NOODLES AND RICE: Stock packets of egg noodles, rice noodles and rice vermicelli, plus bags of fragrant Thai or basmati rice, and perhaps a bag of glutinous or sticky short-grain rice as well.

BE PREPARED

Does it always take a long time to prepare the varied ingredients for an everyday Chinese dish?

It is a fallacy that Chinese cooking needs considerable work ahead of time, even if the cooking process is very quick. Really long preparation is required only for the grand, imperial dishes that few people bother to cook at home anyway.

However, organising even a very simple meal, such as a stir-fry, is easier if some of the work is done beforehand. Slicing the meats in advance allows you to marinate

them, giving a delicious flavour to the finished dish. Vegetables can be washed, dried, sliced and kept in a plastic bag (not soaking in water) until they are needed. Then you can relax, knowing the meal can be cooked in just a few minutes.

PERFECT RICE

How much rice is required for a Chinese meal, and is it best to have a special rice cooker?

In Asia, rice is regarded as a bland base and contrast for richly sauced dishes and it is usually eaten in the ratio of seven parts rice to three parts other food. A typical Asian serving would be 100 g of rice per head. Western diners like a higher ratio of main dish food to their rice, and the usual serving is 60–90 g per person.

In some parts of Asia, electric rice cookers have become very popular. These are worth the expense only if you frequently cook large quantities of rice. The simple and effective way to cook perfect, fluffy rice (below) is to use what many homes already have: a microwave oven. (See also *Rice*.)

Microwave rice

SERVES: *4*
PREPARATION TIME: *5 minutes*
COOKING TIME: *11–12 minutes*

250 g basmati or long grain rice, yielding about 4½ cups of cooked rice

1 Wash the rice, drain and place in a microwave-safe bowl large enough to hold the cooked grains when they have expanded. Add enough fresh cold water to rise 2.5 cm above the surface of the rice.
2 Place in the microwave and cook on High, uncovered, for 18 minutes without stirring, until the water has been absorbed. Rake the cooked rice with a fork to fluff up the grains before serving and season to taste.
VARIATION
For brown rice, add water to a level 3 cm above the rice and cook for 25 minutes.

ROUNDED MEAL

What dishes should I include in a Chinese meal for my family?

Traditionally, most Chinese family meals feature four dishes and a soup, which is drunk throughout the meal and between mouthfuls of the other dishes.

Flavours should be based on the yin and yang concept of contrasts. For example, a typical meal might include deep-fried chicken (which is succulent), steamed fish (light), sweet-and-sour pork (rich and soft) and some water chestnuts (crisp). Dishes are shared, and the ideal menu would feature one dish per person, normally of chicken, fish, pork and a vegetable, generally accompanied by rice or noodles.

Starters are not usually a part of the traditional Chinese meal. If you do want a starter, select something light such as the Hot-and-Sour Soup (right). It lends itself to considerable variations, although the basic seasoning remains much the same. It can be left as a light, spicy vegetable-based soup, or you can add some pieces of chicken, pork or seafood to make it heartier.

Hot-and-sour soup

SERVES: *4 as a starter*
PREPARATION TIME: *10 minutes*
COOKING TIME: *15 minutes*

250 g chicken, pork or green prawns, diced (if using prawns, reserve four to use whole as a garnish)
1 litre chicken stock or water
75 g can Szechwan preserved vegetables
1 egg white, lightly beaten
1 teaspoon cornflour, dissolved in 3 tablespoons water
1-2 red chillies, deseeded and finely chopped
1 teaspoon black pepper
2 tablespoons sesame oil
To garnish: chopped spring onions or crisply fried shallots

1 In a large saucepan, bring the first three ingredients to the boil; simmer for 10 minutes if using chicken or pork, 5 minutes if using prawns.
2 Add the remaining ingredients and stir gently over a low heat.
3 After 5 minutes or so, when the soup has thickened slightly, remove it from the heat, sprinkle with the garnishes and serve in warm bowls.

Hot-and-Sour Soup, here made with prawns, takes its fiery flavour from the spicy preserved vegetables of Szechwan and finely chopped red chillies.

HEIGHTENING FLAVOUR

Why do so many Chinese dishes contain monosodium glutamate?

Monosodium glutamate, or MSG, is glutamic acid, or concentrated salt, used by Chinese cooks to boost the flavour of a dish rather as we use ordinary salt. It is not expensive and keeps indefinitely.

If used well, MSG can do much to improve the flavour of a dish, but it is true that some chefs add too much. In quantity, MSG can cause extreme thirst and other reactions like swollen neck glands, flushes and throbbing headaches. Using salt instead, along with sugar or vinegar, is enough to bring out most flavours in food.

Alternatively, use a tablespoon or two of sesame oil or oyster sauce. These are complete seasonings in that they combine salt and flavouring with the richness of the base product. If you add one or both of these, there is no need to use salt, stock cubes or, indeed, MSG.

CHINESE BREAKFAST

What is yum cha?

Yum cha, also known as *dim sum* and *tien sin*, is a collection of little snacks served to accompany tea. It is a tradition that began in Chinese tea houses around 500 years ago.

Many dishes, primarily breakfast fare but now also lunch and dinner, are served, usually from trolleys piled high with steaming baskets. Popular yum cha dishes include custard tarts, dumplings such as *siew mai* (filled with prawns and pork) and steamed won tons.

EASY DUMPLINGS

Can I make won tons at home?

Stuffed won tons are simple to make at home. The only special ingredients you need are the won ton skins, which are now widely available either frozen or fresh in Asian food shops.

Minced pork and fresh prawns are the essential ingredients for the stuffing. In the following recipe, the use of crunchy water chestnuts and the firm white tops of spring onions in the stuffing provides the right contrast to the soft texture of the won ton skins.

Won ton dumplings

MAKES: 30
PREPARATION TIME: 20–30 minutes
COOKING TIME: 10 minutes to steam, or 15–20 minutes to deep-fry

1 spring onion, green and
    white parts, finely chopped
5 water chestnuts, finely chopped
125 g green prawns, shelled,
    deveined and minced
250 g finely minced pork
1 egg, lightly beaten
A pinch of black pepper
1 tablespoon light soy sauce
1 tablespoon sesame oil
2 teaspoons cornflour
30 won ton skins, each 5 cm
    square

1 Combine all of the ingredients except the won ton skins in a bowl.
2 Test the seasoning of the stuffing mixture by bringing a pan of water to the boil, dropping 1 teaspoon of the mixture into it and cooking it for just a minute. Taste the stuffing and adjust the seasoning as necessary.
3 Take one won ton skin at a time and place 1 heaped teaspoon of the mixture in the centre of each. Then moisten the four edges of the won ton skin, gather up the corners and twist lightly to form a little pouch.
4 Place the won tons on a slightly oiled plate, twisted side up but not touching each other, and steam them in a wok for 10 minutes. Or deep-fry them for 15–20 minutes until crisp.

Dampening the edges of each won ton skin helps to hold the pouches together.

KNOW YOUR CHINESE SAUCES

Tasty sauces are added to most Chinese dishes to enhance their flavour. Matching the right sauce to the ingredients can make a simple dish special.

1 BEAN SAUCE, sometimes known as crushed bean sauce, is made from black or yellow soya beans that have been fermented and blended with flour and salt. Black bean sauce is the saltier of the two and much darker.
2 HOISIN SAUCE is made from soya bean purée, sugar, flour, maltose, salt and spices. This is also known as barbecue sauce because it is used to marinate Chinese roast or barbecued pork. It has a sweet flavour rather than the more pungent taste of Western barbecue sauce. Hoisin sauce is good as a rub for meats and poultry before grilling or barbecuing, and for use in marinades. It also accompanies Peking or aromatic roast duck and mandarin pancakes.
3 CHILLI PASTE is prepared from chillies, soya bean extract, salt, sugar and flour.
4 SESAME OIL is the pure, thick extract of roasted sesame seeds and used as a seasoning or condiment rather than as a cooking oil. It is typically added to soups and stir-fried dishes at the last minute to give a nutty fragrance.
5 LEMON SAUCE includes lemon extract, corn syrup, sugar, rice vinegar, spices and cornflour, and is very good for use in chicken and seafood dishes.
6 OYSTER SAUCE is thick, aromatic and salty. Made from oyster extract and soy sauce, it is used both as a complete seasoning and a stir-fry ingredient.
7 PLUM SAUCE is made from Chinese plums, corn syrup, sugar, rice vinegar, ginger, chillies, spices and cornflour. It is useful for sweet-and-sour dishes, and as a table sauce for barbecued meat or poultry and cold appetisers.
8 SOY SAUCE is a salting agent made from fermented soya beans and comes in a number of varieties, including light, dark, very dark and thick, and salt-reduced. Light soy sauces are used to season almost every Chinese dish. Dark soy sauces are caramelised and sweeter in flavour, so are used more as dips and colouring for soups and stews.
9 BEAN CURD SAUCE is a thick sauce made from fermented bean curd and salt that is used in rich Chinese stews. It comes in two varieties, white or red. There is no difference in flavour between the two, but the red bean curd sauce will make some dishes look much richer.

Chips

HEALTHIER CHIPS

Is there any way to reduce the amount of fat in chips?

Deep-frying by traditional methods trebles the kilojoule content of the potatoes, but there are several ways to control this. Traditional chips are made with floury potatoes that soak up fat; use waxy varieties instead. Do not peel them as the skin helps to reduce the fat and is a good source of fibre. And cut chips in thick wedges rather than thin fries so that there is less surface area and the chips will therefore absorb less fat.

Dripping or lard used to be the traditional cooking medium; but for healthier chips, switch to vegetable oils, such as sunflower or peanut, which are high in mono- and polyunsaturated fats. Be sure the oil is hot enough: when the temperature is too low, the chips will absorb more fat. You can use the recipe below to oven-roast chips, thus completely avoiding the need to deep-fry.

Oven chips

SERVES: 4
PREPARATION TIME: 20 minutes
COOKING TIME: 40-45 minutes

---

500 g large, waxy potatoes
3 tablespoons sunflower oil
Sea salt to taste

---

1 Preheat the oven to 220°C. Scrub the potatoes and pat dry but do not peel. Cut them lengthways into thick chips.
2 Put the chips in a bowl and toss by hand with the oil and sea salt.
3 Spread the chips on two baking trays and bake for 40-45 minutes, turning them three or four times. Swap over the baking trays halfway through cooking for even browning.
4 Remove the chips from the oven, then drain them on kitchen paper towels to remove any surplus oil before serving.

Lightly sprinkling thick-cut potatoes with oil and salt before cooking them in the oven produces chips that not only taste great but are healthier too.

Chocolate

CHOOSING THE BEST

What makes a good chocolate?

The key things to look for are cocoa solids and cocoa butter. The more cocoa solids a chocolate contains, the deeper and more intense the chocolate flavour will be. The wrapping must list the quantity of cocoa solids: any containing less than 50 per cent has little real chocolate taste: one with 70 per cent or more will have a much stronger, finer chocolate flavour.

The amount of cocoa butter listed on the packet will also help you to determine the quality of the chocolate. The more cocoa butter the chocolate contains, the softer it is, melting more easily and having a unique, mouth-feel quality.

But there is a huge demand for cocoa butter for use in cosmetics, which makes it very expensive, and so vegetable oils are substituted for the real thing in cheaper chocolate, reducing the flavour. Cocoa butter does not have to be listed on the packet by percentage, but you can work out how much is present by its position in the ingredients list, since these are shown in order of volume. If vegetable oil comes higher on the list than cocoa butter, it is an inferior chocolate.

As a general rule, the thinner and smaller the pieces of chocolate, the finer the chocolate will be. Another way of identifying good chocolate is how smooth it feels on the tongue. This is because high quality chocolate undergoes a longer period of conching, or stirring, while it is being made. Very fine chocolate with a superior flavour is expensive, but you do not have to use as much to get an intense chocolate taste, so it is a good idea to pay a little more for the best.

GENTLY MELT IT

When I melt chocolate, it occasionally becomes grainy. How can I prevent this happening?

When melting chocolate, remember that you are not heating or cooking it. Chocolate will melt in the heat of your hand, and that is how gentle the melting process should be. Chocolate that is grainy, or turns thick and seizes up in a solid mass, has been overheated.

It is also important that the chocolate be kept dry, as even one drop of water will cause it to seize. When you are melting chocolate in a bowl over simmering water, take the pan off the heat before putting the bowl on top then reduce the heat so that the water simmers gently and does not boil, as boiling water creates droplets of steam that may fall on the chocolate. Do not add any cold liquids to the chocolate until it has melted.

When you are melting chocolate in a microwave, use the Defrost setting and check its progress every 30–60 seconds: the chocolate will retain its shape even though it has softened (see box, page 89).

Save it!

If chocolate seizes, it can be rescued by adding a teaspoon of melted Copha or a pale vegetable oil for each 25 g of chocolate. The resulting chocolate can be used in cakes and desserts.

CHILL WHITE FIRST

Whenever I have tried to melt white chocolate it has turned crumbly. What do I do wrong?

Some types of white chocolate have had some or all of the cocoa butter replaced with vegetable oil and these are extremely difficult to melt. White chocolate should never be directly substituted for dark or milk chocolate. Technically, white chocolate is not chocolate at all as it does not contain any cocoa solids. Should a particular recipe require white chocolate and it has to be melted, check that the type you buy contains a high level of cocoa butter and always chill and then finely grate before very gently melting it. If it seizes, white chocolate is impossible to rescue.

EXTRA SMOOTH

What is 'couverture' chocolate, and what does 'tempering' mean?

Couverture chocolate is a type of chocolate used by professional confectioners. It contains more cocoa butter than ordinary chocolate and so melts and spreads easily. But cocoa butter is composed of fat crystals, and after melting some of these may recrystallise and form grey streaks in the chocolate called bloom which, though harmless, looks unattractive. So couverture chocolate has to be tempered: that is, heated and cooled to precise temperatures to prevent bloom and then spread and worked on a marble slab as it cools to produce a chocolate with a very smooth and shiny texture. All chocolate ideally needs tempering, but for most everyday cooking it is satisfactory to use good plain chocolate.

CAROB STAND-IN

Can carob be used as a substitute for chocolate in recipes?

Not really. Carob is the dried pod of the carob tree and has a sweet taste vaguely like that of the cocoa bean. Chocolate contains caffeine, but carob does not, so some people

MELTING AND DIPPING CHOCOLATE

Great care must be taken when melting chocolate, but it is worth the effort. Melted chocolate can be used in a variety of chocolate desserts, cakes and ice cream as well as in sweetmeats such as truffles. Firm, fresh fruits and whole nuts become doubly tempting when dipped in high-quality melted chocolate.

MELTING ON THE STOVE

1 Chop the chocolate finely with a sharp knife. Fill a saucepan one-third full of water and bring it to the boil, then reduce heat to a simmer. Put the chocolate into a heatproof bowl and place it over the water in the saucepan to melt slowly.

2 The base of the bowl must not touch the water. Leave it standing and stir the mixture occasionally until it is very smooth.

MELTING IN THE MICROWAVE

1 Break the chocolate into small pieces in a microwave-safe bowl. Place on the edge of the turntable. Melt on the Defrost setting for approximately one-minute cycles, stopping and stirring with a plastic spoon after each cycle, until melted.

2 Check amounts over 250 g after 2 minutes, initially; check smaller amounts (50 g) after 30 seconds.

DIPPING IN CHOCOLATE

1 Choose large, perfect nuts, such as almonds, brazils, hazelnuts, macadamias, pecans or walnuts, and dip them one at a time.

2 Place the nut on a small fork then lower it into the cooled, melted chocolate. Lift it straight out again and gently tap the fork on the side of the bowl to remove excess chocolate. Using a toothpick, push the nut gently off the fork and onto a tray lined with nonstick baking paper. Small pieces of fruit can be dipped in the same way, after being peeled, cut, then patted dry with kitchen paper towels.

3 For half-dipped fruits choose those with stems or stalks such as cape gooseberries, strawberries and cherries, or dried or glacé fruits such as apricots, prunes, or stem ginger.

4 Holding the stem or the top of the fruit, lower it halfway into the melted chocolate. Lift it straight out, shake off the excess chocolate then place it on trays lined with nonstick baking paper to set. When the fruits are set, store them in a cool, dry place until you are ready to serve.

prefer to use it for health reasons. Carob can be bought as a powder to use in place of cocoa, and in chips and bars, but it should not be thought of as a substitute for good quality chocolate. Both the flavour and texture of carob are very different from the real thing.

CHOCOLATE SAUCE

What is the best way to make a smooth chocolate sauce?

Use roughly equal amounts of fresh cream and finely grated dark cooking chocolate. For example, put 100 ml of cream into a saucepan and bring it to the boil. Remove it from the heat immediately and leave for 30 seconds to cool. Add 100 g of chocolate and stir well until the sauce is smooth and glossy. You could then add a flavouring such as cherry, coffee or orange brandy if you wish, and use it at once if the sauce is to be served warm. To serve the sauce cold, stir in 2–3 tablespoons of milk and leave it to cool at room temperature, stirring occasionally.

MESSY GRATER

My recipe for chocolate truffles involves grating lots of chocolate, but the chocolate always melts in my hand. I've tried using a food processor but it reduces chocolate bars to a sticky mess. Is there any way to get around this?

The process of grating chocolate generates friction which can melt it and make it sticky. The solution is to use chocolate that has been well chilled. Break off small pieces at a time, leaving the rest in the refrigerator, and chop finely in a food processor with the metal blade attachment. Stop and scrape down with a plastic spatula at intervals.

In the following recipe, grated chocolate is blended with cream, butter and liqueur to make wickedly rich truffles. If you feel particularly extravagant, decorate them with some 24 carat gold leaf, available from art shops. When consumed in tiny quantities, it is edible.

Chocolate dipped truffles

MAKES: *about 35 truffles*
PREPARATION TIME: *45 minutes, plus chilling and freezing time*
COOKING TIME: *5 minutes*

FOR THE FILLING
150 ml fresh cream
350 g dark cooking chocolate, chilled then finely grated
50 g unsalted butter, diced
1-2 tablespoons liqueur, optional

FOR THE COATING AND DECORATION
350 g dark cooking chocolate, cocoa, white chocolate, thin sheets of gold leaf

1 Put the cream into a small saucepan and bring it to the boil. Remove it from the heat then add the grated chocolate and the butter, stirring constantly until the mixture is thick, dark and smooth. Add some liqueur if desired, then transfer the mixture to a small bowl and chill it until it is quite firm.

2 Using a metal teaspoon, shape balls 2.5 cm in diameter. Put them on a tray lined with nonstick baking paper and freeze until solid.
3 Melt the remaining chocolate, then remove half the truffles from the freezer and dip them one by one into the chocolate. Shake off the excess and place the truffles on a tray lined with nonstick baking paper. Dip the remaining truffles.
4 If you want a contrast of smooth and soft surfaces, roll some of the truffles in cocoa straight away, before the coating has fully set. Leave the rest to set completely. Then pipe a little melted white chocolate decoratively onto some of them and, using your fingertip, press a little of the gold leaf onto others. Stored in an airtight container in the refrigerator, the truffles will keep for two weeks, or they can be frozen for a month.

Made from the finest chocolate and decorated with real gold, truffles are the ultimate after-dinner luxury.

CHOICE FOR COOKING

What is the best chocolate for cooking? And when a recipe says dark chocolate what should I use?

The best chocolate for cooking is dark cooking chocolate containing a high percentage of cocoa solids.

Milk chocolate is rarely used in cooking as it does not have the depth of flavour of dark chocolate, but it can be used if it is chilled and then finely grated before melting. These steps are necessary because milk chocolate can easily seize up.

'Chocolate compound' cake coverings or coatings are not chocolate at all. They contain no cocoa solids and most or all of the cocoa butter has been replaced with coconut or palm oil. Although they are very easy to melt and handle, these coatings do not have the flavour or texture of real chocolate. It is a false economy to cook with very inexpensive chocolate or substitutes as the results are disappointing.

Chocolate Cake

CHOCOHOLIC PROBLEM

I love chocolate cake, but have recently learned that I am a coeliac. Can you help me with a suitable recipe?

Coeliac disease is caused by a sensitivity to the protein gluten, found in wheat, rye, barley and oats. These grains are valuable in a normal, healthy high-fibre, low-fat diet, but coeliacs should avoid them. Avoiding gluten in cake recipes is particularly difficult as gluten is in flour, so you need a recipe which substitutes flour with maize-based cornflour, rice flour, soya flour or potato flour. However, the ultimate choice is a flourless chocolate cake. Try this Sephardic Jewish recipe which is part of the suitable non-leavened Passover cake selection. The chocolate icing is a luxurious addition, which transforms the flourless chocolate cake into a special celebration cake.

Flourless chocolate cake

SERVES: 12
PREPARATION TIME: 40 minutes
COOKING TIME: 45 minutes

FOR THE CAKE
250 g dark cooking chocolate
125 g unsalted butter, diced
6 large eggs, separated
125 g (½ cup) caster sugar
250 g (2½ cups) ground almonds

FOR THE ICING
250 g dark cooking chocolate
250 ml fresh cream

1 Preheat the oven to 180°C. Line a 23 cm springform cake tin with nonstick baking paper.
2 Break the chocolate into a heatproof bowl. Add the butter. Melt over a pan of simmering water.
3 Beat the egg yolks and caster sugar with an electric mixer until pale and creamy. Add the melted chocolate mixture and the almonds and stir well.
4 Whisk the egg whites with an electric mixer, at high speed, until stiff peaks form. Fold into the chocolate mixture with a spatula.
5 Pour the mixture into the tin and spread level. Bake for 45 minutes, or until firm and a skewer inserted in the centre comes out clean.
6 Stand the cake in the tin on a wire cooling rack until cool.
7 To make the icing, break the chocolate into a food processor and mix until finely chopped. Transfer to a mixing bowl.
8 Heat the cream in a saucepan until scalded (almost boiling) and pour over the chocolate. Stir until the mixture is smooth.
9 Place the cake on the wire cooling rack over a large plate. Spread about a third of the warm icing over the top and sides of the cake, then leave to set.
10 Place three large triangles of greaseproof paper on a serving plate, covering the edge of the plate. Place the cake on the plate. Rewarm the remaining icing over a pan of simmering water and pour over the cake. Spread over the top and sides. Leave to set, then remove the paper.

DECORATIONS

Elegant adornments made from fine chocolate add the perfect finishing touch to homemade cakes.

SCROLLS AND CURLS

1 Pour melted chocolate onto a marble slab, chilled baking tray or another smooth, cool surface.

2 Spread it with a palette knife to not more than 3 mm thick and leave it in a cool place until it is set but not completely hard.

3 Holding a long, firm knife or scraper at an angle of 45° to the chocolate, push away from you to scrape off long curls. Hold the tip of the knife securely and scrape in a quarter-circle movement.

MAKING LEAVES

1 Use stiff shiny leaves with a short stem. Wash and pat dry. Brush melted chocolate onto the underside of each leaf, using a small brush. Remove excess from reverse side; leave to set. Repeat the process.

2 When the leaves are dry and well set, carefully pull each one from the chocolate by its stem.

THE RICHEST BY FAR

I have made many chocolate cakes but have never achieved a really luscious, sinfully rich result. Is there a particular sort of chocolate that is best for making such a cake?

The quality of chocolate varies, but generally, the more cocoa solids it contains, the better the chocolate (see *Chocolate*). Most large supermarkets now stock good quality dark cooking chocolate. Use the best you can find for the following recipe, such as a dark chocolate with 70 per cent or more cocoa solids. This rich and elaborate cake includes layers of meringue and sponge that can be made the day before, leaving only the mousse and ganache to prepare on the day you want to serve it.

This decadent extravaganza combines rum, cream and chocolate in layers of mousse, meringue and genoese sponge.

Death by chocolate

SERVES: 12
PREPARATION TIME: 1½–2 hours plus about 2 hours chilling
TOTAL COOKING TIME: 2 hours

FOR THE MERINGUE
2 large egg whites
60 g (¼ cup) caster sugar
60 g (⅓ cup) icing sugar
15 g (1½ tablespoons) cocoa

FOR THE SPONGE
6 large eggs
185 g (¾ cup) caster sugar
125 g (1 cup) self-raising flour
30 g (¼ cup) cocoa
2 tablespoons cornflour
75 g unsalted butter, melted gently

FOR THE GANACHE TOPPING
60 g (¼ cup) caster sugar
50 g unsalted butter
500 ml fresh cream
2 tablespoons dark rum
500 g dark cooking chocolate, melted

FOR THE MOUSSE FILLING
125 g unsalted butter
250 g dark cooking chocolate
3 tablespoons dark rum
2 large eggs, separated
300 ml thickened cream
To decorate: chocolate leaves (see page 91) and icing sugar

---

1 To make the chocolate meringue, preheat the oven to 120°C and line a 23 cm springform tin with nonstick baking paper.
2 Whisk the whites until stiff, then gradually whisk in the caster sugar.
3 Sift the icing sugar and the cocoa together and then gently fold them into the meringue.
4 Spread the mixture into the cake tin and bake for 1–1½ hours, or until the meringue is crisp and dry.
5 To make the sponge, preheat the oven to 180°C. Grease a 23 cm springform tin and line its base with nonstick baking paper.
6 Put the eggs and sugar together in a bowl and whisk the mixture

with an electric mixer until it is creamy and thick enough to leave a ribbon-like trail when the beaters are lifted from the mixture.

7 Sift the flour, cocoa and cornflour together then gently fold them into the egg mixture a little at a time, alternating with the melted butter.

8 Spread the mixture into the cake tin and bake for about 30 minutes until the cake is quite firm to the touch in the centre.

9 Turn the cake out of the tin to cool for about 30 minutes and, when it is completely cold, carefully slice the cake in half horizontally.

10 To make the ganache, heat the sugar with the butter, cream and rum until the sugar has dissolved. Stir in the melted chocolate, then chill the mixture for 30 minutes until set.

11 To make the mousse, melt the butter, chocolate and rum in a bowl over a pan of warm water. Let it cool slightly, then beat in the egg yolks and fold in the cream.

12 Whisk the egg whites until they form stiff peaks, then fold them into the chocolate mixture. Leave it to set for 30 minutes to 1 hour.

13 When the mousse has set, assemble the cake. Put a sponge layer on a plate, spread half the mousse on it, then put the meringue layer on top. Spread the remaining mousse on top of the meringue, then top with the other sponge.

14 Spread the ganache over the cake, decorate with chocolate leaves and dust with icing sugar. Serve immediately or chill for a few hours.

Chopping

EVEN-SIZED PIECES

Is there a way of chopping onions that is superior to the others?

The most important thing is to ensure the pieces are an even size so that they all cook at the same rate (see box, above right). If some of the pieces are very small, they may catch and burn before the larger ones are cooked, resulting in a dish that tastes bitter and scorched.

CHOPPING VEGETABLES

When chopping vegetables use a very sharp cook's knife with a secure handle that is easy to grip and will not slip. To lessen tears when chopping onions, try peeling and chopping them sitting down so your face is not directly over the onions, or run the peeled onions under cold water before you chop them.

ROOT VEGETABLES

1 To chop large root vegetables, here a potato, take a slice off one edge, put it cut side down, hold it and slice down firmly, using your knuckles as a guide against the blade of the knife.

2 Stack the slices and slice across them to cut them into sticks. Then pile up these sticks and slice them at right angles to the previous cuts to make chunks. Keep slicing the chunks until they are as thin as you need them for your dish. Keep your fingertips tucked well under all the time that you are cutting the vegetables.

ONIONS

1 Leave the root on to help hold the onion together. Halve lengthways through the core. For finely diced onion, slice once or twice more lengthways, then place it flat.

2 Make a series of parallel cuts across the onion, down to the chopping board, avoiding the root end.

3 Make a second series of parallel cuts at right angles to the first while holding the onion firmly in your hand, keeping your fingers well away from the sharp knife.

CHOPPING BOARDS

What is the best material for a chopping board?

Wood is generally preferred for chopping boards as a thick board made of seasoned wood will last forever and the food does not slide over the surface. Wood also has the advantage of not blunting knives as quickly as other materials.

Doubts have been raised about the hygiene of wood, but in 1993 research at the University of Wisconsin found that wooden boards may be better than plastic for keeping bacteria at bay. A variety of boards were deliberately contaminated and left overnight. Levels of bacteria on the wooden boards were virtually undetectable while bacteria levels had actually risen on some of the plastic boards. The researchers surmised that bacteria may be sucked in by the porous structure of wood and destroyed by the antimicrobial chemicals that protect trees from infection.

Other materials used for chopping boards are polypropylene and toughened glass, both of which can be sterilised easily. In a restaurant or other professional kitchen, these polypropylene boards are often colour coded so that different ones are used for raw meat, cooked meat, fish, fruit and vegetables to avoid cross-contamination.

Whatever material you choose, be sure to scrub your board thoroughly in hot fresh water and soap or an antibacterial cleaner after every use. If the board is washed properly and stored on its edge and not in contact with other surfaces, contamination will be minimal.

USING A MEZZALUNA

What is the best way to chop fresh green herbs?

The easiest way to chop most herbs is with a large, sharp knife. You have much more control and it is quicker than using scissors (except in the case of chives). If you are chopping herbs in bulk, an Italian mezzaluna is a handy tool. This is a double-handed chopper with a semicircular blade that you use with a rocking motion. While these are usually single bladed, they may have up to four parallel blades that can make fast work of large piles of herbs. (See also **Herbs**.)

Chopsticks

CHOPSTICK VARIETIES

There are many types of chopstick available. Which should I buy?

It is best to use bamboo chopsticks, as plastic and lacquered ones are slippery and morsels tend to slide off them. Japanese chopsticks have a pointed end as this makes it easier to pick up pieces of marinated fish, for example. Chinese chopsticks are blunt because in China it is thought unlucky to bring sharp implements to the table.

SUPER STICKS

How are chopsticks used? And are they any better than a fork?

Chopsticks are used mainly to scoop up noodles and to shovel rice from bowl to mouth, holding

---

HOW TO USE CHOPSTICKS

Using chopsticks may seem complicated, but by following these simple steps showing the basic technique, you will find them quite easy to manage.

1 The first chopstick rests between the base of your thumb and the tip of your third finger, near the top third of the chopstick. This chopstick should remain stationary while the second chopstick moves up and down.

2 Rest the second chopstick above the first one, holding it between the base of your first finger and the tip of your second finger. Use this finger and the tips of the others to raise and lower the top chopstick to grasp food.

---

the bowl close to the lips. Chinese people never use chopsticks to pick up rice by the grain to convey to the mouth, as falling grains symbolise bad luck. Except for noodles, most Chinese food is cooked in bite-sized pieces in a sauce, and using chopsticks gives the perfect ratio of morsel to sauce.

Chopsticks have the advantage over forks in that you do not spear pieces of food but slide the chopsticks under and lift them up. This is especially important with deep-fried foods, as piercing the crispy batter before the morsel reaches the mouth will release air and moisture, which causes the coating to deflate and spoils the effect. Turning food with chopsticks when shallow frying also avoids piercing the flesh, which would allow the juices inside the food to escape.

When preparing food such as Japanese tempura, the use of chopsticks to dip the ingredients in batter helps to give a nice, thin coating and the end result is much lighter than would be the case if using a perforated spoon.

Although chopsticks are used exclusively in China and Japan, and among Chinese and Indo-Chinese communities in Southeast Asia, they are not a part of Thai culinary culture unless noodles are being

served. In Thailand, food is always eaten with a fork and spoon, but not as we normally use them in Australia – the spoon is used as a scoop and the fork is employed to push the food onto the spoon.

Choux Pastry

LAST-MINUTE FILLING

How far ahead can I put cream into éclairs or profiteroles without making them soggy?

Once the éclairs have been filled with cream the pastry starts to soften, so ideally they should be eaten within a couple of hours or they will become soggy.

Choux pastry also tastes best on the day it is made but this is not always practical. Instead, the paste can be made the day before, left in a covered bowl and refrigerated overnight. Shape and bake the pastry the following day. Alternatively, unfilled cooked éclairs and profiteroles can be frozen in plastic containers. To thaw, either place the frozen pastries on baking trays and put them into a hot oven for 5 minutes, or leave them out in their containers to thaw at room temperature for an hour or so.

SOGGY RESULTS

My éclairs looked cooked when I took them out of the oven, but on cooling they were wet inside. What should I do next time?

Choux pastry needs a hot oven, so preheat the oven and make sure it has come up to temperature before putting the éclairs inside. To ascertain whether the éclairs are cooked, check the sides and any cracks in the baked pastry; they should look brown, not pale in colour.

When the éclairs are cooked, transfer them immediately to a cooling rack, but do not turn the oven off. They are usually slit so that the steam can escape from inside, as in the recipe below. After the initial cooking, dry them out a little in the oven before filling.

Coffee éclairs

MAKES: about 30 small éclairs
PREPARATION TIME: 50 minutes plus a few hours cooling and setting
COOKING TIME: 25–30 minutes

FOR THE CHOUX PASTRY
60 g (½ cup) plain flour
A pinch of salt
60 g butter, diced, plus extra for greasing
2 large eggs, beaten

FOR THE FILLING
300 ml thickened cream
1 tablespoon caster sugar, optional

FOR THE GLACE ICING
2 teaspoons instant coffee granules
2 tablespoons boiling water
185 g (1 cup) icing sugar, sifted

1 Preheat the oven to 220°C, then line two baking trays with the prepared nonstick baking paper (see box, right).
2 Sift the flour and the salt onto a large sheet of greaseproof paper.
3 Put the butter in a heavy-based saucepan. Add 125 ml water and bring slowly to a rolling boil over a low heat.
4 As soon as the liquid is boiling, take it off the heat, tip in the flour and beat well with a wooden spoon

until it thickens to a paste around the spoon and leaves the sides of the pan clean. Cook the pastry for 2–3 minutes more then leave to cool for a few minutes.
5 Add the egg a little at a time, beating well between each addition, until the paste is as glossy as before and reaches dropping consistency.
6 Spoon the paste into a piping bag fitted with a 1 cm nozzle and pipe out equal lengths of pastry on the prepared baking trays.
7 Bake for about 20–25 minutes until the éclairs are well risen, crisp and golden. Remove the éclairs but leave the oven on. Make a small slit along one side to let the steam escape and then return the éclairs to the oven for a few minutes to dry out. Remove and cool on wire racks.
8 To make the filling, whip the cream and caster sugar until thick. Spoon into a piping bag fitted with a 1 cm nozzle. Split open the éclairs and pipe in a little cream.
9 To make the icing, dissolve the coffee in 1 tablespoon of boiling water. Sift the icing sugar into a bowl, then stir in the dissolved coffee with the remaining hot water until the icing will coat the back of a spoon thickly.
10 Dip the top of each éclair into the icing and leave to set. Keep in a cool place and eat within two hours.

When making choux pastry, beating the mixture thoroughly as you add the egg will help to keep it glossy.

SAVOURY TREATS

Can I use a savoury filling for choux pastry for a change instead of a sweet one?

Crisp choux pastry is very versatile and delicious in savoury recipes. To boost the flavour when making savoury dishes, add a little salt and pepper or some grated cheese to the choux paste before baking it.

Savoury choux buns make good buffet party food, served hot and filled with cheese, ham or mushrooms in a well-flavoured white sauce. Cold éclairs can be filled with chicken, crab, egg or prawn bound with a herb-flavoured mayonnaise. Or make a gougère by piping savoury choux pastry into a circle, baking it, then filling the ring with a flavoursome sauce.

PIPING ECLAIRS

To help you to pipe éclairs of equal length, take a sheet of nonstick baking paper and draw rows of evenly spaced lines, 5–7cm long and 2cm apart, on one side. Then turn it over and use it to line your baking tray.

1 Stand the piping bag in a large jar or jug and turn back the top to form a cuff. Spoon the choux paste into the bag. Do not overfill the piping bag, but allow some room at the end.

2 On the prepared baking trays, pipe out small éclair shapes tracing over the guide lines you have drawn. Cut the piped paste neatly from the end of the nozzle with a dampened knife.

Christmas Pudding

PRESERVING SPIRIT

I once made a Christmas pudding months ahead to give it time to mature. But when I unwrapped it, the pudding had turned mouldy. What did I do wrong?

A good Christmas pudding will keep for up to a year, so long as it is properly wrapped, is kept in a refrigerator in a hot climate, or in a cool, dark, dry place in a cold climate, and is well laced with brandy or some other spirit before storing. The alcohol acts as a preservative, as does the large quantity of dried fruit and sugar.

Once the pudding has been steamed, allow it to cool in its covering. When cold, take off the cover, pierce the pudding in several places with a skewer, and trickle over 2–3 tablespoons of brandy or rum. Wrap the pudding in greaseproof paper, then overwrap it in foil or seal it in a plastic food storage bag. Store as directed above.

Check the pudding occasionally and moisten it with a little more brandy or rum if it looks as if it is starting to dry out, but don't overdo it or it will eventually become too moist. Wrap the pudding securely back in its covers each time you check it.

LOW-KILOJOULE SWEETNESS

Is there any way of cutting down on the kilojoules and the fat in Christmas pudding yet retaining its traditional taste?

You can considerably reduce both the kilojoule and fat content without greatly affecting the flavour.

The following recipe omits the usual sugar and suet, and adds instead grated apple and carrot to a mixture of dried fruit and spices. When serving six people, each portion of this pudding contains about 1510 kilojoules and just under 8 g of fat; in a 'conventional' Christmas pudding of the same size, each portion would contain upwards of 1690 kilojoules and more than 15 g of fat.

The combination of dried fruit and carrot in this pudding is sweet, but it is not sweet enough to act as a long-term preservative, and the pudding should not be matured for more than two weeks.

Low-kilojoule Christmas pudding

SERVES: 6–8
PREPARATION TIME: 30 minutes, plus overnight soaking of fruit
COOKING TIME: 5 hours initially, plus 2 hours before serving

125 g (¾ cup) each raisins, sultanas and currants
125 g (¾ cup) ready-to-eat dried apricots, chopped
90 ml brandy
Juice of 1 orange and 1 lemon
1 teaspoon each finely grated lemon and orange rind
90 g (¾ cup) wholemeal flour
75 g (1¼ cups) fresh wholemeal breadcrumbs
50 g (⅓ cup) blanched almonds, chopped
1 medium carrot, coarsely grated
1 eating apple, peeled and coarsely grated
2 teaspoons ground mixed spice
2 large eggs, beaten

1 Put all the dried fruit, brandy, orange and lemon juice and rind in a bowl and mix well. Cover and leave them to soak overnight.
2 Put the fruit mixture and all the remaining ingredients into a bowl and stir until evenly mixed. Spoon the mixture into a greased 1.5 litre pudding basin, pressing it down, and level the surface.
3 Cover with a double layer of greased, pleated greaseproof paper and foil. Secure them with string and tie a string handle to make it easy to lift the basin in and out of a pan.
4 Put the pudding in a steamer placed over a pan of rapidly boiling water and cover. Steam the pudding over the water for 5 hours - topping up the boiling water as necessary.

5 Let the pudding cool completely. Remove the wrapping and cover with a clean layer of greaseproof paper, then a layer of foil. Store in a refrigerator for two weeks.
6 To finish cooking the pudding, leave it wrapped in its basin and steam as before for 2 hours.
7 Unwrap and turn out onto a serving plate. Serve with Greek-style yoghurt or fromage frais.

Flambéed pudding

A pudding is twice as impressive if you flambé it. Pour some rum, brandy or whisky into a small pan and warm it over a gas flame or electric hotplate – do not let it get too hot or the spirit evaporates. Take the pudding and heated spirit to the table, pour the spirit over the pudding and set fire to it.

MICROWAVE PUDDING

Can I make Christmas pudding in a microwave oven?

Yes. Follow your favourite recipe, replacing all but 2 tablespoons of the spirit with orange or apple juice. Press the mixture into a greased pudding basin. Cover with a plate and cook on Medium for 20–30 minutes until the top of the pudding is just slightly moist. Leave the pudding to stand, covered, for 5 minutes before turning out, or store for up to two weeks.

FIRE RISK

Is it safe to reheat Christmas pudding in a microwave oven?

Never reheat in a microwave oven a Christmas pudding which contains coins or medallions, nor one which has just been laced with alcohol as then it could catch fire.

You can, however, reheat one in a microwave if the alcohol has been incorporated into the pudding mixture. Heat single portions on Medium for 1–1½ minutes; whole puddings on Medium for 3–5 minutes depending on size.

Chutney

PREPARING THE JARS

How do you sterilise jars?

Wash them in warm soapy water, then put them in a pan of boiling water for 10 minutes. You can also sterilise jars in the microwave: half-fill them with cold water, then heat them on High for about 3 minutes or until the water boils. Whichever method you use, then put the jars upside-down in an oven preheated to 140°C and leave them to dry for 10 minutes.

The jars must be clean, dry and warm when the hot chutney is added. As soon as you have filled the jar, cover the chutney with a waxed disc and seal with a glass, plastic or plastic-coated lid. Do not use bare metal as the vinegar in chutney would corrode it.

MOULDY CHUTNEY

The last batch of chutney I made developed mould. What could have gone wrong?

The most likely explanation is that you did not use enough vinegar, as this is the ingredient that preserves the chutney against spoilage.

There needs to be at least 1 litre of vinegar to every 3 kg of fruit and vegetables, as in the following recipe for Tomato and Red Pepper Chutney.

Other possible causes of mould are under-cooking the mixture, so it retains too much moisture, or the use of unsterilised jars.

Chutney with mould growing on its surface should not be eaten, as the mould may have produced toxins within the entire jar.

A chunky tomato and red pepper chutney adds bittersweet 'bite' to cheese sandwiches and cold meats.

Tomato and red pepper chutney

MAKES: about 1 kg
PREPARATION TIME: 30 minutes
COOKING TIME: 1¾–2¼ hours

1 tablespoon yellow mustard seeds
1 tablespoon black peppercorns
1 teaspoon cumin seeds
1 bay leaf
1 kg ripe tomatoes, skinned and
  roughly chopped
4 shallots, chopped
3 red peppers, seeded and chopped
4 cloves garlic, crushed
600 ml white wine vinegar
185 g (1 cup) light brown sugar
Grated rind and juice of 1 lemon
1 tablespoon salt

1 Put the flavourings in a piece of muslin and tie up to make a pouch.
2 Put the tomatoes, shallots, red peppers and garlic into a stainless-steel preserving pan and add the vinegar, sugar, lemon rind and juice, and the salt. Push in the muslin bag containing the flavourings and cook gently, stirring all the while, until the sugar has dissolved.
3 Bring the mixture to the boil, then simmer gently, uncovered, for 1¾–2¼ hours or until the chutney has reduced and thickened, stirring occasionally. The chutney is ready when a wooden spoon run along the bottom of the pan leaves a line that remains clear for a few seconds (see picture, page 98).
4 Remove the muslin bag from the pan. While the chutney is still very hot, spoon it into warm, sterilised jars. Cover each jar of chutney with a waxed disc, then seal it at once with a nonmetallic or plastic-coated lid. When the chutney has cooled, label the jars and store them for a month in a cool, dark, dry place to allow the flavours to mature. Once opened, consume within a month.

PAN CHOICES

Can I use any sort of preserving pan for making chutney?

Only stainless-steel or aluminium pans should be used for chutney. Copper pans, which transmit heat

quickly, are good for making sweet jam but not for soaking fruit or making preserves such as chutney that contain vinegar, as the acids react with the metal.

ONION JAM

I have often seen 'onion confit' on restaurant menus. What is it?

Onion confit is a popular feature in many restaurants, and is easy to make at home. Basically, it consists of either whole button onions or sliced onions, cooked very slowly in oil with spices, vinegar and sugar until they are reduced to a jam-like consistency. Herbs can be added to enhance the flavour.

Its full, rich flavour is especially good served hot with roast meats and game, or served at room temperature with pâtés and terrines.

TEST WHEN READY

How can I tell when a chutney has cooked enough to be bottled?

Chutney is ready when it has reduced and thickened to a jam-like consistency and no excess liquid remains. Long, slow cooking is best for chutneys, so that the ingredients can break down and all the flavour is extracted.

Once cooked and bottled, store chutney in a cool, dry, dark place for at least a month before eating, to allow the flavours to develop and mellow. If kept in the correct conditions, unopened jars keep for up to a year; once opened, consume within a month.

To test whether chutney is ready to be taken off the heat, run a wooden spoon across the bottom of the pan: it should leave a dry channel for a few seconds.

Citrus Fruit

PROTECTIVE COATING

I have been told that all citrus fruits are waxed. Why is this done, and is it unhealthy?

After harvesting, most citrus fruits are washed before being packed. As the washing process removes some of the fruits' natural protective coating, they are given a thin coating of wax to help prevent dehydration, extend storage life and improve their appearance. The waxes used for fruits are made from natural products and are also used to coat jelly beans. They must conform to food standards based on National Health and Medical Research Council (NHMRC) regulations on food additives.

The washed fruit is also treated with preservatives and pesticides to prevent the fruit decaying and protect it against insect damage. These substances are controlled by state and territory legislation and safety assessments, taking account of the fact that the peel may be used for cooking (see also **Zest**).

If these additives make you uneasy, buy organic fruit, which is neither waxed nor treated with fungicides. Seville oranges, used for marmalade, are usually free of

---

PEELING AND SEGMENTING CITRUS FRUIT

The thin skin that separates the segments in oranges and grapefruit can be a little tough. When dividing oranges for inclusion in fruit salad, and when preparing grapefruit, it is best to remove these membranes, as shown below.

PREPARING AN ORANGE	PREPARING A GRAPEFRUIT

1 With a very sharp or serrated knife, cut a thin slice from the top and bottom of the orange, then cut the peel and pith away from the side, cutting from top to bottom.

1 Cut the grapefruit in half across its width, then run a curved-blade grapefruit knife with a serrated edge around the flesh of the fruit, ensuring that all is loosened from the skin.

2 Hold the orange over a bowl to catch the juice and cut down each side of each segment, as close to the white membrane as you can, then ease it out. Squeeze the leftover membrane to extract the juice, which can then be sweetened and used for syrup.

2 Using the tip of a small sharp knife, cut along either side of the grapefruit segments to separate them from the tough white membrane that divides them. Then carefully lift out the membrane by pulling the central stem, leaving the segments in place.

wax and fungicide, but unwaxed lemons (unless they are organic) will have been treated with fungicides. It is best to scrub citrus fruit under a warm tap with a clean nailbrush before use, as the various substances can come off on your fingers and be eaten with the fruit.

RELEASING THE JUICE

How can I tell which oranges or lemons contain the most juice?

It is difficult to tell, but as a general rule, choose smooth, thin-skinned fruit that feel heavy as these are usually juicier than those with a knobbly rind. To get more juice out of a lemon or orange, roll it backwards and forwards under your hand on the work surface a few times before you squeeze it.

If the fruit has gone hard, pop it into the microwave on High for 30 seconds before squeezing.

THE CITRUS FAMILY

The large family of citrus fruits are all widely available. The fruits are invaluable for their juice, in cooking and for healthy snacks. Here is a guide to those you are most likely to find, with some tips on how to use them.

1 *Mandarin* 2 *Lemon* 3 *Pomelo* 4 *Grapefruit* 5 *Ruby red grapefruit* 6 *Lime* 7 *Tangelo* 8 *Navel orange* 9 *Kumquat*

- ORANGES Sweet oranges, available all year round, include juicy Valencias in summer and larger seedless Navels in winter. Bitter Seville oranges, available only in the winter months, are mainly used for making marmalade. Bittersweet blood oranges, with red-streaked skin and flesh, are also used in cooking.
- SOFT CITRUS FRUIT These small, soft-skinned fruits are all hybrids of the Chinese mandarin orange. The range includes locally grown mandarins and, in the northern hemisphere, tangerines and the virtually seedless clementines and satsumas.

- LEMONS AND LIMES The versatility of lemons makes them invaluable to the cook. Their juice can counterbalance oily fish, or sharpen a cream sauce for fish, meat or poultry. Lemon is also the main flavouring in many desserts. Limes are the tropical equivalent of the subtropical lemon. They are smaller but more fragrant in flavour.
- GRAPEFRUIT The two main varieties are white grapefruit, which has a thick skin and pale yellow, sharp-tasting flesh that can be sprinkled with sugar before eating, and thinner-skinned ruby red or pink grapefruit with sweeter pink to

deep ruby-coloured flesh. The pomelo is the much larger ancestor of the grapefruit, occasionally seen in the shops; it is quite sweet. All can be used in salads, savoury dishes and desserts.
- TANGELO A cross between a mandarin and a grapefruit, tangelos have a distinctive bell shape with a bump like a lemon, and a sharp flavour.
- KUMQUATS have tender, sweet, thin skin and tart flesh. Can be eaten whole.
- UGLI FRUIT (not shown) A hybrid of grapefruit and tangerine with knobbly skin and sweet flesh. It can be eaten in the same way as pink grapefruit.

Clams

AUTHENTIC CHOWDER

Can I get the right clams in this country to make an American clam chowder?

Quahogs or hard-shell clams are named in the United States according to size, starting with little necks and cherrystones and going up to the largest sharps or chowder clams, which can measure up to 13 cm. It is these large ones that are minced for chowders, as they have a strong flavour and will withstand long cooking, but you can use any clams and simply add them later in the cooking. Canned clams can also be used in a chowder.

New England clam chowder is rich and creamy; the Manhattan version below is tomato based.

Manhattan clam chowder

SERVES: *4*
PREPARATION TIME: *20 minutes*
COOKING TIME: *25 minutes*

1 kg clams
50 g pickled pork or unsmoked bacon in a piece
25 g lard
1 onion, finely chopped
½ teaspoon dried thyme
1 medium potato, diced
400 g canned chopped tomatoes
Salt and black pepper
3 tablespoons chopped parsley
To serve: French bread

1 Wash the clams in several changes of cold water, scrubbing if necessary, and discard any that are chipped, broken or already open.
2 Put the clams into a deep pan, add 600 ml of water, cover tightly and cook over a high heat for about 10 minutes until they open.
3 Tip the clams into a colander set over a large bowl to catch the liquor, then strain this juice through a sieve lined with muslin. Retain the liquor.
4 Shell the clams, discarding any that are closed and the empty shells. Chop the clam meat and set aside.

5 Dice the pork or bacon. Heat the lard in a pan then add the meat and fry gently until the fat is released and the cubes are crisp. Lift out the meat with a slotted spoon and set aside.
6 Fry the onion and thyme in the lard and meat fat over a very gentle heat for 5 minutes until the onion is soft and transparent.
7 Add the diced pork, the potato, strained clam liquor and tomatoes and their juice. Bring to the boil then simmer for 10–15 minutes until the potatoes are cooked.
8 Add the chopped clams and season to taste, then bring back to the boil. Transfer the soup to a heated tureen and sprinkle with parsley. Serve with crusty French bread.

Cocoa

SWEET RELATION

What is the difference between chocolate and cocoa?

Cocoa comes from the cacao bean, the fruit of the cacao tree, and was one of the treasures Columbus took back to Spain from the New World. The cacao tree originated in the Amazon rain forest and had spread as far as Peru and Mexico in Columbus's time. However, it was Hernando Cortez, while conquering Mexico for Spain, who realised that cocoa was special after he saw it transformed into a chocolate liquid, served in golden goblets, at the court of Emperor Montezuma.

Back in Spain, the cacao bean drink was sweetened and flavoured with vanilla and cinnamon, then heated, and hot chocolate became very fashionable. Special chocolate houses were created for patrons to enjoy socialising while sipping hot chocolate. These spread throughout western Europe to Britain.

During the Industrial Revolution, methods were developed to make the liquid chocolate finer and smoother. In the 1800s, the Swiss added milk to the liquid chocolate and developed the formula for making a solid block of chocolate.

Today, the harvested cacao pods are split open and the wet beans are removed and fermented to develop the rich flavour, then dried. The beans are transported to the cocoa processing factories, where they are cleaned and shelled and the nib is kibbled, roasted and ground to produce cocoa mass. The mass is pressed to extract cocoa fat (called cocoa butter), resulting in a solid block of cocoa, which is ground into powder.

Solid chocolate is produced from cocoa mass, cocoa butter and sugar for dark chocolate; milk solids and milk fat are added to the mixture to make milk chocolate.

Chocolate made in Switzerland is still one of the finest in the world today.

Coconut

WEALTH OF CHOICE

What is the difference between desiccated, flaked, shredded and creamed coconut and how is each one used?

They are all derived from fresh coconuts, but differ in how they are processed. Desiccated coconut is the shredded white flesh of the coconut from which all the moisture has been extracted. It can be bought either flaked or in shredded strands.

Desiccated coconut in all its forms is suitable for both sweet and savoury dishes, but is used mainly in cakes and biscuits. The longer strands and flakes are usually used for garnishing and decorating.

Creamed coconut, sold in cans or as a block, is formed from desiccated coconut that has been ground to an oily paste which thickens and sets when chilled. The block is sealed in plastic, and once opened, can be stored in the refrigerator for many weeks. Simply cut off pieces to use. Add creamed coconut to traditional Southeast Asian and Indian curries, or to stews, casseroles and soups to enrich and flavour them.

FRESHEN UP

If I want to use fresh coconut instead of desiccated, should I use the same amount?

The flavour of desiccated coconut is more intense than that of fresh, so replace desiccated with at least twice the amount of fresh coconut, be it flaked, grated or shredded. Either grated fresh coconut or desiccated coconut can be used for this creamy chicken dish.

Chicken with coconut, Goan-style

SERVES: 4
PREPARATION TIME: 40 minutes; allow extra time if preparing a fresh coconut
COOKING TIME: 1 hour

---

2 teaspoons ground coriander
1 teaspoon each ground cumin, cumin seeds, ground cinnamon, freshly grated nutmeg, paprika and mustard seeds
¹/₂ teaspoon black pepper
A pinch of cayenne pepper
200 g finely grated fresh coconut, or 90 g (1 cup) desiccated coconut
3 tablespoons olive oil
2.5 kg chicken, cut into 8 pieces and skinned
250 g onions, finely sliced
350 g red peppers, thickly sliced
6 cloves garlic, crushed
2 small fresh green chillies, seeds removed and chopped
1 tablespoon grated green ginger
1 tablespoon plain flour
500 ml chicken stock
1-2 teaspoons salt
200 ml natural yoghurt
4 tablespoons chopped fresh coriander
To serve: lemon and lime wedges

---

1 Put all the spices, the pepper and cayenne pepper into a small bowl, mix well together and set aside.
2 Heat a heavy-based frying pan over a medium heat until it has become quite hot. Sprinkle the fresh or desiccated coconut into the pan and stir gently with a fork to keep the strands separate. Heat until it

The flavours of Europe and Asia come together in a mild chicken curry, in which coconut and a wealth of herbs and spices are wrapped in creamy yoghurt.

becomes golden brown, taking care not to let it catch and burn. Remove from the heat and set aside.
3 Heat the oil in a large flameproof casserole or saucepan, then add the chicken pieces, a few at a time, and fry until they are golden brown all over. As the pieces brown, remove them from the pan, put them on a plate and set aside.
4 Add the onion and red pepper to the oil remaining in the pan and cook them gently until they become softened, but not browned. Stir in the garlic, chillies and ginger and cook for a minute, then add the flour and the spice mixture, stir well and cook for a further minute.
5 Stir in the toasted coconut, pour in the stock and bring to the boil. Return the browned chicken pieces to the pan, season well with salt and stir until all the pieces are coated

with the curry mixture. Reduce the heat, cover the pan and cook gently for an hour, stirring from time to time. Leave a serving dish to warm, if necessary.
6 Stir the yoghurt and coriander into the dish and remove it from the heat. If you have used a saucepan to cook the chicken, transfer the meat and curry mixture to the warmed serving dish. Serve with basmati rice, and with wedges of lemon and lime to squeeze over.

ALL CUT UP

How do you cut up the flesh from a fresh coconut?

After cracking open a coconut and cutting the flesh from the shell (see panel, page 102), remove the paper-like brown skin with a small paring knife and shred the flesh in

CRACKING OPEN A COCONUT

The hard shell of a coconut may seem a formidable obstacle, but it will in fact crack open naturally if tapped in the correct places.

1 With a corkscrew, make a hole in each of the coconut's three 'eyes' (the small bare patches at the pointed end). Pour out the liquid from inside the coconut.

2 There is no need to use drastic measures to open a coconut. Coconuts have an invisible natural fault line that runs right around the circumference, just above the centre towards the pointed end. With a small hammer or a heavy kitchen steel, tap the coconut firmly all around the centre and the fruit will split open naturally into two halves, revealing the white flesh.

3 With a small sharp knife, make a series of cuts through the flesh then lever out the portions. Peel off any outer skin that remains attached to portions of flesh.

a food processor or grate it by hand. If you need thin flakes, use the wide cutting blade on a grater or a mandolin cutter.

MILKING A COCONUT

Is coconut milk the liquid in the middle of the nut? And what is the difference between canned coconut milk, creamed coconut milk and coconut milk powder?

The liquid in the middle of a coconut is not coconut milk but coconut water, a delicately flavoured liquid that can be drunk straight out of the shell or added to fruit juices. Coconut milk comes from the flesh of the coconut, shredded or otherwise processed to extract a thick, white liquid. It can be used in both savoury and sweet dishes.

Coconut milk is sold in cans, in which form it is very easy to use. Coconut milk powder is coconut milk that has been dehydrated, and it needs to be reconstituted with warm water. Also available is canned coconut cream, which is slightly thicker and richer, and block coconut cream, which is used to thicken and flavour.

You can get a thin milk from desiccated coconut by soaking it in an equal volume of hot water and squeezing it through a muslin cloth.

HEAT WITH CARE

Is there any danger of coconut milk curdling when you cook it?

Yes, it will curdle if cooked on a high heat or if it is too thick. Never place a block of creamed coconut directly onto a heated surface as it will burn: always melt it down with enough water to cover, either on the stove or in a microwave oven.

When a recipe calls for coconut milk to be added at the end, it is to prevent it rendering down to oil during prolonged boiling. If a dish does not require more than 30 minutes of simmering, it doesn't matter when you add the milk. But once you have added it, do not stir the dish again until ready to serve.

Coffee

CHOOSING COFFEE

I am confused by all the different types of coffee I see in the shops. Can you offer some guidance?

The best coffees are made purely from beans of the arabica strain, or contain a high proportion of them. The shrubs that produce arabica beans are slow to grow and mature, producing a fine flavour. Some coffee blends, particularly espresso blends and some instant coffees, are made with a high proportion of robusta beans. These have a bold, coarse flavour, a very high proportion of caffeine and are much cheaper to produce.

The quality of a particular coffee is assessed by its body, acidity and aroma, each of which will have been affected by the degree of roasting the bean has undergone.

If you enjoy mellow coffee, try Colombian, which is sweet and smooth, or New Guinea, which has a light body. Mild coffees include local Australian and Costa Rican, with a sweet and tangy acidity, and Brazilian, which is described as elegant. Kenya coffee has high acidity and a full flavour, while Java is rich, heavy and spicy. Jamaican Blue Mountain has a flavour that is rich, sweet and mellow.

GROUND RULES

How do I make a decent cup of coffee? Mine often turns out too weak or too bitter.

There are many ways of brewing coffee: in filter pots, plunger pots (cafetières), and electric drip coffee makers to name but a few. You can make consistently good coffee whichever method you choose if you observe the following rules.

Coffee should be stored in an airtight container in the freezer: any contact with air causes loss of flavour. Experiment until you find a blend you like then buy whole beans and delay grinding until the last moment. The finer the beans are ground, the more rapidly the flavour becomes stale and bitter.

Heat water to just under boiling point, about 95°C, or bring the water to the boil and then allow it to cool for 2–3 minutes before pouring it over the coffee. A higher temperature will extract too much of the coffee solids, giving a bitter taste; a lower temperature will not extract enough flavour, resulting in a weak coffee. The coffee should be in contact with the water for about 2 minutes only. Strong coffee is achieved not by allowing the coffee to brew longer, but by using more ground coffee per cup.

To make medium-strong coffee, allow 2 heaped tablespoons of ground coffee per 175 ml of water. If you want weaker coffee, use the same measure of coffee but add more hot water.

STRONG AND THICK

How can I make cups of espresso or Turkish coffee at home?

Espresso (Italian for 'pressed out') is a very strong coffee made by forcing a mixture of steam and water through twice the normal amount of finely ground coffee.

At one time, espresso was available only in cafés and restaurants with enough space to hold professional espresso machines, but there are now many smaller machines designed for home use. In addition, some coffee is labelled espresso for filters and cafetières; this kind will have the strength of an espresso, but without the steam treatment it is not likely to taste the same.

Turkish or Greek coffee is made with finely ground coffee in a long-handled open pot (*ibrik*), or an ordinary small saucepan. Water and sugar are put in the pot and are brought to the boil, the coffee is added and the pot returned to the heat. When the mixture is brought to frothing point the pot is removed until the froth settles. It is frothed and removed twice more, and then this strong, sweet brew is poured into tiny cups to serve.

IRISH ESSENTIAL

Can I make a successful Irish coffee without using sugar?

In a word, no. The combination of sugar and alcohol in the coffee makes the coffee more dense, which in turn allows the cream to float over the surface. If sugar is not used, the cream will mix in with the coffee as soon as it is added.

For each serving, put 1 teaspoon of sugar and 3 tablespoons of Irish whiskey into a warm, tall-stemmed glass and fill two-thirds full with strong black coffee. Stir briefly, then pour fresh cream gently over the back of a teaspoon placed close to the surface, so that the cream does not sink. Serve immediately, drinking the coffee through the layer of cream. The cream often works best when used at room temperature.

RICH FLAVOUR OF MOCHA

What is mocha?

Mocha is a strong-flavoured coffee bean that came originally from Mocha, a port on the Red Sea. The term is now applied to any beverage or confection flavoured with coffee, and is mostly used to denote a mixture of coffee and chocolate flavours used in such foods as cakes, icings and ice creams.

ROASTED ROOTS

What are dandelion coffee and chicory coffee?

Dandelion coffee is made from the dried and roasted roots of dandelions. It is served black, with or without sugar, and has a slightly bitter and nutty flavour.

Chicory coffee is mostly found in France, where most coffee is made from rough-tasting robusta beans. Roasted and ground chicory root is added to mellow the taste of the bean and bulk up the coffee.

REMOVING THE CAFFEINE

How is coffee decaffeinated, and is the process safe?

Caffeine is removed from unroasted coffee beans, either by water or solvent. In the water method, the beans are soaked to bring the caffeine to the surface; the caffeine is then filtered out, removing about 97 per cent of it.

In the solvent method, the beans are soaked in chemicals until most of the caffeine has been leached out. The beans are then washed before drying and roasting. Many people are concerned about solvent residues, but there is no legal requirement for manufacturers to state which method has been used.

IMPROVISING A CAPPUCCINO

In cafés and restaurants, cappuccino is usually made in a special machine, but the milk can also be made frothy with a whisk or in a blender.

1 For two cappuccinos, make 175 ml very strong coffee, using 3 tablespoons ground beans. Heat 150 ml milk until it almost reaches boiling point. Take off the heat and whisk until all the milk is frothy.

2 Divide the coffee between two large cups, top up with whisked milk and spoon some froth onto each one. Sprinkle with powdered drinking chocolate or some finely grated dark chocolate and serve immediately.

Corn

(see panel, page 105)

A QUESTION OF LANGUAGE

I always thought that the word corn referred to wheat, but have recently discovered the word maize. Could you explain?

In Britain, corn is often used to describe all growing cereals, even wheat, but the term used in the United States – maize – is becoming widespread. In Australia, there are two basic types: sweetcorn, which is eaten as a vegetable or dried to form the kernels that become popcorn; and field corn, used as animal feed or processed to make cornmeal, cornflour and corn oil. Blue cornmeal takes its name from the black and blue kernels of a particular American variety of sweetcorn and is used in tortilla chips.

CORN KERNELS

Are hominy and grits the same, and where do they come from?

Hominy is made from corn kernels in a process whereby the outer hull is removed and the remaining kernel left to dry. The dried kernel is then soaked overnight, or cooked for several hours, before it can be added to slow-cooking meat stews.

Grits are made by grinding dried hominy to provide a finer cereal that then needs no presoaking. They require a shorter cooking time than cornmeal, which is made from the whole grain of corn, but grits have less fibre, flavour and texture. The cereal is used throughout the south of the United States, usually cooked to a mush and served with bacon and eggs for breakfast.

MAKE A MEAL OF IT

Polenta appears on many menus nowadays, but seems different in each restaurant. Are there several ways to prepare it?

In northern Italy wet polenta, a savoury corn porridge, is served like mashed potato to soak up the

A comforting alternative to mashed potatoes, polenta's velvety texture is enhanced with butter and Parmesan.

juices from a stew, as in the recipe on the right. Polenta takes a long time to cook, and needs stirring throughout, but instant polenta, taking about 5 minutes to make, is now widely available.

Wet polenta can be a meal in its own right, flavoured with cheese, pepper and a little virgin olive oil. Chopped vegetables, herbs and olives are other good additions.

Polenta is also frequently served in 'cakes', made by allowing wet polenta to cool and set. This is then cut into squares, slices or triangles and grilled or fried (see panel, page 105). These cakes, while also served with stews, can make delicious snacks topped with grilled red peppers, rocket and tomatoes.

For a substantial snack, cut the set polenta into small circles, take two and sandwich with a slice of mozzarella. Coat in egg and breadcrumbs and fry on both sides until the outside is crispy and the cheese is melted in the centre.

Creamy polenta

SERVES: *4-6*
PREPARATION TIME: *5 minutes*
COOKING TIME: *55-60 minutes*

185 g (1 cup) polenta or coarse cornmeal
50 g butter
75 g Parmesan cheese, freshly grated
Black pepper

1 Measure out the polenta and put it in a bowl. Bring 1.25 litres of salted water to a rolling boil in a large, heavy-based saucepan.
2 To avoid lumps forming, sprinkle in the polenta with one hand while beating continually with a wooden spoon with the other, until all the polenta is incorporated in the pan.
3 Cook, uncovered, over as low a heat as possible for 55-60 minutes, stirring frequently. The polenta is cooked when it comes away cleanly from the sides of the pan.
4 Remove from the heat and stir in the butter, Parmesan cheese and pepper. Taste and season with extra salt, if necessary, and serve with a rich meat stew.

POLENTA TRIANGLES

This recipe requires 185 g (1 cup)
instant polenta, which serves
4–6 people as an accompaniment.

1 Bring 1.25 litres of salted water to a rolling boil.

2 Sprinkle the instant polenta into the boiling water while stirring constantly with a wooden spoon.

3 Stir for 3–4 minutes. Remove from the heat, season and beat in 25 g butter and 50 g freshly grated Parmesan cheese.

4 Pour into a greased tin, smooth with a palette knife and leave to set. Turn out and cut into triangles.

5 Brush a heavy-based frying pan with oil. Fry the triangles for 3 minutes on each side until golden.

Corn-on-the-Cob

SIMPLE IS BEST

What is the best way to cook and serve corn-on-the-cob?

In late summer, the whole cobs make a splendid if rather messy starter to an informal meal.

Strip off the outer husk, pull away the silky hairs and trim the stems. Cook them for 15 minutes at a rolling boil without salt, which makes the skins of the kernels tough and spoils the sweet flavour. You can add a pinch of sugar for extra sweetness. Serve them with butter or olive oil, salt and pepper or cayenne pepper. Baby corn cobs can be eaten whole but they lack the sweetness of fully grown corn cobs.

STRIPPING GRAINS FROM THE COB

Raw kernels may be cut from the cob and then simmered. They can also be cut after the cob has been cooked whole, but they may lose their shape in the process.

1 Strip off the outer leaves of the corn ear and pull away the silky hairs around the cob's kernels.

2 Hold cob stem-down. With firm, downward strokes, cut away the kernels using a heavy, sharp knife.

CREAMY COMFORT

I have used frozen corn kernels in rice salads and thick soups. Are there any other uses for them, and could I use canned instead?

When fresh sweetcorn is out of season, frozen corn makes a fair substitute and is better than the canned variety, which tends to lack that special juicy texture.

Frozen corn can be stirred into a thick pancake batter to make corn-cakes (about the size of a pikelet), which are a very good accompaniment to fried chicken and great with a breakfast fry-up. They can also be served hot as a starter: place two or three pancakes in the cupped leaf of a crisp iceberg lettuce and accompany with a spicy salsa sauce.

Alternatively, this soft Corn Pudding (below) can be served as a sauce or a starchy accompaniment to roast chicken, baked ham, or smoked fish fillets.

Corn pudding

SERVES: *4–6*
PREPARATION TIME: *20 minutes*
COOKING TIME: *about 45 minutes*

50 g butter
400 g fresh or thawed frozen
  corn kernels
200 ml fresh cream
250 g egg tomatoes,
  skinned and chopped
Salt and black pepper
A pinch of cayenne pepper

1 Preheat the oven to 180°C. Using half the butter, liberally grease an ovenproof dish.
2 Put the corn and cream into a food processor and process them to a chunky, porridge-like consistency.
3 Stir the chopped tomatoes into the corn mixture. Add salt and pepper.
4 Pour the corn mixture into the prepared dish, dot the remaining butter over the top and sprinkle the dish lightly with cayenne pepper.
5 Bake until the top is browned and crusty (about 45 minutes) then stand the dish in a warm place for 5–10 minutes before serving.

Corned Beef

PRODUCT CONFUSION

What is corned beef and how did it get its name?

In South America and Britain the term refers to beef that has been cured, boiled, heavily pressed and put into cans.

The name, however, comes from an Irish American joint that is known in Australia as corned beef – brisket or silverside cured in brine. The early Irish settlers preserved joints of beef by coating them with grains (or corns) of salt, a process known as corning.

The recipe for Boiled Corned Beef (right) is great for a winter family dinner, and can be served with dumplings.

Corning, followed by a slow simmer in an aromatic broth, turns a potentially tough and tasteless cut of meat into a flavoursome melt-in-the-mouth meal.

Boiled corned beef

SERVES: *4*
PREPARATION TIME: *20 minutes*
COOKING TIME: *2 hours*

---

2 kg joint of corned silverside
1 tablespoon dark brown sugar
1 tablespoon malt or balsamic vinegar
1 bay leaf
12 peppercorns
1 plump clove garlic, halved
1 onion, quartered
1 large carrot, quartered
1 stalk celery, sliced
12 baby onions, to serve
6 slim carrots, to serve

---

1 Rinse the corned beef in cold water and place in a large, heavy-based pan. Add the brown sugar, vinegar, bay leaf, peppercorns, garlic, onion, carrot and celery. Add cold water to just cover the beef.
2 Cover the pan and bring gradually to the boil; remove the scum with a slotted spoon.
3 Simmer, covered, for 1½ hours. Add the extra onions and carrots and simmer, covered, for a further 30 minutes, until the beef is tender when tested with a fine skewer.
4 Remove the quartered onion, carrot and celery and discard. Place the beef on a warm serving plate. Arrange the whole onions and carrots around the beef. Cut the corned beef into slices. Serve hot accompanied with parsley or mustard sauce, a green vegetable and boiled new potatoes.

Alternatively, to serve the corned beef cold, omit the extra onions and carrots for serving and leave the cooked corned beef to cool in the cooking liquor. When cold, wrap the corned beef in foil and store in the refrigerator until required.

Cornflour

KNOW THE DIFFERENCE

What is the difference between cornflour and cornmeal, and can they be used in the same way?

The two differ considerably. Cornflour is ground to a fine chalky white powder and is a valuable thickening agent in sauces. It is also added to some cakes and biscuits.

Cornmeal is much coarser, used to make polenta, muffins and some breads, in particular corn bread.

LUMPY SAUCES

I often have trouble when I use cornflour as it makes my sauces lumpy. What can I do?

When used properly, cornflour is an excellent thickener. Place the required amount of cornflour in a small bowl and stir in a little cold water (1–2 tablespoons) until it is completely blended. Add a little of the hot sauce to the cornflour mixture, blend well and then whisk this back into your main sauce, which should be just below boiling point. Stir the sauce continually until it reaches a steady simmer, then cook it gently for 2 minutes and serve.

See also: *Arrowroot*

Couscous

NORTH AFRICAN PASTA

What is couscous?

Couscous is a pasta made from grains of semolina given a coating of extra fine flour so that they absorb moisture more easily, but it looks like a grain.

Couscous was invented in North Africa, where it is steamed over a stew, allowing the grains to swell and soften as they absorb the steam and the flavour of the stew.

The tagine chicken recipe below, cooked this way, is named after the conical dish in which it is traditionally cooked, but you can use a saucepan with a steamer on top, or put the couscous in a metal sieve over the stew.

Chicken tagine with couscous

SERVES: 4-6
PREPARATION TIME: 30 minutes, plus at least 1 hour marinating
COOKING TIME: 40 minutes

4 tablespoons olive oil
2 cloves garlic, crushed
½ teaspoon chilli powder
2 teaspoons each ground coriander and paprika
1 teaspoon each ground cumin, turmeric and cinnamon
750 g skinless chicken breast fillet, cut in 2.5 cm slices
1 onion, chopped
2 medium potatoes, cubed
2 large carrots, thickly sliced
300 ml chicken stock
300 ml tomato juice
2 tablespoons tomato paste
1 tablespoon chilli sauce
125 g (¾ cup) sultanas
2 tablespoons chopped fresh coriander
Salt and black pepper
350 g (1¾ cups) couscous
To garnish: lemon wedges and sprigs of fresh coriander

1 Put 2 tablespoons of the olive oil in a bowl and stir in the garlic, chilli

A combination of sweet spices, dried fruit and chilli adds an intriguing complexity to the flavour of this North African stew of couscous and chicken.

powder and all of the spices. Add the sliced chicken to the oil mixture, toss well, then cover and marinate it for at least an hour.

2 Heat the remaining oil in a frying pan, add the onion and fry it for 5 minutes, then add the potatoes and carrots and fry for another 5 minutes. Transfer to a saucepan.

3 Remove the chicken slices from the marinade and pat them dry. Put them in the frying pan and stir-fry for 3-4 minutes or until golden.

4 Add the chicken to the vegetables and pour over the stock, tomato juice, tomato paste and chilli sauce. Bring to the boil, cover and simmer for 15 minutes, then stir in the sultanas, coriander, salt and pepper.

5 Place the couscous in a sieve and wash it under cold running water. Put the couscous in a muslin-lined steamer (the holes of a steamer are

too big for the couscous without a cloth) and set it over the stew. Cover and simmer for 8-10 minutes until the couscous is cooked.

6 Serve the couscous on individual plates, topped with the chicken and vegetable tagine. Pour the excess cooking juices into a serving jug to offer alongside the couscous with some wedges of lemon. Garnish the tagine with sprigs of fresh coriander.

SWEET THOUGHTS

Can I use couscous in desserts?

Yes. Steam the couscous over boiling water then top with a generous pat of butter, a few raisins and sprinkle sugar over to taste. Stir in some milk if you like. Alternatively, flavour the cooked couscous with the juice of an orange, chopped dates, and nuts such as pistachios.

Crab

SOME LIKE IT HOT

Is there a way of eating crab hot?

If you are prepared to kill and cook it yourself, you can have hot fresh crab. If you do not want to do this, you will have to buy your crab ready-cooked and therefore cold.

You can, however, use frozen or canned cooked, ready-flaked white crab meat in hot recipes. Add it, with a dash of brandy, to cream sauces to top poached fish, or use it in Thai Crab Cakes (below).

Thai crab cakes

SERVES: 4 as a starter
PREPARATION TIME: 20 minutes, plus 15 minutes chilling time
COOKING TIME: 6–8 minutes

350 g flaked crabmeat, well drained
1 cup cold cooked rice
1 stalk lemon grass, finely chopped
2 cloves garlic, crushed
1 red chilli, seeded and finely chopped
1 coriander root, finely chopped
¼ cup chopped coriander leaves
2 teaspoons fish sauce
1 teaspoon lime juice
1 egg yolk
6 teaspoons cornflour
Extra cornflour, for coating
3 tablespoons peanut oil, for shallow frying

1 Squeeze the flaked crabmeat dry with clean fingers and put into a mixing bowl.

2 Add the rice, lemon grass, garlic, chilli, coriander root and leaves, fish sauce, lime juice, egg yolk and cornflour. Stir together with a fork until evenly mixed.

3 Level the mixture in the bowl with a plastic spatula and divide into 8 equal wedges. With clean cold hands, shape each portion of mixture into a round patty and coat lightly with cornflour. Place the crab patties on a plate and chill in the refrigerator for 15 minutes, or until firmer and easy to handle.

DRESSING A COOKED CRAB

Large-bodied crabs have plenty of body meat, while long-legged crabs have their meat mostly in the legs and claws. The larger the crab, the easier it is to extract the meat. Break open the shell or get the retailer to open a cooked crab for you, and then simply pick out as much meat as you can from the crevices and rearrange it in the shell as shown. The brown meat can be mashed and mixed with breadcrumbs to lighten its flavour. Serve dressed cooked crab with mayonnaise, lemon wedges and crusty brown bread rolls.

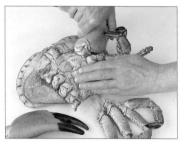

1 Pull off the claws and legs. Crack open the claws with a small hammer and scoop the white meat into a bowl with a lobster pick, skewer or the tip of a small, sharp knife. Keep the legs for a decorative garnish.

2 Twist off the tail flap and discard then stand the crab on its edge and push out the central body chamber from the upper shell using your thumbs. Or crack the body with a knife and pull apart with your hands.

3 Remove the greyish 'dead men's fingers' (lungs or gills) from around the body and discard. Pick up the back shell and remove the stomach sac from just below the head. Check the shell just in case any bits of the grey matter have fallen in and remove if necessary.

4 Use a sharp knife or your hands to split the crab's body into halves or quarters, then carefully remove the white crab meat using a pick or skewer and a teaspoon. Fork it through and discard any small pieces of membrane. Reserve the flesh in a bowl.

5 Spoon the brown meat from the back shell into a separate bowl with any coral meat. Tap the underside of the shell with a small hammer to break back to the natural inner rim. Wash, dry and rub the shell with oil.

6 Season both meats with some salt, pepper and a squeeze of lemon juice. Spoon them back into the shell, placing the white meat on each side and the brown meat down the middle, then garnish with parsley.

4 Heat the oil in a nonstick frying pan over a medium-high heat and fry the patties for 1 minute on either side, turning carefully with an egg slice. Reduce the heat to medium and fry for a further 2–3 minutes on both sides, until lightly browned and cooked through. Drain on kitchen paper towels. Serve hot with sliced cucumber, fish sauce and lime wedges or a salsa, such as Sweet Tomato Salsa (see page 141) or Coriander Salsa (see page 176).

Cranberries

AUTUMN PLEASURES

Are fresh cranberries available in Australia or New Zealand?

No, they're not. Fresh cranberries are in season and at their peak between October and December in the northern hemisphere. However, you can get them frozen all year round for both sweet and savoury cooking, making them into jelly, tarts or piquant sauces to serve with turkey and other meat.

SCARLET SAUCE

Can I use frozen cranberries to make cranberry sauce?

Yes, you can, and they should be cooked while they are still frozen.

Cranberry sauce is most often served with roast turkey, but the recipe below can also be used as a sweet topping for ice cream or cheesecake, as a filling for sponge cakes or little meringue nests, either combined with or topped with whipped cream.

Cranberry sauce

SERVES: 6–8
PREPARATION TIME: 10 minutes
COOKING TIME: 10 minutes, plus 2–3 hours chilling time

1 orange
1 lemon
125 g (½ cup) caster sugar
350 g frozen cranberries
2 tablespoons arrowroot

1 Peel the rind from the orange and lemon, avoiding the white pith, then cut it into fine shreds. Squeeze the orange and lemon and strain the juice into a stainless-steel, nonstick or enamel saucepan.
2 Add the rind, the caster sugar and the frozen cranberries. Cook over a medium heat for 5 minutes or until the cranberries start to pop.
3 Drain the berries through a nylon sieve into a bowl to catch the juice, then put the berries aside. Blend the arrowroot with 3 tablespoons of cold water and stir it into the juice.
4 Return the juice to the saucepan and bring to the boil, stirring continuously, until the sauce thickens. Continue stirring for a minute to cook the arrowroot. Remove from the heat and cool.
5 Put the cranberries into a bowl, stir in the sauce and mix it in well. Allow it to cool completely before covering the bowl with plastic wrap. Chill for 2–3 hours or overnight.

Crayfish

CRUSTACEAN CONFUSION

Is crawfish another name for crayfish or are they different?

They are different. The Australian crayfish is actually a rock lobster. Rock lobsters are also known as crawfish, *langouste* and spiny lobster. They are served as lobster in Australia and also around the Mediterranean. Although they have only small claws with not much meat, the fine white body meat is excellent and there is a good proportion of it in comparison to total weight. They are commonly sold at about 2 kg weight; you should allow 600–700 g shell-on weight per person.

Crayfish, on the other hand, are small freshwater crustaceans found in Britain, Scandinavia and in the bayous of Louisiana, where they feature in Cajun cooking.

You can substitute large prawns or yabbies for freshwater crayfish in most recipes.

Cream

OVERWHIPPED CREAM

How can I rescue my cream if I have whipped it too much?

There is no remedy. Always chill the cream before you start whipping and beat it firmly but carefully and not too fiercely.

ADDING EGG WHITE

Is it possible to make a lighter type of whipped cream?

You can lighten whipped cream by folding in one whisked egg white to every 300 ml of whipped cream.

WHIPPING CREAM

For best results, before whipping chill both the mixing bowl and the hand whisk or the blade attachments of the electric beater, as well as the cream.

1 Whip the cream in the bowl until it starts to thicken.

2 Continue to whip more slowly until the cream stands in soft peaks. If you want stiffly whipped cream, continue whipping slowly until firmer peaks form. The higher the fat content of the cream, the more quickly it will thicken. Do not whip any longer than is necessary, or the cream will become grainy.

NATURAL AND TREATED CREAMS

TYPE	CHARACTERISTICS	MILK FAT CONTENT
NATURAL Rich cream	Rich cream has been homogenised to make it thick for putting on desserts, but it is not suitable for whipping. Also known as double cream.	48% milk fat; 1975 kilojoules per 100 g
Fresh cream	Will double in volume if it is whipped correctly; also suitable for pouring. Use for piped decorations, or for folding into soups and cold desserts to give a light, rich texture. Also known as pure cream.	35% milk fat; 1659 kilojoules per 100 g
TREATED Thickened cream	Made by adding 1% of either gelatine, alginate or rennet to fresh cream. Very good for whipping.	35% milk fat 1447 kilojoules per 100 g
Sour cream	Made by adding selected cultures to pasteurised cream. This process results in a cream that is slightly thicker than fresh cream, with a refreshing but acidic flavour. Used in many dishes including dips, cheesecakes and baked potato toppings, and also for enriching soups, sauces and casseroles.	35% milk fat; 1556 kilojoules per 100 g
Crème fraîche	A blend of fresh and sour cream. In France, crème fraîche is used extensively in cooking. Not suitable for whipping.	48% milk fat; 1975 kilojoules per 100 g
Clotted cream	Very rich, thick yellow cream made by gently heating fresh cream. Used on scones, and can be served with desserts.	48% milk fat; 1975 kilojoules per 100 g
Long life cream	Heated at a high temperature for a short period, then packed in sealed long-life cartons.	35% milk fat, 1659 kilojoules per 100 g
Canned reduced cream	Canned and sterilised. Used for pouring, and for drinks and sauces.	25% milk fat, 1085 kilojoules per 100 g
Aerosol/ Pressure pack	Cream packed with a harmless gas propellant. Used for piping and topping hot and cold drinks.	25% milk fat, 1230 kilojoules per 100 g

This lightened cream must be used within 2 hours as it is less stable than standard whipped cream.

EASY ADDITIONS

Will cream separate if I add another flavouring to it?

No. Just pour the flavouring, such as flower water, spirits or liqueur, into the cream, stir until well mixed, then chill until needed.

GENTLE WARMING

Can I be sure that cream won't curdle if added to hot dishes?

Heat the cream by combining with a little of the hot liquid before stirring into the dish, and do not boil once added. However, cream may curdle if added to a dish that contains a lot of lemon juice, or a much-reduced white wine sauce. To prevent this, reheat it slowly.

FREEZING CREAM

Can cream be frozen?

Yes, as long as it has a milk fat content of 35 per cent or more.

The best results are achieved by half-whipping the cream before freezing. The cream should then be placed in a suitable freezer container, leaving room for expansion. Freeze for up to three months and defrost in the refrigerator.

TANGY FRENCH CREAM

I've heard a lot about crème fraîche recently. Is it possible to substitute it for cream, and use it the same way?

Yes, but it is not suitable for whipping. However, the high fat content of crème fraîche means it does not curdle when heated, and it is therefore suitable for hot dishes such as soups, where it acts as a thickener, and casseroles.

You can also eat crème fraîche with fruit purées or honey. Or serve it with cakes, tarts or any dessert you would usually serve with cream.

FRESH FROMAGE FRAIS

Should I use fromage frais like a cream or like a cheese?

Fromage frais, which means 'fresh cheese' in French, is made from skimmed cow's milk and may have been enriched with cream.

It can be used like cream in both sweet and savoury dishes, but it cannot be whipped, and it curdles easily on heating. Add to a hot dish, off the heat, stir in well and then reheat the dish gently for a few seconds only.

As a dessert, fromage frais can be served fresh with fruit or sugar, or substituted for cream or cheese in cheesecakes. You can also use fromage frais instead of cream for a pavlova. Flavoured fromage frais is widely available.

Fromage frais will keep for up to two months in the freezer; stir it well once it has been thawed and use the same day.

SIMPLY SOURED

Can I turn ordinary cream into sour cream easily?

Yes, you can. Stir 1–2 teaspoons of lemon juice into 150 ml of fresh cream, depending on how thick you like it. Left to stand, the cream will thicken in 30 minutes. The taste and texture will be slightly different, but it is a good substitute for commercial sour cream. To make a lighter version, blend equal quantities of cream and yoghurt.

Creams, fresh and sour, are an ideal base for quick party dips, The following recipes are best eaten on the day they are made.

Serve with raw vegetables, corn chips, bread sticks, crisps, or pita bread, or use to fill baked potatoes.

Sour cream and fresh chive dip

SERVES: *4–6*
PREPARATION TIME: *10 minutes*
COOKING TIME: *none*

100 g cream cheese
150 ml sour cream
3 tablespoons chopped fresh chives
Salt and black pepper
To garnish: cayenne pepper

Mix all the ingredients in a bowl. Transfer to a serving bowl, then sprinkle with cayenne. Cover and chill until needed.

Avocado dip

SERVES: *6–8*
PREPARATION TIME: *20 minutes*
COOKING TIME: *none*

2 ripe avocados, roughly chopped
2 tablespoons lemon juice
1 small onion, roughly chopped
2 cloves garlic
150 ml sour cream
Salt and black pepper
A few drops of Tabasco sauce, optional

Put all the ingredients in a blender or food processor and blend until smooth. This dip should be made at the last minute because the avocado will darken if it is left too long.

Tomato and basil dip

SERVES: *6–8*
PREPARATION TIME: *25 minutes*
COOKING TIME: *none*

100 g light cream cheese
2 spring onions, finely chopped
350 g tomatoes, skinned, deseeded and finely chopped
150 ml thickened cream or thick Greek-style yoghurt
2–3 tablespoons fresh basil, torn with your fingers
Salt and black pepper

1 Cream the cheese with a fork until it is soft and smooth, then stir in the spring onions and tomatoes (and the yoghurt if using) and mix them all together very well.
2 If using cream, whip it until it stands in soft peaks. Fold it into the cheese and tomato mixture, add the basil and season to taste. Transfer to a serving dish, cover and chill.

Blue cheese dip

SERVES: *6–8*
PREPARATION TIME: *20 minutes*
COOKING TIME: *none*

175 g blue vein cheese, crumbled
1 spring onion, finely chopped
150 ml sour cream
2 teaspoons lemon juice
Salt and black pepper

1 Put the cheese, spring onion and sour cream in a bowl and mash them until they are soft. Keep on mashing until well mixed and very smooth.
2 Add the lemon juice drop by drop until the dip tastes sharp but not too acidic. Do not let the lemon become overpowering. Season to taste.

For this dip use a well-flavoured cheese: it is an excellent way of using up slightly over-ripe blue vein which is past its prime; too far gone for serving on the cheese board but too good to let go to waste.

Creamy dips with hearty flavours are unbeatable for parties, and are extremely simple to make. Clockwise from the top: tomato and fresh basil; blue cheese with spring onions; sour cream and chives; and avocado with a dash of tangy lemon.

Crème Brûlée

SKIP THE GRILLING

Can I make crème brûlée if I do not have a proper grill?

Yes. This classic French dessert is made from a thick, baked vanilla custard and sprinkled with caster sugar which is melted to caramel. This is usually done under a grill (as in the recipe, right) but the dish can also be browned in the oven at 200°C for about 15 minutes, until the sugar bubbles.

Alternatively, you can make a caramel topping separately by gently heating 125 g (½ cup) of sugar in 125 ml of water until it dissolves, then boil until it changes to a rich caramel colour and pour it over the custards. Leave for a few minutes to harden, then serve.

Or pour the caramel thinly onto a greased baking tray, allow it to set, then break it into small pieces and sprinkle over each custard.

Banana and ginger crème brûlée

SERVES: 6
PREPARATION TIME: 45 minutes, plus several hours chilling time
COOKING TIME: 1 hour

600 ml fresh cream
1 vanilla pod, split lengthways
4 large egg yolks
125 g (½ cup) caster sugar
2 teaspoons ground ginger
2 bananas, sliced and tossed in
    lemon juice

1 Preheat the oven to 150°C. Put the cream and the vanilla pod into the top of a double saucepan, or into a bowl placed over a pan of simmering water, and heat gently until almost boiling. Remove from the heat and remove the vanilla pod (store it in sugar for use later).
2 Beat the egg yolks with half the sugar until the mixture is light and creamy, then stir in the cream.
3 Sprinkle the ginger over the sliced bananas, then divide them equally between six individual ramekins.

Pour the custard carefully over the bananas, dividing it equally.
4 Put the ramekins in a baking dish and pour in sufficient hot water to come halfway up the sides of the dishes. Bake for 1 hour or until set.
5 Remove the banana creams from the baking dish and leave to cool, then refrigerate them for several hours, preferably overnight.
6 Preheat the grill to a high heat. Sprinkle the remaining sugar over the desserts to form a thin, even layer. Grill for 2–3 minutes until the sugar turns to caramel. Allow it to cool, then chill for 2–3 hours. The creams should not be served until the caramel layer is crisp.

VARIATIONS
You can use other fruits, such as apricots, lychees or raspberries, as an alternative to the bananas, and other spices in place of the ground ginger - try cardamom, cinnamon, mixed spice or nutmeg.

Underneath the 'burned cream' crust of this extravagant dessert is a surprise filling of banana and spicy ginger.

To the rescue!

If you have run out of caster sugar while making crème brûlée, several other sugars are suitable for topping. White, or light and dark brown and demerara, which caramelises more quickly, can all be used instead.

SLIMLINE BRULEE

I love crème brûlée, but worry about it being too rich. Could I make a lighter version?

Yes, by adding thick yoghurt or fromage frais to a custard made from skimmed milk and using gelatine to set it, as in the recipe below.

Light crème brûlée

SERVES: *4*
PREPARATION TIME: *15 minutes, plus 1-1 ½ hours chilling time*
COOKING TIME: *10 minutes*

200 ml skim milk
2-3 drops vanilla essence
3 large egg yolks
40 g (2 tablespoons) caster sugar
1 tablespoon powdered gelatine or 4 sheets gelatine
200 ml Greek-style yoghurt or fromage frais
20 g (1 tablespoon) demerara sugar

1 Bring the milk and vanilla essence to the boil and take off the heat.
2 Whisk the egg yolks and caster sugar together until light. Stir them into the hot milk and return to a low heat, stirring continuously, until the custard coats the back of a spoon.
3 Remove from the heat, add the gelatine, stir until it has dissolved and strain the custard into a bowl. Cool it over iced water until it has set.
4 Whisk in the yoghurt or fromage frais, pour into four ramekins and chill until completely set.
5 Preheat the grill to a high heat. Sprinkle the sugar over the creams and grill until it turns to caramel. Chill for 30-45 minutes.

Crème Caramel

SLOW AND STEADY

Why does my crème caramel contain so many air bubbles?

Crème caramel is cooked in a bain-marie in order to achieve a slow and gentle transmission of heat to the egg mixture. If the egg custard is not cooked in a bain-marie, the oven heat will go directly into the mixture and cook it too quickly, resulting in a custard that contains air bubbles and a grainy or curdled texture. If this does happen there is no remedy. Immersing the dish in cold water will help to stop the cooking process quickly, but it may already be too late for rescue.

Small air bubbles, giving the custard a pitted appearance, can also be created if cold milk was used to make the custard instead of milk that was heated first. You should have no problems with air bubbles if you follow the recipe below, which has a hint of spice from the cinnamon and luxurious warmth from the vanilla.

Orange crème caramel

SERVES: *4-6*
PREPARATION TIME: *45 minutes, plus 3-4 hours cooling and chilling time*
COOKING TIME: *1 hour 10 minutes*

125 g (½ cup) caster sugar
2 oranges and their thin rind (remove all the white pith)
1 stick cinnamon
600 ml milk
4 large eggs
A few drops of vanilla essence

1 Put 90 g (⅓ cup) of sugar in a heavy saucepan with 150 ml of water and heat gently, stirring from time to time until all the sugar has dissolved. Then bring to the boil and bubble rapidly without stirring until the caramel is golden in colour.
2 Pour it into a 15 cm soufflé dish and set aside to cool.
3 Put the orange rind, cinnamon stick and milk in a saucepan and heat gently until almost boiling. Remove the pan from the heat and set aside to infuse for 10 minutes.
4 Preheat the oven to 160°C. Whisk the eggs and remaining sugar together. Strain the milk, discarding the orange rind and the cinnamon, and pour it onto the egg mixture, whisking well. Whisk in the vanilla essence, then strain the custard over the cooled caramel.
5 Stand the dish in a baking dish filled with enough hot water to come halfway up the sides of the dish. Bake for an hour until well set. Meanwhile, peel and divide the oranges into segments, picking off all the pith. Put them in a serving dish, cover and chill.
6 Remove the cooked custard from the bain-marie and set it aside to cool completely. When cold, cover and chill for several hours.
7 Before serving the custard, loosen it around the edges then carefully invert it onto a plate, allowing the caramel to drain out over the baked custard. Stand the baking dish in hot water to soften any caramel that has stuck to the dish, then pour it over the crème caramel on the plate.
8 Serve decorated with the well-trimmed orange segments and, if you wish, a delicate dusting of ground cinnamon and a veil of icing sugar, preferably vanilla flavoured.

Croutons

FAR LESS FAT

How can I make croutons that are healthy but still tasty?

Croutons are usually made by frying 5 mm cubes of bread in oil or butter, which is delicious but rather high in fat. They can also be toasted, which cuts out the fat, but this tends to reduce the flavour. For a reasonable compromise, toss the cubes in a little olive oil, salt and pepper, then spread them on a baking tray and bake them in an oven preheated to 190°C for about 10 minutes, or until they are completely crisp.

Crumble

TIPS ON TOPS

I hate crumble topping that is too thick and chewy. Is there any way to determine how much to add?

The shape and size of the dish you use will determine how much topping you should add. Choose a wide shallow dish rather than a narrow, deep one for a crumble; in a deep dish there will be a little less crunchy crumble showing on top, but plenty underneath which will not become crisp. Using a shallow dish with more surface area will result in a thinner, crispy topping.

Don't worry if some of the juice from the fruit seeps through the crumble. These sticky parts taste sweet and delicious – they are one of the best bits and every crumble should have some. The recipe on the right should provide plenty of crunchy topping and 'gooey bits'.

Add mango for sweetness

If you want to cut down on the sugar in your crumble, add a large sweet ripe mango, peeled and cut into chunks, then mixed with the other fruit.

EXTRA CRUNCH

Are there any variations on the traditional flour, butter and sugar crumble? Sometimes I would like my crumbles to have something more in the way of crunch.

You can add texture in several ways. Sprinkle the crumble topping with 30 g (¼ cup) of coarsely chopped hazelnuts or walnuts, or flaked almonds as in the recipe on the right, before baking. Or use a coarser sugar such as demerara instead of caster sugar, and replace 30 g (¼ cup) of the flour with the same weight of toasted muesli or crushed amaretti biscuits. Add these at the same time as the sugar.

Apricot, orange and almond crumble

SERVES: 5-6
PREPARATION TIME: 30-35 minutes
COOKING TIME: 40-45 minutes

FOR THE FRUIT MIXTURE
1 kg fresh ripe apricots, stoned and cut into quarters
60 g (¼ cup) white sugar
Finely grated zest of an orange
2-3 tablespoons orange juice

FOR THE CRUMBLE TOPPING
185 g (1½ cups) plain flour
125 g unsalted butter, diced, plus extra for greasing
60 g (¼ cup) caster sugar
30 g (¼ cup) flaked almonds, optional
To serve: fresh cream or mascarpone cheese

1 Preheat the oven to 200°C. Butter a shallow 1.5 litre ovenproof dish.
2 Arrange the apricots in the dish and sprinkle each layer with sugar. Add the orange zest and juice.
3 To make the crumble topping, sift the flour into a bowl and rub in the butter until the mixture resembles breadcrumbs. Stir in the sugar and continue to rub in until the mixture begins to cling together in crumbs.
4 Spread the crumble evenly over the fruit and press down lightly. Sprinkle with almonds, if using.
5 Bake for 25-30 minutes, then reduce the temperature to 180°C and continue cooking for a further 15 minutes until the top is well browned and the fruit is tender.
6 Serve the crumble warm, with fresh cream or spoonfuls of thick mascarpone cheese.

VARIATIONS
Blackberries and blueberries, rhubarb, apples and quinces, can also be very successfully cooked in a crumble. Put them into the prepared dish and sprinkle 60 g (⅓ cup) of light brown sugar and 2 tablespoons of water over them instead of the orange zest and juice. Then cover with crumble topping and cook as in the recipe. You can also add 1 tablespoon of fruit-flavoured liqueur or brandy to the filling.

Crystallised Flowers

SWEET BLOOMS

Which flowers are suitable for crystallising? I have a lot of different blooms in the garden, but are some of them better to use than others?

Many highly scented flowers are edible: fruit blossom, jasmine, lilac, wattle, clove-scented pinks, primroses, roses and violets. Never eat flowers that have been treated with pesticides or any that are grown from bulbs as they are toxic. The flowers must be perfect, very fresh and completely dry. Use them as quickly as possible as they will begin to fade and wilt rapidly.

MAKING SUGAR-FROSTED FLOWERS

For elegant decorations use these easy-to-make sugar-coated flowers.

1 Using an artist's soft paintbrush, gently coat a flower all over with a little lightly beaten egg white.

2 Dust the flower all over with caster sugar, using a sieve, and shake off any excess. The flower should have a thin dusting of sugar which should not stick in lumps. Put the flowers on a wire rack and leave in a warm place to dry for several hours or overnight.

DELICATE DUSTING

Is there an uncomplicated way to make decorative sugar flowers?

There are two methods. In the simplest, known as sugar-frosting, the flowers are brushed with egg white and then dusted with caster sugar (see panel, page 114), and this will preserve them for up to two days.

If you want them to last longer you need to use gum arabic (available from cake decorating shops and some chemists) dissolved in rose or orange-flower water. To use gum arabic as a covering, melt 15 g of gum arabic in 2 tablespoons of flower water. The gum must be thoroughly dissolved, so follow the packet instructions.

Using an artist's paintbrush, coat the flowers, petals or leaves on all sides with the gum arabic mixture, then dust them all over with caster sugar. Place the flowers on a baking tray lined with nonstick baking paper and leave them in a warm place for one to two days until they are dry and hard. Stored in a glass jar with a tight-fitting lid, they will keep for up to a year.

As this method takes quite some time and the flowers tend to lose their shape, it is best-suited for petals and flowers that are strongly scented and flavoured and have a good colour, such as gardenia, rose petals or violets. They can be used whole as decorations, or can be crushed and stirred into meringues or whipped cream for a delicate flavouring. Frosted flowers are a pretty touch on a cake or mousse.

The following recipe uses simple frosted rose petals as a decorative and edible touch of colour. For a violet soufflé use candied violets.

The appeal of a creamy rose-flavoured confection is doubled when decorated with powerfully fragrant sugar-frosted rose petals of deep red and vivid pink.

Rose-petal soufflé

SERVES: *4–6*
PREPARATION TIME: *30 minutes, plus 2 hours setting time*
COOKING TIME: *none*

---

1 tablespoon powdered gelatine
3 large eggs, separated
125 g (½ cup) caster sugar or rose-petal sugar (see Sugar)
1 tablespoon rosewater
1–2 drops pink food colouring, optional
300 ml thickened cream
To decorate: 12 sugar-frosted rose petals or tiny rose buds

---

1 Put 3 tablespoons of water into a small bowl standing in a pan of hot water. Sprinkle on the gelatine and stir until it is completely dissolved.
2 Whisk together the egg yolks and sugar until thick and creamy. Stir in the gelatine, rosewater and pink food colouring, if you are using it.
3 Whip the cream until soft peaks form and fold it carefully into the creamed egg yolks and sugar.
4 Whisk the egg whites until stiff and fold them into the mixture.
5 Pour the soufflé into a serving dish or stemmed glasses and leave it to set in the refrigerator for 2 hours. To serve, arrange a few frosted rose petals on the surface of the soufflé or around the individual portions.

Crystallised Fruit

TIME AND SUGAR

I would like to give crystallised fruits as Christmas presents but the cost is prohibitive. Can you tell me how to make them at home?

Crystallised fruits, though expensive to buy, can be made quite cheaply at home and make lovely presents. The fruit is simply saturated in a sugar syrup then left to dry, and although the process takes more than a week, it requires only a small amount of time each day, as the recipe (right) shows. Don't be tempted to hurry the process or the fruit will shrivel and become tough. To finish off the fruit, give it a sparkling crystallised finish or a smoother, shiny glacé coating.

Crystallised fruit

MAKES: *500 g*
PREPARATION TIME: *30 minutes initially, then 10 minutes a day for 7–8 days; plus 30 minutes finishing*
COOKING TIME: *5 minutes a day for 7–8 days*

---

500 g canned fruit in syrup, such as apricots, peaches or pineapple
500 g (2 cups) caster sugar or, for a clearer appearance to the fruit, use half caster sugar and half glucose syrup

---

1 Drain the fruit, reserving 300 ml of the syrup (top up with water if necessary). Remove any damaged fruit, then put the rest of the fruit into a heatproof bowl.

2 Put 250 g (1 cup) of the sugar in a pan with the fruit syrup. Stir the mixture well and heat it gently until the sugar has completely dissolved.

3 Bring the syrup to the boil and pour it over the fruit, which should now remain totally submerged in the syrup. Put a plate over the fruit, if necessary, to prevent it from floating up and being exposed to air. Leave the fruit to stand in a warm, but not hot, place for 24 hours.

4 Drain the syrup from the fruit into a saucepan and add 60 g (¼ cup) of sugar. Bring it to the boil over a low heat, stirring until all the sugar has dissolved. Pour the hot syrup over the fruit again and leave to stand in a warm place for 24 hours. Repeat the next day and again the following day.

5 On the fifth day, strain the syrup into a large saucepan and add 90 g (¼ cup) of sugar. Heat gently, stirring, until sugar has dissolved. Add the fruit and bring slowly to the boil, then simmer for 3–4 minutes. Gently pour the fruit and syrup into a bowl, cover and leave to stand at room temperature for 48 hours.

Everyday fruit is transformed into an exquisite delicacy by a few days' total immersion in a sugar bath.

6 Repeat step 5 once. By the ninth day the cooled syrup should have the consistency of thick honey. (If it does not, boil the fruit and syrup together again until the syrup has thickened, then transfer them to a bowl, cover and leave to stand at room temperature for four days.)

7 Remove the pieces of fruit from the syrup and place them on a wire rack set over a tray to drain. (The leftover syrup can be used for fruit salads or cooking stewed fruit.)

8 The fruit now has to be dried. If the heat is continuous, such as near a hot water tank, the fruit will dry out in a few hours. Drying can also be done in residual heat from the oven, but as the heat should be lower than 50°C, it is best to use it after you have finished cooking, when the oven is cooling down. (Remember to take the fruit out the next time you turn the oven on.) To help the drying process, turn the fruit over now and again. It is ready when all the pieces are dry and not sticky; it can then be eaten as it is or finished further.

9 For a crystallised finish, put a pan of water on to boil. First dip the fruit into the boiling water with a slotted spoon and drain well, then roll each piece in caster sugar and leave on a wire rack to dry for a few hours.

10 For a smooth and shiny glacé finish, put 500 g (2 cups) of caster sugar and 150 ml of water into a saucepan over a gentle heat and stir until the sugar has dissolved. Bring the syrup to the boil and take it off the heat, then cover it to keep it hot. Bring a pan of water to the boil.

11 Pour a little of the syrup into a small bowl. With a skewer, spear one piece of dried crystallised fruit at a time. Dip it first into the boiling water, then drain and dip it into the syrup. Drain on a wire rack.

12 When the coating syrup in the bowl becomes cloudy, replace it with fresh warm syrup from the pan. When the process is completed, the fruit should be shiny but not sticky.

Layer the fruit in an airtight box, with sheets of nonstick baking paper between each layer. Eat within a month or two.

MULTIPLE CHOICE

Can all fruits be crystallised?

Strongly flavoured fruits such as apricots, cherries, mangoes, paw-paw, peaches, pineapple, plums and slightly under-ripe pears are the best choice for crystallising. You can also treat orange, lemon and grapefruit peel, and chestnuts, in the same way. Soft fruits such as berries, kiwifruit and melon are not suitable because they contain too much water and will break up and become mushy. Equally, the large amount of juice in whole oranges and lemons causes them to collapse easily, which makes them difficult to crystallise at home, but tiny kumquats can be preserved by this method.

You can use either canned or fresh fruit but canned fruit is easier to handle, with the exception of canned plums, which soften and disintegrate during the process.

Fresh fruit must be in perfect condition. The first step is to poach it lightly in sugar syrup until just tender. The second stage is to make a crystallising syrup from the cooking water and then the process is the same as for canned fruit (see recipe, left). It needs to be steeped for two to three days longer than canned fruit. Because fresh fruit can break up during the process, it is harder to see when enough sugar has been absorbed so the soaking may be stopped too soon, in which case the fruit could go mouldy.

TOUGH GINGER

Would you crystallise ginger in the same way as fruit?

Commercial preserved or stem ginger in syrup is made from the very youngest shoots of the ginger plant, and these contain very little fibre. The fresh root ginger we can buy is too fibrous to be used for home-made crystallised ginger. To give a subtle flavour of ginger to your own crystallised fruit, add a peeled piece of fresh ginger to the sugar syrup. Steep it with the fruit and discard it when done.

Cucumber

LESS WATER, MORE TASTE

Why do some recipes tell you to salt cucumbers before using?

Salt draws out the moisture which softens the crisp cucumber, resulting in a denser texture and a more concentrated flavour. This method is used for the tangy Greek salad or dip called tzatziki, in which the cucumber is coarsely grated and salted for 30 minutes; it is then rinsed, squeezed dry and mixed into yoghurt with plenty of garlic and a splash of olive oil.

QUICKLY COOKED

Can I cook cucumber and serve it as a vegetable with other dishes?

Hot cucumber makes a light, crisp vegetable dish to go with fish, but it shrinks during salting and cooking so you should allow a whole one to serve two people, or three at the most. You may have to use two pans if you are cooking for a larger number. Choose young cucumbers, which are smaller and have a thinner skin than older cucumbers and are likely to have fewer seeds and softer, more edible flesh.

The recipe on the next page for Hot Buttered Cucumber, flavoured with dill, makes a good side dish for poached or char-grilled salmon.

Leftovers

Cooked or raw cucumber can easily be made into a quick cold and refreshing soup. Process or blend it with a clove of garlic, thick yoghurt, cream or crème fraîche, and mint or tarragon. Serve sprinkled with a tablespoon of the chopped herb and black pepper. A handful of chopped prawns adds colour and flavour.

Cucumber tossed in butter, accented with fresh dill and a sharpening dash of lemon, is a perfect partner for poached or grilled salmon. Instead of dill, you can use mint with trout, and chives, parsley or tarragon with white fish fillets.

Hot buttered cucumber with dill

SERVES: *2–3*
PREPARATION TIME: *5 minutes plus 30 minutes salting time*
COOKING TIME: *5 minutes*

1 large cucumber
2 teaspoons salt
50 g butter
A squeeze of lemon
Black pepper
2 tablespoons finely chopped dill

1 Peel the cucumber and halve lengthways. Scoop out the seeds with a metal teaspoon and discard them. Cut the two halves in sections measuring 2 cm and toss them with the salt in a colander. Leave the pieces to drain in the sink for some 30 minutes, then rinse them under the cold tap and pat them dry.
2 Melt the butter in a wide pan or wok and stir-fry the cucumber until heated through. Season with lemon juice and black pepper and sprinkle on the dill; alternatively, use another herb of your choice.

Custard

GOOD AND EASY

I would like to move on from custard powder to the real thing. Is it difficult to make?

Custard is not really all that tricky but it does need to be cooked carefully. It is worthwhile mastering the technique because not only is the flavour of homemade custard much richer than that made with powder, but rich, smooth custard is the base on which many other desserts are built. For instance, it is essential for a superior trifle; when set with gelatine it turns into a bavarois; and frozen, it is the foundation of the very finest ice cream.

The most important thing when making custard is to cook it very gently and slowly. Trying to cook it in a rush is a mistake as it will almost invariably curdle. It must take its time and must never boil, so the choice of pan is important.

For best results, dessert chefs cook custard in a bain-marie, or water bath, which is a pan of simmering water large enough to hold smaller pans. This makes it easier to control the temperature of delicate mixtures such as custard. A bain-marie is easy to improvise (see box, page 119). Alternatively, make the custard in the top of a double boiler, or in a heavy-based pan on a very gentle heat. In addition, the custard must be stirred continuously while it is being cooked so that hot patches do not form against the side of the pan.

Custard is traditionally flavoured with vanilla. You can either infuse the milk with a split vanilla pod or add a few drops of vanilla essence. It does not have to be vanilla, however; try other flavourings, such as almond, nutmeg or mixed spice.

Once the custard has thickened, (it will never thicken as much as packet custard) take it off the heat and transfer it to a cold jug or bowl, so it does not continue cooking. Serve it immediately if you want it hot. To serve it cold, cover the surface of the custard to prevent a skin from forming on the top, leave to cool completely, then refrigerate.

BAKED IN A MICROWAVE

Baked egg custard is the perfect dish to give to a convalescent, but it takes so long to make. Could I make it in the microwave?

Yes, it is very quick and easy to do, and because you cook the custard at a very low temperature, you do not need to use a bain-marie.

To make four individual custards, put 300 ml of milk in a microwave-safe jug and heat it on Medium for 1½–2 minutes. Whisk two medium eggs, 2 tablespoons of caster sugar and a few drops of vanilla essence together, then pour on the warm milk, whisking continuously. Strain into four ramekins and sprinkle with nutmeg. Microwave the ramekins on Low for 5–7 minutes, stirring occasionally until the custard is just set, then leave it to stand for 1 minute.

MAKING CUSTARD

For perfect custard, you need 600 ml milk; 1 vanilla pod, cut into two lengthways; 2 large eggs, plus 4 egg yolks; and 40 g (2 table-spoons) caster sugar.

1 Reserve 6 tablespoons milk. Put the rest in a heavy-based pan or the top of a double boiler and add the vanilla pod.

2 Heat the milk and vanilla until very hot but not boiling. Take it off the heat and set aside to infuse and cool for about 15 minutes. In a mixing bowl, lightly beat together the eggs, egg yolks and sugar.

3 Discard the vanilla pod and slowly pour the milk onto the egg mixture, whisking well. Then strain through a sieve into a clean heavy-based pan or double boiler.

4 Cook the mixture over a gentle heat, stirring continuously with a wooden spoon, until the custard thickens enough to thinly coat the back of the spoon. Do not allow the mixture to boil as this will make it curdle. Pour the custard into a cold jug and serve it hot or cold.

RESCUE OPERATION

Can I save a curdled custard?

There is no miracle remedy, but it will help to remove it from the heat immediately. You could try straining it into a cold dish sitting in a bowl of ice cubes and beating it vigorously, or you could try to rescue it by blending or processing it. This might restore some of the smoothness, and if it is not too overcooked it can be used, but the flavour will be affected. Another way of partially recovering curdled custard is to whiz it in the blender with a small amount of cooled custard made quickly with about 1 tablespoon of custard powder.

EVEN COOKING

Why do my baked egg custards sometimes leak around the edges?

This is caused by too much heat and suggests the custard has been overcooked or cooked without the use of a bain-marie, or the oven temperature was too high. Any of these could result in pitting, so producing some moisture around the edges, and it cannot be rectified.

Check your oven temperature, and use a bain-marie. The simmering water around the dish lowers the temperature, ensuring a lower, even temperature during cooking.

A bain-marie is not necessary for the Plum Custard Tart, right, as the pastry protects the custard.

Improvising a bain-marie

A baking dish can stand in for a bain-marie, either on the stove or in the oven. Always add the water to the bain-marie after you have put the dish in or it may overflow. When using the baking dish on the stove, put one end over the burner so the water bubbles; position the dish at the other end, away from the direct heat.

A double boiler can also be used on top of the stove to take the place of the bain-marie.

Plum custard tart

SERVES: 6
PREPARATION TIME: *45 minutes, plus 30 minutes resting time for the pastry*
COOKING TIME: *1¼ hours*

---

90 g (¾ cup) wholemeal plain flour
90 g (¾ cup) plain flour
90 g unsalted butter or hard margarine, diced
500 g plums, halved and stoned
60 ml fresh cream or milk
25 g (¼ cup) ground almonds
2 large eggs, beaten
60 g (¼ cup) caster sugar
A few drops of almond essence

---

1 Put the flours in a bowl. Rub the butter or margarine into the flour with your fingertips until the mixture resembles breadcrumbs.
2 Add 2–3 tablespoons of water and make a firm, smooth dough; you may need to add another tablespoon of water. Form the dough into a disc, wrap it in greaseproof paper or plastic wrap and chill it for 30 minutes. In the meantime, preheat the oven to 190°C and lightly grease a 23 cm flan tin.
3 Roll the chilled dough out on a lightly floured work surface and line the prepared flan tin with it. Bake the pastry blind for 15 minutes.
4 Remove the pastry from the oven and reduce the temperature to 160°C. Put the plums, cut side down, in the pastry case.
5 In a mixing bowl, combine the cream and the ground almonds. Beat in the eggs, then beat in the sugar and almond essence. Strain the mixture over the plums and bake the tart in the oven for about 45 minutes until golden brown and just set. Serve warm or cold.
VARIATIONS
You can use other fruit, such as stoned apricots, cherries or sliced kiwifruit, or ripe pears, in place of the plums. For a spicy custard, add a teaspoon of ground mixed spice, some grated nutmeg or a pinch of ground coriander to the custard mixture before baking.

Danish Pastries

PATIENCE MAKES PERFECT

Are Danish pastries difficult to make at home?

Homemade Danish pastries require time and skill to make, but they are especially rich and luscious, as the recipe on the right shows. The yeast pastry is made in a similar way to puff pastry, by rolling butter in between layers of dough. Roll out the pastry so that butter does not break through the paste. If the butter escapes, the pastry will hold less fat and taste heavy.

Roll the pastry with short, light strokes, moving first forwards and up (lifting the rolling pin slightly), and then backwards and up. If your pastry seems too sticky, put it on a plate, dust it with flour then cover it with plastic wrap. Rest the pastry in the refrigerator until firm.

If you prefer, make the dough in advance, then place it in a plastic bag and leave it in the refrigerator for several hours or overnight.

TRICKY CROISSANTS

Why are there so few recipes for croissants?

It is hard to match the flavour and flakiness of a professional baker's croissants, even though homemade Danish pastries, which are similar, can be wonderful.

Croissants result from the special mix of the flour, butter and type of oven used. Any that are baked at home will probably disappoint. Be consoled that even the French rely on bakeries for croissants.

Danish pastries

MAKES: 8 windmills, or 16 small cartwheels, or 8 small crescents
PREPARATION TIME: 1 ½ hours plus about 2 hours resting, chilling and proving
COOKING TIME: 15 minutes

FOR THE PASTRY
175 g unsalted butter
15 g fresh yeast and 75 ml warm milk, or 2 heaped teaspoons dried yeast and 1 teaspoon caster sugar plus 75 ml warm milk, or 10 g sachet rapid-rise yeast
250 g (2 cups) plain flour
A pinch of salt
1 tablespoon caster sugar
1 egg, beaten

FOR THE ALMOND FILLING
25 g (¼ cup) ground almonds
30 g (1½ tablespoons) caster sugar
1 drop almond essence
½ large egg white
NOTE: for cartwheels, you should make double the quantity of almond filling and add 30 g (2 tablespoons) currants for sprinkling
Icing sugar, sifted, for rolling out

FOR GLACE ICING AND DECORATION
125 g (¾ cup) icing sugar
3 teaspoons hot water
30 g (¼ cup) almonds, hazelnuts or walnuts, chopped and blanched, optional
4 glacé cherries, quartered, optional

1 To make the pastry, put the butter between two sheets of greaseproof paper then, using a rolling pin, roll it into a rectangle that measures about 25 × 7.5 cm. Chill the butter for 20–30 minutes.

2 If you are using fresh yeast, blend it with the milk. If you are using dried yeast, dissolve it with the sugar in the milk and leave the mixture until it is frothy, around 10 minutes. If you are using rapid-rise yeast, add it directly to the flour.

3 Sift the flour and salt into a bowl then add the caster sugar. Make a well in the centre and add the yeast and the egg. Using a knife, mix to a soft dough.

4 Add ½–1 tablespoon of water, if this helps the consistency, then knead the dough for 5 minutes until smooth and elastic. Cover with oiled plastic wrap and let it rest in the refrigerator for about 10 minutes.

5 Lightly flour a work surface and roll the dough into a 25 cm square. Place the chilled butter in the centre of the square.

6 Fold over the two sides of dough so that they overlap in the middle and press the edges, to seal. Roll the dough into a strip measuring approximately 45 × 15 cm.

7 Mark the dough into three equal portions. Bring the bottom third up over the middle and the top third down over the first to form a square. Seal the edges with a rolling pin, then wrap the dough in greaseproof paper and chill for 10 minutes.

8 Put the dough on a board with the folded edge on the right. Roll it out into a strip and fold into three as before, then chill. Repeat a third time, again starting with the fold on the right, then chill for 30 minutes.

9 Meanwhile, make the filling: mix the ground almonds and caster sugar in a bowl, then stir in the almond essence and the egg white to make a stiff paste. If you are making pastry cartwheels, add the currants as well.

10 When you are ready to roll and shape the pastries, preheat the oven to 220°C and grease two baking trays.

11 Shape and fill the pastries (see panel, page 121). When they are ready, place them 6 cm apart on the baking trays. Cover the pastries with oiled plastic wrap and leave them to rise for 15–30 minutes at room temperature, until they are puffy.

12 Bake for 15 minutes until risen and golden. Cool on a wire tray.

13 To make the icing, sift the icing sugar into a bowl and add only just enough hot water to make a very smooth, glossy mixture.

14 Brush or spoon the icing over the pastries while they are still warm. Sprinkle with the chopped almonds or walnuts and top with the glacé cherries, if using, before the icing has fully set. Danish pastries are best if served very fresh.

SHAPING AND FILLING DANISH PASTRIES
MAKING WINDMILLS

Roll out the prepared pastry to a rectangle 40 × 20 cm and then cut the dough into eight, neat 10 cm squares. Then cut through the dough from each corner of the pastry to within 1 cm of the centre.

1 Take 1 teaspoon of almond filling, roll it into a little ball and place in the centre of each pastry square.

2 Fold alternate corners of the pastry into the centre to form a windmill, firmly pressing down each corner.

MAKING CARTWHEELS

Start by cutting the prepared pastry in half. Set one portion aside and roll out the other to a rectangle that measures about 23 × 20 cm.

1 Spread the pastry with the almond filling and sprinkle it with currants. Roll the pastry up from the longest side, then cut the roll crossways into slices 2.5 cm thick. Place the cartwheels on a greased baking tray.

2 Flatten the cartwheels lightly with your fingertips to make them about 5 cm in diameter. Then roll out the other half of the pastry, and repeat the rolling up, slicing and flattening process to produce more cartwheels.

MAKING CRESCENTS

Cut the pastry in half and set one portion aside. On a work surface, roll the other portion into a rough circle only a little larger than a 20 cm plate. Place the plate on top of the pastry and use it as a template to cut a neat pastry circle with a knife. Next, cut the circle into four triangles roughly equal in size.

1 Place 1 heaped teaspoon of the ground almond and sugar mixture on each of the four triangles, nearer to the curved edges than the centres.

2 Roll up each triangle from the long end, then bend it into a crescent. When all four have been filled, repeat with the other half of the pastry.

Dates

FRESH FROM FROZEN

In the fresh produce markets I see fresh dates all year round. Are these Australian or imported, and how should they be used?

Commercial date production in Australia is based in and around Alice Springs, but even though the date palms were introduced there by Afghan camel drivers at the time of the early explorers, the industry is relatively new and a date palm takes 15 years to reach full production. (However, once date palms begin to bear fruit, they have been known to continue to do so for up to 100 years.)

Dates are imported from California and Israel. The soft-fleshed Medjool is the most popular variety. After harvesting, they are stored and transported at -15°C. Because of their high natural sugar content, they thaw out perfectly well without any significant alteration to their original texture.

Fresh dates are available all year round, but Australian-grown fresh dates are available in the markets only from February to the end of April, and then usually only in specialist shops.

Try to buy the fresh dates when available. They are not only nutritious, they contain only half as much sugar, and twice as much fibre, as the imported sun-dried boxed variety.

When buying fresh dates, you should ensure that they are deep brown, plump and moist. They will keep well in the refrigerator for up to a week. You can wash the fruit and eat them as they are, or cut the dates in half, remove the stones and chop the flesh into salads.

Dates can be stuffed with soft cheese, almonds and other fillings to serve as savouries. You can also offer them with after-dinner coffee. Fresh dates are also delicious in scones, slices, teabreads, tarts and sticky date pudding.

Deep-frying

CHOICE OF PANS

What kind of pan should I buy for deep-frying?

If you do a lot of deep-frying, an electric model has the advantage of thermostatic control as well as a charcoal-filter lid to prevent odours. Choose a pan with an automatic cut-off facility in case it is left on.

For occasional deep-frying, you can use a heavy-duty saucepan that is deep enough to hold a large amount of oil. You will also need a basket with mesh fine enough to keep the oil free of food particles. A close-fitting lid is essential for cutting off the air in emergencies (see *Safety in the Kitchen*).

PROTECTIVE COATINGS

Why are some foods coated before they are deep-fried?

Foods are subjected to a very high temperature in the deep-fryer. A protective coating prevents a hard, unattractive skin forming on the food while allowing the inside to cook slowly and thoroughly.

If deep-frying is done properly, the coating also creates a seal that stops a food's flavour from tainting the oil, so it can be used again. Sealing has the added advantage of preventing any dangerous spluttering or bubbling of hot oil, which can happen if food juices leak out.

BATTER OR BREADCRUMBS

Recipes say to coat some foods in batter, others in breadcrumbs, before they are deep-fried. Why?

Batter is best for wet foods, such as vegetable or fruit fritters, because it sticks to the surface of these foods once they have been floured. The batter will puff up and seal in the moisture without changing the lightness of the food inside.

Breadcrumbs, which are heavier, are best for foods such as fish and chicken which need to cook longer.

Shake these foods in flour first to dry the surface, then dip them in egg to give an initial seal. Finally, roll the food in breadcrumbs for an outer seal with a crunchy texture.

HEAT TEST

How do I know if the oil is at the right temperature?

The correct temperature for deep-frying is 190°C, which is moderately hot. If your fryer does not have a thermostat, you can test the oil by dropping in a cube of bread. It should take only about 40 seconds for the bread to brown.

If it browns in 10 seconds, the oil is dangerously hot and should be cooled. If it takes a minute, the oil is too cool and the batter will not crisp immediately. This causes the food inside to become soggy.

AVOIDING GREASE

How can I ensure that food inside the batter does not absorb grease?

Cook the food in small amounts. Adding too many pieces at one time to the pan lowers the temperature of the fat so that the coating does not form a crisp crust. The food then absorbs fatl.

WARMING THOUGHTS

How do I keep deep-fried food from cooling off quickly?

If the food must wait a short while before being served, spread it out in a single layer on a hot baking tray or dish. Keep the food warm in the oven, with the door ajar to allow air to circulate. Do not cover or enclose the food, as this will serve to make the crust soggy.

See also: *Frying*

Keep it low

Fill a deep-fryer no more than one-third full of oil. The pan should be no more than half full after all the food has been added.

Dinner Parties

BALANCING TRICK

Can you give me guidelines on putting together a dinner menu?

Try to balance the menu. Include easy dishes as well as complicated ones and vary the ingredients.

Think of the textures, colours and tastes of the dishes you are planning and do not have the same dominant flavouring in more than one course. Also, avoid combining dishes that are similar in colour.

Aim for variety: follow food that is crunchy with something smooth, a mild dish with a sharp-flavoured one. If the main course is heavy, avoid a rich dessert and choose instead a light, simple recipe, such as one based on fruit.

Finally, keep the overall effect of the meal simple. Nothing can better the taste of fresh, well-prepared ingredients. (For detailed guidelines, see *Menu Planning*.)

RELAXED AND PREPARED

How can I give a great dinner party and still find time to enjoy the company of my guests?

Choose recipes that can be made largely in advance and need little last-minute attention. Avoid fiddly recipes that will keep you in the kitchen away from your visitors.

If you have the space, arrange the starter and dessert courses on plates ahead of time. Cover and put them in a cool place and set out cheeses to reach room temperature.

Lay out everything you will need in the way of cutlery and china for all of the courses, including coffee and after-dinner drinks. Make a simple timetable, wearing a watch, and work out a seating plan.

On the next pages are hot main course dishes that will delight your guests while leaving you time to enjoy their company. Choose from the Fillet of Beef with Anchovy Butter (page 124), or the vegetarian crêpes (page 123).

Triple-layered vegetable crêpe cake

SERVES: 6
PREPARATION TIME: 1½ hours
COOKING TIME: 1½ hours

FOR THE CREPES
150 g (1¼ cups) plain flour
175 ml milk
175 ml water
A pinch of salt
3 large eggs
3 tablespoons melted butter, plus
    extra for greasing

FOR THE VEGETABLE FILLINGS
500 g zucchinis, grated
500 g carrots, cut into
    matchsticks
90 g butter
2 tablespoons chopped fresh
    tarragon
3 tablespoons olive oil
2 cloves garlic, finely chopped
4 shallots, finely chopped
500 g mushrooms, finely sliced
Salt and black pepper

FOR THE CUSTARD
175 g ricotta cheese
4 large eggs
125 g freshly grated Parmesan
    cheese
100 ml milk
Salt and black pepper

FOR THE TOMATO SAUCE
1 onion, finely chopped
2 tablespoons olive oil
500 g tomatoes, skinned, deseeded
    and chopped
1 tablespoon chopped fresh basil
Salt and black pepper

1 Whisk all the crêpe ingredients together briefly then let the batter stand for about 10 minutes.
2 Heat a 20 cm crêpe pan and grease it with butter. Pour 3 tablespoons of batter into the hot pan then swirl the pan to distribute it evenly. Cook the crêpe until the underside is lightly browned.
3 Turn the crêpe over and cook the other side, then taste to check. Add a little more water to the batter if it seems too thick. Remove the cooked crêpe to a dish and repeat until you

have made at least ten more (any leftover crêpes can then be frozen).
4 To make the fillings, place the zucchinis in a colander, sprinkle with salt and leave for 20 minutes.
5 Put the carrots in a heavy-based saucepan with two-thirds of the butter, 2 tablespoons of water and a pinch of salt. Cook, covered, over a very low heat until they are partially cooked. Add the tarragon to the carrots and set aside.
6 Heat the remaining butter and 2 tablespoons of oil in a frying pan and add the garlic and two of the chopped shallots. Stir for 1 minute before adding the mushrooms and cooking them until the juices are exuded. Turn up the heat and stir until the liquid has evaporated, then season. Put in a bowl and set aside.
7 Squeeze the zucchinis to get rid of as much liquid as possible. Heat the rest of the oil in the frying pan, add the remaining shallots and the zucchinis and cook, stirring, for a few minutes. Season and set aside.
8 Whisk the custard ingredients together and season. Preheat the oven to 180°C.

9 Lightly grease a loose-bottomed round cake tin 20 × 7.5 cm and line the bottom with a crêpe. Space five more crêpes with their brown sides down around the sides of the cake tin. Arrange these so that they overlap and overhang the tin's edge.
10 Cover the bottom of the tin with the carrots, ladle about a third of the custard mixture over the carrots and top with another crêpe.
11 Next, add the mushrooms with another third of the custard and top with another crêpe. Finally add the zucchinis. Pour over the remaining custard and fold the overhanging crêpes over the filling.
12 Top the cake with one or more crêpes, then cover loosely with foil. Stand the crêpe cake on a baking tray and bake for 1½ hours.
13 To make the tomato sauce, soften the onion in the oil. Add the tomatoes, basil, salt and pepper then heat just enough to warm through.
14 Run a knife around the edge of the cake, turn it over and unmould onto an attractive serving plate.
15 Serve with the tomato sauce passed around the table separately.

Surprise your guests with a savoury layered cake. This vegetarian treat features colourful fillings of vegetables and cheese accompanied by tangy tomato sauce.

Fillet of beef with anchovy butter

SERVES: 6
PREPARATION TIME: 20-30 minutes
COOKING TIME: 25 minutes

1.5 kg piece of beef fillet, cut from
  the thick end, trimmed and tied
  with white kitchen string
Black pepper
3 tablespoons sunflower oil

FOR THE ANCHOVY BUTTER
100 g butter
6 anchovy fillets
1 teaspoon lemon juice
2 tablespoons finely chopped
  parsley
To garnish: fresh parsley, chopped

---

1 Preheat the oven to 230°C.
Sprinkle the meat with the pepper,
heat the oil in a baking dish and
then brown the meat well on all
sides. Place it in the oven and roast
for just 10 minutes.
2 Remove from the oven and place
it on a rack to cool completely.
3 Purée the butter and anchovies in
a blender or a food processor. Scrape
the purée into a bowl and stir in the
lemon juice, parsley and some
pepper. Roll the mixture into a
sausage shape, wrap it in plastic
wrap and refrigerate until firm.
4 When the meat is completely
cold, place it on a piece of foil large
enough to enclose it. Cut away the
string and slice through the fillet of
beef at 5 mm intervals, leaving just
enough meat on the underside to
hold all the slices together.
5 Cut the anchovy butter into slices
and slip one in between every two
slices of meat. Wrap the meat in the
foil and refrigerate it until an hour
before cooking, unless you intend to
use it immediately.
6 Preheat the oven to 220°C. Bring
the meat to room temperature then
roast it in the foil on a baking tray
for 15 minutes.
7 Remove the meat from the foil,
being careful not to lose the buttery
juices. Sprinkle the fillet with some
finely chopped parsley and arrange
it on a warm serving platter. Serve
with spinach and new potatoes.

Dried Beans

A SHORT SOAK

*Do beans and pulses really need
to be soaked before cooking?*

Lentils, peas and many beans do
not need soaking. For those beans
that do, there are some basic rules
to observe. First, rinse them in a
sieve under the cold tap to wash off
any loose, floury matter before
cooking. This minimises the formation of scum during cooking.

Soak dried beans by pouring
boiling water over them to quicken
the process. In hot climate kitchens, a 1-hour soak is safer than
leaving them to sit for a long time.

Alternatively, soak larger beans
in cold water for up to 8 hours, in
the refrigerator if it is very hot
weather. Although the beans absorb water, there is no evidence
that they lose any nutrients.

BOILING FOR SAFETY

*Why are we told to boil beans in
one lot of water, then start again
with fresh water?*

Some dried beans need a prelimi-
nary period of fast boiling because
they contain toxins called protease
inhibitors which interfere with the
digestion of protein. While beans
that have not had this preparation
may taste palatable, the body will
not benefit fully from their protein
unless these toxins are neutralised.

Start by fast-boiling the beans,
then discard the water and complete the cooking in a pan of fresh
water (see chart, page 125).

This fast-boiling is particularly
important for soya beans because
they contain half as much protein
again as most beans and many vegetarians rely on them as a source of
protein. Soya beans should be fast-
boiled for 60 minutes. They should
then be drained, then simmered in
fresh water for another 80–90 minutes, or until tender.

Raw kidney beans contain a
substance that cannot be digested
and which may cause abdominal
discomfort or food poisoning if the
toxins are not extracted. It is essential that you fast-boil red kidney
beans for 15 minutes before use,
then change the water and simmer
them for another 45 minutes, until
they are tender.

TIMELY TIPS

*Why do some beans and lentils
cook in far less time than is
recommended on the pack?*

The recommended cooking times
often reflect the fact that beans and
lentils used to be stored for long
periods before being cooked. This
made them very dry and hard.
Packets now feature 'use-by' dates,
so the dried beans and lentils may
become tender in a shorter cooking time, especially if you follow
these guidelines.

To low-boil beans, cook them at
a boil that is low but continuous,
not at a simmer. The loss of water
in the saucepan through evaporation can be minimised by partially
covering the pan with a lid, but as
water is being absorbed by the
beans as well, you should be prepared to top up the level with
boiling water when necessary.

The scum that rises to the surface
during cooking is not dirt but a
mixture of proteins and starches. It
is best to skim it off, both for the
sake of your pans and to prevent
the liquid boiling over.

Do not salt dried beans during
cooking, or cook them in a liquid
containing salted meat for any
longer than is necessary. This can
toughen their skins and inhibit the
swelling and softening of the
beans. Acidity also impedes their
cooking, so do not add tomato

Record the date

When you store dried beans in a
jar, make a note of the 'use-by'
date. Although older dried beans
will still be quite edible, fresh ones
need less cooking time.

sauces or any others that are acidic until the beans are soft. Herbs and spices may be added early.

The acid to alkaline balance of local water can also affect cooking times. Use the chart (right) as a guide only. Keep testing the beans in the later stages of cooking.

CANS MAY SAVE TIME

Are canned beans as nutritious as dried ones, and which is more economical to use?

Canning does not reduce the nutritional value of beans but canned beans do cost considerably more than dried varieties. For example, 425 g of canned lima beans will give 250 g drained weight only, while 100 g of dried beans bulks up to the same weight after soaking and cooking.

Dried beans work out at less than a third of the price, but lima and some other beans require long cooking. The time and energy saved by using these beans canned may well justify the additional cost.

Whether you choose canned or dried, beans are a good source of protein, fibre and complex carbohydrates. They are low in fat and contain minerals as well as nearly all the vitamins we need.

PEAS AND LENTILS

Are the soaking and cooking instructions for dried peas and lentils the same as for beans?

No, on the whole the cooking process is simpler for peas and lentils. Only chickpeas (garbanzos) need soaking. Place them in cold water for 7–8 hours, then change the water. Fast-boil for 15 minutes and low-boil for 45 minutes.

Neither soaking nor fast-boiling is required for cooking the peas and lentils listed below. They will require only low-boiling for the following times: blue boiler peas for 90 minutes; Puy lentils for 30–35 minutes; split green or yellow peas for 25–30 minutes; brown lentils for 20–25 minutes; and split red lentils for 10–15 minutes.

SOAKING AND COOKING DRIED BEANS

Soaking needs plenty of water. Once the soaking and fast-boiling water is drained off and discarded, cooking should be continued in fresh, cold water. Use this chart as a guide for the timing needed for different kinds of beans:

BEANS	COLD SOAKING	COOKING TIME
Adzuki	Soak for 1–2 hours	Fast-boil for 15 minutes Low-boil for 50–60 minutes
Black-eyed beans/black-eyed peas	Soak for 7–8 hours	Fast-boil for 15 minutes Low-boil for 45 minutes
Black beans	Soak for 7–8 hours	Fast-boil for 15 minutes Low-boil for 60 minutes
Butter beans/lima beans	Soak for 7–8 hours	Fast-boil for 15 minutes Low-boil for 45 minutes
Cannellini/white kidney beans	Soak for 7–8 hours	Fast-boil for 15 minutes Low-boil for 45 minutes
Flageolet/green haricot	Soak for 7–8 hours	Fast-boil for 15 minutes Low-boil for 45 minutes
Haricot/navy/Boston beans	Soak for 7–8 hours	Fast-boil for 15 minutes Low-boil for 45 minutes
Mung beans	No soaking needed	Fast-boil for 15 minutes Low-boil for 25–30 minutes
Pinto beans/borlotti beans	Soak for 7–8 hours	Fast-boil for 15 minutes Low-boil for 45 minutes
Red kidney beans	Soak for 7–8 hours	Fast-boil for 15 minutes Low-boil for 45 minutes
Soya beans	Soak for 7–8 hours	Fast-boil for 60 minutes Low-boil for 80–90 minutes

GLORIOUS SALADS

How do I prepare beans for a mixed bean salad?

Beans make very good salads for parties, whether you use just one variety or a mixture. Combine with fresh or frozen peas or beans. Try to choose different sizes and colourst, as in the recipe below.

Cook the beans according to the times in the chart on the previous page. Garlic, celery and spices – and woody herbs, such as bay and rosemary – can be added to the cooking water. Do not add salt but mix it into a dressing of olive oil and vinegar or lemon juice, with thin slices of red onion and garlic.

Gently toss the drained beans into the dressing while still hot, so they can absorb the flavour. Add the chopped fresh herbs, black pepper and other fresh ingredients when the beans are cold.

Butter, black-eyed and broad bean salad

SERVES: 10–12
PREPARATION TIME: 30 minutes
COOKING TIME: 50 minutes

200 g (1 cup) butter beans, pre-soaked
200 g (1 cup) black-eyed beans, pre-soaked
1 stalk celery, cut into several pieces
2–3 bay leaves
500 g shelled broad beans (about 1.25 kg unshelled), or frozen broad beans, thawed
1 red onion
3 cloves garlic
100 ml olive oil
Juice of 1 lemon
Salt and black pepper
1 teaspoon ground cumin
3–4 tablespoons chopped fresh herbs or herb sprigs (lemon balm, mint or parsley)

1 Fast-boil the butter beans and the black-eyed beans separately in two small pans of water for 15 minutes, then drain and rinse separately.
2 Put the butter beans in a large pan of water, add the celery, bring to the boil and cook for 40 minutes or until the beans are tender. Place the black-eyed beans in another pan of water, add the bay leaves, bring the beans to the boil and cook for 30 minutes.
3 Put the broad beans in a large pan of salted water, bring to the boil and simmer for 5 minutes. Drain and run under the cold tap. When they are cool, peel off the outer skins.
4 Slice the onion finely and chop or crush the garlic cloves. Mix with the olive oil, lemon juice, salt, pepper and ground cumin in a large bowl.
5 Drain the butter beans (removing the celery and bay leaves) and the black-eyed beans. Mix the two types of beans into the dressing and then add the broad bean kernels.
6 Sprinkle the salad with the herbs and serve at room temperature.

Combine butter beans, black-eyed beans and broad beans for a party salad. Onion, garlic, cumin and sprigs of herbs help to make dried beans special.

Dried Fruit

LOSING MOISTURE

Is all dried fruit produced in the same manner?

Most vine and tree fruits, including apples, apricots, grapes, mangoes, peaches and pears, are sun-dried or dehydrated. A few, such as prunes, are dried in ovens. All are dehydrated to about 20–30 per cent of their normal moisture content.

Using different kinds of grapes produces varied results. Currants are dried from a tiny, seedless black grape, sultanas are dried from a sweet, seedless green grape and raisins are dried from several types of grapes, muscat being the largest and sweetest. Store all of these dried fruits in airtight containers and they will keep for up to nine months in a cool, dry place.

Currants, dates, figs, raisins and sultanas are most commonly used in recipes in their dried form. Larger dried fruits, such as apples, apricots, peaches, prunes and pears, are rehydrated by stewing gently, while other dried fruits, such as mango and pawpaw, are sometimes rehydrated beforehand by soaking in cold water for at least an hour.

Some fruits are freeze dried, such as apples; some are snap dried, such as pears. These are usually certified organic products. Similar results can be achieved in your own kitchen by using an electric dehydrator.

Australian dried fruits have an excellent quality, but once opened, the packets should be resealed, refrigerated and the fruit eaten within 14 days.

Some brands of vacuum-packed sultanas and raisins have vegetable oil added. Some dried fruits are packed in oxygen barrier pouches with oxygen absorbers enclosed. Sulphur dioxide is usually added to dried fruits like apples, apricots, mangoes, pawpaw, peaches and pears to preserve the colour.

CLEANING FRUIT

Do I need to wash dried fruit before using it?

It is advisable to wash any dried fruit that has been bought loose. Place it in a colander and rinse well under a cold, running tap.

Dried fruit that is bought in sealed vacuum packs does not need to be washed.

SHORT CUT

Can you suggest a speedy way to rehydrate dried fruit if I have forgotten to soak it?

Rehydrating fruit in a bowl of cold water for at least an hour is easy and produces a good result. However, if you are rushed, put the fruit in a saucepan, cover it with boiling water and then soak it for 15 minutes before cooking normally.

You can also cover dried fruit with water and heat it in a bowl in the microwave on Medium for about 5 minutes.

WILD APRICOTS

I have eaten delicious dried wild apricots while on holidays in Europe. Why are they so different from ordinary dried apricots and why are they so expensive?

Hunza apricots grow wild on trees in an area spanning Kashmir to Iran. They are left on the tree until completely dry and then harvested. As they are not treated with sulphur dioxide, they turn brown and have a deep, rich taste. Their relative scarcity makes them expensive.

An alternative is to buy cheaper unsulphured, sun-dried apricots. Free from preservatives, they turn a chestnut brown, differing from the usual orange fruit. Try any type of apricot you prefer in the tasty dried fruit compote recipe below.

Mixed dried fruit compote with star anise

SERVES: 8-10
PREPARATION TIME: 10 minutes plus overnight soaking
COOKING TIME: 30 minutes

125 g each dried apple rings, apricots, figs, peaches, pears, prunes and dates
150 g dried mango slices
6-8 star anise
Thinly pared zest and strained juice of 1 large lemon
25 g (5 teaspoons) caster sugar, optional

1 Put the dried apple, apricots, figs, peaches, pears and prunes into a large bowl, then pour over 1.5 litres of cold water. Cover the bowl tightly and leave the fruit to soak overnight.
2 Place the fruit and the water in a large saucepan. Add the dates, mango, star anise, lemon zest and juice and the caster sugar (if using).

Stir them together gently and bring the mixture to the boil.
3 Reduce the heat, cover the pan and simmer for 25 minutes. Remove the saucepan from the heat and pour the compote into a heatproof bowl.
4 Serve hot, or let cool, cover and refrigerate for up to seven days.

Duck

VARIATIONS OF DUCK

What is the difference between a duck and duckling, and what are the most common types?

A duckling has not yet reached its second-feather stage, which occurs around the age of two months. Nearly every oven-ready duck you buy is really a duckling, as it is the practice to slaughter commercial birds at about six weeks old. The variations in oven-ready weight, 1.5-3.5 kg, are related to differences in breeds rather than the level of maturity. Ducklings are available either fresh or frozen all the year round.

Nearly 85 per cent of ducklings available locally are the white-feathered Peking ducks. The Chinese community value the Peking duck for its lean meat and skin that will crisp to a fine golden brown colour.

As well as the massive production of Peking ducks, Aylesbury, Lincolnshire and Muscovy ducks are also available. The Lincolnshire is a lovely eating duck, as it has less fat. The Aylesbury and Muscovy are larger breeds of duck.

Few ducks of any kind are kept more than 12 months, except those that are used in France to produce foie gras de canard, a delicacy made from duck liver. It is as good as that made from goose liver.

Ducks are sometimes tricky to cook at home, and many people prefer to consider them a dining-out treat. But for a special, at-home occasion, try the Boned Stuffed Duck (page 128). You can enjoy it either hot or cold.

LOSING THE BONE

Can you bone a duck in the same way as chicken to make it easier to carve at the dinner table?

Yes. Boning a duck takes a bit of time and patience, but it can be done in advance and the stuffing gives you the chance to add texture and flavour, as in the recipe below. You can bone the duck in the same way as a chicken (see *Boning*), or ask the shopkeeper to do it for you.

Boned stuffed duck

SERVES: *4–6*
PREPARATION TIME: *20 minutes (not including boning), plus 1 hour soaking fruit*
COOKING TIME: *2½ hours*

---

60 g (½ cup) dried apricots, chopped
60 g (⅓ cup) dried cherries
125 ml orange juice
90 g (½ cup) wild rice
2 tablespoons vegetable oil
6 spring onions, sliced
2 cloves garlic, chopped
75 g dark flat mushrooms, roughly chopped
500 g pork or veal, finely minced
3 tablespoons chopped fresh thyme and parsley
A pinch of ground allspice
4 tablespoons brandy
Salt and black pepper
1 egg, beaten
1.75 kg oven-ready duck, boned, and its liver chopped

---

1 Soak the apricots and cherries in the orange juice for 1 hour. Cook the wild rice for 45 minutes or until tender. Drain, rinse and let cool.
2 Heat the oil in a small saucepan and cook the spring onions and garlic gently for 3–4 minutes, until soft. Add the mushrooms and the duck liver, cooking for 2–3 minutes or until soft, then cool.
3 Preheat the oven to 180°C. Combine the mushroom mixture with the soaked dried fruit, orange juice, rice, minced pork or veal, herbs, allspice and brandy.
4 Check the seasoning of the stuffing by frying a small patty of the mixture, then tasting it. Add salt and pepper to taste and just enough egg to bind the mixture.
5 Place the boned duck skin side down and place the stuffing down the centre of the bird. Fold over the sides of the bird to form a neat roll and sew with a trussing needle and string, or a needle and strong thread.
6 Wrap the duck tightly in butter-soaked muslin, tying both ends so that it looks like a Christmas cracker. Place the duck on a wire rack over a baking dish and roast for 1½ hours, basting often. After 1¼ hours, you can remove the cloth to help brown the skin.
7 Rest the duck for 15 minutes then serve hot, carved into thick slices, or allow the duck to cool, chill in the refrigerator, and then slice.

For an eye-catching dinner-party dish, serve a tasty boned duck stuffed with a delicious combination of dried apricots and cherries soaked in orange juice.

A TASTE OF THE WILD

Does wild duck have a different taste from ordinary duck?

Wild ducks (such as the mallard, teal and black duck) have a stronger, slightly oilier taste. They can range in size from less than 500 g to 5 kg but most are smaller than domesticated birds.

The mallard is the largest and should be basted while cooking as it can become dry. Black ducks are slightly smaller with dark, oily meat and each will serve one to two people. A teal is a tiny, nice-eating duck and serves only one.

Ordinary duck recipes can be used for wild duck, but you will have to adjust the cooking times and temperatures as wild duck should be cooked rare. It is best roasted whole, at a high temperature of 220°C. The bird should be roasted resting on each leg alternately, then on its back to ensure even cooking.

For a small duck such as teal, allow 12–20 minutes for the whole bird, depending on its size. For a larger mallard, allow 20–30 minutes for the whole bird. Do not prick a wild duck all over before roasting it, as they are leaner than domesticated ducks.

CRISP AND DRY

What is the best way to ensure duck skin becomes really crisp and the flesh is not too fatty?

Make sure the skin is thoroughly dry, as soggy duck skin will never become crisp. Leave the bird unwrapped in a cool place for a couple of hours before roasting to let the skin dry out. Prick the well-dried skin all over with a skewer or fork, being very careful not to pierce the flesh, then rub the bird with fine sea salt.

Weigh the duck and calculate the cooking time, allowing 40–50 minutes per kg. Stand it on a rack in a baking dish. Preheat the oven to 220°C and roast the bird for the first 30 minutes, then turn down the heat to 180°C and complete the cooking. Drain the fat from the baking dish at 20-minute intervals so that it does not burn.

BONY BIRD

I notice that a lot of restaurants serve half a duck per person; this seems a lot. How many people should one duck feed?

It does not feed as many people as you might expect from the size (compared with chicken or turkey) because of the high proportion of bone to meat on a duck: a 2 kg duck will feed only two to three people, a 2.5 kg bird will feed four.

You will need a larger duck, or preferably two smaller birds, to feed six to eight people.

AUTHENTICALLY CRISP

Is is possible to cook Peking Duck at home or is it too complicated?

True Peking Duck uses a special species of bird bred in north China which is roasted and traditionally eaten in three courses. The crispy skin is served first with pancakes, then the meat is stir-fried as a main course and the bones are served next, in a soup. Such a meal is not easy to produce at home. However, it is easier – and acceptable – to serve the meat with the pancakes.

Whatever recipe you use, the duck must be dried thoroughly so the skin is crisp when cooked. The traditional way is to hang the duck in the sun for up to 12 hours. You can also suspend the duck in a warm place for 6–8 hours. A surer solution is to use a hair-dryer.

Turn the dryer to High and blast the duck all over, from a distance of about 15 cm to prevent any scorching. Dry the inside as well. When the skin begins to look parched, the duck is ready to roast.

Thin, pale Mandarin pancakes are essential with Peking Duck. Available from Asian food stores, they can be reheated on High in a microwave for 1 minute.

Dumplings

LIGHTER DUMPLINGS

What is the secret of making feather-light dumplings?

Dumplings are made from suet crust pastry which is traditionally made with self-raising flour, finely chopped suet and cold water. However, suet crust pastry can now be much quicker and simpler to prepare by using a prepared suet mix readily available in most supermarkets. The suet mix is simply mixed with self-raising flour and cold water to make suet crust pastry for pies and roly-polys. It can also be used to prepare traditional steamed suet puddings and dumplings. Once the water has been added, it should be handled lightly to avoid developing the gluten in the flour, which will toughen the pastry

Make the dumplings just before cooking them to ensure they are light. Always simmer them gently as rapid boiling will make them fall apart. A final tip is to serve them immediately while light and fluffy.

The following recipe for savoury herb dumplings can help to make a stew or casserole, or hot corned beef, serve more people.

Herb dumplings

MAKES: 8 dumplings
PREPARATION TIME: 10 minutes
COOKING TIME: 15-20 minutes

60 g (½ cup) self-raising flour
½ teaspoon salt
100 g (1 cup) prepared suet mix
¼ cup chopped fresh parsley
60 ml cold water

1 Sift the flour and salt into a mixing bowl. Add the suet mix and parsley and stir with a round-bladed knife. Add the water and mix to form a soft, scone-like dough.
2 Turn the dough out onto a lightly floured surface and divide it into eight equal portions.
3 With clean, cold, lightly floured hands, roll each portion into a ball, then shake off any excess flour.
4 Add the dumplings to a gently simmering stew, placing them lightly on top and ensuring that they are not submerged in the liquid.
5 Cover the pan or casserole with a lid and continue to simmer for 15-20 minutes, or until cooked through. Serve immediately.
VARIATION
For dumplings to accompany boiled corned beef, sift 1 teaspoon mustard powder with the flour and salt before adding the suet mix.

Use your loaf

To make really light dumplings, substitute white breadcrumbs for half of the flour. This will help to produce a firm but lighter result.

Eggplant

OIL CONSUMPTION

Eggplant seems to absorb an enormous quantity of oil. Is there any way to reduce this?

Instead of frying slices of eggplant, brush the slices with oil and either grill, turning to cook both sides (as in the recipe for Eggplant with Garlic Yoghurt, below), or bake on a nonstick baking tray in a hot oven.

Eggplant with garlic yoghurt

SERVES: 2
PREPARATION TIME: 40 minutes
COOKING TIME: 8–10 minutes

1 large eggplant
Salt
1 clove garlic, crushed
150 ml yoghurt
Black pepper
2 tablespoons olive oil
Mint, shredded, optional

1 Cut the eggplant lengthways in pencil-thick slices, sprinkle each lightly with salt and stack them in a colander. Stand in the sink to drain for 30 minutes. Meanwhile, mix the garlic into the yoghurt and season with salt and black pepper to taste.
2 Preheat the grill to medium hot. Rinse the eggplant slices and pat dry with kitchen paper towels. Brush one side with oil and grill until lightly browned, then brush the other side with oil and grill that. Serve hot or at room temperature, topped with the garlic yoghurt dressing. Garnish, if you like, with fresh shredded mint.

JUST ADD SALT

Why do most recipes recommend salting eggplant slices for half an hour before cooking them? Is this always necessary?

Eggplant grown outdoors in warm climates develops bitter juices, which are drawn out by the salting process. This is sometimes referred to as disgorging. Many year-round eggplant sold are young vegetables and these probably won't be bitter, but the disgorging process does improve the texture of the cooked vegetable. However, it can leave the flesh rather salty, so rinsing is always advisable.

DISPOSABLE SKIN

My children find the tough skin of eggplant indigestible. Can I peel them before cooking?

Eggplant sliced for grilling tends to fall apart without the skins, but it can be peeled for cutting into cubes and adding to stews. Peeled slices make excellent fritters, the flesh soft within a crisp batter coating. For a Mediterranean dip, grill or roast the vegetable until the skin blisters and can be peeled off, then mash the flesh to a cream with plenty of olive oil, lemon juice and crushed garlic, and season to taste. Serve with lots of fresh pita bread or slices of Turkish pide.

LARGE FAMILY

I have sometimes seen rather pale and elongated eggplant. Can these be used in the same way as the dark purple ones?

Yes, they can. Throughout the world, outdoor-grown eggplant come in a wide range of sizes and colours. The choice includes tiny white 'pea eggplant', larger round ones in green, yellow, white or purple, and slender, elongated shapes in shades of violet, often streaked with cream or pale green.

Whatever their shape and colour, always look for unblemished skin, a firm texture and a fresh green calix at the stem.

Eggs

SORTING SIZES

What are the different sizes of eggs and how are they best used?

In Australia, eggs are graded according to size and weight. They range from 500 g to 800 g cartons. The largest carton contains 12 eggs weighing approximately 67 g each. The smallest cartons contain eggs weighing approximately 42 g each. The large eggs used in the recipes in this book are from 700 g cartons which contain eggs weighing approximately 59 g each. The largest eggs are good for breakfast dishes, sponges and soufflés. Small eggs are good for glazing and pastry making.

White or brown shells make no difference; the colour merely depends on the breed of the hen that has laid the egg.

FINE AND FRESH

Is there any way to test an egg for freshness?

An easy way to test for freshness is to put an egg in a bowl of water. If it sinks and lies on its side it is fresh. If it floats with its rounded end on the surface of the water it is stale. If an egg floats in the middle of the water with its rounded end up, it is not stale but it is probably two or three weeks old. Fresh eggs have thick whites that hold the yolks firmly in place.

To the rescue!

If you find you have whisked your egg whites too enthusiastically and they have collapsed, just add one extra white to every four whites already in the bowl. Then whisk them all together for 30 seconds until they are smooth.

KNOW YOUR EGGS

Some of the unusual eggs shown here are sold at butcher shops, specialist food halls, delicatessens and game shops.

Whites from hen's eggs are the best ones for whisking. They have a mild flavour and are the most economical.

1 TURKEY Large and lightly speckled with a delicate flavour, available from some turkey farms. Use as hen's eggs.
2 HEN There is no difference in flavour or nutritional value between brown and white eggs. The colour of the shell depends entirely on the breed of hen.
3 GOOSE Available in spring and early summer, they are excellent for baking. They should be well cooked; hard boiled, they make fine devilled eggs.

4 DUCK Larger than hen's eggs, with a rich, assertive flavour, good for baking. They are best well cooked.
5 PHEASANT Not common but with a fine flavour, often served hard-boiled in salads. Their rich, distinct taste is also very good for baking.
6 BANTAM A breed of chicken, the eggs are similar to hen's, but about half the size, with an almost identical taste. Use them the same way.

7 GUINEA FOWL These eggs with a slightly pitted shell are delicious and rich in flavour, available from farms.
8 QUAIL Tiny eggs, usually hard-boiled and served with salad, but they can be soft-boiled for 1–2 minutes, or fried to serve on small rounds of toast.
9 PARTRIDGE An uncommon delicacy with a good flavour. Like pheasant eggs, they are often hard-boiled and served in salads or used as a garnish.

SCRAMBLED NOT STUCK

How do you stop scrambled eggs from sticking to the pan?

First melt a small pat of butter in the pan to coat the base. Then pour in the eggs and cook very gently and slowly, stirring all the time.

Add a knob of butter or a little cream or milk to the eggs at the end of cooking to reduce the temperature and keep the eggs moist. Take the eggs off the heat when they are still a little runny.

BEAT IN COPPER

What is the best way to whisk egg whites?

Egg whites can be whisked to as much as eight times their volume. It helps considerably if they are at room temperature and only a few days old: stale whites will never whisk properly. Egg whites should always be whisked just before you want to use them otherwise they will begin to collapse and weep very quickly. Adding a pinch of salt or cream of tartar at the start of whisking will help to make the whisked whites stiff.

A balloon whisk and a copper bowl will produce the stiffest egg whites. The copper appears to have an effect on the egg whites, making the beaten foam more stable.

If you do not have a copper bowl, use stainless steel, glass or china and an electric mixer. Whatever utensil you use to whisk the egg white, it must be free from grease and traces of egg yolk.

SEPARATING EGGS

The shell of the egg is a valuable and handy tool for separating eggs, as it cuts easily through the white.

1 Have two or three bowls ready. Tap the egg firmly on the side of one bowl. With your thumbs, break open the egg over the bowl, letting some of the white slip over the edge of the shell into the bowl.

2 Carefully tip the egg yolk back and forth from one half of the egg shell to the other, allowing as much white as possible to drop into the bowl underneath as you do so. Continue until all the egg white has been separated from the yolk.

Put the yolk in the second bowl. If you are separating more than one egg, use three bowls and break each white into the empty bowl before adding it to the others. Then if an egg is bad, you can discard it without ruining the others and if you break a yolk, only one white is spoiled.

3 If some of the yolk slips into the white, remove it with the shell, a teaspoon or a piece of damp kitchen paper towel. The whites will not whisk if any yolk is present.

SIMMER AND SUCCEED

How can I boil an egg without it cracking in the saucepan?

Do not boil the egg, simmer it. The egg should be at room temperature and the water should be gently simmering as you immerse the egg. Another precaution is to pierce the top of the rounded end with a needle before you put the egg in to simmer. To save an egg, should it crack, quickly add 1 or 2 tablespoons of vinegar to the cooking water. This should seal the shell and stop the white leaking out.

EGG STORAGE

How should I store eggs and how long will they keep?

Eggs are best stored in the refrigerator as their freshness deteriorates at the room temperatures that are found in most kitchens. Store them pointed-end downwards to help prevent breakage and minimise dehydration. Eggs are porous and absorb strong flavours and odours, so store them in their carton away from strong-smelling foods.

Eggs should be eaten within two weeks of purchase (check the use-by dates) and should be removed from the refrigerator about 30 minutes before they are used.

Hard-boiled eggs can be stored in the refrigerator and used within two days. Egg yolks placed in a container and covered with water to prevent them from drying out will keep in the refrigerator for up to two days. Whites should be put in a covered container and will also keep well for up to two days.

Egg yolks can be frozen, but they must be creamed lightly with a little salt or sugar (½–1 teaspoon of salt or sugar per two yolks) before being frozen in a covered, rigid container: they will keep for up to three months. The addition of salt or sugar prevents the yolks from thickening and becoming hard.

To freeze egg whites, place them in a rigid container, cover and keep for up to six months. Egg whites can also be frozen in ice cube trays covered with foil. When hard, remove the cubes from the tray and store in a freezer bag.

Once any frozen eggs have been thawed, use them on the same day and do not refreeze them. If you have frozen egg whites and cannot remember how many there were, you can weigh them. For use in recipes calculate that 30 g of egg white equals that of one egg.

POACHING IDEAS

I love poached eggs but find them rather stodgy served on toast. Can you suggest a more interesting way to use them?

Poached eggs make a rich foil for other savoury ingredients such as spinach or smoked fish. Serve this easy dish for brunch.

Poached eggs with smoked salmon and mustard mayonnaise

SERVES: 4
PREPARATION TIME: 5 minutes
COOKING TIME: 4 minutes

---

150 ml mayonnaise
2–3 teaspoons whole-grain mustard
1 tablespoon chopped coriander
100 g smoked salmon, cut into thin strips
8 large eggs
4 English muffins, toasted
To garnish: fresh coriander leaves or snow pea sprouts

---

1 Place the mayonnaise, whole-grain mustard and coriander in a bowl and mix well. Stir in the smoked salmon, cover and set aside.
2 Poach the eggs for 4 minutes or until lightly set.
3 Place two eggs onto a hot toasted muffin on individual serving plates. Spoon some mayonnaise over each egg and serve immediately, topped with fresh coriander leaves or snow pea sprouts.
VARIATIONS
For a lighter sauce, replace half the mayonnaise with sour cream or yoghurt. For a hotter flavour, stir in some Dijon mustard, cayenne pepper or sweet chilli sauce.

Fats

RICH TASTES

Which fat has the finest flavour?

Fats make many foods more palatable because they add flavour, texture, a smooth richness and variety. Goose and duck fat collected from a roasting bird will enrich any roast or fried dish, especially roast potatoes. Chicken fat is popular in traditional Jewish dishes. Beef dripping will add extra flavour when roasting meat or making Espagnole sauce or Yorkshire pudding. Lamb dripping has a very strong flavour and may leave a noticeable and undesirable aftertaste when it is used to fry other foods.

Lard is the rendered version of pork fat (see box, right); however, unrendered pork fat has a better flavour and is used in charcuterie, pâtés and for barding roast meat.

Different brands of butter, margarine and ghee have their own flavour: use the one you like best. Copha is a hard white fat made from coconut oil. It is useful for curries and confectionery.

BUTTER IS BEST

Why do recipes tell you to use butter for greasing baking dishes? Is it better than oil?

Butter is recommended because it does not break down at high temperatures, but will cling to the dish. Oils, and some margarines, become sticky when spread in a thin film so food might stick to them. Butter will give a better-flavoured result.

KEEPING DRIPPING

How long can meat dripping be kept in the fridge?

Like many fats, dripping will turn rancid if it is kept for too long. If you collect the dripping fat from a roast, poured it into a suitable glass or china container; do not use plastic. Allow it to cool, then cover and put it into a refrigerator: fresh dripping may be kept in the refrigerator for up to two weeks and may be frozen for up to six months.

Do not add the dripping taken from one roast to that from another. It will spoil the taste. Pour the second lot into a clean container, label it and store as before: this prevents any cross contamination and lets you keep track of how old the dripping is so there is less danger of keeping it too long.

CARDIAC ALERT

Are some cooking fats healthier to use than others?

Yes. The average Australian diet contains 40 per cent fat, of which a large percentage is saturated. It is now recommended that not only should we reduce our intake of fat, we should aim to replace saturated fats with healthier fats known as monounsaturated and polyunsaturated. One good way to do this is to use olive, canola or peanut oil instead of butter for cooking.

Most vegetable oils are high in polyunsaturates, while olive, canola (also called rapeseed) and peanut oils are high in monounsaturates. Both these types of fats are considered healthier than saturated fats. Coconut and palm oils are high in saturated fats.

Today, margarine spreads are usually made with mono or polyunsaturated vegetable oils, which make them lower in saturated fat than butter. However, some margarines, particularly the harder block varieties, may have animal fats added, so if reducing your cholesterol and saturated fat intake is a concern, read the labels carefully. (See also **Nutrition**.)

HOW TO RENDER FAT

Rendering fat means melting it to separate it from the meat to which it is attached or from the impurities that are thrown off during cooking. Put the fat or meat trimmings in a baking dish and cook in the oven at 150°C until the fat turns to liquid. Carefully strain the melted fat through a fine metal sieve. Cover and cool the fat before storing it in the refrigerator.

Felafel

ALL IN THE SPELLING

Is there any difference between felafel and falafel?

Yes and no!

Felafel are little patties made from chickpeas, burghul, garlic, lemon juice and spices. The mixture can be rolled into small balls with clean, cool hands, but a special utensil is used by Middle East cooks to shape them and slip them into the deep hot oil to cook.

The patties are used in a very popular 'street food' in the Middle East where, although an Arab invention, it is also known as an Israeli hot dog! The patties are tucked into halves of pita pocket bread or rolled up in flat warm pita bread, topped with tomato, lettuce and tabbouleh, then drizzled with harissa or savoury tahini sauce. This whole assembled package is also known as falafel.

The spelling, however, appears to be interchangeable for both the patties and the pita bread package. – which is one of the healthiest and most nourishing fast foods served in Australia today.

Fennel

VERSATILE BULB

How do I cook fennel? Does it go with anything other than fish?

Florence fennel, or fennel bulb, does not have to be cooked; it may be thinly sliced and eaten raw, combined with some rémoulade sauce (see **Mayonnaise**), or tossed with sliced avocado, watercress and French dressing. To prevent cut fennel from turning brown at the edges, put the slices in cold water acidulated with a little lemon juice until it is cooked.

Thin slices of fennel are delicious grilled and added to a warm mixed salad of Mediterranean vegetables. Fennel heads can be quartered and cooked in a sauce, or steamed, poached or braised. If there are any fresh leaves attached to the bulb, reserve them to use as a garnish or toss with salad leaves.

Fennel's mild aniseed flavour matches poultry as well as fish. The following recipe for coarsely chopped fennel cooked in a barley risotto could be served with either. Or it can be scattered with Parmesan cheese to make an original and attractive vegetarian dish that even meat eaters will appreciate.

Fennel with barley and leek

SERVES: 4
PREPARATION TIME: 20 minutes
COOKING TIME: 40 minutes

1 large head of fennel
Juice of 1 lemon
125 g (¼ cup) pearl barley
Salt and black pepper
3 tablespoons olive oil
2 slim leeks, sliced
2 cloves garlic, crushed or
*   finely chopped*
3 tomatoes, skinned and chopped
1 tablespoon chopped parsley

1 Roughly chop the head of fennel and put it into a bowl of cold water with half of the lemon juice.

A new twist on a risotto theme combines the faintly liquorice-like crunch of fennel with braised barley and, for extra colour, finely sliced leek and tomatoes.

2 Wash the barley in a sieve under a cold tap, put it into a saucepan and cover generously with cold water. Bring it to the boil, then drain the barley and discard the water.

3 Rinse the barley and return it to the pan with 1 litre of cold water. Return to the boil, add salt and simmer for 30 minutes, or until the barley is tender. Drain, mix in the remaining lemon juice and keep warm in a serving bowl.

4 Drain the fennel and pat it dry. Heat the oil in a wok or large frying pan and stir-fry the fennel for a few minutes before adding the leeks and garlic. Continue stir-frying them for a further 2 minutes then add the tomatoes and cook for 3–4 minutes.

5 Mix the hot vegetable mixture into the barley, season to taste and scatter the chopped parsley all over.

Figs

FIGGY COLOURS

Is there a difference between green and dark purple figs?

Figs are grown mainly in Greece and Turkey as well as in Australia. Those seen most often have green to purplish-black skins, but they can also be red or yellow, according to the variety. Some figs are much sweeter and more aromatic than others. Ripe figs, with a powdery, white bloom on the surface, have plump, soft flesh and are eaten whole, skin and all. They are perishable and will only keep for a day or two. Do not buy figs that give off a sour odour.

Filo Pastry

LIGHT AND BRITTLE

If a recipe calls for filo pastry, can I use flaky pastry or puff pastry in the dish instead?

Not really. Even though filo pastry (also called phyllo or strudel pastry), flaky pastry and puff pastry are all made with the same basic ingredients of fat, flour and water, the proportion of fat to flour varies and this affects the amount of water used to form the dough and the type of pastry that results. If you use either flaky or puff pastry, both of which are sturdy, instead of the gossamer-thin sheets of filo, the results – although they may be satisfactory – will be completely different in texture.

Filo pastry can be made at home but it takes a great deal of time to beat, stretch, pull and roll the pastry into the characteristic sheets so thin you can read through them. It is much easier to buy it ready-made, fresh or frozen, either from supermarkets or from delicatessens.

Ready-made filo pastry comes in very thin leaves of varying sizes. Thaw frozen filo pastry thoroughly according to the instructions on the packet and let it come to room temperature in its box before you try to use it. The sheets should then be brushed with butter or oil before they are baked to make the pastry layers light and crisp.

CRISPY WRAPPING

How do I make filo parcels?

Crisp, delicate filo pastry makes attractive casings for both sweet and savoury fillings. Cut the filo sheets as you need them and keep the pieces layered under a damp cloth so that the air does not get to them and dry them out.

Use filo in the following recipe for Prawn Triangles, filled with a spicy combination of prawns and coconut. They can be served either as a snack or as a first course.

Prawn triangles

MAKES: 9 starter-sized parcels
PREPARATION TIME: 35 minutes plus 15 minutes chilling time
COOKING TIME: 20-25 minutes

2 tablespoons sunflower oil, plus extra for greasing
1 clove garlic, crushed
4 spring onions, trimmed and chopped (use some of the green part as well as the white)
2.5 cm piece green ginger, peeled and grated
½ teaspoon chilli powder
A pinch each of ground cumin and turmeric
5 teaspoons canned coconut cream
125 g peeled green prawns, deveined, and defrosted if frozen
1 teaspoon cornflour
6 sheets filo pastry
50 g butter, melted
1 teaspoon white or brown sesame seeds to sprinkle, optional

1 In a frying pan, heat the oil over a low heat and fry the garlic, spring onions and the ginger for 5 minutes, stirring occasionally. Add the spices and cook for 1-2 minutes more, stirring the mixture continuously.
2 Remove the frying pan from the heat and stir in the coconut cream. Toss the prawns in the cornflour then stir into the pan.
3 Lightly oil a baking tray. Take two sheets of filo then cut and fill the pastry triangles (see box, right). As each triangle is completed, brush the top with butter, and sprinkle it with a few sesame seeds, if you like. Repeat with the rest of the prawn filling and filo pastry to make nine triangles. Place them on a baking tray and chill in the refrigerator for at least 15 minutes. Preheat the oven to 180°C.
4 Bake the filo parcels in the oven for 20-25 minutes, or until they are crisp and golden brown, then remove them from the oven and drain the parcels on kitchen paper towels.
5 The cooked filo parcels should be served immediately, while they are still very crisp. Once cooked, the pastry quickly becomes soggy. Allow two parcels per person as a starter.

PREPARING FILO PASTRY PARCELS

This extremely brittle pastry dries out quickly, so work with one sheet at a time and keep it away from sunlight. As you work, keep the rest covered with a dampened tea towel. This will keep the waiting sheets of filo pastry moist and pliable until you are ready to use them.

1 Take two sheets of filo pastry and cut lengthways into three equal strips. Brush one strip with melted butter, place another on top and brush it with butter too.

2 Put 1 tablespoon of filling on the end of the double-layered strip, about 2 cm from the end. Gently take hold of one corner of the pastry strip and fold it over the filling, making it into a neat and tidy triangular-shaped parcel.

3 Take hold of this portion and fold it over again. Keep folding the filled portion again and again until the whole strip of pastry is used up and folded over the filling.

Fish

CHOOSING FRESH FISH

I'm not sure I know what to look for when I am shopping for fish. What are the signs of freshness?

If the fish is whole, there are several things to look for: the eyes should be clear and bright, the scales should be shiny, the gills should be a healthy-looking pink or red and the flesh should feel firm and resilient to the touch. Fillets and steaks should also be firm and moist, and the flesh should have a fresh, translucent colour.

A fresh, clean smell is another good sign. Fresh fish should not in fact smell 'fishy', but saltwater fish should smell of the sea.

WHITE AND OILY FISH

What is the difference between white fish and oily fish?

White fish are saltwater fish with oil concentrated mainly in the liver. The two main groups are the cod family, which includes ocean perch, gurnard, ling and whiting as well as cod; and the flatfish family of flounder and sole. Other white fish are barramundi, flathead, garfish, John Dory, parrot fish, red emperor and red mullet, shark, sea bream (or morwong) and snapper.

The oil in oily fish is distributed throughout their flesh. This makes them more nutritious than white fish, but higher in kilojoules. Saltwater oily fish include anchovies, herrings, grey mullet, sardines, pilchards and tuna, while salmon and trout are oily freshwater fish.

KEEPING FISH

Is it necessary to cook fish the same day I buy it?

All fish are highly perishable, especially once they have been cut. It is best to buy fish whole and have the retailer clean or fillet it while you wait, or prepare it yourself just before cooking. Generally, fish is best eaten within 24 hours of purchase. Oily fish go off more quickly than white fish because their oils oxidise, causing the flesh to go rancid. Fish with their guts intact also deteriorate quickly, so gut fish before storing.

To store fish, remove it from its wrappings, rinse it under cold running water and pat it dry. Then rewrap the fish loosely in a sheet of aluminium foil or a clean plastic food storage bag and store it in the coldest part of the refrigerator.

COOKED TO PERFECTION

How can I tell when a fish is ready to serve? I always seem to either undercook or overcook it.

One of the worst things you can do to fish is to overcook it, and as it cooks very quickly it needs to be carefully watched.

Properly cooked fish is moist, tender to the bite and full of flavour. Test the fish when it begins to look opaque. Gently prod it with the prongs of a fork: when the flesh will flake easily, the fish is done.

The moist, delicate flesh of fish becomes tough and loses flavour if overcooked. Keep testing the fish as it cooks for the moment when it will flake easily.

FISH FOR CHILDREN

The only fish my children will eat are fish fingers, because they are worried about bones. Can you recommend any non-bony fish?

Fillets of ling and ocean perch have no small bones that would bother children, only large bones that can be easily seen and removed before cooking. Flatfish, such as fillets of flounder and sole, also have no small bones but have sweet flesh that appeals to children. Fillets of coral trout are also suitable.

Putting the fish into a potato-topped pie is a good idea because you can check for bones when skinning and flaking it. Encasing boned fish in pastry is another option; try cutting the pastry into a fish shape and marking scales on it. Suitable fish are bream or snapper fillets; salmon is particularly good as the rich colour contrasts well with the pastry.

STEAMING FISH

Which is the best fish to choose for steaming, and what's the best way to cook it in a steamer?

Any fish fillet, steak or small whole fish can be steamed – and this is the best way to retain all the natural goodness. Add richness of flavour by using a well-flavoured fish stock or dry white wine instead of plain water in the steamer, and rest the fish on a bed of herbs or seaweed.

Bring the liquid to the boil then turn the heat down to simmering point. Lay the fish in the top of the steamer, making sure they do not overlap or they will not cook evenly, place it over the liquid and cover. Steaming times vary with the size and quantity of fish: allow 5–8 minutes for fillets, 10–15 minutes for steaks and whole fish.

VERSATILE SALTED COD

We tried baccalà recently in a Spanish restaurant. What is it made of?

Baccalà – also known as bacalao – is dried salted cod, which is very popular in the Mediterranean and in the Caribbean. Because of its saltiness, it needs long soaking in water before cooking, and is usually served with pungent ingredients such as garlic.

You can buy baccalà from good Spanish, Portuguese and Italian delicatessens, and in Greek and Turkish shops which sell ethnic foods. It is sold in grey fillets which are hard and dry, and have a light dusting of salt. You need to cut the fillets with a strong knife, then soak them in cold water for one to two days depending on the thickness of the fish, changing the water every 8 hours or so. After draining, baccalà can be cooked exactly like fresh fish, taking about 15–20 minutes to become tender.

In Portugal, baccalà is traditionally boiled, then skinned, flaked and served with boiled potatoes and garlic mayonnaise. It also has a good affinity with tomatoes, and in France it is boiled and puréed with milk, olive oil and garlic, when it is known as *brandade*. Baccalà is also delicious combined with fresh fish, so try adding a few pieces to your usual fish pies and stews.

SOLE DIFFERENCE

What is the difference between sole and flounder?

There are many species of sole and flounder, all flat fish with tiny scales and a white belly. The newly hatched fish have one eye symmetrically on each side of the head. When they grow to 2 cm long, one eye begins to move towards the top of the head, then crosses to the other side to lie adjacent to the other eye. As this happens, the pigment on the opposite side becomes lighter and turns almost white.

Both sole and flounder have a gill cover with another bone in front of it. In a sole these are joined together; in a flounder they are separate and you can insert your fingernail between them.

Both varieties of fish have white, soft flesh with a very fine flake, on a fine-boned skeleton. In most recipes, whether they are used whole or as fillets, sole and flounder are interchangeable.

PAN-DRESSING

My local fish shop has begun to stock what they describe as 'pan-dressed' fish. What is this?

'Pan-dressed' simply means that the fish has been trimmed, scaled, gutted, boned or filleted and is

PREPARING FISH FOR COOKING

Most fish needs some preparation before cooking, even if it is going to be baked very plainly. Fish that is to be served whole is usually trimmed as retaining the fins makes handling and serving difficult. And if a scaly fish, such as grey or red mullet, is being served in its skin, it needs to have the scales removed.

All fish, except very tiny ones such as whitebait, must have their internal organs removed before cooking. Flatfish are usually gutted before being sold, but round fish are sometimes sold whole.

Whether or not you cut the head off the fish before cooking is a matter of taste – and might depend on the size of your cooking vessels.

TRIMMING AND SCALING

1 Using kitchen scissors or a small sharp knife, cut off the fins from both sides of the belly (trout is shown here). Cut close to the skin.

2 Cut off the dorsal fins running along the back of the fish. Always discard the fins after trimming; they should not be used to make stock.

3 Put a large sheet of strong plastic (such as a cut-open bag) over the fish to catch the scales (grey mullet is shown here). Holding the tail of the fish in one hand and working from the tail towards the head, use a serrated knife to scrape the scales off. When finished, rinse the fish thoroughly under cold running water, then feel over the skin with your fingertips to ensure all the scales are removed.

GUTTING

1 Hold the fish on its side, then cut into the underside at the tail end and along the belly until you reach the head (mackerel is shown here).

2 Gently pull the opening apart to widen it, then scrape out the contents of the stomach with a knife or spoon. Discard the entrails.

3 Rinse the cavity thoroughly under cold running water while running the edge of a teaspoon along the backbone. Rinsing and scraping will remove any blood clots which would discolour the cooked fish if left in. Alternatively, rinse the inside of the fish then sprinkle salt in the cavity and, with your fingers, rub away any black skin within. Rinse the salt away under cold running water.

ready to go straight into the pan in the recipe of your choice. This type of preparation is common in quality fish shops and fish markets.

If you choose a whole fish, most fish shops will do all of these things for you, and should do them free of charge, but they may need notice at busy times. And you might need to explain your recipe because certain dishes require skinning as well as filleting.

If you ask your retailer to bone a fish, remember to ask for the bones to use for stock (see *Stock*), as these will not always be included automatically.

Fish in wine sauce

SERVES: 4
PREPARATION TIME: 10 minutes
COOKING TIME: 20 minutes

4 x 200 g white fish fillets, such as perch, bream or sole, skinned
500 ml dry white wine
1 small onion, sliced
1 small carrot, sliced
2 bay leaves
4 peppercorns
125 ml fresh cream
8 spring onions, thinly sliced diagonally
2 teaspoons snipped fresh dill
2 bunches asparagus, trimmed

To garnish: julienne of red capsicum, lime slices and fresh dill sprigs

1 Wash the fish fillets in cold water and pat dry with kitchen paper towels. Remove any bones.
2 Place the wine, onion, carrot, bay leaves and peppercorns into a large frying pan and bring to a gentle boil. Add the fish, cover and poach over a medium-low heat for 8–10 minutes, or until cooked through.
3 Using a fish slice, transfer the fish fillets, in a single layer, to a warm dish. Cover and keep warm.
4 Increase the heat and boil the wine mixture for 5 minutes, or until reduced to ¾ cup. Strain and discard the vegetables, bay leaves and peppercorns. Return the wine to the pan, add the cream, spring onions and dill; heat through gently.
5 Meanwhile, cook the asparagus until just tender.
6 To serve, divide the asparagus between 4 warm dinner plates; place a fish fillet on top of the asparagus and spoon the sauce over evenly. Serve the fish hot, garnished with capsicum, lime slices and dill.

PAPILLOTE AND PAUPIETTES

What is the difference between fish 'en papillote' and 'paupiettes'?

These French terms sound so similar many people confuse the two. Fish en papillote is baked in a parcel. It is traditionally wrapped in greaseproof paper, which puffs up full of steam in the oven, but nowadays foil is often used.

A paupiette (see panel, page 139) is simply a rolled fillet of fish, usually flounder or sole, which is stuffed before being baked, steamed or poached. Paupiette is not a term confined to fish, as fillets of beef, veal, chicken and turkey are also cooked in this way.

The following recipe for Paupiettes of Sole can be prepared in advance up to the stage when the fish goes into the oven. The dish is quite rich and filling, and needs only a green vegetable or salad as an accompaniment.

Delicate, white fish fillets are gently poached, masked with an aromatic wine and cream sauce, and served on a bed of freshly cooked asparagus. You can use any white fish you choose, then highlight it with a colourful garnish.

SKINNING A FLATFISH

If flounder or sole are to be cooked whole, the dark skin is removed by ripping it off. Fresh flatfish can also be skinned with a knife (see page 140).

1 Make a small cut in the dark skin at the tail end. With the point of the knife, ease the skin off the flesh until you can easily grasp it in your fingers.

2 Dip your fingers in salt to help you to grip, then grasp the skin in one hand and the tail in the other. Pull the skin away backwards, not upwards.

MAKING PAUPIETTES

Paupiettes, sometimes described as turbans, transform simple fillets of fish into an impressive dish. The addition of a rich stuffing turns small pieces of fish into more substantial portions.

The fish most typically cooked in this way is sole (pictured here), but any other white or oily fish fillet can be used in its place, provided it is thinly sliced.

1 Place skinned fillets on a board or work surface, skinned side up, and lightly score them with a sharp knife. Put a spoonful of stuffing at the widest end of the fillet and roll the fish up from that side.

2 Stand the filled rolls upright in a buttered dish, placing them close together so they do not unroll during cooking. Alternatively, the rolls can be secured after rolling with a thin strip of lightly oiled greaseproof paper, which is easily removed after cooking.

3 When making a large quantity of paupiettes, a quicker way of preparing them is to roll the fillets up without the stuffing, stand them in the dish and then pipe in the stuffing in the centre. Paupiettes can also be made in long cylinder shapes, by rolling large escalopes of fish such as salmon spread with a stuffing. After cooking, the roll is sliced into attractive pinwheels.

Paupiettes of sole

SERVES: *4*
PREPARATION TIME: *30 minutes*
COOKING TIME: *10-12 minutes*

125 g button mushrooms
50 g butter
1 shallot, finely chopped
1 clove garlic, crushed
50 g (¾ cup) fresh white
  breadcrumbs
1 tablespoon chopped oregano
Salt and black pepper
8 sole fillets, skinned (see panel, above)
Extra 2 tablespoons butter
125 ml dry white wine
125 ml crème fraîche
To garnish: fresh oregano sprigs

1 Preheat the oven to 200°C. Grease a shallow ovenproof dish.
2 Finely chop half the mushrooms. Melt half the butter in a frying pan, add the shallot and garlic and soften. Add the chopped mushrooms and cook over a gentle heat, stirring all the time, until well softened.
3 Transfer the cooked mushroom mixture to a large bowl. Add the breadcrumbs and half the chopped oregano, and season to taste. Mix well with a fork to make a stuffing.
4 Put the sole fillets skinned side up on a work surface, halve them lengthways and score them diagonally with a sharp knife. Put a heaped teaspoon of stuffing at the wide end of each piece, then roll up from that end.
5 Stand the rolls in the dish, close but not too squeezed. Dot each roll with 1 teaspoon of the extra butter, sprinkle with the wine and pepper to taste. Bake for 10-12 minutes.
6 When the paupiettes are done, remove them from the dish and keep warm. Set aside the cooking liquid.
7 Melt the remaining butter gently in the frying pan, add the whole mushrooms and cook over a gentle heat for 1-2 minutes until just softened. Add the fish cooking liquid and the crème fraîche and stir over a high heat for 3-5 minutes until slightly reduced. Add the remaining oregano and adjust the seasoning to taste. Serve the fish with the sauce poured over and around it.

GRILLED FISH

I know that simple, grilled fish is healthy, but what is the best way to cook it so it stays moist?

Grilled fish is not only healthy, it is also very quick and easy to cook. Chopped fresh herbs, a couple of tablespoons of virgin olive oil and plenty of coarsely ground black pepper will greatly enhance the flavour – especially if you leave the fish to marinate in these ingredients for half an hour or so before cooking. Whole oily fish such as mackerel, sardines and trout are

BONING A WHOLE ROUND FISH

Fish can be cooked and served whole with the bones intact, but it makes for neater serving and eating if the bones are removed first. A filleting knife with a flexible blade makes the task easier. The head can be removed if you prefer, but retaining it will help to keep the fish shape intact during cooking. In the pictures below, salmon is shown.*

1 Hold the fish with its open stomach cavity facing you. Taking care not to cut through to the skin, slide the tip of the knife between the rib cage and the flesh on both sides, so that all the ribs are freed down to the backbone.

2 With kitchen scissors, cut through each end of the backbone to release it from the fish. Then start to gently peel it away from the flesh, beginning at the head end. Keep the backbone: it may be used in fish stock.

3 Check that no small bones are still left in the flesh, especially around the edges. If necessary, pull the bones out with a pair of tweezers. The bigger the fish, the bigger the bones will be, so examine smaller fish very carefully.

FILLETING A WHOLE ROUND FISH

A round fish yields two meaty fillets, one on either side of the backbone. A flexible filleting knife is the best tool to use. You will find it easier if you first remove the head and gills but leave the skin on. In these pictures, trout is shown.*

1 Place the prepared fish on its side, with the tail facing you, and cut along the length of its back. Keep the knife parallel to the work surface and cut right through to the backbone, working from the head end to the tail.

2 Starting at the head end, cut the flesh free from the fine rib bones on one side of the fish, keeping the filleting knife close to the bones. Work down along the underside of the fish until the top fillet is detached.

3 Holding the exposed backbone, cut away the remaining lower fillet. Check for any small bones left in the flesh, especially around the edges, and pull these out with tweezers. The backbone may be used in fish stock.

SKINNING ROUND FISH FILLETS

Fish fillets are generally sold with their skins on, but any dark or tough skin is usually removed before cooking. You can ask the fish retailer to skin the fillets, but if you buy them in packets from a supermarket, or if you have filleted the fish yourself, you will have to tackle the skinning yourself at home.

Skinning is a job best done with a sharp, flexible filleting knife. In these pictures, kingfish is shown.

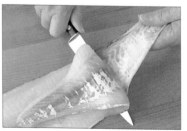

1 Place the fillet skin side down with the tail end towards you. Dip your fingers in salt and grip the tail end. Cut the flesh as close to the tail as possible.

2 Holding the knife flat on the board, work it between the skin and the flesh with a gentle sawing action. Fold the skinned flesh back as you go.

easy to grill because their natural oils baste the fish and keep it moist, as the recipe below shows.

Thick, firm-textured fish fillets and steaks, from fish such as salmon, rainbow trout, swordfish and tuna, can also be grilled in the grill pan or in a ridged, cast-iron frying pan. Do not put them on the grill rack as they may break up.

Grilled fish

SERVES: 4
PREPARATION TIME: 5 minutes
COOKING TIME: 8 minutes

2 tablespoons chopped fresh herbs
2 tablespoons virgin olive oil
4 whole oily fish, each weighing
  375–500 g, trimmed, scaled and
  gutted
Salt and black pepper
To serve: lemon wedges

1 Preheat the grill for a minimum of 5 minutes. In a small bowl, turn the herbs in 1 tablespoon of oil until they are well soaked. With a sharp knife, make three deep slashes at regular intervals on both sides of each fish: this will help the heat to penetrate the flesh and facilitates even cooking. Brush the rack of the grill pan with vegetable oil.
2 Place the fish on the rack, brush with herb oil and season to taste. Put the fish under the very hot grill and cook one side for 4–5 minutes. Turn the fish over, brush that side with the remaining herb oil, season and cook for a further 4–5 minutes or until the flesh is opaque.
3 Serve with lemon wedges or a sauce such as the one on the right.

SAUCE FOR VARIETY

For health reasons, I have started grilling fish but find it a bit dull. Can you suggest a tasty but still nutritious sauce?

The following recipe is based on the Mexican idea of serving hot grilled fish with a chilled fresh sauce (known as *salsa*). The sauce is very low in fat, and the contrast of colour and temperature rejuvenates tired tastebuds.

Fresh cherry tomato salsa, sweetened with a sprinkling of sugar to enhance the sun-ripened flavour, provides a pleasantly chilled contrast to grilled fish.

Sweet tomato salsa

SERVES: 4
PREPARATION TIME: 5 minutes, plus at least 30 minutes chilling time
COOKING TIME: none

250 g ripe cherry tomatoes
  (red and yellow if possible)
½ small onion
1 clove garlic
2 tablespoons virgin olive oil
1 tablespoon white wine vinegar
1 teaspoon sugar
Salt and black pepper

1 Finely chop the tomatoes, onion and garlic and put them in a bowl. Add the olive oil, vinegar and sugar, sprinkle on salt and pepper to taste and stir well to mix.
2 Chill for at least 30 minutes or until you are ready to serve it.
VARIATIONS
Add about six chopped and stoned black olives. Alternatively, flavour the salsa with 1–2 tablespoons of chopped fresh herbs, using whatever herbs were cooked with the fish.

MICROWAVING FISH

I've heard that fish is one of the easiest things to cook in the microwave. Which cuts of fish are the most suitable, and how do I go about cooking them?

Fish is excellent when cooked in the microwave, retaining its texture and shape as well as its natural juices. Because it is cooked with no or little added liquid, there is minimal loss of nutrients.

Fish steaks and fillets are most suitable to cook in the microwave, because they cook quickly and evenly, but whole fish such as whiting and trout weighing up to 500 g are suitable, as are small whole fish such as sardines and pilchards. Microwaved white fish can look bland, but can be made more appetising by basting with soy or other flavoured sauces.

To microwave whole fish, slash the skin in two or three places on both sides so it does not burst during cooking. Then place the fish in a microwave dish and shield the head and tail with small strips of foil. Steaks should be laid in a round dish with their thinner ends facing inwards. Fillets should be placed in a single layer, folding the thinner ends underneath so they do not overcook. Whole or cut, all fish should be covered with a microwave-safe top before cooking and turned over halfway through.

The following recipe for micro-waving salmon steaks can be used for white fish as well and illustrates the simple technique of using soy sauce and similar flavours for a Japanese teriyaki-style marinade.

Fish steaks will cook more evenly in the microwave oven if you place them in a circle, with the thicker end facing out.

Microwaved salmon

SERVES: 4
PREPARATION TIME: 10 minutes, plus 30-60 minutes marinating
COOKING TIME: 5 minutes

4 salmon steaks, each weighing about 175 g
2.5 cm fresh green ginger, chopped
6 black peppercorns
1 clove garlic, chopped
2 tablespoons each vegetable oil, soy sauce and dry sherry

1 Place the salmon steaks in a circle in a deep microwave-safe dish, with the thin ends pointing inwards.
2 Using a pestle and mortar, pound the ginger, peppercorns and garlic to a rough paste. Transfer the paste to a larger bowl, then mix in the oil, soy sauce and sherry.
3 Pour the sauce over the fish, cover with plastic wrap and marinate for at least 30 minutes but no more than an hour, turning the fish over once.

4 Fold back an edge of the plastic wrap so steam can escape then cook on High for 5-7 minutes, turning the steaks over once. Leave to stand for 2 minutes before serving.

CRISP AND LIGHT

Is there a lighter way to cook crispy battered fish?

It is possible to make a light batter with egg whites rather than whole eggs or egg yolks, but the batter still needs to be deep-fried to be crisp. In the recipe below, bread-crumbs replace the batter and the fish steaks are baked, making them a healthy alternative to fried fish. The crust is crispier if the breaded fish is left to chill, uncovered, for up to 4 hours before cooking.

Oven-fried fish steaks

SERVES: 4
PREPARATION TIME: 15-20 minutes
COOKING TIME: 10 minutes

2 tablespoons plain flour
Pinch of cayenne pepper
Salt and pepper
2 tablespoons dried mixed herbs
90 g (1½ cups) fine breadcrumbs
1 large egg white
4 thick white fish fillets or steaks, each weighing 175-250 g, skinned
2 tablespoons peanut oil
To serve: lemon wedges

1 Preheat the oven to 190°C and put a baking tray in it to warm. Mix the flour with the cayenne and salt and pepper to taste. Stir the herbs into the breadcrumbs. Whisk the egg white lightly with a fork until just frothy.
2 Make sure the fish is dry. Coat it in the flour mixture first, then dip it into the egg white and finally the herb-flavoured breadcrumbs.
3 Heat the oil in a large, nonstick frying pan until it is very hot but not smoking. Add the coated fish steaks and fry them over a moderate heat for about a minute each side.
4 Transfer the fish steaks to the hot baking tray and bake for 8 minutes. Serve with lemon wedges.

MIXED FISH STEW

I make the fish stew called bouillabaisse, but the bream and flathead I use often disintegrate. Can you suggest other fish that might be more suitable?

The classic recipe for bouillabaisse from Marseilles in the south of France uses local fish, many of which cannot be found outside the Mediterranean. But you can make a variation without them, as the recipe below shows. The secret is to prepare a rich broth first with trimmings from the fish you buy. Add the fish for the last 5–8 minutes only, to ensure that they will not overcook and disintegrate.

Firm-textured fish such as eel, red emperor, gurnard, jewfish, John Dory, mackerel, morwong or mullet are best, but any similar white or oily fish that are in season will do. It is traditional to leave the fish on the bone as this helps to keep the flesh intact during cooking and also improves the flavour. For extra interest, you could also include squid, and shellfish such as mussels, prawns or scallops.

Pacific bouillabaisse

SERVES: 4
PREPARATION TIME: 35 minutes
COOKING TIME: 1 hour

3 tablespoons virgin olive oil
1 small fennel bulb, thinly sliced
1 onion, thinly sliced
4 cloves garlic, crushed
2 leeks, thinly sliced
4 tomatoes, skinned, seeded and chopped
1 tablespoon tomato paste
300 ml dry white wine
1 litre fish stock
1 strip orange rind
1 bouquet garni
A large pinch of saffron threads
Salt and black pepper
1.5 kg mixed fish, cut into chunks, plus prawns and mussels
2 tablespoons Pernod

1 Heat the oil in a large, heavy-based saucepan and add the fennel, onion, garlic and leeks. Cook over a

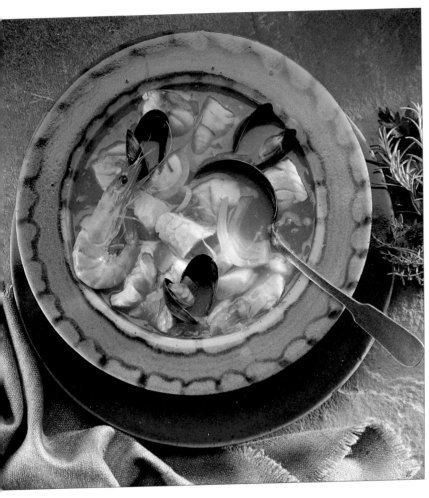

gentle heat, stirring frequently, for about 10 minutes until the vegetables are softened but not coloured.

2 Add the chopped tomatoes, tomato paste and wine to the pan and stir well to mix. Add the stock and bring to the boil over a high heat, then lower the heat and add the strip of orange rind, bouquet garni and saffron. Sprinkle on some salt and pepper to taste.

3 Partially cover the pan and simmer gently for about 30 minutes, stirring from time to time, until the liquid has reduced slightly.

4 Remove the orange peel and the bouquet garni from the soup and discard. Add any firm-fleshed pieces of fish and simmer for 5 minutes, then add the more delicate fish and simmer for a further 2–3 minutes.

5 Pour in the Pernod and stir well. Check the seasoning and adjust if necessary before serving.

A dash of Pernod brings the flavour of the Mediterranean to mixed fish and shellfish in Pacific Bouillabaisse.

SPICY ROUILLE

I was once served some fish stew which came with rouille. What is it, and can I make it myself?

Rouille is a rust-coloured sauce made with cayenne pepper, garlic and breadcrumbs blended with olive oil and fish stock. Spoon it into the soup to thicken it or spread it on toast and serve separately.

To make your own, sweat one or two crushed garlic cloves in a little olive oil, then add about ⅓ cup of crumbled white bread and 100 ml of the fish soup and reduce it all to a thick smooth pulp. Using a balloon whisk, beat in 100 ml of olive oil a little at a time, and season with salt, pepper and cayenne.

WHOLE FISH

I see a lot of different whole fish at the fish market. What could I do with them?

Whole fish are generally very tasty, and are often best simply grilled or baked. However, they can be quite bony and this can put people off – as can their sometimes high price.

The recipe below can be used for any large fish such as flathead, gurnard, leatherjacket or snapper, but many of the whole fish pictured on page 144 could be cooked in this way. For smaller whole fish (about 500 g each), such as bream, John Dory and whiting, allow one fish per person and reduce the cooking time to 20 minutes.

Baked fish

SERVES: *6*
PREPARATION TIME: *20 minutes*
COOKING TIME: *60–70 minutes*

2 red onions, cut into wedges
2 fennel bulbs, cut into wedges
2 red peppers, deseeded and cut
   into wedges
4 large ripe tomatoes, quartered
2 cloves garlic, quartered
3 tablespoons virgin olive oil
1 tablespoon lightly crushed
   fennel or coriander seeds
Salt and black pepper
2 kg whole fish (see above),
   trimmed, scaled and cleaned
200 ml dry white wine
4 tablespoons Pernod, optional

1 Preheat the oven to 230°C. Put all the vegetables in a large baking dish. Mix in the oil and crushed seeds and season to taste. Cover and bake for 30 minutes, turning the vegetables over a few times.

2 Score the fish in two or three places on each side with a sharp knife, and sprinkle inside and out with salt and pepper. Place the fish on top of the vegetables, pour over the wine and Pernod, if using, and cover tightly with foil.

3 Reduce the oven temperature to 190°C and bake for 30–40 minutes until the flesh flakes easily when tested with a fork.

COOK'S GUIDE TO FAVOURITE FISH

Brilliantly coloured fish from around the continent are widely available, either whole or as fillets, cutlets or steaks. | *Whichever one you choose, buy it fresh, cook it with care, and enjoy the wonderful flavour from our rivers and seas.*

1 CORAL TROUT is found around Australia's coral reefs. It is excellent eating with a white, firm-textured, moist sweet flesh.

2 BREAM is a name that covers several varieties, including Yellowfin, Southern and Pikey, also Tarwhine. A popular angling fish found in tidal rivers, estuaries and the ocean, bream is also a fine table fish with a white, sweet flesh.

3 JOHN DORY has a delicate texture and white, moist sweet flesh. Mirror, Silver and King Dorys are similar.

4 SALMON, farmed as Atlantic salmon, is successfully produced in the chilly waters around Tasmania. A large oily fish with firm red flesh, it can be smoked or cooked fresh.

5 RED FISH is a small fish with a red head, back and fins. Caught along the east coast of Australia, it has pale flesh with a medium flake and a mild flavour.

6 FLOUNDER is flat with a white belly. The many species include Greenback

from New Zealand, and the large-toothed, small-toothed and long-snouted flounder from Australian waters. The soft white flesh has a fine flake and a very sweet flavour. Sole is similar.

7 SARDINES are a member of the herring family, found in shoals around the southern half of the continent. They have a dark, oily flesh and are excellent fried or stuffed and baked.

8 TUNA is a large, oceanic game fish, found all around Australia. The flesh is pinkish-red, with a firm oily texture and a strong flavour, popular for Japanese sashimi and for char-grilling.

9 BARRAMUNDI, named by the Aborigines who catch it in rivers around the northern coast, is now farmed so is readily available. A dark bluish colour, it has white, firm, tender, large-flaked flesh and a distinct yet mild flavour.

10 MULLET is a temperate water fish with many species, netted all around Australia. Small to medium in size, it

has large scales and a dark pink, oily moist flesh with a distinct taste.

11 GARFISH is a small, slender, silver-grey fish with a prolonged lower jaw. It lives in warm seas and has a fine-textured flesh with a delicate sweet flavour.

12 RAINBOW TROUT was introduced from California to Australian rivers and lakes, along with the brown trout introduced from Europe. It has an oily pink flesh that can be smoked or cooked fresh.

13 WHITING is a small fish that lives in sandy waters, bays and estauries. All the many varieties have sweet-tasting, tender, fine-textured white flesh.

14 SNAPPER, when mature, develops a bump on the head and a bulge on the snout. One of Australia's best eating fish, it has white, large-flaked flesh.

• Also popular (not pictured) are Blue-eye Cod, Red Emperor, Gurnard, Jewfish, Kingfish, Leatherjacket, Ling, Parrot fish, Swordfish, Trevally, Freshwater Perch and Silver Warhou.

Flambé

HOME FLAMES

My favourite restaurant serves a delicious dessert of fruit flambé. Can I make this at home?

Yes, flambéed food makes a spectacular show and is quite simple to prepare at home. The kirsch used to flambé the cherries in the recipe below intensifies the fruit flavour but if you prefer, use brandy, rum or whisky instead. Other fruits may be substituted for the cherries; for instance, try sliced apples, apricots, bananas, oranges or peaches.

To ensure ignition, heat the spirit before you light it, just long enough to warm it, but not so long that it allows the alcohol to evaporate. Keep your face and hair well away from the pan while you are setting fire to the alcohol and make sure that there is nothing else nearby or above that can catch fire. With practice, and a good spirit burner, you can even flambé the fruit in front of your guests at the table.

Cherries flambéed with kirsch

SERVES: *4*
PREPARATION TIME: *25 minutes*
COOKING TIME: *6–8 minutes*

---

500 ml good-quality vanilla ice cream (either homemade or bought)
25 g unsalted butter
15 cm strip lemon rind pared off with a vegetable peeler
3 tablespoons lemon juice
60 g (¼ cup) caster sugar
500 g ripe, plump and juicy cherries, washed and stoned
4 tablespoons kirsch, poured into a small bowl

---

1 Before cooking the cherries, divide the ice cream between four serving dishes and place these in the coldest part of your refrigerator. Take them out again just before flambéeing.
2 Put the butter, lemon rind, juice and sugar into a wide nonstick or enamel frying pan that is attractive enough to serve the fruit in. Put the pan over a moderate heat and stir until the butter melts and the sugar has dissolved completely. Increase the heat and let the syrup bubble gently until it has thickened slightly.
3 Add the cherries to the pan and cook them over a moderate to high heat for 2–3 minutes, stirring often, until they begin to soften.
4 If the cherries have produced a lot of juice, pour most of it off into a serving jug and set it aside to cool. Leave 2–3 tablespoons of juice in the pan; any more will dilute the spirit and prevent it from igniting.
5 Pour the kirsch into the pan, let it heat for a few seconds and then light it with a long match.
6 Shake the pan gently to and fro over the heat until the flames begin to die down. When all the flames have burnt out, spoon the cherries over the softened ice cream. Serve immediately. The reserved juice in the jug can be used as a sauce.

Dancing flames around a pan of lemon-scented cherries make an impressive finale for a dinner party.

Flan

SHORT FOR SAVOURY

What kind of pastry is best for making a savoury flan?

For a flan with a rich savoury filling like the Pissaladière on page 146, use a basic short crust pastry made with butter and plain flour. The French pastry, pâte brisée (meaning brittle pastry) with a higher proportion of butter than short crust, is also suitable. For pastry to use with sweet fillings, see *Tarts*.

To bake blind, line the uncooked pastry case with greaseproof paper and cover it with a layer of dried beans or rice. This keeps the pastry flat.

FLAN CASES IN ADVANCE

If I want to freeze flan cases to use later, should they be baked?

Bake them blind first, as shown above, then store them for up to three months in the freezer, packed in rigid containers, or keep them in an airtight tin in the refrigerator for a day or two. A prebaked pastry case will stay crisp during cooking, even with a moist filling.

WHICH DISH?

What material should a flan dish be made of for the best result?

A dish which heats up rapidly is best for making flans. Short crust pastry needs a quick burst of heat so the starch grains in the flour will swell and then burst and absorb the melting fat in the pastry mixture. Unless the fat is absorbed quickly the pastry will be limp and soggy. This is also true of pastry which is to be baked blind before being filled.

Metal is a better conductor of heat than ovenproof china or glass, and pastry will cook more quickly in a flan tin or in a metal ring placed on a baking tray. A fluted flan tin with a loose base is easier to use than a fluted ring, which must be put on a baking tray.

China flan dishes are attractive but are not as good for cooking. To make them more effective, put them on a baking tray which has been preheated in a hot oven.

LINING A FLAN TIN

If you and your family enjoy flans it is worth investing in a proper metal flan tin with a removable base. They are not very expensive and using one will make it much easier to remove the flan after it has been baked, when it is ready to be either filled or served.

1 Roll out the dough to a round, using the flan tin as a guide for size. Allow for the depth of the side, plus an extra 1 cm.

2 Using a rolling pin, lift the rolled dough and drape it lightly over the base and side of the flan tin.

3 Gently ease the dough into the corners, being careful not to stretch it. Press it firmly against the side, then roll off the excess dough with the rolling pin to neaten the top edge. Alternatively, trim the edge with a small sharp knife so that it will look professional.

Pissaladière

SERVES: 4-6
PREPARATION TIME: 40 minutes, plus 40 minutes chilling time
COOKING TIME: 55 minutes

FOR THE PASTRY
185 g (1½ cups) plain flour
A pinch of salt
90 g butter, diced
1½ tablespoons water

FOR THE FILLING
2½ tablespoons olive oil
1 large onion, finely chopped
2 cloves garlic, crushed
400 g canned chopped tomatoes in tomato juice
1 tablespoon tomato paste
2 tablespoons sun-dried tomatoes, marinated in oil, drained and thinly sliced
Salt and black pepper
8 fresh basil leaves
3 tablespoons freshly grated Parmesan cheese
50 g canned anchovy fillets, cut into thin strips
50 g black olives, pitted and cut in half

Sun-ripened tomatoes, anchovies, basil, olives and garlic bring the flavours of the Mediterranean to this simple flan.

1 Sift the flour and salt into a large mixing bowl and rub in the butter. Stir in enough water to make a firm dough. On a lightly floured surface, knead gently until smooth then pat into a round. Wrap in greaseproof paper and chill for 20 minutes.
2 Preheat the oven to 200°C.
3 Roll out the pastry and use it to line a 25 cm flan tin with a loose base. Put it on a baking tray and prick the base in several places with a fork. Line the pastry case with greaseproof paper and cover with dried beans. Bake for 10 minutes, then remove the paper and beans and bake for a further 10 minutes. Cool then chill for 15–20 minutes.
4 Heat 2 tablespoons of oil in a saucepan. Add the onion and garlic, cover and cook over a low heat until they are soft but not coloured. Stir in all the tomatoes with a little salt and pepper, bring to the boil, then simmer for about 20 minutes until the mixture is thick. Tear the basil into small pieces and stir it into the mixture. Check the seasoning.
5 Spoon the vegetable mixture into the pastry case, sprinkle Parmesan cheese lightly over it and arrange anchovy strips and olives on top. Brush or drizzle carefully with the rest of the olive oil.

Flour

WHITE OR BROWN?

What is the difference between the various white and brown flours?

Wheat flours are defined by the percentage of bran (the fibrous skin) and wheatgerm (the nutritious embryo of the wheat kernel) that remain after grains of wheat are milled. But most of what is left after grinding is the starchy endosperm, or inside of the wheat.

- WHOLEMEAL FLOUR is made from the whole grain, with nothing added to it or taken away.
- WHITE FLOUR has about 75–80 per cent of the wheat grain.
- MALT FLOUR has been fortified with malted grains which have been sprouted.

Other wheat flours include atta, bakers flour, continental flour, gluten flour, sponge flour and unbleached flour.

Several other cereals, roots and seeds are milled for flour, such as barley, besan, buckwheat, corn, oat, rice, rye and soy.

BAKER'S CHOICE

Which type of flour should I choose for home baking?

Plain flour can be used for short crust pastry, sauces and gravies which do not need a raising agent. Self-raising flour includes baking powder, and is best for most cakes, buns, scones and puddings. It gives a better lift than a homemade mix of plain flour and baking powder (see box, right), though that is suitable for mixes with eggs or egg whites, which encourage rising.

Gluten is a protein in flour that develops and becomes more elastic as the dough is kneaded. Strong flour has a large amount of protein, needed for pasta and bread making.

Use sponge or continental flour, which has less gluten, for light cakes and pastries. Sponges, cakes and scones made with soft, fine flour have a more delicate texture.

LIGHTER BROWN

I like to use wholemeal flour, but find that my pastry turns out very dense when made with it. Is there anything I can do to make the texture lighter?

The fibre and bran in wholemeal flour, which add a nutty flavour to short crust pastry, also make it absorb more water, which produces a closer texture than pastry made with plain white flour.

By combining white flour with wholemeal, either half-and-half or up to a quarter white and three-quarters wholemeal, you retain the wholemeal flavour but the dough is more manageable and easier to roll out, as the following recipe shows.

Wholemeal pasties with vegetable filling

MAKES: 3 pasties
PREPARATION TIME: 40 minutes plus at least 30 minutes standing time
COOKING TIME: 50-55 minutes

FOR THE PASTRY
125 g (1 cup) plain wholemeal flour
A pinch of salt
60 g (1 cup) wheatgerm
100 g butter, diced
Milk to glaze

FOR THE FILLING
2 tablespoons olive oil
1 large onion, finely chopped
1 clove garlic, crushed
1 medium potato, diced
1 medium carrot, diced
½ cup diced pumpkin
1 teaspoon ground coriander
½ teaspoon ground cumin
Salt and black pepper
3 tablespoons chopped parsley
1 tablespoon roughly chopped walnuts, optional
50 g mature Cheddar cheese, grated

1 Sift the flour and salt into a bowl and stir in the wheatgerm. Add the butter and rub in until the mixture resembles fine breadcrumbs. Sprinkle 1 tablespoon of chilled water over the mixture, then use a palette knife to draw it together and the fingertips of one hand to form a firm dough (you may need to add a little more water).

2 Turn the dough onto a lightly floured surface and knead it gently until smooth and free from cracks. Shape into a round, wrap in greaseproof paper and chill for at least 30 minutes.

3 To make the filling, heat the olive oil in a saucepan, add the onion and garlic, cover and cook for 5 minutes over a gentle heat. Add the potato, carrot and pumpkin, cover and cook for 6-8 minutes until they start to soften. Stir in the coriander and cumin and cook for another minute, then remove from the heat.

4 Turn the mixture into a bowl, season well, stir in the parsley and walnuts and leave to cool.

5 Preheat the oven to 200°C and grease a baking tray. Divide the pastry into three equal portions. Using a plate as a guide, roll out a circle 15 cm round, keeping the other portions covered to prevent them drying out. Repeat with the remaining pastry.

6 Divide the filling equally between the rounds, piling it in a strip along the centre of each. Sprinkle each strip with 1 teaspoon of cheese and reserve the remaining cheese.

7 Dampen the pastry edges with water, draw up both edges to meet at the top and press together. Flute the edges and place the pasties on the baking tray. Brush lightly with milk to glaze and sprinkle with the remaining cheese. Bake for about 30 minutes until the pastry is crisp.

To the rescue!

If you run out of self-raising flour you can make a substitute by sifting 2½ teaspoons baking powder into 250 g plain flour. But this will not give quite as high a lift to basic cakes, scones and puddings.

Foil

FOIL SAFE

Is it safe to use foil for cooking and storing every kind of food?

In general yes, perfectly safe. But acid in food can eat into foil, so if you are wrapping, say, a fruit cake laced with spirits, oiling the foil or wrapping the food in greaseproof paper first will prevent this. All food for freezing should be wrapped tightly in foil so it is completely airtight.

Foil should not be used in the microwave (see **Microwave Ovens**), but is fine for using in conventional ovens, when you can put either side, matt or shiny, next to the food. Foil can be used to protect food from burning: for instance, place a piece over the head and tail of a fish, or the breast of a bird, while it is being baked or roasted. If you are wrapping food in foil for cooking, seal the parcel tightly but leave it loose to allow the air inside to circulate and cook the food evenly. And do not stretch foil tight across the top of a dish: put a pleat in the top to allow for expansion.

Food Poisoning

HYGIENE RULES

How should I organise my kitchen to avoid food poisoning?

To avoid contamination of food, store it safely and take care that it is cooked thoroughly. There has been an increase in reported food poisoning cases in Australia in the past decade. Possible causes range from the rise of giant food processing plants, in which a single infection can spread widely, through to declining cooking and hygiene skills in the home. To be safe, here are the golden rules to follow:

- Food should be stored in clean, dry, airtight containers, and raw and cooked foods kept separate.
- Use separate boards when cutting, slicing, chopping or preparing raw and cooked foods.
- Food should be cold or very hot, as bacteria multiply quickly at temperatures between 5° and 65°C.
- Discard any food that is past its 'use by' date, smells unpleasant or tastes as if it may be 'off'. If you have any doubts at all, get rid of it.
- Make sure meat and poultry are fully defrosted before cooking.
- When reheating food, make sure it is piping hot all the way through, and do not reheat it twice.
- Always wash your hands before handling food.
- Disinfect worktops, refrigerators and chopping boards often with an antibacterial cleaner.

GOOD FOOD CARE

What are the common sources of salmonella poisoning, and how can I protect my family?

The foods that are most commonly infected with the salmonella group of bacteria are meat, poultry and other protein foods. Symptoms usually appear in 12 to 48 hours and include tiredness, diarrhoea, high fever, severe abdominal pain and vomiting. If you experience any of these symptoms, you should seek medical attention immediately.

Cooking, providing the centre of the food reaches a temperature greater than 72°C, will destroy the salmonella bacteria. But as some of the bacteria reproduce, they produce toxins which will not be destroyed during cooking and which also cause food poisoning. This is why it is so important not to leave uncooked food lying around in the warm and often moist conditions in which the reproduction of the bacteria takes place.

Take chilled and frozen food home quickly from the shop and put it in the refrigerator or freezer as soon as possible. Store all other food in cool, dry conditions.

To minimise the risk of contamination, it is always wise to reject any eggs that have cracked or blemished shells.

CLEAR, CLEAN WATER

Are water filters worth buying? Or should I use bottled water?

Mains tap water in Australia is safe to drink. If taste is a consideration, then both jug and on-line filters will reduce the taste and smell of chlorine, but it is very important to change the filters regularly.

Bottled water appears to be safe but it is not necessarily free of bacteria. There are standards for the maximum-permitted level of some bacteria for most bottled water in Australia. The bottles may remain on corner shop shelves for up to 18 months in unrefrigerated conditions and overseas tests have shown high levels of bacteria in many still waters.

Sparkling waters generally contain fewer bacteria as the carbon dioxide in the bubbles inhibits the growth of these organisms.

Purchase only what you need at the time. Do not drink directly from the bottle as bacteria from your mouth could contaminate the rest of the water in the bottle.

All water given to babies should be boiled. Some bottled waters contain high levels of sodium which can cause damage to an infant's immature kidneys. Always check the label and choose one which lists a low level of sodium.

HIDDEN POISONS

Is it safe to cut mould off food and eat the unaffected part?

No, because a small number of moulds do produce potentially harmful toxins. It is preferable and desirable to minimise the chance of mould growing on food.

In general, any foods that show mould should be discarded. But some foods, such as cheese stored in the refrigerator, and opened jam stored in a cool, dry cupboard or pantry, may show some mould growth on the surface.

In these cases, if this mould is removed with a generous safety margin, the remaining cheese or jam may still be eaten.

THE SAFE WAY TO STOCK YOUR FRIDGE

Below are basic guidelines regarding hygiene to keep in mind when stocking your refrigerator shelves. Remember that all food should be kept covered.

- The coldest parts of a refrigerator such as the one above are the lowest shelves. But if the fridge has a freezing compartment, the coldest shelves will be those immediately below it.
- Meat should be wrapped and put on the lowest shelf in the coldest area of the refrigerator. Never put raw meat on a shelf high in the refrigerator, in case it drips onto cooked food below. Cooked meat should be separated from raw meat. This is especially important if the cooked meat will not be heated again before it is served.
- Other foods which should be kept on the coldest, lower shelves are fish, prepared salads, leftovers and desserts, in particular those made with cream.
- Foods which can be kept on the less cold shelves, or in the door, are dairy products – including cheese, eggs and butter – and opened jars, cartons and bottles, as well as salad dressings and mayonnaises, both commercial and homemade.
- Salads and most vegetables should be kept in the salad drawer. Store them unwrapped so that air can circulate around them to keep them from spoiling too quickly. If salad greens are left in their plastic wrappings, the top should be opened enough to let air in.
- Fresh fruit will not ripen in the refrigerator, but fruit that is ripe can be stored in the salad drawer to inhibit further ripening and spoilage.
- Cool hot food briefly at room temperature; cover then refrigerate. Modern refrigerators are made to cope with this heat load.

RARE BUG

What is listeriosis, and is it really such a serious risk?

Listeriosis is a food-borne disease caused by a listeria bacterium, but it is very rare. Foods most at risk include pâtés, soft mould-ripened cheeses such as brie and camembert and blue cheeses, ready-to-eat chickens and soft-serve ice creams.

As listeria can multiply at temperatures below that found in many domestic refrigerators, susceptible food should not be stored for more than four days. Listeria is also fairly heat-resistant, so cooked foods should be reheated to piping hot.

Local health authorities advise that pregnant women should avoid susceptible foods, and unpasteurised (or raw) milk and any cheese made from it.

Food Processors

MIX AND CHOP

Which is the most useful machine for everyday domestic cooking, a food mixer or a food processor?

If a choice must be made, the food processor is the more useful. Processors are relatively lightweight and most of the functions are integral to, or built into, the machine. Food mixers tend to be more cumbersome and their attachments take up much more space.

Food processors make light work of laborious tasks such as chopping, grating and slicing, and some machines also have juice extractors. They make excellent pastry, provided the ingredients are not processed for too long. They do not whisk egg whites well because they do not incorporate enough air, but some machines have a separate whisking attachment. Care needs to be exercised with some models when mincing raw meat so that it is minced, not pulped to a mush.

Mixers are usually larger and are good for lengthy beating or kneading bread with the dough hook.

Freezing

QUICK AND SLOW

Why are we told to freeze food quickly and thaw it slowly?

The quicker a food is frozen, the smaller the ice crystals that will form. Large ice crystals damage the cell walls of food so that when it is thawed, liquid is lost, including soluble nutrients. Meat especially loses so much moisture that it will be dry when cooked if frozen too slowly. This is why many freezers contain a fast-freeze compartment for the initial freezing process.

Thawing, however, should take place as slowly as possible since rapid thawing also leads to a loss of moisture and dry, tasteless food.

FULL SAVINGS

Is it more economical to keep the freezer full at all times?

Yes, a full freezer retains more cold when the door is opened. With a half-empty freezer, a lot of cold air will escape whenever the door is opened and more energy is then needed to bring the freezer back down to the right temperature.

Try to freeze small quantities of food at a time, separated out. Once frozen, pack them together closely. Remember to rotate food regularly and label it, or what you lose in wasted food will cancel out what you gain in energy savings.

FANTASTIC PLASTIC

What containers and wrappings are best for freezing food?

Heavyweight plastic or polythene bags are the cheapest and most effective wrappers because they take various shapes of food without creating too many air pockets.

The freezer atmosphere is very drying and direct contact with the icy air may cause 'freezer burn' (dry discoloured patches), so most foods need to be carefully wrapped before freezing. Whatever airtight container you use, it must be robust enough to withstand some rough handling in the freezer.

Pour liquids into plastic freezer bags set in rectangular containers to freeze. Leave 2.5 cm between the top of the liquid and the container to allow for expansion. Once solid, lift the freezer bags out of the containers (which allows the containers to be used elsewhere). The frozen bags of liquid can then be stacked neatly to save space.

Label frozen foods immediately with the contents and the date. Keep a record of what is in the freezer so that you remember what is there and can plan to use the food systematically in date order.

THE BIG THAW

What should I do if my freezer breaks down, or when there is an unexpected power cut?

Check first to see if the plug has been pulled out, a fuse has blown or the thermostat has been misset before calling for maintenance. And keep the freezer door closed while you check. If there has been a power cut, food remains solid and safe for 16–24 hours, providing the door has not been opened.

If you have advance warning of a cut in power, pack out any gaps in the freezer with crumpled newspaper and do not open the door during the cut, or for 2 hours afterwards. Food that is still solid with ice crystals is safe to eat. Foods that have defrosted may be cooked and eaten, but ice cream or foods that contain cream are best thrown away, as are commercially packaged meals near their use-by date. If possible, insure freezer contents.

If your freezer does break down and some of the contents deteriorate, leaving an unpleasant smell, wipe out the inside of the freezer with warm water to which you have added a little bicarbonate of soda or some vinegar or vanilla essence. In addition, a small dish of bicarbonate of soda placed in the refrigerator will help to absorb the smell of strong foods.

THE FRUIT CROP

How should I freeze fruit?

Fruits for freezing must be just ripe, and of prime quality. Wash them only if necessary and dry well. Do not freeze fruit in contact with any metal, including foil.

Soft fruit such as blackberries, black and redcurrants, gooseberries and raspberries are best frozen separately on trays lined with baking paper as they will keep better and defrost easily. When solid, pack them into freezer bags or boxes.

Berries can also be packed with sugar before freezing so that, as it thaws, the fruit and sugar combine to become a syrup. Sprinkle 125 g (½ cup) of sugar over each 500 g of fruit before freezing.

Fresh raspberries, frozen on lined baking trays then packed in freezer bags, extend the summer season.

Apples, peaches, pears and apricots tend to turn brown as they thaw, so freeze them in an acidulated syrup made from 1 litre of water, 500 g (2 cups) of sugar, and the juice of 1 lemon. Allow 300 ml of sugar syrup for each 500 g of fruit.

Whole bananas will turn brown in the freezer; mash them with lemon juice before freezing and defrost to use in cooking.

ONCE IS ENOUGH

Why should you not refreeze food once it has been defrosted?

Freezing will prevent bacteria from multiplying but it does not destroy them. Once frozen food has been thawed, the bacteria may multiply with renewed energy. If food is frozen and thawed repeatedly, bacteria could reach dangerous levels.

You can refreeze food safely if it has been cooked after thawing. However, freezing also results in some loss of moisture and if food is repeatedly frozen and thawed, it will become unpleasantly dry. Fibrous food like meat also loses its texture as it thaws, and will become flabby if it is refrozen and thawed again, say in a casserole.

BLANCH FIRST

Is it really necessary to blanch vegetables before freezing?

To preserve the colour, flavour, texture and nutritional content of vegetables, you must blanch them before freezing (see box, below).

Fresh vegetables contain natural enzymes which help them to grow and ripen. Blanching vegetables – plunging them briefly into boiling water then into cold – inhibits the action of these enzymes, which would otherwise cause deterioration during storage in the freezer.

BLANCHING FRESH VEGETABLES

Fresh vegetables should always be trimmed and blanched before freezing. Use 2 teaspoons salt and 3 litres boiling water for every 500 g vegetables.

Place the trimmed vegetables in a wire basket and plunge it into the boiling, salted water. Quickly bring the water back to the boil and time the cooking according to the chart (right). Then plunge the basket into some water made very cold by the addition of ice cubes. Cool, drain and pack the vegetables for freezing.

PREPARING FRESH VEGETABLES FOR FREEZING

VEGETABLE	VEGETABLE PREPARATION	BLANCHING TIME
Asparagus	Arrange stems of the same length and thickness in bundles.	Thin – 2 minutes Medium – 3 minutes Thick – 4 minutes
Beans	Wash and cut into 1 cm slices. Leave green beans whole. Slice runner beans.	2 minutes
Broad beans	Use young beans only, and pod them.	2 minutes
Broccoli	Trim the heads into even-sized florets and cut away the tough stalks.	Thin – 3 minutes Thick – 4 minutes
Brussels sprouts	Wash, and trim away the outer leaves.	3 minutes
Carrots	Leave young carrots whole, but peel and slice larger ones.	Whole – 3 minutes Sliced – 2 minutes
Cauliflower	Wash and divide it into florets. Add a tablespoon of lemon juice to the boiling water.	3 minutes
Celeriac	Thickly peel off the skin and dice.	4 minutes
Corn-on-the-cob	Remove the husks and silk from the cobs and trim the ends.	Small – 4 minutes Large – 8 minutes
Leeks	Remove the outer leaves. Wash the leeks well and slice if thick.	2–4 minutes, according to size
Parsnips	Choose young parsnips: scrape off the skin with a knife, wash and slice.	2 minutes
Peas	Use young peas only and shell.	1 minute
Spinach	Strip out the tough ribs and freeze only the tender leaves.	1 minute
Zucchini	Cut into 1 cm slices.	1 minute

ICED CREAM

Do cream and yoghurt freeze?

The higher the fat content of the cream, the better it will freeze. Clotted, rich and thickened cream all freeze well and keep for three months. Half-whip the cream before freezing or it will separate on thawing. Adding 1 teaspoon of sugar to 150 ml of whipped cream before freezing will stabilise it. Fresh cream freezes satisfactorily, to use in cooking after thawing. Fruit-flavoured yoghurts and plain yoghurt mixed with honey also freeze well.

BARGAIN JOINT

My butcher is offering half a lamb at a bargain price - but will I be able to fit it into my freezer?

Meat sold at a good discount is worth having, and half a lamb will fit into a small freezer. Ask your butcher to cut the lamb into joints, trimming off the excess fat and removing bones where possible as these take up valuable space.

It is essential to wrap meat well to prevent the fat from turning rancid. Double-wrap the meat using some heavy-duty plastic bags and separate the chops and steaks with layers of plastic freezer film.

FISHERMAN'S CATCH

I have been given a whole trout. Should I gut and scale it before I put it in the freezer?

Yes, it is best to gut fresh fish before freezing. Wash and scale the fish, then gut it and wash the cavity thoroughly under running water. Pat the fish dry and wrap it in foil then place in a sealed strong plastic bag and freeze. Whole freshwater and oily fish can be stored for two months while white ocean fish can be stored for two to three months.

Whole fish are best when thawed slowly to retain their moisture and texture. Fish steaks and fillets are best thawed too, but they may be cooked from frozen if you increase the cooking time by a third.

LUNCH ON ICE

Is it safe to freeze a week's supply of sandwiches and take them to work frozen, letting them thaw out by lunchtime?

It is well worth making sandwiches for the freezer if you eat packed lunches regularly. Use firm slices of bread and spread with softened butter right to the edges. Wrap filled sandwiches in plastic freezer film to keep them separate, then pack in plastic freezer bags.

Use cheese, meat, fish or pâté for the fillings and avoid hard-boiled eggs which can go rubbery, mayonnaise which curdles, and fresh salad which goes soggy.

Keep sandwiches in the freezer for no longer than two months. You can let them thaw in their wrappings for 3 hours or so during the morning. Transport them in a rigid, plastic box to avoid damage.

To the rescue!

Freezer burn is a greyish white patch that appears on frozen food when it is exposed to the air. Its development is due to inadequate packaging. While the burn causes dryness and some loss of colour and texture, the trimmed food is still perfectly safe to eat.

DON'T FREEZE THESE

Are there any foods that cannot be frozen satisfactorily?

Some foods do not freeze well because the texture is ruined. This is particularly true of fruit and vegetables with a high water content, such as bananas, cucumbers, lettuce and watercress, although some may be frozen in purée form.

Whole strawberries keep their colour and flavour well and are excellent for combining in mousses or fools, but the texture deteriorates and they become too soft to

be used whole when thawed. Full-fat milk separates after freezing, but skim and reduced-fat milks that have been homogenised may be frozen for up to a month.

Eggs cannot be frozen in their shells; however, both whites and yolks will freeze well, either lightly beaten together or separated.

Emulsion sauces such as mayonnaise and hollandaise sauce do not tend to freeze well because they will separate when thawed.

Jellies, both savoury and sweet, lose their texture if frozen and would have to be reboiled and allowed to set again after thawing.

Curries freeze well, although after three months the spices will change flavour and may become peppery or fade. The flavour of garlic-laden foods, for example soups and casseroles, will intensify during freezing and can become unpleasantly strong.

Fruit

ORGANIC IS FRESHER

Can I be sure that organic fruit is the same in every shop, and is it really a better purchase?

Fruit that is labelled certified organic has been grown without the use of artificial pesticides or fertilisers and will not have been irradiated. Regardless of where you shop, all the certified organic fruit sold in Australia, is produced to the set of standards established by NASAA, or BFA or Demeter-Biodynamic (see **Additives**).

Growers of organic fruit claim their produce is safer, tastes better and is equally nutritious.

For maximum nutritional benefit, fruit should be eaten soon after picking because its nutritional value declines over time. Organic fruit growers do not use fungicides to preserve their fruit, so it must reach customers quickly. Consequently, organic fruit is generally fresher and could therefore be described as more nutritious.

READY TO ENJOY

How can I tell when fruit is ripe?

A pleasing appearance is only one clue to the ripeness of fruit. Today, many fruits are artificially ripened without reaching their natural stage of maturity. Although these fruits may look attractive, they can nevertheless taste disappointing. It is important, therefore, to also use your senses of smell and touch when selecting the best fresh fruit.

Unwrinkled fruit that feels heavy for its size is likely to have a good juice content and a sweet flavour. Skins should be unblemished, free of bruises, splits and any signs of insect damage. Tough, dry, wrinkled skins on citrus fruits indicate that the rind has lost its essential oils and the zest will not be suitable for use in cooking.

The ripeness of many tree fruits, such as the dessert pear, plum, peach and nectarine, can be ascertained by a light squeeze with the thumb; if the fruit yields to gentle pressure it should be nice to eat.

Berry fruits should be dry and undamaged. Check the packaging of berries for crushing, leakage or signs of mould or wetness.

Test melons, pawpaws and pineapples for ripeness by sniffing the base of the fruit. An attractive, sweet, fresh fragrance indicates the fruit is ripe. Bananas develop 'freckled' skins when ripe.

Over-ripe fruit smells musty and often has soft, dark patches on the skin, indicating that the interior flesh also contains rotten patches.

DELIGHT IN STORE

Can you tell me the best way to store fresh fruit at home?

For the best flavour, you should buy or pick fruit that is ripe and ready to eat. But as fruit cannot always be bought daily, storing it under the right conditions will help to keep it fresh longer.

Grapefruit, lemons, melons, bananas, oranges and pineapple will keep well for several days in a fruit bowl at room temperature,

especially if bought or picked just before they are ripe. However, you must be sure to keep these fruits away from direct sunlight.

Slightly under-ripe apricots, nectarines and peaches can be stored at room temperature to help them ripen, but fruit that is already ripe should be refrigerated. Apples and pears should be stored in the refrigerator to retain crispness.

Loose lemons, limes and passionfruit can be kept for several weeks in the refrigerator. Place them unwrapped in the salad drawer with enough room so that air can circulate around the fruit.

All berries are highly perishable and should be refrigerated as soon as you get them home. Put strawberries in a shallow colander standing on a plate and cover the top with another plate or foil. The holes in the colander will allow air to circulate around the fruit, keeping it dry. When berries become wet, their decomposition accelerates. Blackberries, loganberries and raspberries are best spread out on a large plate. Cover loosely with a lid, some foil or plastic wrap.

Cherries will keep for up to ten days in the refrigerator. Keep them wrapped loosely in a green, long-life storage bag. Ripe, exotic and tropical fruits and grapes are also best kept refrigerated. All refrigerated fruit should be brought back to room temperature before eating to bring out its full flavour.

Some supermarkets now sell fruit such as avocados labelled 'ready to eat now'. However, if you do intend to serve the fruit that very day, it is still best to test it for ripeness before purchase.

SWEET ENOUGH

Is it really necessary for me to use a sugar syrup when making a fresh fruit salad?

No, but sugar syrup is useful when making a fruit salad that contains apples and pears. Adding them to a hot sugar syrup before adding other fruits helps to soften their crisp texture. And slicing bananas

---

HOW TO STORE HOME-GROWN FRUIT

If you are lucky enough to have a glut of home-grown fruit, try storing some of it away carefully and enjoying it a few months later.

1 Winter varieties of apples will keep for several months when placed individually in a plastic bag pierced with air holes (early varieties and windfalls do not store well). Place the wrapped apples, keeping them slightly apart, in single layers in wooden trays and store at an even temperature of about 4°C in a garage or shed.

2 Apples can otherwise be stored unwrapped, in the same storage conditions on slatted wooden trays or greengrocers' fibre trays. If you are using fibre trays, pierce them all over with air holes. Stacking the filled trays saves space and allows the fruit to be inspected easily.

3 Winter pears, too, can be stored unwrapped and in a single layer on a tray or shelf, in a cool room or shed at about 4°C. Ensure the pears do not touch each other.

---

into a cold syrup prevents them browning. Most fruits, however, are naturally quite juicy and sweet, needing only a sprinkling of caster sugar to help draw out their juice. Or you can use a natural fruit juice such as apple, orange or passionfruit juice as an alternative to syrup. Fruit can also be macerated with red or white wine and spirits such as brandy or rum, or liqueurs such as Cointreau or kirsch.

There are no rigid rules for making a fruit salad, the combinations being limited only by the cook's imagination. Simplicity is the key

to success, however, as the salads here show. Try to balance flavours, colours and textures. If you are using mainly soft fruit, add melon or pineapple for a contrasting texture. You could make a salad with a mixture of all citrus fruits, or try a selection of autumnal fruits such as apples, blackberries, pears and plums, or keep the range tropical.

For details of how to select and prepare more unusual fruits, see the feature on pages 156–157.

Golden fruit salad

SERVES: 6
PREPARATION TIME: 40 minutes
COOKING TIME: 10 minutes

FOR THE CARAMEL
250 g (1 cup) white sugar
4 tablespoons water

FOR THE FRUIT SALAD
6 medium oranges
2 grapefruit
3 large, ripe peaches
3 large, ripe nectarines

1 To make the caramel, line a small baking tray with nonstick baking paper and set aside.
2 Make the sugar syrup by putting the sugar and water in a saucepan and heating gently until dissolved, without stirring. Brush down any sugar crystals on the sides of the pan with water. Bring it to the boil and cook until it turns a golden colour.
3 Immediately pour the caramel onto the lined baking tray and set it aside until cooled and set hard. As the caramel will have formed only a thin layer, it should set in 10-15 minutes in a cool place.
4 To make the fruit salad, peel the oranges and grapefruit (see box, page 98), cutting the oranges into thin slices and the grapefruit into segments. Halve, stone and skin the peaches and nectarines, if you wish (see box, page 155), then cut them into neat slices, cutting across the halves for a more attractive slice.
5 Lightly tap the set caramel all over with something heavy until it has broken into several small pieces. Put

Colour-coordinated fruit salads make a pretty dessert. The golden salad is sprinkled with caramel, the green salad with sprigs of lemon balm.

a quarter of the caramel into an airtight container, seal well and set aside until it is needed.
6 Arrange a third of each prepared fruit in the bottom of the serving dish and sprinkle with a third of the remaining crushed caramel. Layer the dish twice more with the fruit and crushed caramel, ending with a layer of caramel pieces.
7 Pour over any remaining orange and grapefruit juice, then cover the dish with plastic wrap. Set the fruit salad aside for 1-2 hours, or until the caramel has dissolved.
8 Just before serving, sprinkle the reserved caramel pieces over the top. Serve the fruit salad with whipped cream or Greek-style yoghurt.
VARIATIONS
Add a few tablespoons of fruit-based liqueur such as Cointreau, Grand Marnier or kirsch to the fruit salad.

Green fruit salad

SERVES: *6*
PREPARATION TIME: *30 minutes*
COOKING TIME: *5 minutes*

60 g (¼ cup) white sugar
3 limes, well scrubbed under warm,
  running water
2 green dessert apples, washed
2 ripe, firm pears, washed
750 g green-fleshed galia
  or honeydew melon
3 kiwifruit
250 g seedless green grapes,
  washed (and halved, if large)
To decorate: sprigs of fresh lemon
  balm, optional

1 Pour 500 ml of cold water into a small stainless-steel or enamel saucepan and add the sugar. Pare the rind from the limes using a zester or peeler and add it to the pan.
2 Stir over a moderate heat until the sugar has completely dissolved, then bring the sugar syrup to the boil and simmer it for 2 minutes. Remove the saucepan from the heat.
3 Squeeze the juice from the pared limes, stir it into the sugar syrup and then pour the flavoured syrup into a large serving bowl.
4 Working quickly, quarter and core the apples and slice them directly into the hot lime syrup. Then peel, quarter and core the pears and slice them into the syrup as well.
5 Cut the melon in half, remove the seeds and then either scoop out the flesh with a melon baller or cut it into cubes. Add the melon and any remaining juice to the bowl.
6 Peel and slice the kiwifruit and add them to the fruit salad with the grapes. Stir the fruits together gently, cover the bowl and leave to chill for 1–2 hours before serving. Serve the salad at room temperature or slightly chilled, decorated with lemon balm, if using.

VARIATIONS
As an alternative to lemon balm, stir a handful of freshly chopped mint leaves through the fruit salad just before serving. For an alcoholic kick, add 1 tablespoon of vodka, either plain or lemon-flavoured, or sweet white wine per person.

Tropical fruit salad

SERVES: *6*
PREPARATION TIME: *30 minutes*
COOKING TIME: *none*

60 g (¼ cup) caster sugar
1 teaspoon ground cinnamon
½ teaspoon ground cardamom
2 passionfruit
1 large, ripe mango
1 large, ripe pawpaw
750 g pineapple
250 g fresh dates
12 lychees or rambutans
4 tablespoons rum
To decorate: a few cape
  gooseberries, optional

1 Put the sugar, cinnamon and cardamom into a small bowl and mix together well.
2 Cut the passionfruit in half and scoop the pulp out into a bowl (see picture, page 157).
3 Peel and slice the mango and the pawpaw. Skin, quarter and core the pineapple then dice the flesh. Halve and stone the dates, and peel and stone the lychees or rambutans (see picture, page 156).
4 Put all of the prepared fruits into the bowl with the passionfruit pulp, sprinkle in the spiced sugar, pour in the rum and gently mix together. Cover and macerate the fruits in the refrigerator for 1–2 hours.
5 Just before serving, transfer the fruits and the flavoured juices to a serving bowl and decorate with the cape gooseberries, which should have their leaves pulled back (see picture, page 157). Serve at room temperature or slightly chilled.

BUSH FRUITS

I notice that there is an increasing interest in using native foods in our cooking, especially in restaurants. Is it safe to use all the bush fruits that grow wild in Australia?

There are many edible fruits available for free in the Australian bush, but it is important that you know what to look for and how to use them. Some bush fruits include the wild orange, wild passionfruit,

STONING FRUIT

With some fruits, you must first remove their stone before cutting the flesh for use in a fruit salad.

To remove the stone from tree fruits such as apricots, nectarines, peaches or plums, carefully cut around the fruit following the natural groove. Gently twist the halves in opposite directions, separate and remove the stone. This method can also be used when stoning avocados.

quandong, wild fig, bush tomato, mistletoe berry, conkerberry, bush banana, mulga apple and bush plum. Some of these fruits are eaten raw, some must be cooked, while others should be swallowed without chewing to avoid sticking to the tongue.

An up-to-date book on bush foods will be a very helpful guide (ask at your local library) or you should contact your nearest Botanical Gardens or Department of Agriculture for further information.

See also: ***Dried Fruit***

Save it!

Over-ripe fruit need not be thrown away. Simply purée it with some caster sugar and a little lemon juice to make a coulis. You can then serve this as a simple fruit sauce to accompany desserts such as ice cream or fold it into whipped cream, Greek-style yoghurt or fromage frais to make a delectable fruit fool.

CUSTARD APPLE (CHERIMOYA)

A heart-shaped green or purplish fruit with either smooth or scaly skin, custard apple has sweet creamy flesh with large inedible seeds. It can be eaten spooned from the skin or used to make desserts.

GUAVA

A good source of vitamin C, a guava can be round or pear-shaped. It is ready to eat when it is yellow and has a fragrant aroma. To eat the fruit, cut it in half lengthways and scoop out the flesh and edible seeds with a teaspoon. Eat it fresh or in tarts, or poach it in sugar syrup, enhancing the flavour with a little lemon juice.

KIWANO (HORNED MELON)

Kiwano's subtle flavour resembles a blend of banana, lime and passionfruit. When ripe, the skin is golden orange.

To serve kiwanos, cut into quarters lengthways and eat the flesh from the skin, as you would a slice of watermelon, or cut them in half and scoop the flesh out with a spoon. The seeds are edible. Kiwanos contain a lot of juice, which can be extracted by pressing the pulp in a sieve over a bowl (see opposite page), then sweetened to taste and drunk, or used for desserts.

KIWANO

EXOTIC FRUIT

◆

Medical advice to eat fresh fruit every day has never been easier to follow as more and more mouth-watering tropical and exotic fruits arrive in the shops. Here's how to enjoy some of the luscious newcomers.

Cinnamon, cardamom and rum add an exotic flavour to a salad made with sweet and fragrant tropical fruit (see page 155).

LYCHEE AND RAMBUTAN

The prickly shell of a ripe lychee can be reddish-brown, deep pink or white depending on the variety. The aromatic pearly white flesh tastes sweet yet slightly acidic. Rambutans, which have soft red or orange spines, are similar to lychees but have less flavour.

To eat lychees, peel away the rough prickly skin with your fingers and eat them like a cherry, discarding the stone. You can serve fresh lychees or rambutans with ice cream and sorbets to add an aromatic flavour, stone them and add them to exotic fruit salads, or liquidise the flesh to make a delicately perfumed drink.

MANGOSTEEN

One of the most delicious tropical fruits. The thick, dark-purple skin conceals segments of juicy, sweet white pulp.

Mangosteens are ripe to eat when their skin turns deep purple, almost black. Slice off the top of the mangosteen with a sharp knife, then cut down deeply through the skin on either side from stem to calyx. Pull the skin carefully away to expose the fruit inside and eat the segments but discard the stones. Alternatively, the mangosteen may simply be cut in half and the flesh scooped out with a spoon.

PAWPAW

Pawpaw (sometimes known as papaya) vary in size, colour and flavour depending on the variety. The dense, firm flesh is highly perfumed, juicy and sweet – something between a melon and a peach. The flesh may be orange, orange-yellow or red. The skin becomes yellow as the fruit ripens. Green fruit has less flavour.

To eat pawpaw, cut it in half lengthways and scoop out the black seeds, then eat the flesh straight from the skin with a spoon. For extra flavour, you can sprinkle lemon or lime juice over it. Pawpaw can also be peeled and cut into slices or cubes to make a sweet addition to a fruit or vegetable salad. Green pawpaw can be grated for a savoury salad.

The flesh can be liquidised to make a rich, sweet drink. Pawpaw can also be used as a marinade to tenderise meat, as it contains an enzyme that breaks down tissue.

POMEGRANATE

PASSIONFRUIT AND GRANADILLA

Passionfruit and granadilla come from the same botanical family. Purple passionfruit has a powerful flavour, yellow granadilla is more subtle and sweeter. Both are ripe when the skin begins to wrinkle.

To eat passionfruit or granadilla, slice in half and spoon out the pulp and seeds with a teaspoon. Eat straight from the spoon, or use the pulp in your favourite recipes.

Passionfruit pulp is sweet yet refreshing when ripe, and is often used to make drinks, ice creams, sorbets and other desserts. To extract the juice, scoop out the pulp into a stainless-steel or nylon sieve placed over a bowl, and push it through using the back of a wooden spoon, discarding the seeds. If you are putting the pulp into a liquidiser, you must pick out the seeds first, as they have a bitter, unpleasant taste when crushed.

CAPE GOOSEBERRY (PHYSALIS)

Pale and papery husks conceal shiny berries with a sweet-sharp flavour. When ripe, the berries are golden-orange.

To eat cape gooseberries, simply pull back the outer husks and bite off the whole fruit. They look attractive used with their leaves curled back as a pretty decoration for cakes and desserts. They look prettier still, and taste even more delicious, if they are dipped first in a caramel, chocolate or fondant coating.

POMEGRANATE

The pomegranate has a tough, brightly coloured skin containing translucent, deep-pink pulpy seeds which have a refreshing sweet flavour.

To eat a pomegranate, slice off the top and bottom and score through the skin from top to bottom in four places with a sharp knife. Gently pull the pomegranate apart, still in its skin, to expose the seeds, and eat them with a spoon. Whether you swallow the inner seeds or spit them out is up to you, but the internal membrane separating the fruit into sections is not pleasant to eat. You can also use the brilliant ruby flesh as a decorative garnish for sweet or savoury dishes.

To extract the juice, gently roll the whole pomegranate in your hand to crush and burst the kernels within. Then make a hole through the skin into the flesh and drain out the juice into a jug.

STAR FRUIT

Shiny and five-sided, the star fruit has a translucent pinkish-yellow colour and tart flesh.

To eat star fruit, wash and dry them and trim off the top edge of the ridges with a potato peeler. Then cut them crossways into thin, star-shaped slices. Star fruit is quite tart, so poach the slices gently for about 30 seconds in sugar syrup before adding to fruit salads or using as a garnish.

TAMARILLO

A shiny red or gold oval fruit, the tamarillo, or tree tomato, has yellow flesh like a plum and purple edible seeds. The sweet-sour flavour is rather an acquired taste, at its best when the fruit is ripe and soft to the touch. Cut it in half widthways and eat it with a spoon, but do not eat the outer skin.

GUAVA

MANGOSTEEN

LYCHEE

TAMARILLO

RAMBUTAN

CUSTARD APPLE

PAWPAW

Fruit Cakes

SUNKEN FRUIT

Why does the fruit always sink to the bottom of my fruit cakes?

Dried fruits are heavy and will sink if a cake mixture is too soft and wet. If the fruit has been washed, spread it out to dry well on a cloth before adding it to the cake mixture. Glacé cherries are particularly heavy and covered in sticky syrup, so always wash, dry and quarter the cherries to make them lighter.

If you find the fruit still goes to the bottom of the tin, toss it first in a little flour or ground almonds, as in the following recipe. This technique should help to spread the fruit evenly throughout the cake.

Rich fruit cake

MAKES: *1 x 20 cm deep round cake (suitable for a family Christmas or celebration cake)*
PREPARATION TIME: *about 1 hour, plus 6 weeks maturing time*
COOKING TIME: *3½–4 hours*

---

100 g (½ cup) glacé cherries
100 g (½ cup) mixed peel, finely chopped
250 g (1⅓ cups) currants
250 g (1⅓ cups) seedless raisins
250 g (1⅓ cups) sultanas
50 g (½ cup) ground almonds
50 g (⅓ cup) whole almonds
250 g (2 cups) plain flour
½ teaspoon salt
1 teaspoon mixed spice
250 g unsalted butter
250 g (1⅓ cups) dark brown sugar
4 large eggs, lightly beaten
1 tablespoon treacle
½ teaspoon vanilla essence
Finely grated zest of 1 orange or lemon
2 tablespoons milk
2 tablespoons brandy

---

1 Preheat the oven to 150°. Grease a 20 cm deep round cake tin and line it with a double layer of greaseproof paper.

Dark from brown sugar, treacle and spice, the Rich Fruit Cake is crammed with fruit and nuts, then laced with brandy to keep it lusciously moist.

2 Wrap a layer of brown paper or newspaper around the outside of the tin and fix it tightly with string.
3 Wash the syrup from the cherries, then pat dry, quarter and place in a bowl. Add the mixed peel, dried fruits, ground and whole almonds.
4 Sift the flour, salt and mixed spice together then add 4 tablespoons to the fruit mixture and toss together.
5 Cream the butter and brown sugar together until very soft, light and fluffy. Then beat the eggs into the creamed mixture a little at a time, adding a teaspoon of the flour with each addition to prevent curdling.
6 Fold in the remaining flour, then add the fruit mixture, treacle, vanilla, zest and milk. Mix well together and turn into the tin. Smooth the batter level and bake for 2 hours, then lower the temperature to 140°C for a further 1½–2 hours, until a skewer or knife pushed into the centre comes out clean.
7 Leave the cake to cool in the tin for about an hour, then turn out

onto a wire rack. When completely cooled, prick the surface with a fine skewer or fork, then brush or spoon the brandy evenly over the top.
8 Leave the cake for about an hour to allow the brandy to soak in.
9 Wrap the cake in a double layer of greaseproof paper, then foil, and seal the wrapping with tape to make it airtight. The paper protects the foil from the acid in the fruit, which can cause corrosion or mould. Store in a dark, dry place for at least six weeks, and leave for longer if possible.
10 Rich fruit cake is almost always covered with marzipan and then iced (see *Icing*). But if you prefer, you could simply brush a glaze of sieved apricot jam on the top and set whole almonds or glacé fruits into this. Clear honey is another possible base for decorative nuts.

VARIATION

For extra richness, soak the dried fruit in brandy for two to three days before baking, as well as brushing the cake with brandy afterwards.

ADDING SPIRIT

Does adding brandy to a fruit cake help it to keep longer?

Adding brandy or other spirits to a rich fruit cake does help it to keep, and gives it a moist texture and mellow flavour. When the cake is cool, skewer the top in several places and spoon or brush the spirit over. Wrap in greaseproof paper and foil, then store at a dry, even temperature. If you can, make the cake at least three months ahead, adding more spirit every month.

HOW MUCH CAKE?

How can I work out what size of wedding cake to make?

The table below shows how many small portions each size cake will usually yield. Use this to work out how many tiers you will need.

Portions	Square	Round
16	13 cm	15 cm
28	18 cm	20 cm
48	23 cm	25 cm
90	28 cm	30 cm
136	33 cm	35 cm

HOW TO ASSEMBLE A TIERED WEDDING CAKE

Wooden dowelling skewers are available from cake decorating shops, or you can cut your own. The skewers should go through the cake to the board, with enough above to reach the top of the decorative hollow pillars that cover them.

1 Cut a circle of greaseproof paper the size of the bottom tier, fold it into quarters and push a pin through about 8 cm from the outer edge to make four evenly spaced pinpricks. Open out the circle on the cake and pierce through the pinholes to mark the position of the supporting pillars.

2 Push skewers into the cake at the marked positions and cover with the decorative pillars. Take another circle of paper the size of the second tier, and fold and mark it as before. It is important to locate the new pillars directly above the ones beneath, so that the cake has adequate support.

HOW TO CUT A CAKE

Use a serrated knife and cut half the cake at a time. Make the long cuts first, 8 cm apart, then short cuts at right angles every 2 cm. Have hot water and a tea towel on hand to clean the knife, which will keep the slices neater.

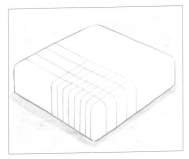

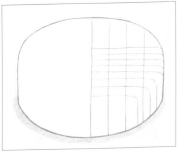

Fruit Drinks

KEEPING JUICE

If I squeeze oranges to make my own fresh juice, how long can I keep it in the refrigerator?

For maximum nutritional benefit, it is best to drink the juice as soon as possible. Orange juice can be kept for up to two days in an airtight container in the refrigerator, but the amount of vitamin C declines.

EXOTIC FRUIT DRINKS

I like unusual fruit juice drinks, but is it worth buying fresh fruit and juicing them at home?

Fresh fruit juices are not difficult to make with the help of an electric juicer, blender or food processor. They are superior to those you can buy, both in flavour and nutritionally, because you need not add any sugar and can avoid artificial preservatives, colours and flavours.

The flesh of mangoes, melons, peaches, pineapples and strawberries in different combinations make good drinks pureéd in the blender, either alone or with added crushed ice. Dilute the juice to taste with mineral, soda or tonic water; use it for milkshakes; or add it to sparkling white wine or champagne. (See also *Juicers*.)

CUTTING DOWN SUGAR

Can I make a fruit cordial that is not as sugary as the bottled ones?

Traditional fruit cordials and syrups are made with a high proportion of sugar which acts as a preservative and enables them to be kept for several months.

Homemade syrups and cordials using the traditional berry fruits can be made using less sugar than is usual. The Christmas Cordial recipe (page 160) is a lower-sugar version that can be stored in the refrigerator for up to three months. It has a slightly sharp flavour but is still sweet enough for most tastes.

Christmas cordial

MAKES: 750 ml
PREPARATION TIME: 30 minutes
COOKING TIME: 20–30 minutes

750 g prepared fruit, such as
   blackberries, boysenberries,
   loganberries, raspberries,
   strawberries, redcurrants or
   blackcurrants
125–250 g (½–1 cup) caster sugar

1 Put all the fruit into a heatproof bowl. If you are using blackberries, boysenberries, loganberries, raspberries or strawberries, add 90 ml of cold water; if using redcurrants, add 200 ml of water; and if using blackcurrants, add 600 ml of water.
2 Place the bowl over a saucepan of gently simmering water and heat for some 20–30 minutes until the juice flows freely. Occasionally crush the fruit with a potato masher to help to extract the juice. When the fruit is very soft, take the bowl off the heat.
3 Scald a nylon or stainless-steel sieve, a large bowl and a large square of muslin with boiling water; drain the bowl and sieve and wring out the muslin. Place the sieve over the bowl and line it with the muslin.
4 Pour the pulped fruit and syrup into the sieve and leave it to drain for about 20 minutes until almost all of the juice has dripped through the sieve into the bowl.
5 Take two opposite sides of the muslin and fold them over the fruit so that it forms a secure parcel. Twist the ends of the muslin tightly in opposite directions to squeeze out all the remaining juice. Once the juice has been extracted, discard the pips and dry pulp remaining in the muslin. This method produces a clear, smooth syrup; for a grainier, more textured juice, you can use a nylon sieve without the muslin.
6 Pour the fruit juice into a clean, stainless-steel or enamel saucepan. Add the sugar gradually, a tablespoon at a time, until sweetened to taste – sweet fruits such as boysenberries, raspberries and strawberries will need about 125 g (½ cup) while the other fruits will require more.

Cordials need not be overly sweet. This pleasantly sharp thirst-quencher combines blackberries, raspberries and redcurrants to make a festive summer drink.

7 Place the saucepan over a low heat and stir until the sugar has completely dissolved, but do not allow the syrup to become too hot.
8 Pour into clean and preferably sterilised bottles (see *Chutney*), seal with a tight-fitting lid and store refrigerated for up to three months.
9 To serve, pour the syrup onto ice and dilute to taste, using about one part syrup to two or three parts mineral, soda, tonic or tap water.

Cordial and convenient

For long-term storage, pour the syrup into ice-cube trays and freeze it. Frozen cubes can be removed as required, put into glasses or a jug, allowed to melt and then diluted to taste. Use three or four cubes for each glass. The syrup will keep in the freezer for up to six months.

Fresh lemonade

SERVES: *6*
PREPARATION TIME: *20 minutes, plus
3-4 hours standing and chilling*
COOKING TIME: *none*

*7 large lemons, well washed
1.25 litres boiling water
60-125 g (¼-½ cup) caster sugar
To serve: ice cubes, optional
To decorate: sprigs of fresh lemon
    balm or mint, optional*

1 Thinly pare the rind from six of
the lemons. Put the rind into a large
heatproof jug or bowl and pour in
the boiling water. Cover and leave to
infuse for an hour.
2 Squeeze and strain the juice from
the pared lemons and pour it into a
large serving jug. Strain the water
from the lemon rind into the jug,
add sugar to taste and stir until the
sugar has dissolved.
3 Thinly slice the remaining lemon,
and add the slices to the jug. Cover
the jug with plastic wrap and chill
in the refrigerator for 2-3 hours.
4 Serve the lemonade as it is or, if
you prefer, add some ice cubes and
decorate with a few leaves of fresh
lemon balm or mint.

Fruit mince

SAFE KEEPING

*How long can I store fruit mince
that I have made at home?*

Fruit mince stored in sterilised, airtight jars will keep for a year in a
cool, dark, dry place. It should be
made at least a month before it is
needed so that the flavour has time
to mature. If it becomes dry, add a
dash of sherry or brandy.

VEGETARIAN OPTION

*I am a vegetarian. Could I make
fruit mince without suet?*

It is possible to make fruit mince by
omitting the traditional shredded
suet and replacing it with cool
melted butter. It must, however, be
stored in the refrigerator and will

keep for up to four weeks. The Vegetarian Fruit Mince (below) should
be bottled in the same way as the
traditional fruit mince and stored in
the refrigerator.

There are also vegetarian fruit
mince recipes that contain no suet
or sugar and simply combine dried
fruits, nuts, fresh fruit or vegetables. Sugar-less fruit mince will not
keep well unless it has a little spirit
added. It should then be stored in
the refrigerator and used within a
week. It makes a good topping for
ice cream or yoghurt.

Vegetarian fruit mince

MAKES: *about 2.5 kg*
PREPARATION TIME: *30 minutes, plus
maturing time of at least 4 weeks*
COOKING: *none*

*350 g (2 cups) seedless raisins
350 g (2 cups) sultanas
250 g (1½ cups) currants
175 g (1 cup) chopped mixed peel
500 g cooking apples (peeled,
    cored and coarsely grated)
250 g butter, melted
350 g (2 cups) dark brown sugar
50 g (⅓ cup) blanched almonds,
    chopped, optional
Finely grated rind and juice of
    1 lemon and 1 orange
3 teaspoons ground mixed spice
1 teaspoon ground nutmeg
150 ml brandy*

1 Pick over the dried fruits and
remove any stalks; wash and dry
only if necessary.
2 Place all the ingredients in a large
bowl and mix together thoroughly.
3 Put the mixture into clean,
sterilised jars then cover, seal tightly
and store in the refrigerator.
4 Allow the fruit mince to stand for
only four weeks before it is used;
this gives it time to mature.
VARIATION
For alcohol-free fruit mince, replace
the brandy with unsweetened apple
juice. This will taste fine, but it will
not have the preservative power of
the brandy, making it necessary to
keep the fruit mince refrigerated.
Alcohol-free mince should be eaten
within a few days.

Frying

SMALL LEAPS

*What is the difference between
shallow frying and sautéing?*

They are both ways of frying food
in a little oil over a medium-high
heat. In shallow frying, the food is
turned with a palette knife or egg
slice; in sautéing, the pan – which
is sometimes covered – is shaken
so the food 'jumps' (the French
verb *sauter* means to leap). Both
are quick cooking methods suitable for small, tender pieces of
meat and other foods.

Bacon and eggs, steak, sausages
and veal and chicken schnitzel are
all shallow fried, for example.
However, a mixture of diced vegetables is sautéed in a covered
pan to develop flavour in the first
stage of making a vegetable soup,
while chicken breast can be
sautéed with onions in a special
sauté pan, then wine, stock and
cream are added and simmered to
produce chicken sauté.

The fat you use for frying or
sautéing food is important, as its
flavour will affect the taste. Olive
oil, butter, lard and beef or bacon
dripping all add their particular
flavour to fried foods; canola, corn,
peanut, safflower and most other
vegetable oils have relatively little
flavour. When choosing a fat,
remember that some of them can
be heated to much higher temperatures than others before they start
to break down and burn. For example, dripping and lard can
withstand more heat than butter or
margarine, while clarified butter
(see *Butter*) can be heated to a
higher temperature than untreated
butter. Copha, which is solidified
coconut oil, must be melted very
slowly on a low heat to avoid
breaking down and burning.

All fats tend to break down if
they are heated too long, causing
them to smoke and give an
unpleasant flavour to any food that
is fried in them.

STAY CRISP

What can I do to prevent fried food from becoming soggy?

Use a wide, uncovered pan because a lid traps the steam so that the food stews or steams instead of frying crisply. Preheat the fat so that the food forms a crisp seal immediately and does not absorb the fat and become greasy.

Fry only a little food at a time, and cook meat quickly so that the outside browns all over. Then lower the heat to medium and continue cooking. Some food with a soft texture, such as fish cakes and croquettes, is coated with egg and breadcrumbs to stop it becoming soggy. To keep fried food crisp, drain well on kitchen paper towels and always serve as soon as you possibly can after it has been cooked. (See also *Deep-Frying*.)

SEASONING SURFACES

What is the best way to season a new frying pan?

Seasoning, or proving, a pan gives a relatively nonstick surface to pans that do not have a nonstick coating. The easiest method is to wash and dry the pan thoroughly and then put it on a high heat with 1 tablespoon of salt and 1 tablespoon of oil. Heat it until the oil is smoking, then wipe the pan clean with a large wad of crumpled kitchen paper towels, using any remaining salt as an abrasive. When the pan is clean, it is seasoned.

A wok is greatly improved by this treatment and may need to be seasoned again if food begins to stick. If possible, use an omelette pan only for omelettes; a crepe pan only for crepes and pancakes, and you should season the pans every time you use them.

DEGLAZING THE PAN

When a recipe mentions the term deglazing, what does it mean?

Deglazing is a term for loosening the browned juices stuck on the bottom of a pan after frying meat.

Tip off the fat, add a few tablespoons of liquid such as cream, stock, water or wine, and bring to the boil, stirring and scraping to dissolve the sediment. The liquid will be full of flavour and can be poured over meat, added to a sauce or stirred into a casserole.

NO-FAT NEWS

What exactly is dry-frying? Surely food will stick if there is no fat in the pan to keep it loose?

In these health-conscious times, dry-frying has become a popular way of cooking fish and meat, especially bacon rashers. First heat a frying pan with a heavy bottom on a high flame until it is hot. Meanwhile, prepare the meat or fish. If it has little fat of its own, drizzle a small amount of oil over the surface and rub it in. However, if the meat has natural fat or the fish is oily, simply season with freshly ground black pepper.

When the pan is hot, add the meat or fish and then leave it. Do not be tempted to move the food around in the pan until a crust has formed. You will then be able to slide an egg slice or palette knife underneath and turn to cook on the other side.

Dry-frying is also used to extract and bring out the flavour of whole spices, seeds or nuts. Fry them without fat in a heavy-bottomed pan over a high heat, shaking the pan from time to time. Continue cooking, watching carefully to avoid burning, until they give off a distinct aroma, and then tip them onto a cold plate.

OIL AND BUTTER

Why do lots of recipes use a mixture of olive oil and butter?

Butter gives a delicious, rich flavour to food, but has a lower burning temperature than olive oil. When the two are heated together, the butter can reach the higher temperature necessary for frying and sealing certain foods, which helps preserve and develop good flavour.

NONSTICK PANS

Is there any advantage in using a nonstick frying pan instead of my regular pan?

It is a very good practice to use a nonstick pan for a healthy low-fat diet. The fat content in most traditional recipes, which start with frying the ingredients – such as onions or meat for a sauté or casserole – may be at least halved if you use a nonstick pan. For some recipes, all you need to do is brush the base of the pan with a little oil or spray the base with some olive oil or canola oil spray.

It is important to take care of nonstick pans by always cooking over a medium heat and by never overheating the pan when it is empty. Use non-metal tools when turning food and stirring, so that the surface is not scratched.

Clean the nonstick interior with a sponge, hot water and liquid detergent and never use wire wool, scouring pads or scouring powder as these materials can cause damage to the nonstick coating.

TRYING FRYING

When I use tongs to turn fish cakes or meat patties, they tend to crack and split open. What is the best utensil to use when frying this type of food?

Tongs are a handy utensil for turning some fried foods, such as bacon rashers, chops or cutlets which have a firm texture. However, the best utensil to use when frying soft-textured food, such as fish fillets, or coated food such as fish cakes or meat rissoles, is ideally a combination of two egg slices (also called fish slices). These are good for loosening, lifting, moving and turning over the frying food without damaging its shape or breaking the coating. Alternatively, you can use two palette knives or use one egg slice in conjunction with a palette knife.

Never use a fork when frying food as this breaks the seal and allows the fat to penetrate the food.

Game

SPORTING FARE

What does the term 'game' mean?

The word game refers to any wild animal, bird or fish hunted for sport or for food, and their flesh. Wild game is rare in Australia, with kangaroos, wild rabbits and wild ducks being the few acceptable species available. Wild venison, however, is the popular game hunted in the mountains of New Zealand. Yabbies and a wide variety of freshwater fish are available in some of Australia's lakes and rivers, while game fishing is a popular sport in tropical waters.

It is permissible to hunt wild kangaroo and wild rabbit in all seasons, but wild ducks are restricted to a shooting season in the wintertime, which allows the birds a time to breed.

The remainder of the game featured on gourmet restaurant menus, and available from game shops, leading butchers and some supermarkets, are all farmed on commercial farms, surrounded and covered by high fences. The table game birds predominantly bred on game farms include guinea fowl, quail, pheasant and squab, which is a baby pigeon. Some game farms also rear poussin or spatchcock and some breeds of duck. White rabbits and red and fallow venison are also farmed in Australia. Farming habits on game bird farms are conducted under compulsory poultry legislation and must meet the strict requirements of the RSPCA. All farmed game is inspected before killing and must be processed in abbatoirs that have been registered by the Australian Quarantine and Inspection Service.

HANGING MATTER

Does all game need to be hung and, if so, for how long?

Game birds produced on game farms are hung for only two days at the most and not as long as is the practice with wild game birds in colder European climates. They are hung before being plucked – suspended by the neck in a cool airy place, not touching each other. This helps to tenderise the meat and develop the flavour. Wild duck, however, needs only one or two days hanging because it can quickly turn rancid.

Wild and farmed rabbit is not hung. Kangaroo and venison, whether farmed or wild, both benefit from a few days hanging to tenderise the meat.

Garlic

KNIFE OR CRUSHER?

Why do some cookery experts prefer not to use a garlic crusher?

Many experienced cooks prefer to use a knife to crush garlic because garlic crushers can be hard to clean and may harbour stale remnants that can taint the next dish. Crushing garlic also releases acrid-tasting chemicals. This is not a problem if the garlic is to be heated, as it is mellowed by cooking, but garlic to be eaten raw has a more refined flavour if it is carefully minced by hand (see panel, right).

EAT MORE, SMELL LESS

Is it true that removing the green shoot from an old clove of garlic prevents 'garlic breath'?

Not necessarily, but the green tip is strong and bitter and should be removed anyway. Some people who eat a lot of garlic claim their

CHOPPING AND CRUSHING GARLIC

For many dishes garlic does not need to be finely chopped. Whole cloves, skinned, can be added and will disintegrate during cooking.

1 To pop the clove out of its papery skin, simply put it on a chopping board and press down firmly with the flat of a large heavy knife.

2 To mince or finely chop a clove of garlic, cut it lengthways into thin strips, then cut widthways.

3 To crush a garlic clove to a pulp, sprinkle it with coarse salt and alternately chop with the blade then mash it with the flat of the knife.

digestive system adapts and the smell of garlic no longer lingers, but this is not proven. The theory that only raw garlic smells, not cooked garlic, is also folklore.

Scientists do agree, however, that garlic, a traditional folk remedy to 'cleanse the blood' of impurities, does have anti-clogging properties. They recommend eating it often for a healthy heart.

SEASONAL SENSATION

Are there different types of garlic, as some bulbs seem to be much more pungent than others?

There are several types of garlic: most is pearly white, but other varieties are streaked with pink and mauve. However, the colour does not noticeably affect the flavour.

The more important distinction is seasonal. The most familiar garlic is sold from late summer, sometimes plaited into skeins to hang in a cool place for winter. It has been dried in the sun, which has firmed up the heads and transformed the skin into a tissue-like wrapping, and the garlic is good if it is firm. It will get stronger in taste as green shoots begin to germinate and sprout in the individual cloves.

As well as locally grown garlic, there is a lot of imported garlic on the market. Also becoming more commonly available are garlic shoots, which are seen from midwinter to spring. The cloves are immature and the stem is thick and fleshy. This green garlic is sweet and mild enough to be treated as a vegetable, and is very good roasted whole with fresh herbs such as thyme, as in the recipe below.

Serve the roasted heads as a starter, with bread and mild goat's cheese, or as an accompaniment to chicken or lamb. Diners squeeze the cloves out with their fingers.

Roast garlic with thyme

SERVES: 4-6
PREPARATION TIME: 20 minutes (for oven to preheat)
COOKING TIME: 45 minutes-1 hour

6 large heads of young garlic
100 ml olive oil
Flaky sea salt
6 sprigs fresh thyme

1 Preheat the oven to 200°C.
2 Using a sharp, large chopping knife, cut the top third from each head of garlic to expose the flesh, then trim off the roots. Pack the whole heads, cut side up, in an ovenproof dish that will hold them tightly in a single layer. Trickle the oil all over, sprinkle with salt and tuck in the sprigs of thyme.
3 Roast, uncovered, for 45 minutes to an hour, basting once or twice with the pan juices. The garlic is done if it feels soft when pressed.

Gelatine

LEAF OR POWDER?

Which is easier to use, leaf or powdered gelatine?

This is a matter of personal preference. Leaf gelatine is sold in sheets which need to be softened in water before being dissolved in a hot liquid. Put the required number of leaves into a bowl of cold water and leave for 5 minutes to soften. Take them from the water, squeeze out excess water and put the sheets in a small pan. Place the pan in a bain-marie, a larger pan half-full of simmering water, and heat until the gelatine has completely dissolved.

Powdered gelatine needs to be reconstituted before use. Measure the liquid into a small bowl and sprinkle the gelatine over the surface. Leave it to soak for 5 minutes, during which time the gelatine will absorb the liquid and the mixture will become spongy. Place the bowl in a bain-marie and heat until the gelatine is runny and clear.

Whichever you use, make sure it does not get too hot. Overheating makes gelatine stringy and can cause it to lose its setting power.

HOW MUCH IS ENOUGH?

If a recipe calls for powdered gelatine and I find that I only have leaves, how do I make up the same quantity of gelatine?

Powdered gelatine is usually sold in boxes of individual envelopes, each holding just over 10 g (3 teaspoons), which sets 600 ml of liquid. Leaf gelatine varies in weight. You need about 7 g to set

Whole heads of garlic roasted with aromatic thyme are a feast for garlic lovers, with their seductive sweet flesh and surprisingly mild flavour.

600 ml, but always check the instructions. If the liquid to be set will contain solid pieces of food, or if the jelly is to stay in a warm room for any length of time, you will need more gelatine. Conversely, if the mixture is to be served chilled, or is already stiff, less gelatine is needed. Note that kiwifruit, paw-paw and pineapple have an enzyme that prevents setting.

SWIRLED NOT STIRRED

Should you stir gelatine if it does not dissolve immediately?

Never stir gelatine as the quantities used are so tiny you will lose half on the spoon. If one or two patches do not absorb the liquid at once, swirl the bowl gently, taking care not to lose gelatine up the sides.

A VEGETARIAN SET

I am a vegetarian. I have always wanted to make savoury set terrines, but cannot use gelatine because it is an animal product. Is there anything else I can use?

Gelatine is derived from the bones of beef. Agar-agar, which is made from seaweed and is used a great deal in commercial food processing for thickening and as a stabiliser, is a common alternative. It is sold in many quality health food shops.

Five grams of powdered agar-agar or dried sponge seaweed sets 750 ml of liquid, but you will never achieve a firm set if your mixture is acidic, for example a mousse with citrus; or if a mixture contains chocolate or spinach. Always dissolve the agar-agar first, then boil it slowly for 15 minutes to activate the setting process. It sets at a higher temperature than gelatine, but the result does not melt so well in the mouth and feels different.

Another vegetarian product that can be used as a substitute for gelatine is Gelozone, which is made from locust bean gum, guar gum and carrageenan, or Irish moss. Follow the instructions on the packet for quantities, and always heat gently before adding it.

Ginger

VENERABLE ORIENTAL

Where does ginger come from, and how is it used?

Ginger comes from Asia where it has been cultivated since ancient times for its warm flavour and is valued as an aid to digestion. The edible part is the rhizome, or root, and it may be used either fresh, dried, pickled or preserved.

In China, India, Japan and Southeast Asia, fresh ginger is very popular and used for a wide variety of savoury dishes such as soups, curries, marinades, pickles and relishes. Western countries have used ground ginger for hundreds of years to flavour dishes such as gingerbread, biscuits and puddings.

To use fresh ginger, first peel the root, then chop it very finely or grate it on a fine grater. If you only want the juice and not the ginger itself for flavouring, crush it in a garlic press.

Fresh ginger is used mostly in conjunction with other flavourings such as garlic, spring onions and chillies, for example in stir-fries. It also goes well with broccoli, red meat, chicken, noodles, rice and shellfish. The following recipe for Ginger Noodle Stir-fry is a spicy accompaniment to grilled fish, chicken or lamb.

Ginger noodle stir-fry

SERVES: *4*
PREPARATION TIME: *15 minutes*
COOKING TIME: *5 minutes plus standing*

---

5 cm piece of fresh green ginger
500 ml chicken stock
185 g yellow egg noodles
2 tablespoons peanut oil
2 cloves garlic, crushed
1 carrot, cut in julienne strips
1 cup sliced spring onions
1 tablespoon salt-reduced soy sauce

---

1 Peel the ginger thinly and chop the root finely.

2 Bring the chicken stock to the boil in a pan. Add the noodles and stir well. Remove from the heat and stand for 5 minutes, or until soft.
3 Heat the oil in a wok on a medium heat. Add the ginger and garlic and stir-fry for 1 minute. Add the carrot and stir-fry for 2 minutes.
4 Carefully add the noodles and stock, spring onions and soy sauce and heat through, stirring constantly. Serve immediately.

ONE OR THE OTHER

Can ground ginger be used in a recipe that calls for fresh ginger?

No, they are not interchangeable. Their flavour is completely different, and one cannot be used as a substitute for the other.

Goat

TASTY AND TENDER

I have seen goat in Indian recipes and kid on a Greek restaurant menu. What are they like to eat?

Goat can have a strong taste, but the flavour is mellowed by being cooked slowly with spices, as it is in Indian and Caribbean recipes. This slow cooking also helps to make the meat more tender.

In Mediterranean countries you are more likely to find lean young goat, called kid. It is very tasty and has the fat on the outside rather than being marbled throughout the flesh. Kid can be ordered locally from specialty butchers and may also be available from Indian and Middle Eastern suppliers. (In the Middle East roasted kid is served with rice and hard-boiled eggs.) If the meat is labelled 'halal', the animal has been slaughtered in accordance with Muslim law, just as 'kosher' meat is killed according to orthodox Jewish religious law.

Cook young goat in the same way you would cook young lamb. Kid is a favourite for spring festivals in France and Greece, roasted with herbs over an open fire.

Goose

PERFECT PARTNERS

How can I work out how many people a goose will feed, and what are some side dishes I can serve with it?

An average goose weighs 4.5–6 kg. There is a high proportion of bone to flesh so allow 750 g per person.

For roast goose, use a traditional sage and onion stuffing. Serve it with gooseberry sauce (see recipe, right), braised red cabbage, roast or mashed potatoes and gravy.

Gooseberries

SHARP SAUCE

How is gooseberry sauce served?

Gooseberry Sauce (right) is a particularly English accompaniment to fatty, savoury foods such as pork, mackerel and goose, which may be how the fruit got its name. The sharpness of the tart gooseberries counteracts the oiliness of the food. To keep the sauce tart, use

A refreshing, pale green sauce of ripe gooseberries makes a pleasantly sharp contrast to deep-fried camembert.

either green gooseberries with only a tiny pinch of sugar added, or the larger, sweeter dessert varieties before they are completely ripe and cook them without any sugar

Gooseberry sauce

SERVES: *4*
PREPARATION TIME: *10 minutes*
COOKING TIME: *15 minutes*

*250 g green gooseberries,
 topped and tailed*
15 g butter
15 g (3 teaspoons) white sugar
*1 tablespoon chopped fennel leaves,
 optional*

1 Place the prepared gooseberries in a saucepan with 1 tablespoon of water, and add the butter, sugar and fennel, if using. Cover and cook them gently, stirring occasionally with a wooden spoon, for about 15 minutes until soft. (Add another tablespoon of water if it seems dry.)
2 Beat well with a wooden spoon to a pulpy consistency and add a little more sugar, if wanted. Serve warm.
VARIATIONS
Retaining the skin and pulpy pieces of fruit adds fibre, texture and colour, but if you prefer a smooth sauce, sieve after cooking. If you use defrosted frozen gooseberries, you should not need to add additional water. They will cook in about 10 minutes; do not overcook.

GREEN FOR FOOLS

What type of gooseberries are best for making gooseberry fool?

The sharper green gooseberries are the best complement to the rich stirred egg custard and cream in a fool. The larger yellow and red gooseberries are sweetest and best kept for eating raw.

Grapes

WAIT TO WASH

Does washing grapes make them rot more quickly?

Grapes should be washed, but only just before they are served or eaten. The pressure grapes put on each other when in bunches can cause bruising which creates moisture, encouraging the fruit to spoil. If they are washed before storing, water is likely to remain between the grapes and can accelerate rotting which will create soft spots.

It is best to buy grapes in small quantities, checking to make sure they are not bruised. Store them, unwashed, in a colander in the refrigerator, which allows the air to circulate and keeps them dry. Use within two to three days.

EASY DESEEDING

I find removing the pips from grapes tedious. Should I just use the seedless varieties?

Seedless grapes are wonderful for eating but are not always what you need for cooking. Some recipes require a sharper tasting grape to counterbalance a rich sauce. You can remove the seeds by cutting the grapes in half, lengthways, and removing with a small sharp knife. However, seedless grapes work well in the following recipe, but do need to be peeled.

To remove grape skins, prick each end, cover with boiling water and leave to stand for 45 seconds. Plunge the grapes into cold water to cool, then peel and cut in half.

Champagne chicken with grapes

SERVES: 4
PREPARATION TIME: 20 minutes
COOKING TIME: 25 minutes

200 g green seedless grapes
4 skinless chicken breast fillets
1 tablespoon plain flour
¼ teaspoon salt
60 g butter
2 white onions, sliced
125 ml champagne
125 ml chicken stock
2 tablespoons ground almonds
1 clove garlic, crushed
¼ teaspoon sweet paprika
½ teaspoon ground turmeric
3 tablespoons cream
To garnish: chopped fresh parsley

1 Skin the grapes, cut in half if very large, and set aside.
2 Rinse the chicken breasts in cold running water and pat dry with kitchen paper towels. Trim off any excess fat or tissues. Place the chicken with the flour and salt in a clean plastic bag. Toss well to coat the chicken lightly.
3 Heat the butter in a large, nonstick frying pan over a medium heat. Add the onions and gently fry for 5 minutes, stirring occasionally, or until soft.
4 Add the chicken breasts and fry on both sides for 2 minutes, or until the colour changes to golden.
5 Add the champagne and stock to the pan and bring to the boil. Cover and simmer over a medium-low heat

Skinless chicken breast fillets are lavishly coated with an elegant champagne and cream sauce enhanced with seedless green grapes.

for 15 minutes or until the chicken is cooked through.
6 Transfer the chicken to a warmed serving plate and keep warm.
7 In a small bowl, blend the ground almonds, garlic, paprika and turmeric smoothly with the cream. Add the almond mixture to the pan and bring to the boil, stirring constantly. Simmer for 3 minutes, to thicken slightly. Stir in the grapes and heat through.
8 Spoon the sauce and grapes over the chicken. Garnish with a little parsley and serve immediately.

Gravy

TRADITIONAL WAY

What is the best way to make really delicious gravy?

Well-flavoured gravy incorporates both the juices and sediment of roasted meat and should be made in the baking dish after the meat has been removed and left to rest on a serving plate.

Once you have moved the joint, pour off most of the fat, except for 1–2 tablespoons which you should leave in the dish with the dark sediment from the roast.

Stir in 1–2 tablespoons of flour, stirring and browning it slowly to the colour you prefer. Then gradually pour in meat stock or vegetable water and stir until the gravy boils and is thick and smooth. Any lumps can be sieved out afterwards.

If any fat remains on top of the finished gravy you can remove it by placing kitchen paper towels on the surface of the gravy.

A thinner gravy can be made by reducing the flour to 1 teaspoon. If it is then too thin, the gravy can be reduced by rapid boiling for a few minutes. Season to taste, transfer to a gravy boat and serve hot.

If you prefer meat gravy to have a slightly lighter texture, you can thicken it with cornflour or arrowroot instead of ordinary plain flour.

DASH OF FLAVOUR

What can I add to gravy to make its flavour more interesting?

The best guarantee of a good gravy is well-flavoured stock. If this is lacking, there are several additions you can make to give the gravy colour as well as flavour.

For children, try a little Vegemite or Marmite. Adults may prefer red or white wine, sherry, brandy, or a dash of liqueur or port.

Adding acidic or sweet flavours in small quantities to gravy will also enhance its flavour. You could try a squeeze of orange or lemon juice, vinegar (in particular a few drops of rich balsamic or sherry vinegar) or even jellies made from mint, redcurrants, rosellas or apples. If you are serving gravy with turkey or pork, meats which benefit from a little sweetness, add a teaspoon or so of plum, cranberry, redcurrant, or similarly sharp-flavoured jelly to the reduced gravy. The jelly melts very quickly when stirred into the hot gravy and gives it an impressive smoothness.

Fresh or dried herbs and spices such as allspice, cayenne, horseradish, mustard, nutmeg and thyme can add a distinctive taste to gravy.

When you are adding alcohol, reduce it first by rapid boiling to eliminate any harsh flavour, then use this to replace some of the water or stock in the recipe.

An excellent way of improving gravy is to pour a glass or two of red wine over the joint halfway through the roasting period. The alcohol will evaporate during the rest of the cooking, the flavour of the meat will improve and the wine will amalgamate with the juices and sediment in the pan.

STOCK QUESTION

What type of stock will make the most successful gravy?

A good homemade stock will taste best. It should ideally match the meat you are roasting, but chicken stock can be used for most gravies.

Giblet stock can be made quickly by simmering the poultry giblets (neck, heart, gizzard, liver) in water for 30 minutes. For a richer gravy, do not add the liver to the stock but instead fry it, finely chopped, in the baking dish before adding the flour.

Supermarkets now sell tetrapacks of liquid stock, which is a good alternative to homemade, and a can of consommé is a good standby. Commercial stock cubes or powders are usually heavily salted and should be used only as a last resort. If you have to use a stock cube, use only half a cube to the amount of water suggested on the pack to reduce the saltiness.

FASTER GRAVY

What can I use to make gravy when I am in a hurry?

The quickest homemade gravy is a *jus* (see panel, below) made from stock and the roasted meat's natural juices. Unlike gravy, it is not thickened with flour. Remove the joint from the baking dish and pour off the fat into a separating jug. Then pour the stock into the dish and bring to the boil, scraping in all the sediment. Add the meat juices that have separated from the fat in the jug and simmer for several minutes. Strain the jus into a gravy boat, season and serve.

DEGLAZING FOR JUS

Jus is an unthickened meat juice gravy made by deglazing the pan in which meat has been roasted. If the juices are not dark enough at the end of the cooking time, reduce them until they are caramelised.

1 Pour the fat from the joint into a jug. A separating jug is ideal for this as it allows you to pour out the meat juices from beneath the fat.

2 With a wooden spoon, scrape all the crusty bits of sediment from the sides and base of the tin. Pour in some stock, vegetable water or wine and continue stirring over a moderate heat. Add any meat juice that has separated from the fat and simmer until rich brown in colour.

Griddle

ANCIENT PAN

What is a griddle?

It is a heavy, flat, cast-iron pan with a small rim and a handle that can be laid flat. It can be used for frying meat and vegetables or cooking pancakes, pikelets, griddle cakes and unleavened bread.

The griddle is an ancient piece of cooking equipment and was originally a large, flat stone heated from below by a fire with the surface used for baking called a griddle, girdle or bakestone.

BEST WITHOUT SIDES

Do I have to buy a griddle pan to make pikelets, or can I use a normal frying pan?

Bannocks, pikelets, oatcakes, tattie scones and Welsh cakes are all best made on a griddle, although it is possible to improvise. You can use a large heavy-based or nonstick frying pan or an electric frypan, but if the sides are too deep, you may have trouble turning the food.

CHARRED LINES

How can I create at home those wonderful brown charred lines that I see on restaurant food?

The brown charred lines on restaurant food are created either by cooking the food on a chargrill or by placing very hot skewers on the cooked food in a trellis pattern.

Charcoal-fuelled chargrills, similar to indoor barbecues, are available for home use from some manufacturers of high quality ovens. These slot into the kitchen bench alongside the stove top. Portable electric 'chargrills' are also available from department stores.

A similar effect can be created by using a ridged griddle or pan (see box, above right). Chicken portions, fish, steaks, as well as eggplants, zucchinis and peppers are delicious cooked in this way.

USING A GRIDDLE

The griddle, a heavy, cast-iron plate or pan, stands over heat for frying. The traditional griddle is flat and is used for pikelets, but some griddles now have ridges, which give an attractive stripe to meat and vegetables as they cook.

Heat the griddle slowly until very hot, then place lightly oiled food onto the surface. Move it after a few seconds, so it does not stick, then leave to brown. Turn and repeat.

Grilling

NECESSARY HEAT

I want to do more grilling as I believe it is healthier than frying. What do I need to know?

Intense heat is the secret of successful grilling. Although this method of cooking requires close attention, the advantages are that the food cooks quickly and the charred surface gives an excellent flavour.

To produce succulent meat that is crisply brown outside and juicy pink inside, it is essential to preheat the grill to its highest setting. This may take 5 or even 10 minutes on a domestic stove.

Under a cooler grill, the meat's surface will not brown quickly and juices will leak out, leaving the meat dry, tasteless and unattractive by the time it is cooked through. If the grill cannot be adequately preheated to ensure that the meat and fish are quickly sealed, it would be better to pan-fry the food instead.

Unlike slow methods of cooking such as braising, grilling will not tenderise meat, so use only tender, choice cuts. For best results, these should not be much more than 5 cm or so thick, otherwise the outside of the meat will be burnt before the inside is cooked.

Ensure the meat is at room temperature before you start grilling otherwise a chilled steak will still be cold inside when the outside is brown and sizzling. This is particularly important if the steak is to be served very rare.

Once the meat has been sealed on both sides, you can reduce the fierceness of the grilling process. It is best to do this, if possible, by lowering the pan a little to increase the distance of the food from the heat rather than by reducing the temperature of the grill itself.

Grilling is considered healthier than frying as the excess fat can drip away during cooking, so it is good for bacon, oily fish, chops, cutlets, kebabs, sausages and steak.

A GOOD TURN

How should you turn food while it is being grilled?

Turn the grilling food with tongs or spoons, not a sharp instrument, which would pierce the meat and allow the juices to escape.

DELAY THE SALT

Why do my recipe books say not to salt meat before grilling?

Salt draws moisture from the meat's cells, so salting in advance may make it dry and tough. Instead, salt meat during or after grilling.

To the rescue!

Brush food for grilling with butter, oil or a mixture of the two to keep it moist and to speed the browning process. This oiling is essential with delicate foods such as fish to prevent them from sticking to the grill pan.

Ham

PRESERVATION TECHNIQUE

What is the difference between ham and gammon?

Ham is a pig's hind leg, first cut off the carcass and then smoked, salted or dried (or a combination of these) for preservation.

Gammon also comes from the hind leg but it is cured as part of a side of bacon and cut off afterwards. (See also **Bacon**.)

Gammon may be smoked separately or left unsmoked but it is not matured long enough to have a strong ham flavour and does not keep for as long as ham, which is generally cured more slowly. While some hams are meant for further cooking, some such as Parma and Bayonne hams are simply eaten in the 'raw' cured state, having been salted and then dried over several months to preserve the flesh.

Hams may also be smoked over a slow fire, and the different types of wood used, such as beech, juniper or oak, will each produce a distinctive flavour. Unsmoked hams are also known as green hams and have a milder flavour.

You can buy an uncooked whole ham to bake as a special dish, but in Australia most ham is sold cooked and sliced, and is used for salads and sandwiches, or included in recipes where it just needs to be heated through. Gammon can be hard to find, but is available from specialist butchers, especially if they sell traditional British cuts. It is sold in joints, rashers or steaks for cooking at home.

BOIL OR BAKE

What is the best way to cook a whole ham at home?

If you want to cook a ham yourself, you will have to order a whole or half joint from the butcher. If the ham is dry-cured and salty it may need soaking overnight in cold water before you cook it, so consult your supplier when you take delivery of the ham.

Hams can be boiled or baked. To boil, put the ham in a large pan of fresh clean water, bring it to the boil, and then simmer it gently for 40 minutes per kg plus 20 minutes extra.

If serving hot, rest the joint for 30 minutes before carving (see panel, below). To serve cold, cool in the water, drain and then remove

Save it!

To prevent cooked ham from discolouring or drying out, wrap it closely in plastic wrap. Joints will keep for up to ten days in the refrigerator, but slices should be eaten within a few days. Alternatively, wrap the ham in a calico ham bag, previously rinsed in cold water and wrung out. Store in the refrigerator.

the skin and press brown breadcrumbs into the fat.

To bake a ham, wrap the joint loosely in foil and place in a baking dish. Cook in a 160°C oven for

HOW TO CARVE A HAM

Because a ham is so large, you need a special long, slim ham knife with a rounded tip to carve it properly. Make sure that it is razor sharp.

1 With the ham lying flat, fat side up, on a board and the knuckle bone pointing towards you, cut even slices along the side of the ham, parallel to the main bone of the leg, using a ham carving knife and fork.

2 After cutting a few slices, you will meet resistance from a small bone located near the knuckle end. Remove this bone with a small pointed knife, then continue cutting slices until you almost reach the main bone.

3 With the ham still lying flat on the surface, cut slices from the large end of the ham - the end opposite the knuckle bone. Continue cutting slices in this direction until the leg's ball and cartilage are fully exposed.

4 Stand the ham on its cut side and slice vertically towards the bone, then horizontally along the bone to release the slices. Grasp the knuckle and trim off the remaining meat by cutting parallel to the main bone.

40 minutes per kg. Thirty minutes before the end of the time, take out the ham and raise the oven temperature to 220°C. Drain off the juices, cut off the skin and score the fat in a diamond pattern. Stud with cloves, spread generously with English or French mustard and then press brown or demerara sugar all over. Return to the oven to finish cooking and then allow the ham to rest for 30 minutes before carving, or leave to cool overnight.

To serve, add a paper frill (see panel, page 173) and serve hot with new potatoes and freshly cooked vegetables or cold with a selection of salads.

Cumberland sauce, either home-made or bought in a jar from a good delicatessen or supermarket, is a traditional accompaniment, as are a selection of hot and mild tasty mustards.

MAKING THE MOST OF IT

Can you suggest some interesting ways for me to make use of any leftover baked ham?

Parsley is a good match for baked ham. Try flavouring aspic or a light jellied stock with parsley and white wine, then pour into a terrine which you have filled with rugged pieces of baked ham. Leave to set in the refrigerator for a few hours, turn out, then slice and serve cold with a green salad.

You could also stir some pieces of leftover ham into a German-style casserole of sausage, beans, cabbage and onion for a hearty winter lunch or dinner.

SUPER STEAKS

My family is very fond of pan-fried ham steaks. Is it possible to cook slices of leftover baked ham in the same way?

Yes, it is. Thick slices of leftover ham can be pan-fried as long as the pan is lightly greased and the ham is just heated through gently. Do not use too high a heat – or cook for too long – as the meat will toughen and dry out.

GLAZING OVER

I have enjoyed glazed leg ham at large buffet parties. Could I glaze a smaller piece of ham at home for a dinner party?

Yes, you can. It is not difficult to make a glaze, and is a good way to make a ham joint look special. The glaze in the recipe (below) uses a mixture of sweet and strong flavours to add a rich, distinctive coating to the piece of ham.

The joint can be eaten hot as soon as it is cooked, or served cold.

Glazed ham

SERVES: 8
PREPARATION TIME: *20 minutes*
COOKING TIME: *1¼ hours for a 1.5 kg joint*

FOR THE HAM
1.5 kg ham joint
4-6 tablespoons dry white wine or stock
Whole cloves

FOR THE GLAZE
1 tablespoon clear honey
45 g (¼ cup) dark brown sugar
1 tablespoon wholegrain mustard
1 teaspoon grated fresh green ginger
2 tablespoons orange juice
Black pepper

A family-sized ham joint, studded with cloves and covered with an aromatic glaze, is transformed into a spectacular-looking party piece.

1 Preheat the oven to 180°C. Place a piece of foil large enough to enclose the ham joint in a large baking dish, put the ham onto it and lift up the sides of the foil. Pour the wine or stock gently over the ham and then fold the foil loosely over it, sealing the edges tightly so moisture does not escape. Bake the ham for 40 minutes per kg – about 1 hour for a joint weighing 1.5 kg.
2 While the ham is baking, stir the honey, sugar, mustard, ginger and orange juice together. Add a good grinding of black pepper
3 When the ham is cooked, remove it from the oven and unwrap it. Turn up the oven heat to 200°C. Using a sharp knife, slice between the skin and fat of the ham, pulling the skin back as you move across the joint, until the skin comes away. Score the layer of fat in crisscross parallel lines spaced about 2 cm apart to form diamond patterns, taking care not to pierce the meat. Then place the ham on a rack in the baking dish.
4 Stud the ham with cloves and brush with the glaze. Return to the oven and bake for 15 minutes. Serve immediately, with the vegetables of your choice, or leave until cold.

Thin slices of sweet, salty prosciutto paired with fruit, asparagus, olives, Parmesan cheese or bread sticks, make sophisticated canapés or starters.

JUST FOR STARTERS

What can I do with prosciutto besides serve it with melon?

Prosciutto (Parma ham), and the other air-dried hams such as Bayonne, can also be served with figs, or try wrapping the paper-thin slices around bread sticks to serve with drinks.

A very simple Italian-style starter involves placing the ham slices flat on each plate, sprinkling them with flakes of Parmesan and dressing with a vinaigrette made of olive oil, lemon juice and seasonings.

Prosciutto is generally wasted in cooked dishes except where it adds a hint of flavour. Try it puréed with ricotta as a filling for homemade ravioli or tortellini.

COSTLY PROCESS

Why are some hams so much more expensive than others?

It is the way ham is produced and cured that most affects the cost. Dry-cured hams are generally more expensive than hams cured in brine as dry-curing takes longer. After salting, the ham may be smoked over fragrant wood and left to age for three months to two years. Traditionally produced dry-cured hams such as Parma (prosciutto) and Bayonne are particularly costly as they take great skill to produce and need more time to mature.

The pigs' feed is another factor affecting the cost and flavour of the finished ham. In the United States, peaches are used for feed in Georgia and peanuts in Virginia, making the hams more expensive.

The following hams are some of the most famous varieties from around the world:

- BAYONNE: French dry-cured ham similar to Parma, eaten raw.
- BRADENHAM: dark red English ham pickled in molasses, juniper berries and spices until the skin turns a distinctive black; strong, sweet flavour; sold cooked.
- COPPA: small, raw Italian ham, air-dried; is similar to prosciutto.
- HAM DE LUXE: a luxury German cut made from the cured loin of lean pork which is smoked.
- JAMBON D'ARDENNES: Belgian ham best sliced thinly; eaten raw.
- KENTUCKY: American ham that is smoked over apple, sassafras or hickory wood; eaten raw.
- PICNIC HAM: not a true ham as it is cut from the shoulder of the pig, but cured in the same way; less expensive; sold cooked.
- PRAGUE: ham from the Czech Republic; smoked over beech; good in hot dishes; sold cooked.
- PROSCIUTTO DI PARMA: Italian ham from pigs fattened on the whey

HOW TO MAKE A PAPER FRILL FOR BAKED HAM

A crisp white frill adds the final touch to a party ham. Use an A4 sheet of paper. The same technique can be used to make smaller frills for lamb cutlets and crown roasts.

1 Lightly fold the paper into halves lengthways. Make 5 mm parallel cuts along the folded edge, cutting two-thirds of the way down.

2 Unfold the cut paper, then fold it back on itself the other way to make the loops open out.

3 Wind the base of the frill round your fingers. Slip off and push up from inside to stagger the loops.

4 Secure the join in the base with a pin or non-toxic glue. Slip the frill over the end of the ham bone.

left over after Parmesan cheese is made; eaten raw.

- SERRANO: Spanish ham matured for about ten months, stronger in flavour than Parma; eaten raw.
- SMITHFIELD: originally from pigs fed on peanuts then cured and processed in Smithfield, Virginia, USA; hickory-smoked and covered with pepper; sold cooked.
- SPECK: smoked ham from Italy; similar to Westphalian.
- SUFFOLK: sweet-cured English ham similar to Bradenham; blue-black skin and rich red-brown meat; sold cooked.
- SUGAR-GLAZED: boneless ham that has been coated with sugar, honey or treacle; sold cooked.
- WESTPHALIAN: German raw ham with a dark coloured rind created by long smoking over beech and juniper twigs; eaten raw.
- YORK: the best-known English ham; mild and usually coated in breadcrumbs; sold cooked.

Hamburgers

HOMEMADE VERSION

My children insist on eating hamburgers. Could you give me a healthy recipe?

The best way to guarantee healthy hamburgers is to make them yourself. Homemade mince has a better flavour and texture than bought mince and you can cut off all fat.

Use a good quality cut of Lean beef as the burgers will be cooked quickly and so need to be tender. Alternatively, try Trim lamb, which also has a lower fat content. Buying your own meat to make into hamburgers also means you can enjoy organic or free-range burgers if that is what you prefer.

Use a food processor fitted with the knife blade or the coarse blade of a mincer to process the meat. Or pile it onto a board and chop it finely (see box, right). The following recipe does not include cereal, so there is no need to use an egg to bind the mixture.

Hamburgers

SERVES: *4*
PREPARATION TIME: *15 minutes*
COOKING TIME: *about 10 minutes*

750 g Lean round or topside steak, trimmed of fat
Salt and black pepper
1 small onion, optional
2 tablespoons chopped parsley
2 teaspoons Worcestershire sauce

1 Preheat the grill and brush the grill rack with oil. Chop the meat.
2 Put the minced meat into a bowl and add salt and pepper.
3 Grate the onion and allow it to sweat lightly in a little oil or butter before adding it to the meat.
4 Add the parsley and the Worcestershire sauce and mix well.
5 With wet hands, form the mixture into even-sized patties 2.5 cm thick, without pressing them firmly together. The mixture will make four to eight hamburgers, depending on the size of the patties.
6 Grill for 4–6 minutes on each side, depending on the thickness of the burgers and how well you like them cooked. Serve with salad and toasted white or wholemeal rolls, or on hamburger buns.

CHOPPING UP MEAT FOR A HAMBURGER

Producing top quality hamburger mince in your own kitchen is easy using two knives and a board.

Chop the meat finely using two large knives, holding them loosely and parallel to each other. Lift each up and down in turn, using a rhythmic movement. Occasionally turn the meat with the flat of the knives. Continue chopping until the meat resembles a fine mince.

HERBS

◆

Nothing improves food so simply and dramatically as a leaf or two of fresh herbs. They offer every sort of flavour from grassy to peppery, aromatic to pungent. They will boost a casserole, add summer to a salad and enhance a sauce. Study this guide to the best culinary herbs for great ideas and partnerships.

GREEN BASIL

PURPLE BASIL

BAY

CHERVIL

CHIVES

CORIANDER

DILL

A yoghurt sauce crammed with aromatic dill and spiced with mustard balances the richness of smoked salmon (see page 178).

ANGELICA
Angelica is rarely used fresh these days, as it cannot be bought raw. The young stems and leaf stalks are picked in the second year to be crystallised and used to decorate cakes and trifles, and this is now done commercially.

You could grow your own, but it is such a large plant (1.8–3 m) it can easily take over a small garden.

BASIL
The three main varieties of basil are the sweet green basil most familiar in Australia, Greek basil which has tiny green leaves, and purple basil. These share a rich, peppery flavour and a powerful aroma.

You can also purchase basils scented with lemon, anise and cinnamon. Basil is particularly good with tomatoes and is frequently used in Italian dishes and in other Mediterranean-style and Vietnamese recipes, especially with vegetables.

BAY
Unlike most herbs, aromatic bay leaves are equally good fresh and dried. Bay forms part of the classic bouquet garni, which is added to fish or meat stocks, soups and casseroles.

BORAGE
The most common use for borage is as a garnish for Pimms. Its vivid blue flowers contribute visual appeal as well as the faint flavour of cucumber to this summer drink.

CHERVIL
This delicate summer herb goes well with eggs, fish, chicken and boiled potatoes. It is a traditional part of the fines herbes mixture.

CHIVES
These bright-green stems have a fresh, oniony flavour and are delicious sprinkled on potato salad, baked potatoes and on vichyssoise soup. They provide a slightly hot contrast for bland creamy dishes.

CORIANDER
A powerfully flavoured herb that looks like flat-leaf parsley, coriander has a special affinity with chillies, garlic, ginger and spring onions, and often adds its heat to exotic food such as Thai dishes, stir-fries and salsas.

DILL
The delicate flavour of dill means it goes splendidly with fish, shellfish, boiled potatoes

and cream cheese. It is also good in sauces and dips made with mustard or sour cream, and it is traditionally used when curing salmon, as in the Scandinavian dish, gravlax.

FENNEL
Fennel is very similar to dill but with a coarser, stronger flavour. It is most often paired with fish and is often burnt under mullet when it is being barbecued to add an unusual smoky flavour.

LEMON BALM
Lemon balm may be used as a substitute for lemon grass or for making tisanes. Its strongly perfumed flavour can be an acquired taste.

LOVAGE
Lovage is a robust plant with an assertive flavour, a little like celery. It is best used sparingly in hearty dishes such as tomato soup or a pasta sauce.

MARJORAM/OREGANO
These two herbs are actually different varieties of the same plant. Sweet or knotted marjoram is the variety usually grown, while wild marjoram (oregano) is used in the Mediterranean for such dishes as pizzas and tomato sauces served with pasta. Marjoram is milder than oregano.

MINT
Mint is frequently used in the Middle East in yoghurt sauces and salads such as tabbouleh. Tea flavoured with mint is a popular drink throughout North Africa and the Middle East. Mint is also used for sauces or jellies to serve traditionally in many Western countries with roast lamb, new potatoes and green peas.

PARSLEY
There are two types of parsley, curly and flat. Choose curly parsley for dishes such as salmon fish cakes and parsley sauce, and for deep-frying to serve as a garnish with goujons of sole. Use the flat variety in Middle Eastern dishes, soups, salads and as a fresh garnish.

ROSEMARY
This has a very pronounced flavour and should be used sparingly. It is best kept for roast or baked lamb, chicken and potato dishes.

SAGE
The dominant flavour of sage goes well with pork, liver, onions and pasta, and the herb is a prime ingredient of the Italian dish of fried calf's liver and onions called *fegato alla Veneziana*. Whole fresh leaves may be fried in butter and scattered over dishes of grilled or baked vegetables.

SALAD BURNET
Less well known than other herbs, salad burnet makes a wonderful flavouring for wine vinegar. It is also good used in salads made with tomato, cucumber and lettuce.

SAVORY
Savory is much used in French cooking, particularly with broad beans. It also acts as a flavour enhancer for other vegetables. Unlike most herbs, its robust flavour develops with long cooking and it is one of the handful of herbs that dries well.

SWEET CICELY
Used mainly in cooking sweet dishes, sweet cicely reduces the acidity of food such as rhubarb and cooking apples without the use of sugar.

TARRAGON
Fresh tarragon has a sweet and spicy flavour well suited to eggs, white fish, chicken, potatoes and cream sauces. The French variety is the one to use; Russian tarragon has little value as a flavouring and tarragon preserved in vinegar makes a better substitute.

THYME
Thyme is easy to grow and can be dried or frozen without any loss of flavour. It is best in Provençal-type dishes, meat or poultry casseroles and with tomatoes, cheese and mustard.

SPECIAL COLLECTIONS
● BOUQUET GARNI consists of three sprigs of parsley, two of thyme and a bay leaf, often tied up with a celery stalk or a section of leek, and added to casseroles and stocks.
● FINES HERBES is a mixture of four fresh herbs – chervil, chives, parsley and tarragon – and is best used for quickly cooked foods such as eggs.
● HERBES DE PROVENCE is a mixture of five or six dried herbs. Rosemary and thyme are always present, plus some marjoram, savory, tarragon and/or basil. It is used in slow-cooked stews.

TARRAGON
THYME
SAGE
MINT

LEMON BALM
ROSEMARY
MARJORAM
BOUQUET GARNI

Herbs

STORING FRESH HERBS

Freshly cut herbs seem to wilt fast. What's the best way to store them?

Wrap herbs loosely in paper towels and put in a green plastic long-life bag; they will keep for five to six days in the refrigerator crisper.

SOFT-FROZEN

Can herbs be frozen?

All the tender herbs, such as basil, chervil and tarragon, freeze well, with the exception of parsley which turns to slush when defrosted. The tougher woody herbs, such as bay, rosemary, sage and thyme, tend to splinter, so it is better to dry these.

To freeze herbs, wrap them in foil or small plastic bags and seal well. It is useful to label the parcels if you cannot see inside them.

PRESERVING IN OIL

Can some herbs be preserved in olive oil instead of being dried?

This used to be done with basil before people owned freezers, but freezing is much more effective.

HOME DRYING

Can I dry my own fresh herbs, and should all herbs be dried in the same way?

Most fresh herbs are easily dried, and the same method applies to all of them, but bay, marjoram, mint, rosemary, sage, savory and thyme dry particularly well.

They should be freshly picked, then quickly rinsed and patted dry before being spread on racks and covered lightly with muslin. Then put them in a warm, dry place out of direct sunlight. They will take about a week to dry.

Most herbs are best stripped off their stems before being stored in sealed jars, but some herbs, such as thyme, may be left on the branch and stored upright in the jar.

TIME TO HARVEST

Can herbs be picked at any time for use in the kitchen?

No, they can be picked only up to the point of flowering. Once herbs have developed buds and flowered, all their energy goes into producing seeds and woody stems, and consequently their flavour is dissipated. For freezing or drying, herbs are best picked immediately before they flower, when their flavour is at its most potent.

Small pots of fresh-growing herbs are frequently available in fresh produce stores throughout the year.

DRIED INSTEAD OF FRESH

Can I substitute dried herbs for fresh ones, and if so, should I use them in the same amounts?

It is hard to give an exact formula for using dried herbs instead of fresh, as the flavour of both is such a variable factor. With fresh herbs, the flavour depends on how fresh they are and how they have been grown: the soil, climate and time of picking. With dried herbs, it depends on how long and in what conditions they have been kept. Assuming both supplies are fresh and in good condition, allow one teaspoon of dried herbs for each tablespoon of fresh.

In some cases, it is possible to replace one fresh herb with a different, dried one. Dried mint can often be used to replace fresh coriander, for instance, as both herbs marry well with cool, sharp, juicy flavours such as cucumber, garlic, tomatoes and yoghurt.

Freshness test

Dried herbs lose their aroma and their flavour quickly. If you think yours may be too old to use in cooking, test with a sniff. Musty herbs do not need to be thrown out, however: you can sprinkle them over the soil of indoor plants to give a fertilising boost.

HERBS IN SALAD

Can you give me a good recipe for a fresh herb salad?

Scatter a mixture of four or five tender herbs – chives, chervil, salad burnet, flat parsley or tarragon, for instance – over the small, tender leaves of mignonette lettuce. Edible flowers such as borage or nasturtium add colour (see also *Crystallised Flowers*). Complement the fresh flavours with a light dressing of olive oil and lemon juice.

CORIANDER: TWO IN ONE

Do the seeds of coriander give the same flavour as the fresh leaf?

Absolutely not. Their flavours are totally different, and they cannot be used as substitutes for each other. Coriander seeds have a gentle, citrus-like aroma, while the leaves are somewhat bitter. The seeds survive long heating well, but the fresh leaves should be added near the end of cooking or sprinkled over the finished dish.

To enjoy the full spicy flavour of the fresh herb, try the following salsa. Its clear, sharp flavour goes well with grilled mixed vegetables, chicken, fish or shellfish.

Coriander salsa

SERVES: 4
PREPARATION TIME: 15 minutes
COOKING TIME: none

---

4 vine-ripened tomatoes, unskinned, cut into quarters
1 bunch spring onions, thinly sliced
1-2 red chillies, deseeded and finely chopped
2 tablespoons lemon juice
2 tablespoons chopped fresh coriander
Sea salt and black pepper

---

1 Put the quartered tomatoes in a food processor and mix until they are reduced to a lumpy texture.
2 Turn the mixture out into a bowl and stir in all the other ingredients. Taste the salsa; if it seems too spicy, add another chopped tomato. Serve cool but not chilled.

FRAGILE BASIL

Why do some people say that it is not advisable to cook basil?

Basil is a fragile herb which suffers some loss of flavour when subjected to heat or drying. In most recipes, you can minimise the loss of flavour by adding basil near the end of the cooking time. However, it is most flavourful when used fresh, as in the Italian sauce pesto, or as a garnish added after cooking, as in this recipe for Grilled Vegetable Salad. The salad is served at room temperature, and is delicious as a starter with some crusty bread to mop up the dressing.

Grilled vegetable salad with basil

SERVES: 4 as a starter
PREPARATION TIME: 45 minutes
COOKING TIME: 50 minutes

---

1 red pepper
1 yellow pepper
1 eggplant
1 head fennel
2 red onions
4 tablespoons olive oil
1 clove garlic, finely chopped
Sea salt and black pepper

FOR THE DRESSING
3 tablespoons virgin olive oil
2 teaspoons white wine vinegar
To garnish: 6-8 leaves basil

---

1 Preheat the grill for 10 minutes. Quarter the peppers and scrape out the seeds. Put the wedges under the grill, skin side up, until the skins have blackened and blistered evenly all over. Let them cool slightly, peel off the skin then set aside.
2 Cut the eggplant lengthways in 1 cm slices, leaving the skin on, and brush with olive oil. Grill until golden brown, turning once. Drain on kitchen paper towels.
3 Cut the fennel lengthways in 1 cm slices. Brush one side with oil and grill until coloured, then oil the other side and grill that.
4 Peel the onions, cut each one into four wedges and brush with oil. Grill until soft and well browned.

The warm flavours of a salad of grilled vegetables are brought to life with a scattering of purple basil leaves and a side dish of spicy coriander salsa.

5 Arrange all the vegetables on a flat dish and scatter the chopped garlic over them, then season with salt and plenty of pepper. Mix the oil and vinegar together and spoon over. If the basil leaves are small, tuck them among the vegetables. If large, tear them in pieces and scatter on top.

SEEDS FOR LONG COOKING

Which are best for using in dishes that require lengthy cooking, fresh herbs or seeds?

Seeds are often better in dishes such as casseroles as most fresh herbs lose their taste when subjected to heat. However, the taste of seeds will be somewhat different. Instead, try finishing the dish with fresh herbs just before serving.

VEGETABLE PARTNERS

How do I choose which herbs to put with vegetables?

All herbs go well with vegetables. It is the nature of the dish, rather than the ingredients, that determines which herb to use. For example, a robust herb such as thyme is a good choice in oily Provençal-type stews or casseroles of mixed vegetables. Dill will add freshness to boiled or steamed carrots, lovage is excellent in hearty vegetable soups, while rosemary goes well with roast potatoes. Basil is the obvious choice for tomatoes and oregano is traditional with mixed Greek salads.

FISHY HERBS

Which herbs go best with fish?

Fennel is served with fish in France, and coriander in Thailand, while curly parsley is also popular.

The Scandinavians usually pair fish with dill, for instance in simple butter sauces or a mustard sauce such as the one below. This usually accompanies cured salmon (*gravlax*), but is also delicious with any cured or cooked fish, with chicken, and even cold boiled beef.

Dill and mustard sauce

SERVES: 4
PREPARATION TIME: 12 minutes
COOKING TIME: none

1 tablespoon Dijon mustard
1 tablespoon olive oil
125 ml yoghurt
Juice of 1 lemon
4 tablespoons chopped dill

1 Put the mustard in a bowl and whisk in the olive oil drop by drop, as if making mayonnaise.
2 When all the oil is amalgamated, gradually stir in the yoghurt. Add lemon juice to taste, sprinkle on the chopped dill and mix well.

VERSATILE PARSLEY

Can curly and flat-leaf parsley be substituted for each other?

Flat-leaf parsley, sometimes called Continental parsley, has a slightly mellower, fuller flavour, and is best used in Middle Eastern dishes (as in the recipe below) and in soups and salads. Use curly parsley for parsley sauce to accompany fish cakes and use as a garnish.

Tabbouleh

SERVES: 6
PREPARATION TIME: 35 minutes
COOKING TIME: None

125 g (⅔ cup) burghul
2 cups chopped flat-leaf parsley
¼ cup shredded mint
¼ cup thinly sliced spring onions
4 tablespoons olive oil
4 tablespoons lemon juice
1 vine-ripened tomato, diced
Salt and pepper

1 Put the burghul in a mixing bowl; add sufficient cold water to cover and leave to soak for 30 minutes.
2 Drain the burghul in a fine sieve, then wrap in muslin and squeeze out as much water as possible.
3 Mix the burghul, parsley, mint, spring onions, oil and lemon juice. Fold in the tomato; season to taste.
4 Cover and chill for 30 minutes before serving.

HERBS FOR CHICKEN

Which herbs go well with chicken?

Rosemary is as good with roast chicken as it is with lamb. Simply tuck a few branches between the wings and the body of the bird, and baste well with oil while roasting. Cook in a fairly hot oven so that the chicken browns well. Serve with roast potatoes and a crisp green salad, sprinkling on a few more rosemary leaves.

Other herbs that go well with chicken are lemon balm, sage, tarragon and thyme. They can either be cooked with the meat or added to a sauce served with it.

HERBAL TEAS

Which are the best herbs to use when making herbal teas?

The most popular herbs to infuse are camomile, hibiscus and peppermint. A mixture of mint and lime flower is very common in France, as is lemon verbena.

An unusual tea can be made with fresh sage. Simply put a handful of freshly gathered sage leaves in a small teapot and pour over about 500 ml of nearly boiling water. Then let it stand, covered, for 4–5 minutes, before pouring into cups. Sage tea is reputed to act as a digestive aid, an antiseptic and a slight stimulant. See also **Tisanes**.

FINELY CHOPPING FRESH HERBS

Herbs can be chopped with a kitchen knife, a two-handled mincing knife, or in a food processor. If using a blade, | *ensure it is sharp or you will crush and bruise the herbs. If using a machine, take care not to overchop into a purée.*

1 Wash and dry the herbs (parsley is shown here) and compress into a ball in the palms of your hands.

2 Chop the leaves coarsely, keeping your fingertips tucked well under, then scrape into a pile with the blade.

3 Hold the knife down at its tip and lever the handle up and down. Keep piling and slicing until finely chopped.

Hollandaise Sauce

CURDLE-FREE SAUCE

How do I stop hollandaise sauce from curdling during cooking?

This butter sauce will curdle if it overheats, so it must be cooked over a very gentle heat, if possible in a bain-marie (see panel, right).

If the hollandaise becomes granular during cooking, immediately remove the basin from the heat, place it in a bowl of cold water and stir the sauce to cool it quickly. Or, remove it from the heat at once and stir in 1 tablespoon of warm water.

To save a curdled sauce, break a fresh egg yolk into a bowl. Stir in 1 teaspoon of water, add a knob of butter and place the bowl over a pan of hot water. Stir the mixture gently until the butter has melted and the egg thickens slightly, then gradually add the curdled sauce, beating until smooth.

QUICKER METHODS

Is there a quick and easy way to make hollandaise sauce?

You can make hollandaise in a food processor or blender: lightly mix the egg yolks and vinegar reduction in the bowl then pour in the warm melted butter in a thin stream while the motor is running and process until thick and smooth.

Hollandaise can also be made in the microwave oven. Heat the butter, egg yolks and vinegar reduction together on High for 10 seconds. Remove from the microwave and whisk. Repeat the 10-second cooking followed by whisking until the sauce is thickened and smooth.

SAUCY DIFFERENCE

What is the difference between hollandaise and béarnaise sauce?

Both butter sauces are based on egg yolks but hollandaise is lightly flavoured with wine vinegar, while béarnaise has shallot and tarragon

added for a more piquant flavour. The Béarnaise Sauce below is delicious with roast fillet of beef, or steak or other grilled food.

Béarnaise sauce

SERVES: *2-4*
PREPARATION TIME: *10 minutes*
COOKING TIME: *15 minutes*

---

4 tablespoons tarragon or white
wine vinegar (or half dry white
wine and half vinegar)
1 shallot, chopped
6 peppercorns, crushed
1 bay leaf
1 sprig tarragon
2 large egg yolks
100 g butter, diced
1 teaspoon chopped tarragon leaves

---

1 Put the vinegar in a small pan and add the shallot, peppercorns, bay leaf and sprig of tarragon. Boil until reduced to 1 tablespoon.
2 Put the egg yolks in a small bowl, strain in the flavoured vinegar and whisk to a light foam. Place the bowl over a small pan of hot (but not boiling) water off the heat, making sure the bowl does not touch the water. Beat the mixture with a hand whisk until slightly thickened.
3 Put the pan and the bowl over a gentle heat. Gradually add the cubes of butter to the mixture, stirring continuously until all the fat has been incorporated and the sauce is thick and glossy. Stir in the chopped tarragon and serve the sauce warm, or at room temperature.

WAITING TIME

How long ahead can hollandaise or béarnaise be made?

Either sauce can be kept warm for up to an hour. Cover the bowl with plastic wrap and stand it over a pan of hot but not boiling water, removed from the heat. Before serving, beat the sauce well as it will have thickened as it cools. If the sauce has cooled too much, reheat the water in the saucepan, then replace the bowl of sauce and whisk it continuously until it is the required temperature.

MAKING HOLLANDAISE SAUCE

Rich and smooth hollandaise sauce is traditionally served warm with delicately flavoured fish, shellfish, asparagus and artichoke.

To make enough sauce for two people, you need 1 tablespoon each wine vinegar and water, 1 bay leaf, 6 peppercorns, 100 g butter and 2 large egg yolks.

1 Boil the vinegar, water, bay leaf and peppercorns together until the liquid is reduced by half. Strain into a bowl or the top of a double saucepan. Gently melt the butter.

2 Put the bowl with the vinegar reduction over a pan of very hot (but not boiling) water and, using a wooden spoon, mix in the yolks.

3 Remove the pan from the heat and gradually stir in the melted butter to give a creamy texture.

4 Return the pan to the heat and continue stirring over a very gentle heat for 8-10 minutes until the sauce becomes light, airy and glossy, and is just thick enough to drip off the spoon. Season to taste.

Honey

HONEY AND SUGAR

Is it true that honey is a healthier sweetener than sugar?

Honey contains a small amount of B-group vitamins and some minerals (calcium, chlorine, potassium and sodium), making it marginally healthier than white sugar, which contains some calcium and potassium but no vitamins at all. Golden demerara sugar contains slightly more minerals than honey does, but fewer vitamins.

In kilojoule content, 100 g honey has 1180–1220 kilojoules, while the same amount of sugar has about 1660 kilojoules. And as honey tastes sweeter than sugar, it is usually used in smaller quantities, reducing kilojoules further.

HONEY FOR COOKING

Can honey be used as a substitute for sugar in recipes?

Honey is good to use in cooking, especially baking, because it absorbs moisture better than sugar. This means that honey will keep breads and cakes moist for longer.

To substitute honey for sugar, use a spoonful of honey to every one-and-a-quarter spoons of sugar stated in the recipe. Note that as honey contains some water, the amount of liquid used in the recipe needs to be reduced slightly.

ORGANIC PRODUCTION

What is organic honey?

Organic honey is produced in areas remote from chemical and artificial sprays, the most notable places being in New Zealand and some forests in Africa, and the hives are not treated with chemicals.

In Australia, hives may be set in relatively pure land, but there can be no guarantees as to its 'organic' quality as bees often fly great distances – up to an 8 km radius – in their search for nectar.

SWEET VARIATIONS

Can I use a thick, set honey where a recipe says to use clear honey, and are some honeys better to cook with than others?

You can use any honey in cooking, but cloudy or set honey should be warmed first to liquefy it so it can be mixed in evenly.

It is generally best to use a light-coloured honey for cooking, as the flavour of darker honeys is too strong. Both the colour and flavour of different honeys are determined by the nectar the bees collect. Acacia honey, for instance, is thin, runny and pale, honey made from heather is thicker and sometimes cloudy, while clover honey is thick and pale amber. Mexican alcahual is almost pure white. Sage honey is very dark and strongly flavoured, as is lavender honey, which is amber with a green caste. Greek Hymettus has aromatic flavours of marjoram, savory and thyme.

A clear, light honey is the best choice for the following ice cream, where it adds richness and depth to a caramelised sugar syrup.

Burnt honey ice cream

SERVES: *4*
PREPARATION TIME: *50 minutes, plus cooling and freezing time*
COOKING TIME: *15–20 minutes*

4 large egg yolks
125 g (½ cup) caster sugar
300 ml milk
300 ml fresh cream, lightly whipped
125 g (½ cup) white sugar
3 tablespoons water
3 tablespoons clear honey

1 Beat the egg yolks and the caster sugar together briskly. Heat the milk until it just comes to boiling point and immediately pour it onto the egg and sugar mixture, whisking well.
2 Return the custard to the pan and heat it gently, stirring continuously until it thickens and just coats the back of the spoon. Strain the custard through a sieve and leave to cool completely, then stir in the cream.

3 Put the white sugar into a small saucepan, add 2 tablespoons of water and heat gently until the sugar has dissolved. Then bring the syrup to the boil and boil rapidly until it becomes a dark golden brown.
4 Remove the pan from the heat, cover your hands well with cloths to protect them and carefully add the remaining 1 tablespoon of water. The mixture will hiss and spit rather fiercely for a few seconds. Stir well, return the pan to the heat and cook for a further 1–2 minutes.

The syrup is ready when a small drop put onto a plate forms a soft ball when rolled between your fingers (dip your finger and thumb into iced water immediately before and after testing). You can also test it with a sugar thermometer, heating until the syrup reaches 115°C.
5 Remove the pan from the heat and allow the mixture to cool slightly, then stir in the honey.
6 When the honeyed syrup has cooled but is still liquid, stir it into the custard. Pour the mixture into a metal or plastic container, cover it, then freeze for 1–2 hours until it begins to harden to a depth of about 2.5 cm around the edges. Whisk the mixture well, then return it to the freezer. Repeat the freezing and whisking process twice more.

CRYSTAL CLEAR

Is crystallised honey usable?

Yes. Crystallisation does not affect either the taste or the nutritional value of honey. If there is only a little crystallisation, a good stir may solve the problem. If most of, or all the honey has become unpleasantly gritty, put the jar in a pan of very hot water and leave it for an hour. For quicker results, gently heat the pan of water containing the jar of honey on the stove. Use the honey while still warm, as it will recrystallise on cooling.

The following recipe for Baklava, the eastern Mediterranean sweetmeat, is a good way to use up gritty honey. The honey is added to a hot syrup which is then poured onto the pastry to seep through.

Baklava

MAKES: *16 pieces*
PREPARATION TIME: *45 minutes*
COOKING TIME: *1 hour*

FOR THE SYRUP
500 g (2 cups) caster sugar
300 ml water
1 tablespoon rosewater
1 tablespoon orange flower water
2 tablespoons lemon juice
4 tablespoons clear, strongly
   flavoured honey

FOR THE FILLING
400 g (3¼ cups) shelled walnuts,
   finely chopped
25 g (5 teaspoons) caster sugar
1 tablespoon ground cinnamon

FOR THE PASTRY
400 g prepared filo pastry
250 g unsalted butter, melted

1 To make the syrup, put the sugar and water into a pan and heat gently until the sugar has dissolved. Bring the mixture to a gentle boil and simmer for about 5 minutes until the syrup is still clear but has thickened enough to coat the back of a spoon.
2 Remove the saucepan from the heat and stir in the rosewater, orange flower water, lemon juice and honey. Leave the syrup to cool thoroughly then chill in the refrigerator.
3 To make the baklava filling, mix together the chopped walnuts, sugar and cinnamon in a small bowl to make a rough paste.
4 Lightly brush a shallow baking tin measuring 33×23 cm with melted butter. Take out the filo pastry but keep the sheets covered with a damp cloth or plastic wrap until you are ready to use them as they dry out very quickly. Preheat the oven to 150°C.
5 Place a sheet of filo in the bottom of the tin and brush it well with melted butter, then repeat until there are six stacked sheets. Spoon on about a quarter of the filling, cover with another five or six layers of buttered filo pastry sheets and then add more filling. Continue layering and filling in this way until you end with a layer of pastry.
6 With a sharp knife, cut the top layer of pastry into strips about 4 cm wide. Cut the strips with diagonal parallel lines 4 cm apart to form diamond shapes.
7 Bake for 45 minutes, then turn the temperature up to 200°C. Cook for a further 5–10 minutes or until the pastry is golden brown and puffed.
8 Remove from the oven and pour the cold syrup all over the baklava. Leave in the tin for at least 24 hours for the syrup to be fully absorbed. When ready to serve, cut into pieces following the original lines. Baklava will keep for up to a week in the refrigerator.

Horseradish

FRESH OR PROCESSED

Can you buy fresh horseradish?

The edible part of the horseradish plant, the small buff-coloured root, is usually found fresh only in good greengrocers, specialist food shops and large supermarkets, throughout autumn and winter. It is more commonly available already processed, finely grated and mixed with citric acid. Horseradish, which is rich in vitamin C, is almost always used in cold sauces like the recipe below, served with hot or cold roast or braised beef or smoked fish such as eel, mackerel and trout.

Horseradish sauce

SERVES: *4*
PREPARATION TIME: *10 minutes*
COOKING TIME: *none*

2 tablespoons fresh horseradish,
   peeled and grated
150 ml lightly whipped fresh cream
1-2 teaspoons lemon juice
Salt and white pepper

Stir the horseradish into the cream, add the lemon juice and season to taste. Keep refrigerated and eat within three days.

A fragrant honey syrup makes a rich treat of Baklava, a Greek speciality in which a sweet, nutty filling is layered between crisp sheets of paper-thin filo pastry.

Ice Cream and Sorbets

HAND-BEATEN

Is an ice cream machine essential for a really good result?

The short answer is no, although machines do make the job considerably easier, as it is essential to beat air into the mixture while it is freezing to break up the ice crystals and create a rich, smooth texture.

To make ice cream by hand, pour the mixture into a metal or plastic container and put it into the freezer for about 1½ hours. When it has started to freeze around the edges, you can either whizz it in a food processor for 20 seconds, or tip it into a bowl and beat vigorously by hand or with an electric whisk.

Return the slushy ice cream to the container and pop it back into the freezer, and repeat the process another two or three times until you achieve the right consistency.

MECHANICAL HELP

There are so many different types of ice cream machine. Can you advise on which one to choose?

The simplest type of machine consists of a container set inside a bucket, which you pack with ice and salt. The ice cream is then churned either by hand or electrically. These machines make very successful ice cream, but they can be messy to clean up.

Sorbetières, used for both sorbets and ice cream, have electric motors; they are designed for use in the

MAKING VANILLA CUSTARD ICE CREAM

Ice cream is easy to make without an electric ice cream machine. The following vanilla ice cream, made with a thick custard base, will serve up to six people. You will need 4 egg yolks, 125 g (½ cup) caster sugar, 300 ml milk, 300 ml fresh or thickened lightly whipped cream and 1½ teaspoons vanilla essence.

1 Beat the egg yolks with the caster sugar. Heat the milk to just under boiling point then whisk it into the egg mixture. Heat the custard gently, without boiling, in a heavy-based pan.

2 Stir the custard continuously with a wooden spoon until the mixture thickens and lightly coats the back of the spoon. Strain through a sieve into a bowl; leave until cold, then chill.

3 With a metal spoon, stir the cream and vanilla essence into the chilled custard. Pour the mixture into a metal or plastic container and freeze for an hour or two until the edges are frozen but give when pressed with a finger.

4 Tip the mixture into a bowl and whisk well, or put into a food processor and beat. Pour the ice cream back into the container and return it to the freezer. Repeat the freezing and whisking process twice more.

freezer, and have a thin power supply cord to enable you to shut the freezer door. Another version has a removable coolant-filled canister which you freeze overnight before churning. These machines are usually quite small.

For people who make ice cream regularly, a large machine with integral refrigeration is worth considering – they are excellent but expensive and take up the same space as a microwave.

SMOOTHER RESULTS

What is the best way to make fresh fruit ice cream?

Ice cream can be made with cream, custard, or a mixture of the two, and recipes with a large amount of butterfat produce the best results when made by hand. Most fruit ice creams are made with a cream rather than a custard base as cream allows more of the fruit flavour to come through. However, a custard base produces smaller ice crystals and will result in a smoother ice cream. If using strawberries, their flavour may be diminished slightly, but can be intensified by adding some strawberry jam.

You can use any berries in the following recipe for cream-based Summer Fruit Ice Cream, but raspberries on their own are watery; it is best to add some other fruit, such as strawberries or blackberries.

Soft fruits such as these need no cooking before being incorporated into ice cream, but you could also use fruit that needs cooking first, such as apples, apricots, pears, plums or rhubarb. Simmer them in a little water, with sugar to taste, until they are just tender, or longer for a purée (depending on how smooth you want your ice cream to be), then continue with the recipe.

A glorious fruit ice cream, made with a mixture of summer berries, is a feast for both the eyes and the palate.

Summer fruit ice cream

SERVES: 8
PREPARATION TIME: 20 minutes plus at least 6 hours freezing
COOKING TIME: none

---

1 kg prepared fresh berries such as
   blackberries, raspberries
   or strawberries
2 tablespoons lemon juice
350 g (2 cups) icing sugar
600 ml fresh cream

---

1 Put the fruit, lemon juice and icing sugar into a food processor and blend until smooth. With a wooden spoon, press the mixture through a nylon sieve into a large bowl, then discard the seeds. Alternatively, if you have no food processor, start by pushing the fruit through a nylon sieve set over a large bowl. Then mix the fruit purée with the lemon juice and icing sugar, stirring well.

2 Whip the cream until it forms very soft peaks, then fold it gently into the fruit mixture.

3 To freeze the mixture without an ice cream machine, pour it into a metal or plastic container, cover and freeze for about 1½ hours until the edges of the ice cream are frozen and the centre is soft. Remove from the freezer and beat until the whole mixture is slushy then return to the freezer. Repeat this process at least twice more. For maximum flavour, eat within two weeks.

VARIATION

For a smoother custard base, mix a few drops of vanilla essence into 500 ml milk and heat gently. Whisk 5 egg yolks with 60 g (¼ cup) sugar and stir this into the hot milk. Heat gently, stirring, until it thickens then leave it to cool. Fold the custard instead of the cream into the fruit purée then freeze.

SMART TURNOUT

What is the best way to turn out a finished ice cream smoothly from a metal mould?

Simply dip a tea towel in hot water, wring it out and wrap it around the mould for a few seconds. Then invert the mould over a plate, give it a good shake and the ice cream should be released. Metal is the best material for ice cream moulds as it conducts cold and heat well.

LUSCIOUS SAUCE

How can I make a fruit sauce to pour over ice cream?

Soft fruits such as blueberries and raspberries are especially good to make into a sauce. Stew the fruit gently in a tablespoon or two of water, with added sugar and a liqueur if you like, until the juices

MAKING A LEMON AND LIME SORBET

Sorbets are made with fruit and a sugar syrup; egg whites can be added to help prevent crystals from forming. For six people, you need 250g (1 cup) caster sugar, the rind and juice of 2 lemons and 4 limes, and 2 egg whites.

1 Put the sugar into a pan with 125 ml water and heat gently, stirring continuously, until the sugar dissolves. Then bring the liquid to the boil and immediately remove the pan from the heat.

2 Add the lemon and lime rind to the hot sugar syrup, then cool the syrup to room temperature.

3 Strain the cooled syrup into a bowl, stir in the fruit juice then pour the mixture into a container and freeze until it resembles slush.

4 Whisk the egg whites to soft peak stage, then add the slushy sorbet in large spoonfuls and gently whisk. Return the mixture to the freezer until it is icy and half-frozen. Remove and stir gently with a fork, then return to the freezer until solid.

run. Then purée the fruit, by hand or in a food processor, and push through a sieve to remove the pips. Serve warm or cold.

WATER ICES

What is the difference between a granita and a sorbet?

Both are based on a sugar syrup but a granita is much coarser, with a consistency somewhat like fluffy snow, whereas a sorbet is smooth-textured. A granita contains much less sugar than a sorbet and should be eaten on the day it is made as the texture deteriorates.

ADDING EGGS TO SORBETS

Is it common for sorbet recipes to include a meringue mixture?

A sorbet does not usually contain any milk or egg. However, some recipes for homemade sorbet add lightly whisked egg whites (see panel, left) to lighten the mixture. This also helps to prevent the formation of crystals and adds an opaque look to the finished ice.

Generally, sorbets are made from a mix of fruit juice or purée and a sugar syrup. The denser the sugar syrup, the smoother and sweeter the sorbet will be.

ADDING YOGHURT

Can you add yoghurt to sorbet?

You can make delicious low-fat ice creams by making a sorbet and adding low-fat yoghurt to the mixture before freezing. Greek-style yoghurt is particularly good for this but has a slightly higher fat content.

SORBETS AS STARTERS

Can you make savoury sorbets?

Savoury sorbets are easy to make from such ingredients as avocados, cucumbers, red peppers and tomatoes. Use virtually any ingredient that will blend well with a sugar syrup, as in the Tomato and Red Pepper Sorbet, right. These savoury sorbets are delicious as starters or as refreshers between courses.

Tomato and red pepper sorbet

SERVES: 8
PREPARATION TIME: 40 minutes plus at least 5 hours freezing
COOKING TIME: 10 minutes

---

2 large red peppers
2 tablespoons sunflower oil
60 g (¼ cup) caster sugar
300 ml water
500 g tomato purée or passata
½ teaspoon salt
Juice of ½ large lemon
1 teaspoon Worcestershire sauce
1 teaspoon soy sauce
A few drops Tabasco sauce
White pepper

---

1 Preheat the grill to medium hot. Cut the peppers into quarters and remove the seeds and membranes. Brush them with 1 tablespoon oil, place skin side up on a grill rack, then grill until the skin is blistered and blackened and the flesh is soft. Allow to cool. Peel off and discard the skin and set the peppers aside.
2 To make the syrup, put the sugar and water into a pan and heat gently, stirring from time to time, until the sugar has dissolved. Bring to the boil and simmer for 4–5 minutes until a thick syrup forms that reaches 115°C on a sugar thermometer. (If you do not have a thermometer, drop a little ball of syrup into a small bowl of very cold water. When gathered together with your fingertips, it should form a soft ball.) Then leave the syrup to cool completely.
3 Put the cold syrup, along with the peppers, remaining oil and all the remaining ingredients into a food processor and blend until smooth.
4 Pour the mixture into a shallow freezer container, cover and freeze for about 1½ hours or until mushy.
5 Remove the soft sorbet from the freezer and beat well, then return to the freezer. Repeat the freezing and beating process twice more.
6 About 30 minutes before serving, move the sorbet into the refrigerator to allow it to soften a little. Serve small scoops in hollowed-out tomato halves or avocado halves, or with a salad garnish and thin crisp toast.

ICE CREAM BISCUITS

How do I make biscuit 'baskets' to use as a container for ice cream?

The easiest way to do this is to make thin, lacy biscuits and press them over oranges while they are still warm and pliable. In the recipe below, chopped almonds add a crunchy texture which is a pleasant contrast to the softness of the ice cream. Note that small shells are most successful as the weight of a larger biscuit can break the shape.

Ice cream shells

MAKES: 16–18 shells
PREPARATION TIME: 25 minutes
COOKING TIME: 8 minutes per batch

125 g (½ cup) caster sugar
125 g unsalted butter
60 g (½ cup) plain flour
50 g (½ cup) chopped almonds
3–4 small oranges for shaping

1 Preheat the oven to 200°C and line two baking trays with nonstick baking paper.
2 Put the sugar, butter and flour in a bowl, beat for 2–3 minutes until well mixed, then stir in the almonds.
3 Put a few rounded teaspoons of the mixture onto the baking trays, leaving a large gap between each one, and flatten with the back of a wet fork. Bake for 7–8 minutes until golden but still slightly pale in the centre, then leave on the trays for no more than a minute to set a little.
4 While the biscuits are still warm, carefully remove them with a palette knife and drape each one gently over a lightly oiled orange, then mould the biscuits around the oranges. (If a shell is now too firm, return it to the oven for a few seconds to soften.)
5 Leave the shells draped over the oranges for a few minutes to let them harden, then lift them off gently and transfer to a wire cooling tray.
6 Repeat the process with the rest of the mixture, then store the shells in an airtight container until ready to use. They will keep for up to ten days. Just before serving, carefully fill each biscuit with a small scoop of ice cream or sorbet and berries.

Icing

CHOOSING WISELY

What is the difference between royal, glacé, ready-made and fondant icing?

Royal icing is a thick paste made from egg whites and sifted icing sugar. It is spread over marzipan-covered fruit cakes, or piped into decorations, and left to dry out. It is mainly used on rich, highly decorated celebration cakes.

Glacé icing is a smooth paste of icing sugar dissolved in a little water, which is spread straight onto the cake and left to dry out. It is ideal for covering cup cakes, tea breads and simple sponges.

Ready-made and fondant icing are the same thing: icing sugar, egg whites and liquid glucose are mixed and kneaded to a soft dough which is rolled out before being smoothed over a cake. Use it on simple cakes, novelty and celebration cakes.

There are many other types of icing, including the rich and creamy frosting in the recipe for Frosted Walnut Cake in *Cakes*.

KEEPING ICING SOFT

How do I stop royal icing from going rock-hard after a few days?

Royal icing becomes hard if it has not been beaten for long enough: it needs at least 15 minutes of beating with an electric mixer (or 20 minutes with a wooden spoon). The mixture should form soft peaks, and a palette knife run through it should leave a clean mark.

Then leave the icing to stand, covered with a damp cloth or in a sealed plastic container, for about 24 hours. This alters the structure of the sugar and makes it easier to spread and pipe. The icing can then be kept in a covered plastic container in the refrigerator for up to a fortnight, but may need further beating to restore to the right consistency. Another way of ensuring that royal icing is soft and spreads

COVERING A CAKE WITH ICING

To achieve a good finish, make sure the cake has a good shape, is placed centrally on a cake board, and is covered with a smooth layer of almond paste, which has been allowed to dry out on the cake for 24 hours.

1 On a clean dry surface sprinkled with sifted icing sugar, knead 1 kg ready-made icing until smooth. Using a rolling pin, roll out the ready-made icing to a round large enough to cover the cake.

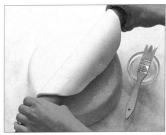

2 Brush the almond paste lightly with boiling water. Working quickly, lift the ready-made icing over the rolling pin, transfer it to the cake and unroll the icing over the top of the cake, with the rolled side uppermost.

3 With an icing paddle or clean, cool hands dipped in icing sugar, quickly rub the icing over the top and down the sides, moulding it to ease in any 'frills' and to stick smoothly to the cake.

4 With a sharp knife, trim off any excess icing from the base of the cake. Use the trimmings to mould some flowers for decoration. Leave the iced cake to dry thoroughly, then seal to the cake board by piping royal icing around the bottom edge before decorating.

easily is to add a teaspoon of glycerine to each 500 g of icing sugar, as in the recipe below.

Royal icing

MAKES: *enough to cover a 20 cm cake*
PREPARATION TIME: *35 minutes*
COOKING TIME: *none*

2 large egg whites
500 g (3 cups) icing sugar, sifted
1 teaspoon glycerine

1 Put the egg whites in a bowl and whisk with a fork until just frothy. Gradually beat in the sugar until the mixture becomes white and smooth.
2 Beat for 15 minutes at a slow speed with an electric mixer, or beat for 20 minutes with a wooden spoon. Add the glycerine, then cover with a damp cloth and leave to stand in a cool place for 24 hours before using.

To the rescue!

If your royal icing dries in the bowl and goes hard, leave it covered with two damp cloths for a few hours or overnight. Pass the dampened icing through a sieve to remove any lumps, then beat briefly to restore the consistency.

DIRECT ACTION

Marzipan is not popular in our family. Could I put royal icing directly onto fruit cake?

Not really. Marzipan, or almond paste (see following recipe), provides a smooth surface for the icing and stops moisture from the fruit coming through to stain the icing. However, you can spread glacé icing (see recipe, right) straight onto a cake that is to be eaten soon after being made.

Marzipan is rolled out, cut to fit the top and sides of the cake and pressed onto the surface. Because it is so smooth, marzipan will not stick unless the cake is covered with a glaze first, traditionally of apricot jam or marmalade. Once pressed onto the cake, marzipan should be left to dry out for at least 24 hours, and preferably a week, before being covered in icing.

Almond paste (Marzipan)

MAKES: *enough to cover a 20 cm cake*
PREPARATION TIME: *20 minutes*
COOKING TIME: *none*

125 g (¾ cup) icing sugar
125 g (½ cup) caster sugar
250 g (2¼ cups) ground almonds
1 teaspoon lemon juice
A few drops of almond essence
1 large egg, beaten

1 Sift the sugars and almonds into a bowl and make a well in the centre. Add all the remaining ingredients and mix to a soft dough.
2 Turn onto a surface that has been lightly dusted with icing or caster sugar and knead briefly until smooth. Wrap tightly in plastic wrap and store in a cool place until needed.

Glacé icing

MAKES: *enough to cover a 20 cm cake*
PREPARATION TIME: *5 minutes*
COOKING TIME: *none*

90 g (½ cup) icing sugar
1 tablespoon warm water

Sift the icing sugar into a bowl and gradually mix in the water, or any variations, until the icing is smooth.
VARIATIONS
• CHOCOLATE ICING: mix 2 teaspoons cocoa in 1 tablespoon boiling water, cool slightly and mix a little at a time into the icing sugar.
• CITRUS ICING: replace the water with 1 tablespoon strained lemon or orange juice, and add a few drops of yellow food colouring.
• COFFEE ICING: dissolve 1 teaspoon instant coffee in 1 tablespoon boiling water, cool slightly and mix a little at a time into the icing sugar.
• ROSE ICING: replace the water with 1 tablespoon of rosewater.

SIMPLE FONDANT

What is the easiest, quickest and neatest way to ice a cake?

Using glacé icing is very simple, as it is quick and easy to make and is spread over cakes with a palette knife. However, if you prefer a smooth, neat finish, use bought, ready-to-roll fondant or ready-made icing. It is rolled out like pastry and can be smoothed over a cake in just a few minutes, either straight onto the cake itself or over a layer of marzipan. It can also be used for modelling decorations or can be cut into letters or numbers for special occasion cakes.

To use ready-made, knead the icing until soft and roll it out onto a surface that has been lightly covered with sieved icing sugar, moving the icing continually to prevent it from sticking. Measure across the top and sides of the cake with string and roll the icing out to a circle 2.5 cm larger.

If you have covered the cake with marzipan first, brush it lightly with boiled water or alcoholic spirit such as brandy so the icing sticks. If you are putting the icing straight onto the cake, brush it with a jam glaze first to enable it to stick.

Holding the rolled icing with both hands, lift it carefully onto the cake and into position. Flute the bottom edges out like fabric but do not pleat or this will leave a line. Smooth the icing over the cake with your palms to remove any air bubbles, then trim the edges with a knife. The trimmings can be used for decorations.

COLOUR TO PLEASE

What is the best way to add colour to ready-made icing?

Ready-made icing is sold only in plain white, which can be coloured or painted with edible food colourings as desired. Liquid food colouring has to be kneaded thoroughly into the ready-made icing to achieve an even depth of colour.

To colour the icing, knead in the colouring until it is mixed through.

Blend it in a little at a time until you achieve the right shade: it is very concentrated.

To paint colouring onto icing, put a drop of the colouring onto a saucer, then mix in 1 teaspoon of water. Paint using a fine brush and then leave to dry.

SHAPING DECORATIONS

I have tried to make fondant cake decorations but the paste turned brittle. Can this be avoided?

Ready-made icing is rolled out to a smooth dough-like paste which can be put over cakes or moulded into shapes such as flowers (see panel, right), but, like Plasticine, it will dry if left exposed to air.

When covering and decorating cakes, keep the trimmings fresh until you are ready to make the decorations. Roll the trimmings into a ball and keep this airtight in a freezer bag or strong plastic bag. When you are ready to make some decorations, break off a little of the icing and return the rest to the airtight bag.

UNBROKEN LINES

When I try to pipe icing from a bag, the lines always break and look ragged. What do you think I am doing wrong?

Piping is usually done with royal icing, and the problem most people have is making the icing to the right consistency.

Stiff icing will be difficult to press out for piping, the strands will break and you will have an aching arm. For best results, use less sugar than you would for a covering icing: beat in only three-quarters of the sugar, until the mixture is like thick cream, and add the rest a little at a time, stopping when the icing is thick but not too stiff.

The easiest way to pipe icing is to place small amounts in a small piping bag (see panel, right) or in a cone made from a rolled-up sheet of greaseproof paper. Piping in small amounts requires less pressure so you have more control.

MOULDING AND PIPING DECORATIVE ICING

Pretty decorations can be made very easily with ready-made icing, using flower cutters. These can be bought at specialist cake decorating shops or through mail order; look for the addresses in specialist magazines or books. To make the flowers pictured here, you will also need royal icing for piping.

Piping decorative shapes onto a cake can take a bit of practice. Success comes from getting the pressure right when pressing out the icing and experimenting with the best angle for holding the bag. Use a small icing bag, as that is easier to handle; if you have only a large bag, fill it halfway.

MAKING FLOWERS

1 Colour some bought, ready-to-roll ready-made icing with edible food colouring and roll it out thinly. Stamp out with flower cutters. To make it easier to bend and shape the flowers, make cuts starting from the side of each rounded 'petal' to within 5 mm of the centre.

2 Holding a flower gently in one hand, mould the petals with the fingertips of the other hand. Place some crumpled foil in the cavities of an egg carton and place the flower in one of the cavities. Shape the petals of another flower and press its centre gently inside the first one to make a double-layered flower head. Shape and assemble the rest of the flowers.

3 Put some royal icing into a piping bag and press out dots of icing into the centre of each flower. Leave the flowers to dry for several hours, preferably overnight. When dry, gently lift each flower out of the egg carton with a palette knife. Arrange them on the cake immediately, or store in an airtight box for up to two months.

PIPING STARS

Put a little royal icing into a small piping bag fitted with a star nozzle, hold the bag vertically and gently pipe out a small amount of icing. Stop pressing and lift the piping bag away.

PIPING SHELLS

Put some icing into a small piping bag fitted with a star nozzle. Hold the bag at a 45° angle, press out a rounded shape, release pressure and pull the bag away sideways. Pipe the next shell about 5 mm away from the first one. As you press out the icing, the shells will touch.

PIPING STRAIGHT LINES

Using a small piping bag fitted with a plain nozzle, press out some icing and gently push it down to secure it to the cake. Then pipe a line, allowing the icing to fall into position.

Indian Cooking

POWDER AND PASTE

What is the difference between curry powder and curry paste?

Both are blends of many spices, but they are used differently. Dry curry powder cannot be fried in hot oil because it burns and turns acrid, so it must be added to foods that are already simmering in liquid.

For fried dishes it is best to use a curry paste. A large variety of good quality Indian curry pastes, with regional flavours, is available in leading supermarkets. Experiment with them in casseroles and soups and decide which you prefer.

Southeast Asian curries, which derive mainly from southern India, will often have fresh ingredients such as lemon grass, sweet basil, galangal (an aromatic root of the ginger family) and garlic added to the ground spices. For example, red and green curry pastes, using fresh chillies with other ingredients, are a central feature of many popular Thai dishes (see *Thai Cooking*).

SPICY DECISION

What is in curry powder, and could I make it myself rather than buy it ready-made?

There is no single recipe for curry powder. It was invented by the British in India as a quick substitute for the thousands of different spice blends and garam masalas that Indian cooks make for themselves. A basic curry powder includes black pepper, chilli, coriander, cumin, ginger and turmeric in varying proportions; it often has fenugreek and oily spices such as cardamom, cinnamon, cloves and mace, and can include asafoetida, cassia leaves, curry leaves, mustard and poppy seeds too. To make your own, experiment until you find a mixture you like.

Some whole spices such as coriander, cumin seed, dried chillies, fenugreek seed and peppercorns,

need to be roasted before being ground and mixed (oily spices do not need roasting). Use a dry baking dish in the oven, or dry-fry them in a frying pan. Use a small coffee grinder or pestle and mortar to grind the spices individually, then mix them together. Store in an airtight glass jar.

HEALTHIER POPPADOMS

Is there a low-fat way of cooking poppadoms so that they are crisp?

The microwave is a blessing for the greaseless cooking of cracker-like poppadoms. Place them one at a time on the turntable of the microwave and cook for 40–60 seconds on High until puffed and crisp. They will not be as fluffy as those that are traditionally fried in oil, but they are considerably healthier.

MYSTERIOUS LASSI

What is in the yoghurt drink that Indian restaurants serve?

Lassi, a traditional Indian drink, used to be made from buttermilk poured into earthenware crocks, with salt added to combat dehydration in the hot climate. It is now made from thin yoghurt, with salt or sugar. To make your own, dilute natural yoghurt with water or milk, add salt or sugar to taste, then blend vigorously with crushed ice.

BALANCED INDIAN MEAL

Are there any rules about what Indian dishes are served together?

Most Indian meals are not formally structured and there are usually a number of dishes for balance. There may be a meat dish, a seafood dish, at least one vegetable dish and perhaps a lentil dish as well. All would be served with fluffy rice and probably a bread such as chapati.

A typical meal you can cook at home includes Chicken Vindaloo and Prawn Korma served with Ghee Rice (see recipes, right). Serve them with mango chutney and cucumber raita, made from sliced cucumbers in yoghurt with

lemon, cumin and fresh mint. A vindaloo is traditionally rather sharp and fiery. The amount of chilli used in the recipe below makes a medium-hot curry. You can add more or less, but keep in mind that a chilli powder made in India may be hotter than a locally made commercial brand.

Chicken vindaloo

SERVES: 4
PREPARATION TIME: 30 minutes, plus 2 hours to marinate
COOKING TIME: 30 minutes

---

1 kg chicken breasts, skinned
300 ml natural yoghurt
1 large onion, sliced
1 tablespoon honey
1 teaspoon salt

FOR THE SPICE BLEND
1 tablespoon ghee or vegetable oil
3 tablespoons chopped onions
1 tablespoon finely chopped garlic
1 tablespoon grated ginger
1 tablespoon hot chilli powder or 3-4 dried red chillies, chopped
1 tablespoon ground coriander
1 teaspoon ground cumin
4 cardamom pods, crushed
4 cm cinnamon stick
2 tablespoons tomato paste
1 tablespoon malt vinegar

---

1 Cut the chicken into large chunks. Mix the yoghurt, sliced onion, honey and salt in a large bowl to make a marinade and soak the chicken in it for 2 hours, turning occasionally.
2 To make the spice blend, heat the ghee or oil in a saucepan and fry the chopped onions, garlic and ginger for 5 minutes. Add the chilli powder or stir in the dried chillies, then add all the other spices to the pan. Stir-fry for a minute or two.
3 Add 300 ml of water, plus the tomato paste, vinegar, the chicken and marinade and mix together well.
4 Cover and simmer for 30 minutes until the sauce has thickened.
VARIATION
For a more substantial dish, you can add a large potato, peeled and diced, to the vindaloo during the last 15 minutes of cooking.

Prawn korma

SERVES: 4
PREPARATION TIME: *5 minutes, plus
30 minutes for prawns to marinate*
COOKING TIME: *20 minutes*

*12 large green tiger prawns, peeled
1 teaspoon ground turmeric
2 tablespoons vegetable oil
2 tablespoons chopped onion
1 teaspoon grated ginger
1 tablespoon seedless raisins
1 tablespoon ground almonds
2 teaspoons sugar
300 ml natural yoghurt
1 teaspoon salt*

FOR THE SPICE BLEND
*1 teaspoon ground cumin
2 teaspoons ground chilli
1 tablespoon ground coriander
3 cardamom pods, crushed*

1 Devein the prawns, rub them with turmeric and leave for 30 minutes.

2 Meanwhile, make up the spice blend with a teaspoon or so of cold water and stir to a soft paste.
3 Heat the oil and fry the onion and ginger for a minute until they have just softened. Add the spice blend and fry for a further 2 minutes.
4 Add the remaining ingredients except the prawns and simmer for about 10 minutes until the sauce thickens. Add the prawns and cook for 5 minutes, or until pink.

Ghee rice

SERVES: 4
PREPARATION TIME: *5 minutes*
COOKING TIME: *20 minutes*

*250 g (1¼ cups) long-grain rice
2 tablespoons ghee
1-2 teaspoons salt*

1 Wash the rice in several changes of water until the water runs clear, then put it in a saucepan. Add 500 ml of water, bring to the boil then simmer for 10 minutes.
2 Add the ghee and salt and rake the rice with a fork. Cover, cook for a further 5 minutes until dry, then rake again to loosen the grains.
VARIATION
To cook in a microwave, prepare as above but add the ghee and the salt at the beginning. Then cook the rice, uncovered, for 18 minutes on High or until the water has been absorbed.

STYLISH VARIATIONS

What is the difference between balti, karahi and tandoori?

Balti and karahi are the same style of cooking, originating in Kashmir, where the curries are made in a cast-iron pan with a rounded bottom and two handles, rather like a Chinese wok. You can use a wok to cook balti-style dishes at home.

Typical spices used in balti curries are aniseed, cardamom, cassia bark, cloves, coriander, cumin, fennel, ginger and the spice blend called garam masala (see **Spices**). Balti curries are often eaten without rice or cutlery, using large, flat breads such as naan instead.

Tandoori cooking, from the Punjab, is named after the tandoor, a clay oven used for roasting or baking. It is shaped like a large jug, and is traditionally sunk into the ground up to its neck. The ovens used today have a plaster layer on the outer walls for added insulation. Burning charcoal is placed in the bottom of the oven and the food to be cooked is hung inside on long spits over the coals.

Before cooking, tandoori meats and seafood are usually marinated in a mixture of chilli, garlic, ghee, ginger, onions, paprika, peppers, salt, spices and yoghurt. The characteristic red stain of tandoori meats once came from cochineal, but now a vegetable colouring is used.

Cooling drinks of lassi are the perfect accompaniment for a fiery Chicken Vindaloo (top), made with spices fried in ghee (right), or a Prawn Korma sweetened with almonds and raisins.

Jam

RIPENESS OF FRUIT

Every year I seem to have a surplus of home-grown fruit that I would like to be able to cook with. When is fresh fruit at its best for making jam?

Use the fruit when it is just ripe or slightly under-ripe. The pectose in under-ripe fruit changes to pectin as it becomes ripe. Pectin is a gummy substance produced by the flesh, skins and pips of fruit and it must be present if jam is to set properly. The amount varies from fruit to fruit, and there is little pectin in any that are over-ripe.

STONY PROBLEM

Do I need to stone fruit before preparing jam?

No, simply wash the fruit carefully. Simmer gently with water in a pan, stirring occasionally, until tender. The stones will float to the surface and can be lifted out.

STRAWBERRY SOLUTION

How can I prevent strawberries from disintegrating when cooked?

To preserve soft-skinned fruit, such as raspberries and strawberries, whole, they should first be covered in sugar. This draws out their juices, leaving them firm enough not to disintegrate during fast boiling.

Hull the strawberries and wipe with kitchen paper towels. Do not wash, as extra moisture dilutes pectin, making the setting more difficult. Layer the fruit in the pan, sprinkle with an equal weight of sugar and leave overnight. Next day, cook the fruit over a low heat until the sugar has dissolved completely. Then bring the mixture to the boil and cook rapidly until it sets (see panel, below).

FROZEN BERRIES

I can't always get fresh berries. Can I use frozen raspberries and strawberries to make jam?

Yes, but the pectin level falls after a few months, so, if the berries have been frozen for some time, use 10 per cent more fruit than specified in your jam recipe to compensate for this loss. Take the fruit straight from the freezer, heating it gently in a pan to defrost.

VARYING TEXTURES

Are there any differences – and if so, what are they – between jams, jellies and conserves?

Jam is basically a cooked mixture of fruit and sugar, made from whole berries or larger fruit that has been chopped. It is usually set, but not hard, and has a very spreadable consistency.

Jellies are made from strained fruit juice and should be firm, but still quivering gently, when they are spooned from the jar.

Conserves are generally richer, sweeter and much more syrupy than jams. Strawberries, raspberries and loganberries are good fruits to use. The fruit is layered with an equal quantity of sugar and left overnight to extract the juices before boiling for a short time. Conserves are superb with thick yoghurt or fromage frais.

RISING PEEL

What can I do to stop all the fruit or the peel from rising to the top of the jar when I make marmalade or jam?

Chunky marmalade and whole fruit jams are particularly susceptible to this problem. After removing the pan containing the mixture from the heat, you should leave it to stand for about 15 minutes.

When it has begun to set, give the blend a stir to distribute the fruit or peel. This precaution will help to ensure that the fruit or peel stays suspended throughout the jar after bottling.

TESTING THE SETTING POINT FOR JAM

The acid, pectin and sugar must all be in the right proportions for jam to become firm. Use one of these two methods to see if yours is ready to set.

TEMPERATURE TEST

1 The most accurate method for testing a set is to stir the jam and then insert a sugar thermometer. Do not let the thermometer touch the bottom or sides of the pan.

2 Keep testing while the jam boils. A proper set should be obtained when the temperature of the jam reaches 105°C.

COLD-SAUCER TEST

1 Remove the pan from the heat to prevent the contents overcooking. Put a small quantity of jam onto a pre-chilled plate and place it in the refrigerator to rest for a few minutes.

2 As soon as the jam is cold enough, push a finger gently through it. If the surface of the jam shows wrinkles, the setting point has been reached.

PREPARING JARS

Is it true you should warm jars in the oven before pouring in jam?

Yes. Warm the jars in an oven preheated to 140°C for about 5 minutes, to ensure that the glass does not crack when you pour in the hot jam. Oven warming also helps to ensure that freshly washed jars are absolutely dry.

TIGHT COVER

What is the best method to use for sealing jam jars?

The best way to seal a jar for long storage is to fill it with hot jam and cover it immediately, using a screw-top or spring-clamp lid.

If the jam is being stored in a cool, dry, well-ventilated place, you can use sealing lids instead. Put a waxed paper disc, waxed side down, on the surface of the jam and smooth it over with your finger to remove any air pockets. Then cover the jar with a cellophane circle made moist by wiping with a damp cloth. Place the cellophane round damp side up over the jar lid and secure it with a rubber band.

Don't wait until the jam is luke-warm before you seal the jar, or moisture will collect inside the lid and the jam may become mouldy. Jams will generally keep for about a year in a dry, cool, dark place.

ADDING PECTIN

Which fruits need to have pectin added when making jam?

Fruits that are low in pectin and in natural fruit acid, which helps the pectin to gel, include cherries, peaches, pineapples, rhubarb and ripe strawberries. Adding lemon juice and pectin, either in liquid form or as a powder, helps the jam to set.

You can buy citrus pectin powder, or make your own pectin extract from sour cooking apples, crab apple or gooseberries. Wash the fruit, then chop apples roughly but leave berries whole. Cover with cold water, simmer for 45 minutes

and then strain through a scalded jelly bag. Add 125 ml of this pectin extract to every 1.5 kg of fresh fruit.

TESTING TIME

How should I test for a set?

Once the sugar has dissolved and the jam is boiling rapidly, it will start to look like jam in about 10 minutes. Test it as soon as you think it is ready as you must not overboil the jam, which could make it dark. If you think it is ready, take the pan off the heat and test with a jam thermometer or in a saucer (see panel, page 190).

Clear jam or jelly will fall from a spoon in a wavy curtain, not a stream, when it is ready.

PREDICTING A SET

How can I tell if my fruit will set?

If you are not sure of the setting qualities of the fruit you are using, take 1 teaspoon of juice from the pan of soft, cooked fruit (before the sugar is added) and put it in a small glass. Add 1 tablespoon of methylated spirit to the cooled juice, shake gently and leave for a minute. If a jelly-like clot develops, the fruit has plenty of pectin. If it does not form a clot, the pectin content is low and extra pectin is needed.

FIRM AND FRUITY

What is the difference between fruit butters, cheeses and curds?

Fruit butters and cheeses are made by cooking fruit to a purée and then adding sugar. They are thicker than jam and often spiced. Fruit butter is set when a spoonful on a saucer does not exude any liquid. Fruit cheese is even firmer when set (see picture, right).

Fruit butters are very tasty spread over toast. Keep unopened jars in a cool place for up to two months. Once open, refrigerate them and eat within two weeks.

Fruit cheeses have a firmer texture than butters, but should be kept in the same way. Blackberry and Apple Cheese (right), can be

potted in small jars and served as a relish with meat, game and cheese.

Curds cannot be called true preserves because they have added eggs and butter. They should be made in small quantities, kept in the refrigerator, and used within two or three weeks.

Blackberry and apple cheese

MAKES: about 1 kg
PREPARATION TIME: 20-30 minutes
COOKING TIME: 1½ hours

---

1 kg blackberries
500 g cooking apples, peeled,
  cored and finely chopped
1.5 kg (6 cups) white sugar
  (approximately)

---

1 Put the fruit into a preserving pan with 600 ml of water and cook gently for about 30 minutes until it is very soft.
2 Press the pulp through a nylon sieve set over a bowl. Measure the resulting purée and return it to the pan, adding 500 g (2 cups) of sugar for each 500 ml of purée.
3 Stir over a low heat until the sugar has dissolved, then bring the mixture to the boil and simmer, stirring often, for 40-60 minutes. Towards the end of the cooking time, check that the fruit cheese is ready (see picture, below).

Fruit cheese is ready when a wooden spoon drawn across the bottom of the preserving pan leaves a clean line.

4 As soon as it is done, spoon the cheese into warmed, clean, small jars, then cover with waxed discs and seal. Alternatively, the fruit cheese can be poured into small ramekins, left to set and then carefully unmoulded for serving.

Japanese Cooking

SUSHI FOR BEGINNERS

Japanese food looks exquisite but appears to be difficult to prepare. Is there anything quick and easy that I could make at home?

Yes, there is. Sushi is made from rice flavoured with *mirin*, or sweetened rice wine, and formed into finger-sized mounds topped with raw seafood or pickled vegetables. It is an art form in Japan, but the basic technique is simple. Sushi rice can also be rolled around a filling and wrapped in sheets of seaweed called *nori*, then cut into bite-sized pieces – but the moulded sushi (right) are easier to make. The seafood toppings are raw and must be absolutely fresh. For the most authentic taste and texture, use Japanese sticky rice.

Sushi rice

MAKES: *about 24 individual pieces*
PREPARATION TIME: *30 minutes, plus 30 minutes soaking rice*
COOKING TIME: *12–15 minutes*

400 g (2 cups) Japanese glutinous
    rice, or risotto rice
2 tablespoons rice vinegar or white
    wine vinegar
2 tablespoons sugar
1 teaspoon salt
2 tablespoons mirin (sweet sake)
    or dry sherry
To serve: 1–2 tablespoons ready-
    prepared wasabi paste
    (Japanese horseradish),
    plus soy sauce, pickled ginger
    and grated mooli (white radish)

FOR THE TOPPINGS
4 medium green prawns
100 g raw tuna, sliced
100 g raw squid, sliced
100 g raw or smoked salmon, sliced
100 g red caviar or salmon roe

1 Put the rice in a saucepan and cover it with cold water up to 4 cm above the level of the grains. Soak for 30 minutes.
2 Combine the vinegar, sugar, salt and mirin in a small saucepan and bring to the boil. Remove and cool.
3 Make a slit along the back of the prawns from head to tail, devein, then put them in boiling water and simmer for 2–3 minutes until they turn pink and open out in a butterfly shape. Drain and set aside to cool.
4 When the rice has soaked, bring it to the boil without changing the water and simmer for 10 minutes until the water is absorbed. Transfer to a bowl and add the cooled vinegar dressing. Stir for about 10 minutes to release the starch and allow to cool.
5 Take handfuls of rice and mould it by patting it firmly into bite-sized oblongs about 4 cm long, 2 cm wide and 3 cm high. Dab wasabi paste on top of each one.
6 Trim the toppings to fit and press them gently down on each piece of moulded rice, using the wasabi to hold them in place.
7 Serve with individual side dishes of soy sauce and wasabi, which each person mixes according to personal preference as a spicy dip, and dishes of pickled ginger and grated mooli.

TEXTURE AND HARMONY

What is distinctive about the style of Japanese food?

Japanese food covers a much wider spectrum than most people realise. The raw fish, called *sashimi*, do not dominate the menu. Japanese cuisine is characterised more by methods of cooking than by particular flavours. There are soups, steamed dishes, raw salads, dishes cooked at the table, deep-fried and quick-fried foods as well as boiled and pickled dishes. There are some

From top to bottom, sushi on the large dish are topped with raw squid, salmon, butterfly prawns and salmon roe. Serve with spicy green wasabi and soy sauce for dipping, bright pink pickled ginger and raw, grated mooli.

complicated recipes and also artful blends of seasonings, but the Japanese generally prefer a stylised minimalist presentation.

The Japanese respect and value freshness above all, so the integrity of each ingredient is enhanced by very few strong condiments or spices, only a little soy sauce, perhaps some grated mooli (white radish) and subtle seasonings such as bonito flakes and some delicate herbs. The strongest condiment used regularly is wasabi.

In the 16th century the Portuguese introduced beef-eating to Japan and this became *sukiyaki*: finely sliced grilled or barbecued beef served with piquant dips. Japanese foods fried in batter are called *tempura* and are also of Portuguese origin.

Noodles are one of the many dishes of Chinese origin, adopted by the Japanese in the 7th century.

Jelly

HEALTHIER JELLY

Packet jelly always seems to taste artificial. Is there any easy way I could use fresh fruit to make a healthier, more natural jelly?

Yes, fresh oranges, lemons and all berries can be easily converted into jelly and the result has a flavour much nicer than any you make from a packet. Children who resist eating fresh fruit often love jelly and making your own helps to ensure that some vitamins are retained. Fresh fruit jellies should be eaten on the day they are made.

Jellies made with boysenberry, raspberry, strawberry or blackberry will still contain a few seeds even after the purée has been sieved. If this coarser texture is not to your liking, you can remove all the seeds by straining the purée through a muslin cloth.

Try making fruit jellies with as little sugar as you can so they are really healthy, and the taste of the fruit comes through.

Fresh berry jelly

SERVES: 4-6
PREPARATION TIME: 30 minutes, plus an hour standing time
SETTING TIME: about 3 hours for moulded jelly; 1-2 hours if set in individual dishes

---

500 g boysenberries, raspberries, strawberries or blackberries, hulled and sliced
Strained juice of 1 lemon
125 g (½ cup) caster sugar
2 sachets powdered gelatine

---

1 Put your chosen fruit into a bowl and add the lemon juice and sugar. Stir well, cover and leave it all to macerate for about an hour.
2 Pour the fruit and lemon juice into a food processor or blender and add 300 ml of water. (If the goblet isn't large enough, the water can be added later.)
3 Process or blend the fruit into a smooth purée then pass this through a fine nylon or stainless-steel sieve to remove the seeds. If you have not already added it, stir the water into the berry purée now.
4 Measure the sieved fruit mixture. The fruit should have produced

This cool strawberry jelly requires no cooking, which means it retains all the flavour and goodness of the fresh fruit.

about 850 ml of purée, but if the fruit is very juicy you may have up to 1.25 litres. Taste for sweetness and add a little more sugar only if necessary.
5 Dissolve the gelatine in 100 ml of water, using one whole sachet plus 1½ level teaspoons of the other sachet for 850 ml of fruit mixture; if you have a larger quantity of purée, use two sachets of gelatine. Leave it to stand for 3-4 minutes, until it has absorbed all the water and looks opaque.
6 Whisk the dissolved gelatine into the fruit mixture and pour the jelly into a 1.25 litre dampened mould, small ramekins or stemmed glasses. Chill for 3 hours or until set.
7 To turn the chilled jelly out, dip the mould up to the rim in hot water for 5 seconds only. Put a plate on top of the mould then invert the two together and give the mould a quick, sharp shake. If the jelly does not come out the first time, repeat the process as many times as necessary. Serve with cream and wafer biscuits.

Jerusalem Artichoke

NO RELATION

Are Jerusalem artichokes related to globe artichokes?

No, they are not. Jerusalem artichokes, also called root artichokes or sunchokes, are actually members of the sunflower family. The name Jerusalem is a mispronunciation of the Spanish *girasol*, meaning 'turn to the sun'. Globe artichokes are members of the thistle family.

The sharing of the name 'artichoke' refers to some similarity of flavour in these vegetables, but they have little in common beyond being pleasantly sweet.

VARIOUS USES

What can I do with Jerusalem artichokes besides make soup?

Jerusalem artichokes are popular for soup as they have a tendency to collapse when cooked. Their sweet chestnutty flavour also makes them good partners for salty foods such as ham or smoked fish, as in the following recipe. You could also lightly poach some slices of Jerusalem artichoke and use them in salads, or try mashing them with potato to serve as an accompanying vegetable with any meal where the mash is a starring partner, or as a topping for meat or fish pies.

Jerusalem artichoke and smoked fish chowder

SERVES: *6 as a starter*
PREPARATION TIME: *30 minutes*
COOKING TIME: *30 minutes*

3 medium-sized floury potatoes
500 g fillet of smoked haddock
  or cod
1 onion, roughly chopped
500 g Jerusalem artichokes
Juice of ½ lemon
2 stalks celery, destrung and diced
50 g butter
600 ml milk
Black pepper
To garnish: chives, snipped

1 Peel the potatoes, boil until soft, then drain, mash and set them aside.
2 Put the fish into a pan with the onion and enough cold water to cover. Bring to the boil and skim. Simmer the fish for 5-7 minutes or until it is just beginning to flake.

3 Drain the fish through a sieve, keeping the liquor and making it up to 500 ml with some fresh cold water. Discard the onion.
4 When the fish is cool, skin, bone and roughly flake it. Stir half of the cooking liquor into the potatoes.
5 Peel the artichokes and slice them thinly into a small bowl of cold water acidulated with the lemon juice.
6 Fry the celery for 2-3 minutes in butter, then add the milk, drained artichokes and the rest of the fish stock. Bring to simmering point, then partially cover and cook for 10-15 minutes until the artichokes are soft.
7 Mix the mashed potato and flaked fish into the vegetable mixture and grind in some black pepper.
8 Heat the chowder again, garnish with the chives and serve as a main meal with hot wholemeal toast.

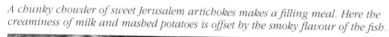

A chunky chowder of sweet Jerusalem artichokes makes a filling meal. Here the creaminess of milk and mashed potatoes is offset by the smoky flavour of the fish.

Juicers

ENDLESS VARIETY

I would like to use my juicer for more than fresh orange juice. Can you suggest some ideas?

Juicers capable of pulping hard vegetables such as carrots and celery will produce highly nutritious, easily digested fruit and vegetable juices very economically and the variety of combinations is endless, depending on your imagination.

Some carrot, celery and tomato seasoned with Worcestershire and Tabasco sauces makes a particularly good version of tomato juice, perfect for Bloody Marys. Cucumber and melon juiced together with a little fresh mint is a refreshing summer drink served with ice.

Juicers also make good bases for milkshakes: try mango and banana, strawberry and peach or pawpaw and kiwifruit, mixed with equal quantities of vanilla ice cream.

Use the pulp left over from juicing fresh carrots as the basis of a delicious carrot cake. You can also use vegetable juices to add flavour to casseroles, risottos and soups instead of adding stock or water.

Kidneys

FROM GRILL TO PIE

Are all types of kidney equally suitable for grilling and frying, or for using in steak and kidney pie?

Lamb's and pig's kidneys are both tender and after preparation (see panel, right) can be grilled, fried, casseroled or used in pies. Lamb's kidney has the more subtle flavour; pig's kidney is somewhat stronger.

Large, multilobed veal kidneys are lightly coloured and delicately flavoured but expensive. They are best quickly grilled or fried in order to optimise their tenderness.

Ox kidneys from mature animals are strongly flavoured and best cooked slowly with other ingredients in casseroles and pies. Many people consider them the first choice for a steak and kidney pie.

The flavour of kidneys combines well with herbs, mushrooms, mustard, olives, peppers, tomatoes and strongly flavoured wines.

SOAK NO MORE

Is it necessary to soak kidneys before cooking them?

In the past, kidneys were often stronger in flavour and soaked to soften their taste. Modern breeding and husbandry methods mean that it is unnecessary to soak calf's or lamb's kidneys. Whether or not you soak the stronger-tasting pig's kidneys is a matter of personal choice. Many people prefer to soak ox kidneys in milk, generally for at least an hour, especially if they are a prominent ingredient in a recipe.

PREPARING LAMB'S KIDNEYS

Lamb's kidneys, with their lighter flavour, are the most versatile and easily available kidneys. The larger ox and pig's kidneys are sliced into chunks before cooking.

1 Cut the lamb's kidneys in half lengthways through the core.

2 Snip out the white core of the kidney with scissors.

3 Using your fingers, peel off the kidney's fine covering skin.

4 To fry a kidney, cut it right through into two. To grill, cut the kidney only three-quarters of the way through so that it can be opened out like a book. Then push a skewer through both halves of the kidney to hold it flat while cooking.

Kiwifruit

VITAMIN RICH

Is it true that kiwifruit have more vitamin C than oranges?

Yes, kiwifruit contain 59 mg of vitamin C per 100 g compared with 54 mg for oranges. So, eating a single kiwifruit or just one medium orange will supply you with more than the recommended adult daily intake of 40 mg of vitamin C. Raw blackcurrants are even better, averaging 200 mg of vitamin C per 100 g.

Once known as Chinese gooseberry, the kiwifruit is an acidic fruit with dark-green flesh and edible black seeds. It has a distinctive flavour and makes a conventional fruit salad more exciting.

Kiwifruit are ready to eat if they yield slightly when lightly pressed. Cut the kiwifruit in half, scoop the flesh out with a teaspoon and eat it straight from the skin. Kiwifruit can also be peeled with a small sharp knife and cut into slices to add to fruit salads or use as a decoration for cakes and desserts.

Knives

ESSENTIAL UTENSILS

I want to buy some new kitchen knives. What should I look for?

Always buy the best quality knives that you can afford. A good set of knives will not only last a lifetime, but will pay for themselves many times over in saved labour. Choose knives that feel comfortable in the hand, are heavy and well balanced. Carefully place the junction of the blade and handle on the side of your open hand. The handle should fall back gently into your palm.

Knives that have a tang (the part of the blade that extends into the handle of the knife) running along the whole length of the handle give the best overall balance and the

HOLDING A KNIFE CORRECTLY

Sharpness is crucial in knives and it is important to choose the correct type of knife for each job. Learning to hold knives correctly will not only improve cutting efficiency but will promote safety in the kitchen as well.

CHOPPING AND SLICING

Hold the knife with your thumb and forefinger either side of the blade just below the handle to prevent it rolling in your hand. Bend the fingertips of the other hand out of harm's way and cut smoothly through the vegetable.

HEAVY-PRESSURE CUTTING

For heavy-pressure cutting of tough vegetables such as cabbage, hold the knife with your hand close to the blade and use the other hand to keep the vegetable steady. Cut through the vegetable firmly, without sawing.

CRUSHING

To use the knife as a mallet to crush foods like lemon grass or garlic, use the flat of the blade and press it down firmly with your fingers.

PRECISION CUTTING

For cutting requiring careful control, or when scraping vegetables, use a small knife and keep your hand low down on the handle.

---

longest life – blades that are not riveted in place this way invariably come loose. The heads of the rivets should be flush with the surface of the handle for easy cleaning.

The best handles tend to be those that are made of wood impregnated with plastic to seal it. Plain wooden handles are nonslip, tough and attractive; the less expensive plastic handles are easier to keep clean but do not provide the same grip.

You can never have too many knives in the kitchen, and there is one for every job you undertake. Build up your selection gradually and, when you can afford it, add specialist knives such as boning and fish filleting knives to your collection. The following are essential knives that should be bought first:

• A large cook's knife with a blade at least 20 cm long.
• A fruit knife with a serrated edge and stainless-steel blade.
• A paring knife with a 8–10 cm stainless-steel blade.
• A bread knife with a rigid 20–25 cm serrated blade.
• A carving knife with a rigid blade at least 20 cm long.
• A palette knife with a flat, round-ended blade.

STEELY LIFESPAN

Are stainless-steel kitchen knives better than carbon-steel ones?

Stainless-steel knives are strong, do not rust and can be used on onions and acidic foods. Unfortunately, they are difficult to sharpen and blunt readily. Carbon-steel knives are easier to sharpen and will stay sharp for a long time. However, they rust easily so they must be wiped clean and dried immediately after use. They also discolour, particularly after contact with onions and highly acidic foods.

Knives made from high-carbon stainless-steel have the advantages of both carbon-steel and stainless-steel knives and yet none of the disadvantages, but they cost more.

CLEAN AND DRY

Should I treat my knives with any special care?

All knives must be looked after carefully. Always wash them and dry immediately after use. Do not put them in a dishwasher. When carbon-steel knives get very stained, clean them with half a lemon sprinkled with salt. If that does not work, use a scouring pad, but only occasionally. To remove rust from a carbon-steel knife, rub the blade with a burnt cork.

Sharpen your knives regularly and do not store them in a drawer, where their blades will get damaged and you may inadvertently cut your hands when reaching for them. Use a wooden knife block or knife magnet to store them instead.

STAY SHARP

What is the best way to use a steel to sharpen my knives?

There are two methods for using a steel. Try both of them to see which is most successful for you.

The first method is arguably the easiest as you have more control of the steel and the angle of the knife. Hold the steel vertically with the tip on a nonslip surface. Put the knife edge where it joins the handle at the top of the steel, with the blade pointing downwards, at an angle of 45 degrees. Bring the knife down the steel, keeping the angle constant and drawing the blade across the steel so that when you reach the bottom of the steel you are sharpening the tip of the blade.

Move the knife smoothly along the length of the steel, parting your hands so that the entire blade is sharpened.

Repeat the procedure, dragging the other side of the blade down underneath the steel, keeping the angle at 45 degrees. Repeat both sequences until the blade is sharp.

Alternatively, hold the steel in one hand, the knife in the other and place the handle ends of each together at an angle of 45 degrees. Keeping your elbows against your sides, raise the steel and the knife, parting your hands so that the blade travels up the steel. Finish with the knife tip near the tip of the steel. Repeat, holding the other side of the knife blade against the other side of the steel. Continue this sequence until the knife is sharp.

Kohlrabi

SPICY CABBAGE

What exactly is kohlrabi and how can I best use it?

Kohlrabi is a round, purple or green stem that looks like a turnip. The leaves, which can be cooked as for spinach, are often trimmed off before the vegetable is sold.

Look for small kohlrabi that are not much bigger than a tennis ball and stuff them, or steam to serve as a hot vegetable accompaniment. If you find leaves attached, trim and shred them, then steam briefly to serve over the halved or quartered globes of the cooked stem.

As it is a member of the cabbage family, the spicy warmth of kohlrabi is best brought out by blanching. The recipe for Kohlrabi and Cress Salad (above right) would go well with pork chops or sausages.

Kohlrabi and cress salad

SERVES: *4*
PREPARATION TIME: *15 minutes*
COOKING TIME: *1 minute*

500 g kohlrabi
Juice of ½ lemon
1 red-skinned apple
4 slim spring onions
Black pepper
1 carton mustard and cress

FOR THE DRESSING
1 tablespoon wholegrain mustard
2 teaspoons cider vinegar
Salt
4 tablespoons olive oil
4 tablespoons natural yoghurt

1 Peel the kohlrabi, then grate it coarsely into a saucepan. Pour on boiling water and cook it just until it returns to the boil. Drain and refresh immediately under a cold tap.

2 Squeeze the lemon juice into a small bowl and half fill it with cold water. Quarter and core the apple then coarsely grate it into the bowl.

3 Drain the apple, mix it with the kohlrabi and dry thoroughly, either in a salad spinner or with a tea towel before transferring it to a salad bowl.

4 Finely slice the spring onions and add to the bowl with some coarsely ground black pepper.

5 Mix the mustard, vinegar and salt in a small screw-top jar and shake until combined. Add the olive oil and yoghurt, shake vigorously again and toss into the salad with another good grinding of black pepper.

6 Cut the mustard and cress and spread over the salad, tossing again immediately before serving.

A dressing of yoghurt and mustard lends piquancy, while the apple adds sweetness to this simple kohlrabi salad.

Lamb

RAISING STANDARDS

I hear so much these days about the conditions under which battery hens are kept. Is all lamb in Australia free-range?

Yes, all lamb is reared naturally outdoors although the sheep are brought inside for lambing in severe climates.

Lamb that has been organically reared complies with a national standard for organic and bio-dynamic produce. Pain and stress are kept to a minimum, and living conditions must consider the natural needs of the lambs.

Several organisations apply special standards to meat produced in Australia, including NASAA, BFA and Demeter-Biodynamic Research Institute (see *Additives*).

GOOD SIGNS

How do I recognise good lean lamb in the shop?

Lean lamb cuts, known as Trim lamb, are now readily available. These cuts contain no bone or selvedge fat. They are available from leading butchers and supermarkets, where they will often display the NHF (National Heart Foundation) approved tick.

New season lamb should be pale pink in colour while older lamb should be brownish-pink, although the colour can vary according to the breed. The colour should never be greyish and the fat should be white, silky and resilient. The flesh should be fine-grained and lean.

YOUTH AND AGE

Is young lamb better than larger, older lamb or mutton?

It depends on the dish. Young lamb (under 3–4 months) has a more delicate flavour and is leaner than older lamb (4 months to 1 year). It is excellent for roasts or cooked quickly as grilled and fried chops, cutlets and noisettes. The stronger flavoured older lamb is more suitable for casseroles where the mild taste of young lamb would be lost.

When a lamb reaches one year of age, its meat is sold as mutton. This is less popular and so less widely available than young lamb, however, you should be able to obtain it easily from a good independent or specialist halal butcher.

DIFFERENT PARTS

What's the difference between a chop, a cutlet and a noisette?

Chops, cutlets and noisettes are all suitable for grilling and frying but are different cuts of meat.

There are two types of chops: chump chops (taken from just above the hind leg), which have a round central bone, and the smaller loin chops (from the middle carcass) with a good eye of meat plus a tail of meat and fat curling round it.

Cutlets come from the best end of neck joint. They have an eye of meat with a short bone on one side and a long one on the other. They are smaller than chops, so you usually need two to three per portion.

Noisettes are cut from the eye of the loin (see panel, below) and are usually about 2–2.5 cm thick. Grill or fry the noisettes until browned on the outside but still pink in the centre. The following recipe partners noisettes with a rich sauce of mushrooms, tarragon and crème fraîche that would be equally delicious served with other cuts of Trim lamb, or with chicken.

PREPARING AND ROLLING LAMB NOISETTES

Noisettes are the eye of the loin, boned, rolled and sliced. They may seem quite expensive, but they generate no waste because they are boneless. Ask the butcher for a trimmed, skinned loin, which will supply four to six noisettes.

1 Cut through the meat on either side of each bone then cut beneath the bone to release and remove it. Cut off the flap at the thin end of the joint.

2 Trim away any excess fat that is on the outer side of the loin, then grip the fleshy end of the joint and roll up the meat tightly towards the thin end.

3 Tie the roll in shape with string at 2.5 cm intervals, knotting each loop separately. Slice it midway between each tie to make the noisettes.

Noisettes of lamb with mushrooms

SERVES: 4
PREPARATION TIME: 5 minutes
COOKING TIME: 15 minutes

250 g mixed shiitake, oyster
and champignon mushrooms, cut
or broken into large pieces
40 g butter
1 tablespoon olive oil
8 noisettes Trim lamb, each about
2.5 cm thick
2–3 teaspoons chopped fresh
tarragon
1–2 tablespoons wine, red or white
90 ml crème fraîche or fresh cream
Salt and black pepper
1 tablespoon lemon juice, optional

1 Fry the mixed mushrooms in the butter for about 5 minutes, stirring occasionally. Using a slotted spoon, transfer the mushrooms to a plate and keep them warm.
2 Add the oil to the frying pan and place over a medium-high heat. Add the noisettes and fry for 3 minutes on each side until they are browned on the outside but still pink in the centre. Using an egg slice, transfer to a warm plate, season and keep warm.
3 Add 2 teaspoons of tarragon and a little wine to the pan and stir to dislodge the sediment, then add the crème fraîche or cream and bring to the boil. Season.
4 Add the mushrooms and any excess meat juices on the plate and stir over a medium heat until it is heated through. Add more tarragon, if preferred, and some lemon juice if necessary to lift the flavour. Serve with the cooked noisettes.

STUFFINGS FOR LAMB

Most stuffings seem to be geared towards poultry. Can you suggest an interesting one that would go with lamb?

Lamb is a very popular dish in the Middle East where it is often served with apricots and spices. This is the basis for the stuffing used with a boned leg (right). Bone the leg of lamb yourself (see **Boning**) or buy an Easy-Carve boned leg of lamb.

Quickly fried lamb noisettes are served accompanied by a rich, chunky sauce of mushrooms and crème fraîche, spiked with the aniseed bite of tarragon.

Stuffed leg of lamb

SERVES: 6
PREPARATION TIME: 1 hour if boning leg otherwise 15–20 minutes, plus soaking of apricots
COOKING TIME: 2 hours

60 g (½ cup) dried apricots,
chopped and soaked for 1 hour
1 tablespoon olive oil
1 onion, finely chopped
1 clove garlic, chopped or crushed
Finely grated zest of 2 oranges, plus
the juice of 1 orange
Juice of ½ lemon
90 g (¾ cup) chopped hazelnuts,
toasted
1 tablespoon ground allspice
75 g (1¼ cups) fresh breadcrumbs
40 g (½ cup) burghul
Salt and black pepper
1 boned leg of lamb weighing
about 2 kg

FOR THE GRAVY
175 ml dry white wine
300 ml chicken stock

1 To make the stuffing, drain the apricots, reserving 100 ml of juice and add it to the stock. Heat the oil in a pan and fry the onion and garlic until softened. Remove from the heat and add the remaining ingredients, except for the lamb.
2 Preheat the oven to 180°C. Pack the majority of the stuffing lengthways down the leg, then roll the meat up and tie it with string at intervals of 2.5 cm. Put the remaining stuffing into a heatproof dish, add 1 tablespoon of hot water, stir and set aside.
3 Weigh the joint and calculate the cooking time, allowing 55 minutes per kg, plus an extra 20–30 minutes for well-done lamb. Place on a rack in a baking dish, sprinkle with pepper and roast.
4 About 30 minutes before the end of cooking, put the dish of stuffing in the oven. When the lamb is done, transfer it to a carving dish, cover and keep warm in the oven, with the heat turned off, for 20 minutes.
5 To make the sauce, pour off the fat from the baking dish. Place the dish over a medium heat and stir in the wine to dislodge the sediment. Bring to the boil, add the stock, and boil briskly until slightly thickened. Season and serve with the lamb.

ON YOUR HONOUR

I have always admired a guard of honour. How do I prepare it?

Guard of honour is one of the most impressive ways to cook new season's tender lamb and it allows you to cut any excess fat off the joint before roasting (see panel, below). Do not overcook the lamb, as it should be served slightly pink. Garnish with a selection of vegetables roasted with the lamb for extra flavour, as in the recipe (right).

PREPARING A GUARD OF HONOUR

The upper rib section (containing seven to nine ribs on each side) is called the best end of neck, or rack of lamb. A single line of ribs may be shaped into a circular crown roast, or two racks of lamb may be interlinked to form a guard of honour.

1 Cut the fat and meat in a straight line across the first rack down to the rib bones, about 2.5 cm from the ends, then remove the fat.

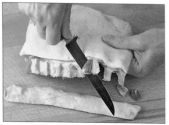

2 Cut the meat from the ends and scrape the bones clean with a knife. Repeat with the second rack.

3 Interlock the two racks of meat with the fat on the outside, and weave string tightly between each set of bones to secure the racks together firmly. Cover the ends of the bones with foil during roasting.

Guard of honour with roast vegetables

SERVES: 6
PREPARATION TIME: 20 minutes
COOKING TIME: 50–70 minutes

---

2 racks of Trim lamb weighing
    750 g–1 kg each
125 g (2 cups) fresh breadcrumbs
1 large egg, beaten
Finely grated rind of 1 lemon
3 tablespoons chopped fresh
    mixed herbs such as basil,
    parsley, rosemary and thyme
1 tablespoon finely chopped black
    olives
3 tablespoons olive oil
Salt and black pepper
6 cloves garlic
2 red peppers, deseeded and cut
    into thick slices
2 eggplants weighing about
    250–300 g each, cut
    into chunks
½ small butternut pumpkin, peeled,
    deseeded and cut into chunks, or
    2 zucchinis, cut into chunks
6 egg tomatoes, halved and
    deseeded
3 sprigs of thyme
3 tablespoons olive oil, or oil
    from a jar of sun-dried tomatoes,
    or a mixture of both
2 tablespoons chopped fresh basil
    or oregano

---

1 Preheat the oven to 180°C. Weigh the lamb and calculate the cooking time: allow 35 minutes per kg plus 15 minutes for pink lamb, or 55 minutes per kg plus 25 minutes for well done.
2 Prepare the racks of lamb and tie them together (see panel, left).
3 Mix together the breadcrumbs, egg, lemon rind, mixed herbs, olives, 1 tablespoon of the oil, and some salt and pepper. Carefully press the mixture in an even layer on the fatty side of the lamb then set aside.
4 Put all the vegetables and thyme into a baking dish, season and pour over the olive or sun-dried tomato oil. Stir to coat all the vegetables.
5 If you prefer your meat well done, place the interlinked racks of lamb upright on top of the vegetables and trickle 2 tablespoons of oil evenly

over the coating, then roast for around 45–50 minutes. If you prefer pink lamb, put the vegetables in the oven for 10–15 minutes, then add the meat and oil and cook for a further 35–40 minutes. Baste two or three times while cooking and cover with foil if the coating becomes too brown.
6 To test, pierce the eye of the meat with a metal skewer. If the juices are red, the meat is rare and if they are clear, the meat is well done.
7 When cooked, sprinkle the basil or oregano over the vegetables, then cover the lamb and vegetables and leave them to stand in the oven, with the heat turned off and the door propped open, for 15 minutes.
8 To carve the guard of honour, remove the string, then separate the racks and cut down between the lamb bones, cutting portions of two or three cutlets per person. Serve with the herb-flavoured vegetables.

Lamingtons

A HOME-GROWN CAKE

What is it about our lamingtons that makes them unique to Australia?

The lamington is a square piece of buttercake (see page 58), or sponge cake, dipped into chocolate icing and then coated with desiccated coconut. It was invented by resourceful bakers in Queensland in an attempt to keep the cake fresh in a hot climate, before the days of home refrigeration. Named in honour of Baron Lamington, a Queensland governor, and his wife, the lamington soon became a feature of fund-raising cake stalls. Lamington drives are still held today to raise money for schools, hospitals, clubs and charities.

For the icing, sift 500 g (3 cups) icing sugar and 30 g (¼ cup) cocoa into a mixing bowl. Add 125 ml boiling water, 30 g unsalted butter and 1 teaspoon vanilla essence; mix well until smooth. This quantity will cover 25 lamingtons.

Lasagne

LESS SAUCE

My lasagne always seems too sloppy. Should I use less sauce?

Yes. Many people enjoy a lasagne that has plenty of sauce but it is not really necessary and can dilute the flavours of the other ingredients.

It is important to use a filling that has a strong taste of its own, such as the ham and mushrooms in the *Lasagne con Prosciutto e Fungi* (below). Add plenty of seasoning because the pasta can also neutralise the flavour of the filling.

Lasagne with ham and mushrooms (Lasagne con prosciutto e fungi)

SERVES: 6
PREPARATION TIME: 1 hour
COOKING TIME: 50 minutes

FOR THE BECHAMEL SAUCE
90 g butter, plus extra for greasing
90 g (¾ cup) plain flour
1.25 litres milk
1 bay leaf
A few gratings of nutmeg
Salt and black pepper

FOR THE FILLING
40 g (1 cup) dried porcini
*   mushrooms*
70 g butter
2 tablespoons olive oil
2 shallots, finely chopped
750 g fresh mixed mushrooms,
*   thinly sliced*
Juice of ½ lemon
500 g lasagne sheets
250 g cooked ham, cut into
*   thin matchsticks*
100 g Parmesan cheese, freshly
*   grated*

1 To make the béchamel sauce, melt the butter in a saucepan, then stir in the flour and cook for a few minutes without allowing the roux to colour.
2 Pour in the milk and whisk until the sauce is thick and smooth. Add the bay leaf, simmer for 15 minutes then season with nutmeg, salt and pepper. Remove the bay leaf and dot the surface of the sauce with butter to prevent a skin forming. Set the sauce aside until needed. Preheat the oven to 190°C.
3 To make the mushroom filling, cover the dried mushrooms with boiling water. Leave for 30 minutes, then rinse and chop finely. Strain the mushroom water through a clean muslin cloth and reserve.
4 Heat 2 tablespoons of the butter with the oil in a large frying pan, sauté the shallots for a few minutes, then add both the fresh and dried mushrooms and lemon juice. Cook, uncovered, until they start to exude juices. Raise the heat to evaporate most of the liquid, add the strained water from the mushrooms, boil for a few minutes, season and set aside.
5 Cook the lasagne sheets, a few at a time, in boiling salted water then remove with a slotted spoon and place in a bowl of cold water. Drain on clean, dry tea towels and continue until all the pasta sheets are cooked.
6 Mix the cooked mushrooms with the béchamel sauce. Lightly grease a shallow, rectangular ovenproof dish about 33 × 25 cm with some of the butter then add a thin layer of mushroom sauce. This makes it easier to get a pie server under the lasagne when you serve it.
7 Arrange a layer of lasagne sheets over the top of the sauce, sprinkle some ham and grated cheese over this layer, then top with some more lasagne and cover it with the sauce (see panel, right). Repeat, finishing with a layer of mushroom sauce, then cover with the remaining cheese and dot with the rest of the butter.
8 Bake for 45–50 minutes, or until well browned and bubbling. Allow to rest for 5 minutes before serving.

SOFT TOUCH

I have tried using those 'no cook' lasagne sheets but they stayed stiff after baking. Why?

'No cook' lasagne sheets will stay stiff unless you layer and cover them with a great deal of fairly thin sauce; even though they absorb it, they can still taste heavy and pasty. In a traditional lasagne, the sauce would be béchamel, but a tomato sauce would also work. Although the lasagne sheets that need precooking are more trouble, the results are superior and demand less sauce. Fresh sheets are now available that need only a little precooking and these are excellent.

LAYERING LASAGNE

Building up layers of pasta sheets, sauce, ham and cheese adds to the varied texture and delicious flavour of this old Italian favourite.

1 Butter a shallow ovenproof dish and cover the base with a layer of mushroom sauce. Arrange a layer of cooked lasagne sheets over the top, without overlapping.

2 Sprinkle a thin layer of ham and cheese over the pasta sheets and cover with another layer of lasagne.

3 Continue to build up the dish, repeating the layers as above and finishing with a layer of the sauce. Cover with grated Parmesan cheese and dot the top with butter.

The simplest dish to make for guests who arrive without warning, or for friends who linger on until they need to be offered a meal, is individual omelettes. They take only a minute or two to make and there is plenty of scope for fillings from things you probably have on hand, such as fresh herbs, grated cheese, chopped tomatoes or crispy bacon.

Another speedy option is pasta, which everyone seems to like, and it is wise to keep a selection of dried pasta on hand. If you also keep some fresh garlic and cans of chopped tomatoes, you have the basis of an impromptu pasta sauce. Just add a can of drained clams, a few olives, anchovies or capers, or some artichoke hearts, capsicum or eggplant, sun-dried tomatoes, or tapenade.

The contents of these cans and jars can also be turned quickly into spreads for toast to serve with drinks, or as a starter, while you make the next course. For instance, try a can of salmon whizzed up in the food processor with a little mayonnaise and sharpened with a few gherkins.

Here are some other recipes for fine-tasting meals you can improvise in a hurry.

*L*AST-MINUTE GUESTS

Friends who turn up unexpectedly are one of life's pleasures – but a challenge to the cook who wants to offer them a welcoming meal. All these simple dishes, however, can be made up in minutes from a well-stocked store cupboard.

Grated potato becomes a star in this gratin mixed with cheese, eggs and herbs, and sandwiched between onions and crispy bacon.

Tuna and bean salad

Tuna and Bean Salad is an Italian classic that fills the bill when you want a nourishing dish that needs no cooking. Keep a variety of ready-to-bake rolls in your freezer or serve it with warm focaccia.

If you don't have cannellini (haricot) beans to hand, you can use other beans such as soy or red kidney beans, or leave them out altogether and add some hard-boiled eggs instead. Or turn the dish into a salade Niçoise: toss the tuna with green beans, tomatoes, canned new potatoes and black olives in a salad dressing.

SERVES: 4
PREPARATION TIME:
10 minutes
COOKING TIME: none

450 g canned tuna
400 g canned cannellini
  beans
½ red onion or several
  spring onions, finely
  chopped
Juice of 1 lemon
3 tablespoons olive oil
Finely chopped fresh parsley
  or other herb, if available
Salt and black pepper

1 Drain the tuna and tip it out into a wide serving bowl, then break the chunks into small pieces with a fork.
2 Drain and rinse the beans and mix them in with the tuna. Add the onion, lemon juice, olive oil and herb. Stir well to mix then season to taste with salt and pepper.

TUNA AND BEAN SALAD

BUTTER BEAN AND SPINACH SOUP

Butter bean and spinach soup

Nourishing Butter Bean and Spinach Soup uses frozen leaf spinach, which is handy to keep as it makes a great addition to a variety of soups. Good homemade stock is another invaluable freezer item, used to upgrade soups and sauces. And a selection of canned beans is a store-cupboard must – for soups, salads and main-course meals.

Follow the soup with some cheese and biscuits, and fresh fruit. Or, if you can find a late-night delicatessen open, buy an array of various cold meats and serve them with bread, pickles and salad to make a more substantial meal.

SERVES: 4
PREPARATION TIME: 5 minutes
COOKING TIME: 15 minutes

2 tablespoons olive oil
1 large onion, chopped
300 g canned butter beans
600 ml chicken stock
250 g frozen leaf spinach
A squeeze of lemon juice
A pinch of grated nutmeg
Salt and black pepper
To serve: grated mature
    Cheddar or Parmesan

1 Heat the oil in a saucepan and gently cook the onion until soft. Rinse the butter beans and add them to the onion along with the stock and frozen spinach. Cover the pan and leave to simmer for about 12 minutes until the spinach is thawed.
2 Season to taste with lemon juice, nutmeg, salt and pepper then mash or blend, leaving some texture to the soup. (A hand-held blender that does its work in the saucepan is useful for this.)
3 Serve the soup sprinkled with a generous handful of grated cheese.

Cheese and bacon potato gratin

This recipe uses the ingredients almost everyone has on hand in the kitchen: bacon, eggs, an onion, potatoes. Even if you don't have cream, you may have some sour cream in the refrigerator, or you can use milk. If you've run out of bacon, you could dice some ham or other cold meat and add that to the grated potato mixture instead.

The gratin does not take long to prepare; then, while it is baking, you can go back to your guests and offer them a drink and a simple starter.

SERVES: 4–6
PREPARATION TIME: 15 minutes
COOKING TIME: 40 minutes

3 eggs
150 ml fresh cream or milk
125 g mature Cheddar or
    Parmesan cheese, grated
750 g potatoes
½ teaspoon dried thyme
½ teaspoon dried chives
Salt and black pepper
1 onion, thinly sliced
250 g bacon

1 Preheat the oven to 200°C. Butter the bottom and sides of a large gratin dish.
2 Beat together the eggs, the cream or milk, and the cheese in a large mixing bowl with a balloon whisk.
3 Peel the potatoes and grate them in a food processor using the coarsest grating disc. Add them immediately to the egg mixture. Add the dried thyme and chives and season with lots of salt and pepper. Turn the mixture over a few times to mix everything thoroughly.
4 Scatter the onion slices over the bottom of the dish and spoon the egg and potato mixture over them, spreading it into an even layer with a knife or spatula. Put it on the top shelf of the oven and bake for 35–40 minutes.
5 Check the gratin is nicely browned, then grill or fry the bacon until crisp (microwave it if you like) and sprinkle it over the top to serve.

Couscous with prawns and peas

Couscous is a versatile grain that is sold already processed and needs only to be moistened and warmed through, rather than cooked. If you have a microwave, the frozen peas and prawns can be defrosted quickly; otherwise, allow an extra 30 minutes.

SERVES: 4
PREPARATION TIME: 10 minutes
COOKING TIME: 10 minutes

375 ml vegetable stock
250 g (1¼ cups) couscous
3 tablespoons olive oil
1 shallot, finely chopped
1 dried chilli, crumbled
250 g frozen peas or
    broad beans, defrosted
300 g peeled cooked prawns,
    defrosted if frozen
A squeeze of lemon juice
2 tablespoons fresh mint
Salt and black pepper

1 Bring the stock to the boil, pour in the couscous and give it a quick stir with a fork before covering it and setting it to one side, off the heat.
2 Heat the olive oil in a frying pan, add the shallot and the chilli and stir for a few minutes. Add the peas or beans and the prawns and stir until heated through.
3 Run a fork through the couscous several times to separate the grains then turn it out into a large bowl. Add the contents of the frying pan along with the lemon juice and the mint, then mix well together. Add a generous sprinkling of salt and pepper and serve warm.
VARIATIONS
Couscous can be an almost instant base for a variety of ingredients. Try leftover cooked meat instead of the prawns, and use canned corn kernels or mushrooms in place of peas or beans.

COUSCOUS WITH
PRAWNS AND PEAS

Leeks

AUTUMNAL TREAT

What can I do with the young slim leeks that are sometimes sold in the shops in early winter?

As they are young and tender, they can be quickly steamed or boiled for a salad dressed with a vinaigrette, as in the recipe, right. This is a good entreé served at room temperature with warm French bread, or an interesting side salad served lukewarm with poached white fish.

You can also cut young leeks into short lengths and add them to mixed vegetable soups, vegetarian casseroles or Asian stir-fries.

Young leeks braised in a peppery dressing, sprinkled with capers and currants, make a tempting dish.

Braised leeks with capers and currants

SERVES: *4*
PREPARATION TIME: *10 minutes*
COOKING TIME: *25 minutes*

75 ml olive oil
4 tablespoons white wine
1 tablespoon white wine vinegar
Salt and black pepper
8 slim leeks
1 tablespoon capers, rinsed
30 g (2 tablespoons) currants
A pinch of cayenne pepper

1 Mix the oil, wine, vinegar, salt and pepper in a pan wide enough to hold the leeks in one layer. Add the leeks, scattering the capers and currants in among them.
2 Bring to the boil, cover and then simmer for 15 minutes, basting once or twice with cooking liquor. The leeks are done when their centres can be pierced easily with a knife.
3 Uncover the pan, raise the heat and boil for 5 minutes to reduce the liquor, basting the leeks regularly. Transfer the leeks and the dressing to a serving dish and sprinkle with a light dusting of cayenne to serve.

GOODBYE GRIT

I wash leeks under the tap but there always seems to be some grit remaining. How should I wash them to get rid of it all?

Supermarket leeks usually come trimmed but homegrown ones can be difficult to clean properly. Remove most of the green tops and make slits in the outer layers to enable you to flush out any grit under the cold tap. If more cleaning seems necessary after you have sliced the leeks, rinse them thoroughly under a running tap or stand them in a bowl of cold water for 15–20 minutes.

VEGETABLE RIBBONS

What is a chiffonade of leeks?

Chiffonade is an old French word for ribbons and refers to finely shredded vegetables used as a bed for fish, lamb or poultry, or as a garnish. Leaves such as endive, lettuce or sorrel are rolled up and cut across to make a chiffonade. Leeks can be cut lengthways (see panel, below) and cooked in a cheese or tomato sauce to serve with pasta.

SLICING LEEKS FOR A CHIFFONADE

This method of cutting leeks results in a coarse shred that makes a useful garnish. The technique can also be applied to rolled-up leaves such as lettuce, sorrel or spinach.

1 Cut the washed and trimmed leeks in half lengthways, then cut into 8 cm lengths.

2 With the cut side down, slice into strips 5 mm wide.

3 Blanch the leek strips in boiling, salted water for a few seconds, then drain well. Serve as desired.

Leftovers

COLD MEATS

Is it safe to freeze leftover meat and poultry and, if so, what is the best way to do this?

Leftover meat can be frozen but do not keep it at room temperature for any longer than necessary. If the meat is still warm, put the plate in the refrigerator to cool quickly and then freeze it immediately so the bacteria that might cause food poisoning have no time to grow.

To freeze a leftover joint, carve the meat and pack the portions separately in foil or airtight plastic freezer bags, or cover the slices in gravy and store in freezer boxes.

Freeze casseroles or curries in plastic boxes or bags. They will keep for up to two months. It is not advisable to refreeze meat that was frozen before being cooked as the texture suffers considerably.

SUPERFLUOUS SAUCE

If I have leftover sauces or gravy, is it all right to freeze them?

Yes, most sauces freeze very well and frozen blocks of sauce or gravy can be reheated in a saucepan straight from the freezer. Egg-based emulsions, however, such as béarnaise, hollandaise and mayonnaise, will separate if they are frozen. Flour-based sauces, gravy and meat sauces such as Bolognese will keep for three months, while vegetable sauces, such as tomato, keep for three to four months. Frozen sauces are good timesavers so it is worth making twice as much as the recipe calls for and freezing half.

NO TO FREEZING

If I don't use all of a can of tuna, can I freeze the rest?

It is not advisable to freeze canned fish or any other canned foods as these products have already undergone heat processing and their structure is affected by cooling

treatments. Canned fish that has been frozen breaks down and becomes flabby and limp when thawed. But canned fish that has been mashed with other ingredients – in a pâté, for example – can be frozen successfully as the flesh has already been broken down.

RECYCLING TIPS

Can you suggest some good ways to use leftover vegetables?

Leftover vegetables can be stored, covered, in the fridge for a couple of days and reheated – for instance in a tomato or curry sauce, or sautéed in herb butter or olive oil. For a family meal, mix them with cooked pasta and cheese sauce in an ovenproof dish, top with breadcrumbs and some grated cheese and bake.

Make vegetables such as green beans, peas or boiled potatoes into a salad by tossing them in a mayonnaise dressing with fresh herbs.

The remains of a roast dinner can be turned into bubble and squeak. To make eight portions, mash 500 g cooked potatoes with 100 g cabbage, carrots or peas, 250 g minced cooked meat, a grated raw onion and 30 g melted butter. Add 2 tablespoons mustard and salt and pepper. Shape the mixture into pieces, coat with flour and fry for 2 minutes on each side.

SECOND APPEARANCE

It seems such a shame to throw away leftover cakes. How can I use them in interesting ways?

Start by removing any icing and almond paste. Rich fruit cake can be fried in butter and brown sugar and served hot with ice cream. Slices of panettone, or yeasted cakes that are only slightly stale, make an excellent base for a very special bread and butter pudding. And stale sponge cake can be used to make a good base for trifles. Put slices in a dish and spread with jam, sprinkle over sherry or fruit juice to moisten, and top with canned fruit, fresh custard and whipped cream.

USING UP EGGS

What can I do with leftover egg yolks and whites, and how long is it safe to keep them?

Separated egg yolks and whites are always worth keeping. Spare yolks can be used to enrich such dishes as omelettes, scrambled eggs or stir-fried rice, as well as to thicken soups or sauces. Leftover whites can be used for a variety of recipes such as meringues and soufflés.

Store egg yolks in a small dish, covered with cold water to stop them drying out, and whites in a lidded plastic box; both can be refrigerated this way for up to two days. Frozen, they will keep for three to six months (see *Eggs*).

Liver

SAME BY ANY NAME

What is lamb's fry?

Lamb's fry is the name most often used in Australia and New Zealand for sheep's liver.

OPTIONAL SOAKING

Why do some recipes tell you to soak liver in milk before cooking?

In the past, liver often had a stronger taste than it does now and it was soaked to soften the flavour. Modern breeding produces liver that has a milder flavour, and lamb's or calf's liver does not need soaking. Whether to soak stronger-tasting pig's and ox liver is a matter of personal taste.

FLASH IN THE PAN

In Italian restaurants the liver is always tender but mine is always tough. What am I doing wrong?

For a start, they always use calf's liver, which is the most tender liver. But it also needs to be cooked correctly, and quickly toughens if it is overcooked. For best results, slice the liver thinly (see panel, right) and cook briefly over a high heat.

When the blood bubbles through on one side, turn it over and cook until it bubbles through on the other side, then serve it immediately. Try the recipe below for a truly tender dish.

Italian liver and onions

SERVES: *4*
PREPARATION TIME: *15 minutes*
COOKING TIME: *45 minutes*

3 tablespoons olive oil
750 g large onions, thinly sliced
Salt and black pepper
500 g calf's liver, prepared and
 very thinly sliced

1 Heat 2 tablespoons of the olive oil in a large frying pan. Add the onions and a little salt and black pepper. Cover the pan with a lid or a sheet of foil and cook gently, stirring from time to time, for 25–30 minutes until the onions are very soft.
2 Put a bowl and a plate to warm. When the onions are soft, remove the cover from the pan, increase the heat to medium and cook, stirring, until the onions are golden brown and caramelised, but be careful not to let them stick to the bottom of the pan. Transfer the onions to the warmed bowl, using a slotted spoon, and leave the excess oil in the pan.
3 Add the remaining oil to the pan and heat over a high heat. Add half the liver in a single layer and cook for 45 seconds–1 minute until it is just browned. Turn the slices over using an egg slice and brown the other side for 45 seconds–1 minute; the liver should still be pink in the centre. Using the egg slice, transfer the slices to the warmed plate.
4 Fry the remaining liver in the same way. Return the onions and the first batch of liver to the pan alongside it and stir both over a high heat for 30–45 seconds to warm through.

TENDER FOR TOTS

Is there any way to cook liver so that my children will eat it?

Most children dislike the strong flavour of liver, and will find it even less appetising if it is tough and

PREPARING LIVER

Very strongly flavoured liver, such as ox liver, can be soaked overnight in milk in the refrigerator, to make the flavour more mellow.

1 Carefully snip and peel away the fine membrane covering the liver (calf's liver is shown here).

2 With a sharp knife, cut the liver diagonally into even, thin slices.

3 Snip out any tough internal tubes with sharp scissors.

overcooked. To lessen both these problems, it is best to braise it very slowly in a casserole with vegetables and flavourings so it is very tender and the flavour is mellowed. Or disguise it by combining the liver with other meats and flavourings. Liver can be buried in meat loaves, patties, burgers, shepherd's pie or with pasta in a tomato sauce.

In any case, children should not eat liver too often; it is such a rich source of vitamin A that just 100 g supplies more than ten times the daily adult requirement, which is too much for children.

OUT OF STOCK

Why should you not include the liver of a bird in giblet stock? What can you do with it?

Poultry livers make stocks cloudy, though this is not a problem if you are using the stock for gravy, and the liver can be mashed up after cooking in the stock to add richness. There are many other ways to use poultry livers; they can be added to stuffing, used to make pâtés, or quickly fried with mushrooms and onions for serving on toast. They can also be used to make an unusual warm salad, as in the recipe below.

Chicken or duck liver and grape salad

SERVES: *4 as a starter*
PREPARATION TIME: *5 minutes*
COOKING TIME: *5 minutes*

4 large handfuls of mesclun (mixed salad leaves such as curly endive, rocket and spinach)
500 g chicken or duck livers
3 tablespoons olive oil
A sprig of thyme
1 tablespoon red wine vinegar
2 teaspoons balsamic vinegar
2 tablespoons walnut oil
125 g seedless grapes, halved
Salt and black pepper
To garnish: fresh herbs or edible flowers

1 Divide the salad leaves between four individual salad bowls or plates.
2 Remove any membranes from the livers and slice them into pieces of roughly equal size.
3 Heat 2 tablespoons of the olive oil in a frying pan, add the livers and thyme and cook briskly, shaking the pan occasionally, for about 2 minutes on each side so the livers are slightly caramelised on the outside but still pink inside. Using a slotted spoon, transfer the livers to the salads.
4 Stir the vinegars and oils into the pan, dislodging the sediment. Add the grapes, season, and gently heat through. Then pour a little warm dressing over each of the salads and garnish with fresh herbs or flowers.

Pan-fried poultry livers on a rainbow-coloured salad of mesclun, marigolds and basil are served with a warm walnut oil and balsamic vinegar dressing.

ENLARGED LIVER

I've heard a lot about foie gras. What exactly is it and can you suggest ways to use it?

Foie gras is the enlarged liver of a force-fed goose or duck. Some connoisseurs think goose foie gras has a smoother, more subtle flavour than that of duck, others prefer the more complex flavour of duck, which also has slightly less fat.

Fresh raw foie gras is produced in France. To serve, it is sliced thickly and sautéed over a high heat until brown on the outside but still pink inside. Gentle baking in a terrine is another way to cook it.

Cooked foie gras is also produced. When labelled *mi cuit* (half-cooked), the liver has been cooked but not sterilised, has a limited shelf life and must be kept refrigerated. It will taste almost as good as the freshly home-cooked liver.

Foie gras in cans, the only authentic foie gras available in Australia, has been sterilised at a high temperature so will not have such a good flavour or texture; *entier* on the label indicates that the liver is whole; pieces of liver are just labelled foie gras.

Truffe on the label means that it contains black truffle, and *pâté de foie gras* contains minced pork.

Foie gras, like all pâtés and terrines, is served cold, often with toast, as an hors d'oeuvre. Liverwurst, a soft spreadable sausage made with cooked liver, can also be served the same way.

Lobster

BEST BUY

Because of its price, lobster for me is a special occasion buy only, so how can I make sure I choose the best lobster?

Lobster has been misnamed in Australia since the days of the early settlers. The species commonly found – with its rough and spiky shell – is, in fact, a rock lobster or crayfish. True lobsters belong to a different family, have two claws like crab claws, and are found in northern hemisphere waters.

Most crayfish sold as lobster in Australia are cooked. When buying a cooked lobster, look for a firm, springy tail and reject any with tails that are limp. They should also feel heavy for their size. Cooked lobsters are perfect to serve cold, or can be used in recipes where the flesh is reheated gently in a sauce, such as Lobster Thermidor (right).

Live shellfish are not easy to buy unless you live near the sea, but live lobsters can usually be ordered in advance from a fish market. Look for one that is still moving and also feels heavy. Lobsters cast their shells to grow larger ones and you don't want to buy a small specimen in a large new shell. A worn shell, and white tracery on the top, are signs of an old shell, which the lobster is likely to have filled out.

KINDLY KILLING

Is there a relatively kind way to kill and cook a lobster?

The traditional way to kill and cook a lobster is to drop it into a large pot with 60 g salt per litre of boiling water. Crustaceans die within a few seconds of being immersed.

A more humane method is to place the live lobster in a plastic bag and freeze it for at least 2 hours before cooking. This will stun the cold-blooded creature so that it is unconscious when it goes into the boiling water.

COOKING AND DRESSING A LOBSTER

Cook for 12 minutes for the first 500 g of weight, 10 minutes for the next 500 g and 5 minutes for each additional 500 g. Remove and hold under the cold tap. Place the cooled lobster on its back and pull away the legs. Break the legs at the central joint and pick out the meat. Twist off the head and put aside.

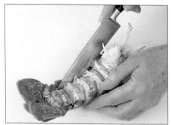

1 With a heavy knife, cut along either side of the underside of the tail, pulling away the covering shell and prising out the column of flesh in one piece.

2 Remove the white gills from below the head and pick out the thin line of intestine running the length of the tail meat. Discard the feathery gills, but keep the grey-green tomalley (liver) from inside the head, and any pink coral (roe).

3 Slice the meat into medallions. Arrange all the meat decoratively on an attractive bed of mixed salad leaves, accompanied by fresh homemade mayonnaise and garnished with the reserved lobster head, well cleaned.

HEAT AGAIN

I can only buy precooked lobster, but would like to serve it in more ways than just cold as a salad. How can I serve it in a hot dish?

To serve hot, ideally a fresh live lobster is killed by splitting it open, then it is simply grilled or baked in olive oil or butter and herbs. But most home cooks would flinch from chopping up live shellfish and prefer to buy a cooked lobster.

Many of the rich classical treatments, such as the recipe for Lobster Thermidor below, use precooked lobster meat that is cut up when cold and then reheated. A sauce is built around the flesh, which is then returned to its shell for a final blaze under a very hot grill to brown the top.

Lobster thermidor

SERVES: 2 as a starter
PREPARATION TIME: 40 minutes
COOKING TIME: 10–12 minutes

---

1 x 750 g cooked lobster
50 g butter
2 shallots, finely chopped
1 tablespoon white wine
1 tablespoon dry sherry
100 ml fish stock
4 tablespoons fresh cream
4 tablespoons finely grated
    Parmesan cheese
1 tablespoon chopped parsley
Salt and black pepper
1 teaspoon mustard powder

---

1 Pull away the legs and crack them open. Twist the head off the lobster. With a heavy knife, cut the tail in two lengthways. Remove all the flesh from both legs and tail, scraping out the tomalley you find in the shell. Cut the meat into slices about 2 cm thick. Scrub the halved shell clean and leave it upside-down to drain. Preheat the grill to red hot.
2 Melt the butter in a saucepan and fry the shallots gently for 3 minutes until softened but not browned. Add the lobster meat and tomalley. Take the pan off the heat and gradually stir in the wine, sherry and fish stock. Return the pan to the heat

Lobster, sherry, Parmesan cheese, cream and a touch of fiery mustard make Lobster Thermidor irresistible.

and simmer the sauce for 3–4 minutes, stirring often, until it is smooth and thick.

3 Pour in the cream and half the Parmesan. Heat gently, stirring often, until the lobster is heated through and the cheese has melted smoothly into the sauce. Add the parsley and season to taste with salt and black pepper, then sprinkle on the mustard powder and stir well.

4 Spoon the mixture into the halved shells, sprinkle over the remaining Parmesan and grill until the surface is bubbling and has turned golden brown. Serve immediately.

VARIATION

For Lobster Newburg, the sauce is made with cream thickened with egg yolk and flavoured with Madeira or sherry. It is sometimes sharpened with a pinch of cayenne powder.

Low-fat Cheeses

SOFT AND LOW

Which cheeses have the lowest natural fat content?

In general, softer cheeses have a lower fat content than hard cheeses because they have a higher percentage of water. Cream cheeses and cheeses labelled double and triple cream are the exceptions as they are particularly high in fat, containing about 47 per cent fat. Hard cheeses made from goat's and ewe's milk are likely to be higher in fat than similar cheeses made from cow's milk, as both goat's and ewe's milk have a naturally higher fat content.

If you are aiming to cut down on your fat intake, it is best to stay with cottage cheese or soft, fresh cheeses such as ricotta and feta. Of the harder cheeses, Edam is a better low-fat choice than Cheddar. Some Australian cheese varieties can be found in reduced-fat versions. These include Edam, Swiss, Cheddar, cream and mozzarella.

Some supermarkets stock a selection of lower-fat alternatives to full-fat cheese in which the saturated butter fat has been removed and replaced with polyunsaturated vegetable oils. These cheeses are particularly useful for those people who want to reduce their saturated fat intake.

The nutritional information supplied by manufacturers can be misleading. The fat content is often expressed as 'fat in dry matter', which means the fat content of the cheese solids after the water has been removed. An ordinary Brie which is labelled a '60 per cent' Brie is not as rich as it sounds because it actually contains half the fat of a regular cream cheese.

AUSTRALIAN CHEESES BY FAT CONTENT

CHEESE	% OF FAT PER 100 g
Cottage cheese (low fat)	1.0
Cottage cheese (creamed)	5.5
Ricotta (reduced fat)	8.5
Cottage cheese (plain)	9.3
Quark	9.6
Ricotta	11.3
Bocconcini	15.2
Haloumi	17.0
Mozzarella (reduced fat)	18.0
Mozzarella	23.1
Fruit	23.3
Cheddar (reduced fat)	24.0
Feta	25.1
Camembert	26.3
Pecorino	27.2
Processed cheese	27.5
Edam	27.9
Romano	27.9
Provolone	28.4
Neufchatel	28.8
Brie	29.1
Tilsit	29.5
Gouda	29.6
Swiss	29.9
Raclette	30.0
Pepato	31.1
Washed rind cheese	32.3
Blue vein	33.5
Cheddar	33.8
Colby	33.8
Cheshire	33.8
Red Leicester	33.8
Cream cheese	33.9
Double Gloucester	34.0
Parmesan	35.7
Havarti	36.5

LEANER CUISINE

Can I use a reduced-fat Cheddar cheese in my usual recipes, or will it behave and taste differently when I try to cook with it?

Modern manufacturing techniques for reduced-fat cheeses are increasingly sophisticated, nevertheless in some situations the performance of these cheeses in cooking is not the same as their full-fat equivalents. A reduced-fat, Cheddar-style hard cheese will melt under the grill, but it will not brown properly. If you want a crusty topping for a baked dish, add breadcrumbs to these reduced-fat hard cheeses.

But in most dishes in which reduced-fat hard cheese is used (such as quiche or pastry), you can expect it to perform in much the same way as its full-fat equivalent.

When making cheese sauces with reduced-fat cheese, make sure you remove the pan from the heat first, and stir the cheese through at the last minute so it doesn't overheat. And when using a reduced-fat cheese for sauces, you may also find it necessary to add a little mustard or some herbs to boost the flavour, as it is usually less rich.

LOW-FAT DESSERTS

Can I use reduced-fat soft cheeses for making desserts?

You can, but be wary as they will work only in some dishes. While hard cheeses made with vegetable oil can be used in cooking like their fattier equivalents, reduced-fat soft cheeses tend to perform poorly in cooking. In particular, they should not be used for icings or dips as the process of stirring will break down the texture of the cheese and the finished product will be disappointingly runny.

Reduced-fat soft cheeses can, however, be used in recipes such as cheesecakes and mousses which contain several other ingredients, but remember to check the flavour level carefully as these cheeses have a less assertive flavour than their full-fat equivalents.

Low-fat Spreads

WHEN THEY WORK

Can all low-fat spreads be used successfully in cooking?

All low-fat or reduced-fat spreads contain less fat than butter or standard block margarine and a great deal more water. This means that while they can be used like butter or margarine as a spread on bread and so forth, they are not always suitable for cooking.

They can be used successfully for all-in-one sauces and cakes, for choux pastry and, if mixed with full-fat butter or block margarine, can sometimes be used for other pastry. To make a cheesecake base, normally done by mixing butter with biscuit crumbs, melt the low-fat spread carefully over a low heat and then add the crumbs.

Low-fat spreads are generally not suitable for shallow or deep-fat frying because they contain too much water. However, they can be used in a nonstick saucepan to fry foods such as onions or mushrooms, as long as it is gently done over a low heat. They are also unsuitable for traditional biscuits and cakes, and preserves such as lemon curd, because they do not set firm.

Very low-fat spreads, which have an even higher proportion of water and contain less than 25 per cent fat, are quite unsuitable for frying or sautéing because they will spit and are liable to burn very easily.

Healthy option

You can use a low-fat spread instead of butter or margarine to make crisp and light choux pastry. Melt the spread with the water over a low heat then add it to the other ingredients and continue with the recipe (see page 95).

LOW-FAT POURING SAUCE

Preparing and cooking this all-in-one sauce will only take about 10 minutes: 5 minutes for preparation and 5 minutes for cooking. It can be flavoured with ingredients such as grated reduced-fat cheese, finely chopped fresh parsley or chopped capers. Stir the chosen flavouring into the sauce after it is cooked.

1 Place 15 g low-fat margarine spread and 15 g (1½ tablespoons) plain flour in a saucepan with 250 ml milk. Heat the mixture, stirring constantly, until the sauce comes to the boil.

2 Simmer gently for 2–3 minutes, whisking all the time until the sauce has become thick, smooth and glossy. Season, add any flavouring and pour into a jug, or over a cooked dish.

FRUITY FAT SUBSTITUTE

Is there any way to lower the fat content of dishes usually made with full-fat ingredients?

Reduced-fat products such as low-fat cheeses and creams may be used to replace full-fat varieties in some recipes. Even more surprisingly, you can reduce the fat, kilojoule and cholesterol contents of some cakes and biscuits by replacing part or all of the butter or margarine with a purée of dried fruit, such as apricot or prune. This will add flavour and texture, as well as reducing the fat.

To make 300 g of purée, place 250 g (1¼ cups) dried apricots or 250 g (1¼ cups) prunes in a food processor or blender with 90 ml water. Blend until smooth, then use in place of the butter or margarine in the recipe.

With many recipes you can replace all the fat with the fruit purée, using the same number of grams of purée. But with other recipes you may find it works better to have half fat and half fruit purée. And note that the purée is not suitable for replacing fat in pastry. The recipe for Apricot and Cinnamon Fruit Bars (right) uses prune purée instead of butter or margarine to make a sweet snack.

Apricot and cinnamon fruit bars

MAKES: *16 bars*
PREPARATION TIME: *35 minutes*
COOKING TIME: *35–40 minutes*

185 g (2 cups) rolled oats
185 g (1½ cups) plain flour
185 g (1 cup) light brown sugar
2 teaspoons ground cinnamon
1 large egg, lightly beaten
300 g prune purée
125 g (1 cup) dried apricots
125 g (¾ cup) sultanas or raisins
250 ml orange juice

1 Preheat the oven to 180°C. Grease a shallow cake tin measuring 28 × 18 cm.
2 Put the oats in a bowl and add the flour, sugar, cinnamon, the egg and three-quarters of the prune purée. Rub the mixture with your fingertips until all is well combined. Spoon half the mixture into the prepared cake tin and spread it evenly.
3 Chop the apricots and put them in a saucepan then add the sultanas or raisins, the orange juice and the rest of the prune purée. Cook over a medium heat for about 5 minutes until the fruit has softened. Take the pan off the heat and allow to cool.
4 Mix the cooled fruit into the remaining oat mixture and spoon it over what is already in the tin. Bake

for about 35–40 minutes or until the mixture is crisp on top.
5 Leave to cool completely in the tin before cutting it into bars.
VARIATIONS
Use muesli instead of rolled oats (or a mixture of half and half), and make the purée from dried apricots.

LOW-FAT SANDWICHES

Can you give me some ideas for tasty, low-fat sandwich fillings?

You can cut kilojoules and reduce the fat content of sandwiches by using a low-fat spread and, if you include well-flavoured ingredients, still make a filling that is satisfying and appealing. You may also find that wholewheat bread sandwiches have not only more flavour but more staying power.

For example, you can use a low-fat spread on brown bread, top it with cottage cheese, scatter chopped sliced canned pineapple over the cheese and then sprinkle it with chopped chives or spring onions. Add a final generous seasoning of sea salt and black pepper.

Another successful combination is flaked cooked or canned salmon and chopped watercress, bound with 2 tablespoons reduced fat mayonnaise, garnished with a sliced tomato and sprinkled with lemon juice to finish. You can also use canned tuna or crabmeat with a handful of freshly chopped herbs and use finely shredded lettuce instead of watercress. Chopped red pepper or canned corn kernels add a crunchy texture.

Instead of sliced bread use muffins, lightly toasted focaccia, a walnut or tomato bread or halved French sticks. To give reduced-fat mayonnaise more zest, stir in a teaspoon or two of good strong mustard. And the addition of fresh herbs, such as basil, coriander or flat-leafed parsley, will help to make sandwiches much more attractive and tempting.

Pungently flavoured foods in unusual combinations can be so interesting and delicious that no one will ever miss the fat.

Macaroons

FRESHLY GROUND

Should I grind my own almonds for macaroons or marzipan?

Yes, because fresh whole almonds usually have more flavour than ground or blanched almonds. To grind your own, first blanch the unskinned almonds in a pan of boiling water, plunge them in cold water, slip off the skins and then grind them in a blender, food processor or coffee mill. You can also pulverise them in a pestle and mortar, but this will take much longer and they will not be as fine.

TINY MACAROONS

What is the difference between macaroons and ratafias?

The only difference is their size. A ratafia is a tiny almond-flavoured macaroon, but in the 18th century, almond-flavoured biscuits, cakes and some homemade liqueurs were also known as ratafias.

A handful of ratafias are a good addition to the base of a traditional English trifle or lemon syllabub. For emergency desserts, sprinkle ratafias with kirsch or brandy, then serve them topped with red berries and cream. They also go well with ice cream and rich chocolate sauce. Finely crushed ratafias can be pressed onto the sides of cold soufflés, or used whole to decorate the tops of creamy mousses.

The recipe for Almond Macaroons on the right can be made into ratafias, but use almond essence, not vanilla, to flavour them.

Almond macaroons

MAKES: *about 15 macaroons*
PREPARATION TIME: *30 minutes*
COOKING TIME: *20 minutes*

2-3 sheets edible rice paper
90 g (¾ cup) ground almonds
125 g (½ cup) caster sugar
1 large egg white
2 drops almond or vanilla essence
To decorate: flaked almonds

1 Preheat the oven to 180°C and line a large baking tray with rice paper.
2 Mix the ground almonds with the caster sugar in a bowl.
3 Whisk the egg white to soft peaks. Using a large metal spoon, carefully fold the ground almonds and sugar mixture plus the almond or vanilla essence into the egg white, stirring until the mixture is smooth.
4 Place a large piping bag fitted with a 2 cm plain nozzle over a jug and turn down the cuff. Spoon in the almond mixture and pipe as many rounds, 4 cm across, as will fit on the lined baking tray. Press a flaked almond on top of each round. Bake the macaroons in the oven for around 20 minutes or until they are very lightly browned then cool them on the baking tray.
5 When the macaroons are cold, lift them and tear away the spare rice paper so that just the base is covered. You can store the cold macaroons in an airtight tin for up to ten days.
VARIATIONS
Instead of a plain nozzle, you can use a straight star nozzle for a fluted appearance. For tiny ratafias, about 1-2 cm, use the recipe above but bake for only 10-12 minutes.

Crunchy macaroons piped into neat rounds need only a simple flaked almond on top for crisp decoration.

Mangoes

TOUCH TESTING

How can you tell when a mango is ripe and ready to eat?

The colour of a mango is no guide to ripeness as the skins vary from one variety to another. A green mango can be as ripe as one that is bright red. You test for ripeness by touch: they should yield when gently pressed. Mangoes that are to travel a long way are picked unripe and can be encouraged to ripen by leaving them out in a warm room or by putting them in a bowl with other fruit: fully ripe bananas are especially effective.

Mangoes can vary considerably in flavour, sweetness, aroma and texture. There are hundreds of varieties, and they are not always labelled, but if they are, one of the most popular mangoes is Kensington Pride, also known as Bowen Special. Others to look for are Kent, Keitt, Palmer R2E2, Nam Dok Mai and Sensation, all of which are rich and melting. The Tommy Atkins variety, which is tougher and more fibrous, is best used for chutney.

MULTIPLE USES

I have often used mangoes in desserts, but is there anything else I can do with them?

Mangoes are more versatile than some other exotic fruits and can be used in many dishes, both sweet and savoury. Diced mangoes can be added to a salad made with rice or vegetables. They also make tasty salsas and cooked chutneys. Ripe mangoes, sliced or cut into chunks, dressed with a squeeze of lime, or fried until slightly caramelised, go well with smoked meats, chicken and turkey. They can be blended with yoghurt, honey and a squeeze of lemon or lime for a revitalising drink. The luxurious prawn salad on page 213 is another original way to use a luscious ripe mango. Serve it as a special dinner party starter.

Mango and prawn salad

SERVES: 4
PREPARATION TIME: *30 minutes*
COOKING TIME: *5 minutes*

1 cup small snow peas
1 large ripe mango
16 large cooked prawns, peeled,
  deveined and halved lengthways
4 spring onions, thinly sliced
  diagonally
2 cups mesclun (salad greens)

FOR THE DRESSING
1 clove garlic, crushed
1 teaspoon chopped fresh ginger
1 teaspoon palm or light brown
  sugar
1 teaspoon chopped coriander root
¼ cup fresh coriander leaves
2 teaspoons fish sauce
1 tablespoon peanut oil
¼ cup lime juice

*Ripe mango, juicy prawns, snow peas
and decorative salad leaves start a
summer meal with colour and flavour.*

1 To make the dressing, put all the
ingredients into a small bowl and
whisk together.
2 Trim the snow peas and steam
for 5 minutes, or until tender-crisp.
Refresh in a bowl of chilled water,
then drain and pat dry.
3 Peel and slice the mango (see
panel, right). Arrange the prawns
and mango on four individual plates.
Sprinkle the snow peas, spring
onions and mesclun evenly on top.
4 Spoon the dressing over the salads
and serve immediately.

VARIATION
For a sweeter dressing, substitute
orange juice for the lime juice, and
add peeled and seeded fresh orange
segments to the salad.

HOW TO CUT UP A MANGO

*Fresh mangoes can be as small as a
peach or as large as a melon.
Inside the tough, leathery skin is
sweetly scented, juicy flesh that can
be sliced or diced for using fresh or
in cooked dishes, sweet or savoury.*

1 Stand the mango on end. With a
small sharp knife, cut through
the flesh lengthways on either side
of the stone, cutting as close to the
stone as possible.

2 To serve the mango cheeks
whole, grip one end of the skin
with your thumb and peel off in
one piece. To serve the mango in
slices, cut lengthways along each of
the cheeks, carefully lifting the
slices away from the skin.

3 To serve the mango cubed, cut
across the flesh of each cheek
several times lengthways, then
widthways. To raise the cubes, press
upwards on the skin side. The cubes
can be cut from the skin, or the
cheek served decoratively as is. The
flesh that remains attached to the
stone can be sucked off as a cook's
perk, very messy but delicious.

Marinade

SOAKED IN FLAVOUR

What is a marinade?

A marinade is a mixture of ingredients in which food is soaked before cooking. It can include fruit juice, herbs, oil, spices, vinegar, wine, yoghurt and other seasonings. Marinades for meat should not contain salt as this draws out too much of the natural juice and colour.

Originally used as a way of preserving meat for a few days, before domestic fridges were common, marinades are now used only to heighten the flavour of food, help to prevent it from drying out and also to have a tenderising effect. The choice of ingredients depends on the food and the type of dish, and how it will be cooked. When grilling, for instance, the marinade is either basted on the food during cooking or reduced and thickened separately to make a sauce.

RAW, COOKED AND DRY

What types of marinade can I use?

There are three main types: raw, cooked and dry. Raw marinades of oils and vinegar, or yoghurt, are used for relatively tender foods such as chicken or fish that only require a short marination time.

An uncooked marinade composed of wine, brandy, vegetables and/or herbs can be used for large joints, game and poultry. Cooked marinades, such as those using red or white wine, are used to give food a fairly strong flavour. They should be properly cooled before being poured over the meat, which is then covered and refrigerated until you are ready to cook it.

The term dry marinades is a slight misnomer, as a little oil and vinegar (or lemon juice or wine) is included. But the spices and other flavourings mixed with the liquid are firstly rubbed into the dry meat and not used as a bath in which the meat is immersed. Dry marinades are more economical, as very little oil or vinegar is used, and the marinade, plus any juices that run from the meat, is frequently used in the final dish. The function of the dry marinade is simply to flavour the meat through prolonged contact.

Whatever method you choose, turn the food frequently while it is marinating for even absorption.

THE RIGHT DISH

What kind of containers should be used for marinades?

Marinades usually contain an acid, such as vinegar or wine, to break down tough food fibres and this affects metals other than stainless steel, including copper and aluminium. Glass or ceramic dishes or bowls or plastic boxes are suitable containers for marinades. Use plastic wrap or a plate to cover them.

OILS FOR MARINADES

Which oil is best for a marinade?

Any oil with a pleasant but not too strong flavour, such as a mild olive, sunflower or canola oil, is fine for a marinade. Oils with a very positive flavour, such as sesame, could drown the flavour of the meat.

If the food to be marinated is particularly bland and needs help, try one of the herb or spice-flavoured oils, such as garlic or chilli, for extra flavour.

BENEFITS OF YOGHURT

When yoghurt is included in a marinade, does it tenderise the meat or simply add flavour?

Both. The yoghurt adds flavour but it also contains active enzymes that act as a tenderiser. Using yoghurt as a marinade is very popular in Indian cookery. The recipe (right) for Chicken Tikka is a typically Indian way of preparing pieces of chicken so that they are tender and aromatic after cooking. In an Indian restaurant this dish would most often be cooked in a tandoor, an extremely hot traditional clay oven, and served with naan bread.

Chicken tikka

SERVES: *4*
PREPARATION TIME: *25 minutes, plus overnight marination*
COOKING TIME: *15-20 minutes*

---

150 ml natural yoghurt
1 teaspoon cornflour
1 small onion, chopped
1 clove garlic, crushed
1 tablespoon finely chopped green ginger
1 fresh chilli, finely chopped
Juice of 1 lemon
2 tablespoons olive oil
2 teaspoons paprika
1 teaspoon garam masala
1 teaspoon ground cumin
2 tablespoons chopped fresh coriander
Salt and black pepper
500 g chicken breast fillets, skinned and cubed

---

1 Put all the ingredients, except the chicken, into a food processor or a blender and process until smooth.
2 Put the chicken pieces into a nonmetallic dish, pour the blended flavourings over them and mix well, ensuring that all the chicken pieces are coated thoroughly. Cover the mixture and leave it to marinate in the refrigerator overnight.
3 Heat the grill to medium. Thread the chicken onto skewers and cook it for 15-20 minutes, turning the skewers occasionally and brushing the chicken from time to time with the remaining marinade until the meat is cooked and tender.
4 Serve the chicken tikka hot or cold with warm naan or pita bread and a cucumber and yoghurt raita.

VARIATION

The threaded chicken pieces can be barbecued and also can be cooked in a baking dish with the marinade in a preheated oven at 200°C for 30 minutes, turning every 10 minutes or so while they cook. If there is any marinade left over when the chicken is done, it can be reduced to a thick sauce by cooking in the baking dish over a high heat while you scrape up all the sediment and pan juices. Stir the sauce then pour it over the chicken before serving.

Tuna steaks taste fresh and tender if they are marinated in olive oil, lime, basil and chillies before being quickly grilled.

TENDERISING TACTICS

If I marinate a tough steak for a few hours, will it become tender?

While the acid content of the marinade will penetrate the meat fibres and make a tough steak softer, it would have to marinate for days to become as tender as fillet steak and this would have a detrimental effect on the flavour of the meat.

FOODS TO MARINATE

Are there any foods other than meat that can be marinated?

Fish and shellfish, game, offal, poultry and vegetables can all be marinated. Thin slices of fish, such as salmon, trout and white fish fillets with a delicate texture, are often marinated from 15 minutes up to 2 hours and served without cooking with a tasty dressing. The tuna recipe below shows how a simple marinade can add a subtle flavour to grilled fish.

Marinated fresh tuna steaks with basil

SERVES: 4
PREPARATION TIME: 15 minutes, plus 2 hours marination
COOKING TIME: 10-14 minutes

---

3 tablespoons olive oil
Finely grated zest and juice of 1 lime
3 tablespoons chopped fresh basil
1-2 whole chillies
Salt and pink peppercorns
4 x 185 g tuna steaks

---

1 Put the oil, lime zest and juice, basil, chillies and seasoning in a bowl and whisk until well blended.
2 Put the tuna steaks in a shallow, nonmetallic dish and then pour the marinade over them so they are evenly coated. Cover and leave to marinate for at least 2 hours in the refrigerator, turning occasionally.
3 Heat the grill to a medium heat. Remove the tuna from the marinade and cook for 5-7 minutes on each side until the fish is lightly cooked and tender. Serve with a spicy salsa or fresh chutney, and some boiled new potatoes or fresh bread.

VARIATIONS

You can also chargrill the tuna over a barbecue or in a ridged iron grill pan over a very high heat.

To bake the fish, loosely wrap the marinated steaks individually in foil, then seal them (with or without a little of the marinade) and cook in a preheated oven at 180°C for 20-30 minutes, until the steaks are just cooked and tender. Allow the tuna steaks to stand in the foil for 10 minutes before serving.

Marmalade

PEEL AND PARE

How should you prepare fruit for making marmalade?

Choose ripe fruit with smooth skin, preferably unwaxed, then scrub and dry them. For fine-shred marmalade, pare off the zest and slice it into very thin strips. For thin-cut and coarse-cut marmalade, cut off and discard the ends, stand the fruit upright and cut away the peel, avoiding the inner pith. Cut each strip of peel into thin strips for thin marmalade or short 3 mm thick strips for coarse-cut.

Cut up the flesh roughly, reserving the juice, pith and pips. You can speed up the job by chopping unpeeled oranges straight into a food processor but the processed peel will be chunky and uneven.

The Ruby Red Grapefruit Marmalade recipe on the right uses thin peel and is surprisingly sweet.

Cooking the pips and pith in a muslin bag with the fruit releases their pectin and helps the marmalade to set.

Ruby red grapefruit marmalade

MAKES: *about 2 kg*
PREPARATION TIME: *30 minutes*
COOKING TIME: *2½ hours*

2 large Ruby red grapefruit
4 lemons
1.5 kg (6 cups) white sugar

1 Scrub the grapefruit and pat dry. Pare the rind from the fruit and slice it into thin, even strips.
2 Remove the pith and roughly cut up the flesh, reserving the pips and any juice. Put the pips and pith on a square of muslin and tie into a bag with a long piece of kitchen string.
3 Put the grapefruit flesh, the juice, rind and 2 litres of water in a large saucepan. Add the muslin bag and tie the string to the handle. Bring the mixture to the boil, then simmer gently for 1–2 hours or until the pared rind is very tender and the pan's contents have reduced by half.
4 Warm the sugar by spreading it on a baking tray and placing it in a very low oven for about 10 minutes.
5 Lift out the muslin bag, squeeze it well to allow the juices to run back into the pan, then discard it. Add the warmed sugar to the pan and stir it over a low heat until it has dissolved.
6 Bring the marmalade to the boil and continue to boil rapidly for 15 minutes or until the setting point is reached. It is ready when your finger leaves a furrow in a spoonful placed on a chilled saucer.
7 Skim the marmalade then leave it to stand for 15 minutes. Stir it well and then pour it into clean, warm jars. Cover immediately with waxed discs, waxed side down, and seal.

Ruby red grapefruit flesh and thin-cut peel make a delectable marmalade to brighten up even a mid-winter morning.

Mayonnaise

SAFETY RULES

Is it safe to eat mayonnaise considering the egg yolk is raw?

It is quite safe as long as strict rules of hygiene and safety are observed. Always use fresh, undamaged eggs from a reputable source, store them in the refrigerator and use them well before their 'use by' date (so the finished mayonnaise can then be stored for up to three days). Bring them up to room temperature by taking them out of the refrigerator about 30 minutes before using.

While eating mayonnaise is safe for most people, raw egg products are not recommended for vulnerable people such as babies, the elderly, pregnant women or anyone who is severely unwell.

KEEPING MAYONNAISE

How long is it safe to keep homemade mayonnaise?

Homemade mayonnaise will keep for up to three days in the refrigerator. The freshly made mayonnaise should be covered immediately to prevent a skin forming, or transferred to a covered container or screw-top jar. Be sure to label it with the date before storing. The flavour will not be satisfactory if it is not warmed to room temperature by removing it from the refrigerator 30 minutes before serving. Mayonnaise does not freeze well as it almost always curdles.

SEPARATE SOLUTION

What can I do if mayonnaise begins to separate?

Rescue it by quickly whisking in 1 tablespoon of warm water. If this fails, the mixture can still be salvaged by starting again. Put a fresh egg yolk, 1 teaspoon of cold water or 1 teaspoon of mustard into a clean bowl then very slowly start whisking in the curdled mixture and carry on until it is smooth.

CHOOSING THE OIL

Is one oil any better than the others for making mayonnaise?

Virtually any edible oil, apart from pumpkin seed oil and sesame oil, can be used as long as the flavour and price are acceptable. Olive oil, as used in the recipe below, is the traditional choice, but some people find the flavour too strong. Instead you can use a mix of olive oil and a milder vegetable oil, or try a light olive oil with a little extra virgin for flavour. Alternatively, mix half nut oil and half mild vegetable oil.

Mayonnaise

MAKES: 300 ml
PREPARATION TIME: 10 minutes
COOKING TIME: none

2 large egg yolks
½ teaspoon Dijon mustard
*   or a pinch of mustard powder*
Salt
300 ml olive oil (or olive and
*   vegetable oil mixed)*
2 tablespoons white wine vinegar
*   or 1-2 tablespoons lemon juice*

1 Put the egg yolks in a medium-sized mixing bowl, add the mustard and a pinch of salt and beat well with a wooden spoon or wire balloon whisk, standing the bowl on a damp cloth to prevent slipping.
2 Add the oil, drop by drop, beating continuously until the mixture has begun to thicken. Continue to add the oil half a teaspoon at a time, still beating well. When half of the oil has been added, beat in the vinegar or lemon juice and keep adding the remaining oil in a thin stream, whisking the mixture all the time.
VARIATIONS
Add what is listed to the 300 ml of mayonnaise (above):
• CHANTILLY MAYONNAISE: add 75 ml whipped cream.
• GREEN MAYONNAISE: add 75 ml chopped fresh herbs such as basil, dill, marjoram, parsley, watercress or blanched and finely chopped fresh raw spinach.
• PRAWN COCKTAIL SAUCE: add 2-4 tablespoons tomato sauce,

MAKING MAYONNAISE IN A BLENDER

This is a quick and easy method for making mayonnaise when it is not so important for the mixture to be really thick and stiff.

Put the two egg yolks (or one whole egg) in the blender, then add the mustard, vinegar or lemon juice and blend for a few seconds. With the motor running, start pouring in the oil through the hole in the lid, drop-by-drop at first, and then in a thin stream until the mixture appears to be thick. This method will produce a slightly thinner and lighter result than hand-mixed mayonnaise.

2 tablespoons cream, yoghurt or fromage frais, and a dash each of brandy and Worcestershire sauce.
• TARTARE SAUCE: add 2 tablespoons each of chopped capers, gherkins and finely chopped chives, parsley, shallots or spring onions to taste.

SAUCE REMOULADE

Is it possible to make mayonnaise without using raw eggs?

Yes. Sauce rémoulade is made with hard-boiled egg yolk, which makes it particularly suitable for anyone hesitant about eating raw eggs.

Mash a sieved large egg yolk thoroughly, add 1 tablespoon of boiling water and stir it to a smooth paste. Gradually add 250 ml of olive oil, beating the mixture continuously. When the mayonnaise has thickened, add 2 tablespoons each of finely chopped gherkins and parsley, 1 tablespoon of drained capers and a dash of anchovy essence. This sauce is often combined with celeriac, as in the recipe for Celeriac Rémoulade (page 218).

Celeriac rémoulade

SERVES: 4-6
PREPARATION TIME: 35 minutes
COOKING TIME: 30 seconds

500–625 g celeriac
250 ml rémoulade sauce
    (see page 217)
1 teaspoon lemon juice or
    wine vinegar
2 tablespoons fresh cream
Salt and black pepper
1 tablespoon chopped parsley

1 Peel the celeriac and cut into thin, julienne sticks, dropping them into water with some added lemon juice as you go, to prevent browning.
2 Blanch the julienne of celeriac in boiling salted water for 30 seconds, then drain and leave the sticks to cool in the sieve or colander.

3 Stir the lemon juice or vinegar and cream into the rémoulade sauce.
4 Place the celeriac in a bowl and fold in the mayonnaise until it is well coated. Season to taste and serve sprinkled with the chopped parsley.
VARIATIONS
Rémoulade sauce goes well with fish and shellfish or cold meats. It can also be added to mixed salads of other grated or sliced vegetables.

GARLIC MAYONNAISE

What is aïoli and how is it made?

Aïoli is a garlic-flavoured mayonnaise that is traditionally served with Mediterranean fish soups. But it also goes very well with other foods such as eggs, fish, salads and vegetables. Follow the recipe on the right to make this superb sauce.

Aïoli

MAKES: 300 ml
PREPARATION TIME: 15 minutes
COOKING TIME: none

2 large egg yolks
2–4 large cloves garlic, to taste
Salt
300 ml olive oil, or olive
    and vegetable oil, mixed
1 teaspoon lemon juice

1 Put the egg yolks in a bowl. Crush the garlic with a pinch of salt, add it to the eggs and beat or whisk well.
2 Start adding the oil, beating all the time. When half of the oil has been incorporated, add the lemon juice, then the remaining oil, whisking all the time until the aïoli is thick and smooth. Aïoli should be stored in the same way as a mayonnaise.

Variations on a mayonnaise theme. Clockwise from left: tangy tartare sauce, green herb mayonnaise and a garlicky aïoli.

Meat

KNOWING YOUR MEAT

What should I look for when choosing a good joint of meat?

It should look and smell fresh, the flesh should be silky, not wet, and the fat should be creamy white. Bright red flesh is not necessarily a sign of freshness or of quality, although many people think it is, and some supermarkets even put extra lights over the meat cabinet to make the flesh look a brighter red. Well-hung meat will be darker, and properly aged beef has a purple tinge. Meat with a greyish tinge should always be avoided.

When choosing boned, rolled and tied joints, look for a neat appearance. They should also be of a uniform thickness so that they will cook evenly. If the meat is still on the bones they should have been cleanly sawn through.

All meat, especially chops and steaks, should be neat and well trimmed of surplus fat. For superior lean cuts and joints of meat, select Lean beef, Trim lamb and New Fashioned pork.

CUTTING TECHNIQUE

Why should you cut across the grain of the meat rather than in the same direction?

Because the meat fibres will be shorter and a piece of meat cut across will be easier to chew, and so seem to be more tender.

LEAN IS BEST

Are more expensive cuts of meat more nutritious or lower in fat?

The nutritional value of all lean meat is absolutely the same no matter what it costs, but weight for weight the cheaper cuts of meat are not quite as good because they contain a smaller amount of nourishing lean meat and more gristle and fat. However, you can buy more of the cheaper cuts for the same money, to allow for wastage, and although they are tough, careful cooking will tenderise them.

GOOD VALUE CUTS

Which cheaper cuts of meat offer the best value for a family meal?

Those that come from the parts of the animal that have done a certain amount of work, such as the legs, are the best value for money. They have developed flavour but not too much waste in the form of fat, gristle or bone; for example, beef chuck and blade steaks, and top rump or round; lamb shoulder and best end of neck chops; pork hand and spring (from the front leg), spare ribs and cuts of shoulder or blade.

However, because these parts of the animal contain the main muscles, they can be tough. To increase their tenderness, beat them or soak for a few hours in a marinade containing an acid, such as lemon juice, vinegar, wine, natural yoghurt or pulped pawpaw. Cook slowly without too much moisture.

JOINTS TO ROAST

Which joints of meat are best for roasting and which for braising or pot roasting? Is size a factor?

The best cuts for roasting are those that come from the parts of the animal that have done the least work, mainly the body, which produces beef fillet, rib, sirloin and top rump; lamb loin; and pork chump end, fillet and loin. But legs and shoulders of lamb and pork, although they contain muscle, are also roasted, since they come from young animals. Large joints roast more successfully than small ones.

Small joints, and joints from the parts of the animal that have been more active, are less expensive and are better suited to more gentle pot roasting or braising, which makes the meat more tender. Suitable joints are beef brisket, silverside, topside and top rump; lamb shanks and shank end of leg; and pork hand and spring.

REMOVING FAT AND CONNECTIVE TISSUE

When you are preparing meat for a casserole or stir-fry, even meat that has already been trimmed by a butcher is likely to need further trimming of fat and connective tissue before it is ready to cook.

1 Using a very sharp knife with a nonslip handle, cut and pull the surrounding fat away from the meat.

2 Cut out the connective tissue, membrane and gristle from each of the smaller pieces of meat.

3 Meat is really a fleshy muscle, with a distinct structure, and should be cut across the grain at right angles or it will tend to fall apart during cooking.

ORGANIC REARING

What is organic meat and where can I buy it?

As community concern for the long-term future of agriculture, and the safety of food, grows in Australia, many tens of thousands of hectares are being converted to organic farming. But it can take years to turn an existing property into an organic farm with standards certified by the National Association for Sustainable Agriculture Australia (NASAA). And virgin bush is not always a viable proposition for development.

Organically produced meat is a precise term that indicates the animals have been raised on a NASAA-certified farm which practises environmentally acceptable, strict production techniques. Where the animals are slaughtered off the farm, the abattoir must also be certified by NASAA before the NASAA label can be applied.

It is currently difficult to find organic meat due to limited supplies and insufficient consistently good-quality product. However, vacuum-packed organic beef is available from some health food shops. Organic chicken, which is much more readily available, is sold by some butchers and most fresh poultry shops.

FRENCH CUTTING

Is French trimming the same as Continental butchery?

Do not confuse the two. French trimming (which almost always applies to lamb) exposes the bone of either a leg, to make carving easier, or a cutlet, to make it easier and cleaner to pick up and chew. For lamb cutlets and racks of lamb or pork, the chine bone is removed and the long ends of the cutlet bones are scraped of all fat and meat about 2.5 cm from the tip of the bone.

Continental butchery, which is also known as seam butchery, produces pieces of meat that are sometimes described as 'Continental cuts'. In seam butchery, the butchers separate the tissues along each muscle instead of cutting across the meat and through the joints. The cuts of meat labelled Trim, Lean and New Fashioned are all examples of seam butchery. Fillet steaks are always seam cut, as is beef rump.

RARE BUT SAFE

With all the worries about food poisoning, is it safe to eat meat that has been cooked rare?

The toxins produced by bacteria prior to cooking are the cause of food poisoning, so storing meat at the correct temperature is the vital factor in food safety.

If the meat has been properly stored, it is safe to leave it rare in the centre. However, if the meat has been pierced or cut in any way, and particularly if it has been boned and rolled, bacteria will have been able to enter the meat, so it should be always well cooked right through.

TAKING THE TEMPERATURE

How can I tell when meat has been cooked enough?

The only way to be absolutely sure that meat has been cooked to your liking is to use a meat thermometer. It should be inserted into the thickest part of the joint, without touching any bones, just before the end of the cooking time. When cooking beef and lamb, the meat will be rare when the temperature reaches 60°C, medium rare when it is 71°C and well done when the temperature reads 80°C. Pork and veal should only be served well done, which means that the temperature should reach 75°C for pork, and 71°C for veal.

If you do not have a meat thermometer, you can insert a metal skewer into the thickest part of the cooked joint and wait for 30 seconds. If the skewer feels cold to the touch when it is withdrawn, the meat is not done; if it feels warm the meat is rare, and if it is hot the meat is well done.

It is wise to take the resting time into consideration when you are testing for doneness because the meat will continue to cook while it is sitting. This is more important for a piece of meat that you wish to serve rare or medium and less crucial if the meat is going to be eaten when it is well done.

COOKING FROM FROZEN

Is it safe to cook meat while it is still frozen?

No, meat should always be completely thawed before it is cooked, as otherwise the centre may not be cooked by the time the outside of the meat looks done, which could be dangerous. This is especially true of large joints of meat.

Whenever possible it is better for meat to thaw slowly in the refrigerator, allowing 6–8 hours per kg for large joints of meat and about 5–6 hours overall for steaks and chops. If you have a microwave oven, follow the instructions.

Another consideration is that the taste and texture of meat, even quite small pieces, cooked from frozen is not very palatable. It is a waste of an expensive item of food to try to cook it without thawing.

DELICATE MINCE

I find mince often goes grey and rubbery when I cook it - what am I doing wrong?

The most probable explanation for pallid rubbery mince is that you are cooking the meat for too long at a temperature that is too high. For better results, the mince should be started over a medium-high heat in a large frying pan. If you use a pan that is too small the mince will stew in the moisture it exudes as it cooks and the texture will not be as firm as it should be. Stir it to break up any lumps and cook it just until it is no longer raw but has not taken on any colour. Then reduce the heat and add the liquid, if you are using any, and continue to cook the meat, keeping it just on the simmering point.

The colour of mince is also determined by the amount of fat it contains. If it is pale it has more fat; lean mince is darker in colour.

For perfectly cooked mince, use the recipe on the right for Mexican Beef with Cornmeal Topping. It is a good dish for a family meal.

See also: *Beef, Lamb, Pork, Veal*

A crunchy cornmeal topping and spicy Latin American seasoning make minced chuck steak into a warming meal.

Mexican beef with cornmeal topping

SERVES: 4
PREPARATION TIME: 15 minutes
COOKING TIME: 1 hour 30 minutes

FOR THE SAUCE
1-2 tablespoons olive or
   vegetable oil
2 stalks celery, chopped
3 cloves garlic, peeled and finely
   chopped
1 onion, finely chopped
1 red pepper, diced
2 teaspoons cumin seeds
750 g chuck steak, fat removed and
   minced
150 ml beef or vegetable stock
   or water
A few drops Tabasco sauce
425 g canned chopped tomatoes
2-3 tablespoons tomato paste
1 tablespoon chopped fresh
   oregano or marjoram
A pinch each of salt, cayenne
   pepper and chilli powder

FOR THE TOPPING
150 g (1 cup) cornmeal
60 g (½ cup) self-raising flour
2 teaspoons baking powder
Salt and black pepper
1 large egg, beaten
60 g butter, melted
185 ml milk

1 To make the sauce, heat the oil in a flameproof casserole over a medium heat. Add the celery, garlic, onion and red pepper and cook until soft and lightly coloured.

2 Stir in the cumin seeds and heat until fragrant, about 30-60 seconds. Stir in the beef and cook it, stirring, over a medium heat until it is no longer pink, but do not let it brown.

3 Stir the stock or water, Tabasco sauce, tomatoes, tomato paste and oregano or marjoram into the meat and heat until bubbles just begin to appear. Cover the casserole tightly and cook the beef at a very gentle simmer for 50-60 minutes, stirring it every so often. Meanwhile, preheat the oven to 220°C.

4 To make the topping, mix the cornmeal, flour, baking powder and seasoning together in a bowl. Stir in the egg, melted butter and milk and stir until it is smooth.

5 When the meat sauce is cooked, season it to taste with salt, cayenne pepper and chilli powder. Spoon on the cornmeal topping. Smooth the top with a spatula and bake the dish for about 15-20 minutes, or until the cornmeal has set. This dish can be made ahead of time and reheated.

Spicy fried patties

Leftover Mexican Beef can be rejuvenated by mixing the meat and topping together in a bowl with a chopped raw onion and a beaten egg. Form the mixture into patties and fry them gently.

MEAT FROM THE DELICATESSEN

Cold meats are a blessing for the busy cook, served thinly sliced in a plate of cold cuts or cut into strips or chunks to boost salads and hot dishes. Here is our guide to the most popular smoked or dried meats and sausages.

Continental meats from the delicatessen counter offer a marvellous range of flavours from mild liver sausage or mortadella to fiery chorizo, spicy pastrami or sweet baked ham, and are ready to use in seconds. Some are made with raw meats, some are cooked, but even those made from raw ingredients have usually been cured, dried or smoked so they need no further cooking.

Heavily smoked or air-dried meats like salami keep almost indefinitely when whole, but dry out once sliced. Lightly smoked meats like bierwurst and mortadella keep less well. Unless you buy a whole pepperoni, salami or teewurst, it is best to eat delicatessen meats within a day or two of purchase. Keep them in the refrigerator, well wrapped, in the meat compartment.

BIERSCHINKEN (Germany)
Made from pork and chunks of ham, bierschinken is studded with peppercorns and pistachio nuts.

BIERWURST (Germany)
Coarse-textured pork, or pork and beef, goes into a bierwurst, which is then highly seasoned with juniper berries and cardamom and sometimes with garlic too.

BOLOGNA (Multinational)
Based on mortadella (from Bologna), this smoked beef and pork sausage is known as

Make perfect antipasto from a selection of cold meats sharpened with olives, gherkins, radishes, celery and a shaving of Parmesan.

boloney in the United States, where it is the second most popular sausage.

BRESAOLA (Italy)
A speciality of Lombardy in Italy, bresaola is an air-dried cut of tender lean beef, very thinly sliced. It is served raw with a vinaigrette dressing or

with a squeeze of lemon, some virgin olive oil and freshly ground black pepper.

CABANOSSI (Poland)
Smoked and spicy, cabanossi, known as kabanos in Poland, is very long and thin. The thicker, shorter version is traditionally cooked with lentils.

CHORIZO (Spain)
A pork sausage, chorizo's hot taste and deep red colour come from a seasoning of paprika. There are different types and it is often added to dishes of beans, soups and a Spanish vegetable stew.

COPPA (Italy)
This large sausage is made from air-dried raw ham marbled with extra fat.

GARLIC SAUSAGE (Multinational)
In Australia, this is a soft 'devon-like' or 'fritz-like' product, similar to frankfurter, with a garlic flavour and a short, squat shape.

GYULAI (Hungary)
Pork is mixed with sweet red peppers to make gyulai.

HAM (Multinational)
Ham, simply the cured hind leg of the pig, often air-dried; many countries have their particular versions (see *Ham*).

JAGDWURST, SCHINKENJAGDWURST (Germany)
Minced pork with chunks of pork fat, produces a sausage similar to bierschinken.

JERKY (Australia)
Jerky, originally from the United States (or biltong from South Africa), was originally strips of game dried in the sun to provide long-lasting rations for travellers. Now you can buy both beef and venison

CHORIZO

GYULAI

MORTADELLA

CABANOSSI

METTWURST

LIVERWURST

varieties. To eat, simply cut off thin slices and chew hard.

KIELBASA (Poland)
A highly seasoned mixture of pork and beef, kielbasa can be smoked or fresh, cooked or uncooked. It is used in *bigos*, a Polish hunters' stew.

LANDJAGER (Germany)
Air-dried or smoked, this sausage is made of beef with a little pork, and flavoured with caraway seeds and garlic.

LIVERWURST (Multinational)
German and Latvian leberwurst are the best known, but many other countries in Europe have their own. It is a smooth spreadable mixture of well-seasoned pork and pig's liver, onions and seasonings, steamed inside a thick casing.

LOUKANIKA (Greece)
Small and knobbly loukanika is made from minced lamb and pork seasoned with coriander and marinated in red wine. It is a popular ingredient of Greek hors d'oeuvre.

METTWURST (Germany)
A lightly smoked mixture of pork and beef, mettwurst can be either a smooth uniform pink or coarsely minced to resemble salami.

MORTADELLA (Italy)
Much bigger than other sausages, mortadella is made from pork and contains large chunks of fat, whole black peppercorns and sometimes green pistachio nuts.

PASTRAMI (Italy)
Pastrami is brisket of beef cured in a dry mixture of sugar, spices and garlic, then smoked – which gives it a dark exterior. Like corned beef, it is excellent in sandwiches made with rye bread.

PEPPERONI (Italy)
Coarsely chopped pork and beef flavoured with red pepper and fennel, pepperoni is often served on pizza.

PLOCKWURST (Germany)
Also known as schinkenplockwurst, this is a large, coarsely chopped smoked ham. It is also sold in another version known as pfefferplockwurst, which is square and coated with crushed peppercorns.

SALAMI (Italy and other European countries)
There are countless different salami, all made from coarsely minced pork and pork fat, with beef and veal sometimes included. Flavourings include coriander, fennel, garlic, paprika, peppercorns and wine.

They are slowly air-dried or smoked to produce a long, mottled sausage. The casing may be smoke-blackened, covered in white mould or coated with herbs or crushed peppercorns.

Italian salami are often considered the finest. Danish salami is cheaper but is fatty, salty, and has a bright red colour.

SAUCISSON FUME (France)
The French equivalent of salami is made with smoked or dried pork, pork fat and garlic. The best-known are saucisson Jésus and Rosette de Lyon.

SILVERSIDE (Australia)
Corned silverside of beef is cooked commercially and served sliced; the joint is first wet-cured in a brine with salt, sugar and spices.

SMOKED CHICKEN (Multinational)
Smoked chicken is ready-to-eat and has a mild, bacony flavour. It is good dressed in mayonnaise in sandwiches or salads. Smoked turkey is also available, and can be used in the same way. Both are also available pressed and rolled.

TEEWURST (Germany)
This highly spiced sausage combines very finely minced pork and beef mixed together and cooked to form a pink spreadable paste similar to liverwurst. It looks small and stubby and comes in a smooth, inedible casing.

WIEJSKA (Poland)
A pure pork sausage with a hint of garlic, tied into a horseshoe. Typically sold cut into chunks, wiejska is eaten cold or can be served hot, either boiled, grilled or stewed.

ZUNGENWURST (Germany)
A large reddish blood sausage, zungenwurst contains substantial chunks of fat and slices of tongue (zunge).

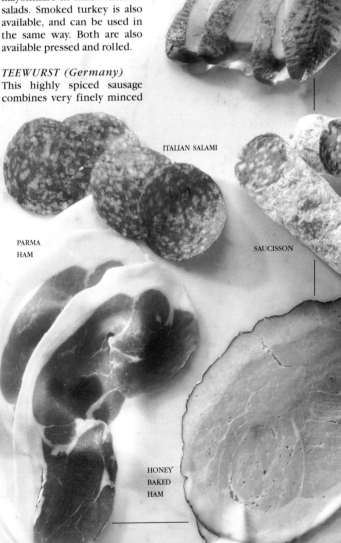

SMOKED CHICKEN

ITALIAN SALAMI

SAUCISSON

PARMA HAM

PASTRAMI

HONEY BAKED HAM

Melons

TEST FOR RIPENESS

When buying melons, how can I tell if they are ripe and sweet?

A ripe melon should give slightly when pressed gently at one end. For rockmelon, press at the stalk end. For honeydew, press at the end opposite the stalk. You should also sniff the melon: a ripe one has a strong scent and there will be little scent if it is unripe.

A ripe watermelon sounds hollow when tapped. If buying by the slice, choose those that are bright red with shiny black seeds.

Freezing can dull the flavour of any melon, so adding a little lemon juice will help to sustain the melon flavour, as in the recipe, right.

MAKING MELON BALLS

Shaping melon flesh into balls is an attractive way to present the fruit.

1 Cut the melon in half and scoop out the seeds with a spoon. To catch any juice retained among the seeds, put them into a stainless-steel or nylon sieve placed over a bowl to drain. The recovered juice can then be added to a fruit salad.

2 Press a melon baller, open side down, into the flesh and twist it to remove a neat, round sphere of melon. Tap the melon ball out into the bowl. Repeat this process until all the flesh of the melon has been removed. Each time you insert the baller, place it as close as you can to the previous cavity.

Scrape out the ragged pieces of melon with a spoon and liquidise to make a refreshing drink.

A scintillating granita made with lush, ripe rockmelon and white wine is layered with kirsch-soaked raspberries, scoops of perfumed honeydew and cool mint.

Melon granita with raspberries

SERVES: 4
PREPARATION TIME: 30 minutes plus 4–5 hours freezing
COOKING TIME: 5 minutes

For the granita
60 g (¼ cup) white sugar
1 rockmelon, weighing about 600 g
2 tablespoons lemon juice
90 ml medium-sweet white wine

TO SERVE
1 medium honeydew melon
175 g fresh raspberries
1 tablespoon caster sugar
1–2 tablespoons kirsch
Fresh mint leaves
1 teaspoon icing sugar, for sifting

1 To make the granita, put the sugar into a saucepan with 90 ml of water, and stir over a medium heat until the sugar has dissolved. Bring to the boil and continue boiling for 1 minute, then remove from the heat and allow to cool.

2 Cut the rockmelon in half and discard the seeds. Scoop out all the flesh, put it into a food processor and blend to a purée. Add the cooled sugar syrup, lemon juice and wine. Blend the mixture together for a few seconds, pour it into a plastic or metal bowl then put it into the freezer to harden.

3 After an hour, stir the granita with a balloon whisk to break up the stiff crystals around the edge. Freeze for another hour and whisk it again, then cover the granita and return it to the freezer until it is completely frozen. (Granita is best served as soon as it is ready so that the texture is light.)

4 Twenty minutes before serving, take the granita from the freezer and leave at room temperature to soften.

5 Cut the honeydew melon in half and dice the flesh or shape it into balls (see panel, page 224).

6 Put the raspberries into a small bowl, sprinkle with the caster sugar, add the kirsch and mix gently. Cover and set aside.

7 Chill four large serving glasses in the freezer for a few minutes. Just before you are ready to serve, break up the granita with a fork and spoon it into the chilled glasses, alternating the granita with the honeydew melon and the macerated raspberries.

8 Decorate each glass with a few sprigs of mint, sift icing sugar over the leaves and serve immediately.

Menu Planning

KEEP IT SIMPLE

Can you suggest some tips to put together a successful menu?

However large or small the occasion, try to keep the menu simple, and aim to have at least two-thirds of the cooking and preparation done in advance. The meal should also be feasible. It is no use planning two courses that will require oven space at different temperatures if there is only one oven, or trying to stir-fry all the vegetables while at the same time assembling a complicated main course.

Match the food to the guests and try to stay with one style. For example, serving an Italian starter, followed by a main course from southern France, and ending with a Spanish dessert is fine as these are all Mediterranean. It would be considerably less appealing to serve French moules marinière, followed by Thai green curry, and ending with an American pecan pie.

Balance is also crucial because you do not want your guests to feel bloated. If the first and second courses contain little fat, then an indulgent coffee cream mousse or a pavlova that tastes wickedly rich will be greeted with pleasure instead of half-hearted enthusiasm.

Avoid repetition. For example, do not have a melon starter and then fruit as the dessert. No two courses should contain similar meat or fish, and try to vary the colours, textures and cooking processes as well. If a first course is vichyssoise, do not then serve mashed potato or puréed parsnips with the main course, as they all have a similar smooth texture and rather bland colour.

On the whole, sauces tend to be very popular, so be generous in the amounts being offered, and if they are served separately the guests can help themselves.

Check that the wines, if served, are in the right order, so that more dominant flavours follow delicate ones and match the food. In general: red wines should follow white wines, older wines should follow younger ones and strong wines should follow light ones. Usually, white wines are a good match to fish, white meats and poultry, while reds go with cheese, game, red meats and robust poultry dishes. (See also *Wine*.)

COLOUR AND TEXTURE

Should I always offer two or three vegetables with the main course, or is one enough?

Offering a varied selection of vegetables adds colour and texture to meals, but is not always necessary. Try to achieve a balance to the meal by offering one starchy dish, such as pasta, polenta, potatoes or rice, and one crisp, fresh vegetable. Alternatively, serve a mixture of vegetables cooked in advance, such as roasted root vegetables, or braised fennel and celery, plus a quickly cooked green vegetable or a green salad. If your main course consists mainly of vegetables (a vegetarian stew, for example) you may decide potatoes or rice, plus a salad, is more than enough.

PLANNING QUANTITIES

How can I work out how much food people will probably eat?

Professional caterers work on the basis that the more people there are being served, the less food per person is needed. With a larger group, everyone has more people to talk to and there is less time to eat; people also tend to eat less when they are standing up. Here are some guidelines on how much raw food to allow per person for a gathering of four to six people:

- CHICKEN AND TURKEY: 500 g if it is on the bone.
- CUTS OF MEAT: **Lamb cutlets:** three or four. **Loin chops:** two. **Pork chops:** one. **Fillets:** two for three or four people.
- ROAST MEAT: **Beef, on the bone:** 375 g. **Beef, boned and rolled:** 185–250 g. **Beef, fillet:** a 2 kg piece will feed ten people. **Leg of lamb:** 1.5 kg for three or four people, 2 kg serves four or five people, 3 kg for seven or eight people. **Crown roast:** 3 cutlets. **Leg of pork:** 200 g loin, off the bone.
- STEWED MEAT: **Beef and lamb:** 250 g boneless and trimmed. **Venison:** 175 g lean meat.
- FISH: **Whole large:** uncleaned, with head, 350–450 g. **Whole small:** with head, 250–350 g. **Cutlets and steaks:** 185 g. **Prawns:** 90–125 g.
- VEGETABLES: assuming that two vegetables, as well as potatoes, are being served with a main course: 125 g of each vegetable, except green beans and peas: 90 g; spinach: 350 g.
- SOUP: 250 ml.
- CHEESE: 50–60 g.
- SANDWICHES: **Bread:** assume an average 20 slices of bread in a medium sliced loaf. **Butter:** 30 g butter or soft mayonnaise will cover eight large slices of bread. **Cucumber:** one makes 15 rounds. **Egg:** one hard-boiled egg per round. **Tomatoes:** 500 g for nine rounds. **Smoked salmon:** 20 g per round. **Canned tuna:** 200 g plus 4 tablespoons mayonnaise for five sandwich rounds.

Meringues

PERFECT RESULTS

How can I make wonderful, foolproof meringues?

Begin with a bowl that is clean and completely free of grease. It should be either copper, stainless steel, glass or china, not aluminium or plastic. Using either an electric or a balloon whisk, whisk the egg whites until they are very stiff. Gradually add half the sugar, whisking well after each addition and then, using a metal spoon or a plastic spatula, lightly fold in the rest of the sugar.

Use the frothy meringue mixture immediately, piping or spooning it onto nonstick baking paper placed on baking trays. Bake in a 110°C oven for 2½–3 hours. The meringues will be firm and crisp but still white. They will actually be drying out in the oven rather than cooking. Leave the meringues to cool on a wire rack, then carefully remove the baking paper. Once cooled, the meringues should keep fresh for up to three weeks if stored in an airtight container.

WEEP NO MORE

I use the same recipe every time, but sometimes my meringues weep terribly. Why is this?

Meringues tend to weep if the uncooked meringue mixture is left standing too long before baking. The meringue then begins to liquefy or separate and this may result in the meringues exuding droplets which stick to the upper surface and edges and look unsightly. Once you have made the meringue mixture, especially a simple one of egg whites and caster sugar, you should bake it immediately.

Meringues that are baked at too high a temperature may also weep. Always ensure that they are baked at a very low heat for the correct amount of time, which will be indicated in your particular recipe.

SOFTENING THE MIXTURE

Why is vinegar added to some meringue recipes?

In meringue recipes such as the Summer Pavlova (below), a small amount of vinegar and cornflour is added so that the baked meringue has a crisp outside and a soft, textured centre, which makes a soft bed for the mixed fruit.

Summer pavlova

SERVES: 6-8
PREPARATION TIME: 30 minutes
COOKING TIME: 1 hour

3 large egg whites
185 g (¾ cup) caster sugar
A few drops of vanilla essence
½ teaspoon white wine vinegar
1 teaspoon cornflour
300 ml fresh cream
350 g mixed berries such as blackberries, blackcurrants, raspberries and strawberries, fresh not frozen

1 Preheat the oven to 150°C. Draw an 18 cm circle on a piece of nonstick baking paper and place this on a baking tray with the marked side of the paper down.
2 In a large bowl, whisk the egg whites until stiff. Gradually add half the sugar, whisking well. Fold in the remaining sugar with the vanilla, vinegar and cornflour.
3 Spread or pipe the meringue over the circle on the paper, piling it up at the edges to form a rim. Bake for about 1 hour until the meringue is crisp and dry. Transfer to a wire rack to cool, then remove the paper and place the pavlova on a serving plate.
4 Whip the cream until it is stiff, then pile or pipe it on top of the pavlova. Arrange the fruit over the top and serve immediately.

VARIATIONS
Use other fruits such as apricots, nectarines, peaches or mangoes in place of the mixed berries.

Light brown sugar may be used to make the meringue instead of caster sugar and will turn it brown. You can also add a teaspoon or two of ground mixed spice to the mixture.

Benefits of maturity

Egg whites that are a few days old whisk better than egg whites that are very fresh, as some of the water in the white will have evaporated. The drying makes the albumen stronger. Egg whites that have been frozen also whisk well.

VARIATIONS ON A THEME

What is the difference between Swiss meringue, Italian meringue and meringue cuite?

Swiss meringue, also known as plain or simple meringue, is made by whisking and folding caster sugar into stiffly whisked egg whites at a ratio of 60 g (¼ cup) per egg. This mixture has to be used immediately. The resulting meringues are light and fragile but have a delicious, sticky texture.

Italian meringue is made by beating hot sugar syrup, boiled to the hard ball stage, into whisked egg whites. The hot syrup partially cooks the whites, enabling them to hold their shape for much longer. Italian meringue is impossible to overwhisk and, when uncooked, is more stable than a Swiss meringue, holding its shape well for as long as two days. Italian meringue also cooks faster than Swiss meringue, making brilliant white meringue that forms a powder when the meringue is crushed. Because it holds its shape in the oven, Italian meringue is suitable for shaping as baskets and vacherins (shells).

Meringue cuite, also known as cooked meringue, is the most robust. It is made by whisking egg whites and sugar together over a pan of steaming water to form a smooth, fluffy paste. This process, used mainly by professional chefs, takes time and is hard work when performed by hand. It is used for intricate work and as an uncooked frosting for various pies and cakes.

The Hazelnut Meringues recipe that follows shows how easy Swiss meringues can be to make.

Hazelnut meringues

*MAKES: either 20 single meringues
or 10 pairs*
PREPARATION TIME: 30 minutes
COOKING TIME: 2½–3 hours

*50 g (½ cup) hazelnuts, toasted
3 large egg whites
185 g (¾ cup) caster sugar
150 ml fresh or thickened cream*

1 Chop the toasted nuts by hand
because using a food processor
would make them very oily which
will affect the meringue. Preheat the
oven to 110°C.
2 In a large clean bowl, whisk the
egg whites until they are stiff.
Gradually add half the sugar,
whisking well after each addition.
Lightly fold in the remaining sugar
and the chopped hazelnuts, using a
metal spoon.
3 Pipe 20 small mounds of the
meringue onto baking trays lined
with nonstick baking paper and bake
for 2½–3 hours, until crisp.
4 Transfer them to a wire rack to
cool, then whip the cream until it is
quite thick. Sandwich the meringues
together in pairs with the cream and
serve immediately.

VARIATIONS
You can use other varieties of nut,
such as chopped or ground almonds,
in place of the toasted hazelnuts.

Light brown sugar may be
substituted for the caster sugar.

If you prefer, the meringues may
be sandwiched together with plain
fromage frais or thick Greek-style
yoghurt in place of the cream.

Chopped hazelnuts add a light crunch to these delectable meringues.

Mexican Cooking

MARVELLOUS MEXICAN

*The dishes listed on the menus of
Mexican restaurants confuse me.
Could you please explain them?*

Mexico's culinary heritage reaches
back a thousand years and Mexican
food is still popular today because
of its simplicity, as well as its
colour and spicy flavour. The Mexican cuisine is based on two staple,
nourishing foods – tortillas (Mexican bread), which are round flat
discs like pancakes, made from
cornmeal, and beans, which are an
excellent source of protein.

The tortilla can be folded and
crisply fried and filled with a spicy
beef mixture, topped with lettuce,
tomatoes and cheese, to make a
taco. The tortilla also can be served
flat and crisp, topped with refried
beans, chicken or beef, lettuce,
tomato, cheese, sour cream, guacamole and spring onions, as a
tostada. It also may be used soft
and filled with savoury beef or
chicken, then rolled and coated
with enchilada sauce and baked to
produce an enchilada. A crisp corn
tortilla folded over cream cheese,
onions and taco sauce is called a
quesidilla. The cornmeal dough is
used also to encase a spicy meat
filling, which is then steamed to
make a tamale.

Fresh tomato and onion salsas
help to enliven many dishes, and
chillies are often in evidence,
including in chilli con carne (the
famous beef and bean dish).

While a Mexican meal can be a
very casual occasion, there are a
small range of main-course dishes
available. As meat is not very plen-
tiful, poultry is very popular. One
of Mexico's more unusual dishes is
Mole poblano – turkey baked in a
sauce made with chocolate, nuts,
chillies and spices.

Most main dishes are washed
down with beer; to follow, there
are few desserts, but Mexican
cakes are very sweet.

Microwave Ovens

VIBRATING MOLECULES

How do microwave ovens differ from conventional ovens?

A microwave oven uses an electronic device, the magnetron, to convert electrical energy into high-speed waves. These are deflected off the oven's metal walls directly into food to a depth of about 4 cm. These microwaves are then absorbed by molecules of moisture in the food, causing them to vibrate rapidly, which creates intense cooking heat. With larger pieces of food, the centre is cooked by conduction, in the same way as in an ordinary oven.

Microwaves pass through china, glass, paper, pottery and some plastics, but metal deflects the microwaves so metal containers are not suitable to use.

PROS AND CONS

What are the good and bad features of a microwave oven?

Apart from reheating cooked food, thawing frozen food and cooking raw foods like fish and vegetables, the microwave is an invaluable cook's mate. Use it to soften butter, heat sauces and melt chocolate. Microwaving is very fuel-efficient and fast, taking a quarter to a third of the time needed in conventional cooking. Both oven cleaning and washing up are usually reduced.

As microwaves stop when the oven door is open, and the oven itself is not hot, there is less risk of anyone being burnt. This is especially helpful with children, the elderly and the disabled. The chances of food boiling over or burning are reduced as the oven is set to switch off. Microwaving is also healthier in that less fat, oil and liquid are needed and more nutrients are kept in the food.

Microwave ovens are very useful but have disadvantages with some types of recipes. Anything which needs hot air to rise, such as puff pastry, will fail as the air inside a microwave does not get hot. Roasting is also less successful, but you can brown meat by frying or grilling it briefly before or after microwaving. A combination oven can work as a microwave and convection oven simultaneously, and speeds up cooking while also giving food a brown, crisp finish.

LEARN THE RULES

How can I be sure to use my microwave oven safely?

Do not use metal containers, china with a metallic trim or wire twists as metal may cause damage to the component parts. However, very small pieces of foil can be used, as on a chicken where the wings are cooking too quickly. Secure the foil with toothpicks as it must not touch the walls.

Use only microwave-safe plastic containers. You can use plastic cooking bags designed to withstand roasting or freezing, but make a slit in the bag to allow steam to escape. To cover food, use a perforated plastic lid or microwave-safe plastic wrap folded back at one corner.

Cooking eggs in their shells causes a build-up of pressure and they may explode unless cooked in a special microwave egg-boiler. Foods such as potatoes or apples should be pricked all over for cooking in their skins. Membranes like egg yolks need pricking too.

BASIC TECHNIQUES

What is the best way to arrange food in a microwave oven?

Microwaves are generally focused around the oven edges with less energy present in the centre. Arrange individual items around the outside of the turntable in a circular fashion, with thinner parts placed towards the centre.

Be guided by the instruction manual for your oven and consult microwave cookbooks for good tips and handy information.

REHEATING DRINKS

Is it possible to successfully reheat cups of cold tea or coffee in a microwave oven?

You can reheat coffee and tea by microwaving for a minute or two (check the manual with your machine). For best results, use a safe cup with a sloping side and stir it midway. Do not boil or the drink will become bitter.

Middle Eastern Cooking

BONDED TOGETHER

How many countries make up the Middle East cuisine?

The cooking of the Middle East is very distinctive. It is difficult to agree where the geographical boundaries of the Middle East are, but – for the purposes of studying its cuisine – nine countries are usually included. These are Greece, Turkey, Lebanon, Syria, Jordan, Israel, Iraq, Iran and Egypt.

Many dishes overlap from one country to another; many of the countries have their own culinary style, but certain foods and how they are treated bind these countries together in a Middle Eastern cuisine. Think of eggplant, lamb, yoghurt, olive oil, burghul, chick peas, lemons, rosewater, orange flower water, walnuts, pine nuts, pistachios, honey, quinces, melons, figs, pomegranates and dates and you have the foundation ingredients of Middle Eastern cooking.

A typical Middle Eastern dinner could start with hummus (chick pea) and baba ganoosh (eggplant) dips served with pita bread, and dolmathes (stuffed vine leaves); follow with a cold Cacik soup made from yoghurt and cucumber; then a main course of shish kebab, kibbi, moussaka or Arabian roast chicken stuffed with currants and pine nuts, served with pilau or pilaf and tabbouleh or a Greek salad, with

Baklava and maybe some fresh melon for dessert; the meal would end with Turkish coffee.

The following recipe for a low-fat Moussaka is adapted from a Middle Eastern classic.

Moussaka

SERVES: 4
PREPARATION TIME: 30 minutes
COOKING TIME: 1 hour

1 eggplant, about 500 g, sliced
   1 cm thick
Olive oil cooking spray
2 onions, thinly sliced
2 cloves garlic, crushed
500 g finely minced Trim lamb
2 tomatoes, chopped
½ cup tomato paste
250 ml chicken stock
1 tablespoon chopped fresh
   oregano
Freshly ground black pepper
1 large egg
250 ml Greek-style yoghurt

1 Preheat a grill to medium and line a grill pan with foil. Place the eggplant slices on the grill pan and spray lightly with olive oil. Grill the eggplant for 5 minutes, or until soft. Turn the slices over; spray with more olive oil and grill the other side until soft.

2 Preheat the oven to 180°C. Spray a nonstick frying pan with olive oil. Place over a medium heat and fry the onions and garlic for 5 minutes, or until soft, stirring frequently.

3 Add the lamb to the pan and cook over a medium-high heat, stirring frequently, until browned.

4 Stir in the tomatoes, tomato paste, stock and oregano and bring to the boil, stirring frequently. Add pepper to taste.

5 Place a third of the eggplant in a single layer in the base of a ceramic baking dish. Spoon half the lamb mixture over the top. Repeat the layers, then top with the remaining eggplant slices.

6 Beat the egg and yoghurt together until smooth and pour over the eggplant. Bake for 1 hour, or until tender and bubbling hot. Serve with a green salad.

Milk

PROCESSING TECHNIQUES

In what way do pasteurised and homogenised milk differ?

They are two different processes. Many countries have laws that require milk to be pasteurised so that harmful bacteria are destroyed. The milk is heated to almost boiling, held at this temperature for several seconds then cooled.

After being pasteurised, some milk is homogenised, which disperses the fat evenly throughout the milk. If it is not homogenised, the cream will float to the top.

LONGER LIFE

What is UHT milk and can I use it in my cooking?

UHT, ultra heat treated or long-life, milk has been ultra-pasteurised by being heated in a sealed container to 138°C for a few seconds. It is packaged in sealed cartons and can be stored without refrigeration for up to three months.

The ultra-pasteurisation affects the taste, making it less appealing to drink. It is probably best used for cooking, where it will behave just like ordinary milk. Once it is open, UHT milk must be kept in the refrigerator like fresh milk.

BUTTERMILK OPTIONS

What is buttermilk and is there a substitute I could use in cooking?

Traditional buttermilk is the liquid whey left behind when milk has been churned and all the fat is extracted as butter. Commercial buttermilk is produced by adding a special bacterial culture to either low-fat or skim milk.

Buttermilk contains an acid that reacts with bicarbonate of soda and releases gas to raise the dough in soda bread, scones, biscuits and some pancakes. If no buttermilk is available, use half sour cream or yoghurt with half fresh milk. Alter-

natively, you can mix 1 teaspoon of lemon juice with fresh milk and the dry ingredients.

REDUCING THE FAT

If I were to use skim milk in place of whole milk in recipes, would the reduced-fat content affect the result?

Skim milk has a much thinner consistency than whole milk and a flavour that is less full and rich than whole milk. Skim milk performs acceptably in cooking but the dish will have a thinner flavour.

If you would like to give your family a milkshake with less fat but without losing its popular appeal, boost the flavour with fresh fruit.

Strawberry milkshake

SERVES: 1
PREPARATION TIME: 5 minutes

300 ml skim milk
75 g strawberries
2 tablespoon vanilla ice cream
   (low-fat, if preferred)

Place all the ingredients in a blender or food processor and blend until smooth. Pour the milkshake into a large glass and serve immediately.

FREEZING MILK

Is it all right to freeze milk?

Milk can be frozen in either waxed cartons or plastic containers (not bottles) that allow enough space for expansion. Skim milk freezes better than whole fat milk, which tends to separate on thawing. They can both be frozen for up to a

Healthy option

Fortified skim milk can be used just like ordinary milk. It is made by adding extra vitamins and calcium to the milk after the cream has been skimmed off.

month and then thawed slowly in the refrigerator. If the milk is going to be heated, the thawing process may be speeded up by heating it slowly from frozen.

AVOIDING BURNING

How do I stop my milk-based recipes from burning?

Milk scorches easily because of the sugars and proteins which fall to the bottom of the pan when it is heated. To avoid scorching, place the milk in either a heavy-based saucepan or a double-boiler and cook over a low or medium heat. You can also try rinsing the pan in cold water before adding the milk.

CONDENSED VERSION

What is the difference between evaporated and condensed milk?

Evaporated milk (available either whole or skimmed) has had its water content reduced so that it is almost twice as concentrated as ordinary milk. Condensed milk is evaporated milk with added sugar, which makes it thicker. Both milks may be used in cooking, but some recipes are clearly better made with one or the other.

The high heat of the canning process gives evaporated milk its very distinctive cooked flavour. Evaporated milk, well-chilled, may be whipped like fresh cream for use in desserts, poured over fruit and other desserts as a topping, or made into a delicious fudge.

Condensed milk is rich, thick and syrupy and is especially suited to making toffee and other kinds of confectionery, including the sticky coconut sweetmeats made in India.

The toffee and banana pie which follows makes delicious use of the special taste of condensed milk.

Sliced bananas and grated chocolate crown this regal Banoffee Pie in style. Condensed milk is the key ingredient.

Banoffee pie

SERVES: 6-8
PREPARATION TIME: *20 minutes, plus 45 minutes cooling and chilling*
COOKING TIME: *10 minutes*

---

150 g unsalted butter
185 g granita biscuits, crushed
1 teaspoon ground mixed spice
60 g (⅓ cup) light brown sugar
2 tablespoons milk
250 g condensed milk
5 small bananas
Juice of ½ lemon
150 ml fresh or thickened cream
To decorate: grated chocolate

---

1 Carefully melt half the butter, remove it from the heat and stir in the crushed biscuits and mixed spice. Press evenly into the base of a 20 cm flan dish and then refrigerate for at least 30 minutes.
2 Put the other half of the butter and the sugar in a small, heavy-based pan and heat it gently until the butter melts and the sugar dissolves. Bring the mixture to the boil and allow it to simmer for a minute.
3 Take the pan off the heat and stir in the milk and the condensed milk. Bring back to the boil and bubble for 2 minutes or until the mixture turns to a very thick golden sauce, stirring continuously so that it does not burn. Remove it from the heat.
4 Peel and slice four of the bananas and then brush them lightly with some of the lemon juice.
5 Arrange the banana slices over the prepared biscuit base, then spread the warm sauce over the banana slices and leave it to cool.
6 Whip the cream until it is stiff and spread or pipe it over the filling.
7 Peel and slice the last banana, brush the slices with lemon juice and arrange them decoratively over the cream. Sprinkle the chocolate over the top and serve.
VARIATIONS
Use crushed chocolate biscuits or gingernuts in place of the granita biscuits. You can also leave out the mixed spice if you prefer a pie shell with a milder flavour.

Millet

I thought millet was simply birdseed. Is it also for cooking?

Yes, it can be used to thicken soups, or cooked in milk to make a breakfast cereal or added to breads and teabreads to boost their texture and flavour. While it is not a gourmet ingredient, millet can be tasty and is a good source of proteins as well as carbohydrates.

Since Roman times at least, millet has been widely grown in North Africa, Asia and the Mediterranean countries. It is an important food for many of the world's poor, and is often fermented to make beers.

The dried grains are tiny, about the size of a pinhead, and coloured pale yellow with a darker brown spot on one side. They swell considerably during cooking so it is important not to add too much to dishes such as soups. Millet flakes cook faster than the whole grains and are also used to thicken soups.

Unless whole millet grains are cooked in plenty of liquid, they should be presoaked as shown in the following recipe for flapjacks. The millet adds a fine texture to these delicious treats. Serve the flapjacks warm with lusciously melting strawberry butter as a sweet surprise for afternoon tea.

Flapjacks with strawberry butter

MAKES: 6 cakes
PREPARATION TIME: 10 minutes
COOKING TIME: 45 minutes

FOR THE FLAPJACKS
15 g (1 tablespoon) millet grains
250 g (2 cups) plain white flour
½ teaspoon cream of tartar
½ teaspoon bicarbonate of soda
30 g (1½ tablespoons) caster sugar
1 large egg
375 ml milk
Vegetable oil, for frying
To serve: fresh strawberries and crème fraîche

Fresh strawberries and crème fraîche brighten these flapjacks made with millet. Spread them with strawberry butter for an unusual sweet treat.

FOR THE STRAWBERRY BUTTER
125 g unsalted butter, softened
1 tablespoon good quality strawberry conserve

1 Wash the millet, place it in a small pan and cover well with cold water. Bring to the boil and simmer for about 25–30 minutes until the grains are swollen and tender. Drain the millet well and set aside.

2 Meanwhile, make the strawberry butter by beating together the butter and the strawberry conserve until they are thoroughly combined. (It is worth using the best quality conserve you have to add maximum flavour.) Chill this mixture well until it is required.

3 Sift the flour, cream of tartar and bicarbonate of soda together into a bowl. Stir in the sugar and gradually beat in the egg and milk to form a smooth batter. Stir in the cooked millet and mix thoroughly.

4 Lightly brush a griddle or heavy-based frying pan with the oil and bring it to a medium heat. Using a ladle, pour on a spoonful of batter. Cook for about a minute until very small bubbles begin to appear on the surface. Gently flip the flapjack and cook on the other side for a further minute, or until puffed and golden.

5 After cooking, keep each flapjack warm in a low oven and repeat the frying process with the rest of the batter until you have made a total of six flapjacks.

6 Serve the flapjacks at once, spread with some of the strawberry butter and decorated with a few fresh strawberries. Add some generous spoonfuls of crème fraîche to the warm flapjacks for a delicious creamy topping.

Mousse

SEPARATE PROBLEM

My mousses always separate while chilling. What am I doing wrong?

If you are using gelatine to set the mousse, do not fold the gelatine mixture into the cream until it is cool, as this may cause the mousse to separate. The thickened mixture should be of a similar consistency to the cream before the two are stirred together. Stir the mousse mixture continuously while combining the gelatine mixture with the cream so it does not sink to the bottom, giving a layered effect.

If the mousse is being made with whisked egg white instead of, or as well as, gelatine, fold it in gently so as not to lose the air bubbles which hold up the mousse.

If a mousse does separate, there is no remedy. However, it should be perfectly edible, even if it is less attractive than intended.

FISHY CHOICE

What is the best fish for mousses?

Fresh salmon is a popular choice because it has a good flavour and an attractive colour. It is particularly nice combined with shellfish for a luxurious dinner party starter.

Smoked fish such as mackerel, salmon, trout and even kippers work well because they, too, are strongly flavoured. They can be combined with some cream, cream cheese or mayonnaise and lemon to make a rich, tasty mousse.

Remove all the bones before working the flesh in a food processor. The resulting purée should also be checked for small bones before being combined with other ingredients. Fish bones in mousse are unpleasant and can be dangerous.

Try this quick recipe for Smoked Salmon and Taramasalata Mousse (right) which has no fish bones at all. Buy a good quality, mild and creamy taramasalata, or make your own (see recipe on page 322).

Smoked salmon and taramasalata mousse

SERVES: 4
PREPARATION TIME: 20 minutes, plus 4 hours chilling
COOKING TIME: none

---

1 teaspoon powdered gelatine
250 g taramasalata
Black pepper
375 g thinly sliced smoked salmon
To garnish: black olives, lemon wedges and coriander sprigs
To serve: hot pita bread

---

1 Sprinkle the powdered gelatine over 2 tablespoons of water in a heatproof bowl and let it soak for about 5 minutes until spongy.

2 Stand the bowl in a small pan of gently simmering water and heat until the gelatine dissolves. Leave it to cool slightly, then slowly stir the gelatine into the taramasalata in a thin stream. Add pepper to taste and stir again until evenly mixed.

3 Line four small ramekins or timbale moulds with the smoked salmon slices, allowing them to hang over the edges a little. Spoon in the taramasalata, dividing it equally between the ramekins, and fold the salmon slices neatly over the top.

4 Leave to chill in the refrigerator for at least 4 hours, then turn the mousses out onto plates and serve with hot pita bread. Garnish, if you like, with some black olives, lemon wedges and sprigs of coriander.

This stunning parcel of taramasalata with smoked salmon wrapping will impress dinner guests. It looks complicated to make but in reality is quick and simple.

MOUSSES AND FOOLS

What is the difference between a mousse and a fool?

A mousse is a light, foamy mixture that usually contains a cold set mixture made with egg yolks, cream, whisked egg white or gelatine, and flavouring. A fool is a cold dessert of sweet fruit purée mixed with whipped cream. It does not contain eggs and is not set.

In the following recipe for a Minted Blackberry Mousse, the mixture is lightened with whipped cream and set with gelatine.

Minted blackberry mousse

SERVES: 6
PREPARATION TIME: 45 minutes, plus 3–4 hours chilling time
COOKING TIME: none

500 g fresh blackberries, poached lightly and cooled, or frozen blackberries, thawed
A small bunch of fresh mint sprigs
1 tablespoon powdered gelatine
3 large eggs
125 g (½ cup) caster sugar
300 ml fresh cream
To decorate: mint sprigs

1 Put the blackberries in a blender or food processor. Strip the leaves off the mint sprigs, add them to the blender and process until smooth. Press the blackberry mixture through a fine nylon sieve, then discard the seeds.
2 Sprinkle the powdered gelatine over 2 tablespoons of cold water in a small bowl and leave it to soak for about 5 minutes. Place the bowl over a pan of simmering water until the gelatine has dissolved, then set aside until it has cooled.
3 In a large bowl, whisk the eggs and sugar until they are thick, pale and creamy. Gradually whisk the blackberry purée into the egg mixture, then stir in the gelatine.
4 Whip the cream until softly stiff and fold with a metal spoon into the egg and fruit mixture carefully but thoroughly. Pour the mousse into one large serving dish, or into six individual dishes and chill for

3–4 hours or until it has set. Decorate the mousse with the fresh mint sprigs before serving.
VARIATION
For an alcoholic kick, try folding 2 or 3 tablespoons of a blackberry or a blackcurrant liqueur into the egg mixture just before adding the whipped cream.

Healthy option

When making a mousse you can replace the cream with plain fromage frais, a mixture of fromage frais and Greek-style yoghurt, or whipped reduced-fat cream to create a healthier version.

Muffins

CAKE CONFUSION

What is the difference between an American muffin, an English muffin and a fairy cake?

Fairy cakes are small buttercakes made by the creaming method and often topped with coloured icing. American muffins are a cross between a scone and a fairy cake, but bigger. They are made with a thick batter mixture rather than a dough and are raised with baking powder. American muffins are not as sweet or as rich as fairy cakes.

Americans use the term 'English muffins' to describe what the English call crumpets; however, the authentic traditional English muffin is different and uses dough made from strong white flour and yeast cooked on a griddle or hot plate. The muffin is torn apart when cooked and eaten immediately with sweet or savoury toppings.

American muffins are both quick and easy to make, as the following recipe shows. They are best eaten the day they are baked.

American muffins

MAKES: 10–12 muffins
PREPARATION TIME: 10 minutes
COOKING TIME: 20 minutes

250 g (2 cups) plain flour
3 teaspoons baking powder
½ teaspoon bicarbonate of soda
90 g (½ cup) light brown sugar
1 large egg
250 ml milk
60 g unsalted butter, melted and cooled

1 Preheat the oven to 200°C. Place 10–12 large, deep, paper cases in muffin tins.
2 Sift the dry ingredients into a bowl and make a well in the centre.
3 Beat together the egg and milk and add to the dry ingredients with the melted butter. Lightly stir the mixture together with a fork.
4 Fill the paper cases three-quarters full, then bake for 20 minutes until the muffins are well risen, golden brown and cooked through. Leave them in their tins for a few minutes then transfer to a wire rack to cool.
VARIATIONS
For blackberry, blueberry, cranberry or raspberry muffins, add 75 g fresh or partly thawed frozen berries and a few drops of vanilla essence to the mixture after adding the melted butter.

For double chocolate chip muffins, add 4 tablespoons of cocoa powder and 100 g chopped dark, milk or white chocolate.

For banana, bran and cinnamon muffins, add two mashed bananas, 50 g natural bran and ½ teaspoon of ground cinnamon.

BERRY CHOICE

My favourite muffins contain blueberries, which sometimes are unavailable. Can I use other fresh berries instead?

You can include any other berry fruit such as raspberries or blackberries in muffins, but use them half-thawed if they have been frozen. This will keep them firm when baked and give better results.

Mushrooms

CAREFUL STORAGE

What's the best way to store and prepare mushrooms?

Fresh mushrooms have a sponge-like density that either absorbs moisture or sweats it out to become slimy in storage, so it is important to keep them dry. Wrap mushrooms in kitchen paper towels and store in a brown paper bag in the refrigerator crisper drawer.

Washing mushrooms impairs their texture and peeling diminishes their flavour: there is no need to do either. Brush off any surface grit or growing medium with a clean, dry pastry brush or some kitchen paper towel if necessary.

WILD AND CULTIVATED

Can wild mushrooms be used in place of cultivated ones in recipes, and when is it best to use large mushrooms rather than the smaller button variety?

Wild mushrooms are a rare treat. Although they can always be substituted for other mushrooms in recipes, they are best when simply fried in butter with shallots, or in olive oil with garlic.

Button mushrooms make dainty garnishes and have a firm texture that is good thinly sliced and served raw or marinated in salads; however, they can also look attractive when cooked whole in stews.

Large flat mushrooms have a much fuller flavour that makes them the best choice for a breakfast fry-up, or to use in meaty stews or creamy sauces as in the paprika-spiced Hungarian recipe (above right). This can be served on toast as a snack for four, or with rice as a vegetarian light meal for two, or as a vegetable accompaniment to some plainly grilled meat or fish.

Chunky paprika-spiced mushrooms gently pan-fried make a deliciously creamy topping for hot toast.

Mushroom paprika

SERVES: *4*
PREPARATION TIME: *10 minutes*
COOKING TIME: *20 minutes*

---

1 large, white onion, finely chopped
A good pinch of dried thyme,
*   optional*
3 tablespoons olive oil
2 teaspoons paprika
250 g field or large flat mushrooms,
*   sliced*
Salt and black pepper
300 ml light sour cream or Greek-
*   style yoghurt*

---

1 Gently fry the onion, with the dried thyme if using, in the oil over a very low heat for at least 10 minutes or until the onion is soft and golden, stirring occasionally. Stir in the paprika, sliced mushrooms and salt. Add 200 ml of water.
2 Raise the heat a little and bring the sauce to the boil. Cover and cook for 2–3 minutes until the mushrooms collapse, releasing their liquor.

3 Remove the lid, raise the heat higher still and cook the mushrooms for around 5–6 minutes, shaking the pan regularly (stirring would break up the mushrooms), until the sauce is thick and sticky.
4 Carefully stir in the sour cream or yoghurt. Season with pepper, then spoon the mushrooms over toast.

HOME DRYING

Can I dry mushrooms myself, and how should they be stored?

Yes, you can dry mushrooms and they are a useful addition to the store cupboard. To dry your own, place the mushrooms on racks in a very low oven for several hours or overnight. Large, fleshy flat mushrooms can be sliced before drying.

The dried mushrooms are ready for storage when they are dry but still just pliable rather than crisp. If stored in airtight containers, the dried mushrooms can be kept and used for up to 12 months.

COOKING FROM DRIED

How do I cook dried mushrooms?

Dried mushrooms should be reconstituted before use: soak them in warm water, perhaps with a splash of sherry or wine in it, for up to 20 minutes depending on their size, then use in stews, risottos or pasta sauces. The liquid in which they were reconstituted can be incorporated into sauces and stock.

Mussels

STAYING SAFE

How can I tell when is it safe to eat fresh mussels, and how do you prepare and cook them?

Traditionally mussels were eaten during the colder winter months because they were at their cheapest and best in the cool weather. However, fish farming, refrigerated transport and air transportation have made them available virtually throughout the year, and refrigeration keeps them safe.

Mussels are sold while still alive, and although they are now sold much cleaner than they used to be, it is important to follow careful preparation procedures (see panel, right), and particularly to ensure you discard uncooked mussels that gape open or have chipped shells.

LIVE STORAGE

How long can I store live mussels I have gathered myself?

If you gather your own mussels, you must make sure they come from safe sites, from wide estuaries or coasts facing out to sea and away from sewage outfalls or other possible sources of pollution. It is best to take local advice if you do not know the area, and safest of all to buy mussels in the fish market or from reliable fish shops.

Live mussels may be stored in a damp hessian bag or in a bucket of water, in a cool place, for 1–3 days. Discard any that open.

CLEANING AND COOKING MUSSELS

Before mussels can be opened, they must be properly cleaned. Once the shell has been opened, the mollusc must be cooked or eaten immediately.

1 Scrub the mussels in a sinkful of cold water, scraping off barnacles with the back of a small knife. Pull away the beards. Discard any mussels with broken shells or open mussels that don't close when tapped sharply.

2 Cover the bottom of a large pan with white wine then add parsley stems and garlic if you like. Bring the wine to the boil, place in the cleaned mussels, then cover and cook them for 2–3 minutes over a high heat.

3 Transfer the opened mussels with a slotted spoon to a sieve placed over a bowl. Cook any that have not yet opened for another minute, then discard if they are still closed. Dish up the mussels, straining the liquid from both the pan and the bowl over them.

4 Eat the mussels with your fingers, using an empty mussel shell to scoop out the meat. Accompany the mussels with French bread and place a large bowl on the table for discarded shells. When you have finished eating the mussels, drink the broth.

VARIETY OF RECIPES

I see moules marinière on many menus, but what are some other ways of cooking mussels?

Mussels are found in many of the world's waters so there are plenty of different treatments for them. Mussels spill delicious juices as they open and most of the popular cooking methods incorporate this liquor in the sauce.

When mussels are to be served in their shells to eat with the fingers, it is best not to include sticky or fatty ingredients, but mussels can be shelled and their juices then enriched with cream.

For an excellent starter, large mussels can be opened over heat (see panel, above), shelled and then returned to their half shells, topped with some garlic butter and breadcrumbs, then grilled. Eat the mussels with a fork.

Alternatively, try using the technique from the basic recipe for Moules Marinière (page 236) but adapt the ingredients to create several simple, well-flavoured mussel dishes. Add some chopped fennel and shallots, for instance, or for a Provençal flavour add tomatoes, garlic and thyme with white wine and a dash of an anise-flavoured liqueur such as Pernod. You could also thicken the juices slightly with beurre manié or a little cream.

Mussels with similar cream, wine or tomato-based sauces are highly delicious when served with freshly cooked pasta such as spaghetti.

Moules marinière

SERVES: 4
PREPARATION TIME: 30 minutes
COOKING TIME: 6-8 minutes

2 kg live mussels
2 onions, chopped
2 cloves garlic, chopped
4 large sprigs parsley
200 ml dry white wine
Salt and black pepper

1 Clean the mussels (see details in panel on page 235).
2 Put the onions and garlic into a large pan with the parsley stalks (not the leaves) and the wine. Bring to the boil and simmer for 5 minutes.
3 Raise the heat and add half the mussels. Cover the pan with a lid and cook the mussels for 3 minutes.
4 Use a slotted spoon to transfer the opened mussels to a sieve placed over a bowl. Cook any unopened mussels for a minute more, but if any remain shut they must be discarded. Warm a serving bowl while cooking the next batch of mussels.
5 Chop the parsley leaves. Transfer the mussels to the serving bowl. When you have transferred them all, season the cooking liquor to taste.
6 Allow the liquid to stand for 1-2 minutes so that any grit settles on the bottom of the pan, then strain it over the mussels. Scatter with the chopped parsley and serve.

Fresh mussels from the market are a gourmet treat best cooked simply, as in this recipe for Moules Marinière.

Mustard

SPICY PLANT

What is mustard made of?

Mustard is made from the crushed seeds of a family of plants. Some mustard plants are grown for their leaves, which are widely eaten as a vegetable in the East; others for their seedlings, often eaten with cress as a salad or sandwich garnish.

Three sorts of seed – black, brown and white – were once used in the manufacture of mustard powder but black seeds are no longer grown commercially. Mustard powder has been used in Britain for centuries, but French-style wholegrain mustard, Dijon, German, American, Australian and flavoured mustards have all become popular in recent years.

FEEL THE HEAT

Why is English mustard so much hotter than other mustards?

Largely because this is what the English desire of it. English mustard is made with equal quantities of white and brown mustard seeds; while the white give heat on the tongue, the brown give a volatile heat in the back of the throat. It is usually sold dry and then simply mixed with cold water, which adds to its strength of flavour.

French Dijon mustard is made from brown mustard seeds only, diluted with white wine and spices to make it less hot than English mustard. The sweeter, smoother German and American mustards are made with white mustard seeds, their flavour softened by additions such as sugar or herbs.

FLAVOUR IMPROVER

Is it true that a pinch of mustard powder added to cheese recipes makes the cheese easier to digest?

True or not, it certainly improves the flavour. Mustard has been credited with digestive powers, and it has always been eaten with rich, fatty foods, such as ham, pork, sausages or cooked cheese. The simple Mustard Sauce below adds spice to grilled pork or veal chops, chicken, rabbit or hard-boiled eggs.

Mustard sauce

SERVES: 4
PREPARATION TIME: 5 minutes
COOKING TIME: 30 minutes

40 g butter
2 tablespoons plain flour
300 ml chicken stock
1-2 tablespoons smooth Dijon mustard, to taste
150 ml sour cream
Salt and black pepper
2 tablespoons chopped chives

1 In a saucepan, melt the butter, add the flour and cook over a medium heat for 1 minute, stirring continuously.
2 Add the stock and bring to the boil, stirring constantly. Simmer gently for 5 minutes, then whisk in the mustard and sour cream.
3 Season to taste then cook gently for 1-2 minutes without boiling. Remove from the heat and add the chopped chives before serving.

Noodles

IN THE SOUP

What sort of noodles should I use in chicken noodle soup?

The traditional noodle for chicken noodle soup is a narrow, square tube rather than a rounded noodle, but any small, narrow egg pasta would be an acceptable substitute.

The word 'noodle' is confusing because although it was used in the past to describe hollow, macaroni-type pasta, today it is used when referring to long, flat Italian pasta such as fettuccine, pappardelle, tagliarini, tagliatelle or tagliolini.

To complicate matters further, Chinese noodles are generally thin and round, like spaghetti.

WORLDWIDE STAPLE

What are Chinese noodles?

There are two basic types of Chinese noodles, wheat flour noodles which are yellow, and rice flour noodles which are white. Many shapes are available and their texture varies, with the addition of egg for instance. The translucent vermicelli or cellophane noodles are made from mung bean flour.

Throughout the Asian world, noodle dishes take on myriad guises. There are curried noodles (such as Singapore's *laksa*), plus Indonesian spicy fried noodles (*bahmi goreng*), Vietnamese beef noodles (*pho*), complex recipes cooked with choice ingredients, and humble vegetarian dishes. There are also dozens of varieties of instant noodles available.

SIMPLE COOKING

What is the best way to cook Chinese noodles?

This depends very much on the type of noodle. Generally, all dry noodles, whether made from rice, wheat or mung bean flour, should be softened by blanching or boiling before cooking with other ingredients. Fresh noodles, such as rice sticks and wheat noodles, can be cooked without preparation.

Throughout Asia, noodles are eaten as much for symbolic reasons as for taste, texture and their versatility – which explains why they are always disconcertingly long. It will not do to cut them as the action shortens your life span!

One of the best-known Asian dishes in the Western world is chow mein (literally, 'fried noodles'). Leftover cooked chicken, beef and pork are excellent ingredients to use with fresh vegetables in the following recipe, which could be served as a meal in itself or as part of a Chinese menu.

Leftovers are never more enticing than when fried with Chinese noodles to produce the popular chow mein.

Quick chow mein

SERVES: 4
PREPARATION TIME: 10 minutes
COOKING TIME: 10 minutes

500 g wheat or rice noodles
2 tablespoons vegetable oil
1 large onion, sliced
125 g bean sprouts
125 g fresh vegetables, such as baby corn, peppers (sliced or chopped) and snow peas
250 g roast chicken, beef or pork, thinly sliced
2 tablespoons light soy sauce
2 tablespoons oyster sauce
300 ml chicken or beef stock
To garnish: 2 tablespoons chopped fresh coriander

1 Cook the noodles according to the packet instructions; drain well and set aside.
2 Heat the oil in a wok and stir-fry the onions for 5 minutes until soft.
3 Add the vegetables and stir-fry for around 2–3 minutes. Add the meat, noodles and remaining ingredients and stir-fry for 5 minutes until well blended and the stock is nearly all absorbed. When cooked, the noodles should be moist. Serve immediately, garnished with coriander.

Nutrition

VARIETY IS THE KEY

I feel battered by the conflicting advice on healthy eating. Are there some simple rules to follow?

Yes. Eat a variety of different types of food and try to regulate your intake to keep your weight within the healthy range for your height.

Study the diagram opposite, of the Australian Healthy Diet Pyramid, which is based on the dietary guidelines for Australians, and was formulated by the Australian Nutrition Foundation. The pyramid shows at a glance what proportion of our diet the foods from each food group should constitute to maintain good health. Most of our food should come from the groups that include vegetables, fruit, cereals, legumes and bread; we should eat least of the sugar, salt, butter and oil at the top of the pyramid.

Make the most of poultry and fish, choose lean cuts of meat and limit fried foods, snacks containing hidden fat, pastries and biscuits. Take advantage of lower-fat alternatives, use salt sparingly and drink alcohol only in moderation.

A GOOD DIET IS BEST

Do my children really need to take multivitamin pills?

Although children do not generally need larger amounts of vitamins in absolute terms, they have high requirements in relation to their energy needs and body weight. Vitamin supplements may be a convenient 'insurance policy' but are not really a substitute for a good diet, in children or adults.

PRESERVING VITAMINS

What is the best way to cook fresh fruit and vegetables with the least possible loss of vitamins?

The cooking of fruit and vegetables always results in some loss of vitamins: water-soluble vitamins may be leached into the cooking water and some vitamins are destroyed when exposed to air. The loss of water-soluble vitamins can be very large if the vegetables are completely covered in water while being cooked – they may lose up to 80 per cent of their vitamin C.

Steaming reduces this loss, but the destruction of vitamin C may be increased. Microwaving and pressure cooking both help to reduce the loss of essential vitamins, as less water is used and the cooking time is shorter.

FAT IN PERSPECTIVE

Would it be harmful to cut fat from my family's diet completely?

Although we need to avoid eating too much fat, cutting all the fat from your diet is not wise. We need fat because it gives us energy, provides the essential fatty acids which enable the body to absorb the fat-soluble vitamins, A, D, E and K, and makes foods more palatable.

Fats are particularly important for children under the age of five, who need to have sufficient energy and nutrients for rapid growth. If very young children are given the bulky, low-fat diets recommended for adults, their small stomachs are quickly filled without providing them with the amounts of energy and nutrients they need.

BUTTER OR MARGARINE?

What are the pros and cons of butter and margarine?

Butter and traditional margarine contain the same number of kilojoules. However, many vegetable oil-based spreads now contain less fat than previously. Butter naturally contains vitamins A and D and, by law, these vitamins are added to margarines and spreads. But they differ in other ways. Butter contains more saturates (54 per cent) and less polyunsaturates (5 per cent) than soft margarines and spreads (which contain 16–26 per cent saturates and more than 40 per cent polyunsaturates). As most people need to limit their consumption of saturated fats while increasing their intake of polyunsaturates, margarine is the healthier choice. However, cooking margarines can contain up to 35 per cent saturated fat and only a small amount of polyunsaturates.

The differing cholesterol contents of butter and margarine may also be important to people concerned about heart disease. Most spreads made from vegetable oils are almost cholesterol-free.

TRANS FATTY ACIDS

What are trans fatty acids?

Trans fatty acids have been linked to heart disease because, like saturated fats, they raise blood cholesterol levels. They are created when polyunsaturated and mono-unsaturated oils are hydrogenated, either naturally or industrially. Trans fatty acids occur in butter (5 per cent) and in some margarines and spreads (0–10 per cent). However, about half the margarines and spreads on the market in Australia are now virtually free of trans fatty acids.

If you are concerned about heart disease and your blood cholesterol level, choose food products that are low in trans fatty acids.

OILY FISH

What are omega-3 and omega-6 fatty acids?

Omega-3 and omega-6 are generally known as essential fatty acids and are found in some foods such as oily fish, seeds and seed oils.

Believed to be essential for brain and eye development, omega-3 is also useful to the body for reducing inflammation and lowering the tendency for blood to clot.

Omega-6 appears to help regulate blood pressure and the body's water balance. It also improves our nerve and immune functions.

There is some evidence to suggest that people who eat oily fish, such as mullet, mackerel and sardines, twice a week may have lower rates of heart disease. Certainly, it is an easy and inexpensive way of increasing your intake of omega-3 fatty acids. The seeds of pumpkin, sesame and sunflower are good, tasty sources of omega-6.

JUICE IS BETTER

I have heard that drinking tea with food, or shortly before eating, inhibits our absorption of iron. Is this true?

Yes. Only a small amount of the iron in the foods we eat is absorbed and it varies according to the type of food, and whether other factors help or hinder its absorption. For example, about 20–40 per cent of the iron in red meat is absorbed, compared with only 5 per cent from some vegetable sources.

Vitamin C improves the body's absorption of iron while the tannins in tea and, to a lesser extent, coffee interfere with this process. So to boost iron absorption, a glass of orange juice is a better accompaniment to a meal than tea or coffee.

IRRADIATION WORRIES

Is irradiated food harmful? And is there any danger of my buying it without knowing?

Irradiation involves exposing food to a source of radioactivity that inhibits the continued growth or ripening of the food. This makes it an effective preservation process, but it does cause chemical changes in the food, and some destruction of vitamins may occur.

The irradiation process can form new compounds called 'radiolytic products' in the food. Even though these may be present in very small amounts (only one or two parts per million), questions have still been raised about the possible harmful effects.

The flavour and texture of foods can also be adversely affected by irradiation; for instance, vegetables may become soft and spongy, and irradiated meats have often been described as having an unpleasant 'goaty' or 'wet dog' flavour.

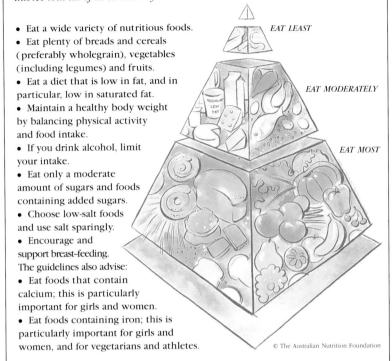

THE BALANCE OF GOOD HEALTH

The current dietary guidelines for Australians were drawn up by the Commonwealth Department of Health and constitute essential basic dietary advice that all of us should try to adhere to.

- Eat a wide variety of nutritious foods.
- Eat plenty of breads and cereals (preferably wholegrain), vegetables (including legumes) and fruits.
- Eat a diet that is low in fat, and in particular, low in saturated fat.
- Maintain a healthy body weight by balancing physical activity and food intake.
- If you drink alcohol, limit your intake.
- Eat only a moderate amount of sugars and foods containing added sugars.
- Choose low-salt foods and use salt sparingly.
- Encourage and support breast-feeding.

The guidelines also advise:
- Eat foods that contain calcium; this is particularly important for girls and women.
- Eat foods containing iron; this is particularly important for girls and women, and for vegetarians and athletes.

EAT LEAST

EAT MODERATELY

EAT MOST

© The Australian Nutrition Foundation

There is no permission granted currently in Australia either to manufacture or to sell irradiated food. This prohibition also applies to imported foods – so it is not, in fact, possible to find yourself buying it without knowing.

SALT AND BLOOD PRESSURE

Food tastes so bland without salt. Why is its consumption said to be bad for you?

There is some concern about the amount of salt used in Western diets because of the links between sodium and high blood pressure (hypertension), a condition which increases the risk of heart attack, stroke and kidney failure.

We need sodium (salt is sodium chloride) for proper cell, nerve and muscle function, but the danger of consuming too much comes partly from the hidden salt in processed foods and the habit of oversalting

food at the table. While many of us consume about 3000–4600 mg of sodium daily, the recommended ntake is no more than 2300 mg.

There are two ways of reducing your salt intake. Limit your intake of foods, such as smoked and cured meats or fish, cheese, salty snacks, packet soups and stock cubes. Secondly, reduce the amount of salt you add to food, both when cooking and at the table.

POTASSIUM CONCERN

Is reduced-sodium salt better for you than ordinary salt?

While using reduced-sodium salt can help you eat less sodium, the amount of potassium in these products makes them unsuitable for diabetics, and sufferers of kidney disease. Moreover, the level of salt we use is largely a matter of habit and using substitutes does not help to re-educate our taste buds.

Nuts

STORING NUTS

What is the best way to keep nuts really fresh and full of flavour?

Because of their high fat content, nuts turn rancid quite quickly in warm or damp conditions and they are best bought only when you intend to use them, and in small quantities. They can be stored in the refrigerator or freezer, providing they are kept very dry, or in airtight plastic containers.

Nuts sold in vacuum-sealed packs showing a 'use-by' date are the best to buy, as they will keep in a cool, dry cupboard until you are ready to use them. Once the packet has been opened, however, the nuts should be kept in an airtight container and eaten quite quickly.

RICH IN PROTEIN AND FAT

Some people say nuts are very healthy, while others say they are high in fat: who is right?

Both statements are correct. All nuts, but particularly peanuts and almonds, are a good source of protein, and play an important part in a vegetarian diet. They are also a good source of B-group vitamins.

However, all nuts except chestnuts are high in fat and therefore high in kilojoules, so anyone on a low-kilojoule diet should avoid them. Macadamias, pine nuts and walnuts are highest in fat; pine nuts and hazelnuts contain less saturated fat than other nuts.

NUTS OR SEEDS?

Are pine nuts really nuts?

No. Although pine nuts resemble nuts and are used like nuts, they are in fact the seeds, or kernels, of the stone pine, a tree native to Mediterranean countries and especially common in Italy. In that country, pine nuts are an essential ingredient for the basil, garlic and Parmesan sauce, pesto (see *Oils*).

SHELLING AND SKINNING NUTS

Nuts that are to be used in cooking should have their thin inner skin removed first. Prepared nuts in packets are available, but nuts are best when used fresh.

BLANCHING AND SKINNING ALMONDS

1 Crack open the shells and remove the kernels. Put the almonds into a saucepan and cover with cold water. Bring to the boil and immediately pour the almonds into a sieve to drain.

2 As soon as the blanched almonds have drained and while they are still warm, pop the nuts out of their thin papery skins by squeezing them between your thumb and forefinger.

ROASTING AND SKINNING HAZELNUTS

1 Crack open the shells, remove the kernels and put the hazelnuts on a baking tray. Roast them in a moderate oven for 5–10 minutes or until their skins begin to split open and the nuts turn golden brown. Remove from the oven and tip onto a clean tea towel.

2 Rub the roasted hazelnuts together firmly in the tea towel to remove their thin papery skins, then pick the skinless nuts out of the tea towel. If necessary, put any nuts still covered in their skin back into a moderate oven for a few more minutes.

MELLOWING WALNUTS

I find the flavour of some walnuts rather bitter. Is there anything I can do to counteract this?

The flavour of walnuts can vary depending on their freshness and country of origin. If you have bought some which you find bitter, their flavour can be mellowed by blanching them. Crack open the nuts and put the kernels in a small saucepan of boiling water. Boil gently for a minute, then drain and dry before using.

For the best flavour, make sure that walnuts are absolutely fresh. To test the freshness of shell-on nuts, weigh them in your hand individually – each one should feel heavy and not rattle when shaken. If the nut rattles, the kernel inside will have dried and shrivelled.

If, after blanching, you still find the flavour too bitter, you could use mellower pecan nuts instead, which are from the same family.

NUT-FREE STUFFING

I have an allergy to all types of nuts; can you suggest an easy alternative to add to a stuffing?

Burghul makes a great alternative to nuts as it has a similar taste and texture. First soak the uncooked grains in cold water for 30 minutes to swell and soften them, then add them to the stuffing and cook as stated in the recipe.

Oats

FABULOUS FIBRE

I have heard that oats are good for the heart. Is this true?

Generally speaking, oat grains are a highly nutritious food: they contain carbohydrates, protein and fat as well as iron, potassium and most B-group vitamins. Oats also contain soluble fibres that turn into a jelly-like consistency when cooked; these have been connected in various studies to cholesterol-lowering activity in the body. Though there is not enough firm evidence to confirm this, oats are regarded as very beneficial in the diet.

SUPERIOR PORRIDGE

I have always made porridge with rolled oats, but on a recent trip to Scotland I had delicious porridge made with oatmeal instead. Which is best?

In Scotland, where it originates, porridge is traditionally made with oatmeal. Although it takes longer to cook, the flavour and texture of oatmeal are far superior

The easiest and quickest way to make porridge, however, is to use rolled oats, as they cook in only 3–4 minutes against 20 minutes or more for oatmeal. To make two portions, put 125 g (1⅓ cups) of rolled oats into a pan. Pour in 600 ml cold water or, if you prefer, half water and half milk. Bring to the boil and continue simmering, stirring continuously, for 3–4 minutes. When the porridge is as thick as you like it, season with a little

Rich and crumbly rolled oat Crunchies are some of the easiest biscuits to make. They are always a favourite with children and anyone with a sweet tooth.

salt. Serve with milk, butter or cream, and brown sugar, honey or golden syrup.

GROUND OR ROLLED

What is the difference between oatmeal and oatflakes?

Both are processed from the oat cereal, but oatmeal is ground from the whole kernel while oatflakes are made from steamed and rolled oats. Oatmeal is graded according to how finely it is ground; the largest is pinhead oatmeal, followed by coarse, medium and fine.

Both oatmeal and oatflakes can be used in sweet or savoury dishes. Because oatflakes (also known as rolled oats or porridge oats) have been lightly steamed, they cook faster than oatmeal. Oatmeal is used in stuffings and coatings instead of breadcrumbs; it is also added to breads, although it cannot be used on its own for this purpose as the gluten content of oats is too low. Traditionally, rolled oats are used in biscuits (right).

Crunchies

MAKES: 8-12 fingers
PREPARATION TIME: 5 minutes
COOKING TIME: 15-20 minutes

100 g unsalted butter
3 tablespoons golden syrup
60 g (¼ cup) caster sugar
185 g (2 cups) rolled oats

1 Preheat the oven to 190°C. Grease a shallow 18 cm square cake tin and line the base with nonstick baking paper.
2 Put the butter, golden syrup and sugar in a small pan and heat gently until the butter is melted. Stir in the rolled oats until evenly combined.
3 Spoon the warm mixture into the prepared tin and smooth the surface level. Bake for 15-20 minutes.
4 Remove from the oven and leave to cool for a few minutes, then mark the top into fingers. Leave to cool in the tin before turning out.
5 When thoroughly cool and crisp, cut out the individual portions and serve. The biscuits will keep in an airtight tin for three to four days.

Offal

INTERNAL PARTS

What does the term offal include?

It covers all edible, internal parts of animals, such as kidneys and liver, also brains, cheeks, ears, stomachs, sweetbreads, tripe and tongue.

FRESH AND FREEZING

Can I freeze offal?

Offal must be absolutely fresh before freezing. Look for moist, shiny meat, and avoid buying any that has a greenish colour, slimy surface or an unpleasant smell.

Liver can be frozen either in large pieces or sliced. Calf's kidneys should be chopped up, but lamb's kidneys can be frozen either whole or halved. Sweetbreads are best frozen whole, after blanching.

BLANCHING NEEDS

What kinds of offal should be blanched before cooking and why?

Brains, sweetbreads and tripe have to be immersed in boiling water before cooking to remove all traces of blood and to give them a better texture. First soak the offal in cold water for 1–2 hours. Then put it in a pan of fresh cold water and bring to a gentle boil. Simmer for a few minutes, drain and rinse well.

COOKING CHOICE

What is the best way to cook each type of offal?

Brains and parts of the stomach are poached in a well-flavoured court bouillon (water, sometimes with added white wine, and herbs) with vinegar or lemon juice to tenderise the meat. Braising in the oven, using a low, even temperature, is better for tougher types of offal such as heart and tongue.

More tender offal, such as sweetbreads, kidney and liver, can be sliced and sautéed in butter (see also **Kidneys** and **Liver**).

Oils

BEST FOR COOKING

Can I use any variety of oil in cooking, or are some unsuitable?

There are more than 20 different culinary oils available, including avocado and pumpkin seed oils; in addition, there are many varieties of olive and flavoured oils.

Oils which are fairly neutral in flavour and can withstand high temperatures, such as those made from corn, grapeseed, peanut, rapeseed (canola) and sunflower, are best for cooking. Others, such as almond, hazelnut, sesame and walnut oils, are more suitable for flavouring foods. Some oils, such as olive, may be used for both.

STORING OILS

What is the best way to store oils?

They should be stored, well sealed, in a cool, dark, dry place to prevent the oil from oxidising and developing a rancid taste. Some deterioration is inevitable over a period of time, so buy oil in small amounts and replace it frequently.

REHEATING OIL

How long can I keep reheating frying oil before it goes off?

Oil that is frequently reheated in a deep-fryer is likely to become rancid in time. Its vitamin content also reduces, the flavour may become unpleasant, and it is possible for harmful substances to be produced if the oil is overheated. Discard any frying oil that smells unpleasant, produces too much foam when heated, creates smoke easily and has become dark in colour.

In general, you should reheat oil two or three times only before discarding it. Each time it is used, the oil should be allowed to cool completely, then be filtered through a fine sieve. Once you have cooked a specific type of food in a batch of oil, re-use the oil for that food only.

EXTRA PURE

What is the difference between ordinary and virgin olive oil?

Olive oils are classified according to their level of acidity. The first cold pressing of a high grade of olives produces the finest olive oil, with a maximum acidity level of only 1 per cent and this is called

---

MAKING PESTO

Pesto sauce, usually served with pasta, blends the aromatic flavours of basil, garlic, pine nuts, Parmesan cheese and virgin olive oil.

1 In a mortar, put 50 g torn fresh basil leaves, 3 chopped garlic cloves, 2 tablespoons pine nuts and some salt and pepper.

2 Grind the mixture with a pestle until it forms a rough paste. Add 50 g finely grated fresh Parmesan cheese and mix well.

3 Gradually trickle over and beat in 100 ml virgin olive oil, using the pestle or a wooden spoon. Pesto can be kept for up to a week; store it in a sealed jar in the refrigerator. It also freezes well.

VARIATION: Pesto may be made using a blender or food processor instead. Put all the ingredients except the Parmesan cheese in a blender or processor and blend at high speed until creamy. Transfer to a bowl, add the Parmesan and mix well.

extra-virgin olive oil. Further processing by heat produces more oil, which decreases in quality and flavour. Fine virgin olive oil contains a maximum acidity level of 1.5 per cent; ordinary virgin olive oil of 3 per cent. Plain olive oil, sometimes called pure olive oil, is made from a blend of refined oil and one of the grades of virgin oil.

Olive oil is healthy and versatile, and it is worth buying the best quality that you can afford. It is important to use virgin olive oil in sauces such as pesto (see panel, left). The following recipe for Bruschetta, a simple crispy snack or starter, calls for the best extra-virgin olive oil, but this may be too strong for some other recipes.

Bruschetta

Serves: 4 as a starter
Preparation time: 10 minutes
Cooking time: 10 minutes

4 thick slices of Italian or French
*   country bread*
2 large cloves garlic
Extra-virgin olive oil
Sea salt
To serve: slices of prosciutto or
*   grilled tomato slices, optional*

1 Preheat the grill and toast the bread on both sides.
2 While the bread is hot, rub cut garlic over both sides of each slice. Drizzle some oil over each slice and sprinkle with sea salt. If you like, top with prosciutto or slices of grilled tomato. Serve immediately.

Adding Flavour

Flavoured oils are lovely but quite expensive. Could I make my own?

Oils can easily be infused with a variety of herbs or spices to add extra taste and colour, as the following recipes show.

Chilli Oil is strongly flavoured, good for stir-fries, marinades, and for drizzling over noodles. Herb and Saffron Oil makes a light and subtle salad dressing, or it can be brushed onto fish or chicken before grilling or barbecuing.

Chilli oil

Makes: about 250 ml
Preparation time: 5 minutes, plus 12 hours infusing
Cooking time: 11–12 minutes

2 teaspoons Szechwan or whole
*   mixed peppercorns*
8–10 dried red chillies, blanched
250 ml peanut oil
1 tablespoon sesame oil

1 Heat a heavy-based pan, then add the peppercorns and eight of the chillies. Dry-fry them over a medium heat for a minute or two, stirring all the while so they do not catch and burn. Reduce the heat to very low, pour in the peanut oil and cook for 10 minutes more. Leave to cool.
2 When cold, stir in the sesame oil. Cover the pan and set aside to infuse for about 12 hours or overnight.
3 Strain the flavoured oil through a muslin-lined sieve into a sterilised jar or bottle. Add the two remaining chillies if you like, for decoration. Seal well then store in a cool, dark place for up to three months.

Herb and saffron oil

Makes: about 750 ml
Preparation time: 10 minutes
Cooking time: none

2 sprigs fresh rosemary
2–4 sprigs fresh thyme
1 teaspoon dried oregano
2 cloves garlic
1 teaspoon fennel seeds, crushed
A generous pinch of saffron strands
750 ml extra-virgin olive oil

1 Wash the fresh herbs; pat dry thoroughly with kitchen paper towels, then lightly bruise them with the flat side of a knife to release their aroma.
2 Place all the dry ingredients in a sterilised jar or bottle and cover completely with oil. Seal well, then shake to mix. Store in the refrigerator for at least a week and use within two weeks. You might prefer to strain the oil before using.

Oils flavoured with herbs and spices such as chilli, garlic and rosemary add a touch of drama to simple dishes.

Okra

JUICY FINGERS

Is okra the same as the 'ladies' fingers' I have eaten in Indian restaurants? If so, are there any other ways of cooking it?

'Ladies' fingers' does refer to the tapering shape of okra's seed pods. Inside the pods, the seeds are set in sticky juices and this is what thickens the soups and stews that are part of southern American cuisine. In the Cajun dishes of Louisiana okra is usually sliced up so the sticky juices are released, and it is often smothered in a peppery tomato sauce like the one on the right. Lard would probably be used instead of olive oil. However, in this recipe the pods are left uncut.

Choose okra that is bright green and velvety, with no brown tinge along the outside ridges. Serve this dish as a hot accompaniment to grilled meat or oily fish. Or, for a vegetarian meal, offer it with bean dishes and cornbread or corn muffins made with green chillies.

Cajun smothered okra

SERVES: 6
PREPARATION TIME: *10 minutes*
COOKING TIME: *35-40 minutes*

500 g okra
3 tablespoons olive oil
1 red onion, thinly sliced
1-2 cloves garlic, crushed
1 teaspoon dried oregano
400 g canned chopped tomatoes in juice
3 tablespoons red wine
Salt, black pepper and cayenne pepper or Tabasco sauce

1 Trim off the stem ends of the okra. Avoid cutting into the seed pod, as this would make the dish very sticky.
2 Heat the oil in a frying pan then fry the onion, garlic and oregano for 2-3 minutes. Add the tomatoes with all their juices, and the wine. Gently stir the mixture and cook at a low boil for about 10 minutes until it becomes a thick sauce.
3 Season the tomato sauce with salt, then stir in the okra. Put a lid on the pan and continue cooking over a low heat for about 25 minutes. Check halfway through the cooking and add a little hot water if the sauce seems to be drying out.
4 When the okra are soft, season with black pepper and sprinkle on cayenne pepper or Tabasco sauce.

A colourful dish of spicy okra from the southern United States is smothered in a garlic, tomato and red wine sauce.

Olives

COLOUR DIFFERENTIAL

What is the difference between black and green olives?

They are essentially the same fruit, picked at different stages of ripeness: unripe olives are green, black are fully ripe, and those with a violet tinge are picked sometime in-between. Black olives have a fruitier taste than the green and are more often used in cooking.

Olives are one of the oldest processed foods known to man, and there are many regional varieties and preferences. In Spain, there are smooth, green table varieties, from large queen olives to the refined manzanilla often sold stoned and stuffed with red pepper, anchovy, orange rind or almonds. Purple-black Kalamata olives from Greece have an intense flavour, especially those allowed to ripen on the tree. The shiny Niçoise olives from Provence are small, black and wrinkled with an almost creamy taste and are often sold in jars. Kalamata and Niçoise olives are the ones most often used in cooking.

HOW TO STORE

How long do olives keep, and how should they be stored?

Fresh olives are very bitter and must be 'cured' or pickled in brine to render them edible, so they are naturally long-keeping. However, when removed from their brine they will begin to go soft and deteriorate in flavour.

Once the jar or can has been opened, or if bought loose in their brine, olives should be stored in the refrigerator and eaten within a few days. Those stored in olive or some other cooking oil will keep for about two weeks in the refrigerator, as long as they are completely submerged in the oil. The oil will take on some flavour from the olives and this delicately flavoured oil is very pleasant for cooking.

Omelette

SECRET INGREDIENTS

Is the secret of a good omelette in the cooking or in the pan?

Both. Omelettes, to be soft and runny in the centre while smooth on the surface, should be cooked very quickly over a heat that is brisk but not too fierce. If cooked slowly, they become flat and tough and similar to scrambled eggs.

To ensure even cooking, use a small, heavy-based nonstick frying pan. Better still, invest in an omelette pan, in which the base meets the side in a gentle curve to make it easier to fold the omelette and slide it out. After use, do not wash an omelette pan but simply wipe it clean with kitchen paper.

LIGHTEN UP

How do I make an omelette that is really light and fluffy?

Traditional omelettes are not fluffy, but a fluffy soufflé omelette can be made by folding whisked egg whites into beaten egg yolks. These soufflé omelettes may be savoury, like the bacon, cheese and tomato recipe on page 246, or sweetened by whisking sugar into the egg whites before they are added to the yolks.

MAKING AN OMELETTE

Heat and speed are essential to make perfect, soft omelettes. To serve several people, make individual omelettes like the one below rather than one large one.

1 Break two eggs into a bowl, add salt and black pepper to taste and beat lightly with a fork until the egg just passes through the prongs.

2 Place the pan over a brisk heat and add a little oil or some clarified butter. When the oil or butter is very hot, quickly pour in the beaten eggs.

3 Shake the pan to and fro and stir the eggs with the back of the fork until they start to thicken. Then tilt the pan, lifting the cooked egg at the side and allowing the uncooked egg to flow underneath. When the eggs have cooked enough so that only the centre is still just moist (about 1–2 minutes), draw the pan off the heat.

4 To transfer the omelette to the plate, fold a third of the egg from the side to the centre, sliding the omelette towards the edge of the pan. Fold the open third back towards the centre, forming a cigar shape. Press the ends together so that all the juice remains in the omelette and does not leak when it is turned onto the plate.

Smoked bacon, cheese and tomato soufflé omelette

SERVES: 1
PREPARATION TIME: 20 minutes
COOKING TIME: 15 minutes

50 g bacon, diced
1 tomato, peeled, deseeded and
roughly chopped
2 teaspoons chopped fresh mixed
herbs or spring onions
2 large eggs, separated
Salt and black pepper
15 g salted butter
50 g Cheddar cheese, grated or
finely chopped

1 Cook the bacon in a saucepan or small frying pan for about 5 minutes until crisp, then add the tomato and cook for a further minute to soften. Stir in the herbs or spring onions, then keep the mixture warm while you make the omelette.
2 Put 2 tablespoons of water with the egg yolks, whisk well and season. Whisk the egg whites until stiff.
3 Preheat the grill. Melt the butter in an omelette pan over a gentle heat. Meanwhile, fold the egg whites into the yolks, using a metal spoon.
4 Pour the mixture into the pan and cook over a medium heat until the underside is golden brown. Then put the pan under the heated grill and cook until the omelette is puffed up, set and pale gold on top.
5 Loosen the omelette around the edges and make an indented line across the middle to help you fold it. Spoon the bacon mixture over the omelette, sprinkle the cheese on top, then fold the omelette in half and slide it onto a warmed plate.

FRITTATAS AND TORTILLAS

What is the difference between a frittata and a tortilla?

They are very similar: both are flat, round, firm omelettes in which the eggs are cooked without stirring over a low heat and served hot or cold. Tortillas are from Spain and Mexico, while frittatas come from Italy, but both make excellent fare for picnics or packed lunches as they are chunky, sturdy and very easily transported. They also make a good family weekend lunch and are usually cut into wedges for serving. Choose a lively red or white wine from the Mediterranean, their home ground, to drink with them.

Tuna and zucchini tortilla

SERVES: 4
PREPARATION TIME: 20 minutes
COOKING TIME: 20 minutes

1 tablespoon olive oil
1 onion, sliced
1 clove garlic, crushed
275 g zucchinis, thinly sliced
350 g boiled potatoes, diced
4 large eggs
3 tablespoons milk
2 teaspoons chopped tarragon
Salt and black pepper
180 g canned tuna in oil,
drained and flaked
75 g Red Leicester or Cheddar
cheese, grated

1 Preheat the grill. Heat the oil in a large nonstick frying pan, then add the onion, garlic and zucchinis and cook for 5 minutes, stirring once in a while. Add the potatoes and cook for 3 minutes, still stirring.
2 Meanwhile, beat the eggs, milk, tarragon and seasoning together, add the tuna and mix well. Add the egg mixture to the frying pan and cook over a medium heat, without stirring, until the eggs begin to set and the tortilla is golden brown underneath.
3 Sprinkle the cheese over the top and place the tortilla under a very hot grill until the cheese has melted and the top is golden brown.
4 Cut the tortilla into wedges and serve it with crusty bread. A good accompaniment would be a salad of mixed leaves topped with a garlic dressing and croutons, and perhaps some capers, olives or anchovies.

A substantial tortilla with eggs, tuna, zucchini, potato and tarragon is given a golden glaze of grilled cheese.

The other tortilla

In Latin America, tortillas are also a popular form of flatbread (see **Mexican Cooking**). The pancakes are made from corn or maize flour and are dry-fried. They can be served fresh, or folded, fried and filled. Small stale pieces are deep-fried to make tortilla chips.

SERIAL COOKING

Could I make omelettes for a lunch party one at a time and let them sit while I make more?

No. If omelettes are left to stand, or kept warm for even a short period of time, they will dry out and be tough and leathery. Have every-thing prepared, and warm a plate ready to serve the omelette as soon as it has been cooked. Make them in swift succession for your guests and insist that they start eating the omelettes as soon as they are done.

Onions

VARIOUS TYPES

Are some kinds of onion better suited to certain methods of cooking than others?

Yes. Red onions and big, sweet golden Spanish onions have the mildest taste and can be sliced raw into salads or gently fried. Spring bulb or salad onions are also excel-lent raw, or cooked quickly in stir-fries so that they do not collapse.

Medium-sized brown onions, which have a stronger flavour, are delicious peeled and roasted whole, and basted as they cook. This will transform their flavour into a mellow sweetness. Shallots are usually fried briefly and then finished in wine or stock.

For braising, choose pickling or small, evenly sized white onions no larger than a golf ball, so that they all cook at the same rate, as they do in the recipe on the right.

Succulent braised onions, cooked with raisins, fresh rosemary and bay leaves, have a hint of sweet and sour flavour that goes well with roast meat or poultry.

Onions braised with raisins and rosemary

SERVES: 4-6 as an accompaniment
PREPARATION TIME: 10 minutes
COOKING TIME: 40-45 minutes

12-18 small white onions, peeled
3 tablespoons olive oil
3 tablespoons red wine vinegar
Salt and black pepper
1 teaspoon sugar
2 bay leaves
6-8 short sprigs rosemary
2 tablespoons raisins
1 teaspoon balsamic vinegar

1 Put the onions in a pan in a single layer. Add the oil and fry gently for about 5-8 minutes, shaking them regularly, until patched with brown.
2 Pour in cold water almost to cover the onions and add the vinegar, some salt, the sugar, bay leaves, four sprigs of rosemary and the raisins. Partially cover and simmer for 10 minutes. Then remove the lid, increase the heat and cook just below the boil for 25-35 minutes, shaking the pan regularly to turn the onions. They are done when they look translucent and feel soft when pierced with a knife. The braising liquid will have reduced to a sticky brown sauce.
3 Sprinkle on the balsamic vinegar and pepper to taste. Serve garnished with the remaining rosemary sprigs.

NO TEARS

What is the best way to chop an onion without crying?

The trick is not to stand over the onion, where the rising fumes can enter your nose and tear ducts. Sitting down to slice or chop your onion is the simple answer.

TAKE YOUR TIME

Why do fried onions sometimes taste terribly bitter?

They taste bitter if they are not fully cooked. Many cooks do not realise that it takes a good 10 minutes of slow frying and stirring to caramelise and soften one medium onion; allow 20–30 minutes for two or three onions. And frying onions for only 5 minutes before adding any liquid will result in slimy pieces of half-cooked onion lurking in the finished dish.

Skinning small onions easily

Small onions can be fiddly to peel. Pouring boiling water over them in a heatproof container and draining them after a minute or two will make the skins slip off more easily.

Ovens and Hotplates

FUEL FOR THOUGHT

I am trying to decide whether to cook by gas, electricity or solid fuel. What factors should I take into account when I choose?

- GAS produces heat quickest and is easiest to control: when you turn down the flame on the gas jet there is an instant reduction in temperature. Gas ovens are hotter at the top than the bottom, which is preferable when it is convenient to bake several dishes in the oven at the same time but at slightly different temperatures. The central shelf is usually closest to the temperature the oven is set at, while the top shelf is a few degrees hotter and the bottom shelf a few degrees cooler.

- ELECTRIC OVENS AND HOTPLATES create no fumes, and ceramic halogen hotplates are almost as quick to heat and easy to control as gas hotplates are. Some electric hotplates can be set at a hand-hot temperature for long periods of time. Like gas ovens, conventional electric ovens do not provide an even heat, but the difference is less acute than with gas. Some electric ovens also offer the option of an automatic timer, which can be set to turn the oven on and off when you are away from the kitchen.

- FAN-FORCED OVENS give perfectly even heat throughout an electric oven by means of a fan mounted on the back wall of the oven (which is not practical with gas). This makes the transfer of heat to the food more efficient, so it is cooking at a higher temperature than in a conventional oven. Take this into account when setting the oven temperature.

- SOLID FUEL STOVES such as Agas and Rayburns use fuel such as wood or coal. They are usually left on all day, ready for use.

WIDE RANGE

What sorts of features should I be looking for in a new oven?

After deciding on the fuel to use, the choice is between a traditional, free-standing stove or a separate hotplate and oven. An all-in-one stove is often cheapest. The advantage of separate units is that you can install them in different parts of the kitchen; the oven can be positioned higher than it is in a free-standing stove to eliminate stooping; and you also have the option of using different fuels, possibly gas for the hotplates and electricity for the oven.

With a separate oven, the grill may be placed either above the hotplate at eye-level, below it or inside the oven itself. Decide how much grilling you do and how inconvenient it would be if the grill were inside the oven. If you have only one oven, it cannot be used for any other cooking, such as baking, while you are using the grill.

There are useful extras which are worth considering. You might want a self-cleaning or stay-clean oven, a motorised rotisserie or an integral charcoal-style grill. There are also built-in wok stands, or deep-fryers connected to extraction units to eliminate smells. Some ovens have optional bread or pizza stones which fit exactly into the oven, heat up with it and provide an ideal surface on which to bake breads and pizza.

DOUBLE THE CHOICE

Is it worth having a double oven?

If you do a lot of cooking, a double oven is more useful than a single one because you can bake and roast at different temperatures at the same time. Fitted oven units with a lower main oven and smaller top oven housing the grill allow the grill and oven to be used at the same time. But you may have to reconsider cooking the Christmas turkey, as double ovens are often smaller than single ones.

TEMPERATURE CHECK

I have an old stove, and lately a lot of my dishes have come out of the oven not properly cooked. Could it be the oven's fault?

In an old stove, the temperature control may well have become less accurate over the years. If you have doubts, use an oven thermometer to check the heat being produced at a specific setting on your oven so you can then adjust the cooking times in recipes accordingly.

You need a thermometer able to withstand temperatures as high as 260°C. While thermometers with dials are tougher, they have fewer markings and give less precise readings than those of spirit thermometers. To test an oven, put the thermometer on a middle shelf while preheating it and take the reading when the oven is up to temperature. Check with the manufacturer if you have any queries.

HOTPLATE CHOICE

What are the different types of hotplates to choose from, and what are their advantages?

Electric stoves that have sealed hotplates with the electric element embedded in them are easier to clean than radiant rings, but you may not be able to tell at a glance when the plate is hot. Ceramic tops, which hold the radiant elements under glass, often have 'hot' signals which stay on until it is safe to touch the rings.

Some hotplates have halogen areas which heat up and cool rapidly, but they must be used with saucepans that have dull, flat bases because shiny bases reflect the light back into the hotplate. Another type, the induction hotplate, can heat the contents of a steel or iron pan while the plate itself stays cool to the touch.

Most gas hotplates still have the traditional burners, but with different sizes and innovations such as a revolving oval burner that produces a gentle, simmering heat. And several manufacturers offer a special wok ring which produces the very high heat needed to stir-fry. Some gas hotplates also have a long central plate, which is used mainly for cooking in a fish kettle.

SAFETY FIRST

I worry about grilling in my oven with the children playing in the kitchen. Is there any oven that is considerably safer to use?

Some fan-forced ovens have a system that lets you keep the door closed while grilling, which is useful for homes with young children. There are also ovens with doors that stay cool while the oven is hot inside, which is another safety feature. These options often do not add much to the cost of the stove.

See also: *Microwave Ovens*

Oysters

WHEN TO EAT OYSTERS

What is the difference between Sydney Rock oysters and Pacific oysters, and when is the best time of year to enjoy them?

The famed Sydney Rock oyster (*Saccostrea commercialis*), has a smaller, rougher, longer shell than the Pacific or Japanese oyster (*Crassostrea gigas*). Both varieties, which are farmed commercially, are available and are good to eat all year round.

A third variety, becoming increasingly available, is the Native Flat oyster (*Ostrea angasi*) which is also grown commercially.

Oysters from natural oyster beds, found along Australian sea shores and estuaries, have the best flavour in the cooler months. Pacific oysters breed differently, so they taste agreeable all year round.

CLEAN LIVING

Is eating oysters ever risky?

There is very little chance of eating a contaminated oyster as long as you choose ones with their shells tightly shut. Oysters grown commercially in New South Wales undergo a cleansing period in purified water for 36 hours. This requirement is not needed in the other Australian states.

Fresh oysters that are tightly shut can be kept in the refrigerator for up to a few days. Wash off any mud before storing them, but do not soak them. Oysters that have been opened are best eaten straightaway but can be stored in the refrigerator for up to 2 to 3 hours.

Always buy opened oysters from a reputable fish market or retailer.

Oysters are a very concentrated form of protein and some people find them difficult to digest for this reason. As oysters are often eaten on festive occasions, they may be consumed with more alcohol than usual, which can also contribute to adverse side effects. Oysters do seem to cause particularly severe problems if mixed with spirits, so it is better to drink chilled white wine or champagne, or even cold dark stout, with them. These are better suited to their taste.

Oysters are most often served raw, topped with black pepper and a squeeze of lemon juice. They may also be grilled lightly in the half-shell, or topped with breadcrumbs or garlic butter. They can also be gently cooked in soups.

THE SAFE AND EASY WAY TO OPEN AN OYSTER

When opening or 'shucking' oysters, use a knife with a finger guard and take care to hold it and the shell securely. This job needs concentration, not speed.

1 To open oysters, hold the oyster firmly on a board, rounded shell down, with a tea towel wrapped around your hand in case the knife slips. Using an oyster knife, work the point into the hinged end, then twist the knife and break the shell open.

2 Cut through the muscle holding the shell closed and the muscle fixing the meat to the shell. Serve in the deep shell, with its liquor. Pacific oysters are harder to open because of the crumbly 'apron frill' around the shell but the same rules apply.

PACKED LUNCHES

Whether you are filling a child's lunch box, snatching a bite at your desk, or setting off into the outdoors, a well-planned packed lunch can become a personal treat. Here are great ideas for recipes that are portable and memorable.

Just a few simple touches in preparation and presentation can make all the difference to a successful packed lunch. For instance, make or buy whole small pies or quiches: they are more robust than a slice from a larger one. To accompany a flask of soup or a carefully packed salad, rolls travel better than slices of bread. And sandwiches will stay fresh for longer if they are lined with lettuce and well wrapped in plastic wrap.

Always add some refreshing extras to the meal, such as a dozen cherry tomatoes or a stalk of celery, and a whole fresh fruit. And if you know the lunch will be eaten alone, include a cheering sweet treat, even if it is only a chocolate bar or some biscuits.

Wide-mouthed flasks are best for hot stews, but bear in mind that the food will go on cooking. This suits some soups and curries, but is not kind to fresh herbs, fish, pasta or rice, and has a specially bad effect on anything creamy. Soups thickened with pulses or a vegetable purée are best.

Wrap cutlery in a paper napkin so it doesn't stray into the depths of the box, and pack twists of salt and pepper so food can be seasoned to taste.

Vegetable and barley broth, a wholegrain roll, some mayonnaise and crudités to dip, make a filling lunch for a hungry child.

A CHILD'S LUNCH BOX
Nourishing vegetable soup can be enhanced with the addition of barley for added interest. Make enough soup for at least four servings and freeze the rest for another day.

Pack a small, buttered wholegrain roll to eat with it. Cut some crisp raw celery and carrots into little sticks and, for a dip, add a small tub of mayonnaise, coloured a rich pink with tomato sauce to make it more tempting. As a special treat, finish off the meal with a few chocolate wheatmeal biscuits.

(This menu is suitable for vegetarian children also.)

Vegetable and barley broth

SERVES: 8
PREPARATION TIME: 30 minutes
COOKING TIME: 35 minutes

1 onion, diced
1 leek, thinly sliced
2 carrots, diced
40 g butter
2 cups diced swede
2 litres vegetable or beef stock
1 teaspoon Vegemite
50 g (¼ cup) barley
250 g Brussels sprouts, shredded

1 Place the onion, leek, carrots and butter in a large, heavy-based pan. Cover and sauté over a medium heat for 2–3 minutes, shaking the pan occasionally while still in contact with the heat.
2 Add the swede, stock and Vegemite and bring to the boil. Meanwhile, wash the barley in cold water, drain well and add to the pan. Cover the pan and gently boil for 30 minutes.
3 Add the Brussels sprouts, stir well and simmer for another 1–2 minutes.
4 Pour the hot soup into a pre-warmed vacuum flask and cover immediately. The remaining soup can be frozen in 250 ml (1 cup) quantities, then thawed and reheated in a microwave oven for several more packed lunches.

SNOW PEA AND BACON
SALAD WITH HAZELNUTS

THE OFFICE LUNCH PACK

Salads are often favoured by office workers who don't want a higher kilojoule intake than they can work off in the course of a day at the desk.

Green salads wilt if dressed too long in advance, but some salads actually improve in their dressing. Try grated carrot and sultanas, dressed in olive oil and orange juice and scattered with sesame seeds; potato salad with chopped onion and a little mayonnaise, eaten with some separately wrapped slices of cooked ham or smoked chicken; or a well-herbed snow pea salad, like the one below.

Pack cherry tomatoes and a crunchy bread roll to eat with the salad. Add some Brie, sandwiched between crackers, and finish with a fruit yoghurt.

Snow pea and bacon salad with hazelnuts

SERVES: 1
PREPARATION TIME:
10 minutes
COOKING TIME: 10 minutes

1 tablespoon olive oil
2 rashers streaky bacon, cut
    into small strips
1 shallot, chopped
125 g snow peas, topped
    and tailed
1 teaspoon hazelnut oil
1 teaspoon red wine vinegar
Salt and black pepper
1 tablespoon roughly
    chopped hazelnuts

1 Heat the oil in a frying pan and fry the bacon strips until the fat runs off and the bacon becomes crispy. Before the bacon is fully cooked, add the shallot and fry for 2 minutes.
2 Meanwhile, bring a small pan of salted water to the boil and cook the snow peas for about 3 minutes. Drain well and tip them into a bowl.
3 When the bacon is cooked, remove the frying pan from the heat. Add the hazelnut oil and vinegar, stir to scrape off any sediment then pour the mixture over the snow peas.
4 Season to taste, toss in the hazelnuts and leave to cool.
5 When cold, transfer to a covered container.

BACKPACKER'S PICNIC

Spending a day in the fresh air is a hungry business and, more than any other packed lunch, backpackers' food should be satisfying, tasty and easy to eat in the hand.

For a hearty treat, cook and cool a couple of pork sausages, split them open and smear with mustard or chutney. Then cut the thick ends from four stalks of crisp celery and sandwich each sausage between a pair for transit. Add a few spring onions, a vine-ripened tomato and also a hard-boiled egg.

To follow, pack a big square of fortifying sticky Ginger Cake (see right) wrapped in greaseproof paper. Add a small jar of moist and refreshing home-made apple sauce, to spread over it before eating.

Remember to include some munchies that will fit in the pocket: make up small packets of nuts, dried fruit or a couple of sturdy biscuits. And don't forget to pack plenty of water, as exercise is thirsty work.

Ginger cake

SERVES: 4-6
PREPARATION TIME:
20 minutes
COOKING TIME: 45 minutes

185 g (1½ cups) plain flour
2 teaspoons ground ginger
2 teaspoons baking
    powder
200 ml milk
1 teaspoon bicarbonate of
    soda
60 g (⅓ cup) light brown
    sugar
60 g soft margarine
1 tablespoon treacle
1 tablespoon golden syrup
2 large eggs

1 Preheat the oven to 160°C. Line an 18-20 cm square cake tin with nonstick baking paper, letting it stand 2.5 cm above the rim of the tin.
2 Sift the flour, ginger and baking powder together.
3 Put the milk into a pan, sprinkle the bicarbonate of soda over it and swirl over a low heat until it dissolves and the milk is warm.
4 In a bowl, beat together the sugar, margarine, treacle and syrup until the mixture is much paler. Beat in the eggs one at a time, adding a tablespoon of the spiced flour mixture after each egg.
5 Add the remaining flour mixture and the milk mixture, and beat briefly until smooth. Pour into the tin and bake in the centre of the oven for 45 minutes or until springy in the middle.
6 Gently turn the cake out of the tin onto a wire cooling rack and leave it to cool in its lining paper.
7 When the cake has cooled completely, peel off the paper. Cut into slices and wrap them individually.

GINGER CAKE
AND APPLE SAUCE

Pancakes

THIN AND LIGHT

My pancakes always seem to turn out stodgy. How can I make a really light batter?

Pancake batter can be used as soon as it is made, but it is best to allow it to stand in a cool place for 15–30 minutes before using. This makes the starch grains in the flour soften and expand in the liquid, which results in lighter pancakes. The following recipe is for some delicious stuffed pancakes, which are sprinkled with cheese and then baked for an ideal light dinner dish.

Chicken, mushroom and broccoli pancakes

SERVES: *4 (2 pancakes per person)*
PREPARATION TIME: *20 minutes, plus 15-30 minutes standing time*
COOKING TIME: *45 minutes*

8 *pancakes*
100 g *broccoli florets*
60 g *salted butter*
100 g *mushrooms, sliced*
30 g *(¼ cup) plain flour*
300 ml *milk*
185 g *boneless chicken breast, cooked and diced*
2 *teaspoons fresh or dried tarragon*
Salt and black pepper
75 g *Cheddar or Gruyère cheese, grated*

1 Prepare the batter and cook the pancakes (see panel, right). Preheat the oven to 180°C.
2 Cook the broccoli in a saucepan of boiling water for 5 minutes, then drain the florets and set aside.

3 Melt one-third of the butter in a pan and cook the sliced mushrooms for 3 minutes, stirring occasionally. Remove from the heat and set aside.
4 Melt the remaining butter in a saucepan over a medium heat, stir in the flour and cook for 1 minute, stirring continuously. Remove from the heat and gradually add the milk, stirring until smooth. Bring slowly to the boil, stirring constantly, until the sauce thickens, then simmer gently, stirring occasionally, for a further 5 minutes.
5 Stir in the broccoli, mushrooms, chicken, tarragon, salt and pepper.
6 Fill the cooked pancakes with the mixture and fold or roll them. Place in a single layer in an ovenproof dish. Sprinkle with grated cheese and bake for 20 minutes, or until the cheese is melted and bubbling.

VARIATIONS

Substitute 1 cup of chopped walnuts for the chicken, and parsley for the tarragon.

Substitute 185 g can of tuna or salmon for the chicken and 2 peeled and chopped tomatoes, sautéed in butter, for the mushrooms.

Or use a selection of cooked fish and school prawns instead of the chicken and broccoli. Substitute parsley for the tarragon.

THINNER BY FAR

Is 'crêpe' just a fancy French word for ordinary pancakes?

Crêpes is the French term for delicate pancakes, which are thinner than ordinary pancakes. They may be served on their own or rolled or folded with a sweet or savoury filling. A little sugar is often added to the batter for sweet crêpes.

Crêpes are best cooked quickly in a crêpe pan for about a minute on each side. If cooked slowly, they will become tough and leathery.

Unfilled crêpes can be layered in between sheets of greaseproof paper, then covered and stored in the refrigerator for up to three days or in the freezer for two months. Filled crêpes can be kept covered in the refrigerator for two days and frozen for up to two months.

MAKING PANCAKES

To make enough batter for eight pancakes you need 125 g (1 cup) plain flour, a pinch of salt, 1 large egg and 300 ml milk.

1 Sift the flour and salt into a bowl and make a well in the centre. Add the egg and beat it well with a whisk. Gradually beat in the milk, incorporating all the flour to make a smooth batter. Cover and chill the mixture for 15–30 minutes.

2 Pour a little oil into an 18 cm crêpe pan or heavy-based frying pan, running it round the base and sides. Pour off any surplus.

3 Ladle in just enough of the batter to coat the base of the pan. Cook it for 1–2 minutes, until it is golden brown underneath and set on top.

4 Turn the pancake with a palette knife, or toss it, and then cook the second side until it is golden.

5 Transfer the cooked pancake to a plate and keep it warm. Make more pancakes with the remaining batter, layering them when cooked with greaseproof paper.

Parsnip

HARD CENTRE

Do I need to remove the core of a parsnip before cooking it?

Parsnips, especially when they are large or flabby, can be woody in the middle. Then it is wise to cut them into chunks and remove the centres. When they are smaller, removing the core is not necessary. While available all year round, parsnips are at their best in winter.

TASTY MASH

I love the taste of parsnip, but I find that when mashed, they seem to be lacking in something. How do I make a great parsnip mash?

Mashed parsnips can make a lovely vegetable accompaniment but do need rich additions to improve both the texture and flavour. Dry the cooked pieces carefully before mashing, then add plenty of butter or cream, black pepper and sweet spices such as nutmeg. Some dry mashed potato can also be mixed into mashed parsnip to lighten it and this makes a good topping for shepherd's or cottage pie.

Carrots and parsnips mashed together make a tasty and colourful dish to go with plain grilled meats.

NEW IDEAS

Are there better ways of cooking a parsnip than to purée it?

Being sweet, parsnips are excellent roasted, a process that caramelises their sugars. Scrub, trim off roots,

A pretty presentation of root vegetables, Parsnip and Carrot Wheel is garnished with parsley and sage and tastes sweetly of caramelised butter and spices.

then peel. If liked, cut in halves or quarters. Blanch in salted water for 5 minutes, dry, then roast with hot dripping in a 190°C oven for 45 minutes, or cook alongside a joint of meat that is being roasted.

They also make good alternative chips, can be diced to add to vegetable soup, or can be layered with other root vegetables to form a stylish dish such as the one below.

Parsnip and carrot wheel

SERVES: 6–8
PREPARATION TIME: 20 minutes
COOKING TIME: 1¼ hours

---

125 g butter, melted
1.5 kg parsnips
500 g carrots
A pinch of ground allspice
Salt and black pepper
To garnish: sprigs of fresh parsley and sage

---

1 Preheat the oven to 190°C. Line a 25 cm diameter fixed-bottom cake tin, at least 5 cm deep, with foil and brush generously with melted butter.

2 Try to choose parsnips and carrots of a similar medium size. Peel the parsnips and slice them thickly lengthways, then drop them into a large pan of salted, boiling water and after the water returns to the boil, cook them for 3 minutes. Drain the parsnips thoroughly. Peel the carrots and halve them lengthways.

3 Line the tin with parsnips, tips inwards, sprinkle them with melted butter and season with the allspice, salt and pepper. Put a layer of carrots of the same thickness on top of the parsnips, then butter and season. Continue layering the vegetables, making the top layer parsnips.

4 Cover the wheel with foil and bake for about 1-1¼ hours, or until the vegetables feel soft when pierced with the point of a knife. Remove the wheel from the oven and allow it to stand for 5-10 minutes.

5 Remove the foil cover, place a plate larger than the tin on the top, grip both firmly and invert. Lift the tin off and peel away the lining foil. Decorate the wheel with fresh sprigs of parsley and sage.

PASTA SHAPES

Pasta is universally popular, quick and easy to cook and a valuable source of complex carbohydrate. A versatile food, it can be boiled quickly until al dente and tossed with simple, light sauces or richer, chunky ones. It can also be stuffed, layered and baked, added to soups, or used for high-fibre salads.

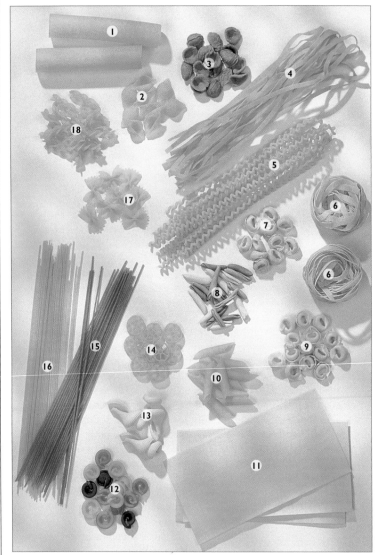

1 CANNELLONI – large round tubes for stuffing. **2** COCCIOLE – shell shapes. **3** ORECCHIETTE AGLI SPINACH – spinach-flavoured, hollow discs, literally 'little ears'. **4** TOMATO FETTUCINE – tomato-flavoured, flat, ribbon-shaped strands. **5** FUSILLI BUCATI LUNGHI – long, hollow twists. **6** TAGLIATELLI – long flat ribbons. **7** TORTELLINI WITH MUSHROOMS – little round shapes filled with either meat or vegetables. **8** FUSILLI TRIS – short twists, 'screws', in three flavours. **9** TORTELLINI WITH CHEESE –

little round shapes, filled with cheese. **10** PENNE ZITONI – quill-shaped short hollows. **11** LASAGNE – flat sheets for layered baked dishes. **12** CAPPELLETTI WITH SPINACH AND TOMATO – similar shape to tortellini with a savoury filling. **13** CAMPANELLE DI PUGLIA – little, rolled bell shapes. **14** ROTELLE – small wheels. **15** WHOLEMEAL SPAGHETTI – round, thin strands, 'thin string'. **16** VERMICELLI – very thin spaghetti. **17** FARFALLE – bows, literally 'butterflies' **18** SPIRALI – short twists.

Pasta

HEALTHY PASTA

Is pasta fattening?

Not necessarily: 25 g of dried pasta contains about 117 kilojoules. A generous 75 g helping of cooked pasta with a tomato and cheese sauce makes a satisfying dish of about 1045 kilojoules. Served with a salad and fruit for dessert, it makes a well-balanced meal. And pasta's low fat content means it is useful for people on diets. Remember, however, the richer the sauce, the more fattening the dish will be.

The following recipe for Fettucine with Summer Vegetables is a perfect example of a low-fat, tasty pasta dish that can be prepared with a minimum of fuss.

Fettucine with summer vegetables

SERVES: 4
PREPARATION TIME: 20 minutes
COOKING TIME: 12 minutes

---

1 tablespoon olive oil
3 shallots, finely chopped
1 each small red and yellow pepper, cut into 2 cm squares
1 medium carrot, peeled and thinly sliced
2 cloves garlic, crushed
¼ teaspoon black pepper
¼ cup vegetable or chicken stock
1 medium zucchini, sliced
1 cup cherry tomatoes, halved, or 2 medium tomatoes, cut into 2 cm cubes
375 g green (spinach) fettucine
1 tablespoon each finely chopped fresh basil and parsley

---

1 Heat the oil in a nonstick frying pan over a medium heat. Add the shallots and cook for 1 minute. Add the peppers, carrot, garlic and black pepper; cook for 1 minute.
2 Add the stock, bring to the boil, lower the heat and simmer, covered, for 3 minutes.
3 Stir in the zucchini and tomatoes, and cook, covered, for 1–2 minutes

or until the tomatoes are heated through and the vegetables are tender.
4 Meanwhile, bring a large saucepan of water to the boil. Add the pasta and cook for 5 minutes or until tender but still firm to the bite.
5 Drain, transfer to a warm serving bowl, add the vegetable mixture, basil and parsley. Toss well.

WELL WORTH IT

Is it worth making fresh pasta when it is widely available?

Using commercial pasta is fine when you need tagliatelle or other noodles. But homemade pasta is worth the effort when preparing a stuffed or baked dish such as ravioli or lasagne, because you can achieve a lightness and texture no commercial products can match.

It is not difficult to make pasta at home if you have a hand-cranking machine (see panel below). If you eat a lot of pasta, it is worthwhile investing in a pasta maker.

WHAT TYPE OF FLOUR?

I've noticed that much of the fresh pasta sold in shops is advertised as being made from durum wheat. Do I have to use a special flour to make pasta at home?

You can make pasta with a variety of flours including plain white flour or strong white flour. In Italy they would use flour made from durum (or hard) wheat and you should be able to find this in some health food shops and the larger, quality supermarkets.

You may also find farina in Italian food stores. Also called '00' (double zero) flour, this is a specially refined durum wheat flour and is used for the most delicate, handmade egg pasta.

You can use ordinary plain flour if you cannot find durum wheat flour, but plain flour makes a fluffier pasta. The recipe below lets you choose.

Homemade egg pasta

MAKES: *375 g*
PREPARATION TIME: *20 minutes*
COOKING TIME: *5 minutes*

3 large eggs
310 g (2½ cups) plain, strong or farina flour
A pinch of salt

1 Mix the eggs, flour and salt in a bowl, using a fork, and then work the dough with your hands until it just forms a mass. The dough should not be too moist – if it is, add a little more flour.
2 Take a lump of dough the size of a lemon and feed it through the rollers of the pasta maker, which should be set at the widest opening (see steps, below). Crank the piece through.

Fold it in half, end to end, and feed it through the rollers again six or seven times until the pasta is smooth and quite rectangular. If the dough sticks to the machine, brush it with flour.
3 Place the pasta sheet on a clean cloth or lightly floured surface. Taking a lump of dough as before, repeat the rolling process with the remaining dough.
4 Reset the rollers to the next setting (narrower) and, starting with the first strip, crank it through the rollers once. Do the same with the other pasta strips, keeping them in the same order to allow them to dry.
5 When you have fed all the dough through, reset the machine to the next setting and repeat the rolling. Do this twice more, resetting the machine on each occasion. The strips of pasta will become longer and will need to be cut in half to facilitate handling.
6 When the strips have reached the desired thinness, they are ready to be cut into the required shape, or to be fed through the cutters and made into noodle shapes such as spaghetti or tagliatelle. Be sure the strips have dried enough (without becoming brittle) to prevent them sticking once they have been cut. If you are using sheets of pasta for lasagne or stuffed pasta, proceed without drying.
7 Cook the pasta for 2–3 minutes or until it is al dente (cooked but firm).

ROLLING FRESH PASTA BY MACHINE

As a general rule, use 1 cup flour per egg to make pasta. You will need 310 g (3 cups) flour and 3 eggs to make enough pasta for four people. To prevent the dough sticking to the machine, dust the rollers with flour before use.

1 Set the rollers of the machine fully open and crank the dough through six or seven times until it is smooth.

2 Reset the machine to the narrower setting and crank again. Repeat three times, lowering the setting each time.

3 To make the pasta strips (tagliatelle is shown here), feed the dough through the appropriate cutters.

DRYING OUT

Should I let homemade pasta rest for a while before cooking?

Just-made pasta can be sticky and should be left to dry out slightly before being cut. Once cut, pasta can be cooked immediately but you can also make it in advance and place the cut strips on a baking tray between sheets of greaseproof paper.

Alternatively, sprinkle the fresh pasta with a few tablespoons of semolina and refrigerate for about 24 hours. You can also freeze strips of cut pasta, first loose on trays, then packed together.

SHAPES AND SAUCES

How do I know what shaped pasta to add to what sauce?

Thick pasta shapes are best with meat sauces. Long thin pasta, such as spaghetti, goes well with olive-oil based sauces that allow the strands to remain separate. If you are layering a dish with a sauce, large flat sheets of lasagne are the obvious choice. There are, however, no strict rules, and you can use whichever pasta is your favourite to go with the quick sauces below.

Pasta with sardines

SERVES: 4
PREPARATION TIME: 5 minutes
COOKING TIME: 20 minutes

3 tablespoons olive oil
½ small onion, finely chopped
50 g anchovy fillets, drained
400 g fresh or canned chopped
    tomatoes
50 g (¼ cup) raisins
240 g canned sardines in oil,
    drained
Black pepper
350 g dried pasta
2 tablespoons finely chopped
    parsley, optional
60 g (½ cup) dried breadcrumbs

1 Heat the oil in a large frying pan and sauté the onion and anchovies until softened but not browned.

2 Add the tomatoes and raisins and cook for 10 minutes. Then add the sardines, simmer the sauce gently for 5 minutes and season to taste.
3 Cook and drain the pasta, add to the sauce and toss together. Stir in the parsley, breadcrumbs and serve.

Pasta with sun-dried tomato sauce

SERVES: 2
PREPARATION TIME: 15 minutes
COOKING TIME: 15 minutes

2 tablespoons olive oil
5 ripe tomatoes, chopped
12 sun-dried tomatoes in olive oil
A handful of stoned olives, sliced
1 fresh green chilli, deseeded and
    finely chopped
175 g dried pasta

1 Simmer the olive oil, fresh and sun-dried tomatoes, olives and chilli for 10 minutes in a small saucepan.
2 Bring a large pan of salted water to the boil. Cook the pasta, drain and serve it with the sauce.

The robustly flavoured sardine pasta sauce (left) and sun-dried tomato sauce (right) are quick and easy to make.

PLENTY OF WATER

How much water do I need for cooking pasta, and is it the same for dried and fresh pasta?

Allow 1 tablespoon of salt and 1.5 litres of water for each 100 g of dried pasta, and remember that you will need a large saucepan, even if you are cooking a small amount of pasta. Once the water has come to the boil, add the salt and then the dried pasta.

This large amount of water will prevent the pasta sticking together and enable it to return to the boil more quickly once the pasta has been added – this is important to achieve a firm yet cooked result.

If you leave the lid off while the pasta boils it will be easier to prevent the water boiling over. Use the timing instructions on the packet as a guide but test the pasta a few minutes before the given time. Remove a piece of pasta and bite into it. It should be tender yet still have a slight resistance.

The rules for cooking fresh pasta are the same except that it will cook in just a few minutes and requires about 25 per cent less water because fresh pasta does not expand to the same degree.

If you are cooking pasta for a salad, do not let it drain too thoroughly, and immediately toss it with a few tablespoons of olive oil. For hot pasta dishes, add the sauce just before serving so the pasta does not sit in it and become soft.

PASTA WILL WAIT

What is the best way of keeping pasta warm if I have to wait for my guests? I usually keep it warm over a very gentle heat, but it sometimes sticks together.

Pasta can be kept warm, covered, in a low oven. It can be reheated in a microwave or conventional oven, also covered, or over a low flame with a little added water to prevent it from sticking together. If you have to keep it for some time, leave a little of the cooking water with it, as you do with pasta for salad.

QUICK AND CONVENIENT

Is fresh pasta always better than dried? What is the difference between fresh and dried pasta?

Each kind has its virtues. Fresh pasta has more flavour because it always contains eggs, but dried pasta, which except for noodles is made without eggs so is more neutrally flavoured, is preferable for some dishes. Fresh pasta is quicker to cook but dried pasta is more versatile as it comes in many different shapes. Dried pasta can be stored indefinitely and is therefore a very convenient store cupboard item.

WHEN AND HOW?

If I am adding pasta shapes to soup, what sort of soup should I add them to, when do I add them and in what quantity?

Thick vegetable-based soups such as minestrones are enhanced by shapes such as shells, bows or macaroni. They should be added to the simmering soup, allowing enough time for them to cook as if in water. Pastina is the general term for a group of tiny pasta varieties normally used in clear broths.

Pasta expands with cooking so you need only very small amounts: a tablespoon or two is enough for a soup that feeds four or six people.

HOLD THE CHEESE

Should I always sprinkle pasta with grated cheese? A waiter once told me that you don't put it on fish sauces like vongole.

There are many pasta sauces that are served on their own without the addition of grated cheese. Seafood sauces are traditionally served plain, as are many of the sauces based on olive oil, such as *olio, aglio e peperoncino* (oil, garlic and chilli). Pesto sauce, which contains Parmesan, does not require additional cheese, although you can always add more if you enjoy the flavour.

See also: ***Cannelloni, Lasagne, Ravioli, Spaghetti, Tagliatelle***

Pastry

CHILL OUT

I don't have the cool hands needed for shortcrust pastry nor a mixer. What can I do?

You do need to keep everything cool when you are rubbing fat into flour for shortcrust pastry, but even if your hands are not naturally cool (and few people's are) you can keep everything else cool. Chill the mixing bowl for about 30 minutes beforehand and use iced water to make the dough. A marble slab is excellent for rolling out pastry as the surface remains cold.

You could also buy an inexpensive gadget called a pastry blender that rubs in the fat for you. Hold the handle and draw the rack of rounded metal blades across the flour and fat until the mixture resemble breadcrumbs. The water can then be added and mixed in with a round-bladed knife or fork. Grating the chilled butter into the flour also reduces the rubbing time and hence the heat generated.

Or try a quick-mix pastry where you do not have to use your fingers. Sift 250 g (2 cups) plain flour into a bowl with a pinch of salt. Using a fork, cream 150 g butter at room temperature with 1½ tablespoons of water and half the flour until well mixed. It takes about 30 seconds. Stir in the remaining flour to form a firm dough, then knead it on a lightly floured work surface until smooth. Or use frozen pre-rolled pastry sheets.

Fast shortcrust

To make shortcrust pastry in a food processor or mixer, sift the flour into the bowl. Add the diced butter. Mix until the mixture resembles breadcrumbs, then add the water and process until it just binds together to form a firm dough. Chill for 20 minutes.

SHORT WORK

Which makes the better pastry: butter, margarine or lard?

Butter gives pastry a fine flavour, golden colour and a crisp texture. For rich pastries, such as puff or pâte sucrée, or sweet short crust pastry, where flavour is important, it is best to use butter.

Firm margarine can be used to make plain types of pastries such as shortcrust pastry. Some soft mono-unsaturated and polyunsaturated margarines can also be used for pastry: check the label and follow the manufacturer's instructions. Use the margarines straight from the refrigerator for easy handling.

Lard gives shortness to pastry but not much flavour so a mixture of equal quantities of butter and lard is often preferred. An exception is the lard pastry used in Chinese egg (custard) tarts served at yum cha.

DELAYED REACTION

Why should pastry be rested before I have finished making it?

Gluten, the protein present in flour, begins to react when it comes into contact with water during mixing, and during resting it becomes firm and elastic. This makes the dough much easier to roll out.

Resting pastry in the refrigerator is particularly important during the folding and rolling process of rich layered pastries such as puff and flaky, because it firms up the fat in the pastry, making it easier to roll, and protects the layers so they will rise evenly during cooking.

LIQUIDATE THE LIQUID

How do I stop the pastry in my pies going soggy?

There are several possible causes of soggy pastry. One is that oven temperatures vary and the only way to be sure your oven is the correct temperature is to use an oven thermometer. A pie that is soggy inside may not have been cooked for long enough; or a precooked filling may not have cooled sufficiently before being covered with pastry.

Too much liquid in the filling can wet the pastry lid. Fruits combined with sugar require only a little water as they will exude juice during cooking. If you are layering fruit with sugar, make sure the last layer is fruit before the pastry lid is added: if the sugar comes directly into contact with the pastry, it will make it soggy. A hole or cross cut in the top of the pie allows steam to escape from a covered pie and keeps the pastry crisp.

QUANTITY MATTERS

If a recipe states that I should use 250 g of pastry, is this the amount of flour I should use, or the quantity of finished pastry?

Pastry quantities given in recipes indicate the amount of flour used to make the pastry. Care should be taken when using bought puff pastry in a recipe. It is sold by weight, so a 500 g pack of puff pastry will be equivalent to 250 g of home-made pastry made with equal quantities of flour and butter.

HEALTHY CRUST

Is it possible to make a healthy pastry, one low in saturated fat?

Yes, you can make a flan case using light olive oil. This pastry is not as short as traditional short-crust and will have a firm texture that needs careful handling.

Sift 250 g (2 cups) of plain flour into a bowl with a pinch of salt and make a well in the centre. Whisk 4 tablespoons of light olive oil and 4 tablespoons of water in another bowl until blended.

Gradually add the oil mixture to the flour, mixing until it forms a firm dough. Knead quickly until smooth then line a 23 cm flan tin; bake it blind. Should a slight crack appear during baking, brush it over with a little lightly beaten egg white and return to a hot oven for 1–2 minutes to dry out. This helps to seal the crack and prevent the filling seeping out.

DECORATING A PIE

After sealing, the edges of pies can be decorated using a fork, pastry pincer, knife or even your fingers. Deep fluting is the most appropriate technique to use for fruit-filled pies, which might leak juice.

1 Cut off the pastry edge level with the edge of the dish, using a sharp knife. Hold the knife at an angle, with the handle pointing towards the edge of the dish.

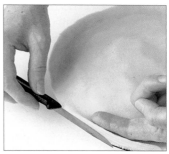

2 Gently mark the pastry edges with the back of a knife to neaten them and give an attractive flaky finish to pies and tarts.

3 To decorate, pinch around the outer edge of the pastry lid with your fingers to shape the dough.

4 Or press your thumb on the top outer edge, then draw the edge towards the centre using the back of a knife. Repeat around the edge.

Deep dish fruit pies with a buttery pastry crust are a traditional favourite. Add a twist with unusual fruit combinations, such as nectarines and redcurrants.

STAY PUT

What makes the tops of single-crust pies come away from the side and slip into the filling?

It happens because the lids have shrunk during cooking. Pastry that has been chilled for 20–30 minutes before rolling will relax and shrink less. Short, light strokes are also important when rolling out pastry as pushing the rolling pin heavily will stretch the pastry and it will shrink during baking.

Pies made in deep oval dishes are always made with a single crust as the shape makes it difficult to line the dish properly. But there must be sufficient filling to mound above the rim of the dish and support the pastry lid. The fruit pie (right) is baked in just such a deep dish with a single crust of short crust pastry, so there is more of the luscious fruit filling than pastry.

Nectarine and redcurrant single-crust pie

SERVES: *5–6*
PREPARATION TIME: *40–45 minutes, plus 30 minutes resting*
COOKING TIME: *45–50 minutes*

FOR THE PASTRY
250 g (2 cups) plain flour
125 g unsalted butter, diced
20 g (1 tablespoon) caster sugar
To glaze: 1 egg white, beaten, and caster sugar

FOR THE FILLING
7 ripe nectarines, peeled, stoned and cut into thick wedges
125 g redcurrants, rinsed and stripped off their stalks
60 g (¼ cup) caster sugar
1 tablespoon lemon juice

1 Preheat the oven to 200°C. Sift the flour into a bowl, add the butter and rub into the flour until the mixture looks like fine breadcrumbs. Add the sugar and 3–4 tablespoons of cold water and, using a knife, mix to form a stiff dough.

2 Using your fingertips, knead the dough gently on a lightly floured board until smooth. Then wrap it in greaseproof paper and leave it to rest in the refrigerator for 30 minutes.

3 Have ready a 1 litre oval pie dish. On a floured surface, roll the pastry to a shape 4 cm larger all around than the top of the dish. Then cut out the centre of the pastry about 2.5 cm in from the edge. Reserve the outer strip to line the rim of the pie dish.

4 Spread layers of nectarines and redcurrants into the dish, sprinkling each with a little caster sugar and finishing with a layer of fruit. Add the lemon juice. The fruit should be piled well above the top of the dish to hold up the pastry lid.

5 Lightly brush the rim of the dish with beaten egg and lay the pastry strip on it neatly with no overlap. Dampen the pastry strip with water or beaten egg then lift up the pastry lid on a rolling pin and cover the pie, pressing gently to seal.

6 Trim then knock up the pastry edge by making horizontal dents on the outside edge with the back of a knife, and decorate by pinching (see panel, page 258). Make a small hole in the centre to let the steam escape.

7 Roll out the pastry trimmings, cut three or four leaves, draw on veins with a knife and arrange on the pie.

8 Brush the pie with egg white and sprinkle with caster sugar. Put the pie dish on a baking tray and cook the pie for 20 minutes. Then reduce the heat to 180°C and continue baking for a further 25–30 minutes until golden brown.

LAYERED FOR LIGHTNESS

What is the difference between puff and rough puff pastry?

The aim with both pastries is to form thin layers of fat between very thin layers of dough to produce a pastry which rises well.

Puff pastry is the richest and lightest of the two, and usually uses

ROLLING AND FOLDING PUFF PASTRY

The rolling and folding process is a simple one and creates the light layers characteristic of puff pastry.

1 Roll out the dough into a strip 38 × 13 cm, then form the butter into a rectangle around 13 × 10 cm and place it in the middle. Fold the bottom third of the dough up and the top third down to enclose the butter. Press the edges firmly with the rolling pin to seal.

2 Give the dough a half turn clockwise so that the folded edge of the dough is on your right. Roll into a strip three times as long as it is wide. Mark the strip into three. Fold the bottom third of the dough up and the top third down.

3 Seal the edges again with the rolling pin and give the dough a half turn clockwise. Roll the pastry into a strip then fold and seal again.

4 Press the top of the dough with your fingertips to remind you of how many rolls and folds the pastry has had. It is easy to forget! Then chill the pastry and repeat twice.

equal quantities of fat to flour. Some of the fat is rubbed into the flour, as in shortcrust pastry, but then the rest is added in a single piece and distributed through the dough by a lengthy process of rolling and folding, which builds up the number of layers and the subsequent lightness of the pastry.

If the butter is cut into pieces instead of formed into a compact slab, and if the folding process is shortened, the result is flaky pastry, which does not rise quite as effectively as puff pastry.

Rough puff pastry uses less fat than puff pastry and is easier to make. The fat is cut into small pieces and added all at once to the flour. Rough puff pastry also needs less rolling and folding.

COOK'S CHOICE

Is it really worth the effort of making homemade puff pastry when you can buy it prepared?

Making puff pastry takes time and practice, but once you have the skill, making puff pastry may be fitted in with other cooking and will seem less of a chore.

Is it worth the effort? That is for you to decide. Homemade puff pastry will taste rich, light and buttery because it is usually made with equal quantities of butter and flour. Frozen puff pastry tastes less rich but there is no denying that it is convenient to store, easy to use and gives good results.

It really all depends on how much pastry cooking you do, and whether making your own puff pastry gives you immense satisfaction or simply becomes a burden.

STEAM HEAT

I seem to have mixed success whenever I use puff pastry on top of a savoury pie. Is there any way to make sure puff pastry will rise evenly?

A steamy atmosphere inside the oven will help the layers of puff pastry to rise evenly. Half fill a baking dish with hot water and place on the bottom of the oven during cooking. This and a wetted baking tray will create the steam to help the pastry rise evenly. Try this method with the following recipes for homemade puff pastry, which can then be made into a giant vol-au-vent case filled with mixed mushrooms in a creamy sauce.

Puff pastry

SERVES: 4-6
PREPARATION TIME: 1 hour plus 1½ hours chilling time, plus overnight chilling; then from 30-60 minutes resting time
COOKING TIME: 65 minutes

250 g (2 cups) strong plain flour
A pinch of salt
250 g butter, at room temperature
About 6-8 tablespoons iced water
2 teaspoons lemon juice

1 Sift the flour and salt into a large mixing bowl. Work the butter on a plate with a palette knife until it is softened. Cut off about 1 tablespoon of butter and rub it into the flour until it resembles breadcrumbs.
2 Sprinkle the surface of the dough with 6 tablespoons of the iced water and the lemon juice. Mix to a soft but not sticky dough – add the extra water if the mixture is dry.
3 Transfer the dough to a lightly floured surface and knead it for about 5 minutes or until smooth and elastic. Sprinkle it with flour, wrap it in greaseproof paper and leave it to rest in the refrigerator until cool and firm, about 20 minutes.
4 Lightly flour a work surface. Shape the dough into a small rectangle and then roll and fold it, enclosing the butter, as described in the panel on the left. For best results, always roll the dough away from you with short strokes of the rolling pin.
5 Roll and fold the pastry four more times, putting the pastry in the refrigerator to chill for around 20-30 minutes after each two rollings and foldings, or after each if the pastry becomes sticky.
6 Wrap and chill the finished pastry for at least 20 minutes before using, or refrigerate overnight.

A selection of earthy mushrooms glistening with Madeira sauce makes a superb chunky filling for a mammoth vol-au-vent case made with buttery puff pastry.

Giant mixed mushroom vol-au-vent

SERVES: 4 – 6
PREPARATION TIME: *30 minutes, plus 2½ hours resting time*
COOKING TIME: *40 minutes*

FOR THE VOL-AU-VENT
250 g homemade puff pastry, (see left), or 500 g frozen pre-rolled puff pastry, thawed
1 large egg, beaten with a pinch of salt for brushing

FOR THE MUSHROOM FILLING
15 g dried mushrooms
150 ml Madeira
60 g unsalted butter
3 shallots, finely chopped
500 g mixed fresh mushrooms, cleaned, quartered or sliced
Juice of ½ lemon
3 teaspoons arrowroot
100 ml crème fraîche or sour cream
Salt and black pepper

1 Remove the puff pastry from the refrigerator and leave it to rest for an hour before rolling out.
2 Roll the pastry out to about 1 cm thick. Using a sharp knife, cut two circles from the pastry using an 18 cm plate as a guide.
3 Cut a 10 cm circle from the centre of one of the circles: this will be the lid. Leave the uncut circle, the circle with the hole and the lid, covered with some plastic wrap, in the refrigerator to rest for 30 minutes.
4 Put the uncut pastry circle on a wetted baking tray. Brush the edge with beaten egg and carefully place the cut ring of pastry on top.
5 Knock up the sides of the pastry. Brush the top of the ring with the beaten egg, avoiding the knocked up edges or they will stick together and prevent the pastry rising properly.
6 With the back of a knife, mark lines to form a star pattern around the border of the pastry ring.

7 Place the lid on another wetted baking tray and knock up or flake the edges. Brush with beaten egg and mark a trellis pattern on the top of the pastry with the back of a knife. Cover each piece of cut pastry with plastic wrap and leave them in the refrigerator to rest for an hour.
8 Preheat the oven to 220°C. Half fill a baking dish with hot water and place it in the bottom of the oven.
9 Put the pastry case near the middle of the oven and the lid on the shelf below, allowing room for it to rise, and bake for 30–35 minutes or until the case and lid are well risen, cooked and golden brown.
10 Meanwhile, start to make the filling. Rinse the dried mushrooms to remove any grit then soak them in warm water for 20 minutes, or until they are plump and soft. Drain the mushrooms and reserve the liquid.
11 Pour the Madeira into a small saucepan and boil for 5 minutes or until reduced by half.
12 Melt the butter in a frying pan, add the shallots and fry gently for around 2–3 minutes until softened but not browned. Add the dried and fresh mushrooms, sprinkle with the lemon juice, then cover and cook for about 5 minutes until softened.
13 Measure out 150 ml of the reserved mushroom water, blend with the arrowroot and add to the mushroom mixture. Cook gently, stirring, for 3 minutes or until the sauce has boiled and thickened.
14 Remove the vol-au-vent from the oven and cool slightly. Remove any soggy pastry from the centre of the case and return the vol-au-vent to the oven for 5 minutes to dry off.
15 Add the reduced Madeira and crème fraîche to the mushrooms and cook the mixture over a low heat for about 2–3 minutes. Season to taste with salt and pepper.
16 To serve, pour the mushrooms into the hot pastry case and put the lid on top at an angle. Use a large knife to cut the vol-au-vent into four wedges at the table and place on serving plates, ensuring each person has a generous portion of pastry and mushroom filling. Accompany the vol-au-vent with a spinach salad.

LEAVE IT OUT

Should the butter be used straight from the refrigerator when making flaky or puff pastry?

No. To make flaky or puff pastry easy to roll, the butter should be the same temperature and consistency as the dough, at normal room temperature. (Do not attempt this pastry in hot weather as it can become sticky.) If the butter is hard it can break through the dough; if it is too soft it will not keep the layers apart, making the rolling sticky and hard to manage. If the dough becomes sticky, wrap it in grease-proof paper and chill until firm enough to continue.

Save it!

Rolled trimmings of puff or flaky pastry can be rerolled two or three times but you must not roll them into a ball as this will destroy the light layers of the pastry. Instead, stack the trimmings on top of each other as neatly as possible and then roll.

BETTER BOUGHT PASTRY

How can I make sheets of bought puff pastry fit my recipes?

Packets of frozen puff pastry are a freezer must.

Most 1 kg packs of frozen, ready-rolled sheets of puff pastry contain 6×25 cm sheets, which are convenient to use. If you need a larger piece of rolled pastry, brush one edge of a pastry sheet with cold water, overlap a second sheet by 10 mm, press down gently to join the pastry together, and use according to the recipe directions.

Alternatively, place a pastry sheet on a lightly floured surface; lightly brush with cold water, place a second pastry sheet on top, then roll out the layered pastry to the required size.

RAISE THE HEAT

How can I stop butter from seeping out of puff pastry while it is cooking?

You need to use a hot or very hot oven, usually 220°C. If the oven is not hot enough, the butter will run out of the pastry layers before it is absorbed by the starch. If the butter runs at this oven setting, check the temperature of your oven or use a higher setting. If you are using bought pastry, check the oven temperature on the pack and be sure you preheat the oven for long enough: at least 20 minutes.

Some recipes advise reducing the oven temperature after the initial cooking. This allows time for the filling of the dish to cook sufficiently while preventing the pastry from cooking too quickly.

PASTRY LEAVES

I always admire attractively decorated pies. What's a simple way to make pastry leaves?

The trick is to gather the pastry trimmings, after covering your pie, and layer them, then roll out to a thin strip. Using a sharp knife, cut the pastry into 2.5 cm wide strips, then cut across diagonally to make diamond shapes. With a small sharp knife, mark veins on each diamond; twist to give a natural leaf 'look', and attach to the pie with chilled water or beaten egg.

SWEETER PASTRY

The pastry used in French tarts seems to taste richer than my normal short crust. What is it?

For fine pâtisserie the French often use pâte sucrée, which is enriched with egg and icing sugar, instead of short crust pastry. To make pâte sucrée, rub 125 g of unsalted butter into 250 g (2 cups) of plain flour, stir in 60 g (⅓ cup) icing sugar, then mix in 2 egg yolks to form a dough, adding a little chilled water if necessary. Shape into a disc, wrap in greaseproof paper and chill for 30 minutes before rolling.

WEIGH THE FLOUR

What quantity of pastry do I need to make if I want to line a 25 cm tart tin?

For a 25 cm tart tin you will need 250 g of short crust pastry – that is, pastry made with 250 g of plain flour. This will also do for a 28 cm tart tin. For a 23 cm tin you will require a 185 g quantity of pastry.

SEASONAL ZEST

I would like to jazz up my mince pies this year. What kind of pastry would complement the flavour of the fruit mince?

Oranges are frequently associated with Christmas time. Try this recipe which uses concentrated orange juice instead of water to make the basic shortcrust pastry, traditional for mince pies. The grated zest of an orange is then added to the fruit mince. For an extra kick, you could add a few tablespoons of an orange liqueur.

Orange mince pies

MAKES: *about 18 pies*
PREPARATION TIME: *30-35 minutes plus 20-25 minutes resting time for the pastry*
COOKING TIME: *25 minutes*

---

375 g (3 cups) plain flour
185 g unsalted butter, chilled and diced
2-3 tablespoons concentrated orange juice
Grated rind of 1 small orange
500 g fruit mince
Milk for brushing pastry
To decorate: icing or caster sugar

---

1 Sift the flour into a mixing bowl. Add the butter and rub into the flour until the mixture resembles fine breadcrumbs.
2 Add sufficient orange juice, using a round-bladed knife, to mix to a firm dough.
3 Using your fingertips, knead the dough gently on a lightly floured board until smooth, then wrap it in greaseproof paper and leave it to rest

in the refrigerator for at least 20-25 minutes before using.

4 Preheat the oven to 200°C. Lightly grease two tartlet tins, enough for about 18 pies.

5 On a lightly floured surface, roll out two-thirds of the dough thinly. Using a 7.5 cm round fluted cutter, stamp out as many rounds as you can. Reroll the pastry trimmings and cut out more rounds.

6 Carefully line the tartlet tins with the cut rounds of pastry.

7 Roll out the remaining portion of pastry and cut out 6 cm rounds to make lids. Using a small star-shaped cutter, 3 cm in diameter, cut out shapes from each pastry lid. Or, if you prefer plain lids, cut two slits in the top of each lid with a sharp knife or scissors.

8 Stir the grated orange rind into the prepared fruit mince and put 1 teaspoon of the mixture in the centre of each lined tartlet case.

9 Dab some water onto the pastry edges. Place the lids over the filled tartlets and press the edges together to seal. Glaze the lids with milk.

10 Bake the pies for 25 minutes or until the pastry is golden.

11 Sprinkle the cooked pies lightly with sifted icing or caster sugar and serve warm with some brandy butter or cream. Alternatively, cool the pies on a wire cooling rack and when cold, store in an airtight tin. They will keep for up to ten days in a cool place.

To reheat the pies, preheat the oven to 180°C. Put them on a baking tray and heat for 8-10 minutes or until warmed through.

Pâtés and Terrines

ROUGH OR SMOOTH?

What is the difference between a pâté and a terrine?

The line dividing pâtés and terrines is a very thin one. They are both most commonly made with minced or pounded meat, poultry or vegetables, highly seasoned and then cooked in a very slow oven. Pâtés tend to have a smoother texture and, apart from fish and vegetable pâtés, are predominantly made of liver, served from the container in which they are cooked, and eaten spread on bread or toast.

Terrines often, but not always, have a coarser texture than pâtés, with definite pieces. They are usually pressed after cooking and then served sliced as a first course. Terrines do not have to be made from meat. Layered terrines of seafood or vegetables set with aspic are very attractive.

The word terrine is also used to describe some very smooth fish, seafood or vegetable mixtures that are set in a terrine tin, turned out and served sliced.

SEALED WITH BUTTER

What does it mean when a food is described as 'potted'?

Cooks have been potting meat and fish since the 16th century as a way of preserving it. Potted meat or fish is seasoned and cooked until tender, then either pounded to a paste, pressed into a pot and covered with melted butter, or left whole in its cooking pot and covered with melted butter. The butter sets into an airtight seal so that the contents can be stored in a refrigerator for up to two months.

Once opened, potted food is eaten within two days. This preserving method is largely a thing of the past, but potted shrimps are still popular in English restaurants and recipes can be found in traditional British cookbooks.

Peaches and Nectarines

SUMMER SEASON

At what time of year are peaches and nectarines at their best?

The best time to buy peaches and nectarines is during the summer months, from November through to the end of February, when they are in season and readily available. Peaches and nectarines that appear in the shops around Christmas time are perfect to eat fresh in the hand or use in refreshing desserts. Look out for white-fleshed peaches also as these are considered to have a better flavour than the yellow-fleshed varieties.

Peaches and nectarines are close relations: the nectarine is not, as is widely believed, a cross between a plum and a peach. The only difference between them is that peaches have a fuzzy skin while nectarines are smooth. Before they are eaten, peaches and nectarines should be rinsed under a cold running tap to rid them of any fungicides.

SWEET RELATIONS

Can peaches and nectarines be used interchangeably in recipes?

Yes. Peaches and nectarines are completely interchangeable in recipes, although nectarines can be a little sweeter so may require less additional sugar than peaches.

Raw and ripe, both peaches and nectarines are perfect for making fruit salads – combined with just one other fruit such as fresh raspberries (with which peaches and nectarines have a natural affinity) or with a mixture of other fruits.

Poached in a light sugar syrup, they can be served hot with cream or ice cream, or chilled and used to top a flan or gâteau. They can also be spiced, baked, or grilled, cooked with pan-fried ham steaks and pork fillet, or added to casseroles, curries and stews.

Pears

COOKING AND EATING

Which varieties of pears are best for cooked recipes?

Virtually any variety of pear can be used for cooking, provided the pears are firm and not too ripe. For eating, it is best to buy pears that are not quite ripe unless you want to eat them immediately as they deteriorate quickly after reaching their peak. Keep them in a warm place to ripen and they should be ready to eat in two to three days. For the Boozy Pears recipe below, choose a large, firm variety of pear.

Boozy pears

SERVES: 8
PREPARATION TIME: 30 minutes
COOKING TIME: 30-40 minutes, plus overnight standing; next day: 15 minutes plus 2-3 hours chilling

1 large orange and 1 large lemon
185 g (¾ cup) white sugar
750 ml sweet white wine
8 large, ripe Comice, Packham or Josephine pears
2-3 tablespoons Grand Marnier
1 tablespoon chopped pistachio nuts
To serve: whipped cream, optional

1 Wash the orange and lemon and pare off the rinds in thin strips. Put these into a large stainless-steel or enamel saucepan that will hold all the pears comfortably.
2 Add the sugar and the wine, then stir over a medium heat until the sugar dissolves.
3 Bring to the boil and remove from the heat. Squeeze the orange and lemon, adding the juice to the pan.
4 Cut off the dried flower bud from the bottom of each pear and peel them, leaving the stalks. Place the pears in the wine syrup and return the saucepan to the heat.
5 Bring to the boil, then reduce the heat. Cover the pan and gently cook the pears for 30-40 minutes until only a slight resistance is felt when they are pierced with a knife. Turn

Thin strips of orange and lemon rind make a colourful decoration for this pear bathed in white wine and Grand Marnier. Pistachio nuts provide some crunch.

the pears frequently to ensure they are well coated with the wine syrup.
6 When the pears are cooked and translucent, take the pan off the heat and let the pears stand in the syrup overnight at room temperature.
7 Next day, remove the pears from the wine syrup with a slotted spoon and arrange them upright on a serving dish. Cover and set aside.
8 Bring the wine syrup to the boil and simmer it for 15-20 minutes or until it has reduced by about half

and become rich and heavy. Remove the saucepan from the heat and allow the wine syrup to cool.
9 Stir the Grand Marnier into the cooled syrup, then pour it over the pears. Cover the dish with plastic wrap and chill in the refrigerator for 2-3 hours.
10 Just before serving, spoon the syrup from the bottom of the dish over the pears and sprinkle with the chopped nuts and strips of rind. Serve with whipped cream, if liked.

KEEPING GOOD COLOUR

How do I stop pears from turning brown during preparation?

Use a stainless-steel potato peeler and put the peeled pears into a bowl of cold water. Add the juice of a large lemon or 2–3 tablespoons of bottled lemon juice.

Alternatively, depending on the recipe you have chosen, the pears can be put directly into a wine or sugar syrup to keep them from discolouring. For the most appealing presentation, try to choose either Comice, Conference or Packham varieties that are a standard size and have a true pear shape.

Peeled pears may be poached, stewed, baked or even pickled in a wide variety of recipes. They are delicious with fish and poultry.

Peas

CLOSE RELATIVES

Are snow peas and sugarsnap peas similar to garden peas?

They are all the same family of pea, but they are sold at different stages of maturity. Snow peas are flat with barely formed peas inside. Sugarsnaps contain more developed, plump peas, but are not as mature as garden peas. Both snow peas and sugarsnap peas are grown for their crisp, sweet edible pods.

For peas eaten whole, a good helping is about 125 g for each person. Garden peas should yield just under half their unshelled weight. For two people, allow about 500 g of unshelled peas, unless you are serving them with other vegetables or using them in a salad, such as the one on the right.

This is a good salad for a summer buffet table or barbecue because the peas and lentils stay firm in the dressing. Soft fruits are in season at the same time as peas, so you can sprinkle over some redcurrants as a colourful decoration. A splash of raspberry vinegar will lend another subtle summer aroma to this salad.

Pea and puy lentil salad in mint dressing

SERVES: 6-8
PREPARATION TIME: 15 minutes
COOKING TIME: 30-35 minutes

350 g (1¾ cups) puy lentils
2 bay leaves
750 g unshelled peas
1 teaspoon sugar
Salt and black pepper
1 teaspoon ground cumin
4-6 spring onions
3-4 sprigs mint
2-3 sprays redcurrants, optional

FOR THE DRESSING
90 ml olive oil
1 tablespoon white wine vinegar
1 teaspoon raspberry vinegar

1 Put the lentils into a pan with the bay leaves and cover them well with cold water. Bring to the boil, skim, then turn down the heat and simmer for about 30-35 minutes or until tender. Drain, rinse and leave them to drain further in a colander.

2 Meanwhile, shell the peas and put them in a small pan. Add the sugar and enough water to cover. Simmer the peas for 7-10 minutes, or until they are soft and sweet.

3 While the peas are cooking, put the ingredients for the dressing into a small screw-top jar and shake well.

4 When the peas and lentils are done, mix them together in a bowl. Season with the salt, black pepper and ground cumin and stir in the salad dressing. This can be done a few hours in advance if you like.

5 Shortly before serving, wash, trim and shred the spring onions, then shred the mint and toss them both into the pea and lentil salad. Garnish with redcurrants if you like, or add an extra sprig of mint to decorate.

Bright redcurrants enliven the green peas, spring onions and puy lentils in this distinctive salad. Fresh mint and ground cumin add an exotic flavour.

Peppercorns

COLOUR VARIATIONS

What is the difference between black, white, green and pink peppercorns?

Black, white and green peppercorns all come from the fruit of the same Asian tropical vine. However, they are picked at different stages and processed differently, which affects their flavour. Black peppercorns are the most pungent variety, followed by white, then green.

The vine bears green berries, which may be canned in their unripe state. These green peppercorns give a pepper flavour but without much heat. They can be used in subtle ways, such as scattered over strawberries, and will not overpower poultry or fish.

If these green berries are dried rather than canned, they darken to form the familiar black peppercorns. If, instead, they are left for longer on the vine to ripen, they turn bright red. White peppercorns are made by taking the ripe, red berries and removing the skin and pulp. The inner white seeds are then dried in the sun. White pepper is more expensive and less aromatic than black, but it is preferred for use in some sauces where black pepper would look unattractive.

Pink peppercorns are the berries of a different tropical bush. They are picked ripe and then dried. Pink peppercorns have a fruity heat and spicy flavour that is reminiscent of both cinnamon and allspice, but must be used sparingly as they are toxic when eaten in large quantities. Try a smattering of pink peppercorns in pickled peaches to add attractive colour to the presentation.

All dried peppercorns should be freshly ground in a mill to maintain their flavour, which is quickly lost after processing. An opened can of green peppercorns can be transferred to an airtight jar and stored for six weeks in the refrigerator.

DAMPEN THE FIRE

What can I do if I have added too much pepper to a dish?

There is not much to be done, beyond trying to lessen the impact of the pepper by increasing the other ingredients. In some cases you may be able to add a bland ingredient to the dish, such as mashed potato, rice or cream. There are some recipes, however, where pepper is the primary flavouring ingredient, such as in the classic French dish Steak au Poivre.

Steak au poivre

SERVES: 2
PREPARATION TIME: 3 minutes
COOKING TIME: 6 minutes

---

2 teaspoons black peppercorns
2 sirloin steaks, cut 1.5 cm thick
1½ teaspoons olive oil
Sea salt

---

1 Crush the peppercorns briefly with a pestle and mortar.
2 Rub the steaks lightly with the oil then press the crushed peppercorns firmly into the meat.
3 Heat the grill, or grill pan, until very hot. Cook the steaks quickly for about 2 minutes on each side.
4 Sprinkle the steaks with coarse sea salt and serve immediately with Coriander Salsa (see page 176).

Peppers

THE NAME GAME

Are peppers the same as capsicums?

Yes. Green, red and yellow peppers are members of the same capsicum family as chillies and are also known as capsicums.

SWEETER WHEN SKINNED

Do all peppers taste the same regardless of their colour?

No, they do not. Red peppers are distinctly sweeter than green, which are simply unripened red

GRILLING AND ROASTING PEPPERS

Grilling or roasting peppers makes them sweeter, more succulent and considerably easier to digest.

1 Put the peppers under a hot grill until they are well blistered and browned. Cover for 5 minutes. Or put them in the oven at 200° C for about an hour, turning once. When cooked, put them in a covered dish.

2 When the peppers are cool enough to handle, pull away the skin with your fingers.

3 Halve the peeled peppers on a plate to catch as much juice as possible. Remove the core, seeds and pith then slice the flesh of the peppers as required. It is worth saving the juices to add to a salad dressing.

peppers. Yellow peppers are mild. The flavour of all peppers will be even smoother and sweeter if they are grilled or roasted (see panel, left). If you want to peel the peppers but do not want to cook them, a sharp potato peeler will take off almost all the skin. The following recipe shows how delicious roasted peppers can be.

Salad of roasted peppers and shallots

SERVES: 6
PREPARATION TIME: 20 minutes
COOKING TIME: 1 hour

6 peppers of assorted colours
12 shallots
8 large cloves garlic, unpeeled
3 bay leaves
2-3 tablespoons olive oil
2 canned anchovy fillets
2 tablespoons walnut oil
1 tablespoon red wine vinegar
2 tablespoons chopped walnuts
Salt and black pepper

1 Preheat the oven to 200°C. Halve the peppers and place them, cut side down, on a baking tray on the top shelf of the oven.
2 Peel the shallots, letting them fall into their natural segments. Place in an ovenproof dish with the garlic.
3 Halve the bay leaves lengthways and scatter them over the shallots, then sprinkle with 1 tablespoon of olive oil. Place the shallots on the shelf beneath the peppers and roast both for about 30 minutes until the peppers are blistered and brown.
4 Remove the skin, seeds and pith from the peppers, saving as much juice as possible. Slice the peppers into long strips, on a plate to collect their juices, then transfer the strips and juices to a shallow serving dish. Add the roasted shallots, discarding the cooked strips of bay leaves.
5 Squeeze the garlic pulp out of the skins, mash it into the anchovies and beat in the remaining oils and vinegar, adding more vinegar if there is a lot of sweet pepper juice. Pour the dressing over the salad, scatter with walnuts and mix gently. Season with salt and black pepper.

PICKING PEPPERS

Peppers are available all year but are they better in some months?

As peppers respond well to good cultivation, they are grown all year round. However, their natural season is late summer, when they are at their tastiest and cheapest. Look for bright, shiny peppers that look full and firm and avoid any peppers that are wrinkled, limp or brown around the stem.

Pestle and Mortar

STILL GOOD

Is a pestle and mortar still useful as kitchen equipment?

A pestle and mortar is invaluable for jobs like crushing and grinding small amounts of spice. You are able to control the grinding very accurately and the weight of the pestle helps with the process. This fine grinding is used in Indian and Southeast Asian cooking where freshly ground spices are preferred.

A pestle and mortar is excellent for lightly crushing soft herb leaves such as mint and basil to release their fragrance for use in dressings and pestos (see *Oils*).

Making garlic mayonnaise is also easier with a pestle and mortar. Soak a slice of white bread in water, squeeze and then crush it in the mortar. Add two peeled cloves of garlic, a pinch of coarse rock salt and pound into a smooth paste. Gradually add a lightly flavoured olive oil in drops, mixing vigorously with the pestle.

When the mayonnaise has become sufficiently thick, season it with a little lemon juice.

The better bowls

Marble, glass and porcelain are good materials for mortars as they do not absorb flavours. All will work best when less than half full.

HOW TO USE A PESTLE AND MORTAR

The ancient pestle and mortar is one of the best tools for pounding spices to release their aroma.

Hold the pestle upright and push down firmly, moving it in a circular motion around the mortar bowl.

Pheasant

PLUCKY BIRD

A friend who lives near a pheasant farm is bringing me some birds. What should I do with them?

Check with your friend if the birds have been hung and are ready to eat. If not, you will have to hang them yourself for two days.

For pheasants that are still 'in the feather', you will also need to dress them.

First, pluck the feathers by pulling them out in the direction in which they grow, then cut off the head. Make a slit in the neck lengthways, take hold of the neck bone and twist, then cut off the neck close to the body of the bird.

Turn the pheasant around and make a slit at the rear vent. With your fingers, work around the cavity loosening the innards, which you should draw out in one motion. Take care not to break the gall bladder, which is the green sac attached to the liver, as its bitter juice would taint the meat. Do not rinse the cavity as you would lose much flavour; simply wipe the inside with damp paper towels. Discard the lungs, intestines and

The robust flavours of pheasant and red wine combine beautifully with the crunch of the walnut halves and the crisp clean taste of the apples and grapes.

cut the gall bladder away from the liver. Keep the neck, gizzard, heart and liver to make giblet stock.

Finally, cut through the feet and pull them off, twisting to pull out the sinews from the legs. The bird can be frozen at this stage.

SEX DISCRIMINATION

Why do recipes often specify a hen pheasant rather than a cock?

The hen pheasant is smaller than the male but has a plumper breast and finer flavour. If you buy a brace of pheasant, you usually get a cock and a hen. One pheasant will serve two people.

Pheasant can be used in robust recipes for chicken and guinea fowl and using a chicken clay pot gives good results. Cook the pheasant for 1½ hours, putting the clay pot into the cold oven and then setting the temperature to 230°C. Young, tender birds are best plainly roasted, while older birds are best made into pâté or casseroled, as in the following recipe.

Pheasant casserole with apple and walnuts

SERVES: *4*
PREPARATION TIME: *25 minutes*
COOKING TIME: *1 hour 35 minutes*

6 dessert apples
250 g seedless red grapes
300 ml red grape juice
1 tablespoon green tea leaves
300 ml boiling water
2 tablespoons olive oil or butter
2 pheasants, plucked and
 dressed
1 tablespoon soy sauce
250 ml red wine
2 teaspoons balsamic or white wine
 vinegar
Salt and black pepper
185 g (1½ cups) walnut halves
To garnish: sautéed apple slices and
 extra grapes

1 Peel, core and roughly chop the apples into a bowl. Whizz the grapes roughly in a food processor with the grape juice and mix with the apples.
2 Put the green tea leaves in a bowl, pour over the boiling water and leave it to steep for about 5 minutes. Strain the tea, reserving the liquid.
3 Preheat the oven to 180°C. Heat the oil or butter in a casserole and fry the birds until browned. Pour on the fruit mixture, tea, soy sauce, wine and vinegar. Season and bring to the boil.
4 Cover tightly and transfer to the oven for 1¼ hours or until one of the birds' legs will wobble when pushed. Alternatively, test by pushing a skewer into the meatiest part of a thigh. If the pheasants are cooked, the juices should flow clear.
5 Transfer the birds to a warmed serving platter and keep warm in the oven while you finish the sauce.
6 Bring the juices in the casserole to the boil and then fast-boil them for about 10 minutes. Strain the liquid into a saucepan, pressing the juice through with a wooden spoon.
7 Stir the walnuts into the sauce, then bring to the boil and simmer for 10 minutes or until it has reduced to about 500 ml. The sauce should be slightly syrupy. If it is not, reduce further then season to taste.
8 Joint the pheasants into four and arrange on a dish. Spoon the walnuts around the birds and garnish with sautéed apple slices and grapes. Pour the sauce into a warmed sauceboat to serve separately.

FATTY PROTECTION

How do you keep the tender breast meat from drying out when you are roasting a pheasant?

As the flesh of game birds is very lean, the breast must be protected. Cover it with a layer of pork fat or streaky bacon to prevent it drying out in the oven. The birds should also be basted from time to time during roasting with the cooking juices and melted fat. Remove the pork fat or bacon 10 minutes before the end of cooking to let the breast brown. If the skin is not brown and crisp enough at the end of cooking, put the bird under a hot grill for a minute or two before serving.

Using oven roasting bags also helps to retain the moisture when cooking a game bird.

Pickling

WELL PRESERVED

Does it really matter what type of vinegar I use to make pickles?

You should use only high quality vinegar with an acetic acid content of at least 5 per cent, which includes all wine vinegars and most others. Malt vinegar, which was once the staple of the traditional homestyle pickle, is the most economical but it has a distinctive taste. Brown malt vinegar has the best flavour.

White distilled malt vinegar, with its concentrated acidity, is useful for pickling watery vegetables such as cucumber, but there are more subtle, less harsh alternatives you can use as well, such as cider vinegar and red or white wine vinegar. Sherry vinegar and balsamic vinegar can be used half and half with wine or cider vinegar in order to impart their special flavours.

When choosing a vinegar, try to complement the vegetable or fruit that is being preserved. Think about the colour and flavour you wish to create. For example, white vinegar gives a better appearance to light coloured pickles, such as those made from gherkins, cauliflower or cucumber, whereas dark red wine vinegar is best for pickled beetroot or red cabbage. Cider vinegar, with its apple base, is particularly good for sweet pickles. Sherry vinegar, which is a deep caramel colour, has a very mellow flavour. It is perfect for giving a boost to pickled shallots.

ADDING SPICE

What else besides vinegar can I use to give pickles more flavour?

Sugar, herbs, and hot and sweet spices can be added to pickling vinegar to give extra flavour. Sweet pickles are produced by adding a spiced sugar and vinegar syrup to the ingredients. The vinegar must rise above the pickling ingredients by 1–2.5 cm to allow for evapora-

tion. When crisp vegetables such as onions are pickled, cold vinegar is used. For softer pickles, such as peaches or walnuts, the vinegar should be heated.

GIFT WRAPPING

Can you give me some ideas for pretty or unusual pickles I could make as Christmas presents?

Homemade preserves, like Pickled Quail's Eggs, Pickled Shallots and Sweet Pickled Peaches (see recipes, following) make good Christmas presents. They taste superb with ham and cold meats, cheese, or freshly baked sausages. The best time to make them is when you can obtain a large quantity of ingredients at bargain prices, which is usually in the summer.

Put the pickles into attractive jars and decorate with labels that state the contents, when the pickles were made, how they should be stored, the date by which they should be eaten and some serving suggestions. Make little hats or collars for the jars and tie the tops with pretty coloured ribbon. The following recipe for Pickled Quail's Eggs would make an especially dainty and sophisticated present.

Pickled quail's eggs

FILLS: 500 ml jar
PREPARATION: 20 minutes, plus
2 hours infusing
COOKING TIME: 10 minutes

---

1 teaspoon whole mixed
*   peppercorns*
2 dried red chillies
Small piece fresh ginger, peeled and
*   finely chopped*
1 blade mace
A pared strip of orange zest
1 teaspoon yellow mustard seeds
1 teaspoon sea salt
600 ml white wine vinegar
24 fresh quail's eggs

---

1 Put all the pickling ingredients except the eggs into a pan. Bring them to the boil, then remove from the heat and leave for at least 2 hours or until cold.

2 Hard-boil the eggs for 3 minutes, plunge them into cold water, and peel them when cool. Pack the eggs into a sterilised jar (see *Chutney*).

3 Strain the spiced vinegar through muslin, then pour it over the eggs so that it covers them completely.

4 Seal with nonmetallic vinegar-proof lids and store in a cool, dark place for a week before using. It is best to use them within a month.

Pickled shallots

FILLS: 2 x 1 litre jars
PREPARATION TIME: 30–40 minutes,
plus 2 days wet brining and
2 hours infusing
COOKING TIME: 10 minutes

---

125 g (½ cup) sea salt
1 kg shallots
600 ml white wine vinegar
300 ml sherry vinegar
2 blades mace
2 dried red chillies
4 allspice berries, lightly crushed
1 cinnamon stick
6 black peppercorns
1 bay leaf

---

1 Using a large, nonmetallic bowl, dissolve the salt in 1.25 litres of water, then add the trimmed and peeled shallots with the root end intact. Rest a weighted plate on top of the bowl to keep the shallots submerged. Leave them for two days, stirring the shallots occasionally.

2 About 2 hours before you are ready to start pickling, bring the vinegars, spices and bay leaf slowly to the boil in a large pan. Remove from the heat and leave the mixture to stand for 2 hours or until cold.

3 Rinse the shallots under cold running water, drain well and pat dry with kitchen paper towels. Pack the shallots into sterilised jars.

4 Strain the spiced vinegar through muslin, then pour over the shallots so that it covers them completely.

5 Seal the jars with nonmetallic vinegarproof lids then leave them in a cool, dark place for at least a month before using. This resting period will allow the flavours to develop. The shallots will be at their best when eaten within a year.

Using attractive glass jars makes these pickled shallots, peaches and shelled quail's eggs particularly welcome presents.

Sweet pickled peaches

FILLS: 1 litre jar
PREPARATION TIME: 30 minutes
COOKING TIME: 25 minutes

---

375 g (1½ cups) white sugar
2 teaspoons coriander seeds
1 teaspoon whole mixed
  peppercorns
5 cm piece cinnamon stick
8 cloves
4 green cardamom pods, lightly
  crushed
2 tablespoons lime juice
600 ml white wine vinegar
10 ripe but firm peaches

---

1 Put all of the ingredients, except the peaches, into a large saucepan. Heat gently, stirring, until the sugar has dissolved.
2 Meanwhile, bring a saucepan of water to the boil. Halve the peaches, remove the stones, then drop them into the boiling water a few at a time for 30-40 seconds, depending on their ripeness. Remove them with a slotted spoon and slip off the skins, using a potato peeler if necessary.
3 Add the peeled peach halves to the vinegar and sugar mixture, bring them to a simmer then poach for about 5-10 minutes, or until tender when pierced. Transfer the peaches to a warmed, sterilised jar.
4 Boil the syrup rapidly over a high heat to reduce it by half. Strain the syrup and pour it over the peaches, making sure the fruit is completely covered and there are no air pockets. If necessary, weigh the peaches down with crumpled greaseproof paper, removing it after a week.
5 Seal with a nonmetallic vinegar-proof lid and store in a cool, dark place for six weeks before using.

CAREFULLY SEALED

What is the best way to seal jars used for pickles?

Lids with plastic-coated linings or specialised preserving jars with glass tops and rubber sealing rings are essential. Never use paper or cellophane covers for pickles (or chutneys) as the jars need to be completely airtight. If the jars are not adequately covered, the vinegar will evaporate and expose the ingredients to the air and harmful bacteria. The preserve will shrink and the top will dry out.

Avoid using metal tops for jars as the vinegar in pickles will corrode them, leading to possible rust and contamination. If the vinegar does evaporate during storage, top it up with more as the ingredients in the container should stay covered.

Pineapple

SWEET SMELL OF RIPENESS

How can I tell if a pineapple is ripe before I buy it?

The easiest way is to smell it – a ripe pineapple will have a sweet yet distinctive fragrant smell.

SIMPLE PREPARATION

What is the best way to prepare a fresh pineapple?

First cut off the top with its spiky green plume and then take a thin slice from the base; stand it upright.

With a large knife, cut the skin downwards in wide strips. Then, with the tip of a knife, remove the hard brown eyes from the surface of the pineapple flesh.

If you want to serve the pineapple in rings, cut it into slices of the required thickness. For wedges or cubes, cut the fruit lengthways into quarters, slice off the core from each piece, then cut up the flesh.

Pineapples can also be hollowed out to act as a container for sorbet, ice cream or fruit salad. First, slice off the top of the pineapple leaving a good wedge of skin attached to the green plume, then cut a sliver from the base and stand it upright. With a pointed stainless-steel knife, carefully cut down into the pineapple just inside the skin. Work the knife right round the pineapple. Make several cuts across the flesh and remove as much of it as you can. Continue cutting until all the flesh has been removed.

A note of caution

If you are adding fresh pineapple to dessert mixtures that contain gelatine, such as cheesecake, jelly or mousses, poach the fruit gently in a little sugar syrup beforehand. Otherwise the pineapple's enzyme will break down the gelatine and prevent the mixture from setting.

SUMMER SALAD

Can you help me with a savoury pineapple salad recipe I can make in advance?

The following salad is great to make a day ahead of serving and is suitable for a main meal when accompanied with a tossed green salad and warm crusty bread rolls.

Pineapple and rice salad

SERVES: 6–8
PREPARATION TIME: 20 minutes, if the rice is cooked
COOKING TIME: 10 minutes, for the rice

4 cups cold cooked long-grain rice
  (1⅓ cups uncooked rice)
2 cups diced fresh pineapple
1 Lebanese cucumber, seeded and diced
8 spring onions, thinly sliced
6 radishes, thinly sliced
250 g cooked leg ham off the bone, cut into 5 mm julienne strips
To garnish: whole radishes and fresh mint sprigs

Summer in a salad bowl, with ever-popular sweet pineapple and ham, offset by crisp cucumber and radish.

FOR THE DRESSING
250 ml Greek-style natural yoghurt
80 ml light sour cream
1 tablespoon wholegrain mustard
2 teaspoons lemon juice
¼ cup shredded fresh mint leaves
Salt and white pepper

1 If the rice is not cooked, place it in a heavy-based pan with 4 cups of boiling salted water. Boil rapidly, uncovered, for 10 minutes, or until the rice grains are tender. Pour into a colander and hold under cold running water to rinse off the excess starch. Drain well and cool, then chill, covered, in the refrigerator for at least 30 minutes, or overnight.

2 In a large bowl, combine the cooked rice, pineapple, cucumber, spring onions, radishes and ham. Fold together lightly.

3 To make the dressing, place the yoghurt, sour cream, mustard, lemon juice and shredded mint together in a bowl. Stir gently until evenly combined. Season to taste.

4 Add the dressing to the pineapple and rice mixture and fold together gently. Transfer the salad to a serving bowl, cover and chill for 30 minutes.

5 Serve the salad chilled, garnished with radishes and fresh mint sprigs.

Pipis

BURROWING SHELLFISH

I've seen pipis in the fish market but don't know what to do with them. How do you serve them?

A pipi is a very small shellfish with a smooth, polished, triangular-shaped shell. Its colour can vary from yellow to pink or green. It burrows beneath the sand of ocean beaches. Pipis are always sold enclosed in their shell. Do not buy them if the shells are open.

To cook pipis, poach in stock, white wine or water just until the shell opens or grill or barbecue them until they open. Remove the pipis from the shells immediately, and add them to a potato chowder, or a marinara pasta sauce, or a vegetable stir-fry, and heat through before serving.

Pizza

MORE HEAT

Why does my homemade pizza base come out soft and not crisp?

Most likely the baking surface was not hot enough. The oven and the cooking surface must be preheated to the highest temperature. The dough should then be put straight onto a preheated pizza stone or tile (many kitchen shops sell them) or a large, preheated, unglazed tile. This is the closest home cooks can get to a traditional pizza oven.

A wooden pizza paddle with a long handle makes moving the pizza easier. If you do not have one, put a baking tray (or tile) on the top rack of the oven and pre-heat. Then put the dough on a thin pizza tin, oiled and floured, and put it on the preheated surface to bake.

You can also buy a special non-stick two-piece pizza pan which has a perforated disc on which the pizza cooks, so that air circulates underneath ensuring a crisp crust.

FAMILY FAVOURITE

Can you recommend a pizza topping that my whole family will enjoy?

When catering for a range of ages and taste buds, it's a good idea to divide your pizza topping into halves or quarters. You can then use substantial ingredients with robust flavours to please the adults – such as ham and olives, chicken and anchovies, and prawns and capers – and select milder flavours for the children – such as tomatoes, mushrooms and cheese. Place the combinations in quarter segments on a base of bottled Italian tomato sauce on the pizza dough as in the following recipe.

Family pizza

MAKES: 2 x 30 cm pizzas
PREPARATION TIME: 30 minutes
COOKING TIME: 15–20 minutes each pizza

Basic Pizza Dough (see recipe, right)
Italian tomato sauce
4 egg tomatoes, thinly sliced
125 g mushrooms, thinly sliced
250 g cooked ham, chopped
125 g skinless chicken breast or thigh fillet, cooked and chopped
8 black olives, stoned and sliced
8 large green prawns, shelled, deveined and halved lengthways
1 tablespoon capers
250 g mozzarella cheese, thinly sliced
4 tablespoons freshly grated Parmesan cheese
2 tablespoons olive oil

1 Preheat the oven to 240°C. Make the pizza dough and leave it to rise for 15 minutes.
2 Roll out half the dough into a circle with a 30 cm diameter. Repeat with the other half of the dough.
3 Spread the tomato sauce evenly over the pizza bases, leaving a 1.5 cm rim of dough around the edge. Lightly score into quarters.
4 Divide the tomato and mushroom slices evenly over opposite quarters, on both pizza bases. Sprinkle the

ham, chicken and olives evenly over the remaining quarters; top with the prawns and capers.
5 Arrange the mozzarella cheese over both pizzas. Sprinkle half the grated Parmesan cheese over each pizza. Brush the edges of the dough with oil and drizzle any remaining oil over the top of the pizzas.
6 Bake as for the Basic Pizza Dough recipe, one by one, or together if the oven is large enough. Serve immediately, cut into quarters.

CHEESE CHOICE

Are there any cheeses I can use on pizza that will melt well but make a change from mozzarella?

Yes, there are several. Gorgonzola, Cheddar, Fontina, Gruyère and goat's cheese all melt well and are very suitable for pizzas. Or try placing spoonfuls of ricotta on top of a pizza and sprinkle them with a little Parmesan. The recipe below uses a stylish combination of tangy goat's cheese and walnuts.

Basic pizza dough

MAKES: 2 x 30 cm pizzas
PREPARATION TIME: 20 minutes
COOKING TIME: 15 minutes

10 g fresh yeast or 7 g sachet dried yeast or 10 g sachet instant rapid-rise yeast
125 ml lukewarm water
250 g (2 cups) plain flour
½ teaspoon salt
1 tablespoon olive oil

1 Preheat the oven to 240°C. Put a pizza tile, a layer of unglazed ceramic tiles or a flat baking tray on the oven's top rack.
2 Dissolve the fresh or dried yeast in the lukewarm water. Put the flour into a large bowl with the salt and the rapid-rise yeast, if using. Make a well in the centre, then add the oil and the yeast mixture or water. Stir the mixture first with a fork, then by hand, until a dough is formed.
3 Knead on a floured surface for around 5 minutes or until soft and smooth. Divide into two balls, put on a floured board, cover with a

Mild red onions add an attractive colour and delicious sweetness to this pizza baked with goat's cheese, walnuts and rosemary.

cloth and leave to rise for 15 minutes or until doubled in volume.

4 Roll out one ball of dough on a floured surface, rolling it from the centre until you have a circle about 30 cm in diameter. Flour a pizza paddle and put the pizza round on top. Or shape the pizza with your hands on a round, lightly oiled and floured tin, or press gently into a nonstick pizza pan.

5 Quickly add the topping and, if you are using a pan, put it immediately into the hot oven. If you are using a pizza paddle give it a few shakes, back and forth, to be sure the dough is not sticking and then slide the pizza from the paddle onto the hot tiles or baking tray with a sharp jerk. Bake the pizza for about 15 minutes.

If you want to make more than one pizza at a time, you can partially bake each one separately first for

about 7 minutes with a thin layer of thick tomato sauce, if using, and set them aside. Then, when you need the pizzas, add the various toppings and finish off the baking, together if you have room, or one at a time.

Pizza with onions, goat's cheese and rosemary

MAKES: 2 x 30 cm pizzas
PREPARATION TIME: 40 minutes
COOKING TIME: 15-20 minutes each pizza

30 g butter
2 tablespoons olive oil
4 large red onions, thinly sliced
A pinch of sugar
Salt and black pepper
Basic Pizza Dough (see recipe, left)
175 g firm goat's cheese, chopped
90 g (³⁄₄ cup) walnuts, chopped
1 teaspoon very finely chopped rosemary

1 Heat the butter and oil in a large frying pan. Add the onions and sugar, season with salt and pepper and stir for several minutes.

2 Cover and cook over a gentle heat for about 30 minutes. Uncover and continue to cook until the onions start to take on a little colour. Taste and adjust the seasoning.

3 Preheat the oven to 240°C. Make the pizza dough and leave it to rise for 15 minutes.

4 Roll out one ball of dough into a circle about 30 cm in diameter. Spread half the onions over the pizza base and sprinkle with half of the cheese, walnuts and rosemary. Bake as for the Basic Pizza Dough recipe, about 15 minutes. Repeat with the remaining dough and filling for a second pizza.

Plastic Wrap

PLASTIC SAFETY

Is plastic wrap safe for all kitchen use, or does it affect some foods?

Plastic wrap is indispensable in the modern kitchen, but there have been fears in recent years that some of the substances used in its manufacture could migrate into foods, particularly those with a high fat content such as fried meats, pastries and some cheeses. The manufacturers have carried out research into the matter and now give consumers the following advice.

All plastic wraps, as well as food wraps that contain PVC (polyvinyl chloride) or PE (polyethylene), are suitable for use in contact with all foods, except almost pure fat, such as lard, oil or foods in an oily medium (for example, tuna or meat that is being marinated). If plastic wrap is in direct contact with these, a small migration of substances will occur.

Never use plastic wrap on warm food, or where it may melt into it, such as in a conventional oven. When reheating or cooking food in a microwave oven, do not let the plastic wrap touch the food.

Plums

PLUM JOBS

Which are the best plums to eat fresh and which need cooking?

Most plums can be eaten fresh; only a few are too tart to be eaten raw and are best used for cooking.

Dessert plums are at their best when they have a bloom on their skin and are plump and firm to the touch. Disregard any that are damaged, shrivelled or poor in colour.

Varieties to look out for include President, Black Amber, Donsworth Lewis, Mariposa (blood plum), Narrabeen, Tegan Blue and Santa Rosa. Dessert varieties of plum, such as the greengage, can also be used for cooking if they are bought slightly underripe.

Of the cooking plums, damsons are the best known, especially for making jam. Angelina is another cooking variety available. These are excellent for French-style fruit tarts or flans.

SKIM THE STONES

Is it necessary for me to remove the stones of the fruit when making plum jam?

No. After the sugar has been added and the jam is brought to a full boil, the stones will rise to the surface and can be skimmed off easily with a slotted spoon. The stones should be removed, however, when making a stone fruit compote, as in the recipe below.

Plum compote

SERVES: 6-8
PREPARATION TIME: 10 minutes
COOKING TIME: 15-20 minutes

---

1 kg plums
125 g (½ cup) caster sugar
250 ml dry white wine
250 ml water
1 cinnamon stick
2 teaspoons arrowroot

---

1 Wash and dry the plums. Cut into halves and remove the stones.
2 In a large pan, dissolve the sugar in the wine and water over a medium heat. Bring to the boil, add the cinnamon stick and boil the syrup for 5 minutes.
3 Place the plums in the syrup, reduce the heat to medium-low and simmer gently for about 10-15 minutes, or until tender.
4 With a slotted spoon, transfer the fruit to a serving bowl. Blend the arrowroot with 1 tablespoon cold water in a small bowl. Add to the syrup and return to the boil, stirring constantly with a wooden spoon.
5 Cool the syrup, remove the cinnamon and pour over the plums.

GOOD GAGES

What is the difference between plums and greengages?

The greengage is one of several varieties of plum. It is an old variety, more tender and lavishly scented than others. Gages can be either the original green-skinned variety with green flesh, or the newer yellow-skinned gage with yellow flesh.

Gages are a dessert plum but are also used for cooking. They are particularly good in tarts, fruit pies and compotes but especially they make excellent preserves.

The wonderful summery flavour of perfectly ripe plums takes a starring role in this stone fruit compote that is enhanced with only the gentlest of spices.

Poaching

GENTLE COOKING

What is the difference between poaching and boiling?

Poached chicken or fish has a juicy tenderness not found in boiled food. For food to be poached it must be submerged, or partly submerged, in a flavoured liquid (such as syrup or stock), and cooked so that the liquid barely moves. It is an excellent way to cook delicate fruit.

Foods can be cooled in their poaching liquid, which stops them drying out, but the poaching pan should be stood in cold water so that the contents cool quickly. This is to prevent the food going bad, as it might if kept too long in a warm, steamy atmosphere.

Pork

SAFE STORAGE

Does pork go off quicker than other types of meat? If so, how should I store a Sunday joint of pork before cooking?

In the past pork was particularly susceptible to contamination by trichinella cysts, rather than the usual food poisoning bacteria. But today modern husbandry and stringent inspection ensure that pork is unlikely to be infected. The only pork that might go off slightly quicker than other types of meat is very fatty pork, but most New-fashioned pork is so lean that there is no risk of the fat becoming rancid.

As with all meat, pork should be stored loosely wrapped in the coldest part of the refrigerator, where the temperature should be 0–5°C. If it is placed in a rigid plastic container with a sealed top, this should not be opened until required. Otherwise, discard the original wrapping from the meat, rewrap it loosely in greaseproof paper or foil, and put it on a plate to catch any blood that comes out of the meat. You can then keep the pork for up to two days. Always store raw meat well away from cooked foods in the refrigerator.

LESS FAT

When I tried grilling lean pork leg steak, it turned out tough. What's the best way to cook it?

Lean cuts, such as pork steaks, which do not have much natural fat, need some lubrication if they are not to be dry, tasteless and tough. This is best done by marinating them in oil and vinegar so that you replace some of the missing pork fat with a healthier fat. Add other ingredients to give extra flavour, such as fruit juice, wine or yoghurt, plus herbs or spices.

Pork leg steaks, schnitzels or escalopes cut from a lean leg, can be beaten and then quickly pan-fried.

WELL COOKED

How long should a pork chop be grilled or fried to make sure it is cooked through?

It depends on the chop's thickness, shape and size, the temperature of the grill or the hot plate, and the temperature of the chop. For best results, meat should always be cooked from room temperature rather than straight from the refrigerator, so take it out 5–10 minutes before you need it.

Allow 4–5 minutes a side for a chop that is 2.5 cm thick and at room temperature before cooking. To test whether the pork is cooked, pierce the thickest part with the point of a thin knife or a fine skewer – when the juices run clear the meat is done.

Another way to cook pork chops that takes a little longer, but is a reliable way of making sure they are well cooked, is to bake them, as in the recipe below. This also provides an opportunity to give the chops a strongly flavoured spinach and mushroom filling.

Pork chops stuffed with spinach and mushrooms

SERVES: 4
PREPARATION TIME: 25 minutes
COOKING TIME: 20-25 minutes

---

4 pork chops 4 cm thick, each weighing about 250 g
1 tablespoon oil
1 small onion, finely chopped
2 cloves garlic, crushed
125 g large flat mushrooms, finely chopped
250 g frozen leaf spinach, thawed
50 g cream cheese
1 tablespoon snipped fresh chives
1 teaspoon wholegrain mustard
1 tablespoon fresh breadcrumbs
Salt and black pepper

---

1 Preheat the oven to 180°C. Cut a deep large pocket in each chop (see panel, above right).
2 Heat the oil in a frying pan, add the onion and garlic and fry until softened. Add the mushrooms and

STUFFING PORK CHOPS

As pork is becoming leaner all the time, a stuffing is useful to help keep the meat moist and tender while it is baking in the oven.

1 Trim off any excess fat from the chops, then cut horizontally into the fat side to make a pocket.

2 Pack the stuffing into the pocket you have made, then tie some kitchen string around the chop to hold in the filling during cooking.

continue to cook the mixture until the mushrooms are tender.
3 Drain the spinach and squeeze out as much water as possible. Stir into the frying pan and continue cooking for about 2 minutes.
4 Remove the pan from the heat; stir in the cheese, chives, mustard, breadcrumbs and seasoning.
5 Divide the mixture between the pockets in the chops. Season the outside of the meat, then place the chops in a shallow baking dish and bake for 20-25 minutes.

VARIATIONS
Make an apricot-flavoured stuffing with 1 small onion, 6 reconstituted dried apricots, 2 tablespoons pine nuts, 4 tablespoons fresh white breadcrumbs, 1 clove garlic and some fresh sage, chopped and mixed together. Or try prunes and walnuts instead of apricots and pine nuts.

DRY AND CRISP

How do you get perfect crackling?

Make sure the skin is completely dry and, if necessary, remove any remaining hairs by singeing the rind with a flame or shaving it with a disposable razor. Just before roasting the joint, score the rind.

Carefully scoring the skin and fat of the pork joint at regular intervals before roasting it will help to give delicious, crispy pieces of golden crackling.

Rub the rind generously with salt. Cook the meat on a rack in a shallow baking dish and refrain from basting it during cooking.

For crackling that is particularly crisp, remove the whole rind about 30–45 minutes before the end of roasting and continue cooking it beside the joint, as in the recipe below, which includes an accompaniment of baked apples.

Roast leg of pork

SERVES: 6
PREPARATION TIME: *20 minutes*
COOKING TIME: *about 2 hours*

Fillet end of pork leg weighing about 2 kg
Salt
3 crisp dessert apples, washed
2 tablespoons lemon juice
2 tablespoons clear honey
6 small sprigs of fresh sage

1 Preheat the oven to 200°C. Score the rind of the pork and rub it generously with salt.
2 Put the pork leg onto a rack in a shallow baking dish and then roast it, without basting, for 55 minutes per kg.
3 About 30–45 minutes before the end of the roasting, take the pork

Liven up a simple roast leg of pork with accompaniments such as apples baked with honey and sage, sugarsnap peas and a parsnip and carrot purée.

out of the oven. Using a sharp knife, slice off the rind. Put the rind next to the pork on the rack and return them to the oven to finish cooking.
4 Halve and core the apples. Place the halves cut side down on the work surface and slice them thinly without cutting completely through.
5 Place each half on a square of foil and spoon over the lemon and honey. Add a sage sprig then bring up the edges of the foil and twist the edges together to seal. Place the parcels

on a baking tray and cook for 5-10 minutes, until the apples are tender. Test by opening a parcel and piercing the apple with a knife.
6 Transfer the pork joint to a warm carving plate and leave to rest in the oven with the heat turned off and the door propped open, for about 10 minutes. Carve the pork, cut the crackling into pieces, and serve it with the baked apples, sugarsnap peas, parsnip and carrot purée and gravy, if you care to make it.

Pot-roasting

BAKED IN A POT

What is the difference between roasting and pot-roasting?

Pot-roasting is not really roasting at all, but an old, economical way of baking food in a pot, either over a low heat or in the oven. Roasting proper is a faster, dry method, used for cooking choice, tender cuts of meat, poultry and sometimes game.

Pot-roasting is used for cheaper cuts that are cooked in their own juices and it could be considered a simpler version of braising. The meat is first browned in oil or butter to give a 'roasted' appearance and then cooked with little or no extra liquid in a casserole with a tight-fitting lid. Moisture from the meat provides the liquid during cooking, though with poultry a few spoons of liquid are usually added after browning.

A traditional technique in pot-roasting is to cook the browned meat on a piece of pork rind. This adds flavour and richness, and prevents the meat scorching on the bottom of the pot. Coarsely cut root vegetables are sometimes put under the meat for the same purpose. They can be raw, or browned in the same fat as the meat, though the meat should be removed while you are browning the vegetables. When cooked, the vegetables are served alongside the meat.

For more tender and subtly flavoured meats, try this variation on pot-roasting that could be called 'gentle roasting'. Small cuts, such as best ends of lamb or even whole small birds, are seasoned, rubbed with butter and set on a bed of root vegetables in a deep pot with a lid. The lid is removed in the latter stages of cooking to brown the meat lightly, and a sauce is made by pouring off the fat and adding a good stock and some wine or spirit to the meat juices. The sauce is then simmered and thickened with arrowroot if necessary.

Potatoes

WHAT YOU SEE

Is there any way to tell simply by looking at a potato whether it will be waxy or floury?

Alas no, but retailers are increasingly offering advice as to the suitability of potatoes for various cooking methods. The new baby chats or first early Coliban or Sebago varieties available in spring and summer are waxy and good for boiling to eat hot or in salads. Winter maincrop potatoes tend to be floury and good for mashing, but the red-skinned Desirée and Pontiac varieties and Tasmanian Pink-Eye with its red skin and yellow flesh, are firmer and are better for boiling.

Good waxy potatoes to look for in winter are Bintje and Kipfler, both of which have a fine flavour. New potatoes are reliably waxy and are good for salads such as in the recipe below.

Waxy and floury varieties of potato all cook very successfully in the microwave oven.

New potatoes in watercress and walnut vinaigrette

SERVES: *4*
PREPARATION TIME: *10 minutes*
COOKING TIME: *20-30 minutes*

60 g (½ cup) walnut halves
1 bunch watercress
4 spring onions
500 g small, waxy potatoes
3 tablespoons olive oil
2 tablespoons walnut oil
1 tablespoon red wine vinegar
Salt and black pepper

1 Crush half the walnut halves in a mortar or food processor; set the remaining halves aside. Trim and chop the watercress and then finely shred the spring onions.
2 Wash the potatoes but do not scrape them. Leave the tiniest ones whole but cut larger ones to the same size as the smaller ones. Cook in boiling salted water until tender.
3 Put the crushed walnuts into a jar with the oils, vinegar, salt and pepper and shake it well to combine.
4 Drain the cooked potatoes. Shake the dressing again and stir it gently through the potatoes. Leave to cool.
5 Scatter the watercress and spring onions over the salad, mix again and then serve the salad scattered with the uncrushed walnut halves.

SUPERB ROAST SPUDS

What is the secret of perfect roast potatoes, brown and crunchy outside and meltingly soft inside?

There are three golden rules to perfect, crunchy roast potatoes. First, choose a floury, maincrop variety such as King Edward or, when you can get them, Golden Wonder or Kerr's Pink. Then parboil the potatoes for 5–7 minutes before roasting, shaking them gently in the pan after draining so that the outside surface becomes soft and flaky. This will allow them to absorb the fat better, essential for a good crust. Alternatively, you can rough up the surface of parboiled potatoes with the tines of a fork.

Roast the potatoes in meat dripping rather than oil and start them in a little lard or dripping, adding fat from the joint as it collects in the baking dish. Regular turning of the potatoes in the fat is important for a good crust – do it every 20 minutes, as you baste the meat.

It is a sad fact that there is no vegetarian alternative to perfect roast potatoes; oil tends to toughen the outside more than animal fats.

Temperature and timing are not crucial – both can be adapted to suit what is required for the meat the potatoes will accompany. If they are to go with small joints it may be advisable to start roasting the potatoes before the meat and allow at least an hour in all.

The most luxurious potatoes of all are those roasted in goose fat. Keep the fat from the dish in which you have roasted a goose or if you remove any solid fat from the bird before roasting, melt it slowly and then store it in a covered container in the refrigerator. Goose fat is also sold in cans, and you can save the surplus fat from a can or jar of Confit d'Oie (goose preserved in its own fat). Duck and pork fat are almost as good as goose fat. The recipe here for roasted potatoes is excellent with roast chicken.

Roast potatoes with a sesame seed crust

SERVES: *6*
PREPARATION TIME: *20 minutes (while oven preheats)*
COOKING TIME: *about 1½ hours*

1 kg floury maincrop potatoes, peeled
Salt
3 tablespoons sesame seeds
100 g lard, dripping or chicken fat

1 Preheat the oven to 200°C. Cut the potatoes into evenly sized pieces then bring them to the boil in a large pan of salted water and keep at a low, rolling boil for 5 minutes. Drain and leave until cool enough to handle.
2 Pull the tines of a fork over the surface of each potato to score it. Roll each potato in sesame seeds.
3 Melt the fat in a large baking dish in the hot oven. Turn the potatoes in the fat a few times then roast them for about 1½ hours, turning the potatoes again every 20 minutes or so until they are brown and crispy.

FEWER KILOJOULES

Are there any low-fat fillings for jacket potatoes that sink into the flesh instead of just sit on top?

Sadly, no. It is fat that sinks into the flesh, softening it and giving flavour. Low-fat yoghurts or cottage cheese are just not as effective or as delicious as butter. However, there are some good fillings that turn a jacket potato into a meal.
• A poached or a soft-boiled egg slipped inside a split baked potato makes a satisfying supper, as the yolk spills nicely into the flesh. For a more elaborate treatment, spoon

out the cooked potato flesh, then season and mash it. Separate a raw egg, beat the yolk into the mashed potato (with some cheese, too, if you like), then whisk the egg white firmly and fold in. Spoon back into the potato shells and return to a hot oven to rise soufflé-style.
• For vegetarians, baked potatoes can be topped with cucumber and celery in sour cream or yoghurt and sprinkled with chopped nuts.
• Smoked cod in white sauce is good in baked potatoes, as is taramasalata with diced cucumber.
• Scoop out the flesh from split baked potatoes, then mash diced grilled bacon into it plus chopped red onion. Spoon back into the shells, top with grated cheese and return to the oven to heat through and melt the cheese. Serve with hot beetroot or green vegetables.
• Baked jacket potatoes to accompany a stew can be split and served with a spoonful of the meat juices or gravy to moisten and flavour them.
• Olive oil and mashed anchovy makes a pungent filling, or try sour cream with some chopped onion in it and a topping of caviar.

QUICK OR CRISP?

Why are potatoes baked in the microwave so disappointing?

It is not possible to truly bake a potato in a microwave oven. When a potato is properly baked, the heat of the oven reaches the skin first, drying it and sealing in the potato's natural moisture so that the flesh steams as the skin crisps. This delicious contrast of textures cannot be achieved in a microwave oven, which merely cooks the potato.

You can bake small-sized baking potatoes relatively quickly, in about 30 minutes, in a hot oven; they will cook even quicker if you push a metal skewer through them. Alternatively, if you own a convection microwave, compromise and use the combination facility. For best results and to achieve a delicious contrast between crisp skin and soft interior, rub the potato skins

with sea salt while they are still damp from washing. Baked potatoes are done when you can press them and feel that the flesh inside is soft and yielding.

TWICE-COOKED POTATOES

What are the potato skins I see on restaurant menus, and can I make them at home?

Dishes based on potato skins are a good way for restaurants to make use of the skins left over from making mashed potatoes. It is time-consuming to make potato skins at home, but they are delicious.

A good method is to bake potatoes in the oven until soft, let them cool, then cut them in half and scoop out most of the flesh. The skins can then be cut into pieces and shallow fried until crisp, or oven-roasted in a little oil until well browned.

Serve with salsa, cheese or sour cream and snipped chives.

SKINS ON

What is the best way to boil potatoes?

It is always best to boil potatoes in their skins, even if they are to be mashed. Not only does this help to prevent the flesh from absorbing too much cooking water, it also conserves vitamins which are concentrated in or just below the skin. Serve the potatoes whole in their skins or, for mashing, peel them as soon as the cooked potatoes are cool enough to handle.

An alternative, particularly at the end of the season when they tend to absorb more moisture, is to oven-bake the potatoes in their skins and then mash them. This is a common practice commercially.

It is always worth making extra mashed potatoes as the leftovers are very good for thickening soups, making potato scones, fish cakes, bubble and squeak or hashes, or for topping shepherd's and fish pies. Alternatively, blend leftover mashed potato into the following small, hot, savoury cheese puffs.

Whisked egg whites lighten this savoury mixture of cheese, potatoes and spring onions, which is cooked in patty cake tins.

Cheese potato puffs

SERVES: 4-6 as a snack, with salad garnish as a first course, or with grilled sausages for a main course
PREPARATION TIME: *20 minutes*
COOKING TIME: *15 minutes*

---

500 g mashed potatoes
4 spring onions, finely shredded
50 g mature Cheddar cheese, finely grated
3 tablespoons milk
30 g butter
Salt and black pepper
Grated nutmeg, to taste
2 large eggs, separated

---

1 Preheat the oven to 220°C and generously butter a nonstick patty cake tin, also greasing the sections between the holes.
2 Mix the mashed potatoes, spring onions and cheese in a bowl.
3 Warm the milk and butter with salt, pepper and nutmeg, swirling the saucepan to help melt the butter. Heat to just below boiling point, then beat the milk into the potato mixture and beat in the egg yolks.
4 Whisk the egg whites to form soft peaks, mix a spoonful or two into the potato mixture to loosen it, then fold in the rest as lightly as possible.
5 Spoon the mixture into the patty cake tins and bake for about 15 minutes until golden brown and well risen.

HAND BEATEN

What is the secret of perfect mash with no lumpy bits? Can I use a blender or processor to keep my arms from aching?

No, unfortunately all electric tools seem to produce mashed potatoes with the gluey texture of wallpaper paste. The easiest way to a lump-free mash is some hard work with a potato masher, or to put the pota-toes through a food mill. Additions such as olive oil, cream, butter and milk should be added while the potatoes are warm, along with sea-sonings of salt, pepper and nutmeg. Vigorous beating is what lightens the mash and at the final stage you could possibly use an electric beater set on a slow speed.

As an alternative to mashing, try riced potatoes, positively lump-free. A potato ricer, available from catering shops and good kitchen-ware departments, looks rather like a giant garlic press and crushes whole, cooked potatoes, extruding them in a light snow.

Rice the potatoes directly into the serving bowl, adding butter and seasonings to the layers as you go. Riced potatoes can be reheated in their bowl, but stirring will sacri-fice their lightness. You can mash or rice the potatoes for the gnocchi recipe on page 280.

Potato gnocchi in Gorgonzola sauce

SERVES: *4*
PREPARATION TIME: *15 minutes*
COOKING TIME: *30-40 minutes*

500g King Edward or other floury
    maincrop potatoes
1 large egg, lightly beaten
150g (1¼ cups) plain flour
3 tablespoons milk
30g butter
150g Gorgonzola cheese, cubed
125ml fresh cream
4 tablespoons finely grated
    Parmesan cheese
Black pepper and freshly grated
    nutmeg
To garnish: basil leaves

---

1 Boil the potatoes in their skins in salted water, or bake in the oven until tender. Drain and skin as soon as they are cool enough to handle.
2 Mash or rice the potatoes and beat in the egg and most of the flour.
3 Spread the remaining flour thickly on a work surface and gently knead the potato dough on it, gradually incorporating all of the flour.
4 Divide the kneaded dough into two and lightly roll each section into a cylinder about 36 cm long.
5 Cut each cylinder of dough into pieces 1.5 cm long. Flatten each one slightly with the tines of a fork to create some ridges.
6 In a small saucepan warm the milk, butter and Gorgonzola, stirring steadily, swirling the pan to melt the cubed cheese. Add the cream and half the Parmesan. Bring to the boil, season with pepper and nutmeg, reduce the heat and keep warm.
7 Heat a serving dish in the oven. Bring a large pan of water just to simmering point (do not let it boil). Cook the gnocchi in two or three batches, lifting them out using a slotted spoon 15-20 seconds after they float to the surface.
8 Transfer to the warmed serving dish and trickle some cheese sauce over each batch, stacking them on the dish as they are cooked. Scatter over the remaining Parmesan and garnish the dish with basil just before serving.

TROPICAL TUBERS

Is there a difference between a sweet potato and a yam?

Yes. Sweet potatoes and yams are members of two different botanical families. Sweet potatoes (*Ipomoea batatus*) come from the tropical areas of the Americas and have a distinctive sweetness, particularly the pink-skinned, orange-fleshed variety, also known as kumara. There are also some sweeter white or yellow-fleshed varieties grown in the tropics.

Though sweet potatoes are native to tropical America, they also found their way to New Zealand and Asia, and hot baked sweet potatoes are sold in winter on the streets of many Chinese and Japanese cities.

The yam (*Dioscorea*), is a large, brown-skinned starchy root that can weigh over 5 kg. Its bland yellow or white flesh is a perfect partner for spicy stews in the parts of Africa, Asia and the Caribbean where yams are a staple ingredient.

NICE AND SWEET

When I boil sweet potatoes, why do they sometimes go mushy and taste disappointing?

Sweet potatoes are less firm than ordinary white potatoes and lose much of their flavour into the cooking water when boiled. They also have a tendency to absorb a lot of water when cooked this way, making them heavy and soggy.

They are much better when they are baked like ordinary baked potatoes, although sweet potatoes will cook more quickly. Split them and serve oozing with butter, salt and plenty of black pepper or paprika. Baked sweet potatoes also tend to benefit from the addition of a little cinnamon and brown sugar. Try baking then mashing them to make a topping for shepherd's pie.

Sweet potatoes make very good chips, either deep-fried or oven-baked, and can be sliced thickly, brushed with butter and grilled, a treatment which is very good with venison steaks or duck breasts.

Prawns

RAW PRAWNS

I thought all prawns were sold already cooked; is this true?

Not always. In Australia, most prawns are sold cooked in their shell, but some are cooked and shelled before sale. Prawns that are sold raw, or uncooked, are known as green prawns, and are usually still in their shell.

When buying green prawns, look for a firm body, a pleasant sea smell and no blackness. When buying cooked prawns, look for firm flesh, tight shells, no blackness and a pleasant smell.

Prawns that have already been cooked only need heating through when they are added to a dish.

WHOLE DELICACY

Peeling small prawns seems very fiddly. Is it always necessary?

Not always. One of the nicest ways to eat small pink prawns, known as school prawns, is as the Greek islanders do: fried in unsalted butter and olive oil. You bite off the body and eat it shell and all, discarding only the head. Small prawns must be peeled for potted prawns, which are sealed under a thick layer of clarified butter (see recipe in *Preserving*).

NICE LOOKS, FINE TASTE

Is it better to buy large prawns for Asian recipes?

It depends on the recipe. If visual impact is important, the large seawater prawns, usually called king prawns or tiger prawns, look spectacular and are impressive grilled.

However, smaller river, bay and estuary prawns have a finer flavour. Use them in fish stews and curries where size is less of an issue, such as in the following recipe for Thai Prawn Curry. Here the prawn shells are also used to contribute to the flavour of the stock.

Thai prawn curry

SERVES: 4
PREPARATION TIME: 25 minutes
COOKING TIME: 30 minutes

---

750 g cooked prawns in their shells
7.5 cm piece fresh green ginger
2 stems lemon grass, bruised and
    chopped
Salt
100 g creamed coconut block,
    grated, or 200 ml canned coconut
    cream
1 onion, chopped
3 cloves garlic
1 teaspoon ground coriander
1 teaspoon ground cumin
1 teaspoon ground turmeric
3 tablespoons cooking oil
3 large green chillies, deseeded
    and cut into long, thin strips
Juice of 1 lime
2 tablespoons chopped coriander
    leaves
To serve: boiled rice, prawn crackers

---

1 Shell the prawns and put the shells into a small saucepan. Peel the ginger and add the peel to the shells. Set the remaining ginger aside.
2 Add the lemon grass and a little salt to the prawn shells with cold water just to cover. Bring to the boil and simmer the shells, uncovered, for 15 minutes. Strain the stock through a sieve, mashing the solids with a spoon to extract the flavour before you discard them.
3 Put the grated coconut or coconut cream into a measuring jug and stir in enough hot prawn stock to make 500 ml. Stir the mixture until the coconut is dissolved.
4 Put the peeled ginger, onion, garlic, coriander, cumin, turmeric and half the oil, plus 3 tablespoons of cold water, into a food processor and blend to a paste.
5 Put the remaining oil into a large pan. Add the chillies and spice paste, and stir-fry gently for 2–3 minutes until it becomes more aromatic.
6 Stir in the coconut liquid and lime juice and cook the sauce at a low boil, stirring it regularly, for 10–15 minutes until the sauce has thickened. Add the prawns and cook just until heated through.

You can use full-flavoured cooked prawns for this spicy blend of green chillies, coriander and coconut. Accompany the curry with rice and prawn crackers.

7 Adjust the seasoning and serve the prawn curry scattered with some chopped coriander and accompanied by rice and prawn crackers.

NEW IDEAS

I enjoy prawns in starters but would like a change from prawn cocktail. Have you got any ideas?

Prawns work very well with Asian flavouring ingredients and can be quickly stir-fried or grilled on skewers with flavourings such as chilli, garlic, honey and soy sauce. A seafood kebab, perhaps with bacon, is another way the flavour of prawns can be highlighted.

Stirred with a few tablespoons of tomato-flavoured mayonnaise, prawns make a good filling for avocados or omelettes. Alternatively, scatter them over a fanned avocado half and serve with a vinaigrette dressing, or use in a salad with mango slices, lettuce and tomato.

Preserving

PRESERVING IN OIL

I love red peppers preserved in oil; is it safe to preserve my own?

Vegetables preserved in the Mediterranean fashion, using olive oil, are safe provided you take strict precautions as there is a slight risk of botulism with food preserved in oil. Botulism is caused by a bacteria that lives in the soil; it does not penetrate the vegetable, but could be present in any soil particle clinging to it and thrives in the absence of air. So foods to be preserved in oil must first be washed carefully. Any that grow underground, such as garlic, are most at risk of being contaminated.

After washing, the foods must be processed in some way to remove their excess water, otherwise they will deteriorate. Baby artichokes are cooked in a vinegar solution; eggplants are salted then cooked in a vinegar solution; mushrooms can be dried or cooked; olives are salted; peppers are roasted; and tomatoes are dried.

Even after the foods have been processed, it is important to bring all the ingredients to boiling point. A squeeze of lemon juice or splash of vinegar, which are acidic, also lowers the risk of contamination. Commercial preparations, such as sun-dried tomatoes in oil, are all ultra heat treated (UHT).

Always use sterilised jars (see **Chutney**) and seal them tightly, and store the preserves in the refrigerator for no more than two months. Refrigeration may cause the oil to solidify, but it will clear again when left at room temperature. Once the preserve has been eaten, the flavoured oil can be used for drizzling over bread or salads, or for basting grilled meats and fish.

Unlike vegetables, cheese does not need cooking before being preserved; feta and goat's cheeses are favourites for preserving in this way, as the following recipe shows.

Goat's cheese with herbs

MAKES: 2 x 750 ml preserving jars
PREPARATION TIME: 10–15 minutes
COOKING TIME: none

---

750 g fresh, firm goat's cheese
½ teaspoon finely crushed
* black peppercorns*
4 teaspoons dried mixed herbs
Whole peppercorns, sprigs of herbs
* and 1–2 bay leaves, optional*
750 ml olive oil
150 ml walnut oil

---

1 Cut the goat's cheese into 2.5 cm chunks. Sprinkle over the peppercorns and herbs; pat lightly. Transfer the cheese into sterilised jars, adding more peppercorns, herbs and a bay leaf or two if liked.
2 Mix the olive and walnut oils well, then pour over the cheese, making sure it is completely covered.

3 Seal the jars tightly and store in the refrigerator. Take the jars out of the refrigerator about an hour before you are ready to serve the cheese to bring it to room temperature.

The cheese is best eaten within one month.

POTTED FOR STORAGE

What exactly are potted fish and meats?

Potting is a technique in which cooked meat, fish and shellfish are preserved in fat in small earthenware pots for a wintertime treat. The meat or fish is spiced and then puréed or finely chopped before potting. It is then encased in clarified butter or fat to exclude air and moisture, which would encourage the growth of bacteria. Unopened jars can be stored in the refrigerator

Herb-dusted goat's cheese preserved in olive oil brings a touch of sunshine to the table. Mixed peppercorns, sprigs of herbs and bay leaves add extra piquancy.

for up to a fortnight depending on the meat or fish used. Once the fatty seal has been broken, the contents should be consumed within one or two days.

Although most potted meat or fish is puréed, baby prawns are often left whole, as in the recipe below. If you cannot get tiny prawns, use the larger ones and chop them roughly.

Potted prawns

SERVES: *4*
PREPARATION TIME: *5 minutes, plus 1-2 hours cooling and chilling*
COOKING TIME: *15 minutes*

250 g unsalted butter
375 g baby prawns, cooked and peeled
½ teaspoon ground mace
A generous pinch each of cayenne pepper and freshly grated nutmeg
A pinch of salt

1 Melt 185 g of the butter in a saucepan. Remove from the heat and leave to stand for a few minutes to allow the sediment to settle. Pour off the clear liquid into a clean pan, leaving as much of the sediment as possible in the first pan.
2 Stir the spices into the clarified butter, cover and heat gently for 2 minutes. Remove from the heat; add the prawns and allow them to soak up some of the spiced butter. Sprinkle on salt to taste.
3 Put an equal amount of prawns and clarified butter into four sterilised ramekins and set them aside to cool thoroughly. When completely cold, chill until the butter is firm.
4 Melt the remaining butter, let it stand for a few minutes to allow the sediment to settle and pour the clear liquid over the prawns to seal. Leave to cool, then chill once more until the butter is completely set. Cover with foil or plastic wrap, then store in the refrigerator for up to a week.
5 Before serving, leave the mixture to soften at room temperature for about 30 minutes. Serve the potted prawns with thinly sliced buttered brown bread, toast or warm damper, and lemon wedges.

FRENCH PRESERVES

What are rillettes?

Rillettes are a type of preserved meat. The meat is gently cooked in fat, strained, shredded into a coarse pâté, packed into jars or terrines and covered with a fresh layer of fat. Originally from south-western France, rillettes may be made from pork, goose or rabbit, though pork is the most common. Rillettes will keep for a month unopened in the refrigerator, and improve in flavour during that time. Eat with French bread and small pickled gherkins.

Pumpkins and Squashes

SEASONAL VARIATIONS

What is the best way to cook pumpkins and squashes?

This large family of vegetables has both summer and winter varieties. Summer squashes such as zucchinis, marrows and the small patty pan squashes generally have thin green or yellow skins and moist, subtly flavoured white flesh. They need only light steaming, grilling or stir-frying and a sprinkling of salt, pepper and fresh herbs.

Winter varieties, which include both small and large pumpkins, have dense yellow or orange flesh within their hard skins. They respond well to vigorous flavours. Add to a casserole, or use in well-spiced, thick winter soups, such as the one that follows.

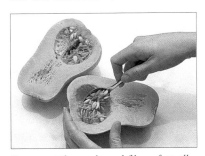

Scoop out the seeds and fibre of small pumpkins, then cut up and peel the flesh before cooking if you like.

Spiced butternut and millet soup

SERVES: *6*
PREPARATION TIME: *20-25 minutes*
COOKING TIME: *35 minutes*

1 kg butternut pumpkin or other winter squash or pumpkin
3 tablespoons vegetable oil
1 large onion, finely chopped
2-3 cloves garlic, finely chopped
5 cm piece green ginger, grated
2 dried red chillies, crumbled
2 bay leaves
1 teaspoon mustard seeds
1 teaspoon cumin seeds
50 g (¼ cup) millet
Salt and black pepper
3 tablespoons tomato sauce
Juice of 1 lemon
2 teaspoons garam masala
To garnish: 1 bunch watercress, chopped

1 Cut the pumpkin in half, remove and discard the seeds and fibre, chop the flesh into chunks and peel them.
2 Heat the oil in a heavy-based pan and fry the onion, garlic, ginger and chillies over a low heat for 5 minutes.
3 Add 1.75 litres of water to the pan. Grate the pumpkin and add with the bay leaves. Bring to the boil and simmer for 10 minutes, or until the pumpkin is soft, then mash.
4 Dry-fry the mustard, cumin and millet over a medium heat until the millet looks mildly toasted and the mustard seeds have mostly popped.
5 Tip the spiced millet into the soup, sprinkle on some salt and simmer for about 15 minutes until the millet is soft. Remove from the heat and leave to stand for at least 10 minutes.
6 When you are ready to serve the soup, remove the bay leaves and stir in the tomato sauce, lemon juice, garam masala and a generous sprinkling of pepper. Stir in the watercress, reheat, and serve.

VEGETABLE PASTA

What is spaghetti squash?

Spaghetti squash, sometimes also called vegetable spaghetti, looks like a yellow-skinned marrow with a harder rind. When it is cooked and split open the flesh falls into a mass of tangled strands.

To cook it, break off the stem and pierce that end deeply to stop the squash bursting during cooking, then boil or bake for about 40 minutes until the flesh feels tender when pierced with a skewer. Split the squash lengthways and fork out the strands. Serve with a meat or tomato-based sauce as you would pasta.

YOUNG, TENDER MARROW

A neighbour occasionally gives me one of his home-grown marrows, but I can't find any interesting recipes for them. Can you tell me how to make them flavoursome?

Marrows are often allowed to grow too large, and end up watery and bland. Smaller marrows, measuring less than 30 cm, have much more flavour. They can be stuffed with rice or minced meat and baked in a moderate oven for 30–45 minutes, or cut into small pieces, gently fried in olive oil with some garlic and sprinkled with parsley.

Large marrows can be made into well-spiced and fruited chutneys or combined with ginger to make a surprisingly good jam.

SWEET AND FILLING

I have tried pumpkin scones. Is that the only way to turn savoury pumpkin into something sweet?

Pumpkin scones are a traditional Australian favourite, while pumpkin pie is – for many people – even more American than apple pie. To make a spicy yet supersweet dessert pie, you can use any pumpkin you prefer in the following recipe.

Spicy pumpkin pie

SERVES: 8
PREPARATION TIME: 45 minutes
COOKING TIME: 50–55 minutes

---

250 g pâte sucrée (see page 354)

FOR THE FILLING AND TOPPING
125 g (⅔ cup) light brown sugar
1 teaspoon ground cinnamon
½ teaspoon ground ginger
¼ teaspoon ground nutmeg
2 large eggs
150 ml fresh cream
250 g (1 cup) mashed cooked
    pumpkin
Icing sugar, to dust
200 ml thickened cream
To decorate: grated nutmeg and
    chopped pecans

---

1 Make the pâte sucré according to directions and chill for 30 minutes. Preheat the oven to 200°C.
2 For the filling, combine the sugar, cinnamon, ginger and nutmeg in a small bowl and mix well. Beat the eggs until smooth. Stir in the cream. Add the pumpkin and sugar mixture and stir gently until combined.
3 Roll out the pastry on a lightly floured surface to a round large enough to line a 23 cm loose-bottomed flan tin. Trim off the excess pastry by rolling over the top of the tin with a rolling pin.
4 Prick the base of the pastry case and line with greaseproof paper and a layer of baking beans. Bake blind for 10 minutes. Remove the paper and beans. Reduce the oven temperature to 180°C.
5 Pour the pumpkin filling into the pastry case. Bake for a further 40–45 minutes, or until the filling is set. Stand the flan tin on a wire cooling rack to cool completely.
6 Just before serving, dust the pie with icing suger.
7 Whip the cream in a chilled bowl until soft peaks form. Spoon a dollop of the cream on top of each slice and sprinkle the nutmeg and pecans over the cream to decorate.

Simple yet sensational: the humble pumpkin is combined with traditional sweet spices in this dessert pie.

Punch

WELL-MIXED DRINK

How much punch should I allow per person, and what will the alcohol content of each glass be?

When punch is served as a welcoming drink to arriving guests, one or two 250 ml glasses will be sufficient. If punch is to be the only alcoholic drink served, guests will probably drink three to four glasses each. But because most punches are sweetened, people tend not to go on drinking them all night, usually preferring to switch to wine, beer or spirits, given the chance.

The alcohol content will depend on whether the punch is made with wine alone or has added spirits, and on how much – or how little – the alcohol has been diluted. Note that a cold punch, such as the one below, will be more intoxicating than a hot one made with the same amount of alcohol, as some of the alcohol will have cooked off the hot one during the heating.

Chilled, as above, or mulled, this fruity and powerful punch is welcome at any time of the year. Cinnamon and cloves spice the blend of brandy, rum and wine.

Chilled wine punch

MAKES: 8 glasses
PREPARATION TIME: 30 minutes, plus 3 hours chilling time
COOKING TIME: 5 minutes

---

1 large orange
2 large lemons
600 ml water
125 g (½ cup) white sugar
7.5 cm stick cinnamon
4 cloves
185 g fresh pineapple, cubed or cut into wedges
150 ml brandy
150 ml rum
1 lime, thinly sliced
750 ml full-bodied red wine, such as a shiraz, chilled
12 ice cubes

---

1 Wash the orange and lemons under warm running water. Pare the rind of the orange and one of the lemons finely, then squeeze and strain their juice. Thinly slice the other lemon.

2 Pour the water into a stainless-steel or enamel pan. Add the orange and lemon rind, sugar, cinnamon and cloves and stir over a medium heat until the sugar has dissolved, then bring to the boil and boil for 2 minutes. Take the pan off the heat, cover and allow to cool. When cold, chill for 3 hours.

3 Put the pineapple into a jug. Add the orange and lemon juice, brandy, rum and the lemon and lime slices, and stir well. Cover the jug with plastic wrap and chill.

4 One hour before serving, strain the spiced sugar syrup through a nylon sieve into the jug. Pour in the wine, stir and chill. Just before you serve the punch, add the ice cubes.

VARIATIONS

For an alcohol-free version, use the juice of two lemons instead of one, and 1 litre of grape juice instead of the wine and spirits.

For a hot punch, allow the sugar syrup to infuse at room temperature for an hour then strain it into a large pan. Add all the remaining ingredients, stir well and heat until the punch becomes very hot, but do not allow it to boil. Serve in punch cups or heatproof glasses.

If you do not have any heatproof glasses, put a metal teaspoon into ordinary glasses before pouring the hot punch: the metal will absorb the heat and prevent the glass cracking.

COCKTAIL EGGS

What is the difference between eggnog and egg flip?

Eggnog is a very rich, chilled punch made with egg, sugar, whisky (or rum or brandy), milk and cream (or all cream), with the egg whites whisked separately and folded in. In the United States, it is traditionally served at Thanksgiving and Christmas, topped with grated nutmeg. Egg flip is a much simpler drink: a whole egg is mixed with sugar and some wine or spirit, and is then strained into a glass and topped with grated nutmeg. It can be made with brandy, Madeira, port, rum, vodka or whisky.

WINTER WARMER

What is a hot toddy?

It is a hot drink made from whisky, brandy or rum and boiling water, with or without added spice, sugar, lemon or orange rind and juice.

Hot toddies are normally thought of as a remedy for colds and flu, but they make a wonderful warming drink to have on any chilly evening. You certainly should not wait until you get a cold to make the following toddy.

A twist of lemon and a cinnamon stick add a sharp bite to sweet hot toddy, the ultimate alcoholic winter warmer.

Hot toddy

SERVES: 2
PREPARATION TIME: 5 minutes
COOKING TIME: none

90 ml brandy, whisky or rum
2 teaspoons dark brown sugar
2 teaspoons runny honey
2 cinnamon sticks, each measuring about 7.5 cm
A strip of thinly pared rind and strained juice of 1 lemon or orange
600 ml boiling water

1 Pour the spirit into two heatproof glasses. Add 1 teaspoon of sugar, 1 teaspoon of honey and 1 cinnamon stick to each glass.
2 Cut the lemon rind in half and add a piece to each glass. Divide the juice between the glasses and top up with boiling water. Stir and serve immediately.

Purées

VEGETABLE VARIATIONS

I love parsnip purée. Can you give me some ideas for other interesting vegetable purées?

Almost any cooked vegetable may be puréed, and the resulting dishes are often lighter, and more attractive and sophisticated than the whole ingredients. First cook the vegetables, either by boiling, steaming, roasting, frying or sweating, then purée them in a food processor or blender, or work them through a sieve. Season well and beat in some butter, cream, white sauce or another vegetable purée.

You can create some interesting combinations, but cook the vegetables separately to retain their full flavour, then purée each individually before mixing together. Some purées, for example carrot, celeriac or spinach, can be rather wet; drive off the excess moisture by cooking them gently while stirring, or add a little mashed potato to stiffen. Purées reheat very well and can be made in advance. Try some of the following combinations:

• BROAD BEAN with butter and chopped fresh summer savory.
• CARROT with pepper, sugar and a touch of grated ginger.
• CAULIFLOWER AND POTATO with a light sprinkling of curry powder, or with cream and nutmeg, baked in a dish with a cheese topping.
• CELERIAC AND POTATO with an added trickle of rich truffle oil.
• MUSHROOM AND ONION mixed with breadcrumbs and baked in scooped-out tomatoes.
• PEAS AND GREEN BEANS with onion, garlic, mint and sugar.
• PUMPKIN or squash with garlic, pepper and sour cream.
• SPINACH AND PEAR with nutmeg and cream, reduced a little.
• SWEETCORN AND POTATO, mixed with egg and grated cheese and fried as pancakes.
• TURNIP, CARROT AND POTATO with butter and garlic.

Quail

TINY TREAT

Quail are so tiny, are they really worth preparing and eating?

The flesh of quail is pale and delicate, and is certainly worth trying. The birds, which are tender and juicy, weigh 125–185 g each. They look small but, like pigeon, have a lot of meat on the breast. Some people find eating whole quail very fiddly, and some butchers and supermarkets are selling part-boned quail, ready for stuffing or already stuffed, which makes them a bigger mouthful. These part-boned quails have the breast bone and rib cage removed but have the legs intact so that when stuffed they will retain the original shape of the bird.

WORKING OUT PORTIONS

How many quails should I allow per person as a main course - or are they simply unsuitable for a main course?

A boned stuffed quail would serve one person, as there really is quite a lot of meat on the breast. However, if not stuffed, allow two per person as a main course. It is worth being generous as quail is equally delicious served cold as a leftover.

Quails are suitable for roasting (as in the following recipe), casseroling, grilling and barbecuing (most chicken recipes will suit them), and will cook in 30 minutes. Serve them with a purée of potato mixed with mashed parsnip or carrot, or golden potato croquettes.

Quail with apples and raisins

SERVES: 4
PREPARATION TIME: 15 minutes, plus 1-2 hours soaking time
COOKING TIME: 30 minutes

75 g (⅓ cup) seedless raisins
2 tablespoons brandy
2 small apples
1 teaspoon fresh thyme leaves
8 quails
185 ml unsweetened apple juice
300 ml chicken stock
Black pepper

1 Place the raisins in a basin, pour over the brandy and leave to soak for 1-2 hours, until plump.
2 Preheat the oven to 220°C. Core and chop the apples, leaving the skins intact. Add the apples to the raisins with the thyme and mix well. Use this mixture to stuff the quails; place the birds in an ovenproof dish.
3 Pour over the apple juice and stock and season with pepper. Roast the birds for 30 minutes, basting two or three times with the liquid. Preheat a serving dish.
4 Transfer the birds to the serving dish, then cover and keep warm. Strain the cooking liquid into a pan and boil rapidly to reduce by half. Pour it around the quails and serve.

Quenelles

SOFT AND TENDER

What are quenelles?

Traditionally, quenelles were small portions of savoury fish mousse, traditionally shaped like an elongated rugby ball with a flat bottom, poached and served as a starter or light meal. The term is occasionally used for sweet confections, but is usually reserved for savoury mixtures of fish, poultry or vegetables. In the recipe (right), delicate spinach and cheese quenelles are served on a robust tomato sauce.

When cooking quenelles, it is important to poach them gently so that they will not break up.

Spinach and ricotta quenelles

SERVES: 6 as a starter
PREPARATION TIME: 20 minutes, plus infusing time
COOKING TIME: 10 minutes

FOR THE QUENELLES
175 g spinach
250 g ricotta cheese
50 g Parmesan cheese, finely grated
1 large egg, lightly beaten
Salt and black pepper
A pinch of freshly ground nutmeg

FOR THE SAUCE
125 ml virgin olive oil
2 cloves garlic, flattened but not crushed
8 egg tomatoes, peeled, deseeded and finely chopped
1 bunch basil, finely chopped, reserving a few leaves for garnish
Salt and black pepper

1 To make the sauce, gently heat the oil and garlic together in a pan. Before the oil gets very hot, remove it from the heat and leave to infuse for 10 minutes to 1 hour, depending on how strong you want the flavour.
2 To make the quenelles, rinse the spinach, put it into a pan with no added water and cook for 3 minutes. Drain well, pressing out as much liquid as possible, and chop finely.
3 Put a large pan of salted water to heat and bring up to simmering point. Mix the spinach, cheeses and egg together in a bowl and add salt, pepper and nutmeg to taste.
4 Using two dessertspoons, form the mixture into 12 ovals resembling small Cornish pasties. Lower them gently into the barely simmering water until the pan is comfortably full (poach two batches if you need to). Poach them very gently until they float back up to the surface, in about 3-4 minutes. Remove from the pan with a slotted spoon, drain off any excess liquid, and keep warm.
5 To complete the sauce, remove the garlic from the oil. Stir in the tomato and basil and season to taste.
6 Pour the sauce onto six plates and place the quenelles on top. Garnish with the reserved basil and serve.

Quiche

VERSATILE SAVOURY

What is the difference between a quiche and a flan and a tart?

Quiche is the French name for an open savoury flan or savoury tart. A quiche, a flan and a tart are much the same thing as they all require a crisp pastry shell to enclose the filling. A flan or tart, however, can have a savoury or a sweet filling, whereas a quiche usually has only a savoury filling.

The recipe for Quiche Lorraine that follows is a classic from which many variations can be made. The custard remains the same.

Quiche Lorraine

SERVES: *4–6*
PREPARATION TIME: *30 minutes, plus 30 minutes chilling time*
COOKING TIME: *45–50 minutes*

FOR THE PASTRY
185 g (1½ cups) plain flour
90 g butter, diced
1½ tablespoons chilled water

FOR THE FILLING
6 rashers bacon
1 teaspoon butter
2 large eggs
2 egg yolks, extra
250 ml cream
¼ teaspoon salt
¼ teaspoon white pepper
125 g Swiss cheese, grated
Fresh herbs to garnish

1 Sift the flour into a mixing bowl. Add the butter and rub in with the fingertips until the mixture resembles fine breadcrumbs. Add sufficient of the chilled water to mix to form a stiff dough. Shape into a flat disc; wrap securely in greaseproof paper and chill for 30 minutes.
2 Preheat the oven to 200°C.
3 For the filling, cut the rind and the excess fat from the bacon. Cut the bacon into 5 mm squares with kitchen scissors. Heat the butter in a frying pan and cook the bacon over a medium heat until crisp and golden. Drain on kitchen paper towels and set aside.
4 Whisk the eggs, egg yolks, cream and salt and pepper together. Stir in the grated cheese.
5 Roll out the pastry and use to line a 20 cm loose-bottomed flan tin (see *Flans*). Line the pastry with greaseproof paper and a layer of baking beans. Bake the pastry blind for 10 minutes, remove the greaseproof paper and beans, return the pastry to the oven and bake for a further 5 minutes.
6 Sprinkle the bacon over the base of the pastry case. Carefully pour the egg mixture over the bacon. Reduce the oven temperature to 190°C and bake for 25–30 minutes, or until the filling is set and puffed. Serve immediately, garnished with the fresh herbs.

Quinces

MYSTERIOUS FRUIT

What are quinces, and what can I do with them? Can I buy them in the shops, or do I have to grow them myself?

The large, golden-yellow, apple or pear-shaped quince is thought to have originated in western Asia, although it is now also grown in Europe. It has yellow flesh that is slightly tart and turns pink when cooked. Because the flesh is too hard to eat raw, quinces must be cooked for about 30–40 minutes in a sugar syrup. They can then be eaten as plain poached fruit or used as a pie filling.

Quinces are very high in pectin, so are ideal for jam and jelly making. Quince jelly is an excellent accompaniment to pork, poultry and game, or cold meats.

When they are in season, from March until about June, quinces can be bought from good greengrocers and large supermarkets. Of course, if you grow your own, the supply is guaranteed.

SOMETHING DIFFERENT

I was served quince paste recently with a cheese platter at a restaurant, and enjoyed the combination. Can I make this paste at home?

Yes. Quince paste is a Persian delicacy usually served as a sweetmeat or petit four with after-dinner coffee, but it also goes exceptionally well with cheeses.

The paste is available ready-made from continental delicatessens and good food shops, but is easy to make at home. Serve it cut in thin slices on the cheese platter with a few fresh dates to emphasise the Middle Eastern theme.

Quince paste

SERVES: *8*
PREPARATION TIME: *30 minutes, plus drying time*
COOKING TIME: *approximately 30 minutes*

1 kg quinces
500 g (2 cups) white sugar
Juice of 1 lemon

1 Wash and dry the quinces, then cut into quarters and place in a saucepan. Add 60 ml water and cook, covered, for about 30–40 minutes or until soft.
2 Meanwhile, put the sugar, lemon juice and 125 ml water into a saucepan; place over a low heat until dissolved. Simmer for 5 minutes, or until the syrup is thickened.
3 Rub the quinces through a fine strainer and discard the skin and the core.
4 Add the quince purée to the syrup and cook over a very low heat, stirring constantly, until the paste is thick enough to come away from the base of the pan, about 15 minutes.
5 Spoon the paste onto a baking tray and spread out evenly. Leave the paste to dry in a warm sunny spot for several days, or in a very low oven, until set like a very firm jelly.
6 Wrap in plastic wrap or foil and store in a cool, dry place. Serve the paste with cheese or coffee at the end of a meal.

Quinoa

HIGH-PROTEIN SUPERGRAIN

I have recently seen a food I did not know called quinoa. What is it, and how is it cooked?

Quinoa is a small grain indigenous to South America. It has a very high protein content, which has led to it being described as a 'supergrain', but you might find its flavour slightly bitter. When cooked, the grains swell to double their size.

Quinoa makes a good substitute for rice, can be added to stuffings, served in a salad (as in the recipe, right) or sweetened with sugar as a breakfast cereal. It tends to become soggy when cooked immersed in boiling water. It is best to soak the grains for a few hours, preferably overnight, and then steam them for 8–12 minutes depending on how long they have been soaked.

Spiced quinoa salad with grilled peppers

SERVES: *4*
PREPARATION TIME: *20 minutes, plus overnight soaking*
COOKING TIME: *25 minutes*

250 g (1½ cups) quinoa
2 large red or yellow peppers
90 ml olive oil
1 onion, chopped
1 clove garlic, crushed
1 small red chilli, deseeded and chopped
1 teaspoon ground coriander
1 teaspoon ground cumin
½ teaspoon ground cinnamon
2 tomatoes, peeled, deseeded and chopped
2 tablespoons red wine vinegar
2 tablespoons chopped fresh coriander
Salt and black pepper

1 Wash the quinoa, then transfer it to a bowl, cover it well with cold water and leave to soak overnight.

2 The next day, grill the peppers for about 15-20 minutes, turning them often until charred all over. Transfer them to a dish, cover and set aside until cool enough to handle.

3 While the peppers are under the grill, drain the quinoa and transfer it to a muslin-lined steamer. Cook it, covered, over simmering water for about 10 minutes until the grains are puffed up and tender, then set aside.

4 Heat 2 tablespoons of the oil in a frying pan and fry the onion, garlic, chilli and spices for 5 minutes until tender. Transfer to a bowl and stir in the tomatoes and quinoa.

5 Peel and deseed the peppers over a bowl to catch the juices. Chop the flesh and stir it into the quinoa, then add the pepper juices, the rest of the olive oil, the vinegar and chopped coriander, and season to taste. Serve warm or allow to cool.

Protein-rich quinoa is the basis for an aromatic salad, where the grain's slight bitterness is balanced by sweet peppers.

Rabbit

PORTION SIZE

How much meat is there on a rabbit? How much do I need to buy to feed four people?

A medium-sized farmed rabbit will weigh around 1.25 kg and will serve up to three people. If you want to serve four generously, allow 350 g of meat on the bone for each person. If you cannot find a large enough rabbit, cook two small ones, or buy extra joints. Wild rabbits are usually slightly smaller than farmed ones.

STRENGTH OF FLAVOUR

How can I make the most of the flavour of rabbit?

Farmed rabbit does not have a strong flavour at all but tastes rather like chicken and can be cooked using most chicken recipes. Rabbit also cooks very well in a clay pot where it will benefit tremendously by being cooked with strong flavourings such as garlic, herbs, onions, red wine and tomatoes. Mustard is another good partner, as the recipe on the right shows.

Wild rabbit, however, has a more gamy flavour and is better suited to long, slow, gentle cooking with strongly flavoured sauces. As wild rabbit tends to be dry, it is wise to marinate it in ingredients such as olive oil, red wine and herbs for at least 4 hours before cooking.

Tender fresh rabbit makes a warming casserole with shallots, fresh thyme and a creamy French mustard sauce.

Mustard rabbit

SERVES: 4
PREPARATION TIME: 10 minutes, plus 1 hour marinating
COOKING TIME: 1½ hours

1.25–1.5 kg rabbit joints, cleaned and skinned
4 tablespoons Dijon mustard
600 ml dry white wine
1 bay leaf
2 teaspoons chopped fresh thyme
60 g butter
12 shallots, peeled
300 ml fresh cream or crème fraîche
Salt and black pepper
2 tablespoons chopped fresh parsley

1 Spread the rabbit joints with half the mustard, then cover and leave them to marinate for at least an hour.
2 Preheat the oven to 220°C. Place the rabbit pieces in a shallow flameproof casserole (it is not necessary to add any oil) and roast, uncovered, for 30 minutes.
3 Remove from the oven and reduce the temperature to 180°C. Pour the wine over the rabbit and stir well to loosen any sediment. Add the bay leaf and thyme, bring to the boil, cover and return the casserole to the oven for 30-40 minutes, or until the meat is very tender.
4 Meanwhile, in a separate pan, melt the butter and fry the shallots until golden. Set aside.
5 With a slotted spoon, remove the rabbit from the casserole, put it on a warm serving dish, cover and keep warm while you make the sauce.
6 Bring the casserole juices to a boil and cook for 10 minutes or until reduced by half. Lower the heat and stir in the shallots, the remaining mustard and the cream. Simmer the sauce for 10 minutes, or until it has thickened, then remove the bay leaf. Season to taste, stir in half the parsley and pour over the rabbit.
7 Sprinkle the dish with the rest of the parsley then serve with buttered noodles and steamed broccoli.

Radishes

LOOK AT THE LEAVES

Which are the best radishes?

Radishes are at their best during their natural season, summer. They can be red and round, or elongated and white-tipped. The latter are widely preferred for their peppery crunchiness. Solid red radishes can be good if they are not too bloated.

Choose bunched radishes with their leaves attached, as the leaves are a good indicator of freshness. Radishes can be sliced thinly for a green salad, but are perhaps best served in the French manner, as a first course with French bread, unsalted butter and flaky sea salt. They also go well with cold cooked or processed meats.

VERSATILE DAIKON

What is daikon? How is it used?

Daikon is a variety of radish and tastes similar to the red varieties. Also called mooli, white or winter radish, in size and appearance it is more like a parsnip.

Peel and grate or shave it into very thin slices to eat raw in salads. Pickled daikon is popular with Japanese food. Serve daikon as a hot vegetable by cutting it into slices, sprinkling with salt and draining for 30 minutes to remove some of the harshness. Then steam or simmer it until tender and serve hot, tossed with butter or olive oil.

Save it!

Radishes that are just beginning to become soft can be firmed up by a short soak in a bowl of iced water. But if the radishes are very limp, starting to wrinkle and losing their lustre, they are beyond redemption.

Ravioli

SIMPLE BUT NECESSARY

Do ravioli need a sauce?

Ravioli do benefit from being served with a sauce, as otherwise they can be rather dry. The sauce need only be as simple as melted butter to which you have added a few chopped fresh sage leaves, or it can be a combination of cream and butter melted together. This can be made richer with a little cheese, such as Gorgonzola, which has a very pungent flavour and creamy texture. A light tomato sauce is also good and goes with most stuffings. The hearty ravioli in the recipe below, however, stuffed with butternut pumpkin, have enough flavour to need only a simple sauce of melted butter and some freshly grated Parmesan cheese.

Ravioli stuffed with butternut pumpkin

SERVES: 4–6
PREPARATION TIME: 1 hour
COOKING TIME: 10 minutes

FOR THE FILLING
500 g butternut pumpkin, peeled, deseeded and chopped
50 g Parmesan cheese, freshly grated
1 large egg yolk
½ teaspoon freshly grated nutmeg
1 tablespoon fresh white breadcrumbs
½ teaspoon salt
Black pepper

FOR THE PASTA
375 g homemade pasta, thinly rolled into sheets (see Pasta)
To serve: melted butter and freshly grated Parmesan cheese

1 Steam the pumpkin for 10 minutes or microwave it until tender. Drain and press out as much liquid as possible.
2 Mix the pumpkin in a bowl with the cheese, egg yolk, nutmeg, breadcrumbs, salt and pepper.

FILLING RAVIOLI

Making your own fresh ravioli with homemade pasta is easy once you have mastered the technique.

1 Place a sheet of pasta on a work surface and put half-teaspoons of filling at 5 cm intervals.

2 Brush around the filling with water before placing a second sheet of pasta over the top.

3 Press down between the mounds of filling with the side of your hand and cut the sheets into squares using a special fluted pastry cutter.

3 Depending on the size of your pasta sheets, you can either make two rows of small ravioli or one row of bigger ravioli. Fill the ravioli as shown in the panel above.
4 Cook the ravioli uncovered in a large saucepan of boiling salted water for about 5 minutes or until tender. Remove with a slotted spoon and serve with melted butter and grated Parmesan cheese.

VARIATION

Make mushroom ravioli by replacing the pumpkin with 250 g mushrooms which you have chopped and fried with 4 thinly sliced spring onions in 60 g butter for about 10 minutes, or until soft. Stir in 125 g crumbled goat's cheese and black pepper to taste. Add a tablespoon of dried breadcrumbs to the filling mixture to make it firmer.

LEAKPROOF RAVIOLI

If I increase the size of my ravioli, are they more likely to fall apart while they are cooking?

If you seal the edges of your ravioli well, by using water and pressing the edges together firmly, it will help to keep them intact and the size should not make any difference. It is also helpful to roll the pasta as thin as you can and use a fairly thick stuffing. You can always add a few dried breadcrumbs, if necessary, to firm up the filling.

The most usual size for ravioli, and the most practical, is 4–5 cm square. If possible, have the salted water gently boiling in a wide shallow pan and cook the ravioli uncovered. When they are ready, carefully remove them with a slotted spoon rather than turning them out into a colander.

INSIDE INFORMATION

My family is getting bored with the conventional meat filling. Could you suggest some other fillings I could make for ravioli?

A popular Italian combination that will fill 375 g of pasta is made with 300 g of fresh spinach and 150 g of ricotta cheese, 2 tablespoons of grated Parmesan cheese and ½ teaspoon of salt. Wash the spinach and cook it covered, with only the water that is still clinging to the leaves, for 5 minutes. When cool, squeeze out as much liquid as you can and chop finely. Mix with the other ingredients and then use. Any leftovers can be used to stuff large, ripe tomatoes or flat mushrooms and then baked in the oven.

Another simple filling is made with 150 g of ricotta, 40 g freshly grated Parmesan cheese, an egg yolk and 2 tablespoons of finely chopped parsley, mixed together.

If you have any left over once the ravioli have been filled, the mixture can be made into patties or small sausage shapes and gently fried for a minute or two in a little olive oil that has been heated with a garlic clove.

Refrigerators

NEVER ENOUGH

What is the best way to choose and use a new refrigerator?

Buy the largest model that you can afford and that will fit into your kitchen; you can never have enough refrigerator space. Models that defrost automatically are a tremendous bonus, as are frost-free ones where cold air is constantly circulated so frost is never deposited.

• The ideal internal temperature of a refrigerator is 4°C. Some models have different temperature zones to store different foods. For example, the fruit and vegetable section has a higher temperature than the area for meat.

• Most kitchens have only one refrigerator, so it is important that you observe some basic rules of elementary hygiene.

• Always store raw meat and fish in the special meat and/or fish container, or place it on the bottom shelf so that if there are any drips or leaks they will not contaminate food stored below.

• Cover all food, to avoid cross-contamination. This will also stop strong-smelling food from tainting any other foods stored nearby.

• Cool hot food briefly before putting into the refrigerator. (See also **Food Poisoning**.)

HOW TO CHILL

If a recipe says to chill something after cooking, how can I do this as safely as possible?

Food cools more quickly when fresh air can circulate around it, so do not leave it to cool in its hot cooking vessel covered with a tightly fitting lid. Transfer the food to a cold dish and cover it loosely with a clean tea towel until cold, or put a large upturned bowl over it. If you want to stop it drying out or prevent a skin from forming, put wet greaseproof paper, which is thin enough not to hinder cooling, flat

on the surface of the food. Do not wrap hot food in plastic wrap, as this can leave spaces between the food and the plastic which create pockets of hot air where the climate is ideal for bacteria to breed.

Cool casseroles and large pans of food fast by standing the container in a bowl of ice or cold water or stand it in the sink with the cold tap running to keep it cool. Place cooled food into the refrigerator as soon as possible.

Rhubarb

LIGHT AND DARK

What is the difference between the pink rhubarb I can sometimes buy and darker rhubarb?

Bright pink, early rhubarb is tender and considered to be superior in quality and flavour to the later maincrop rhubarb, which is reddish-green in colour, is far tougher and has a stronger flavour. As the stems are so tender, early rhubarb does not require stringing: simply cut off the leaves and the root end of each stalk, then wash them and cut into pieces ready for cooking. Maincrop rhubarb often has a stringy covering that is best peeled and discarded.

Rhubarb is a cool weather crop available in the winter months, and is produced using horticultural techniques that have hardly changed since Victorian times. Harvesting is done by hand.

When buying rhubarb at any time look for firm, bright stems and avoid those that are clearly limp, bruised or split. The part of the plant that is edible is the leaf stem (rhubarb is actually a vegetable and not a fruit) and when it is limp, it can be refreshed by standing the stems, root end down, in a jug of cold water.

It is imperative that you always remove and discard the leaves from rhubarb. They must not be eaten as they contain oxalic acid and are extremely poisonous.

PINK AND SWEET

I know rhubarb is usually served stewed, with custard or cream, or made into a pie, but is there any other way to use it as a dessert?

Rhubarb goes especially well in a crumble, and the following charlotte recipe is a brilliant combination of rhubarb, cooking apples and breadcrumbs. During late summer, when the first of the season's cooking apples are available, you should be lucky enough to find some slender stalks of pink rhubarb in fresh produce stores.

For convenience sake, you can also make the charlotte with canned rhubarb pieces and canned pie apples.

Rhubarb charlotte

SERVES: 8
PREPARATION TIME: 1½ hours
COOKING TIME: 1–1¼ hours

---

1 kg trimmed rhubarb, cut into
*   2.5 cm pieces*
300 g (1¾ cups) dark brown sugar
1 kg cooking apples, peeled, cored
*   and sliced*
185 g (¾ cup) white sugar
250 g (4 cups) fresh breadcrumbs
125 g unsalted butter
1 teaspoon ground cinnamon
1 tablespoon icing sugar
To serve: whipped cream

---

1 Preheat the oven to 180°C.
2 Put the rhubarb pieces and 250 g (1½ cups) of the brown sugar into a heavy-based, stainless-steel or nonstick saucepan and cover with a tightly fitting lid. Put the sliced apples with the white sugar into a similar, separate saucepan. Cook them both over a medium heat for about 25–30 minutes until both fruits have been cooked enough to soften, but have not completely broken up. Stir them occasionally to prevent sticking. (The apples will not exude much juice as they cook but the rhubarb will.)
3 Meanwhile, put the breadcrumbs on a baking tray and dry them in the oven, without browning, for 10–15 minutes. Stir gently with a

Buttery toasted breadcrumbs with dark brown sugar and cinnamon form crunchy layers for a charlotte of rhubarb and tangy cooking apples.

fork occasionally. Remove the crumbs from the oven and set aside to cool.
4 Put two large nylon sieves over two large bowls. Pour the cooked rhubarb into one of the sieves and the apples into the other then leave the fruit to drain for 20 minutes so that the juice drains off, but the fruit does not become too dry.
5 Mix the drained rhubarb and the apples together gently and set aside. Pour the rhubarb juice into a jug and reserve to serve as a sauce.
6 Melt the butter in a large frying pan, add the dried breadcrumbs and cook over a gentle heat, stirring constantly, until they turn a golden brown colour. Take the breadcrumb mixture from the heat and stir in the cinnamon and the remaining sugar.
7 Butter a 20 cm round, springform cake tin and line the base with a circle of nonstick baking paper. Spread a third of the buttered crumbs in the bottom of the tin and spoon on half of the fruit mixture. Add another third of the crumbs and

then the remaining fruit. Cover the charlotte with the rest of the breadcrumbs.
8 Place the cake tin on a baking tray and bake in the centre of the oven for 50 minutes – if the crumbs start to overbrown, cover the cake tin loosely with foil. Remove the charlotte from the oven and allow it to cool for about an hour to room temperature before serving it or, alternatively, allow it to cool then cover and chill it overnight.
9 Run a palette knife around the charlotte to loosen it from the tin, then open out and remove the side of the cake tin. Put the charlotte on a flat serving plate and sift the icing sugar evenly over the top. Cut the charlotte into wedges and serve it on individual plates.
10 Thicken the rhubarb juice with 1 tablespoon arrowroot blended with 2 tablespoons cold water. Bring to the boil, stirring constantly. Pour the sauce into a jug to serve with the charlotte. Accompany with whipped cream.

LESSEN LEAKS

Why does my rhubarb pie always leak all over the oven?

Rhubarb has a high water content and exudes considerable juice as it cooks. To help prevent the juice overflowing, toss the cut rhubarb in a little flour before putting it into the pie dish: the flour will thicken the juice as the pie cooks and help to keep it contained. Use a level tablespoon of plain flour to each 500 g of prepared fruit, and mix it with the sugar before tossing with the rhubarb.

Also, when making the pie, ensure that the pastry edges are well sealed. Make a small hole in the top of the pie to let the steam escape – this will prevent the steam forcing the sealed edges apart and will allow some of the juice to evaporate. As a final precaution, always stand the pie dish on a baking tray to catch any juice that could overflow and burn on the bottom of the oven.

Rice

EASY PERFECTION

Is there a fail-safe method for cooking light, fluffy rice?

There are many different types of rice grown all over the world and each of them requires a slightly different method of cooking. If you use more than one type of rice in the kitchen, you may have to experiment to find the exact proportion of rice, water and cooking time that works for each variety as they all have different absorption qualities. The following recipes for cooking white and brown rice are very reliable. The most widely available variety of rice is white long-grain. White rice has been polished to remove the outer husk. Brown rice is considerably more nutritious as the outer layer of bran is left on the grain, adding valuable fibre and more vitamins and protein to the diet than white rice.

Perfect white rice

SERVES: 4
PREPARATION TIME: 2 minutes
COOKING TIME: 15 minutes, plus 10 minutes standing time

---

250 g (1¼ cups) white long-grain rice
A pinch of salt

---

1 Put the rice into a heavy-based saucepan (you will need one with a tight-fitting lid), add 500 ml of cold water plus the pinch of salt and bring the pan to the boil. Stir the rice once, return it to a gentle simmer, then cover and continue to simmer it over a very low heat for 10 minutes.
2 Remove the pan from the heat but do not remove the lid. Leave the pan undisturbed for 10 minutes, then remove the lid, fork through the rice and serve it immediately.
VARIATIONS
If you are using white basmati rice, put the rice in a deep bowl and add plenty of cold water. Drain off the water and repeat this process two or three times until the water in the bowl is clear, then drain off all the water. When you are cooking white basmati rice, boil it for only 8 minutes before letting it sit for another 10 minutes.

Perfect brown rice

SERVES: 4
PREPARATION TIME: 2 minutes
COOKING TIME: 35–40 minutes

---

250 g (1¼ cups) brown rice
Boiling water, for topping up the saucepan as necessary
A pinch of salt

---

1 Place the rice in a large saucepan, cover with 500 ml of cold water and add the salt. Stir the rice once to prevent it from sticking to the bottom of the pan.
2 Bring the rice to the boil and then simmer it, uncovered, for 30–35 minutes, or until the rice is cooked through, adding more boiling water if the pan becomes too dry. When the rice is cooked, drain well and serve.

UNSTICKING THE GRAINS

What do I do if I lift the lid and find my rice has stuck together?

Transfer the rice to a large sieve and rinse it thoroughly with boiling water over the sink. Shake off the excess liquid, return the rice to the cleaned saucepan, cover and leave for 5 minutes. Remove the lid, fork through the rice and serve.

PRESTEAMED RICE

Is easy-cook rice really easy?

Easy-cook rice, which is sometimes called parboiled or converted rice, is steamed before it is milled. The whole grain is steamed under pressure, which hardens it so that it will not break down during cooking.

Easy-cook rice cannot be overcooked and the grains will always remain separate. But, in general, this rice is considered inferior in taste to ordinary long-grain rice varieties because some people find the texture unpleasantly chewy.

There are, however, some nutritional benefits to this process: all the mineral and vitamin content of the outer layers of the grain that are normally removed in the milling process are pushed into the centre of the grains.

INDIAN SPECIALITIES

Which is the best rice to serve with an Indian curry?

In India two main types of rice are used to accompany curries. The rice chosen will depend on the region, the dish and the occasion.

Basmati rice, the most superior, is grown in the foothills of the Himalayas in India and Pakistan. It is served on special occasions because of its lovely aromatic flavour.

All-purpose long-grain rice, usually the patna variety, is used in many Indian dishes where herbs, spices and other flavourings may be added to the rice for extra flavour. Whenever possible, spend a little more and use basmati rice, which is available in both brown and white varieties.

WHEN TO RINSE

Some books say you should wash all rice, some say never wash it. Which of these is correct?

The reason for washing rice is to remove any excess starch from the grains; it is the starch in the grain that gives the rice a sticky quality, so whether or not you need to wash it will depend on the type of rice you use and the recipe.

Basmati rice needs to be washed before cooking in plenty of water. Stir the rice well then drain off the cloudy water. Repeat until the water that runs off the rice is clear.

Risotto, on the other hand, needs starch to give a creamy texture to the finished dish so risotto rice should never be washed.

All-purpose long-grain rice is processed and does not generally need washing, though it may need to be soaked if the cooking method in the recipe requires it.

STIRRING STORY

Why are you warned not to stir rice while it is cooking?

Stirring rice while it is cooking makes it more sticky as the action releases the starch in the grain. You should only stir rice once, at the beginning of cooking, to prevent it from sticking to the bottom of the pan. However, when you cook a risotto, which needs to be sticky, it is important to stir the grains continually, which releases the starch as the rice cooks and absorbs the liquid in which it is cooking.

NOT THE SAME

Are risotto and pilau the same dish with different names?

No, there is very little similarity between risotto and pilau dishes, although both are savoury and often combined with a mixture of meat or fish, spices and vegetables.

The Italian risotto is authentically made with a long, large-grained Italian rice called superfino, a variety that includes the arborio and canaroli rices, though a fino rice called vialone, a long and tapering grain, is also used. These can be found in well-stocked delicatessens and some supermarkets.

Risottos, such as the one on the right, are cooked in a heavy-based pan to which simmering stock is added a little at a time. The rice is stirred continually as it cooks so that it absorbs the liquid, becoming creamier and stickier as the starch in the grain is released. The risotto is cooked when the rice grains have swollen to about three times their original size and are still slightly crunchy in the centre.

Pilau is Indian in origin although many Middle Eastern and North African countries cook pilaf, which is similar. The rice (usually basmati) for a pilau or pilaf should be washed and then left to soak in plenty of cold water for an hour or so before cooking to remove the excess starch and soften the grains, so that they do not stick together. The rice is first fried in butter or oil, then as soon as the liquid is added the rice is left undisturbed until the grains are cooked through.

Pilaf can be cooked either in a pan on top of the stove, as in the recipe overleaf, or in a casserole dish in the oven, with the ingredients arranged in layers so that they cook evenly. In either case, use a pan with a tight-fitting lid.

Simple basil risotto

SERVES: 4
PREPARATION TIME: 5 minutes
COOKING TIME: 35-40 minutes

---

4 tablespoons olive oil
1 onion, chopped
2 cloves garlic, crushed
350 g (1¾ cups) Italian risotto rice
1.25 litres chicken or
*   vegetable stock*
150 ml white wine
50 g Parmesan cheese,
*   freshly grated*
2 tablespoons fresh cream
4 tablespoons chopped fresh basil
Black pepper

---

1 Heat the oil in a deep frying pan or large saucepan, fry the onion and garlic until soft but not coloured, then add the rice. Continue frying for a minute, stirring all the time, until the rice is translucent and each grain is well coated in oil.
2 Bring the stock up to a steady simmer. Add the white wine to the rice and boil until reduced. Add a ladleful of the simmering stock to the rice, stirring constantly over a low heat until the liquid is absorbed.
3 Continue adding the stock to the rice, one ladleful at a time, and stir constantly for about 25 minutes until the rice is al dente. Just before serving, stir in the Parmesan cheese, cream, basil and pepper.

MAKING AN ITALIAN RISOTTO

Start the risotto by gently frying first the flavouring ingredients and then the rice. Stir the rice until it is transparent and then begin to add the stock, which should be just simmering and close by the pan so that it can be added easily.

1 Add the simmering stock a ladleful at a time, stirring constantly until most of the liquid has been absorbed. Then repeat with the remaining stock.

2 After about 25 minutes, when the risotto has thickened and the rice is cooked but al dente, quickly stir in the Parmesan cheese and basil.

Layered pilaf

SERVES: 4
PREPARATION TIME: 20 minutes,
plus 30 minutes soaking and
15 minutes standing time
COOKING TIME: 55 minutes

---

250 g (1¼ cups) long-grain rice
75 g (⅓ cup) seedless raisins
2 tablespoons olive oil
500 g Trim lamb, diced
1 onion, chopped
2 cloves garlic, crushed
2 carrots, diced
2 stalks celery, sliced
2 teaspoons ground mixed
   spice
25 g (2 tablespoons) almonds,
   blanched and lightly toasted
1 litre lamb or chicken stock
To garnish: toasted pine nuts or
   flaked almonds, and chopped
   coriander, mint or parsley

---

1 Soak the rice and the raisins, separately, in water for 30 minutes. Drain the rice and rinse it under running water until the water runs clear. Drain the raisins and set aside.
2 Heat the oil in a frying pan and fry the lamb over a high heat for a few minutes until browned. Remove from the pan to a plate.
3 Fry the onion, garlic, carrots, celery and mixed spice in the pan for 5 minutes. Add the raisins and almonds to the pan and stir well.
4 In a straight-sided, heavy-based saucepan, stir a quarter of the rice into the lamb. Add a layer of one-third of the vegetables, then one-third of the remaining rice, and repeat the layers ending with a layer of rice.
5 Bring the stock to the boil. Pour it slowly down the side of the pan.

When making pilaf, pour the stock down the side of the pan carefully to avoid disturbing the layers.

6 Cover the pan and cook, without stirring, over a low heat for 35–40 minutes until the liquid is fully absorbed.
7 Remove the lid and cover the pan with a layer of foil. Replace the lid and allow the pilaf to sit undisturbed for another 15 minutes. Invert onto a serving dish. Sprinkle pine nuts or flaked almonds over the top of the pilaf and finish with a scattering of chopped parsley, mint or coriander.

WARM UP

How can I keep rice fluffy if it has to be kept warm for some time? And can I heat up leftover rice?

One of the best ways to keep rice warm is to put it in a large heat-proof dish or platter, fork it through well, cover it with a tent of foil and keep it warm in a preheated oven at 140°C until ready to serve.

Leftover rice can be steamed in a muslin-lined steamer for 5 minutes or so, stirring regularly until it is heated through, or put into a large pan of boiling water, brought back to the boil and drained immediately. Alternatively, stir-fry the rice for a few minutes or heat it in a microwave just before serving.

CALCULATING QUANTITIES

Should I allow the same amount of rice per person for different dishes, or does it vary?

As an accompaniment to a curry or a stew, 60–90 g of uncooked rice per person is the accepted norm. A rice salad for two people will require a greater quantity of rice, as much as 125 g per person.

For a risotto or a paella, such as the one on the right, where the rice makes up the greatest part of the dish with extra meat, fish and vegetables added, the quantity of rice required could also be as much as 125 g per person. In Spain the rice traditionally used for paella is a creamy variety from Valencia. It is not easy to find outside the region, although some quality supermarkets and specialist food stores stock it. You can use arborio rice instead.

Seafood paella

SERVES: 4–6
PREPARATION TIME: 40 minutes
COOKING TIME: 1½ hours

---

250 g large green prawns
1 litre fish stock
A pinch of saffron strands
4 tablespoons olive oil
1 large onion, chopped
1 large red pepper, deseeded and
   chopped
2 cloves garlic, crushed
1 small red chilli, deseeded and
   chopped
2 teaspoons paprika
350 g (1¾ cups) Valencia or
   arborio rice
150 ml dry white wine
250 g blue-eyed cod fillet, skinned
   and cubed
12 fresh mussels, scrubbed
250 g squid, cleaned and sliced
   into rings
125 g frozen peas
2 tablespoons chopped fresh parsley
Salt and black pepper
To garnish: lemon wedges

---

1 Shell and clean the prawns, then put the prawn heads and shells into a saucepan with the stock. Bring to the boil, cover and simmer for 30 minutes. Strain the stock, add the saffron strands and set aside.
2 Heat the oil in a large wide frying pan and fry the onion, pepper, garlic and chilli for about 5 minutes. Add the paprika and rice and stir-fry for 2 minutes. Pour in the wine and boil rapidly until evaporated.
3 Reheat the stock until simmering, then add 150 ml to the rice and simmer gently, uncovered, for 10 minutes or until absorbed. Add the remaining stock to the pan and leave to simmer for 20 minutes, stirring occasionally. Add extra stock or hot water if the pan becomes dry.
4 Add the prawns, cod, mussels, squid and peas to the pan. Cover the pan loosely with foil and cook for a further 10–12 minutes or until the rice is tender, the liquid is absorbed and the seafood is cooked through. Sprinkle with chopped parsley, salt and pepper, and garnish the paella with lemon wedges.

NO ORDINARY RICE

What makes wild rice different from ordinary rice?

Wild rice is actually not a rice at all. It is an aquatic grass with thin black grains that is indigenous to Canada and the northern United States.

Wild rice absorbs four times its volume of liquid during cooking and takes much longer to cook than ordinary rice; anything from 35–60 minutes. It has an intriguing nutty flavour and is extremely nutritious as it contains all nine of the essential amino acids. Wild rice is also a good source of fibre, is gluten free and low in kilojoules and cholesterol.

In the following recipe for an exotic salad inspired by the exciting flavours of Californian cooking, wild and white rice are combined with fresh crab meat and diced pawpaw. If you use a freshly cooked crab you will need one weighing about 1.5 kg. Reserve the brown meat to use in another dish. Some fish shops sell vacuum-packed fresh crab meat or frozen crab meat. You could also use well-drained canned white crab meat.

Another unusual, colourful rice is the red rice from the Camargue region of France, which is stocked by specialist food shops. Cooked in the same way as brown rice, it has a distinctive flavour that makes it a good alternative to wild rice.

Wild rice salad with crab and pawpaw

SERVES: 6
PREPARATION TIME: 15 minutes
COOKING TIME: 40 minutes

---

90 g (½ cup) wild rice
125 g (¾ cup) white long-grain rice
100 ml extra virgin olive oil
1 clove garlic, crushed
2 tablespoons lime juice
½ teaspoon clear honey
Salt and black pepper
500 g white crab meat
1 ripe pawpaw, deseeded and diced
1 small red onion, thinly sliced
50 g (½ cup) flaked almonds, very lightly toasted
2 tablespoons finely chopped fresh coriander

---

1 Cook the wild rice for 35–40 minutes in plenty of boiling water until just tender. Meanwhile, cook the long-grain rice separately in salted water for 12–15 minutes.
2 In a small bowl, combine the oil, garlic, lime juice, honey, salt and pepper to make the dressing.
3 Drain the cooked rices and mix together in a bowl, then add the crab meat. Stir in the dressing and leave the mixture to cool.
4 Add the pawpaw to the rice and crab mixture along with the onion, almonds and coriander. Stir until well combined and serve at once.
VARIATIONS
Use brown rice, boiled for 25–30 minutes, instead of wild rice. Or replace the fresh coriander with mint, chervil, garlic chives or the green tops of spring onions.

Wild rice, white crab meat, sharp red onion and vivid pawpaw are tossed in a colourful salad with a zesty lime and honey dressing.

Rice Pudding

SOFTLY SOFTLY

Is there a quick way to cook a smooth rice pudding?

Not really. Rice pudding is always best cooked slowly, so that the rice will absorb all the milk and soften. It is normally baked at a low temperature for a couple of hours, but may also be simmered on the hotplate in a covered saucepan, as long as the heat is kept low and the mixture is stirred frequently.

The only way to speed up the process is to use a microwave oven but it will still take about an hour, and care must be taken as milky puddings have a tendency to boil over in the microwave.

The following recipe is a lovely example of a creamy rice pudding baked in the oven, and may be eaten hot or cold.

Fresh lemon rice pudding

SERVES: 4
PREPARATION TIME: 15 minutes, plus 30 minutes standing time
COOKING TIME: 2–2½ hours

50 g (⅓ cup) short-grain rice
600 ml whole milk
Finely grated rind of 1 lemon
25 g (5 teaspoons) caster sugar
15 g butter

1 Grease an 850 ml ovenproof dish. Wash and drain the rice, then put it in the prepared dish. Pour on the milk and gently mix in the lemon rind, and allow the mixture to stand for 30 minutes. While the rice softens, preheat the oven to 150°C.
2 Stir the sugar into the milky rice and dot the surface of the pudding with shavings of butter.
3 Bake for 2–2½ hours, stirring after 30 minutes, until the pudding is thick, creamy and golden brown on top. For a creamier pudding without a skin, fold the skin in after about 1½ hours cooking. Serve hot or cold with fresh or canned fruit such as peach slices or raspberries.

Spoon through the crisp, golden skin to reach a soft and creamy sweet rice pudding. A hint of lemon brightens up this traditional comfort-food dessert.

CREAMY SUCCESS

My rice puddings tend to be a bit thin. How can I rectify this?

Too much milk can make the pudding thin and runny. You may also be using the wrong rice. Short-grain rice, also known as pearl, round or pudding rice, contains more starch than long- or medium-grain rice so that it absorbs a large quantity of liquid and becomes quite sticky and very soft.

To enrich the mixture, replace some of the milk with the same quantity of fresh cream, and dot 2 teaspoons of butter over the top before baking. You will also achieve a creamier result if you stir in the skin 30 minutes into the cooking time, and again about two-thirds of the way through.

Rissoles

CRISPY COATING

What is the difference between a rissole and a croquette?

They are very similar: both are made with chopped or minced ingredients bound together, often with a well-seasoned white sauce (in the case of croquettes) or a thick brown sauce (rissoles) but sometimes with mashed potato. The mixture is then coated with egg and breadcrumbs and fried.

The terms are sometimes used interchangeably, but rissoles are generally thought to have meat or poultry as their main ingredient, while croquettes are more often made with vegetables. Mixtures containing fish as a main ingredient are mostly called fish cakes.

Whatever they are called, when cooked they should be crisp and golden on the outside yet remain moist and creamy inside. The mixture should be thick enough to hold together during cooking, but not so thick that the finished result is dry, so it is advisable to chill rissoles and croquettes thoroughly before cooking to firm the mixture up.

VERSATILE DISH

What sort of ingredients could I use to make rissoles?

Rissoles are a good way to use up leftover meat or vegetables, but they are also worth making from scratch. Served on a bed of salad, or with a spicy sauce, they make a good starter or light weekend lunch.

A few simple ideas might include a mixture of chopped ham, grated cheese and finely chopped sage; a selection of cooked, diced root vegetables sprinkled with crumbled goat's cheese and finely chopped celery; or pieces of crispy bacon with blue vein cheese.

Season the mixture to taste, mix with a white sauce and shape into patties (see panel, above right). Alternatively, shape teaspoons of the mixture into flat rounds and cover them with stiff mashed potato. In either case, dust them with flour, dip in egg and coat in breadcrumbs, and fry gently to ensure the inside is heated through.

LUSCIOUS FISH CAKES

What kind of fish should I use for making fish cakes?

Any firm white fish is suitable, and you can use either raw or cooked fish, though raw will take a little longer to cook. First flake the fish and mix it with mashed potato, or with a strongly flavoured cheese sauce and plenty of chopped parsley. Then shape, coat and cook.

For a more unusual flavour, add some chopped garlic, grated ginger, lemon grass and spring onion.

SHAPING RISSOLES

Creamy rissoles or croquettes are shaped by hand, dusted with flour, dipped into egg and breadcrumbs then fried for a crisp exterior.

1 For every 500 g minced dry ingredients (minced poultry is shown here), mix in some 200 ml thick white sauce.

2 Shape the mixture, using wet hands, into flattened balls. Dust with flour, coat in beaten egg and breadcrumbs, chill thoroughly till firm, then fry gently until golden.

Roasting

TURNING POINT

What is the difference between roasting and spit-roasting?

Roasting is a method of cooking food, usually meat, in the oven with no liquid other than fat. The food is regularly basted to prevent the upper part of the meat drying out, and to enhance the flavour.

In spit-roasting, meat is skewered onto a rod and cooked in front of or above an open fire, being turned regularly to ensure cooking throughout and to run the fat and meat juices over the surface. Nowadays some ovens or grills have electrically operated spits, known as rotisseries, built into them.

RELAXING MEAT

Why should meat and poultry be rested after roasting, and how long should they be rested for?

Resting meat after roasting allows the fibres of the meat to relax. The juices, which expand during roasting, shrink as the meat cools so the joint deflates and the fibres consolidate. The meat is then firmer and easier to carve. If you try to carve it straight from the oven, the slices will be ragged and steam from the hot juices can cause scalding.

Large joints weighing more than 2 kg should be covered in foil and rested for 20–30 minutes. Small roasts need 10–15 minutes and can be rested uncovered.

SMALL IS BEAUTIFUL

I enjoy a roast, but there are only two of us in our household. Are small joints worth cooking?

Joints of meat and poultry that weigh under 1.5 kg are now commonly available, reflecting the growing number of small households. These joints need extra care to be successfully roasted. Although small, they still need time to cook through, and as there is not enough fat and juices to keep the meat moist, they could become dry and tough. The answer is to bard them (see page 300), and baste often.

Making gravy from small joints is another problem, because they will not provide enough of the vital sticky juices. But you can create the basis of a good gravy by roasting the meat on a bed of sliced onion and carrot and pouring 150 ml of stock, wine or water into the baking dish at the start.

TROUBLE-FREE ROASTING

How do I ensure my roasts are always successful?

Roasting should be trouble-free, but here are some general rules:
• Weigh the meat to calculate cooking time (see page 300), but remember that cooking times are meant only as a general guide, and

a long, thin piece of meat will take less time to cook than a thick, round one of the same weight.

• Before putting the meat on to cook, allow time to preheat the oven to the required temperature: this may take 15 minutes or more.

• Put the meat on a wire rack or trivet in a baking dish. This keeps the meat off the bottom of the tin where the melting fat accumulates, and allows the heat to penetrate the meat more evenly as it circulates around it.

• Beef and lamb should be cooked at 230°C for 20 minutes first, to brown them. The temperature is then reduced and roasting completed according to the chart below. Roast pork does not need this initial browning as it is cooked at a higher temperature to ensure crisp crackling.

• Halfway through the cooking time, check the meat. If it is well browned on top, turn it over and baste it with the melted fat and juices in the bottom of the pan.

• Lamb and beef must reach an internal temperature of 60°C to be rare, 71°C to be medium pink and 80°C to be well done. Pork and chicken must reach 85°C. A meat thermometer inserted directly into the centre of the meat eliminates guesswork. It should be positioned when the roasting is almost complete, and should not touch any bones or the baking dish as both of these conduct heat.

• When the cooking time is up, stand the roast on a warm serving platter in a warm place to relax and firm up, or leave it to rest in the turned-off oven with the door ajar while you make the gravy.

ADDING FAT AND FLAVOUR

What is the advantage of barding and larding over basting?

Very lean meats, such as veal and game birds, and very small joints of any meat, need extra fat when they are roasted or they become dry and tough. Continual basting is time consuming, and opening the oven door lowers the temperature. The answer is to make a roast 'self-basting', by barding or larding it.

Barding involves covering the joint with a layer of fat, which melts over the meat as it cooks. Pork back fat is the most suitable as it does not have a strong flavour, but some game birds are barded with streaky bacon, tied into place.

Larding involves threading strips of pork back fat through the meat with a larding needle. It is particularly suitable for large joints which need a long cooking time as the fat slowly dissolves, basting the meat internally and adding extra richness to the meat juices.

Barding dry meat, such as quail, with bacon keeps the flesh moist, enriches the flavour and produces rich juices.

ROASTING CHART

This is general guie to the most popular joints of roasting meat and poultry. Bear in mind that long, narrow joints need less roasting time weight for weight than large round ones, and joints on the bone cook faster than boned joints.

MEAT	OVEN TEMPERATURE / COOKING TIME	INTERNAL TEMPERATURE
Beef (sirloin, rib or topside)	180°C	
Rare	30 min per kg + 15 min	60°C
Medium	35 min per kg + 20 min	71°C
Well done	40 min per kg + 30 min	80°C
Lamb (leg, loin or shoulder)	180°C	
Rare	35 min per kg + 15 min	60°C
Medium	40 min per kg + 20 min	71°C
Well done	50 min per kg + 25 min	80°C
Pork (leg or loin)	200°C	
	60 min per kg	85°C
Chicken	200°C	
	30–40 min per kg + 15–20 min	85°C
Turkey	180°C	
	45 min per kg + 20 min	71°C

Rolls

HOMEMADE READY-BAKE

I find the 'ready-bake' rolls I buy from the supermarket invaluable. Could I make my own?

Ready-bake rolls, or prepared but undercooked rolls that need only brief reheating or baking, are easy to make: simply bake any bread roll recipe in the usual way but remove them from the oven about 15 minutes before the total baking time. They can be made in the morning and finished off that evening, or frozen and kept for a later date, then cooked straight out of the freezer as required.

The following unusual savoury rolls have the advantage of being different from most 'ready-bake' rolls you can buy.

Sun-dried tomatoes and chopped black olives give a Mediterranean flavour to a cluster of rolls, the perfect foundation for a filling snack or cheese course.

Sun-dried tomato and olive rolls

MAKES: 8 rolls
PREPARATION TIME: 20 minutes
RISING AND COOKING TIME: 3 hours

500 g (4 cups) strong, unbleached white flour, plus extra for kneading
2 × 10 g sachets instant rapid-rise yeast
2 teaspoons salt
250 ml lukewarm water
6 sun-dried tomatoes packed in olive oil, finely chopped
12 black olives, stoned and finely chopped
40 g butter, melted

1 Mix together the flour, yeast and salt in a bowl. Make a well in the centre and stir in the water, first with a spoon and then with your hand until a soft dough is formed. Do not knead the dough at this stage; just cover with a cloth or plastic wrap and position in a warm place for 1–2 hours, until doubled in volume.
2 When the dough has risen, knock it down and knead until it is smooth.

Knead in the tomatoes and olives, sprinkling on more flour if the dough becomes sticky.
3 Form the dough into a long tube and cut it into eight equal pieces. To shape the rolls, cup the palm of your hand over each piece of dough and rotate your hand continuously until it gathers up into a small ball.
4 Grease a 23 cm shallow cake tin and dust it with flour. Set the balls in the tin, cover and leave to rise for 30–40 minutes until doubled in volume. Meanwhile, preheat the oven to 230°C.
5 When the rolls have risen, brush them with melted butter and bake for about 15 minutes or until lightly browned. Remove the tin from the oven and leave the rolls in the tin to cool. Cover with a cloth if the baking is to be completed later that day. To freeze, seal the rolls in a plastic freezer bag.
6 When ready to serve, preheat the oven to 230°C and cook for 10–15 minutes until crisp and browned. Cool on a wire cooling rack. To serve, pull off individual rolls by hand as needed.

Rosewater

DELIGHTFULLY DELICATE

What is rosewater, and are there many dishes that I can use it in?

Rosewater is a clear liquid with a delicate flavouring derived from scented rose petals. When made for its scent, to freshen pillows and sheets for instance, it is made from plain water, but for cooking purposes it is made from the distilled essence of rose petals.

Rosewater is used a great deal in Middle Eastern dishes and Balkan confectionery, and in some Indian cooking. It can be added to sweet syrups for poaching fruit, serving with fritters or pouring over sponge cakes to moisten them, or mixed into icings, milk puddings, cream, ice creams and cold soufflés. Some savoury rice dishes, such as pilau, also contain rosewater.

The other commercially available flower water is orange flower water, which is made from the flowers of the bitter Seville orange. It is used in cooking in the same way as rosewater. Commercial rosewater and orange flower water are both distilled, so it is not possible to make your own at home.

Rye

FOREIGN FLOUR

I like the sharp taste of rye bread as a change from wholemeal. Could I make my own?

The rye grain is ground to produce a dark greyish flour, used in various sour-tasting Eastern European breads. You can make a successful light rye bread by using a mixture of half rye flour and half plain flour, adding some caraway seeds for extra flavour and consistency. You can also use rye flour to make pancakes similar in appearance and taste to buckwheat pancakes.

Safety in the Kitchen

BURN TREATMENT

What is the best first-aid action to take if I burn myself in the kitchen?

Never apply butter, lotions or ointment to a burn, as these trap the heat and intensify the problem. Instead, run cold water over the affected area for at least 10 minutes. Remove any rings, watches or tight clothing before any swelling starts, then cover the burn with a sterile dressing or any other clean, non-fluffy covering.

If the burn is large, or the skin looks charred and grey, or there is clothing stuck to the burnt area, the injury may be serious. Cover it with plastic wrap or a clean plastic bag to prevent infection and reduce dehydration of the area, and cool the burn by running cold water over the film or bag. Do not touch the affected area, burst any blisters or remove anything sticking to the burn. Seek immediate medical help for any burn larger than a 10 cent coin.

MOUTH BURNS

I am terrified that my young child will get hold of something very hot and put it in his mouth. What should I do if this happens?

This type of accident can result in rapid swelling of the throat and inflammation of the air passages, leading to a serious risk of suffocation. Loosen clothing around the neck, give the child cold water to sip and phone for an ambulance.

CHEMICAL DANGERS

I am aware that some common household cleaning agents contain potentially dangerous chemicals. What should I do if one of these comes into contact with the skin, or if my child swallows some?

Chemical burns are different from other burns: the onset is slower and there is a fierce stinging pain. Look for redness or staining of the skin, and blistering followed by peeling. Wash the affected area under cold running water to remove traces of the chemical and reduce the heat, then the person should be taken to hospital immediately.

Dangerous chemicals should be kept out of the reach of children. However, even seemingly innocuous substances, such as liquid soap, can be dangerous if swallowed. If the child swallows a household substance, such as bleach or cleaning fluid, and is conscious, give milk or water to sip. An unconscious victim should be laid on their front, face sideways and chin tilted up to keep the airway open. In either case, call an ambulance and, if possible, take a sample of the chemical with you to the hospital.

CUTS IN THE KITCHEN

What should I do if I cut myself while preparing food?

If possible, your hands should be clean before dealing with a wound. Rinse the cut under cold water then gently dry it with a clean or sterile swab and apply a plaster. A kitchen cut is most likely to affect a finger or hand, which you should then keep covered to prevent infection getting in. Your hands are likely to become wet and dirty as you cook, so change the dressing regularly and use water-resistant plasters.

COPING WITH GAS LEAKS

What should I do if I walk into my kitchen and smell gas?

If you smell gas, extinguish any naked flames immediately, but do not turn any electrical switches on

To the rescue!

Make your kitchen safe by keeping this equipment to hand:
- First-aid kit containing plasters, sterile dressings and bandages, safety pins, scissors and tweezers.
- Plastic wrap or large plastic bags in case of large burns.
- Fire blanket to smother flames.
- Dry-powder fire extinguisher labelled 'for kitchen use'.

or off. Open the door and windows to let the gas disperse. Turn off the gas supply to the stove and any other gas appliances such as a gas fire, either at the tap that supplies it, or if it does not have one, at the main tap next to the meter. When the lever is parallel with the pipe the gas is on, when it is at right angles to the pipe the gas is off.

If you cannot turn off the supply, or the smell continues after the gas has been turned off, ring your area's gas supplier immediately. Their 24-hour emergency service number is listed in the phone book.

OIL FIRE

What should I do if oil catches fire in a deep-fryer or saucepan?

Never throw water on an oil fire as it will cause an explosion of hot fat. Turn off the heat but do not move the pan as the flames could blow towards you. To deprive the flames of oxygen, cover the pan with a fire blanket, or use a damp towel or a metal lid or tray. When approaching the burning pan, keep the cloth or lid between you and the flames.

Leave the pan covered for at least 30 minutes; do not uncover it sooner as it could reignite. To minimise the risk of an oil fire, never fill a pan more than half full of oil.

If you feel unable to cope with fire, shut the doors and windows to contain the flames, leave the room and call the fire brigade. Do not go back into the room.

ELECTRICAL FIRE

What should I do if there is an electrical fire in the kitchen?

Turn off the power and pull out the plug, if possible. A small fire will probably go out once the power is cut. If it persists, it is best to use a dry-powder fire extinguisher on a small electrical fire: conveniently sized extinguishers of dry chemical powder marked 'for kitchen use' are sold by hardware shops. Never use water on an electrical fire.

If the source of a fire is in the socket rather than the appliance, it may indicate a fault in the wiring. In the event of a socket fire, do not attempt to fight it yourself. Close the doors and windows, leave the room and call the fire brigade.

Saffron

FLOWER POWER

Is saffron added directly to dishes, or do I have to prepare it first?

Saffron, which comes from a flower of the crocus family, is sold either as whole strands or in powdered form. Strands should be toasted briefly, just for a few seconds, in a dry frying pan over a gentle heat, then pounded in a mortar and steeped in a little hot liquid, stock, milk or water, in order to disseminate their flavour and colour more freely. Powdered saffron can be added directly to dishes.

LIMITED ALTERNATIVES

Saffron is very expensive. Is there any other way to give dishes that wonderful, warm colour?

Nothing can duplicate the orange hue of saffron, or its subtle and aromatic flavour. Turmeric produces a vivid yellow colour, has an agreeable flavour and is cheaper and easier to find, but it cannot be fairly compared with saffron.

Saffron is essential for this cool, golden, spicy sauce, which makes any fish dish very special.

A light and fragrant mayonnaise, made with added yoghurt and flavoured with saffron and other spices, is perfect with grilled or poached fish and vegetables.

Cold saffron sauce

SERVES: 4
PREPARATION TIME: 10 minutes
COOKING TIME: none

---

1 large egg yolk
A pinch of sea salt
⅛ teaspoon powdered saffron
¼ teaspoon ground cumin
¼ teaspoon ground coriander
150 ml sunflower oil
1½ teaspoons white wine vinegar
1½ teaspoons lemon juice
150 ml natural yoghurt

---

1 Beat the egg yolk in a bowl, then mix in the salt and spices.

2 Pour in the oil drop by drop as if making mayonnaise, beating with a wooden spoon until each addition has been amalgamated. After half the oil has been beaten in, the rest can be added a little more quickly.

3 When all the oil is amalgamated, stir in the vinegar and lemon juice, then fold in the yoghurt. Serve with grilled salmon steaks, trout, or poached white fish.

VARIATION
For a more robust flavour, replace the ground cumin and coriander with ½ teaspoon of mild curry powder. Toast it briefly in a metal spoon over a flame before adding it to the egg.

SALAD LEAVES

Healthy food has never been as quick to prepare or as pretty to look at as it is now with all these gorgeous salad leaves. Balance colours and flavours and add a simple garnish, and your own salad dressing, for a feast of fresh goodness.

COS

RED AND YELLOW WITLOF

CRISP LETTUCE

CHINESE CABBAGE

FRISEE

ICEBERG

Leaves of different colours and flavours, dressed with nut oil and fruity raspberry vinegar, draw the eye and tempt the palate.

You need only one salad leaf to make a plain green side salad: cos, for example, with a few shavings of Parmesan cheese. For a more elaborate salad bowl, three different leaves are usually enough: try to balance taste and shapes, mixing a crunchy leaf like iceberg with sharp rocket, witlof or watercress and a pretty leaf like green coral.

Keep a selection of toppings in the refrigerator to add a sharp taste or crunchy texture to salads: fresh herbs, olives, slivers of roasted pepper, lardons, croutons, toasted pine nuts or sesame seeds.

The best way to keep salad leaves fresh is to leave them unwashed and still attached to their stem, in a plastic box or long-life, green plastic storage bag in the refrigerator crisper. Use a sharp knife to cut the leaves as it minimises damage to the cell structure and the consequent loss of vitamins.

There is a great deal of name-switching in salad leaves, with new terms from overseas usurping the names of traditional varieties, and stores giving their own 'brand names' to identical lettuces. Here are the leaves you are most likely to find.

BABY COS
A miniature cos, this little lettuce is usually sold in quality fresh produce shops. Known also as little gem, its leaves are so densely packed you can slice straight across the head for salads, while the single leaves fit into a sandwich.

BUTTERHEAD
Once the lettuce of the summer salad patch but now available all year, it has soft, green leaves and is ideal for lining a dish of sandwiches or cold meats. It is also good inside sandwiches, keeping them moist without drawing attention to itself. The crinkle-leaved mignonette is a smaller variety of butterhead.

CHINESE CABBAGE
A refined member of the cabbage family, the tender leaves can be used all year round - it is much the best cabbage to use for coleslaw. Heads are large, but they keep well and can be used also in a stir-fry.

COS
Also known as romaine, cos is a classic, crisp, long-leaved lettuce, whose head plumps out considerably in summer though it does not have much heart. The leaves are packed with assertive flavour, and it is essential for Caesar salad.

CRISP LETTUCE
This has leaves that bend over backwards to show off its big heart. It is a junior member of the iceberg clan, weighing in at about 200 g.

DANDELION
Dandelion leaves are a feature of salads in many parts of Europe in spring, when youth

softens their bitterness. But gather them from your own garden, where you can be sure they are not polluted.

ENDIVE
Sometimes known as escarole, or broad-leaf batavian endive, this leaf began life as a coarse-leaved winter salad, but to-day is a tender, loose-leaved lettuce with well-flavoured, crimp-edged leaves.

FRISEE
A raggedy-leaved salad, frisée is the bistro favourite topped with bacon bits and croutons. Called chicorée in France and chicory in the United States, frisée has a pleasing bitterness and a texture sturdy enough to stand up to hot dressings.

GREEN CORAL AND RED CORAL
Both have wonderfully pretty frilled leaves; the green coral is a dainty pale green, while the leaves of the red coral are flushed with bronze at the edges. Glamorous but delicate, these leaves are best included in a mixed salad for their looks alongside others with more texture and flavour.

ICEBERG
This is subsuming older names such as Webb's Wonderful as the generic term for all crisp, tightly packed, pale green lettuces. Its juicy leaves keep better than most. Iceberg makes a big bowlful of salad for a buffet, but needs other elements added to compensate for its bland flavour.

LAMB'S LETTUCE
Also known as mâche and corn salad, lamb's lettuce is related neither to lettuce nor

corn. It is expensive, but a few sweet little leaves will go a long way as a garnish for first courses or incorporated into a mixed salad.

MESCLUN
This salad is a mixture of fresh herbs, edible flowers and young baby salad leaves such as rocket and lamb's lettuce or baby spinach leaves.

OAK LEAF LETTUCE
This is tender, mild flavoured and handsome, with serrated and variegated leaves coloured from brownish green through to deepest bronze. It makes a highly pleasing salad mixed with peppery greenery such as rocket or watercress.

RADICCHIO
A ruby-leaved Italian chicory that is now grown in Australia, radicchio is firm, bitter and beautiful, and mixes particularly well with pale green contrasting additions such as sliced avocado. It is sometimes cooked, but this darkens its leaves to brown.

ROCKET
Halfway between a herb and a salad leaf, rocket – also known as arugula – has a strong, peppery flavour that goes a long way. Mix a few leaves into green salads to add piquancy, or use as a garnish.

WITLOF
In Australia, witlof means the tight, pointed heads that the French call endive and the English call chicory. They are sold blanched and pale green, or occasionally red. The mildly bitter leaves cook well and are especially good teamed with citrus.

SALAD DRESSING (VINAIGRETTE)
- PROPORTIONS: traditionally, a salad dressing comprises three parts oil to one part vinegar (or other acid element such as lemon juice), but you can use up to six parts oil. Measure the ingredients into a screw-top jar, or pour into a bottle and shake to emulsify.
Green salads will wilt if they are left sitting in a salad dressing too long. Either offer the dressing at the table, or toss it in at the last minute.
- OILS: use your best oils, such as extra virgin olive oil, for simple vinaigrettes; but if you find this too heavy, mix it with a lighter oil such as grapeseed. For a nut-flavoured dressing, one part of hazelnut, macadamia or walnut oil can be mixed to two or three parts of olive oil. For an Asian dressing, use one part sesame oil to four parts peanut oil, and season with soy sauce instead of salt.
- VINEGAR: the classic acid element of salad dressing is red or white wine vinegar. Balsamic vinegar has a strong, sweet flavour and, like sherry vinegar, is rich and powerful; use both in small quantities. Cider vinegar is assertive and good for winter salads. Fruit and herb-flavoured vinegars can be added by the teaspoon for an elusive background flavour, while for an Asian dressing try using rice wine vinegar. Or don't use vinegar at all - lemon juice makes a refreshing change.
- FLAVOURINGS: add sea salt, pepper, crushed garlic, some finely chopped shallot or a pinch of sugar to taste, and a teaspoon of French mustard to thicken the dressing.

BUTTERHEAD

RADICCHIO

ROCKET

OAK LEAF LETTUCE

OLIVE OIL

BALSAMIC VINEGAR

GREEN CORAL

RED CORAL

LAMB'S LETTUCE   BABY COS

HAZELNUT OIL AND RASPBERRY VINEGAR DRESSING WITH MUSTARD

Salmon

HOT AND COLD

When poaching whole salmon, how do I calculate the cooking time? Some books say 2 minutes, some say 20. Which is right?

A whole poached salmon can be served either hot or cold, and the cooking method varies accordingly. This accounts for the wide variation in cooking times given for whole salmon in recipe books.

For a salmon that is to be served cold, as in the recipe on the right, put the fish into cold water or court bouillon, cover and then bring it to the boil, skimming off any scum that forms. Turn off the heat as soon as it reaches the boil and leave the salmon in the liquid to cool completely before dressing it with your chosen garnishes. It is not necessary to set the trimmings in an aspic glaze. If preferred, fresh herbs can simply be arranged decoratively on top.

For a salmon that is to be served hot, pour enough court bouillon or water to cover the fish into a fish kettle, but do not add the salmon. Bring the liquid to the boil, and then add the fish. Return it to sim-mering point and poach the salmon gently, allowing 10 minutes per kg. Remove the fish from the liquid, then cover and leave it to rest for 5 minutes.

To accompany the salmon, serve tiny new potatoes, freshly made mayonnaise, and a cucumber salad made with fresh dill or mint, thick natural yoghurt and black pepper.

Whole dressed salmon

SERVES: *8 as a main course*
PREPARATION TIME: *20 minutes, plus cooling time for court bouillon*
COOKING TIME: *40-45 minutes, plus several hours or overnight cooling*

Whole salmon, about 2.5 kg, gutted and cleaned

COURT BOUILLON
6 litres cold water
150 ml white wine vinegar
1 onion, sliced
1 carrot, sliced
1 stalk celery, sliced
2 strips lemon zest
3 bay leaves
A small bunch each of thyme sprigs and parsley stalks
A pinch of peppercorns
To garnish: thinly sliced cucumber, aspic jelly (optional), plus sprigs of fresh dill and lemon wedges to decorate the serving platter

1 To make the court bouillon, put all the ingredients in a fish kettle and bring them to the boil. Cover and simmer gently for 15 minutes.
2 Leave the court bouillon to cool and then strain off the flavourings, reserving the liquid.
3 To cook the salmon, lower the fish into the cold court bouillon (cut the head off to fit, if necessary, but add it to the pan for flavour). Bring to the boil over a medium heat, skim off any scum, then turn off the heat, cover the fish kettle and leave to cool for a few hours or even overnight.

TO DRESS THE SALMON
1 Remove the fish from the liquid then trim off the skin, fins and grey flesh, and the head if you wish.
2 Transfer the salmon to a serving dish or board. Decorate the top of the fish with cucumber slices. If liked, the fish may then be coated in a layer of aspic jelly (made according to packet directions).
3 Cover and leave the fish in a cold place until required. It is better not to chill it if possible; however, if the fish has to be prepared more than several hours in advance, or if it is being served on a hot day, keep it refrigerated until about 30 minutes before serving. Do not add the fresh garnishes until just before you are ready to serve the salmon.

The freshest and lightest of garnishes – a neat row of thinly sliced Lebanese cucumber – decorates the length of a whole salmon. The fronds of dill and lemon wedges complete the simple summery decoration for this quintessential party dish.

IMPROVISED FISH KETTLE

I do not have a fish kettle or even a pan large enough to hold a salmon – what can I do?

If you do not want to go to the expense of buying a fish kettle that will be used only rarely, you can hire fish kettles from some catering suppliers and large hotels for a special occasion. It is also possible to use a baking dish as described in the panel on the right.

Alternatively, you can bake the fish on a large baking tray in the oven. Preheat the oven to 160°C. Brush a large piece of strong foil with oil or melted butter and put it on a baking tray. Put the gutted and cleaned fish in the centre (if it is too big the head and tail can be cut off), season it inside with salt, pepper, slices of lemon or herbs if you want to, and wrap it loosely in the foil, folding over the edges to seal the parcel.

If the salmon is to be served hot, cook it for 30 minutes per kg. Remove the fish from the oven and leave it to set, still wrapped in the foil, for 5 minutes.

If the fish is to be served cold, cook it for 20 minutes per kg, then remove it from the oven. Keep the fish wrapped in the foil until it has cooled down completely.

IN A PICKLE

Can you suggest a variation on smoked salmon as a starter for a dinner party?

Raw salmon can be pickled with alcohol, such as vodka or tequila, and flavoured with herbs and spices, or marinated in lemon or lime juice. This has the same effect as cooking the fish because the acid in the alcohol or juice coagulates the protein, making it opaque.

In South America this marinated fish dish is known as ceviche and is flavoured with chillies, onions and garlic. The following recipe also uses lime or lemon juice but takes inspiration from Sweden's famous cured salmon dish – gravlax – by flavouring the fish with dill.

IMPROVISING A FISH KETTLE

Fish kettles are convenient for cooking a large whole fish but if you do not have one, here are two ways to improvise. To cook a fish that is too large for a small baking dish, cut off the head and tail, poach them separately, then reassemble after cooking, covering the joins with garnish. Or curl the fish to fit in the tin.

IN A BAKING DISH	*COOKING IN FOIL*

Measure the length of the fish and choose a baking dish that will hold it comfortably. (You could also measure your baking dish and choose a fish that will fit in it.) Place an oiled rack in the tin, set the fish on the rack and pour in salted water, stock or court bouillon according to the recipe. Cover the whole of the tin loosely with foil and cook the fish on top of the stove or in the oven.

Alternatively, cut and fold a double or triple thickness of strong foil slightly larger than the fish. Place the fish on the foil and put it in the cold cooking liquid in a baking dish. Cover the tin with foil and cook according to the recipe. When the fish is cooked, it can be lifted out easily by lifting the edges of the foil beneath it. Then transfer the fish to a serving platter for the final decorating and garnishing.

Pickled salmon and cucumber

SERVES: 4–6 as a starter
PREPARATION TIME: 15 minutes, plus several hours marinating
COOKING TIME: none

½ small cucumber
2 teaspoons salt
500 g very fresh thick salmon fillet, skinned and chilled
4 tablespoons lime or lemon juice, or white wine vinegar
1 teaspoon caster sugar
Coarsely ground black pepper
1 tablespoon chopped fresh dill
To garnish: sprigs of fresh dill and thin slices of lime or lemon

---

1 Score the skin of the cucumber lengthways all the way round, then slice it as thinly as possible. Place the slices in a plastic sieve and sprinkle them with the salt, shaking to distribute the salt evenly.
2 Place the sieve over a bowl and leave the cucumber to drain at room temperature for an hour, shaking it occasionally, until 4 tablespoons of juice has drained off. Rinse the salt from the cucumber in cold water and then drain well.
3 Slice the salmon fillet very thinly, as you would smoked salmon (see panel, page 308). The colder the fillet, the easier it is to slice.
4 Put the slices in a bowl. Pour over the lime or lemon juice or vinegar then add the sugar, pepper, dill and cucumber and mix gently by hand.
5 Cover and chill for 30 minutes, turning occasionally so that all the salmon is thoroughly coated with the marinade. The acid in the marinade will 'cook' the salmon, changing it from bright pink to a pale opaque colour, as it would be if heated.
6 When ready to serve, arrange the slices of salmon and cucumber neatly on individual plates and then garnish with sprigs of dill and slices of lime or lemon. Serve the pickled salmon with slices of brown or dark rye bread, plain or spread with butter.

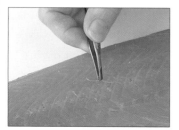

SOMETHING SMALLER

We are very fond of fresh salmon but a whole fish is usually too much for my family. What are the best cuts to buy?

If you have fish left over from a poached or baked whole salmon, it is delicious served cold with a flavoursome mayonnaise, with some crusty fresh bread and a salad on the side.

However, for those times when you can't find a whole fish small enough for your needs, larger farmed salmon are sold cut into steaks, cutlets and fillets. The tail end of salmon has moist flesh, while the larger middle cuts can be a little dry, so care should be taken to avoid overcooking them. All cuts of salmon benefit from either being cooked with moist flavourings, or served with a luscious sauce. The classic Beurre Blanc (see the recipe on page 55) is a traditional partner for salmon.

Try also Steamed Salmon Steaks (see **Wok**) and Microwaved Salmon (see **Fish**), both of which use simple Asian flavours with quite spectacular results.

Salt

EARTH AND OCEAN

What is the difference between ordinary salt and sea salt, and is one better for cooking?

Most ordinary salt is rock salt, the residue of ancient oceans mined from underground, which comes finely ground or in large crystals. Some cooks prefer to use coarse rock or sea salt (which has been evaporated from sea water, or from salt marshes), as these do not need the anti-caking additives used in many brands of finely ground salt. Sea salt is a good choice for both cooking and the table. One of the finest is Maldon salt from Essex, in England, with large soft flakes that can be crushed by the fingers.

OVERSEASONED

What can I do if I have put too much salt in a dish?

It depends on the dish. In the case of a semi-liquid dish like a soup or stew, you can add a couple of peeled and sliced potatoes to soak up the salt: cook them until tender, then discard before serving. Alternatively, you may add a couple of spoonfuls of rice or pasta pieces, but these will have to stay in the dish after cooking. Other thick, bland foods, such as cream or yoghurt, can be added to help reduce the saltiness. The damage is harder to counteract in dishes which have a thicker consistency. The only solution is to cook a second batch of half the quantity of the recipe without salt, and then to combine it with the oversalted lot.

SALT REDUCTION

How much will it affect a recipe if I cut out all the salt?

You can cut the salt out altogether but it will affect the taste of the dish. People who need to go on salt-free diets soon learn to live without it but, for most of us, entirely salt-free food is unacceptable. One solution is to reduce the amount of salt you use in cooking, perhaps adding only half as much as formerly, and putting good sea salt on the table for diners to help themselves. (See also **Nutrition**.)

Samphire

BEACH VEGETABLE

What is samphire?

Samphire is a native Australian plant that grows in marshes, at the back of mangrove swamps, also in the outback in low-lying areas affected by salt. There are a number of species, related to, but different from, the European variety. Gather some yourself, for it is delicious. Its soft, salty flavour goes well with fish in white sauce, and also makes a fine first course, served like asparagus with melted butter. It needs rigorous washing to get rid of any sand, but samphire should be cooked for only about 1 minute. It is done when you can suck the flesh away from the fibre in the middle of the stem.

Samphire, with its unique salty flavour, tastes equally good hot or cold.

Satay

TENDER CUTS

What is satay, and how do I go about preparing it?

Satay is an Indonesian dish of pieces of marinated meat grilled on wooden skewers and served with a spicy peanut sauce. Traditionally, the meat used in satay is not cubed but minced and moulded around the satay sticks. However, delicious satay can also be made with tender cubes of meat: leg or rib of pork with a little fat; skinless breast or upper thigh of chicken; sirloin or rump steak (fillet is too dry); best end of lamb or lamb chops.

Marinating the meat for a few hours before cooking, as with the chicken in the recipe below, will tenderise as well as flavour it. Use bamboo satay sticks, which should be soaked in water for a few hours before using so they will not burn. They should be about 20 cm long to allow the meat to be skewered along half the length, leaving a 'handle' to grasp during grilling.

Grilled chicken satay

MAKES: 20–30 sticks
PREPARATION TIME: 20 minutes, plus at least 2 hours marinating
COOKING TIME: 35 minutes

1 kg chicken breast
2 tablespoons ground coriander
1 tablespoon ground cumin
2 teaspoons ground turmeric
1 tablespoon each finely minced garlic and green ginger
1 large onion, finely chopped
2 tablespoons sugar
3 tablespoons vegetable oil
2 teaspoons salt
To use as basting brushes: 3 stalks lemon grass, bruised at the base
To serve: satay sauce (see recipe, page 310)

1 Cut the chicken into 2 cm cubes and flatten them a little.
2 Combine all the other ingredients in a bowl then stir in the chicken,

For an authentic Asian taste, serve homemade satay with a sauce of freshly ground peanuts pungently flavoured with chilli, shrimp paste and galangal.

making sure all the pieces are well coated. Refrigerate the chicken for a few hours or leave overnight.
3 When you are ready to cook the chicken, preheat the barbecue or grill until red hot. Thread the cubes of meat onto the presoaked bamboo skewers and press as much of the marinade onto the meat as possible.
4 Grill the satay for 5 minutes per stick, turning once or twice during cooking and basting the meat often using the bruised lemon grass as a brush. Serve with satay sauce.

VARIATION

Whole, scored chicken breasts steeped in the same marinade can be grilled and served as a main course, with satay sauce alongside, plus rice and a salad or stir-fried vegetables.

PREPARING AHEAD

Can I make satay ahead of time and keep them warm?

Satay can be prepared one day ahead. Marinating for longer results in even more succulence and a richer flavour than meat not treated in this way. The satay can also be grilled or barbecued in the morning to serve in the evening, but should then be covered with plastic wrap to prevent the meat drying out.

To reheat, put the satay in a shallow baking dish without crowding or overlapping, and warm through in an oven that has been preheated to 150°C. The satay is ready when the oil has taken on a sheen.

SEAFOOD FOR SATAY

Is is possible to make fish or seafood satay?

Yes, but only a few fish stand up to being skewered in this way. Use fish with firm flesh, such as ling and jewfish. These can be cut up in the same way as meat and poultry, but the pieces should be slightly larger so that they do not fall apart when threaded onto the skewer. Prawns should be shelled and left whole. Thread one king or two medium green prawns onto each stick. Scallops can be used whole, while green lobster should be cut into medallions about 2 cm thick and then threaded onto the skewer.

SPICY PEANUT SAUCE

Do I have to buy the peanut sauce that is served with satay, or can I make my own?

The peanut sauce, also called satay sauce, is widely available but making your own is more satisfying and will taste more authentic. Most commercial brands of satay sauce leave out shrimp paste, a fundamental ingredient, because it does not have a long shelf life.

Ready-made satay sauce tends to be very thick as the ground nuts absorb some of the liquid over time. You can thin it by adding a little water or coconut milk, heating the sauce until lukewarm, and then stirring to make it smooth.

Leftovers

Leftover satay sauce should be used within a day or two. It makes an excellent topping for grilled chicken, or a dressing for gado gado, the Indonesian cucumber, bean sprout, green bean and bean curd salad. It can also be used in vegetarian dishes, for instance mixed with rice, peas and carrots, or as a dip for crudités.

When making the following satay sauce, it is better to buy unsalted peanuts that have been shelled and roasted and then grind them yourself at home. The simplest way to crush peanuts is to put them into freezer bags, one inside the other, and pound them with a rolling pin until fine. Alternatively, you can use some thick chunky peanut butter, preferably unsweetened.

Satay sauce

MAKES: *about 1.25 litres*
PREPARATION TIME: *15 minutes*
COOKING TIME: *15 minutes*

2 stalks lemon grass
1 tablespoon chilli powder
2.5 cm cube shrimp paste
2 large onions, chopped
6 candlenuts or macadamia nuts
2 cloves garlic
3 slices galangal or ginger
250 ml vegetable oil
75 ml tamarind concentrate
40 g (2 tablespoons) white sugar
2 teaspoons salt
750 g (4½ cups) peanuts,
  finely ground, or 500 g crunchy
  peanut butter

1 To make the spice mixture, cut off the bulbous white root ends of the lemon grass stalks and discard their green shoots. Cut the root ends into thin slices. Put them, along with the chilli powder, shrimp paste, onions, nuts, garlic, and galangal or ginger into a mortar, or coffee grinder, and pound or grind them to a purée. You could use a blender or a food processor, but you will not get the very smooth texture that is best for this sauce.
2 Heat the oil and fry the mixture over a medium heat for 10 minutes, stirring all the time. When the spice mixture releases its aroma and the oil has become rich and red, add the tamarind and 750 ml of water. Bring the mixture to the boil and simmer for 5 minutes.
3 Add the sugar and salt, adjusting them to taste, then add the ground peanuts or peanut butter, and stir well. Remove the sauce from the heat and allow to cool and thicken.

Sauces

SMOOTH SAUCE

I'm familiar with the basic roux for making white sauces but mine are sometimes lumpy. How can I make a sauce with no lumps?

The first step when making a white sauce (see panel, right) is to combine equal quantities of plain flour and melted butter, oil or margarine to form a pale golden roux – this is usually problem-free. The lumps come when the liquid is added, often to a roux that is too hot, so remove the pan from the heat and allow the roux to cool slightly before adding the liquid.

Lumps can be smoothed out by whisking the sauce briskly, or by blending it or sieving it. However, if you leave too many lumps in the strainer, the sauce will be thinner than you intended.

TIME SAVER

What is an all-in-one sauce?

The all-in-one sauce is a useful timesaving method of making a white sauce in which all the ingredients are put into a saucepan and whisked continuously over a medium heat until the sauce boils and is thick and very smooth.

Another option is to put all the ingredients into a blender and blend for about 30 seconds, and then transfer the mixture to a saucepan and bring it to the boil, stirring continuously. The sauce should then be simmered for about 3–5 minutes, a little longer than a traditionally made sauce, to ensure the flour is well cooked.

MORE BUTTER AND FLOUR

How do I make a binding sauce?

A binding sauce, such as that used in making croquettes or rissoles, is made in the same way as a white sauce (see panel, right) but with 60 g butter and 60 g plain flour per 300 ml of liquid.

MAKING A BASIC WHITE SAUCE

The basic white sauce often used for savoury dishes is made with a liquid, such as stock or milk, and thickened with a cooked mixture of flour and butter. The finished sauce is often given an added flavouring such as cheese or parsley.

These flour-based sauces can be made either in a saucepan or a microwave. In many ways the microwave is easier to use as its exact timings and temperatures mean the sauce can be left for a while at any stage, if there is something else to attend to, without the risk of it overcooking or turning lumpy.

IN A SAUCEPAN

1 Melt 30 g butter in a small saucepan; stir in 30 g (¼ cup) plain flour with a wooden spoon. Stir until the mixture forms a smooth ball in the base of the saucepan.

2 Cook the roux over a medium heat, stirring, for 1-2 minutes until it has a sandy texture but has not changed colour. Allow to cool slightly before adding the liquid.

3 Gradually add 300 ml hot milk to the cooked roux over a low heat, stirring until it boils and is thick and smooth, then simmer gently, stirring constantly, for about 3 minutes.

IN THE MICROWAVE

1 Melt 30 g butter in a jug on High for 20-40 seconds. Remove from the microwave and stir 30 g (¼ cup) plain flour into the butter to make the first stage of the sauce, the roux.

2 Add 300 ml milk to the roux, and whisk it constantly until the mixture is well blended, most of the lumps have disappeared and the sauce is quite smooth and thick.

3 Return the sauce to the microwave and cook on High for 1-3 minutes. Take it out every minute and whisk it well until the sauce is smooth and as thick as you want it to be.

JAZZ IT UP

What can I add to white sauces to make them more interesting?

There are several ways in which a basic white sauce can be altered to give a tastier result:

- CHEESE SAUCE: stir in 60 g of grated cheese (mature Cheddar, Gruyère or Parmesan) just before serving – the heat of the sauce will melt the cheese. If you are making the sauce to pour over cooked fish or vegetables, the cooking liquid may be used instead of some or all of the milk. Add a sprinkling of cayenne, mustard, nutmeg or hot paprika for a piquant flavour.
- MUSHROOM SAUCE: sauté 60–100 g of thinly sliced fresh mushrooms in 20–30 g of butter then stir them into the white sauce. Season with nutmeg and serve with fish or meat dishes.
- ONION SAUCE: sauté a medium to large chopped onion in butter or oil before adding to the white sauce.
- PARSLEY SAUCE: stir in 2–3 heaped tablespoons of finely chopped parsley (or basil, chives, oregano, tarragon or watercress for other herb sauces) just before serving with fish, ham, or a selection of boiled or grilled vegetables.

LIQUID OPTIONS

What liquids can I use for sauces? Should they be added hot or cold?

The liquid you choose depends on the dish, but it should have a good flavour. A rich, homemade stock is good for many savoury sauces, but the water in which a particular vegetable has been cooked is the most appropriate liquid to use for a sauce that is to be served with, or poured over, that vegetable.

Milk is often used for white sauces and the classic Béchamel (page 312) is given extra flavour by infusing the milk with onions, herbs and seasonings.

Whether you add hot or cold liquid to the roux should not affect the finished sauce, but if you use cold liquid the sauce will take longer to come to the boil. If hot liquid is added to the roux, the mixture must be stirred vigorously because it will thicken much faster.

Other liquids used for sauces include wine, a mixture of stock and white wine or cider, and dessert wines, which are often used in sauces to accompany puddings.

Béchamel sauce

MAKES: *300 ml*
PREPARATION TIME: *5 minutes, plus at least 10 minutes to infuse*
COOKING TIME: *5–10 minutes*

300 ml milk
1 small onion, peeled and studded with cloves
1 bay leaf
A few parsley stalks
6 peppercorns
30 g butter
30 g (¼ cup) plain flour
Salt and black pepper

1 Pour the milk into a small pan and add the onion, herbs and peppercorns. Slowly bring the milk to simmering point then remove it from the heat and stir.
2 Cover and leave to infuse for at least 10 minutes, but preferably 30 minutes or longer, then strain.
3 Melt the butter in a saucepan. Add the flour to make a roux and cook over a medium heat for 1–2 minutes, stirring with a wooden spoon.
4 Gradually add the milk, stirring until the sauce is thick and smooth. Bring to the boil, stirring constantly, then simmer for 3 minutes and season to taste.
VARIATIONS
• MORNAY: stir in 60 g of grated Gruyère, Cheddar, or fresh Parmesan cheese, an egg yolk and a few tablespoons of fresh cream. This sauce goes well with egg dishes, chicken or white fish.
• SOUBISE: stir a purée of simmered onion into the béchamel. Serve with meat or vegetables.
• VELOUTÉ: make in the same way as béchamel, but use stock instead of milk, and cook the roux until it is pale brown. Whisk in some cream before serving to make a richer sauce. Serve with poultry or fish.

FAT FREE

Is there any way to thicken a sauce without using a roux?

Yes, you can use cornflour to make a white sauce, using vegetable stock for a savoury sauce, or water and wine for a sweet sauce. It is a useful method for people on low-fat diets. A sweet cornflour sauce, such as the one in the following recipe, goes especially well with traditional steamed puddings.

Cornflour sauce

MAKES: *300 ml*
PREPARATION TIME: *5 minutes*
COOKING TIME: *10 minutes*

20 g (2 tablespoons) cornflour
300 ml sweet white wine (or half wine and half water)
1 split vanilla pod

1 Put the cornflour in a medium-sized bowl and stir in 2 tablespoons of the wine to make a smooth paste.
2 Heat the remaining wine with the vanilla pod to just below boiling point, then strain onto the cornflour paste. Save the vanilla pod for use another time and stir the sauce well.
3 Return the sauce to the pan and bring it to a boil, stirring constantly, until it is smooth and thick. Simmer gently for 1–2 minutes, then serve.
VARIATIONS
Replace the vanilla with cinnamon, ginger, mace or nutmeg. To make a savoury sauce, use stock or stock and wine, sprigs of herbs plus a bay leaf and some peppercorns.

QUICK BUTTER SAUCE

I find flour-based sauces too heavy. Is there an alternative?

Many professional chefs now rarely make roux-based sauces, preferring to use reduced stocks and wine as the basis of well-flavoured sauces, sometimes with the addition of butter or cream. These sauces have a lighter texture than flour-based sauces and do not cloy the palate, although they are still rich. It is essential when making butter or cream sauces to balance

the flavour with a little lemon juice, vinegar or wine, to provide acidity, as in the recipe below.

Tomato butter sauce

MAKES: *about 300 ml*
PREPARATION TIME: *5 minutes*
COOKING TIME: *10 minutes*

1 large shallot, finely chopped
185 g unsalted butter, diced
2 large egg tomatoes, quartered
100 ml white wine
A squeeze of lemon juice
Salt and black pepper
Chopped fresh herbs such as basil or chives, to taste

1 In a saucepan, sweat the shallot in 1 tablespoon of the butter, then add the tomatoes and wine, bring to the boil and simmer for 5 minutes.
2 When the tomatoes are cooked, beat the sauce vigorously until quite smooth then gradually whisk in the diced butter a piece at a time.
3 Pass the sauce through a fine strainer, pushing through as much of the tomato pulp as possible.
4 Whisk the sauce a final time, then taste it and adjust the acidity with a little lemon juice as necessary. Season with the salt, pepper and herbs.

KEEPING IT WARM

Can I make a sauce in advance and reheat it when I need it?

Most sauces can be made ahead and kept warm in a bain-marie for up to an hour. When you need the sauce, raise the heat, stir it until heated through and smooth, then simmer for a minute. Sauces can also be reheated in a microwave oven set on Medium-High; whisk the sauce every minute until well heated, thick and smooth.

Sauces can be chilled for several days, or frozen for one to two months, and then reheated. However, by the time you have thawed, reconstituted and stirred a frozen sauce back to the right texture, you could have made it from scratch. Egg-based sauces, such as custard, should not be frozen because they usually curdle after thawing.

VEGETABLE VARIETY

I'm a vegan. Are there any interesting sauces that don't use meat stock or dairy products?

Sauces made with vegetable stock can be made more lively by the addition of strong flavourings such as chilli, garlic, ginger, plenty of fresh herbs or a splash of wine, and thickened if you wish with puréed vegetables. The versatile vegan tomato sauce below is one of the most popular of all Neapolitan sauces. It is full of flavour, easy to make and delicious whether hot or cold. Serve it with rice, polenta or any grain dish, or with stuffed, grilled, or boiled vegetables.

Salsa pizzaiola

MAKES: 500 ml
PREPARATION TIME: 10 minutes
COOKING TIME: 30–45 minutes

1 tablespoon olive oil
1 medium onion, chopped
1 large clove garlic, crushed
750 g fresh ripe tomatoes (preferably egg) skinned and chopped
2 tablespoons chopped fresh basil or oregano, or 2 teaspoons dried
1 teaspoon sugar
Salt and black pepper

1 Heat the olive oil in a medium saucepan and fry the onion gently for 5 minutes until lightly golden. Add the garlic and cook, stirring, for a further minute.
2 Add the chopped tomatoes with all their seeds and juice, then add the herbs, sugar, salt and pepper.
3 Bring the sauce to the boil, then cover the pan and simmer for 30–45 minutes, stirring occasionally until the sauce is thick and chunky. You can cook it longer if you want it to be thicker and less runny.
VARIATION
For a smoother sauce, the mixture can be puréed in a blender or sieved. If you plan to do this, there is no need to skin the tomatoes first. You can also used canned tomatoes instead of fresh. Fresh herbs can be stirred in or sprinkled on top.

SKINLESS

How can I stop a skin forming on a sauce after cooking?

Stir the sauce frequently while it is cooling, or cover the surface of the hot sauce with buttered greaseproof paper, buttered side touching the sauce, or some foil or plastic wrap. A knob of butter added after cooking, or a few tablespoons of the liquid kept back and floated on the surface, can also prevent a skin forming, and can be stirred in when the sauce is reheated.

OLD FAVOURITE

My family want to try some bread sauce with their Christmas turkey. Is it difficult to make?

Not at all. Smooth, creamy and subtly spiced, it is one of the easiest sauces to make (see recipe, right). It is traditionally served in a sauce boat with roast chicken, turkey and game birds. Make it in a double boiler or a heavy-based saucepan but be sure to watch it carefully.

Bread sauce

SERVES: 4–6
PREPARATION TIME: 15 minutes, plus at least 15 minutes infusing
COOKING TIME: 15 minutes

4 cloves
1 small onion
300 ml milk
1 bay leaf
1 blade mace, optional
A pinch of salt
4 peppercorns
60 g (1 cup) fresh breadcrumbs
30 g butter
2 tablespoons cream, optional

1 Stick the cloves into the surface of the onion. Pour the milk into a small saucepan and add the onion, herbs and spices. Bring to the boil slowly, remove from the heat, then cover and leave to infuse for 15 minutes.
2 Strain the milk and return it to the saucepan. Add the breadcrumbs and butter and cook over a gentle heat for about 15 minutes, or until the breadcrumbs absorb the milk and the sauce is thick and creamy.

Pizzaiola is a chunky vegetarian sauce full of the zesty flavour of fresh garlic, ripe egg tomatoes and basil. It can be used to liven up a variety of dishes.

Wine-braised sausages

SERVES: 4
PREPARATION TIME: 20 minutes
COOKING TIME: 50 minutes

---

2 tablespoons olive oil
500 g sausages
250 g baby onions, peeled
1 small red pepper, deseeded and
  coarsely chopped
100 g pancetta or thick-cut streaky
  bacon, diced
1 clove garlic, crushed
2 teaspoons plain flour
150 ml red wine
100 g mushrooms, thickly sliced

---

1 Heat the oil in a large, flameproof casserole. Add the sausages (do not prick them first) and when lightly browned all over, transfer to a plate.
2 Add the onions, red pepper, bacon and garlic to the pan and cook until all are lightly browned. Stir in the flour, then gradually add the wine.
3 Place the sausages on top, cover and simmer as slowly as possible for 30 minutes. Stir in the mushrooms and cook for a further 10 minutes.

HEALTHIER SAUSAGES

Are there some sausages that are more nutritious than others?

Sausages with more meat and less fat are better for you: a high price should reflect a high meat content. Australian pork sausages must, by law, contain at least 50 per cent fat-free meat. Beef, or pork and beef sausages, also need contain only 50 per cent fat-free meat. The rest is made up of herbs, rusk, spices and water, with antioxidants, polyphosphates and preservatives. Continental sausages are made of pure meat with flavourings added.

NO BANGS

I thought you were supposed to prick sausages before cooking them. Is this true?

After the Second World War, when meat was still scarce, sausages contained so much water that they exploded when cooked, which is why they were nicknamed bangers.

Sausages

Choose an earthy red wine for this colourful family meal of sausages with peppers, onions and mushrooms.

WORLD OF CHOICE

Sausages make a good quick meal but my family gets bored with the same old ones. Are there some new varieties I could try?

Almost every part of the world has its own variety of sausages. You might like to look out for some of the following types.

German *bratwurst* are large, long and pale, as they often contain veal or milk. If you like spicy sausages, try the ruby-red Spanish *chorizos*, Lebanese *m'anak* made of lamb and studded with pine nuts, or Algerian *merguez*.

Italian versions, called *salsiccie* (sausage), are flavoured with herbs and sometimes whole peppercorns. A speciality from northern Italy is the long, unlinked *luganega*.

One of the best-known French sausages is the pure pork *saucisse de Toulouse*, a substantial, coarsely textured sausage which is also often unlinked. The small French *andouillette* has a stronger flavour as it is made of pig's tripe and offal and is salted and then smoked.

Gourmet sausages with a high meat content, made from pork, lamb, veal, beef, chicken and turkey, and flavoured with herbs, are available in leading delicatessens and specialist food shops. There are also sausages made with kangaroo, emu and venison.

If you want to try a new way to cook sausages, which is very good for most of the Continental-style sausages or the newer Australian ones with a high meat content, try the recipe, above right.

Pricking was an attempt to prevent this, but now it should not be done as it just allows the juices to escape.

Sausages will burst if cooked at too high a temperature. Fry them gently for about 10 minutes, turning until golden brown all over, or grill them not too close to the heat.

SAUSAGE NICKNAMES

Why do my American friends call frankfurters hot dogs or wieners?

The popular American smoked sausage in a roll has two nicknames because it is similar to two German sausages: the frankfurter, which was originally made in Frankfurt, and the wiener from Wien (Vienna). When a cartoonist drew a tail, legs and a head on the frankfurter to make it look like a dachshund, it was christened the hot dog and has remained so ever since. They can be made of beef, pork or poultry with added fat and need no cooking, just heating.

SMOKED PORK SAUSAGE

Are saveloys sausages?

The word saveloy is a corruption of the French term *cervelas*, which originally meant a sausage made with brains (*cervelles*). Now saveloy is a fat sausage made from smoked pork, found battered in fast-food shops. There it is heated up by plunging it into the hot oil, but it usually tastes better if poached in hot water like the French original.

SCOTTISH DELICACY

What exactly is haggis?

Haggis, a popular Scottish speciality, is a large, spicy sausage encased by a sheep's stomach. It is made from the animal's liver, lungs and heart, minced and mixed with oatmeal, onion, suet and seasonings, and is served accompanied by mashed potatoes and bashed neeps (swedes) on festive occasions such as Burns Night. The taste is rich and quite meaty.

Haggis is available from delicatessens specialising in Scottish

imports; it is already cooked but needs reheating by steaming for around 45–60 minutes. To serve the haggis, cut a hole in the skin and scoop out the contents.

CHINESE BANGERS

Are there any Asian sausages?

Yes, Chinese food shops stock *lap cheung* or *ap yeung cheung*, both suitable for grilling or frying (*cheung* is the Chinese word for intestine). They are small, knobbly looking pork sausages, flavoured with soy sauce and a small amount of alcohol. *Lap cheung* is fresh and is coloured bright red with paprika. *Ap yeung cheung* is air-dried and the Chinese usually steam it over a pan of boiling rice.

VEGGIE VERSIONS

Are there any meat-free sausages suitable for vegetarians?

Vegetarian sausages, based on soya bean products, are widely available, and many speciality sausage shops are now selling innovative vegetarian sausages.

CUSTOM MADE

I would like really lean, chunky sausages. Can I make my own?

Making your own sausages is easy and appealing because it allows you to use a high proportion of lean meat, and you can vary the texture and flavouring to suit your own taste by adding different herbs and spices. A good butcher should be able to sell you sausage casings.

Some kitchen shops sell a mincer with plastic sausage nozzles or you can use a funnel with a large opening. Slide the end of the sausage casing onto one end of the funnel and push the meat mixture into it with a pestle or the handle of a wooden spoon.

The homemade sausages in the following recipe should be cooked and eaten within 24 hours of being made; unlike commercially made sausages, the only preservative they contain is salt.

Pork and herb sausages

SERVES: 4
PREPARATION TIME: 30 minutes
COOKING TIME: 10 minutes

1 m sausage skins, soaked in warm
    water for 10 minutes (or as
    instructed by the butcher)
1 tablespoon olive oil
1 small onion, finely chopped
500 g lean pork, such as leg steaks
1½ tablespoons chopped mixed
    fresh herbs, such as oregano,
    parsley, rosemary, sage or thyme
1 tablespoon Dijon mustard
Salt and black pepper
Olive oil for basting

1 While you leave the sausage skins to soak, heat the olive oil in a small frying pan, add the onion and fry it gently until it has softened but not coloured. Transfer the onion to sheets of kitchen paper towels and leave it there to drain as it cools.

2 Trim and dice the pork, then pile it onto a chopping board. Chop it finely by holding two sharp knives loosely and parallel to each other. Lift each knife in turn up and down to chop in a smooth rhythmic movement (for details, see *Hamburgers*). Put the chopped pork into a bowl and stir in the onion and seasonings with a fork.

3 Drain and dry the sausage skins. Tie a secure knot in one end, then slide the loose end onto a hand-held sausage maker or the sausage making attachment of a food mixer, gently ruffling up the skin so that the knotted end is at the opening of the attachment. Pack the meat mixture into the sausage maker and pipe it into the skins, smoothing it so that there are no air bubbles. Twist the skins at about 10 cm intervals to make the sausage links. Tie the loose end securely.

4 These sausages are better grilled than fried. Preheat the grill and then brush the sausages lightly with oil. When it is very hot, grill them for about 10 minutes.

For a simpler recipe, shape the mixture into 8 flat patties and fry them in 1 tablespoon oil for 10-12 min-utes, turning once.

Scallops

CORAL DELICACY

Are there different kinds of scallops and how do I cook them?

Scallops, classified by their shell size, range from 7.5–10 cm up to the great scallops available in the northern hemisphere, which can grow as large as 15 cm. The coral, or roe (eggs), is prized for its sweet creamy taste and striking colour.

Scallops can be sliced in half horizontally if large but Australian scallops are generally left whole. They need only very brief cooking: 1–2 minutes deep-fried, grilled or poached; 2–3 minutes sautéed. Heat the coral for a few seconds at the end of the cooking time.

DO NOT BUY WATER

Are fresh scallops really that much better than frozen? They are a lot more expensive.

Fresh seafood is always preferable to frozen. With scallops it is particularly important to buy them on their shells: frozen scallops often absorb water during freezing, making them swell to double their size, but they shrink the instant they hit the pan.

PREPARING SCALLOPS

Shelled raw scallops should be kept for no more than 24 hours; cooked, they can be kept for up to two days.

Fresh scallops are usually sold ready-dressed with the white meat and the coral together on the half shell. Cut the small strip of muscle from the white part and discard it, then separate and set the coral aside. The white scallop meat can be halved through the middle or sliced if large.

Scampi

OCEAN SHELLFISH

Are scampi just large prawns?

No. Scampi, which are also called langoustines, are actually a cross between a small lobster and a prawn, but there is virtually no flesh in their claws. The confusion arises because they are known as Dublin Bay prawns in Britain as well as Norwegian lobsters. They are trawled in the ocean near Western Australia, and are also found in the Atlantic from Iceland to Morocco and in the Mediterranean. The scampi resembles the yabby in appearance but is an ocean shellfish whereas the yabby is a freshwater shellfish. The tail meat is delicious, simply cooked by boiling or barbecuing in the shell.

Scones

HIGH AND TIDY

What is the secret of well-shaped and beautifully risen scones?

Ideally, scones should double in size when cooked but they will not rise well and will be poorly shaped if the dough is rolled out thinly and unevenly.

Pat out or roll the dough 2 cm thick, using even pressure on the rolling pin. Dip the cutter in flour before cutting the scones out, and push straight down. If you twist, they will be ragged or slanted. Bake immediately in a hot oven as the raising agent starts to work the minute any liquid is added. Bicarbonate of soda and cream of tartar used with plain flour give a better lift than self-raising flour (see recipe, above right).

Plain classic scones

MAKES: 12 scones
PREPARATION TIME: 10 minutes
COOKING TIME: 8–10 minutes

---

250 g (2 cups) plain flour
1 teaspoon bicarbonate of soda
2 teaspoons cream of tartar
A pinch of salt
40 g butter, diced
40 g (2 tablespoons) caster sugar
150 ml milk

---

1 Preheat the oven to 220°C. Grease a baking tray.
2 Sift the flour, bicarbonate of soda, cream of tartar and salt into a bowl. Rub in the butter with your fingertips until the mixture resembles fine breadcrumbs, then carefully stir in the sugar.
3 Make a well in the centre, pour in the milk and mix with a round-bladed knife to form a soft, but not sticky, dough.
4 Turn the dough out onto a floured surface and knead lightly for a few seconds to smooth it. Pat out, or using a floured rolling pin, roll it out to a thickness of 2 cm. Then, using a 5 cm cutter, cut out as many rounds as you can. Make a ball with the trimmings, reroll the dough and cut more rounds.
5 Place the rounds on the baking tray and dust the tops with flour. Bake immediately for 10–12 minutes until well risen and light brown. Cool on a wire cooling rack for 15 minutes.

ADDING FLAVOUR

What ingredients can I add to a plain scone mix for a change?

For fruit scones, add 60 g (⅓ cup) of mixed dried fruit to the recipe above, and ½ teaspoon of ground cinnamon; or 60 g (⅓ cup) chopped dates and the grated zest and juice of an orange. For cheese scones add 50 g of grated Cheddar cheese, ½ teaspoon of mustard and a pinch of cayenne pepper. Half a teaspoon of mixed dried herbs is better for making savoury scones than fresh herbs, which can produce green streaks.

Seaweed

HIGH NUTRITION

Why does anyone eat seaweed?

Seaweed is quite delicious, with a pleasant fresh saltiness reminiscent of the sea. Vegetarians have always recognised the importance of sea vegetables, which are a valuable, and inexpensive, source of concentrated essential vitamins and minerals. They also rely on carrageen or agar-agar, seaweed used for thickening and gelling, instead of animal-derived gelatine.

Asians have always been more ready to eat sea vegetables than Westerners, and seaweed is particularly popular in Japan with its long jagged coastline. The proliferation of Japanese restaurants in Australia's capital cities has spurred interest in sea vegetables, and there is a wide variety of dried marine vegetation now on sale in Asian food stores and health food shops.

Seaweeds are eaten as vegetables, are used as garnishes and in dressings, and add a distinctive salty flavour to soups and snacks such as crispy rice crackers.

Versatile nori, like all seaweed, is rich in minerals and is sold both in handy sheets or ready-flaked.

SEASIDE PROVENDER

Can I eat seaweed gathered straight from the beach?

In theory you can, but you must collect it from a shoreline free of pollution. Laver weed, also called red laver or tangle, is used to make laver bread in Britain. It is the same variety called *nori* in Japan and sold dried in sheets. But it can take 8 hours boiling to make it edible. Purple fronds of dulse can be cleaned, brushed with egg, coated with flour or oatmeal and deep-fried until it is very crisp.

NAME THAT SEAWEED

What are the different sorts of seaweed, and how are they used?

• ARAME has a particularly high calcium content and can be bought already shredded in a dark-green tangle. Very strongly flavoured, it is used in Japanese miso soup and a small amount makes an exciting addition to mushroom or seafood risottos as well as Asian rice dishes. It needs a 5-minute soak and then 30 minutes cooking.

• DULSE, which is available fresh and dried, is good in soups and in vegetable or grain dishes. You can eat it deep-fried or, after a brief soak to soften it, shred it into salads or their dressings, for example the Asian salad dressing on the right. This can be poured over cooked fish or grilled prawns, or served as a dipping sauce: you can also use prawn crackers to scoop it up.

• KOMBU is valuable in vegetarian stocks. A strip of kombu cooked with dried beans both speeds up their cooking time and contributes flavour – even a strip that has been simmered for 20 minutes in stock.

• NORI is one of the most common seaweeds. It is sold in sheets which can be lightly toasted for additional flavour and then used in sushi (see *Japanese Cooking*) or crumbled over rice or vegetables. Nori also comes ready-flaked, so it can be either sprinkled, uncooked, over rice dishes, or added to pancake or tempura batters for extra flavour.

Dulse, ginger and spring onion dressing

SERVES: 4
PREPARATION TIME: 10 minutes
COOKING TIME: 1–2 minutes if using fresh dulse; none if using dried dulse

---

90 g fresh dulse or 30 g dried dulse
4–6 spring onions, chopped
5 cm piece cucumber, finely diced
5 cm piece green ginger, peeled and grated
1 teaspoon Thai fish sauce, optional
1 tablespoon lemon juice
1 tablespoon soy sauce
1 teaspoon dark brown sugar
1 tablespoon peanut oil or sunflower oil
1 teaspoon sesame seed oil

---

1 If using dried dulse, soak it for a minute in cold water then drain. If using fresh dulse, rinse it, put it into a pan with boiling water to cover and cook for 30 seconds. Drain and set it aside to cool.
2 Press the drained dulse with your hands to squeeze out all the liquid, compressing it into a ball. Put it on a board and shred it, then mix in the spring onions and cucumber.
3 Mix the ginger, fish sauce, lemon juice, soy sauce and sugar in a bowl and stir to dissolve the sugar. Whisk in the oils, then toss in the dulse mixture. Use as a dressing or dip for spring rolls or won ton dumplings.

Seeds

EATEN NOT SOWN

In the shops, seeds are sometimes on the spice racks and sometimes, like sunflower seeds, they are with the nuts. Are they spices?

The difference between seeds and spices is a hazy one, as many spices are themselves seeds. The distinction seems to be made between those that impart their flavour to other foods (for example, caraway, celery and mustard), which are regarded as spices, and those that retain their own flavour (for example, poppy seeds). All seeds, especially pumpkin, sunflower and sesame, are rich in essential minerals and vitamins, and they are also exceedingly high in kilojoules.

Black seeds, such as poppy seeds, come in useful for adding a colour contrast to pale dishes. Both black mustard seeds and black (unhulled) sesame seeds can be bought in Indian shops, as can small black seeds called *kalongi*, which have a pleasant, earthy flavour.

SEED GUIDE

How do I use all the different seeds I see on sale?

• CARAWAY SEEDS are favourites in Central Europe where they are used with pork and potatoes, and in sausages and breads such as rye and pumpernickel. Sprinkle them over pork chops before frying, then add a drop of kummel, the caraway-flavoured liqueur, and a tablespoon of sour cream to the pan juices to make a sauce. The most popular Western use is seed cake spiced with caraway.

• CELERY SEEDS are good added to winter soups and stews. Celery salt is a traditional English seasoning for hard-boiled eggs. To make it, simply pound five parts lightly roasted celery seed with one part sea salt. Put the mixture into a jar, then seal tightly to store.

• MUSTARD SEEDS (yellow and black) are widely used in India to thicken and flavour. The yellow is milder than the black. Both are usually fried quickly in hot oil until they pop, at the start of cooking, or added as a garnish at the end.

• POPPY SEEDS pounded into a paste and sweetened with honey, or sprinkled generously over bagels and dumplings, are a feature of Jewish cooking. Try tossing them, alone or with breadcrumbs, in butter to dress egg noodles.

• PUMPKIN AND SUNFLOWER SEEDS are popular additions to vegetarian dishes as they are nutrient-rich, and are also served as a snack.

• SESAME SEEDS are the most widely used and many people enjoy their nutty flavour. They come in three different colours: beige (unhulled), black (found in Asian shops) and pearly white. In the Middle East, sesame seeds are made into a paste called tahina, pounded with chickpeas to make hummous. They are also the basis of the Greek sweetmeat halva.

Like most seeds, sesame seeds benefit from being gently dry-fried for 2–3 minutes. Scatter them over boiled carrots or a salad of raw grated carrots, or make a nutritious open sandwich by topping buttered wholemeal bread with mixed bean sprouts and sprinkling it with some toasted sesame seeds.

Sesame seeds are ground into two forms of oil: a light, almost tasteless oil for frying, and a dark toasted oil used in small quantities as a flavouring condiment.

Semolina

HARD HEARTED

What is semolina made from?

Semolina is a coarse flour, usually of wheat or maize, which is left behind when the finer flour has been sifted out. Durum wheat semolina is used in Italy to make commercial pasta. It is too hard to use on its own at home, where it needs to be used in conjunction with either pasta or bread flour, usually in a ratio of one part semolina to three parts pasta flour.

As well as making pasta with it, Italians also use semolina to make gnocchi or small dumplings, which can be made either with potatoes or ricotta cheese.

Another good way to use semolina is to substitute it for some of the flour in cakes and biscuits, where the slightly gritty grains add a crisp texture. Semolina was traditionally used to make a rather bland baked milk pudding, the kind of food that is regarded as suitable for toddlers and invalids.

Shellfish

SEA SALTY

When recipes say to boil shellfish in salted water, how much salt do I need to use?

The aim is to emulate sea water: use 150 g (⅔ cup) of salt for every 4 litres of water. Shellfish should always be cooked in a generous quantity of well-salted water.

HOME FREEZING

Do shellfish freeze well?

It is not a good idea to freeze shellfish at home. The freezing process damages shellfish more than many other foods, and even commercial freezing – which is much faster than anything that can be achieved in a domestic freezer – causes considerable deterioration in flavour and texture. While frozen shellfish may be preferable to none at all, they are always much better when eaten fresh and in season.

LAVISH PLATTER

Is it possible to assemble a spectacular dish of fruits de mer in this country like the one I had on holidays in France?

Of course it is. Choose whatever seafood or shellfish is best in the fish market, including at least three, and preferably five, different varieties in a mixed price range: mussels and pipis as well as crab, lobster, oysters and prawns. Also, look for Balmain or Moreton Bay bugs, clams and cockles, periwinkles, scallops, scampi and the freshwater yabbies. The smooth-shelled yabby is a small species of delicious freshwater crayfish. Larger varieties include the Western Australian marron, and the Murray River and Tasmanian crayfish.

Prepare the shellfish you choose according to the instructions given for each in this book. The larger ones, especially lobsters, are often halved to make sure there is

The nicest way to eat fresh shellfish is from a lavish iced platter. Choose from as wide a selection as possible, including scallops, prawns, rock lobster, blue swimmer crab, scampi, sand lobster, Balmain bugs, oysters, mussels, pipis and cockles.

enough to go around. To approximate the French effect – where the food is set out on dramatic elevated platters – arrange the shellfish on a wide plate or round tray lined with washed seaweed and cracked ice and set this in the middle of the table. Surround the platter with halved lemons or limes.

Serve the shellfish with plenty of French bread, crab crackers and lobster picks, the largest white cloth napkins you can find, and finger bowls for each person.

Chilled white wine is probably best to drink with cold seafood. Time, however, is the most essential element when eating a platter of fruits de mer – it is a treat to relax over, not to be rushed through.

Shortbread

BREAKING BREAD

Why does my shortbread break straight out of the oven?

It could be because the dough was worked too much, which can make it tough and brittle. When making shortbread, the dough should be handled as little as possible.

You can also ensure that it does not break up by marking it into wedges before baking. Once cooked, cool the shortbread briefly in the tin then transfer to a rack to cool a little more. While it is still warm, put the shortbread on a hard

surface and cut along the lines you have marked, using a bread knife and a sawing action.

Shortbread almost always breaks if you cut it after it has cooled completely. It is also brittle when it is cooked for too long. When it has been properly baked, shortbread is a pale golden colour, never brown.

GROUND RICE FOR CRUNCH

Why do some shortbread recipes contain ground rice?

Ground rice, rice flour or semolina are frequently added to shortbread dough to give it a fine-grained yet crunchy texture. The recipe for Foolproof Shortbread on page 320 includes ground rice or rice flour.

Foolproof shortbread

MAKES: *8 wedges*
PREPARATION TIME: *30 minutes*
COOKING TIME: *30–40 minutes*

125 g salted butter, softened
60 g (¼ cup) caster sugar
125 g (1 cup) plain flour
A pinch of salt
60 g (½ cup) ground rice
    or rice flour
Caster sugar for dredging,
    optional

1 Preheat the oven to 180°C. Grease a baking tray. Put the butter and sugar in a bowl and beat until pale and fluffy. Mix in the flour, salt and ground rice or rice flour and stir until the mixture has just begun to bind together.
2 Knead the mixture lightly to form a smooth, pliable dough. Transfer the dough to the prepared baking tray and shape it quickly and lightly into a round 1 cm thick; do not overwork the dough. Alternatively, it may be pressed into a special wooden shortbread mould then turned out onto the baking tray.
3 Prick all over the surface of the dough with a fork, mark into eight equal wedges and flute or crimp the edges decoratively. Bake for 30–40 minutes, until the shortbread has cooked to a pale golden colour.
4 Allow the shortbread to cool on the baking tray for a few minutes, then transfer to a wire rack to cool a little. While it is still warm, put the shortbread on a hard surface and cut or break into the marked wedges, then leave it on the wire rack to cool completely.
5 Dredge with caster sugar before serving. The shortbread can be stored for up to a week, wrapped in a layer of greaseproof paper in a biscuit tin.

Ground rice gives this heavenly shortbread body and texture without making it brittle, while dredging it with sugar adds sweetness and a delicate crunch.

Silverbeet

DOUBLE THE USE

There seems to be almost as much stem as leaf on silverbeet. How much stem should I discard?

The whole of silverbeet's white stem, which looks a bit like a celery stalk, is wonderfully juicy and some people consider it to be the best part of the vegetable. It should be cooked separately from the leaf. Cut away the leaf with scissors, peel and de-string the stems, cut into 10 cm batons and steam or poach until just tender. Serve hot as a starter with a creamy sauce.

The leafy part is rather coarser than spinach but can substitute for it. Silverbeet leaves can also be used in a meatloaf or terrine. The Silverbeet and Pork Terrine (below) is useful as part of a buffet or picnic spread and leftovers can be served sliced with French bread or in sandwiches.

Silverbeet and pork terrine

SERVES: *12*
PREPARATION TIME: *20 minutes*
COOKING TIME: *about 1¼ hours*

1.5 kg belly pork (rind removed and
    reserved), minced
150 g streaky bacon in a piece,
    diced
1 teaspoon each ground mace and
    celery salt
½ teaspoon each salt and black
    pepper
Green leaf from 500 g silverbeet
To garnish: fresh bay leaves or
    sprigs of rosemary

1 Ask the butcher to derind and mince the pork and to give you the rind. (If doing it yourself, cut off the rind and set it aside.) Dice the meat and process it to a coarse mince.
2 Mix the pork with the streaky bacon, sprinkle on the mace, celery salt, salt and pepper and work in by hand. To check the seasoning of the meat, fry a teaspoon of the mixture

on both sides, then taste it and adjust the seasoning as necessary.

3 Wash the silverbeet and pack it into a pan. Cover tightly and simmer for 5 minutes, then drain.

4 Preheat the oven to 160°C and grease a 2 litre terrine tin.

5 Press the silverbeet into a ball and squeeze out the liquid with your hands. Put the ball on a board and slice across at 1 cm intervals. Turn and cut again at right angles.

6 Using your hands, mix the silverbeet into the meat mixture then pack it into the tin. Cut the reserved pork rind into rectangles and press it, fat side down, on top.

7 Cover the tin with foil, stand it in a baking dish in the middle of the oven, then pour in boiling water to come halfway up the terrine. Bake for about 1¼ hours – the exact time will depend on the shape of the tin.

8 Lift a section of rind and insert a skewer into the terrine, then press to squeeze out some juice; it is ready when the juice runs clear.

9 Remove from the oven and leave to stand for 5-10 minutes. Uncover, then remove the covering rind. If there is a lot of liquid, pour off a little and set aside.

10 Cool the terrine completely in the tin. Turn out onto a serving plate, cover with plastic wrap and store in the refrigerator. The liquid you have reserved will set to a jelly which can be warmed to brush onto the chilled terrine as a glaze. Serve garnished with bay leaves or rosemary sprigs.

Slices

LIGHTEN YOUR LOAD

I have been asked to cook for the school fete. Any suggestions?

The best way to approach the cooking is to bake slices in large trays and freeze some of them. Start a few weeks ahead, baking and freezing a batch at a time.

The Caramel Slices and Mango Muesli Slices will keep in the freezer for up to three months. Sell the Apple Cheese Slices fresh!

Cook up a storm for the fete and choose from a selection of slices: old-fashioned caramel (back left), mango and muesli (centre) and apple with cottage cheese.

Caramel slice

MAKES: 12
PREPARATION TIME: 30 minutes
COOKING TIME: 20-25 minutes, plus cooling

---

185 g (1½ cups) plain flour
45 g (½ cup) desiccated
*   coconut*
125 g unsalted butter
90 g (½ cup) light brown sugar

FOR THE CARAMEL AND TOPPING
400 g can sweetened condensed
*   milk*
3 tablespoons golden syrup
125 g (½ cup) caster sugar
60 g unsalted butter
175 g dark cooking chocolate

---

1 Preheat the oven to 180°C. Grease a shallow 20 cm square cake tin and line with nonstick baking paper.

2 Sift the flour into a mixing bowl. Add the coconut. Combine the butter and brown sugar in a saucepan and stir over a medium heat until the butter is melted and the sugar dissolved.

3 Add the butter mixture to the flour mixture and stir until combined. Press into the prepared tin, with the back of a metal spoon. Bake for 20-25 minutes, or until firm and golden. Stand the tin on a wire cooling rack and leave to cool.

4 For the caramel, put the condensed milk, golden syrup, caster sugar and butter into a heavy-based saucepan. Stir over a low heat until the mixture boils. Pour over the base and bake for 20 minutes. Cool completely.

5 For the topping, break the chocolate into a heatproof bowl set over a pan of barely simmering water. Allow to melt, then spread over the caramel with a palette knife. Leave to set. When cool, cut into slices and freeze.

Mango muesli slice

MAKES: 18
PREPARATION TIME: 15 minutes
COOKING TIME: 25-30 minutes

250 g unsalted butter
250 g (1 cup) caster sugar
2 tablespoons honey
250 g (2½ cups) rolled oats
60 g (²/₃ cup) desiccated coconut
30 g (½ cup) wheatgerm
75 g (½ cup) pepitas
100 g (1 cup) sun-dried mangoes
90 g (½ cup) chopped pitted dates

1 Preheat the oven to 160°C. Grease a shallow 30 × 20 cm cake tin and line the base and sides with nonstick baking paper.
2 Place the butter, sugar and honey in a pan. Stir over a low heat until the butter is melted and the sugar dissolved. Remove from the heat.
3 Combine the remaining ingredients in a mixing bowl. Stir well with a wooden spoon. Add the butter mixture and mix thoroughly.
4 Press the mixture into the tin and level the top with a spoon. Bake for 25-30 minutes, or until golden.
5 Cool in the tin for 15 minutes, then cut into neat slices and transfer to a wire cooling rack to cool completely. Cut into slices and freeze.

Apple cheese slice

MAKES: 12
PREPARATION TIME: 15-20 minutes
COOKING TIME: 45-50 minutes

2 sheets frozen shortcrust pastry,
    thawed

FOR THE TOPPING
2 large eggs
185 ml fresh cream
250 g cottage cheese
125 g (½ cup) caster sugar
1 tablespoon cornflour
400 g can pie apples, chopped
Extra 1 tablespoon caster sugar and
    ½ teaspoon ground cinnamon

1 Place a pastry sheet on a lightly floured surface; brush lightly with cold water and place the second pastry sheet on top. Roll out the layered pastry to a rectangle and use to line a 26 × 16 cm shallow cake tin. Chill the pastry for 15 minutes.
2 Preheat the oven to 200°C and heat a baking tray.
3 Beat the eggs lightly in a small bowl then beat in the cream. Combine the cottage cheese, caster sugar and cornflour. Add the egg mixture and stir well.
4 Arrange the apples over the pastry base. Pour the cottage cheese mixture over and spread level. Mix the extra caster sugar and cinnamon together; sprinkle over the top.
5 Place the tin on the preheated baking tray and bake for 20 minutes; reduce the oven temperature to 180°C and bake for a further 25-30 minutes, or until lightly set.
6 Cool in the tin standing on a wire rack. Cut into slices to serve.

Slow Cookers

REMOTE COOKING

I work all day; is there any way I can cook when I'm not at home?

Yes, with an electric slow cooker. The heat is gentle so you can leave the food for long periods without ever having to stir it.

Slow cookers are perfect for the tougher, cheaper cuts of meat. But meat with a high fat content should be trimmed and browned first, and then the fat drained off.
. Because the cooking temperature is so low, the cooking liquid must be brought to the boil before adding it to the slow cooker.

As well as casseroles and stews, slow cookers can be used for fruits, chutneys, jams and porridge.

Smoked Fish

HOT AND COLD

Why does some smoked fish need to be cooked and others not?

It all depends on the treatment.

Hot-smoked fish and seafood such as eel, kippers, mackerel, mussels, oysters, trout and tuna has dry, firm flesh and looks as though it has been cooked. It does not need further cooking.

Cold-smoked fish, for example cod and haddock, has the translucence of fresh seafood and almost always needs to be heated. But delicate cold-smoked salmon is eaten uncooked. (See also **Salmon**.)

SMOKED COD'S EGGS

I see smoked cod's roe everywhere but what can I do with it?

Smoked cod's roe may look like a strange lump, but it is simple to handle. Just scrape the delectable salty inner flesh from the tough outside membrane, then mash it or slice it thinly to serve on toast or water biscuits as a snack.

Alternatively, you can make the Greek purée called *taramasalata*, which will have a fresher, deeper flavour than the bright pink versions you can buy in the shops.

Taramasalata

SERVES: 6-8 as a starter
PREPARATION TIME: 15 minutes
COOKING TIME: none

60 g white crustless bread
4 tablespoons milk or water
250 g smoked cod's roe
1 clove garlic, crushed
200 ml olive oil
2 tablespoons lemon juice
1 tablespoon hot water
Black pepper

1 Put the bread in a bowl, pour on the milk or water and leave to soak.
2 Scoop the cod's roe out of its skin and put it in a mixing bowl. Squeeze the bread with your hands to press out all the water and add it to the roe with the garlic. Beat well with a wooden spoon or electric mixer.
3 Add the oil, drop by drop, as for a mayonnaise, beating all the time to make it into a thick, creamy paste.
4 Gradually beat in the lemon juice and hot water and season with black pepper. Chill until ready to serve.
5 Serve with hot pita bread, crispy toast or crudités.

Soufflé

HIGH RISE

How do I bake the perfect soufflé?

Soufflés are relatively easy to make as long as a few basic rules are followed. To produce a hot soufflé, egg whites are stiffly whisked and folded into a thick, flavoured sauce then cooked in a straight-sided dish.

The consistency of the panade, the thick basic sauce, is crucial. It must be soft enough so that the whisked egg whites can be folded easily into it. If it is too thick, the soufflé will not rise properly. If it is too thin, it will knock air out of the whisked egg whites and again the soufflé will not rise properly.

Under or overwhisking the egg whites will also result in a poorly risen soufflé. Follow the instructions below for a savoury soufflé.

This Cheddar-topped soufflé cooks to puffy, golden brown perfection. Add a little Dijon mustard to highlight the savoury cheese flavour of the basic sauce.

Cheese soufflé

SERVES: 4
PREPARATION TIME: 1 hour, plus
30 minutes for infusing the milk
COOKING TIME: 30 minutes

250 ml milk
1 slice of onion
1 small carrot, sliced
½ celery stalk, sliced
1 bay leaf
4 peppercorns
30 g salted butter, plus extra
   for greasing
1 tablespoon Parmesan cheese,
   finely grated
30 g (¼ cup) plain flour
½ teaspoon Dijon mustard
4 large eggs, separated, plus
   2 extra egg whites
125 g Cheddar cheese, finely grated
Salt and black pepper

1 Put the milk, onion, carrot, celery, bay leaf and peppercorns in a small saucepan and bring them slowly to the boil. Remove from the heat, cover and set aside to infuse for around 30 minutes. Strain and reserve milk.
2 Brush a 1.5 litre soufflé dish all over with melted butter, taking it right up to the top, and sprinkle the Parmesan cheese over the base and sides of the dish.
3 Preheat the oven to 180°C. Melt the butter in a saucepan over a medium heat, stir in the flour and cook gently for a minute or two, stirring continuously. Remove the pan from the heat and stir in milk.
4 Return the pan to the heat and bring the sauce slowly to the boil, stirring continuously. Continue to cook the sauce for 2 minutes, until it thickens, then lower the heat, stir briefly and simmer the sauce gently for around 3 minutes.
5 Remove the pan from the heat and allow to cool slightly. Beat the mustard, egg yolks, Cheddar cheese and salt and pepper into the sauce, reserving a tablespoon of the cheese.
6 In a large bowl, whisk the egg whites until they form stiff peaks. Fold 2 tablespoons of the whisked egg whites into the cheese sauce, then carefully fold in the remaining whisked egg whites, using a cutting and folding action. Be careful not to overmix, but make sure there are no visible flecks of egg white.

7 Gently pour the soufflé mixture into the prepared dish. Using a table or palette knife, pierce the surface of the soufflé 2.5 cm in from the edge of the dish and carefully move the knife in a circle around the edge of the mixture to release any trapped air bubbles and ensure that the soufflé crowns and rises evenly.
8 Sprinkle the reserved cheese over the top of the soufflé and bake for about 30 minutes, until the soufflé is well risen, golden brown and just firm to the touch: the centre may be slightly soft. Do not open the oven door to check on the soufflé for at least 25 minutes. Serve immediately.

VARIATIONS
Add 1-2 tablespoons of chopped fresh mixed herbs with the cheese, or use blue vein instead of Cheddar.

For a spinach soufflé, replace the cheese with 250 g of cooked, chopped and drained spinach then gently fold in 2 tablespoons of grated Parmesan and a pinch of nutmeg.

For a seafood soufflé, add 200 g of drained and flaked canned salmon or tuna and 1-2 tablespoons of chopped fresh tarragon.

FORWARD PLANNING

How far ahead can I make the base of a soufflé, and how many eggs should I use?

The panade, or basic sauce, of the soufflé can be made in advance and kept in the refrigerator for several hours before using. It should then be reheated gently before folding in the whisked egg whites.

If the whisked egg whites are folded into a cold base, the volume of the soufflé will be lost, as the sauce will be much stiffer and it will be difficult to fold the whites in lightly. It is important that once the egg whites have been folded in, the soufflé is baked immediately.

To serve four people, you need four large whole eggs, plus an extra two egg whites. The amount of filling depends on the type of flavouring being added.

KEEP IT CLOSED

Is it an old wives' tale that you should not open the oven door when baking a soufflé?

Opening the oven door is unlikely to be a disaster unless your kitchen is very draughty, but you are much more likely to make a successful soufflé if you keep the oven door closed during cooking. The soufflé should increase in volume by at least half and sometimes as much as double and to do this it must cook at the correct temperature. Opening the oven door will cause a sudden drop in temperature.

BURNT OFFERINGS

My soufflés always burn on the outside - what can I do to stop this happening?

Baking in too hot an oven will result in a creamy-centred soufflé that is well risen but burnt on the outside. Check first with an oven thermometer if your oven settings are above normal; if so, choose a slightly lower setting.

To test how well a soufflé is cooked, open the door a little, put your hand through and give the dish a sharp nudge. If the soufflé is very steady, it will be dry in the centre; if it trembles a little, it will have a slightly set centre; in either case it is done. If it wobbles easily, the soufflé will still be liquid in the centre and you should leave it in the oven for a few minutes longer.

Put it on ice

You can make individual soufflés in advance and freeze uncooked until required. Preheat the oven to the temperature specified in the recipe and cook them from frozen, adding 5 minutes to the cooking time.

CLINGING TO THE SIDE

Should a soufflé dish always be buttered and lightly floured before the mixture is poured in?

Yes, because the combination of grease and dusting, with flour, caster sugar, finely grated cheese or very fine breadcrumbs, provides the right surface for the soufflé to cling to as it rises in the dish.

NECESSARY FRILLS

Do I really have to bother with a paper collar? My soufflés seem all right without them.

A hot soufflé may be baked without a collar, but as the mixture is delicate, it could rise unevenly or with a crown in the centre. This does not affect the taste.

Cold soufflés, which are not cooked but set, need a collar to support the mixture until it chills and sets, otherwise it will simply flow over the sides of the dish. The greaseproof paper collar should stand at least 2.5 cm above the rim of the soufflé dish.

The 'collar' area of a cold soufflé is often decorated with ingredients such as chopped nuts or grated chocolate and the stunning visual effect of the chilled mixture rising above the dish after the collar has been removed is what distinguishes a cold soufflé from a mousse.

Soups

TOO MUCH SALT

What can I do to rescue a soup that is too salty?

Add some unsalted stock, milk or cream, which will dilute the flavour as well as the saltiness, or add a large peeled and halved potato and simmer for 20 minutes: the potato will absorb some salt as it cooks. Remove the potato before serving.

Over-seasoned soup is quite a common problem, especially if you use stock cubes, which are very highly seasoned. It can also be a problem with homemade stocks if they contain salt, as soups are often boiled until reduced, concentrating the seasoning. It is best to leave the seasoning of stocks and soups until the end, or if you are using a stock cube, use half a cube to the prescribed amount of water.

GIVE IT BODY

How can I rescue thin soup?

The easiest solution is to reduce the soup by simmering it without the lid to evaporate some of the liquid, but this can take some time and could concentrate the seasoning too much. Alternatively, thicken it with beurre manié, cornflour, or arrowroot (as you do for a sauce).

If the soup contains cooked vegetables, all or some of these can be puréed (by mashing, sieving or blending) and then stirred back into the soup to thicken it. Alternatively, add some finely chopped vegetables which will cook quickly in the soup and can also be puréed.

WHICH FAT?

Does it matter whether I use oil or butter to cook the vegetables for soup, and what do I do if the soup is very greasy?

Any oil or fat can be used to sauté the vegetables for soup. Butter, meat or poultry dripping, olive oil or vegetable oil, will all give their individual flavours to the soup. Margarine does not provide such a good flavour and low-fat spreads are not suitable for frying because many of them are almost half water.

After sautéeing the vegetables, a little flour can be stirred in to soak up any excess fat and form a roux, and the resulting soup should not be greasy. If you do end up with a greasy soup, pour or spoon off any oil that comes to the surface, or if you have time, chill the soup so that the fat solidifies on the surface and can be easily lifted off. For a fat-free version, the oil or fat can be eliminated and the vegetables just simmered in the stock.

The substantial spiced vegetable soup below is cooked with very little oil and, with the exception of a green pepper, can be made with ingredients in the store cupboard.

Chilli vegetable soup

SERVES: 4
PREPARATION TIME: 20 minutes plus soaking and cooking beans
COOKING TIME: 30–40 minutes

---

250 g (1¼ cups) mixed dried beans (such as black-eyed, butter, chickpea, haricot, kidney, pinto)
2 tablespoons sunflower or olive oil
1 large onion, chopped
1 large green pepper, deseeded and chopped
1 clove garlic, crushed
2 tablespoons plain flour
½–1 teaspoon chilli powder, to taste
400 g canned tomatoes with juice, roughly chopped
500 ml vegetable or chicken stock

FOR THE GARLIC TOAST
1 loaf French bread
30 g butter, softened
1 clove garlic, crushed

---

1 Prepare the beans you have chosen according to the chart in *Dried Beans*. When they are ready for their final low-boil, put those that require a longer cooking time into a saucepan with 1 litre of fresh unsalted water. Bring it to the boil,

A colourful selection of beans and a buttery garlic toast topping make this chilli-flavoured vegetable soup a satisfying choice for winter evenings.

reduce the heat, then cover the pan and simmer, adding the other beans according to the bean cooking chart. When all the beans are just tender, drain and set aside.
2 Heat the oil in a medium-large saucepan and sauté the onion for a few minutes. Add the pepper and garlic and fry for 2 minutes. Stir in the flour and the chilli powder and then cook, stirring, for 1 minute.
3 Add the tomatoes and the stock, bring to the boil, and stir until lightly thickened. Add the cooked,

drained beans, then cover the pan and simmer for 30 minutes until the beans are very tender.
4 Preheat the grill. Cut the bread into 2 cm slices, put them on a baking tray and grill on one side until lightly toasted. Mash the butter and garlic together. Turn over the bread, spread the untoasted sides with garlic butter and grill until they are lightly browned.
5 Place the soup in bowls and top each with two pieces of the hot garlic toast. Serve immediately.

CLEVER GARNISHING

Can you suggest some interesting new garnishes for soups?

Garnishes should look attractive, be edible and complement the flavour of the soup. Some typical examples include a sprinkling of fresh herbs or spices on a thick, rich soup, or more robust croutons or cheese on a lighter soup. Here are some more ideas:

- Whole sprigs of herbs, such as basil, dill, marjoram, mint, parsley, or thyme, or chopped leaves.
- Shredded lettuce, cress, spring onion or watercress, or diced or sliced raw vegetables, such as cucumber or tomato.
- Chopped, shredded or sliced vegetables, blanched or cooked, such as cabbage, carrot, zucchini, leek, mushroom or green beans.
- Whole edible perfumed flowers, such as borage, chive and thyme, or marigold petals.
- Croutons of fried bread or toast, slices of French bread, dumplings.
- Cream, sour cream, fromage frais or natural yoghurt, swirled on in an attractive pattern.
- Cooked and finely chopped or shredded meat, ham or poultry, or pieces of crispy bacon.
- Thinly shredded smoked salmon, smoked trout or salmon roe.

EGG ENRICHED

I have heard you can thicken a soup with egg. How do you do it?

Adding egg to thicken a soup is a little tricky as it will curdle or scramble if overheated. Beat one or two egg yolks (or whole eggs) in a bowl and stir in a little of the hot soup. Then strain this into the pan and stir over a gentle heat until thickened; do not allow it to boil.

This method can be used for a hot soup or one to be served cold (which will thicken further on cooling). For a richer soup, the eggs can be mixed with cream. The Greek recipe (above right) is for one of the most famous egg-thickened soups, based on chicken stock and flavoured with lemon.

Mixing egg yolks and cream with a little of the soup then gently pouring it back into the pan will give a delicious thick and velvety texture to this lemon-flavoured chicken soup.

Avgolémono

SERVES: 4
PREPARATION TIME: 10 minutes
COOKING TIME: 20 minutes

---

1 litre homemade chicken stock
Salt and black pepper
60 g (⅓ cup) long-grain rice
2 large eggs
2 tablespoons lemon juice
To garnish: lemon slices and sprigs of thyme or parsley

1 Pour the stock into a saucepan, bring to the boil and season with salt and pepper to taste. Add the rice and simmer gently for 10–15 minutes or until the rice is tender.
2 Beat the eggs and lemon juice in a small bowl. Add 150 ml of the hot stock, beat well, then stir it into the soup. Reheat very gently, stirring constantly to give a thick, creamy soup (do not allow it to boil or the soup will curdle).
3 Pour the soup into serving bowls and garnish with lemon slices and sprigs of thyme or parsley.

NO STOCK

If I want to make a quick soup and have neither homemade stock nor cubes what can I use?

You do not have to have stock to make soup as long as the other ingredients provide flavour. You can also make a quick stock to use in a specific recipe. Chop a selection of vegetables such as carrots, celery, leeks, mushrooms, onions or potatoes. Sauté them in butter first, or just simmer them until tender in water with flavourings such as herbs, citrus peel, vegetable juice or wine. The stock can be strained, or the vegetables may be puréed with the stock by blending or sieving to give a thick soup.

If you want to use a stock base, good-quality stock is now available in tetra-packs that can be kept in the store cupboard with cans of consommé, which can also be diluted and used instead of stock. Chilled fresh stock is also sold by some quality butchers and deli-catessens; it can be kept in the refrigerator for two or three days, or frozen.

The following recipe for Gazpacho, the celebrated cold Spanish soup that needs no cooking, is a good example of a highly flavoured soup that is nevertheless made without stock. (See also **Stock**.)

Gazpacho

SERVES: 4
PREPARATION TIME: 1 hour (or 15 minutes using a blender) plus 30 minutes soaking
COOKING TIME: 5 minutes for the crouton garnish

---

1 thick slice white bread, crusts removed
2 large cloves garlic, crushed
2 tablespoons red wine vinegar
4 tablespoons olive oil
500 g ripe tomatoes, skinned, deseeded and finely diced (reserve juice)
1 large red pepper, quartered, deseeded and finely diced
1 large green pepper, quartered, deseeded and finely diced
1 medium red onion, grated
1 large cucumber, peeled and finely diced
½ teaspoon salt
Black pepper to taste
1 sprig fresh basil or marjoram
250 ml ice-cold water
To garnish: 50 g croutons

---

1 Cut the bread into small cubes and put them in a large mixing bowl. Add the garlic and vinegar and crush together with a fork. Gradually add the olive oil, mashing it all to a paste. Stir the tomato pulp and juice into the bread mixture.

2 Set aside a quarter of the diced peppers then put the rest of them, the grated onion and the cucumber into the bowl with the bread and tomato pulp mixture. Add the salt, the pepper to taste plus the basil or marjoram and stir well to combine. Cover and leave for 30 minutes, allowing the flavours to amalgamate and the juices to seep out.

3 Rub the soup through a sieve into another bowl, pushing down on the vegetables with a wooden spoon until you get about 600 ml of smooth, thick purée. Stir in the iced water and chill until required.

4 Alternatively, for a soup that is thicker and crunchier, the iced water can be blended with the vegetables remaining in the sieve, sieved again and then added to the soup.

5 To serve, pour into soup bowls and sprinkle the croutons and the reserved chopped peppers on top, or hand them round separately in small bowls. Crushed ice cubes can also be added just before serving.

VARIATION

For a quick but equally delicious version of gazpacho, put all the ingredients, roughly chopped, in a blender (in batches if necessary), purée and then rub through a sieve and chill until required. There is no need for you to skin and deseed the tomatoes when using this method.

THICK AND RICH

How do you make cream soups?

By mashing, blending or sieving the soup to a 'cream'. Cream soups do not necessarily contain cream. They may be thickened by purée-ing vegetables (especially starchy ones such as potato or root vegetables) with stock and these can then be sieved for a smoother texture.

Soups are also often thickened with flour, in the form of a roux or beurre manié. Cream can be added to enrich the soup and should be stirred in at the end of cooking. The following soup recipe is thickened with flour and fresh cream.

Cream of mushroom soup

SERVES: 6–8
PREPARATION TIME: 15 minutes, plus 10–30 minutes standing time
COOKING TIME: 40 minutes

---

500 ml milk
1 small onion, sliced
1 small carrot, sliced
1 stalk celery, sliced
1 bay leaf
3 parsley stalks
1 blade of mace
6 black peppercorns
60 g butter
1 medium onion, chopped
250 g mushrooms, sliced
500 ml beef, chicken or vegetable stock
½ teaspoon salt
Black pepper
30 g (¼ cup) plain flour
150 ml fresh cream
2 tablespoons chopped parsley

---

1 Pour the milk into a saucepan and add the sliced onion, carrot, celery, bay leaf, parsley stalks, mace and the peppercorns. Heat gently until just simmering, then remove from the heat, cover and leave to stand for at least 10 minutes, but preferably for around 30 minutes or longer.

2 Melt half of the butter in a large saucepan and sauté the chopped onion gently for 2 minutes. Add the mushrooms and sauté for 5 minutes, stirring occasionally. Add the stock, bring to the boil, cover and simmer for 10 minutes. Blend well to a smooth, thin purée and reserve.

3 Melt the rest of the butter in a large, clean saucepan, stir in the flour and cook gently to a sandy textured roux. Gradually add the strained, flavoured milk, stirring well until thickened and smooth, then simmer gently for 20 minutes.

4 Add the reserved mushroom purée and stir well over a gentle heat. Cook the soup at simmering point for another 2 minutes.

5 Stir the cream into the soup then reheat it gently, without boiling. Check the seasoning and then serve sprinkled with chopped parsley.

Smooth and warming, this mushroom soup is enriched with cream and sprinkled with fresh parsley. Serve it with crusty bread for a light lunch.

Spaghetti

BEEFING UP BOLOGNESE

I find bottled Bolognese sauces taste quite bland. Is there an authentic recipe with more zip?

Many bottled sauces lean heavily on tomato purée and leave out ingredients with stronger flavours used by Italian cooks, such as chicken livers and fresh chilli. As the recipe below shows, these additions, along with fresh vegetables and herbs, combine to make a memorable sauce. This is a substantial dish and does not need anything more than a salad of mixed leaves dressed with a well-seasoned vinaigrette to follow it.

Spaghetti alla Bolognese

SERVES: *6*
PREPARATION TIME: *30 minutes*
COOKING TIME: *1¼ hours*

---

1 tablespoon olive oil
30 g butter
50 g bacon, cut into 5 mm strips
1 medium onion, finely chopped
1 stalk celery, finely chopped
1 small carrot, finely chopped
1 clove garlic, finely chopped
500 g finely minced beef
60 g chicken livers, roughly chopped
150 ml red or white wine
250 ml stock
2 tablespoons tomato paste
250 g tomatoes, skinned and chopped
1 chilli, deseeded and finely chopped
1 bay leaf
A pinch of dried oregano
Several stalks of parsley, chopped
Salt and black pepper
A pinch of grated nutmeg
600 g spaghetti

---

1 Heat the oil and butter in a heavy-based pan and cook the bacon until it starts to brown. Add the vegetables and garlic and cook together, stirring, for a few minutes until they begin to soften.
2 Add the minced beef and lightly brown, breaking it up with a wooden spoon at the same time. Add the chicken livers and cook for a minute or until they lose their raw look.
3 Add the wine and boil rapidly until it evaporates. Add the stock, tomato paste, chopped tomatoes, chilli, bay leaf, oregano, parsley and some salt and pepper to taste. Cook, covered, over a very low heat for at least 1 hour. For best results, the sauce should barely simmer.
4 Add some grated nutmeg, taste for seasoning and adjust if necessary, then remove the bay leaf and parsley.
5 Ten or fifteen minutes before the sauce has finished cooking, while it is still simmering, cook the spaghetti. When cooked, drain and toss with the sauce. Serve the spaghetti accompanied with a bowl of freshly grated Parmesan cheese.

Two of the best-loved pasta sauces are meaty Bolognese, right, and creamy carbonara, left, with bacon and egg.

HOW MUCH SAUCE?

What is the correct proportion of sauce to spaghetti?

There are no hard and fast rules. Italians like their pasta with very little sauce, just enough to thinly coat it as the spaghetti itself has a good flavour. In Australia people like to add far more sauce. But if the sauce has a very strong, concentrated flavour you will need less of it. To feed four people who like a lot of sauce, allowing about 375 g of spaghetti, a sauce made with 500 g of fresh vine-ripened tomatoes, or 250 g of sun-dried tomatoes, would be ample.

TOMATO-FREE ZONE

Do all Italian dishes include tomatoes? I'd like a change.

Italians do love their sun-ripened, richly flavoured tomatoes, but they do not use them in every recipe. One of the most popular dishes in northern Italy is spaghetti with bacon and egg, called *spaghetti alla carbonara*. This is fairly new, and it is said to have been invented when American servicemen arrived in Italy during the Second World War and handed over their breakfast rations of bacon and egg to bemused Italian cooks. The recipe below uses quick-cooking spaghettini, a thin version of spaghetti.

Spaghettini alla carbonara

SERVES: *4*
PREPARATION TIME: *20 minutes*
COOKING TIME: *15 minutes*

---

2 tablespoons olive oil
175 g bacon, cut into 5 mm strips
4 tablespoons white wine
1 large whole egg plus 2 egg yolks
50 g butter, softened
4 tablespoons fresh cream
100 g Parmesan cheese, freshly grated
Salt and black pepper
375 g spaghettini

---

1 Preheat the oven to 140°C. Heat the oil in a frying pan, then add the bacon and sauté until crisp. Pour in the wine and let it bubble up then take the pan off the heat and set aside.
2 Warm a serving bowl which is large enough for the pasta and put in the egg and egg yolks, butter, cream, half the Parmesan and some salt and pepper. Mix well and put it in the oven for about 10 minutes to just warm through without cooking.
3 Meanwhile, cook the pasta. When it is cooked, drain it and mix it with the egg sauce. The heat from the pasta will just set the eggs.
4 Quickly reheat the bacon and wine and pour over the pasta. Pass the remaining Parmesan separately.

Spices

HOME GROUND

Is it better to buy whole spices and grind your own?

Yes, because ground spices deteriorate rapidly, although some, like fenugreek, are so hard that they are almost impossible to grind at home. It is probably best to buy a selection, in small quantities, and grind them a little at a time. One advantage of buying whole spices is that you can roast them before you grind them (see below). You can grind spice in a stone mortar and pestle, or in an electric coffee mill. If using the latter, be sure to keep it for spices and have a separate one for grinding coffee beans.

DRY FRY

Indian recipes often call for spices to be fried lightly at the start of cooking. What does this do to the flavour of the spices?

This is dry-frying, and only applies to whole spices. They are heated gently for 2–3 minutes in a heavy frying pan without any oil, shaken now and then, until the seeds start to change colour. This has a beneficial effect, especially with certain spices such as cumin, for it draws out the flavour remarkably well. Most of the spices in commercial curry powders, and other mixtures such as garam masala, are treated in this way before being ground. In Indian cookery it is very important that the spices do not taste raw.

REPLACE OFTEN

How long do ground spices keep?

It depends on how fresh they were when you bought them. Those you grind yourself will almost certainly keep longer, as long as they are tightly sealed. All ground spices, even the home-ground ones, should be replaced with new ones after six months when they have lost their savour and begin to taste dusty.

NUTMEG COVERING

What is the difference between nutmeg and mace?

Not a great deal in terms of flavour, though mace is more powerful and has traditionally been used in savoury dishes. Nutmeg is used in sweet and savoury recipes. Both spices lie within the fruit of the nutmeg tree, as a peach's stone lies within its flesh; mace is the lacy covering that encloses the nutmeg.

ALL OR MIXED?

What is the difference between allspice and mixed spice, and are they interchangeable?

Although they are near enough in flavour to stand in for each other sometimes, allspice is in fact one single spice, the berry of an evergreen tree growing wild in South America and the West Indies. It got its name because it resembles a mixture of four spices: cinnamon, cloves, mace and pepper.

The term 'mixed spice' is a vague one which usually means a mixture of cinnamon, cloves, ginger, nutmeg and sometimes cumin.

PERSONAL BLEND

I had a homemade garam masala in India which was superb. Can you give me a recipe?

Garam masala is a mixture of aromatic spices which, unlike curry powder, does not need heating to mellow the flavour. It is usually added to dishes at the end of cooking or sprinkled on top just before serving to brighten the flavour.

To make 100 g of garam masala, simply dry-fry in a small pan 2 tablespoons of coriander seeds, 1 tablespoon each of mace and black peppercorns, 1 teaspoon each of cloves and cardamom seeds and a 6 cm piece of cinnamon stick broken into pieces. When the spices smell rich and pungent, grind them together in a coffee grinder or pound finely in a mortar. Store the garam masala in an airtight jar, away from heat and light.

SPICES: WHAT THEY LOOK LIKE AND HOW TO USE THEM

After more than a century of relative neglect, spices are back in favour in the West, boosted by the subtle ways of spicing | *for flavour and colour that we have learnt in recent years from the many Asian cuisines. Here are some of the best.*

1 STAR ANISE has a flavour halfway between aniseed and liquorice. It is an ingredient of Chinese Five Spice powder.
2 CORIANDER SEED has a warm, citrus-like flavour. Use it alone or combined with other spices. It is always included in curry powder and garam masala.
3 FENUGREEK is an unusual spice, most identifiable as curry-like. It is not often used in the West, but is extremely popular in India. The squarish, hard seeds are crushed and roasted, then cooked with meat, fish and vegetables, and in curry powders. The leaves,

which have a strong, almost bitter taste, are used as a herb, both fresh and dried.
4 CARDAMOM has tiny, highly aromatic black seeds inside the loose pod. Green cardamom (pictured above) is best, but brown or white are also good. It is used in India in curries and in the Middle East to perfume coffee.
5 CUMIN is delicate and mild, and goes especially well with coriander. It is best bought as seeds and then gently toasted before use, whole or ground.
6 TURMERIC, usually sold ground, is perhaps the easiest spice to recognise,

because of its bright yellow hue. Often used for its colour as a cheap substitute for saffron, its flavour is actually fairly unremarkable and slightly bitter.
7 CINNAMON is the inner bark of an evergreen tree, sold either in papery rolls that resemble quills, or ground. Its fragrant sweetness can be used in both savoury and sweet dishes, such as rice pilafs, hot cross buns and apple tarts.
8 NUTMEG is best bought whole and grated when required. It is good used in cheese and vegetable dishes, milky sauces, junkets and rice puddings.

OUT OF THE LIGHT

Is it true that direct sunlight gradually destroys the essential oils in spices? Why are they sold in glass jars if light harms them?

Sunlight destroys chlorophyll, the plant's pigment, causing the structure to disintegrate. All herbs and spices should be stored in a cool dark place – the refrigerator is ideal – but attempts to package them in tinted glass have proved unsuccessful. Most people prefer to see what they are buying.

HOME GROWN

Which spices can be grown in Australia? Can I dry them?

Very few spices grow successfully in Australia, but cinnamon, cloves and nutmeg can be grown in northern Queensland. Ginger and turmeric are cultivated successfully, also in Queensland. Those that can be grown in a temperate climate, such as coriander seed, grow in the wheat-producing areas of South Australia and western New South Wales.

Curry trees (*Chalcas koenigii*) can be grown, if you can find them in a nursery. The small shrubby tree has aromatic leaves that are used in Indian cookery. To dry the leaves, place them on a rack, cover with muslin and leave in a warm dry place for a week to ten days until they are completely dry.

A juicy stem of fresh lemon grass may be potted up and grown under glass or in a sunny garden. The stalks are dried in the same way as curry leaves, but for longer.

Dill and fennel seeds can be collected from the growing herbs and dried like curry leaves.

EASY-GOING PAPRIKA

If I'm adding paprika to a casserole or goulash, should it be fried first to release the aroma?

No, paprika is one of the most accessible of spices and can be treated like salt or pepper, and added without any treatment.

SPICY AND CRUNCHY

Using breadcrumbs for coatings is useful but so bland. Can I jazz them up with spices?

Ground spices may be mixed with breadcrumbs (or sifted flour) for coating fried foods, or with butter and flour as a crumble topping for fruit desserts. For instance, try using a pinch of saffron, turmeric or curry powder mixed with flour for coating fish cakes, croquettes or potato cakes, and ginger or cinnamon mixed with the topping for an apple crumble. Add a large pinch of ground nutmeg to a creamy cheese sauce or mashed potatoes. And mace will perk up bread sauce, spinach purée or creamed onions.

Spinach

SALAD LEAF

Can I use spinach in salads?

Young, tender spinach leaves make splendid salads and mix particularly well with fruit; try them with grapefruit and orange segments or dried fruits. Spinach is good with dressings pungent with garlic or thickened with nuts and, since it can be cooked, is the perfect leaf for wilting with warm dressings. With added bacon, chicken liver and egg, poached or soft-boiled, these salads make lively substantial dishes to serve at lunch.

GREEN AND CRUNCHY

A local restaurant serves delicious crispy spinach which has been deep-fried, but is very light. Is it possible to do this at home?

Yes, it is, though it takes care. Spinach intended for deep-frying should be very fresh and very dry. After washing, pick it over carefully, removing any coarse stems and discoloured sections. Spin it in a salad dryer, then tip it onto a tea towel and toss it about gently until it is completely dry. Shred the spinach finely and fry a generous handful at a time in very hot oil over a medium to high heat for about a minute. Tip the spinach into a strainer placed over a bowl, and while the oil reheats for the next batch, tip the cooked spinach onto a double layer of paper towels and shake with flaky sea salt.

This makes a dazzling garnish for fish or poached poultry, or in a tangle on top of a salad. However, the spinach should be used on the day it is cooked, and do not deceive yourself into thinking that crisp equals light and fat-free. Like all deep-fried foods, it will absorb a great deal of oil during cooking.

COOK FROM FROZEN

Can I use frozen spinach without thawing it first?

Frozen spinach is one of the most versatile and easy of all frozen vegetables to use, and is a very handy standby. Unlike many green vegetables, spinach stands up well to freezing and loses very little flavour and texture on thawing or cooking.

Chopped spinach can be added straight from the freezer to enrich hearty soups. With poached eggs and a creamy sauce it makes eggs Florentine, and it adds a colourful green layer to a fish pie. But it is best to thaw it before blending it into a root vegetable purée, then heat the purée for a few minutes to warm through quickly.

SHOPPING LIST

How much raw spinach will be enough for four people?

Spinach loses about half its weight in cooking: to serve four people as a side vegetable, you need 1 kg of washed fresh spinach to get 500 g of cooked spinach. Freshly cooked spinach made into a roulade, such as the one on the next page, is a smart and colourful starter and is ideal for entertaining since most of the work can be done in advance. It will taste even better if you make your own taramasalata for the filling (see the recipe on page 322).

Fresh spinach and taramasalata roulade

SERVES: 6
PREPARATION TIME: 45 minutes
COOKING TIME: 20 minutes, plus
3 hours resting time

625 g spinach, washed
30 g butter
Salt, black pepper and nutmeg
50 g Parmesan cheese, finely grated
5 large eggs, separated
200 g cream cheese
2–3 tablespoons crème fraîche
  or Greek-style yoghurt
150 g taramasalata

1 Remove the coarse stems and discoloured sections of the spinach leaves. Pack the spinach into a large pan with just the washing water clinging to the leaves, cover and cook for 4 minutes over a medium heat. Remove the lid, turn the spinach over and continue cooking for a further 2–3 minutes until the leaves have wilted thoroughly. Turn into a colander and leave to drain.

2 Line a 33 × 23 cm Swiss roll tin with some nonstick baking paper or buttered greaseproof paper.

3 When the spinach has cooled a bit, squeeze out the moisture with your hands and chop it finely. Return it to the pan and add the butter, salt, pepper, a good grinding of nutmeg and two-thirds of the Parmesan. Keep stirring gently until the butter melts and all is warmed through, then take the pan off the heat.

4 Preheat the oven to 180°C. Whisk the egg whites to soft peaks. Beat the yolks briskly until creamy, then pour them into the spinach mixture and mix well. Gently fold in about 2 tablespoons of the whisked egg whites to loosen the mixture, then fold in the rest. Pour the mixture into the prepared tin, spreading it gently into the corners. Bake for 20 minutes until the top is just firm to the touch.

5 Leave the roulade to cool in the tin, then chill it for 2 hours. Remove from the refrigerator, cover with a just-damp tea towel and rest for at least an hour at room temperature.

6 Put a board or tray over the cloth-covered tin, then invert the tin to turn the roulade out onto the cloth. Peel off the paper.

7 Beat the cream cheese and crème fraîche or yoghurt together to a spreadable mixture. Spread it over the spinach base, then spread the taramasalata over the cheese. Add salt and pepper and roll up the roulade, lifting the cloth to help shape it.

8 Serve the roulade within an hour of rolling. To serve, transfer it to a serving dish and sprinkle with the remainder of the Parmesan.

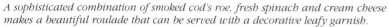
A sophisticated combination of smoked cod's roe, fresh spinach and cream cheese makes a beautiful roulade that can be served with a decorative leafy garnish.

Spirits and Liqueurs

PRESERVED FRUIT

Can any fruit be preserved in spirit, or do some produce better results than others?

Fruit preserved for a month or more in alcohol makes wonderful, easy-to-make winter desserts. Most fruits are suitable, with the exception of very watery ones such as melons as these dilute the alcohol, which may result in mould growth or fermentation.

For the best results, use ripe, unblemished fruit: berries should be hulled; currants, gooseberries and grapes stripped of their stalks; nectarines, peaches, apricots and plums should be halved and stoned; pineapples should be peeled, cored and sliced or cubed; cherries and kumquats should be pricked and kept whole; apples and pears should be peeled, cored and sliced. Firmer fruit such as peaches, apples and pears are better if they are poached in a sugar syrup first.

Pack the prepared fruit into clean jars, layering it with sugar as you go, then cover with alcohol such as rum, brandy, kirsch, vodka or any flavoured liqueur, as in the recipe below. Cooked fruits are packed with their cooled sugar syrup plus an equal quantity of alcohol. With either raw or cooked fruit, spices such as cinnamon, ginger, star anise or vanilla can be added for extra flavour. Seal the jars tightly; as long as the fruits are kept covered by the alcohol, they should keep for about a year.

Pineapple in kirsch

MAKES: 1 litre
PREPARATION TIME: 20 minutes
MATURING TIME: at least a month

---

1 medium-sized ripe pineapple
250 g (1 cup) caster sugar
About 300 ml kirsch
1 cinnamon stick, broken into
*   three pieces*

---

1 Peel the pineapple and cut the flesh crossways into thick slices, then remove the central core from each slice. Cut the flesh into small chunks. Put alternating layers of pineapple pieces and sugar in a large clean jar, dropping in the pieces of cinnamon stick as you go.
2 Pour in enough kirsch to cover the pineapple completely. Seal the jar and leave in a cool, dark place for at least a month before using. Give the jar a shake occasionally to make sure all the sugar dissolves.
3 When ready, serve the fruit with a large spoonful of the steeping syrup. If you like, top with whipped cream, or some vanilla ice cream.

ALCOHOLIC FLAVOUR

When recipes include spirits, is it for the taste or the alcohol?

If the recipe is for preserving fresh fruit, both the flavour and the alcoholic content are absorbed by the fruit. But when spirits are added to cooked dishes or flambéed, they are used only for their flavour as the alcohol will evaporate during cooking or burn off when it is ignited. It is also usually for the flavour alone that alcohol is added to cold desserts, fruit salads, cakes

and cream fillings for pastries, as the quantity used is not large enough to have a significant alcoholic effect. If too much is added the dish will be too thin and watery and the taste overpowering.

FULLY COVERED

How do I stop the fruit from bobbing up out of the alcohol when I am trying to preserve it?

Fruit that is being steeped in alcohol needs to be totally immersed in order to save it from the damaging effects of air. Inevitably, however, the fruit will float to the top, exposing enough of the flesh to start the fermentation process.

To keep the fruit fully immersed, place a few balls of loosely crumpled greaseproof paper over them in the jar to weigh them down. Alternatively, if the opening of the jar is wide enough, cover the fruit with plastic wrap and put a plate or saucer over that (see panel, right).

FRUIT, GLORIOUS FRUIT

How long does it take to make a rumtopf from start to finish?

This fruity dessert (named after the German for rum pot), can be eaten after four to six weeks of steeping in alcohol, but if you have the patience, it is at its best if it is left in a cool dark place for at least three months to mellow and mature.

Rumtopf is made up of layers of stoned, stemmed and cut-up fruit steeped in spirit, and the time you actually spend on making it will depend on how many different types of fruit you put in it. Each addition takes about 30 minutes to prepare, plus an hour of standing time, before it is added to the jar. Traditional rumtopf jars are made of glazed ceramic (to keep out the light) but any large glass jar with a closely fitting lid will do.

Begin with the first fruits of the summer (usually strawberries) and keep on adding layers of other fruits as they come into season. Peaches, pears and plums are best. Because a rumtopf can be made

MAKING A RUMTOPF

For the first layer in the jar, you should use equal weights of fruit and sugar, and add about 750 ml of dark rum or brandy to every 500 g of fruit. For the subsequent layers, add 500 ml of spirit to every 500 g of fruit and use only half the weight of sugar.

1 Put the fruit (strawberries are shown here) and the measured sugar into the rumtopf jar, mix gently and leave it to stand for an hour. Then pour in enough rum to cover the fruit by 2.5 cm.

2 It is essential that the fruit stays submerged, so cover it closely with plastic wrap and put a small plate over that. Put more plastic wrap over the jar then seal tightly.

3 Continue to layer in more fruit: prepare the next batch (peaches are shown here) by soaking it in sugar for an hour, then add it to the jar and pour on more rum to cover the fruit by 2.5 cm. Continue to add sugar-soaked fruit and rum until the jar is full. Cover it well and if necessary, weigh the fruit down with a ball of greaseproof paper.

with any amount of different types of fruit, there is no precise recipe (see box, page 333).

When you are choosing fruit, bear in mind that those with a high water content can cause fermentation so avoid apples, melon and oranges. Neither is it advisable to use sharply flavoured fruits such as blackberries, gooseberries and rhubarb as they will dominate the more delicate taste of the others.

SAY WHEN

If a recipe says to add 'a little' spirit, how much should I use?

Generally, it means anything from 1–4 tablespoons or until it tastes right. Start with a small amount and keep tasting as you add more.

FRUIT FLAVOURS

I like sloe gin, but sloes are not available in Australia. Is there any other fruit I can use instead?

Yes, you can flavour a delightful summer gin with raspberries, boysenberries or strawberries (see recipe, below), and with berries it is ready to drink much sooner.

Strawberry gin

MAKES: *about 750 ml*
PREPARATION TIME: *15 minutes*
MATURING TIME: *a week*

About 250 g strawberries, hulled
750 ml gin
About 125 g (½ cup) caster sugar

1 Lightly crush the strawberries with a fork. Place them in a clean jar, then pour in the gin to cover.

When the gin is ready to drink, it is strained through a layer of muslin, bottled and tightly sealed for storing.

2 Seal tightly and leave to mature in a cool, dark place for at least a week, shaking the jar every now and again to disperse the fruit.
3 Strain the flavoured spirit through a funnel lined with a double layer of clean muslin into a clean jug. Stir in the sugar well to dissolve it. The gin is ready to drink when the sugar has dissolved. Pour it through a muslin-lined funnel into a clean bottle and seal with a cork. Store in a cool place.

Serve as a liqueur, or over ice, or sprinkled over fresh strawberries.

FINE FLAVOURED VODKAS

I like flavoured vodkas, but they are quite expensive to buy. Can I make some of my own?

Yes, not only is flavoured vodka easy to make, but the results can be more interesting than those you can buy commercially.

For example, a dried chilli makes a rose-coloured vodka in a very short time. Roast the chilli in a hot oven for 5 minutes, then stuff it down the neck of a bottle of vodka, or put it into a wide-mouthed jar with the vodka and seal tightly. The vodka takes on colour and flavour within a day but it will need at least a week to develop a strong flavour.

Vodka can also be flavoured with strips of grapefruit, lemon or lime peel and it needs only two weeks to mature.

ALCOHOLIC ICES

I've been told you can't make ice creams and sorbets with alcohol. Is this always true?

No, it is not, but do not add any more than is necessary to give a good flavour. Alcohol affects the way food freezes because it freezes at a lower temperature than water, so ice creams and sorbets containing alcohol freeze more softly than those without. Add just 90–125 ml of spirit or liqueur to 600 ml of cream for ice cream, or to syrup for a sorbet.

Wine is somewhat less of a problem in ices because it has a much lower alcohol content.

FLAMING IDEAS

I notice a lot of restaurants use alcohol in their recipes and I am especially fond of flambé desserts. What spirits and liqueurs are best to use for cooking?

Along with table wine, fruit liqueurs and spirits such as brandy, whisky and rum are often used in cooking – together with port, sherry, vermouth and beer. Diluted vermouth, in fact, makes a good substitute for wine (see also **Wine**).

Spirits are often added, for example, to dishes of sautéed meat or poultry at the beginning of cooking. Liqueurs and spirits are also added to sweet sauces.

As a general rule of thumb, if a recipe doesn't specify a particular liqueur or spirit, be guided by the main flavours in the dish. Use a cherry liqueur with cherries, an apple brandy with apples, and so on. Liqueurs also add a zing to cold fruit desserts and, as only a small amount of alcohol is needed, it's worth experimenting with combinations of flavours. Kirsch, for example – a cherry liqueur – goes especially well sprinkled over slices of sweet, fresh pineapple, while Grand Marnier and Cointreau, with their distinctive orange flavour, perk up fresh fruit salads.

You can also turn everyday desserts into dinner party delights. Fruits such as apples, cherries, peaches, pears, plums and quinces can be poached in a simple sugar syrup (see page 346 for recipe) enhanced by the addition of some grated lemon or orange rind, a few cloves, a cinnamon stick or a vanilla pod. When the fruit is cooked, sprinkle over some brandy, port, sherry, kirsch or your favourite fruit liqueur. Serve when cold with thick cream.

Spirits are also used to flame (*flambé*) dishes. The spirit is spooned over food simmering in a shallow pan and, once it is really hot, set alight. Always let the flames die down before serving.

To flame a Christmas pudding, see the box on page 96.

BLITHE SPIRITS

What spirits, other than gin and vodka, can I use to make my own special drinks, and what could I use to flavour them with?

Almost any clear spirit, such as inexpensive brandy, kirsch or rum can be infused with fruit to make drinks such as plum brandy or rum. Soak the fruit in sugar and the spirit and then strain off the alcohol. For best results, allow the flavours to blend together for at least three months before straining. The flavoured spirits can then be drunk, although if stored unopened in a cool, dark place they will keep almost indefinitely.

You can also experiment with other flavourings such as herbs and spices. For example, a half-dozen crushed cumin seeds, a sprig of rosemary and a few cloves, steeped in a bottle of brandy, make a delightful digestive drink. Expansively flavoured spices such as cinnamon or star anise go well with heartier-flavoured fruit such as plums, and vanilla will enhance the flavour of almost any fruit.

Vanilla-scented fruits are best steeped in rum or brandy rather than gin or vodka.

The following recipe for Cherry Brandy produces a richly coloured spirit that is ideal for flavouring cream or creamy desserts as well as being drunk on its own. It looks most festive spooned over vanilla or pistachio ice cream and can also be mixed with soda water or lemonade to make a party drink or a refreshing sparkling cocktail.

Cherry brandy

MAKES: about 750 ml
PREPARATION TIME: 15–20 minutes
MATURING TIME: 3 months

---

500 g fresh dark cherries, such as morello
75 g (⅓ cup) caster sugar
600 ml brandy

---

1 Wash the cherries and pat them dry with kitchen paper towels. Remove the stalks but do not stone the fruit, then prick each cherry all over with a clean needle or skewer.
2 Put alternate layers of cherries and sugar in a large clean jar. Pour in the brandy to cover the cherries completely, weighing them down with balls of crumpled greaseproof paper if necessary.
3 Seal the jar tightly and leave it in a cool, dark place for three months, shaking the jar occasionally until the brandy has taken on a deep rich colour from the cherries.
4 Strain the flavoured spirit through a funnel lined with a double layer of clean muslin into a clean bottle. (You may find it easier to strain the brandy into a clean jug first, and then pour it into the bottle.) Seal tightly with a cork or screw top. Drink immediately, or store in a cool, dark place.

Dark cherries and a little sugar give a bottle of brandy a dramatic colour and a delicate summery flavour.

Squid

EASIER THAN YOU THINK

How should I prepare squid, and how do I cook it?

Squid is now often sold cleaned and prepared, fresh or frozen, and is one of the easiest seafoods to tackle, as it has no readily identifiable innards (see panel, below). It is available in a range of sizes, from 10–25 cm, although any that measure more than 18 cm will be very rubbery. The Southern Calamari is the most tender species.

Medium-sized squid can be sliced for frying, either shaken in flour or in a light batter. Smaller ones can be served in seafood salads and stir-fries as they require scarcely more than blanching to cook, as in the recipe on the right. Larger ones are usually quite tough and chewy, but can be stuffed and baked.

Spicy squid salad

SERVES: 2 as a starter
PREPARATION TIME: 15 minutes
COOKING TIME: 5 minutes

---

2 tablespoons cooking oil
1–2 cloves garlic, finely chopped
2.5 cm piece fresh ginger, grated
1 fresh green chilli, deseeded and finely sliced
200 g small squid, prepared
2 teaspoons soy or fish sauce
1 tablespoon lime juice
2 teaspoons sesame oil
Salad leaves
6 leaves of mint or basil

---

1 Heat the oil in a pan, then fry the garlic and ginger over a high heat for about 30 seconds. Stir in the chilli, squid and soy or fish sauce and cook for a further 2 minutes, then remove the pan from the heat.

2 Stir in the lime juice and sesame oil. Divide the warm salad between two plates dressed with salad leaves, and scatter with mint or basil leaves.

CLEANING AND PREPARING SQUID

The pouch, fins and tentacles of a cleaned squid can be chopped, sliced into bite-sized pieces or left whole.

1 Pull the head of the squid and the soft innards that are attached to it, including the ink sac, gently out of the body. You can save the dark ink to use in the poaching liquid or cook it in a sauce to serve with cooked squid.

2 Cut off the tentacle cluster attached to the head and set it aside, then discard the rest of the head.

3 Pull out the clear central quill from inside the body of the squid and discard it. Cut off the wing-like flaps from either side of the body, but keep them. Peel away the thin, greyish membrane that covers the body - it should slip off easily - and discard.

4 The hollow body section can now be turned inside out and washed clean of any loose matter. Then turn it right side out. Use it whole for stuffing, or cut it into rings. The tentacles and the side flaps can be left whole or cut in half, depending on the recipe.

Starch

POTATO AND RICE FLOURS

I have seen references in some recipe books to potato and rice flour as thickening agents. Could I use them instead of cornflour?

Potato flour, or *fécule de pomme de terre* as it is called in France, is the pure starch that is leached out by soaking potato gratings in water. The liquid is drained off, leaving behind the starch, which is then dried. Similar to cornflour and used in the same way, potato flour needs only to be simmered gently for 1–2 minutes and should be added at the end of cooking; cook it any longer and the sauce will thin out again. It makes a good thickening agent and is better than cornflour for use in fruity or delicate sauces as it is both colourless and tasteless. It is available in Australia at good health food shops.

Rice flour is finely ground rice and is used in some Asian countries to make thin rice noodles. In common with potato flour, it thickens sauces and stews without flavouring or adding colour to them, and is available in Asian food stores.

FINE PEA FLOUR

What is besan flour? I have seen it mentioned in Indian recipes.

Besan flour, also known as gram flour, is used in Indian cooking and it is actually made from ground chickpeas (*chana dhal*). It is a very fine, soft flour, pale creamy yellow in colour, and is used to thicken soups and curries or made into a batter to coat vegetables or fish. But it must be stirred well or it will turn lumpy. This nutritious flour is also used in Provence and northern Italy to make crêpes, soups and special pastries. It is available from health food shops, Asian specialty food stores and the larger supermarkets. For flavour and also for texture, there is really nothing that is an adequate substitute.

Steak and Kidney Pie

FILLING PIE OR PUDDING

Is steak and kidney pie very different from steak and kidney pudding? Can I use the same dough and filling for both?

The fillings for both are similar; it is the way the filling is cooked that differs. Steak and kidney pudding is always made with a suet-crust pastry, and the uncooked mixture is spooned into the pastry before the pudding is steamed. For a steak and kidney pie, the meat filling is usually cooked before being put into a pie dish which is then covered with pastry and baked. Sometimes the filling is cooked under the pastry and, on these occasions, rump steak is used.

The traditional pastry used for a steak and kidney pie is suet-crust pastry but puff, flaky or short crust pastry are equally popular today, and give deliciously good results.

Steak and kidney pie

SERVES: 4–6
PREPARATION TIME: 45 minutes
COOKING TIME: 2½ hours

FOR THE FILLING
750 g stewing steak, blade or chuck, trimmed and cut into 2 cm cubes
250 g lambs' kidneys, skinned, trimmed and cut into 1 cm cubes
20 g (2 tablespoons) plain flour
1 teaspoon salt
½ teaspoon pepper
1 onion, chopped
125 ml water or red wine
2 tablespoons chopped fresh parsley

FOR THE PASTRY
2 sheets frozen pre-rolled butter puff pastry, thawed (approx 25 cm square)
To glaze: 1 small egg, beaten

1 Preheat the oven to 150°C.
2 Place the cubed steak and kidneys in a bowl. Sprinkle with the flour, salt and pepper, then stir well until evenly coated.
3 Place the steak and kidney mixture, the onion and water into a casserole. Cover and cook in the oven for 2 hours, or until the meat is tender.
4 Transfer the cooked filling to a bowl and leave to cool.
5 To make the pie, increase the oven temperature to 220°C. Place a pastry sheet on a lightly floured surface. Brush the pastry lightly with cold water and cover with the second pastry sheet. With a rolling pin, roll the layered pastry very lightly, just to seal, but do not roll larger.
6 Place a 1 litre oval pie dish, upside down, on the pastry. With a sharp knife, cut around the edge of the pie dish to make the top of the pie. Cut a 1 cm wide strip of pastry around the pie dish. Reserve the corner trimmings for decorations.
7 Turn the pie dish upright and spoon the filling into the dish, piling the centre up in a dome-shape. Brush the rim of the dish with cold water and cover it neatly with the strip of pastry, joining it with cold water if required.
8 Brush the pastry strip with cold water. Lift the remaining pastry top over the rolling pin and unroll over the top of the pie.
9 Gently press the pastry top onto the pastry strip to seal. Trim off any excess pastry around the edge, holding a small sharp knife at an angle of 45 degrees.
10 With a round-bladed knife, flake the edge of the pie horizontally to seal and also to raise the edge. Mark scallops around the edge of the pie. Make slits at each end of the pie between the pie dish and the pastry to allow steam to escape.
11 Place the pie dish on a baking tray. Make some leaves with the pastry trimmings and use to decorate the top of the pie. Brush the pastry with beaten egg, but do not brush the flaked edge. Bake for 30 minutes, or until the pastry is golden brown and well risen.
12 When cutting the pie to serve, top up the juices with 125 ml hot

PREPARING A STEAK AND KIDNEY PIE

Covering the top of a steak and kidney pie properly can be tricky, but taking care ensures that the filling stays rich and tender and the pie looks attractive.

1 Using the upside-down pie dish as a guide, cut out the top from the pastry, then cut a 1 cm strip to fit all round. Spoon the filling into the dish. Brush the rim of the dish with cold water and cover with the strip of pastry, pressing on gently, and joining with water if required.

2 Unroll the pastry, from a rolling pin, over the top of the pie. Press onto the pastry strip to seal.

3 Trim the edge of the pie with a sharp knife held at an angle. Flake the edge with a round-bladed knife, then mark into scallops.

stock or red wine, if liked. Serve hot accompanied with freshly cooked carrots and a green vegetable such as green beans, Brussels sprouts or broccoli and a small portion of creamy mashed potatoes.

Steamed Pudding

LEAKS AND SPILLS

If water has accidentally leaked into my steamed pudding, is there anything I can do to save it?

It depends on the quantity of water. If a lot of water gets into a steamed pudding while it is cooking, it will be soggy. If only a small amount of water has leaked in, the pudding may be affected only in a small area and will still be palatable.

The best advice is to try to stop water getting into the pudding by covering it properly. Traditionally, steamed puddings are cooked in a deep bowl or basin that is covered with a piece of greased greaseproof or baking paper, pleated in the middle and topped with a cloth, or a piece of pleated foil tied securely with string. The pleats allow room for expansion when the pudding is cooked. The covering is needed to keep the pudding well protected from the boiling water beneath, so that it is cooked in the steam and is moist but not sodden.

When steaming puddings, do not let the water boil too furiously as this will make it lap over the top. Keep it at an even rolling boil, or boil the pudding in a slow cooker.

TIME SAVER

Can you cook steamed puddings in a microwave oven?

Yes, they can be made quickly and easily in a microwave oven and the result is a light, spongy texture, as the following recipe shows. Cooking your steamed pudding in the microwave not only means you save on time, you also avoid having a lot of steam in the kitchen.

A cup of hot water placed in the microwave next to the pudding will introduce some steam to the microwave oven and help to keep the pudding moist. This is also a good practice to follow when you are reheating precooked steamed and sponge puddings.

Take the fast lane to pleasing the family by cooking one of their favourite desserts in the microwave. It saves time and also some of the washing-up.

Choc-hazelnut and lime puddings

SERVES: 6
PREPARATION TIME: 30 minutes
COOKING TIME: 4 minutes per batch, plus 1 minute standing time

Melted unsalted butter and caster sugar, for coating
6 thin slices of lime, halved
12 teaspoons lime marmalade, warmed
100 g dark cooking chocolate
4 large eggs, separated
125 g (½ cup) caster sugar
1 teaspoon vanilla essence
90 g (¾ cup) hazelnuts, toasted and ground
60 g (1 cup) soft white breadcrumbs
Orange wedges, to garnish

FOR THE SAUCE
100 g dark cooking chocolate
30 g (2 tablespoons) icing sugar, sifted
125 ml fresh cream, at room temperature
1 tablespoon orange-flavoured liqueur

1 Brush a six-hole microwave-safe muffin tray with melted butter and coat with caster sugar. Tap out the excess. Place a half slice of lime and 1 teaspoon of lime marmalade in the base of each muffin hole.
2 Break the chocolate into a microwave-safe bowl. Melt in the microwave on Defrost for 2 minutes; stir, then melt on Defrost for another 2 minutes. Continue this process until all the chocolate is melted.

3 Beat the egg yolks and caster sugar together until thick and creamy. Stir in the melted chocolate and vanilla essence.
4 Whisk the egg whites until soft peaks form. Fold the hazelnuts, breadcrumbs and egg whites into the chocolate mixture.
5 Spoon half the mixture evenly into the muffin tins. Place on a rack on the microwave turntable and cook on Medium power for 4 minutes. Cover with paper towels and stand for 1 minute. Turn out and keep warm while cooking the remaining puddings as directed.
6 To make the sauce, break and melt the chocolate as directed for the puddings. Add the icing sugar, cream and liqueur and stir well.
7 Place 1-2 puddings on individual plates. Serve warm with the sauce and orange wedges on the side.

Steaming

PRESERVING VITAMINS

In what way is steaming a better method of cooking than boiling, frying or roasting?

Steaming is the cooking of food in hot vapour rather than in liquid. As the food never touches the liquid, the loss of vitamins is significantly reduced. And as steamed food is cooked without fat, it is more digestible and highly suitable for invalids and those on low-fat diets.

You must, however, ensure that you always choose excellent quality ingredients for steaming – there is no help to be had from the flavour of butter or oil, nor does the food caramelise during cooking, so the raw materials must taste good without such assistance.

ESSENTIAL EQUIPMENT

I would like to steam more of my food for a healthy diet. Do I need any special equipment?

It is probably quite possible to improvise a steamer by using your existing kitchen equipment, but if you are intending to do a lot of steaming, it is worth investing in a dedicated steamer of some sort.

A variety of special equipment for steaming is available. Most common are oval or round steamers, which are rather similar to double boilers, except that the top layer has holes in its base. Steam from the boiling water in the lower pan rises through the holes to cook the food, while the lid on the upper pan keeps in the steam.

Another popular steaming device is a stainless-steel, plastic or aluminium basket that opens and folds shut, rather like a fan. This can be used with an ordinary lidded saucepan. The basket stands on its own short legs to keep it clear of the boiling water; it fits inside most saucepans and is particularly suitable for quick-cooking foods as the water underneath the basket would have to be replaced often.

If you want to steam a large fish, a fish kettle is ideal: place the fish on the rack carefully and lower this onto upturned ramekin dishes to hold the rack out of the water.

Small pieces of fish can be plate-steamed: put the fish on a lightly buttered plate, season and set the plate on a pan of simmering water or on a trivet inside a frying pan half full of water. Cover the pan and cook the fish for 8–10 minutes.

Chinese cooking also employs steaming. Fish, shellfish and tender cuts of meat, often wrapped in thin pastry or vegetable leaves, and dumplings, are steamed in rattan baskets stacked over a wok of boiling water. (See also **Wok**.)

Stew

CRUCIAL FIRST STEPS

Are there any golden rules for making a perfect stew?

Good stews are made or lost in the early stages of their preparation. In many stews the meat is fried first (sometimes with onions, carrots, leeks, whole or sliced mushrooms, peppers or shallots), to give a rich flavour and to add colour to the sauce, which will be made with the browned sediment and dried juices that stick to the pan after frying.

If the sauce is not to look too pale and taste insipid, you must fry the meat until each piece is a good even brown colour. Fry the pieces a few at a time, so as not to crowd the pan, and keep the temperature high so that the meat browns and fries rather than sweats.

If the bottom of the pan begins to get too brown, you can deglaze it between batches of meat by pouring in a few tablespoons of stock, wine or water. Stir it vigorously to loosen the sediment, taste the liquid, and, if it is not burnt, reserve it to add to the stew. It will not taste delicious at this point but as long as it has not burnt it will enrich and colour the stew.

THE RIGHT TEMPERATURE

The meat in my stews is always stringy. What am I doing wrong?

Stews are a perfect way to use the tougher, cheaper cuts of meat. Long, slow cooking makes the meat tender and full of flavour. But tough, stringy meat can be the result of overcooking, especially if it is cooked at too high a temperature so that the liquid boils and breaks up the fibres of the meat.

The temperature at which the stew cooks should be no higher than 150°C, and this should be maintained for at least 2 hours. The aim is to achieve a very gentle simmering, with only the occasional bubble breaking the surface of the liquid. A heat diffuser made of wire mesh and placed between the hotplate and saucepan can prevent the stew cooking too quickly.

The pan should be heavy with a tight-fitting lid that keeps in the moisture. A pan that is too thin or buckled can cause the stew to burn at the bottom. Your pan should also be the appropriate size; small quantities of stew in a large pan will dry out very quickly, while too much food in a small pan might boil over.

VARIABLE QUANTITIES

How much meat should I allow per person in a stew?

As a general rule, allow 175–250 g of boned meat per person depending on the proportion of meat to other ingredients. When you are catering for a large group, use the smaller amount of meat as people tend to eat less at big functions.

A mainly meat stew will be rich and will need a carbohydrate side dish (bread, pasta, potatoes or rice) and a green vegetable or salad. Or the stew can contain everything for a complete meal. The traditional French recipe below, featuring lamb, haricot beans and tomatoes, is a good example of a hearty stew.

Navarin of lamb with haricot beans

SERVES: 4-6
PREPARATION TIME: 20 minutes, plus 30 minutes soaking the beans
COOKING TIME: 3 hours

200 g (1 cup) dried haricot beans
3 tablespoons olive or
   sunflower oil
1 kg boned lamb, cubed
500 g onions, sliced
20 g (1 tablespoon) white sugar
20 g (2 tablespoons) plain flour
500 ml meat or vegetable stock, or
   375 ml stock and 125 ml dry
   white wine
500 g tomatoes, skinned, deseeded
   and roughly chopped
1 bouquet garni
1 teaspoon salt
½ teaspoon black pepper
1 large clove garlic, crushed
To garnish: sprigs of fresh thyme

1 Cover the dried beans with water and soak for 30 minutes. Drain, put in a pan of fresh water and rapidly boil the beans for 15 minutes. Drain, return the beans to the pan with fresh water to cover and simmer for 1¼ hours. Drain again and set aside.
2 Heat the oil in a large saucepan or flameproof casserole and fry the lamb over a medium heat, until it is browned all over. Remove the meat and drain any oil back into the pan.

A tender stew of lamb, haricot beans, sliced onions and tomatoes cooked with stock and herbs makes a warming meal for wintry evenings or weekend lunches.

3 Add the sliced onions and sauté over a medium heat for 5 minutes, stirring occasionally. Add the sugar and stir over a medium heat for a further 5 minutes until the onions are well browned, then stir in the flour and cook for another minute.
4 Add the stock and bring to the boil, stirring until thickened. Add the chopped tomatoes, the bouquet garni, salt and pepper, then the fried lamb with any juices, and return to the boil. Reduce the heat, cover and simmer very gently for 1-1½ hours.
5 Stir in the drained beans and the garlic and return to the boil. Cover the pan and simmer very gently for another hour until the meat and beans are tender but not mushy. Stir the stew occasionally so that it does not stick to the pan.
6 Remove the bouquet garni before serving the stew hot, garnished with sprigs of thyme and accompanied by a steamed green vegetable such as spinach and some rice or potatoes.

CAREFUL TRIMMING

Should I cut off all the fat and gristle from stewing steak before it goes into the pot?

Always remove any obvious gristle from stewing steak as this will not dissolve during cooking the way ordinary fat does. A little fat may be left on to add moisture and flavour to the stew, or trimmed off.

A good compromise is to trim off any pieces of fat surrounding the meat but leave any marbled fat between the meat tissue as this will melt and add flavour to the dish. If you want to remove all the fat, make the stew a day ahead, chill and when cold, lift off any fat that has set on the surface. If you intend to trim off all the fat, remember to buy a larger quantity of meat.

Cooking your chosen meat on the bone, or adding the meat bones to the stew, will also give extra flavour and texture to the stew.

Stock

PATIENCE IS A VIRTUE

Why does stock always take so long to make?

Meat or poultry stock needs long, slow cooking in order to extract as much flavour as possible from the bones. But vegetable stocks can be made quickly or slowly and fish stocks are always made quickly.

Cooked bones can be used for stock and do not need blanching, but will have lost some of their flavour and are not as good as raw bones. For poultry or game stock, use the carcass from a roasted bird. Avoid using lamb bones, which give an unpleasant flavour.

It is often better to place raw bones in a pan of cold water, bring them to the boil, then drain and refresh before using them to make stock. This will remove impurities that would give the stock a tainted taste and unpleasant grey colour.

Do not boil stock during the cooking process as this will make it cloudy. But after the bones and vegetables have been strained off, the stock may be returned to the pan and boiled to reduce it.

Raw beef bones can be used for an all-purpose Meat Stock like the one featured below.

Meat stock

MAKES: *1 litre*
PREPARATION TIME: *5 minutes*
COOKING TIME: *3-4 hours*

750 g-1 kg raw beef bones, chopped
1 onion, chopped
1 carrot, chopped
1 stalk celery, roughly sliced
1 mushroom, sliced
1 bouquet garni
6 peppercorns

1 Put the bones in a large saucepan with 2.5 litres of cold water. Bring to the boil, skim off thoroughly any scum that rises to the surface, then add the vegetables, bouquet garni and peppercorns.

2 Half cover the pan so the lid is tilted, reduce the heat and simmer gently for 3-4 hours until the liquid has reduced by more than half.
3 Remove the saucepan from the heat and strain the stock, discarding the bones and vegetables. Leave the stock to cool then skim off the fat that has risen to the surface. Use the stock immediately, or store in the refrigerator for up to four days.
VARIATIONS
For a brown stock, the dry bones and vegetables can first be roasted in a very hot oven for 30-40 minutes, until browned at the edges, then transferred to the stockpot with the water. Alternatively, put the bones in a saucepan and cook over a gentle heat, turning occasionally, for 10 minutes until the fat runs. Add the vegetables and continue cooking over a medium heat for 15 minutes, turning regularly until they are well browned, then add the water.

Carefully skimming off all the scum that rises to the surface during boiling leaves a clear and tasty stock.

SIMPLY THE BEST

Can you suggest a good, fast recipe for chicken stock?

Chicken stock is one of the easiest and quickest stocks to make and it can be used whenever a well flavoured stock is required in a recipe. You will get the best flavour if you use a raw chicken carcass plus the giblets, but if you have cooked a roast chicken, you can use the leftover carcass from that instead. Include any uneaten pieces of chicken wing or drumstick in the stockpot; they will help to give the stock extra flavour.

Chicken stock

MAKES: *1 litre*
PREPARATION TIME: *5 minutes*
COOKING TIME: *2 hours*

1 chicken carcass (raw or remains from a roasted chicken)
Chicken giblets, but not the liver, optional
1 onion, roughly chopped or sliced
1 carrot, roughly chopped or sliced
1 stalk celery, roughly sliced, optional
1 leek, sliced, optional
1 mushroom or a few stalks, roughly chopped, optional
1 bouquet garni
6 peppercorns

1 Break up the carcass into several pieces and put it in a large saucepan. Add 2 litres of cold water and bring it to the boil. With a slotted spoon, remove any scum that rises to the surface of the stock, then add the vegetables and flavourings.
2 Half cover the pan, reduce the heat and simmer gently for 2 hours until the stock has reduced by half.
3 Remove the saucepan from the heat and strain the stock, discarding the bones and vegetables. Reduce the strained stock if necessary then leave it to cool before skimming off any fat that rises to the surface. Use the stock immediately or store it, chilled, for up to four days.

COOL JELLY

My stock never seems to thicken even though I simmer it for hours. What am I doing wrong?

Stock is not supposed to thicken while it is still cooking, but a well concentrated meat stock should gel on cooling and any fat can then be scraped easily off the top.

When the collagen that is contained naturally in the meat bones dissolves during cooking, it forms the gelatine that later sets the stock. To make a really good jellied meat stock, try to get hold of a raw veal knuckle, calf's foot or beef marrow bone, and simmer it in plenty of water with vegetables and flavourings for about 4 hours before straining and cooling. If this stock is then reduced even further, it will form a syrupy glaze called a glace that is often used in classic French sauces. Glace can be frozen in ice cube trays for convenience.

STOCK FROM FISH

How does fish stock differ from a fumet or court bouillon, and how should they each be used?

Fish stock is made in the same way as meat stock in that the fish bones, heads and tails (and the shells of shellfish) are simmered in water with vegetables and flavourings. But fish stock is cooked for only 20–30 minutes as lengthy cooking will make it bitter. Once the stock has been strained it can be concentrated by further boiling. A glass of dry white wine added to the stock improves the flavour considerably.

After straining, the stock can be boiled slightly to reduce it to a more intensely flavoured fumet. Fumet can be used in fish sauces, soups and stews.

Court bouillon is the liquid used for poaching fresh fish such as salmon. It is made from water, white wine (or lemon juice or vinegar) and flavourings, but unlike fish stock, it does not contain any fish trimmings. Court bouillon is rarely featured in the finished dish.

A bouquet garni of bay leaf, celery, parsley and thyme adds a fresh note to meat, chicken and fish stocks.

Fish stock

MAKES: 1 litre
PREPARATION TIME: 5 minutes
COOKING TIME: 30 minutes

500 g white fish trimmings (heads, bones, tails, etc)
1 onion, roughly chopped or sliced
125 ml dry white wine
1 bouquet garni
1 tablespoon lemon juice

1 Put the fish trimmings in a large saucepan (breaking or folding over if necessary), add the onion and sweat them over a low heat for 10 minutes.
2 Pour on 1.25 litres of cold water and the wine, then bring to the boil. Remove any scum that rises to the surface, then add the bouquet garni and lemon juice.
3 Half cover the pan so that the lid is tilted, reduce the heat, and then simmer for 30 minutes only.
4 Remove the saucepan from the heat and strain the stock, discarding the bones and other solids. Use it immediately or cool and chill.

MAKING IT LAST

How long will stock keep?

Stock should be cooled then kept, covered, in the refrigerator for four days (two days for fish stocks) or in the freezer for up to three months (two months for fish). It is best to reduce the stock by rapid boiling to get a concentrated stock for freezing. Frozen stock can be defrosted or reheated straight from frozen, but should be simmered for at least 10 minutes; it can also be diluted.

VEGETABLE VARIETY

I am vegetarian – can you suggest an all-purpose vegetable stock?

The following recipe can be used in cooking for vegetarians, as well as for anyone following a low-fat diet. Vegetarian stocks can be as bland or as strong as you like: the greater the variety of vegetables and herbs you use, the better the stock will taste. Because they do not contain any meat bones, vegetarian stocks do not set to a jelly.

Vegetable stock

MAKES: 1 litre
PREPARATION TIME: 5 minutes
COOKING TIME: 1–1½ hours

750 g–1 kg selection of vegetables: beans, broccoli, cauliflower, celery, fennel, leeks, mushrooms, onions and any root vegetables, cleaned, trimmed and roughly chopped
Selection of herbs such as bay leaf, dill, marjoram, parsley stalks, rosemary, tarragon, thyme
Large strip of lemon rind, optional
Blade of mace, optional
6 peppercorns

1 Put all the ingredients in a large saucepan, add 1.5 litres of cold water and bring the stock to the boil. Reduce the heat, half cover the saucepan so that the lid is tilted and simmer gently for 1–1½ hours until reduced by nearly half.
2 Remove the saucepan from the heat, strain the stock and discard the vegetables. Leave to cool, then store in the refrigerator for up to four days.
VARIATION
A darker vegetable stock may be made by including eggplant in the vegetable mixture and adding clean onion skins or mushroom stalks.

STALKS FOR FLAVOUR

Why do stock recipes use parsley stalks? Is it considered a waste to use the florets or do they give the stock a bitter taste?

Recipes for stock often specify the use of parsley stalks because they have more flavour than the florets, which will turn bitter if cooked for several hours. This is also economical as the parsley leaves can then be used for garnishing.

Other herbs suitable for adding to stocks are the woody ones that will stand up to prolonged cooking: sprigs of marjoram, tarragon and thyme, as well as bay leaves. A slice of lemon or pared lemon rind is a good addition to chicken stock and onion or tomato skins can also be added to give a strong golden colour and extra flavour.

Storage

KEEP IT FRESH

What is the best way to store fresh food in the home?

The modern methods of chilling, freezing, wrapping and transporting food should mean that we buy produce at its very best: fruit and vegetables brought to perfect ripeness, meat and fish at the peak of freshness. Sometimes, however, the freshness is an illusion created by packing and refrigeration technology, and when you get the food home, spoilage will be rapid unless some of the professionals' techniques are employed.

Almost all vegetables store well in the refrigerator, where the low temperature prevents spoilage. If space cannot be found in the refrigerator for all the vegetables, use a cool, dark place instead as warmth and light will hasten their spoilage. Do not store them in clear plastic bags or airtight containers as the warmer temperature will make them sweat and rot. Keep potatoes in a dark place or they will go green and be inedible.

Never store bananas or unripe avocados in the refrigerator, as both develop black skins if refrigerated and their ability to ripen is impaired. Ripe avocados, however, can be stored for a few days in the salad compartment of the refrigerator. Keep strong-smelling fruit such as cut pineapple or melon well wrapped in the refrigerator, or their fragrance will affect the flavour and smell of dairy foods such as butter, cheese and milk.

In the refrigerator, cheese is best stored in waxed paper or foil which, unlike plastic wrap, do not cause it to sweat. Very strong cheeses, however, are best kept in a plastic box so that their aromas do not taint other foods.

Fish does not improve with storage. If it is to be kept for more than 12 hours, even in the refrigerator, scatter cracked ice over it, replac-ing the ice as necessary, and cover the container to prevent the smell of fish tainting other food. Shellfish perishes particularly quickly and for this reason it is generally sold alive, or else precooked or frozen. If you are in any doubt about the length of time a quantity of shell-fish has been stored, do not eat it.

All meat and poultry should be chilled; meat should be eaten within four days, poultry within three days. If you buy your meat from a butcher, store it loosely wrapped in greaseproof paper or foil as a plastic covering will cause the meat to sweat and then become slimy and decompose. However, most meat sold in supermarkets is wrapped in sealed packets; these are best left unopened until the meat is needed.

THE BREAD LINE

Does keeping fresh bread in the refrigerator prevent it from going mouldy, or does this make it go stale more quickly?

The answer is yes on both counts. Using the refrigerator will prevent mould development, but as it is a very dry environment it also makes bread go stale very quickly.

The best way to store bread for long periods of time, is to slice it and keep it in the freezer. Slices can be toasted from frozen very successfully, and they can be defrosted in very little time if they are to be eaten untoasted.

KEEPING EGGS

How should fresh eggs be kept? I thought I should refrigerate them, but supermarkets never do.

Eggs can be stored perfectly safely in any cool spot, although they will keep for longer in a refrigerator and should always be refrigerated in hot climates. The cartons carry a 'use by' date, so it is easy to keep track of their age. If you store them in the refrigerator, take them out an hour or so before using: cold eggs will crack when you boil them and room-temperature eggs will whisk to a greater volume than cold ones.

STORAGE LIFE

How do I store dried foods such as beans, herbs, spices and coffee?

Dried pulses and beans should be bought from a shop with a rapid turnover to ensure fresh stocks. There is a great difference between beans dried last season and those from two or three years ago. Store dried pulses and beans in airtight containers in a dark place and try not to buy more than two months' supply at a time. Although stored beans will be safe to eat, they do go stale and their skins will toughen.

Dried herbs and spices also have a relatively short storage life and although they look attractive in glass jars on a spice rack, this is the worst way to store them. To ensure complete freshness, store them in a cupboard or a dark airtight container and use within two months.

Coffee, both beans and ready-ground, will go stale in a cupboard within days. Store it in the refrigerator or freezer and use it from frozen for a perfectly fresh cup.

Stuffing

USED FOR CENTURIES

Are stuffings and forcemeats the same thing?

These two words are often used interchangeably, and there is some confusion about their exact meanings, probably because forcemeat, which is finely chopped and usually made of spiced meat or poultry, is often an ingredient in stuffings. Both are used to fill meat, poultry and vegetables and have been used for centuries, especially to make roast meat go farther and to add flavour and moistness.

The staple ingredients for stuffings are breadcrumbs, which add bulk, and egg, which binds the stuffing mixture together. This can be confusing for cooks because it is natural to think that breadcrumbs will make stuffings stodgy, and that the egg will make it creamy because it visibly loosens the mixture when added to it. But, in fact, a high proportion of breadcrumbs will give a soft and tender stuffing, while using too much egg makes a stuffing stodgy once it has been cooked and the egg has set.

TAKE CARE WITH CAVITIES

I have heard that there is a risk of salmonella poisoning if I stuff the cavity of a bird. Is this true, and if so, is it safe to stuff it at all?

Meat and poultry are highly vulnerable to salmonella and the bacteria is only killed by thorough cooking (see **Food Poisoning**).

With a large bird, such as a turkey, it is safer not to stuff the entire cavity, especially if you use a sausage meat stuffing. This is because there is a risk that by the time the rest of the bird is cooked and ready, the heat will not have penetrated to the centre of the substantial amount of stuffing used to fill a large bird, so it will not have cooked enough to kill off any bacteria. It is safe to stuff the neck end, which holds a lot of stuffing, as there is less meat between the source of the heat and the stuffing and there is a better opportunity for thorough cooking.

It is completely safe and also simpler to put an onion studded with cloves, a lemon, or a handful of peeled chestnuts into the body cavity of the bird to add flavour.

With a small game bird, such as pheasant or quail, you could stuff the entire bird as it takes less time for the heat to cook the smaller quantity of stuffing, providing you do not pack it too tightly.

There is some risk of salmonella in wild game birds as well as in farmed game birds and chicken and turkey. If you are going to stuff any bird, it is important that both the meat and the stuffing are thoroughly cooked to guarantee safety.

If you want to be completely assured that there is no risk of salmonella, cook the stuffing separately. Place in a buttered dish, cover, then put in the oven for the last 30 minutes cooking time.

Suet

RICH, PURE FAT

Where does suet come from?

Suet is the hard, concentrated, white fat that surrounds beef and sheep kidneys. It is now less often sold in solid form from butchers for grating at home – in supermarkets you will find suet sold already shredded and floured in a mix ready for use.

A rich, pure fat that contains a high percentage of saturated fatty acids, beef suet is traditionally used for cooking many dishes including dumplings, fruit mince, suet crust pastry and steamed puddings.

Lamb suet is not widely available although butchers will be able to order it for you; it has a stronger flavour than beef suet and is therefore less adaptable in cooking and a poor choice for sweet dishes such as steamed puddings or pastry.

LIGHTEN IT

Why is my suet pastry heavy?

There are several reasons why suet pastry may be heavy and stodgy. Check that you have measured your ingredients accurately and do not undercook or overcook the pastry. When you are steaming a suet pudding over a pan of water, ensure that water does not seep into the pudding as this too can cause the pastry to become heavier in texture. The following recipe for a Blackberry and Apple Suet Pudding combines suet and autumnal fruits for a sweet pudding with a delicious taste and texture.

Blackberries lend their rich colour to this luscious suet pudding. Combined with apples, they give moistness and flavour to the comforting pastry mixture.

Blackberry and apple suet pudding

Serves: 4
Preparation time: 20 minutes
Cooking time: 1½-2 hours

250 g cooking apples, peeled, cored
    and sliced
30 g (2 tablespoons) light brown
    sugar
125 g blackberries, washed
250 g packet suet mix
1 teaspoon baking powder
60 g (¼ cup) caster sugar
1 egg
125 ml milk

1 Put the apple slices in the base of a lightly greased 1.25 litre pudding basin, sprinkle with brown sugar and top with the blackberries.
2 Put the suet mix, baking powder and caster sugar in a bowl and stir until mixed. Make a well in the centre and add the egg and enough milk to produce a soft dropping consistency, mixing well.
3 Spoon evenly over the fruit and level the surface of the pudding.
4 Cover the pudding with a double layer of pleated, greased, greaseproof paper or foil and tie securely with kitchen string. Make a string handle across the basin top.
5 Place the pudding in a steamer over a pan of boiling water. Cover and steam for 2 hours, topping up the pan regularly to prevent it from boiling dry. Turn the pudding out onto a warmed serving plate and serve with custard or cream.

Variations
Use some other soft fruits, such as raspberries or mulberries, in place of the blackberries. You can sprinkle 1 teaspoon of ground cinnamon or mixed spice over the fruit before steaming. Add the finely grated zest of a lemon to the pudding mixture before spooning it over the fruit.

Vegetarian suet

Is there a vegetarian alternative to using beef suet?

Vegetarian suet is not available in Australia; however it is produced and marketed in the United King-dom. It is made from hard or hydro-genated vegetable oils or solid white vegetable fat. It may be used as an alternative to and in the same way as beef suet and, unlike beef suet – which is coated with wheat flour – vegetarian suet tends to be dusted with rice flour, making it appropriate for people who are allergic to wheat or those on gluten-free diets. Low-fat vegetar-ian suet has 25 per cent less fat.

As an alternative, you can use the same quantity of finely ground Brazil nuts, a highly nutritious veg-etarian substitute that can be used in all recipes containing suet. Brazil nuts melt in the same manner as suet and will provide a pleasing, rather grainy, texture. They contain 68.2 per cent fat with only 16.4 per cent of that being saturated fat – the rest is half monounsaturated and half polyunsaturated fat.

Sugar

Fine line in sugars

If a recipe calls for caster sugar and I've run out, can I substitute ordinary white sugar instead?

It depends on the recipe. In cakes made by the rubbing-in method, you can use the white sugar as it is. If you need a finer sugar, it is pos-sible to grind white sugar in a blender or coffee grinder: the result is more like icing sugar than caster sugar but it would be acceptable for making biscuits, pastry, icings and so on. Home-ground sugar is not, however, suitable for creamed cake mixtures as the volume of sugar will be reduced and result in a cake with a hard crust.

Low-kilojoule substitute

Can low-kilojoule sugars be used in cooking in place of ordinary sugars?

Generally, artificial sweeteners and sugar substitutes are much sweeter by volume than sugar and cannot be directly substituted for them in

cooking. However, some brands of white sugar substitutes are specifically designed to be used in exactly the same quantities as ordinary sugar in cooking, so check the instructions given on the packet.

SYRUP RATIO

Does sugar syrup always require the same ratio of sugar to water?

No. Sugar syrup is simply a solution of sugar dissolved in water, and different concentrations are used for different recipes. A thin syrup is three parts water to one part sugar; a medium syrup is two parts water to one part sugar; and a heavy syrup is equal volumes of water and sugar. In simple, clear syrups, the sugar and water are stirred over a low heat until the sugar has dissolved, the mixture is boiled for a minute then removed from the heat (see panel, right).

If any of these syrups are boiled for a longer time, more water evaporates, the temperature of the syrup increases and the sugar changes colour, deepening from pale yellow to dark brown and eventually turning into caramel. There are various stages to which the sugar syrup can be boiled (see list, next column) and different recipes will require different stages of caramelisation.

TESTING TIME

What is the best way for me to test whether sugar syrup is ready?

It is best to use a sugar thermometer to test sugar syrup. First, put the thermometer in a bowl of hot water for a few minutes so it is warm before going into the syrup. Take it out of the water, dry it and place it into the pan containing the hot syrup. Make sure the bulb of the thermometer is covered by the syrup but not touching the base of the pan or you will get a false reading. If the quantity of syrup is small, tilt the pan to one side so that you can immerse the bulb.

When the syrup has reached the desired temperature (see the following list), remove the pan from

the heat and place the thermometer back in the bowl of hot water to make cleaning the bulb easier.

Although a sugar thermometer is recommended for taking the temperature of your syrup mixture, do not worry if you do not have one. You can use the simple tests listed below to ascertain what stage your sugar syrup has reached.

- THREAD STAGE for thin syrups: 103°C. Thread test: dip two spoons into the syrup, back to back. Pull gently apart until a thin thread forms and then breaks almost immediately.
- PEARL STAGE for fondants and icings: 105°C. Pearl test: small pearl-like globules appear on the surface of the syrup, and if the thread test is repeated, the thread formed will be thicker.
- BLOW STAGE for ices: 110°C. Blow test: use a metal skewer with a small ring at one end. Dip the ring in the syrup then blow on it gently – a small bubble of syrup should appear.
- SOFT BALL STAGE for fondants and soft fudges: 115°C. HARD BALL STAGE for hard fudges: 120°C. Soft and hard ball test: drop a little syrup into a small bowl of cold water. Then gather it together with your fingers and it should form a soft or hard ball.
- CRACK STAGE for soft toffees: 136°C. HARD CRACK STAGE for hard toffees and spun sugar: 149°C. Crack and hard crack test: drop a little syrup into cold water and the pieces will become brittle and snap easily between your fingers. Crack is not quite so brittle as hard crack.
- CARAMEL STAGE for caramel coatings, decorations and praline: 170°C. Caramel test: the colour of the syrup will change from pale gold to dark brown.

STICKY BUSINESS

How do I avoid ruining my pan when making caramel?

As caramel is usually made in fairly small amounts, it is important to use a small pan as then it is easier

to control the degree of heat and prevent the caramel from sticking. In a large pan there is the danger that the sugar will caramelise quickly, burn and stick to the pan.

The pan should also have a heavy base: a thin pan will buckle, then heat will not be evenly distributed and, again, the caramel will burn. If the caramel does stick to the base of the pan, the easiest way to clean it is to add some cold water, return the pan to a low heat and stir gently; the hardened burnt caramel should gradually dissolve. Repeat this process until the pan is thoroughly cleaned.

BROWN OR WHITE?

Is brown sugar any healthier to eat than white sugar?

Most brown sugar is refined sugar that has been treated with colour and flavour, and so there is no evidence to suggest that brown sugar is healthier than white.

Golden demerara sugar and the light and dark brown sugars have traces of minerals and vitamins, so it could be claimed that they are marginally healthier than other sugars. However, to gain any benefit from these minerals and vitamins you would have to eat an enormous amount of sugar, which would not be healthy.

CRUNCHY MICE

I remember in my childhood being given sugar mice as a special treat. Can I make them at home myself?

Yes, very easily. Sugar mice take only a short while to make, keep for a long time, and are very popular with young children, who love to suck on the hardened shapes.

Sugar mice

MAKES: *8 mice*
PREPARATION TIME: *30 minutes*
COOKING TIME: *none*

500 g (3 cups) icing sugar
1 large egg white
2 tablespoons golden or corn syrup
Edible food colourings, optional
Silver confectionery balls
Shoelace liquorice or fine string

1 Sieve 350 g (2 cups) of the icing sugar into a bowl. Add the egg white and the golden or corn syrup and mix with a wooden spoon.

2 Gradually add more icing sugar until the sugar paste is of a similar consistency to pastry (you may not need to add all the sugar). Divide the sugar paste into separate bowls, one for each colour, and stir in a few drops of food colouring.

3 To shape the mice, divide the sugar paste into nine roughly equal portions and set one portion aside. Roll the other eight pieces into balls then pinch one end of each ball to make a teardrop shape.

4 Pull small bits of paste from the remaining portion, flatten them to make ears and, using a little water, attach them to the narrow end of the mice. Press in the silver balls to make some eyes, and add a liquorice tail to the rounded end.

5 Leave the mice to dry overnight on nonstick baking paper and store them for up to a month in an airtight container.

With their liquorice tails and silver ball eyes, these candy-coloured Sugar Mice look as sweet as they taste.

SHADES OF BROWN

I get confused by all the different brown sugars – what are they used for and can they simply be substituted for white sugar?

It depends on the sugar. There are various types of brown sugar, with different levels of coarseness and colours that range from pale beige to deep dark brown – the darker the colour of the sugar, the richer its flavour will be.

Demerara has a crunchy texture and is good for making chutneys, for grilling as a topping on crème brûlée and for glazing baked ham. It should not be used when a quick-melting sugar is needed, or for jellies, as it will make them cloudy; for these, use white sugar instead.

Light and dark brown sugars can be used in fruit cakes and other moist cakes, some biscuits, fudge and chocolate icings, toffee and fudge, chutneys and some sauces (barbecue, sweet and sour, chocolate and so on). As these sugars are moist they should not be used in light cakes which need creaming or whisking, or in light icings where the additional flavour and colour would not be desirable.

Black or very dark brown sugar (also called Barbados sugar) contains molasses; the darker the colour is, the more molasses and therefore the stronger the flavour. It is used in the same way as light and dark brown sugars and is perfect for Christmas cakes and puddings, but take care it does not mask delicate flavours.

To the rescue!

If your brown sugar has hardened in the cupboard, wrap the pack in a damp tea towel and microwave it on Medium for a minute or two or until the sugar begins to soften. You can then use it as normal.

KEEP IT FLOWING

How can I ensure that sugar does not go hard in my cupboard?

Sugar should be kept in an airtight container in a cool dry place, and once opened, packets should be resealed between use.

Moist light and dark brown sugars are the ones that tend to go hard and lumpy, as exposure to air dries them out. Adding a slice of apple or bread to the container in which the pack is stored for a couple of days should restore moisture.

If you want to use the hardened sugar immediately, blend it in a food processor and then sieve it, or heat in a microwave oven (see box, below left).

NUTTY LUXURY

How do I make sugared almonds?

They are very difficult for the home cook to make, as you need to achieve a very smooth, very hard fondant. This delicacy is best treated as a shop-bought luxury.

Swede

ROOT CONFUSION

I have heard swede referred to as 'neeps'. Is it the same as turnip?

No, it is not. Swede is a larger, rounded winter root vegetable with coarse, pale orange flesh. 'Neeps', or Swedish turnip, is what swede is called in Scotland. In the United States swede is called rutabaga.

Although they are different from each other, swede can be substituted for turnip in recipes. Choose smaller swedes for cooking as large ones tend to be tough.

BUTTER AND SPICE

Is there a way to make the strong, coarse flavour of swede gentler and more sophisticated?

Swede, like the other winter roots, needs butter and loves spices. An excellent way to serve swede is to peel it thickly and cut it into slices before being parboiled and grilled, then lightly spread with tapenade. Bacon is another tasty accompaniment. Parboil chunks of swede, drain them well then stir-fry in olive oil with chopped bacon and a teaspoon of cumin seeds.

Slow roasting brings sweetness and a soft texture to the vegetable and so pieces of swede are best roasted around a meat joint for 1–1½ hours. Alternatively, roast them on their own in a little olive oil and, 10 minutes before the end of cooking, top them with slices of Cheddar, Gruyère or mozzarella cheese and return to the oven.

Swede is also good served as a purée, often mixed with other root vegetables (as in the following recipe), and this can help to soften its flavour.

Mashed swede and carrot with allspice

SERVES: 6
PREPARATION TIME: 25 minutes
COOKING TIME: 20 minutes

---

500 g swede, cut into chunks
400 g large carrots, cut into chunks
75 g butter
4 tablespoons fresh cream or thickened cream
150 g mashed potatoes
1 teaspoon ground allspice
Salt and black pepper

---

1 Put the swede into a large pan of water, bring to the boil and simmer for 10–15 minutes until soft.
2 Meanwhile, cook and drain the carrots, then put them into a food processor with the butter and cream.
3 Drain the swede, then return it to the dry pan, and shake over low heat to encourage evaporation.
4 Add the chunks of swede to the carrots in the food processor and purée them together.
5 In a large bowl, stir the mashed potato and the purée of swede and carrot together by hand. Season with allspice, salt and black pepper.
6 Spread the purée in an oven dish and serve immediately, or reheat in the oven when required.

Sweet and Sour Sauce

KITCHEN PHILOSOPHY

Why do I find sweet and sour dishes on every Chinese menu?

Chinese culture is based on the yin-yang concept of universal balance and absolute harmony. Sweet and sour are only two of the many opposite elements which symbolise this philosophy, but they are the most commonly encountered.

The permutations of sweet and sour are endless as long as you stick to the fundamental principle, balancing honey and wine vinegar, honey and malt vinegar, even marmalade with balsamic vinegar or tomato sauce and pineapple juice. It is a matter of ingenuity and the ingredients you use are less important than achieving a sauce that is a harmonious blend.

Traditional Chinese sweet and sour dishes are made with plum sauce and rice wine, vinegar or lemon juice. The authentic sauce (right) is easy to reproduce. You can make a large batch, omitting the cucumber and the onion, and refrigerate it for up to a week. Add the vegetables just before cooking.

If you are using previously fried, battered pork or chicken, simply combine the sauce and coated meat in a wok or pan and stir to blend. Pork cubes are best floured and refrigerated for a few hours before being deep-fried for a sweet and sour dish as this makes them crisp.

Sweet and sour sauce

MAKES: 175 ml
PREPARATION TIME: 5 minutes plus 1 hour standing
COOKING TIME: 10-15 minutes

½ cucumber
1 teaspoon salt
3 tablespoons plum sauce
2 tablespoons malt vinegar
1 tablespoon tomato sauce
1 teaspoon sugar
1 tablespoon vegetable oil
½ large onion, sliced

This authentic Sweet and Sour Sauce is a harmonious blend of plum sauce and malt vinegar. Add vegetables and deep-fried cubes of meat for a complete dish.

1 Peel the cucumber, discarding the soft central seeds, then cut it into slices 1 cm wide. Sprinkle it with salt and set aside for an hour. Squeeze the cucumber to remove as much moisture as you can, then set it aside for later use.

2 Place 150 ml of cold water in a saucepan with the plum sauce, vinegar, tomato sauce and sugar and bring the mixture to a simmer.

3 In a separate pan or wok, heat the oil and fry the sliced onion over a high heat until the edges begin to brown. Add the cucumber and stir rapidly for a minute or two.

4 Transfer the cucumber and onion to the simmering sauce and cook for a minute or two. The sauce can now be combined with other ingredients, such as chicken, pork or seafood, to make a superb sweet and sour dish.

VARIATIONS

To give a sharper taste to the sauce, use Chinese lemon sauce (a bottled sauce that can be found in Asian supermarkets and some speciality food stores) instead of plum sauce.

Omit the tomato sauce but add a skinned and quartered tomato. Omit the cucumber and substitute a small can of drained pineapple chunks.

Use two stalks of spring onions, cut into 2.5 cm lengths, in the sauce instead of the large onion. Or omit the cucumber and add a green or red pepper cut into 2 cm cubes.

Swiss Roll

ROLL-UPS

What is the difference between a Swiss roll and a roulade, and how should they be rolled up?

Swiss rolls are made from a light sponge mixture that contains flour. Roulades are based on a whisked egg mixture and contain very little or no flour, and are moister and softer than Swiss rolls.

To prevent a Swiss roll cracking when rolled, trim off its crusty edges then, while it is still warm, put it on greaseproof paper dusted with caster sugar. Roll it up loosely, rolling the paper with it, and leave it to cool in its wrapping. Then gently open up the roll slightly, remove the paper and spread the interior with jam, lemon or lime curd or cream.

Roulades are easier to roll, so can be filled before rolling up, as in the following recipe. They do usually crack when being rolled, but look attractive when dredged with icing sugar and decorated.

Chocolate and coffee roulade

SERVES: 8
PREPARATION TIME: *20 minutes, plus overnight cooling*
COOKING TIME: *20 minutes*

1 tablespoon instant coffee granules
100 g dark cooking chocolate
4 large eggs, separated
125 g (½ cup) caster sugar

FOR THE FILLING
300 ml fresh cream
1 tablespoon brandy or orange liqueur
To decorate: fresh berries or thin orange slices

1 Preheat the oven to 180°C. Grease a Swiss roll tin measuring 33 × 28 cm and line it with nonstick baking paper. Dissolve the coffee granules in 1 tablespoon of boiling water and stir to a smooth paste.
2 Break up the chocolate and melt it in a heatproof bowl set over warm water, or in the microwave oven, then remove from the heat.
3 Whisk the egg yolks and sugar together in a large bowl until thick and pale, then stir in the cold coffee paste and melted chocolate.
4 Whisk the egg whites until stiff. Fold 2 tablespoons of the egg white into the chocolate mixture to loosen it, then fold in the rest.
5 Spread the mixture into the tin and bake for about 20 minutes or until it springs back when lightly pressed with a finger.
6 When the cake is cooked, remove it from the oven and put the tin on a wire rack. Cover the cake with a clean tea towel and leave it to cool for a few hours or overnight.
7 Sprinkle some caster sugar over a sheet of greaseproof paper, then turn the cake out onto this and trim off the crusty edges.
8 Whip the cream lightly, fold in the brandy or liqueur and spread it over the cake. Roll up the cake, using the paper to help you lift it. Dredge with icing sugar and decorate with fresh berries or thin slices of orange.

Cool whipped cream, delicately flavoured with a dash of liqueur, is rolled up in a light and moist chocolate roulade. A hint of coffee adds depth of flavour.

Syrup

REFINED SWEETNESS

Are molasses, treacle and golden syrup the same thing?

No, they are not. Molasses is the syrup left over after sugar has been refined and crystallised from sugar cane. It is sold in several grades, from sweet and refined 'first' or light molasses, to thick, dark and slightly bitter blackstrap molasses. Treacle is a form of molasses, one that has been blended to produce a sweeter syrup which is less prone to becoming gritty. Golden syrup, which is sweeter than treacle, is made from refined white sugar.

Molasses has a dominating taste that gives a powerful flavour to sticky, moist cakes: gingerbread and fruit cakes are probably the best known. It is also used for making toffee and fudge, and its slightly bitter taste can enhance savoury dishes such as pork and dried bean casseroles, gravies and American-style barbecue sauces.

Golden syrup is used as a sweetener in baking, or as a topping for ice cream or steamed puddings.

SWEET LIQUID CORN

I have a recipe that calls for corn syrup – what is this, and can I use anything else instead?

Corn syrup is a clear, thick, sweet syrup with little taste, derived from corn kernels. It is very useful in cooking, as its moisture-absorbing qualities help to keep cakes and other baked items very moist.

There isn't really an exact substitute for corn syrup, which is widely used in the United States. There, it is available both in its clear form and with added colouring and flavouring to give it a flavour similar to molasses. In Australia, many of the larger supermarkets stock the clear version, but if you have difficulty finding it you could substitute golden syrup (although the flavour will be different) or glucose syrup.

TREE SUGAR

What is maple syrup, and how should I use it?

Maple syrup is produced from sap tapped from maple trees in early spring, when their sap is rising. The fresh sap is then boiled to reduce it to sugar or a reddish-brown, relatively thin and very sweet syrup with a positive flavour. Pure maple syrup is quite expensive; some brands are blended with cheaper corn or cane syrup, so check the ingredients on the label.

Most maple syrup is imported from Canada, whose national emblem is the maple leaf; in North America it is typically served with pancakes and waffles. It may also be poured over thick plain yoghurt or vanilla ice cream, or over a pudding such as the one that follows.

Pilgrim pudding

SERVES: *8-10*
PREPARATION TIME: *15 minutes*
COOKING TIME: *1½ hours*

---

750 ml milk
100 g (⅔ cup) fine cornmeal
  (polenta)
50 g unsalted butter, softened or
  diced
4 tablespoons black treacle or
  molasses
60 g (¼ cup) white sugar
60 g (⅓ cup) dark brown sugar
2 large eggs, beaten
1 teaspoon ground cinnamon
¼ teaspoon ground allspice
90 g (½ cup) seedless raisins,
  optional
To serve: whipped cream or vanilla
  ice cream and maple syrup

---

1 Put 500 ml of the milk into a saucepan and bring to the boil. Sprinkle in the cornmeal, stirring continuously. Cook over a low heat, stirring continuously, for 15 minutes until the mixture is very thick and will hold its shape. Remove from the heat and stir in the butter. Mix well.
2 Preheat the oven to 160°C and butter a shallow ovenproof dish about 25 × 23 cm.
3 Warm a metal spoon in very hot water and measure the black treacle or molasses into the cornmeal. Add all the remaining ingredients and mix thoroughly. Gradually stir in the remainder of the milk and mix well to blend it thoroughly.
4 Pour the cornmeal mixture into the prepared dish and spread it level with a knife. Bake for 1-1¼ hours until firm to the touch in the centre. Serve warm or cold, with whipped cream or ice cream and maple syrup.

SUGAR CRYSTALS

When I opened my tin of golden syrup I found that it had crystallised. Is it safe to use?

Crystallisation, where syrup develops gritty particles, is a natural process which sometimes occurs after long storage at cool temperatures or even because of air bubbles in the syrup, but it is quite

harmless. If you discover that your syrup has developed crystals that you think would spoil a dish, simply warm the can gently in a pan of hot water to dissolve them and then use as specified in the recipe.

While it is not necessary to store opened cans of golden syrup in a cool place, as long as the container is sealed, it is best to keep black treacle where it will stay cool.

Tagliatelle

MULTICOLOURED PASTA

Can I make different colours and flavours of tagliatelle myself?

Yes, certainly. Tagliatelle is easy for the home cook to make, and is the pasta most commonly coloured and flavoured. A basic egg pasta dough is simply rolled out and cut into strips about 1 cm wide and 25–30 cm long. To add colour and flavouring, mix the appropriate ingredients with the egg before mixing it into the flour, as in the following recipe.

Spinach tagliatelle

SERVES: 4
PREPARATION TIME: 30 minutes
COOKING TIME: 5 minutes

50 g spinach
310 g (2½ cups) plain, strong or
   farina 00 flour
A pinch of salt
3 large eggs

1 Wash and drain the spinach. Cook it gently for a few minutes in just the water that clings to the leaves. Drain, squeeze it very dry then chop finely.
2 Put the flour and salt in a bowl and make a well in the centre. Mix the eggs with the chopped spinach then pour the mixture into the well. Mix first with a fork, then use your hands until it just forms a solid mass. The dough should not be too moist – if it is, add a few more tablespoons of flour to the dough.
3 Take a portion of dough the size of a lemon and feed it through the pasta machine rollers, which should

Add flavour and colour to plain tagliatelle (bottom row) with saffron (top left), tomato (top right), cuttlefish ink (centre left) or spinach (centre right).

be set at the widest opening. Fold the strip in half, end to end, and feed it through the rollers again six or seven times until it is rectangular.
4 Place the pasta sheet on a clean cloth or a lightly floured surface and repeat with the remaining dough.
5 Reset the rollers to a narrower setting and crank the strips through the rollers once. Reset the machine to the next setting and repeat, then do this twice more, resetting the machine each time. The strips will become longer and will need to be cut in half to facilitate handling.

6 When the strips have reached the desired thinness, they are ready to be fed through the cutters and turned into thin tagliatelle strips.
7 In a large saucepan, heat some water to a rolling boil. Add the pasta, stir briefly and cook for 2-3 minutes or until al dente (cooked but firm).
VARIATIONS
• SAFFRON TAGLIATELLE: replace the chopped spinach with ½ teaspoon powdered saffron.
• TOMATO TAGLIATELLE: replace the chopped spinach with 2 tablespoons concentrated tomato paste.

INKY BLACK

Will anything other than cuttlefish ink make pasta black?

No. Traditionally, cuttlefish ink has been used in Italy for colouring and flavouring risottos containing either squid or cuttlefish, rather than in pasta. Black pasta is a more recent innovation, and cuttlefish ink is the only satisfactory way of colouring it: add 2–3 teaspoons of ink to the eggs before mixing into the flour. Bear in mind that it will give the pasta a fishy taste so it is best served with a complementary fishy sauce. Cuttlefish ink is available from specialist fishmongers.

THE RIGHT SAUCE

What are the best types of sauces to serve with tagliatelle?

There are no hard and fast rules. Tagliatelle and most other egg pasta shapes are frequently served with tomato-based sauces (see *Pasta*), but in northern Italy, an area noted for its dairy and meat produce, tagliatelle is traditionally served with cream or meat sauces. Two common examples are mushroom and cream, with a little flour added to thicken the sauce, and the following chicken liver and ham recipe.

Chicken liver and ham sauce

SERVES: 4
PREPARATION TIME: 10 minutes
COOKING TIME: 10–15 minutes

250 g chicken livers
1 tablespoon olive oil
30 g butter
2 shallots, finely chopped
100 g cooked ham or lean bacon, diced
1 tablespoon fresh sage or 1 teaspoon dried sage
75 ml chicken stock
3 tablespoons brandy
Salt and black pepper

1 Remove any discoloured pieces and fat from the chicken livers. Dry them thoroughly on kitchen paper towels and cut into small morsels.

2 Heat the oil and butter in a frying pan and gently sauté the shallots for a few minutes until translucent. Stir in the ham or bacon and the sage, and cook for a further minute. Add the chicken livers and cook for a further 2–3 minutes, stirring from time to time, until they have lost their raw colour and become soft.
3 Add the stock to the pan, stir well and cook gently for a few minutes until the liquid has slightly reduced and thickened. Then add the brandy, season to taste and take off the heat.
4 Cook the pasta and drain. Place it in a warm bowl, reheat the sauce if necessary and toss with the pasta.
VARIATION
For a rich creamy sauce, add 150 ml fresh cream to the livers with the brandy.

Tapioca

ROOT STARCH

What is tapioca, and what kind of dishes is it used in?

Tapioca is a starch extracted from the root of the tropical cassava plant, also known as manioc. The starch has to be detoxified before the tapioca can be sold commercially as some fresh manioc roots contain a toxic substance that is destroyed by a heat process. Tapioca is sold either as granules or flakes; both can be hard to find but most good health food stores and larger supermarkets stock either one or the other.

Tapioca is a useful, easily digestible starch. Flaked, it has similar thickening properties to cornflour and arrowroot, so is good for thickening sauces. The grains are best used like rice or barley to bulk out soups and stews.

Many people associate the grains with a rather bland milk pudding, but tapioca pudding is anything but bland when the milk is flavoured with cinnamon and enriched with cream or coconut milk, as in the following recipe for an unusual variation on crème brûlée.

Coconut tapioca brûlée

SERVES: 4–6
PREPARATION TIME: 10 minutes, plus 2–3 hours chilling time
COOKING TIME: 30 minutes

60 g (⅓ cup) granular tapioca
300 ml milk
300 ml canned coconut milk
½ teaspoon ground cinnamon
60 g (¼ cup) caster sugar
300 ml fresh cream
2–3 tablespoons demerara or dark brown sugar
To garnish: summer fruit or berries

1 Put the tapioca, milk, coconut milk and cinnamon in a saucepan. Bring to the boil then simmer over a low heat for 10–15 minutes until the grains are tender. Stir in caster sugar and set aside to cool.
2 Preheat the grill and lightly butter a 1.25 litre heatproof dish. Whip the cream until it holds its shape, then fold it into the tapioca.
3 Spoon the tapioca mixture into the prepared dish. Sprinkle a layer of demerara sugar over the top to cover the surface. Put the dish under the hot grill until the sugar caramelises. Remove it from the heat, let it cool and then chill for several hours.
4 When ready to serve, crack the crispy layer of sugar with a spoon, and decorate with summer fruit or berries, such as raspberries.
VARIATION
For a plainer flavour, leave out the coconut milk and cinnamon. Cook the tapioca in 600 ml milk with half a vanilla pod. Remove the vanilla then stir in the caster sugar and leave it to cool, then continue with the recipe as above.

PALM STARCH

Is there a difference between tapioca and sago?

They are indeed similar, but sago is extracted from the pith of the tropical sago palm. It is sold in granular form, and its pearl-like appearance explains why it is often called pearl sago. Sago is a particularly easily digestible starch and is often used in dishes for the sick and elderly.

Tarts

STICKY PROBLEM

Why do my tarts always stick to the bottom of the tin?

There are two possible explanations. First check the state of your flan or tartlet tins: the surface of cheaper ones, even those labelled nonstick, may become scratched or pitted after a time and this can cause sticking. Good quality tins are a worthwhile investment.

Second, don't allow tarts to cool in their tins for too long after removing them from the oven: they may stick if the pastry contains any sugar or fruit juice. Just leave the pastry case in the tin for a few minutes and, when it is firm enough, slip it out carefully and leave it on a wire tray to finish cooling.

GLAZED OVER

How can I make a professional-looking glaze for a fruit tart?

Glazes add a sheen to the fruit which prevents the surface from becoming dry. Many people like to use jam or jelly made from the same fruit for the glaze, but a contrasting flavour and colour can enhance the taste and appearance of the tart. Apricot jam and redcurrant jelly both make attractive, general-purpose glazes.

For pale fruits such as apples and pears, an apricot glaze is best. To glaze a 23 cm tart, put 100 ml of apricot jam in a pan and stir in 1 tablespoon of water. Bring to the boil, stirring gently all the while, and boil for 1 minute. Pass the jam through a sieve, let it cool slightly then brush it over the tart and leave it to set.

A clear redcurrant glaze looks attractive on red berries, as in the recipe for Strawberry Tartlets on the opposite page. The jelly should not be allowed to boil or it will discolour. It sets fairly rapidly as it cools in the pan, so you have to work quickly or reheat it gently.

Turn simple strawberries into a bite-sized luxury in a crispy glazed tartlet. For a professional touch, arrange them on a cushion of luscious crème patissière.

PASTRY CUSTARD

What can I do if crème patissière does not thicken?

Crème patissière, or confectioner's custard, is thickened with both egg yolks and some starch, which is usually flour but sometimes a mixture of flour and cornflour. When making crème patissière, it is essential that the mixture does actually come to the boil, since it is only at boiling point that the starch grains will burst and thicken the custard.

CRUMBLY PASTRY

My fruit tartlets always end up crumbling when picked up. Could I use a firmer pastry?

You could try using pâte sucrée, a crisp, sweet pastry used in French patisserie. In the traditional recipe, the flour is sifted onto a work surface, and the butter, sugar and egg yolks are added in the centre and mixed with the fingertips to form a soft dough. The following recipe uses a simpler method.

Strawberry tartlets

MAKES: 20 tartlets
PREPARATION TIME: 45 minutes, plus
1½ hours chilling time
COOKING TIME: 20 minutes

FOR THE PATE SUCREE
250 g (2 cups) plain flour
125 g unsalted butter, chilled and
* diced*
60 g (⅓ cup) icing sugar,
* sifted*
2 egg yolks

FOR THE CREME PATISSIERE
1 large egg yolk
25 g (5 teaspoons) caster sugar
15 g (6 teaspoons) plain flour
125 ml milk
15 g unsalted butter
A few drops of vanilla essence
* or orange flower water, or*
* 1 teaspoon kirsch, rum or*
* sherry*

FOR THE TOPPING
500 g small ripe strawberries or
* other fresh berries*
185 ml redcurrant jelly

1 To make the pâte sucrée, sift the flour into the bowl of a food processor. Add the butter and mix for 1 minute, or until the mixture resembles fine breadcrumbs.
2 Add the icing sugar and egg yolks and mix for a few seconds, until a soft dough forms which leaves the side of the bowl.
3 Gently knead the dough, working it with the base of the hand a few times just until it becomes smooth. Wrap it securely in greaseproof paper and, for easy rolling, leave to chill for an hour before use.
4 While the dough is chilling, make the crème patissière: put the egg yolk and caster sugar in a mixing bowl and beat well with a wooden spoon until smooth and creamy. Mix in the flour.
5 Heat the milk to just under boiling point, then add it to the egg mixture bit by bit, stirring until smooth.
6 Pour the mixture into a small, clean saucepan. Place it over a gentle heat, stirring continuously, until the mixture comes to the boil

and thickens. (If any lumps develop during cooking, take the pan off the heat and beat until smooth.)
7 When the crème patissière has thickened, remove it from the heat, beat in the butter and add the vanilla or other flavouring. Pour the mixture into a bowl. Wet some greaseproof paper, cover the crème patissière with it and set aside until cold.
8 To make the tartlets, roll out half the pastry thinly on a lightly floured surface. With a 7.5 cm cutter, stamp out ten rounds and use them to line ungreased tartlet tins. Prick the bases well with a fork and chill for 30 minutes. Use the remaining pastry to line a further ten tins, and chill those. Meanwhile, preheat the oven to 190°C.
9 Bake the chilled tartlets in their tins for about 10 minutes or until the pastry is pale golden. Leave them in their tins for 1–2 minutes to harden slightly, then slide them out carefully with a knife. Cool on a wire rack.
10 When the pastry cases are cold, spread a teaspoon of crème patissière in the bottom of each one, then top with a few strawberries.
11 To make the glaze, push the jelly through a sieve placed above a small pan. Heat gently, without stirring or boiling, for 1–2 minutes until clear.
12 Leave the jelly to cool slightly, then brush the fruit with it and leave it to set. The tartlets are best when eaten within 2 hours of filling.

AVOIDING SOGGINESS

How can I stop the pastry shell of a fruit tart from going soggy?

There are several easy preventive measures. As soon as the baked tart case comes out of the oven, brush the inside with some lightly beaten egg white: this will cook and harden on the hot pastry to form a seal. Also, use small to medium sized fruits and berries rather than big ones which need to be cut, as cut surfaces create more juice, and wipe berries clean with kitchen paper towels rather than rinsing. Finally, don't fill the tart more than a few hours before serving it.

Tea

CHOOSE YOUR BREW

What is the difference between black and green tea?

Although there are many types of tea, they all come from the same plant, *Camellia sinensis*. The differences arise because of the area where they are grown and how they are processed.

Black teas, the most commonly known in the West, have a rich aroma and flavour and are in fact reddish to dark brown in colour. The leaves are picked and allowed to wither in the sun, then bruised and left to ferment, during which time their colour, flavour and astringency develop. The leaves are then dried to stop the fermentation process and preserve them.

Green teas have less aroma and flavour than black ones and are paler. The leaves are first steamed after harvesting to retain some of the colour and stop the fermentation process. They are then lightly rolled before drying.

Oolong tea is a cross between black and green tea as it is semi-fermented. Sometimes sold on its own, it is mostly used in blends.

TIME FOR TEA

Is there much difference between the various types of tea?

Different teas do have very different characteristics, and this can affect not only how they are drunk, but at what time of day.
- ASSAM tea, from north-east India, is strong and dark and, blended with a Ceylon and often an African tea, it makes up the 'breakfast' blends. Best drunk with milk.
- CEYLON tea is crisp and strong and distinguished by its amber colour. Best drunk with milk.
- DARJEELING tea varies in taste and price depending on when it has been harvested. Tea from the first 'flush', or harvest, is very delicate, the second flush is more mature

and the autumn harvest produces a thicker tea. You can buy all three from tea merchants, but Darjeeling bought in a supermarket will be a blend of second flush teas. Its delicate aroma and flavour make Darjeeling the perfect tea to have after lunch, and it is best drunk without milk or sugar.

• SCENTED teas such as jasmine, or Earl Grey which is flavoured with bergamot, a citrus fruit, are good in the afternoon and evening, drunk without milk or sugar.

• LAPSANG SOUCHONG, the smoked black China tea, is very refreshing as an afternoon drink. It is drunk without milk or sugar.

• GUNPOWDER, a Chinese green tea, and OOLONG, from Taiwan or China, are very light and should be drunk without milk. They contain less tannin and caffeine than black teas, so are good after dinner.

SERVE IT CHILLED

How do I make iced tea?

Iced tea is extremely easy to make, but there are two things to bear in mind: always use good quality tea leaves and not tea bags or instant tea; and choose a tea that is suitable for drinking without milk, such as Earl Grey, as iced tea is served with slices of lemon or orange.

Make the tea in the normal way and when it is brewed to your taste, strain it into a jug, leave it to cool then chill it for an hour or so. Sweeten the chilled tea to taste and put some crushed ice in tall glasses. Pop in a slice or two of lemon or orange, add a few mint leaves, and pour the tea over the lot.

There's more to tea than a breakfast cuppa: a refreshing glass of iced tea is just the thing for summer afternoons.

COOKING WITH TEA

Are there any recipes in which I could use my favourite brew?

Tea can form the base of fruit and alcoholic punches, but it can also add flavour and colour to both savoury and sweet dishes. It can be surprisingly good in meat casseroles and pâtés, for instance, and scented teas can be used in ice creams. Use ordinary leftover tea for soaking dried fruits, especially prunes, for a compote, or for soaking mixed dried fruits for rich fruit loaves, as in the following recipe.

Fruit loaf with tea

MAKES: 1 x 1 kg loaf, roughly 18 slices
PREPARATION TIME: 15 minutes, plus overnight soaking
COOKING TIME: 1½–1¾ hours

---

500 g good-quality mixed dried fruit (currants, sultanas, seedless raisins, cherries, dried apricots, glacé pineapple and mixed peel)
250 ml strong tea, such as Assam or Ceylon, cooled and strained
250 g (1½ cups) soft brown sugar
2 large eggs, beaten
250 g (2 cups) self-raising flour
2 teaspoons mixed spice
1–2 tablespoons clear honey

---

1 Put the fruit and tea into a bowl, cover and leave to soak overnight.
2 Preheat the oven to 160°C and line a 1 kg loaf tin with nonstick baking paper. Stir the sugar into the fruit and tea mixture and leave to dissolve for 5 minutes, stirring once or twice.
3 Stir in the beaten eggs. Sieve the flour and mixed spice over the bowl and mix well together till smooth.
4 Pour into the prepared tin and bake in the oven for 1½–1¾ hours or until a skewer inserted into the centre comes out clean. Cover with foil if the top browns too much.
5 Remove the cake from the oven. While it is still warm, trickle the honey all over it and spread with a pastry brush. Leave in the tin until cold. To store, wrap the loaf in foil.

Thai Cooking

DIFFERENT CURRIES

What is the difference between the curries of Thailand and other Southeast Asian countries and the curries of India?

The range of Asian curries is wide. Some use dry ground spice mixtures similar to those used in Indian cooking, but just as many use only fresh ingredients, such as chillies, coriander roots, galangal, garlic, ginger, lemon grass, shallots and sweet basil as in Thai curries.

Some of the best curries use a combination of dried and fresh ingredients, so a korma prepared with dried spices may be given an aromatic top note with fresh coriander, mint and sweet basil. A typical Thai curry that uses fresh spices is the green curry below. It can be made with chicken, pork or prawns instead of vegetables.

Thai vegetable curry

SERVES: 2
PREPARATION TIME: 20 minutes
COOKING TIME: 15 minutes

6 baby eggplants or 2 zucchini
1 carrot
1 teaspoon sugar
2 green chillies, deseeded and
  roughly chopped
1 small bunch fresh coriander with
  roots, thoroughly cleaned, or
  pound the whole stalk and leaves
1 large onion, roughly chopped
2 cloves garlic, chopped
1 teaspoon shrimp paste
1 stalk lemon grass
2 thin slices galangal
2 kaffir lime leaves
3 tablespoons vegetable oil
500 ml coconut milk
20 green beans, trimmed
2 tablespoons fish sauce

1 Peel and cut the baby eggplants diagonally into slices 2 cm thick; if using zucchini instead, peel and slice them. Peel and slice the carrot diagonally.

Fresh green herbs and spices such as coriander leaves and roots, green chillies and kaffir lime leaves add pungency to this Thai curry of vegetables.

2 Finely grind the sugar with the chillies, coriander, onion, garlic, shrimp paste, lemon grass, galangal and kaffir lime leaves in a pestle and mortar, coffee grinder, or food processor (the mixture will be dry).
3 Heat the oil and fry the spice paste over a low heat for 5 minutes until it smells powerfully aromatic. Add the coconut milk, green beans and other prepared vegetables and bring the mixture to the boil.
4 Add the fish sauce, then lower the heat and simmer for 8 minutes. Adjust the seasoning and serve the curry hot with plain boiled rice.

JUICY FRUIT

Is tamarind, popular in Indian cooking, used in Thai cooking?

The juice of the pulp around the seeds of the tamarind, sometimes called the Indian date, is used to give a fruity, sour flavour to many Asian curries and spicy dishes. Those that do not contain coconut milk tend to be cooked in tamarind juice. Generally, tamarind is used with seafood while coconut accompanies meat and poultry dishes.

Tamarind is available in several forms, the most common being brown or black blocks of concentrated pulp, which must be soaked in hot water before using. When the liquid has reached the desired acidity, like very strong lime juice, it is strained and used for cooking. In Thailand, a sweeter variety of tamarind is eaten fresh as a snack.

Some Asian food shops sell bottled tamarind concentrate in a thick liquid form that needs no further straining. The concentrate is very tart and should be diluted in the proportion of one part tamarind concentrate to two parts water. If you cannot find any tamarind, you can substitute fresh lime juice instead. In the following recipe for fish with tamarind and Asian spices, choose whichever is the most convenient for you.

Fish in tamarind

SERVES: 4
PREPARATION TIME: 15 minutes, plus
30 minutes salting time
COOKING TIME: 15 minutes

500 g blue-eye cod fillet
2 teaspoons salt
1 teaspoon chilli powder
1 teaspoon ground turmeric
2 cloves garlic, finely chopped
1 large onion, finely chopped
2 tablespoons prepared tamarind
    pulp or concentrate, or
    2 tablespoons lime juice
1 stalk lemon grass, lower stem
    bruised

1 Clean and skin the fish, cut it into large chunks, rub with salt and set aside for about 30 minutes.
2 Pound the chilli powder with the turmeric, garlic and onion in a pestle and mortar. Mix with the tamarind, lemon grass and 600 ml water in a wok or small saucepan and bring to the boil.
3 Simmer for 10 minutes, add the fish then cook for another 3 minutes. Serve immediately with rice.

THAI-TASTING

I have bought some pre-prepared stir-fry vegetables, but would like to make a Thai sauce to add to them. Can you suggest a recipe?

There is no standard stir-fry sauce for Thai dishes as such. Thai cooking has adapted the basic Chinese stir-fry sauces by adding chillies to give the flavour a little kick.

The basic seasoning in Chinese stir-frying is soy sauce. Thai cooks will generally use fish sauce (also known as *nam pla*) instead, which is basically soy sauce infused with fermented fish extracts taken from various fish. *Nam pla* tastes salty, very much like strong anchovy sauce, and can be found in Asian shops and some supermarkets.

Like the Chinese, Thai cooks use sesame oil, garlic and ginger to season their stir-fries. The following recipe is for an all-purpose sauce that you can use to give your usual stir-fry dishes a Thai taste.

Thai stir-fry sauce

MAKES: enough to season
500 g vegetables, fish or meat
PREPARATION TIME: 5 minutes
COOKING TIME: none

1 tablespoon sesame oil
2 teaspoons chilli paste
1 teaspoon palm or brown sugar
½ teaspoon black pepper
2 cloves garlic, very finely chopped
2 teaspoons finely chopped green
    ginger
2 tablespoons fish sauce

1 Mix together the oil, chilli paste, sugar, pepper, garlic and ginger.
2 Add some cooking oil to the wok according to your usual recipe, then add the sesame oil mixture. When it comes to the boil, add the fish sauce, then your other stir-fry ingredients and cook in the usual way.

GREATER GINGER

What is galangal?

Galangal looks very like its relative the ginger root, but has a paler, pinkish colour. It cannot be eaten raw and is usually ground up with other ingredients to make a paste.

There are two varieties of galangal, the greater and the lesser. Both are used a lot in Thai cooking but it is the lesser that is the most flavoursome. Galangal is sometimes available in fresh produce markets and you can buy it in Asian stores.

PERFUMED LEAVES

What are kaffir lime leaves?

These are the leaves of a lime tree native to tropical Asia. The leaves are shaped like a figure eight, with two leaves held together from the tip to the base. The small fruit of the kaffir lime can also be purchased from Asian food stores.

Imparting their full, fresh, citric flavour, both the aromatic leaves and the bitter rind are used in Thai cooking, primarily in chicken and fish dishes. To use, slice the kaffir lime leaves finely, which will give a stronger flavour, or crush them as you would bay leaves.

THAI SWEETS

Are there any Thai desserts?

Generally most Asian meals do not end with desserts. Sweet things tend to be eaten as snacks during the day and desserts, if served, are reserved for special occasions.

Thai desserts are usually based on grains such as rice, sago and sweetcorn, as well as coconut milk and tropical fruits such as bananas, jackfruit and oranges.

Many Thai desserts are sweetened with palm sugar, also known as jaggery, or coconut sugar. This comes in hard cylinders that have to be grated, cakes that can be broken up, or as a thick treacle in tubs. If palm sugar is unavailable, use some demerara or dark brown sugar melted with a little water for this popular Thai dessert instead.

Sticky rice and mango pudding

SERVES: 4
PREPARATION TIME: 25 minutes, plus
at least 4 hours soaking time
COOKING TIME: 20 minutes

250 g (1¼ cups) sticky rice
1 teaspoon salt
140 g (¾ cup) palm sugar
500 ml coconut milk
2 large sweet mangoes, peeled and
    sliced

1 Wash the rice and add water to just cover, about 1 cm over the top of the rice. Soak overnight or for at least 4 hours.
2 Drain the rice and stir in the salt. Steam the rice for 20 minutes over a saucepan of boiling water, then set aside to keep warm until needed.
3 Melt the palm sugar with a little water in the microwave, or in a bain-marie, until completely dissolved: do not do this over direct heat as the palm sugar will burn easily.
4 Mix the melted sugar and coconut milk well together in a bowl.
5 To serve, place a few tablespoons of rice in each bowl, top the rice with the sliced mangoes and drizzle on the coconut milk and palm sugar mixture, dividing equally.

Tisanes

HERB AND FLOWER DRINKS

Can I use any type of flower or herb to make tisanes?

Any unsprayed, edible flower or herb can be used in tisanes, or herbal teas or infusions, but some are more flavourful than others. Herbs and flowers commonly used in this way include bergamot and camomile flowers; caraway leaves (caraway seeds give a stronger tea); dill leaves; elderflowers; fennel leaves, flowers and seeds; hawthorn and hibiscus flowers; lemon balm; lemon grass; lemon verbena; lime flower; mint (all varieties); rose petals or hips; and rosemary.

In addition, you can use angelica leaves (diabetics should be aware of their sugar content) and raspberry leaf (said to help with labour pains). Sage makes a refreshing tea, but it should not be drunk regularly for more than a week or two at a time, as the plant's antiseptic properties can cause potentially toxic effects. Thyme is also good as a tisane, but it is advised not to drink thyme tea during pregnancy.

Tisanes can be made with either a single herb or flower (as in the panel on the right), or a mixture of several, with spices added, as in the recipe for Dill Tisane below. Whichever method you choose, they make a pleasant, caffeine-free alternative to tea and coffee. All tisanes should be drunk without milk and may be sweetened with honey or sugar if desired.

Dill tisane

SERVES: 3-4
PREPARATION TIME: 8-10 minutes
COOKING TIME: none

2 teaspoons fresh chopped dill
4 green cardamom pods, lightly crushed
¼ teaspoon fresh chopped mint
1 thin slice fresh ginger
600 ml boiling water
To serve: thin slices of lemon

MAKING A TISANE

Either fresh or dried herbs and flowers can be infused to make a refreshing tisane. In the pictures below, dried camomile is shown.

1 Pour a little very hot water into a teapot, preferably made of glass and kept for making tisanes. When the pot is warm, discard the water.

2 Put a teaspoon or two of dried herbs, or 2-3 teaspoons of fresh ones, into the warmed pot and pour on 500 ml freshly boiled water. (If your water contains a lot of chlorine, use boiled still mineral water instead.) Leave to infuse for 3-5 minutes, depending on how strong you like it – the deeper the colour, the stronger the flavour.

3 When the tisane is ready, pour some into a cup, using a strainer if the teapot has not got one built into it. Serve with a little honey and a slice of lemon if desired.

---

1 Warm the teapot by pouring in a little very hot water, then leave for a minute or two and discard the water.
2 Put the herbs and spices into the pot and pour on the boiling water. Leave to infuse for about 5 minutes.
3 Strain into cups and serve with a thin slice of lemon in each.

VARIATION
For a fruitier drink, add some grated zest of an unwaxed orange. To give a delicate hint, use ¼ teaspoon, or ½ teaspoon for a stronger taste.

Tofu

PROTEIN-PACKED SOYA

I was recently given a recipe which calls for tofu; is this the same as bean curd?

Yes, it is. The word tofu is the phonetic translation of the Chinese 'dau foo', which means 'mash of bean curd'. It is also sometimes called soya cheese. Whatever it is called in recipes and on packets, tofu is a protein-packed, easily digestible product made from the extract of soya beans. In recent years in the West, it has become one of the basic ingredients for people on a vegetarian diet.

TYPES AND USES

What does tofu look like, and how do I use it?

Tofu comes in many guises: it is available fresh as large, silken and soft white cubes, or in firmer, pale cream-coloured pressed blocks; dried in cubes of about 2 cm or in 7 cm squares; and in UHT long-life packs. There is also brown, dried tofu skin, used for wrapping food into little parcels or for soaking in stews, usually sold in 60 cm folded rounds. Many supermarkets now sell tofu in one form or another; large Chinese supermarkets will have the full range.

Tofu has little taste of its own but it absorbs the flavours of sauces, spices and other ingredients, especially if marinated before cooking. How you use it depends on the kind of tofu you have. Dried tofu is treated as a substitute for meat in stir-fries, curries and spring rolls, and can be stuffed much like pita bread. Fresh tofu is used to bulk out minced meat and seafood, or as a substitute for them in vegetarian dishes. It is also often diced or shredded and added to soups like the Japanese miso soup, or mashed and mixed with chopped mixed vegetables, or deep-fried as in the recipes overleaf.

Tofu cutlets

SERVES: *4 as a starter or snack*
PREPARATION TIME: *25 minutes,
plus optional 30 minutes chilling
time*
COOKING TIME: *10 minutes*

300 g soft, fresh white tofu, cubed
1 large boiled potato, mashed
4 green beans, finely chopped
2 tablespoons finely grated carrot
1 spring onion, finely chopped
2 tablespoons sesame oil
1 large egg, lightly beaten
1 teaspoon salt
½ teaspoon black pepper
Cornflour, for dusting
Oil for deep-frying

1 Put the tofu in a mixing bowl and
mash it finely with a fork. Mop off
any liquid with paper towels.
2 Mix in all the other ingredients
except the cornflour and frying oil.
Mix well to a soft consistency,
adding a tablespoon or two of water
if the mixture is dry and crumbly.
3 Divide the mixture into four equal
portions and press them to make
lightly rounded, burger-like patties.

Dust the cutlets with cornflour. You
can cook them immediately, but
they will firm up a little if you chill
them for 30 minutes beforehand.
4 Heat some oil in a deep-fryer or
wok and fry the cutlets until they
are golden brown and crisp. Drain
on paper towels. Serve with sliced
tomatoes and a chilli sauce dip.

Tofu balls

SERVES: *4*
PREPARATION TIME: *25 minutes*
COOKING TIME: *10–12 minutes*

375 g firm tofu
30 g finely chopped pecans or
  almonds
1 large egg, beaten
1 tablespoon miso paste
1 white onion, finely chopped
¼ cup chopped flat-leaf parsley
Finely grated rind of 1 lemon
15 g (¼ cup) wholemeal
  breadcrumbs
¼ teaspoon white pepper
2 teaspoons sesame oil
Vegetable oil for shallow frying
To serve: sweet and sour sauce and
  brown rice

1 Drain the tofu and squeeze dry
with clean hands. Place in a
mixing bowl and mash well with a
fork, or place in the bowl of a food
processor and process just until
crumbled finely.
2 Add all the remaining ingredients
and mix well to a firm consistency.
If necessary, add a little plain
wholemeal flour to bind together.
Flatten the mixture and divide into
16 equal-sized pieces.
3 With clean cold hands, roll
the mixture into balls. Chill for
15 minutes, if time allows, then
reroll to neaten the shape.
4 Heat sufficient vegetable oil in a
heavy-based frying pan over a
medium heat. Add the tofu balls and
fry for 5–6 minutes, turning
frequently, until sealed all over, then
reduce the heat to medium-low and
fry for a further 5–6 minutes until
the balls are cooked through. Drain
well on kitchen paper towels.
5 Serve the tofu balls hot. For a
well-balanced vegetarian meal,
accompany them with a sweet and
sour sauce (see page 349) and
freshly cooked brown rice.

SOFT, DELICATE SKINS

*I've cooked with firm white
tofu before, but how do I use
tofu skin?*

Cut the tofu skin up and cook it
in soups, stews and casseroles just
like meat, or soak it until soft to
form the basis of many Chinese-
style dishes.

You can also use it to make delicate spring rolls quite unlike
conventional wheat-flour rolls,
which were created by Chinese
cooks in Western countries when
tofu skins were hard to come by.
To make them, sprinkle a savoury
spring-roll stuffing over the skins,
then simply roll up and deep-fry
them until crisp. The rolls are quite
mild in flavour but are usually
dipped in a hot chilli sauce as you
eat them.

Tofu skins dry out and crack in
time. Test whether they are still
good by pressing gently; they
should be soft and not brittle.

*Mashed potato and crispy chopped vegetables add substance to these golden fried
tofu cutlets, a protein-rich vegetarian starter for the whole family.*

Tomatoes

LET THE SUNSHINE IN

How can I choose a tomato with flavour? So many of them look good but taste bland.

Left to themselves, tomatoes are a seasonal vegetable (or more accurately, fruit), but they are now very widely grown all year round. Consumer demand has resulted in the production of vine-ripened tomatoes, and these have more flavour than those picked under-ripe for long transportation to the market.

It is best to keep recipes that are dependent on good, fresh tomatoes for summer, when they are in season locally, and ripened on the vine before picking, so have a better flavour. In winter, some smaller varieties such as Tom Thumb or cherry tomatoes have enough flavour to contribute to a sandwich; for cooked winter dishes it is often better and cheaper to use canned tomatoes, a paste or concentrate, or sun-dried tomatoes.

To serve whole with a stuffing as in the recipe below, use the biggest ripe tomatoes you can find.

Stuffed tomatoes

SERVES: 4
PREPARATION TIME: 20 minutes
COOKING TIME: 1½ hours

8 large tomatoes
4 tablespoons olive oil
1 onion, chopped
1 teaspoon dried marjoram
2 cloves garlic, chopped
250 g finely minced beef
1 tablespoon tomato paste
90 g (½ cup) long-grain rice
Salt and black pepper
½ teaspoon ground allspice
3 tablespoons chopped fresh parsley

1 Slice the tops off the tomatoes and set them aside. Scoop the tomato pulp and seeds into a bowl, rub a bit of salt round the inside of the shell and leave upside down on plates to drain. Chop the tomato pulp finely.

2 Fry the onion and marjoram in half the oil over a low heat for some 8–10 minutes until the onion is soft and golden, adding the garlic for the last 2 minutes of cooking.
3 Add the minced beef and stir, mashing with a fork to break up the granules of meat. When the meat is browned, stir in half the tomato paste and half the pulp from the tomatoes, cover and simmer over a very low heat for 20 minutes.
4 Rinse the rice, drain it well and add it to the meat. Stir in 75 ml cold water. Season with salt, pepper and allspice, stir well and simmer for a further 10 minutes.
5 Preheat the oven to 190°C. In a small mixing bowl, blend the remaining tomato paste with 4 tablespoons cold water, then add the remaining tomato pulp and the juices that have run off from the upturned tomatoes. Season the mixture to taste and spread it in a baking dish large enough to hold all the tomatoes tightly in a single layer.
6 Stir the parsley into the meat and rice mixture and adjust the seasoning to taste. Spoon the still semi-liquid stuffing into the tomatoes, filling them about three-quarters full only to allow for swelling as the rice completes its cooking. (Any surplus can be stirred into the sauce at the bottom of the dish.)
7 Arrange the stuffed tomatoes in the dish, put their tops back on and trickle the remaining olive oil over them. Bake for 45 minutes or until the tomatoes are very soft and the stuffing has expanded to fill them. Check the sauce halfway through the cooking time and stir in a few tablespoons of water if it threatens to dry out. Serve immediately, giving two tomatoes to each diner.

CONCENTRATED FLAVOUR

What, if any, is the difference between tomato purée, passata, paste and concassé?

In theory, purée and passata mean the same thing – that the flesh of the fruit or vegetable has been passed through a sieve to rid it of pips and make it smooth.

MAKING TOMATO CONCASSE

Freshly diced tomato flesh is useful in a variety of soups, stews and sauces. The tough skin is removed first, using boiling water.

1 Place the tomatoes, which should be very ripe, in a heatproof bowl and cover with boiling water. Stand for 1–2 minutes until the skin splits. Drain, refresh and pull off the skins.

2 Cut the skinned tomatoes in half horizontally and, cupping each half in your hand, squeeze out the seeds and surrounding liquid.

3 Put each half cut side down on a wood or marble board and cut the flesh up into small dice.

Tomato purée is available in cans in most supermarkets. Passata has become a supermarket term for pasteurised and sieved tomato sauce, and is sold by the jar or carton. It is usually imported from Italy and is an excellent convenience product for all kinds of tomato soups and sauces, both cooked and uncooked.

Tomato paste is an intensely flavoured concentrate of tomato. It is sold mainly in cans, foil pouches and tubes, and is usually used to boost the flavour of cooked tomato dishes, to intensify flavour in casseroles, or to contribute tomato flavour to mayonnaise or cream-based sauces

In addition, sun-dried tomato paste is now widely available. It is slightly more granular and a bit sweeter than plain tomato paste, but is used in the same way.

Concassé refers to the chopped flesh of tomato without seeds, pulp or skin. It is popular with chefs and easy to make at home (see panel on page 361). Use it as the basis of cooked sauces, salads and raw salsas, or stir it into warm seasoned cream to dress vegetables or pasta.

A combination of both fresh tomatoes and concentrated tomato paste is used in the following recipe for a classic pasta and pizza sauce.

Napoletana sauce

SERVES: 4
PREPARATION TIME: 20 minutes
COOKING TIME: 20–30 minutes

---

2 tablespoons olive oil
2 onions, chopped
2 plump cloves garlic, crushed
1 kg ripe tomatoes, cored and roughly chopped
4 tablespoons tomato paste
1 tablespoon chopped fresh oregano
1 tablespoon shredded fresh basil
1 bay leaf
1 teaspoon sugar
2 teaspoons salt
Freshly ground black pepper

1 Heat the oil in a heavy-based pan over a medium heat and fry the onions and garlic, stirring occasionally, for 5 minutes, or until soft and transparent looking but not browned.

2 Stir in the tomatoes, tomato paste, oregano, basil, bay leaf, sugar, salt and pepper to taste.

3 Bring the mixture to the boil, stirring occasionally, then reduce the heat to medium-low and simmer, covered, for 30 minutes, or until thick. Remove the bay leaf and adjust the salt and pepper to taste. If the sauce is too thin, simmer for a few minutes longer without the lid, until reduced and thickened.

4 Spoon the sauce over freshly cooked pasta and top with Parmesan cheese for a simple, tasty Italian meal.

VARIATIONS

The sauce may be spread over pizza bases before topping with the flavouring ingredients. (Try it instead of the commercially bottled tomato sauce on the Family Pizza on page 272).

It is also delicious served with pan-fried veal steak or chops, sautéed chicken breasts and grilled lamb chops.

For a summer lunch, serve as a dipping sauce alongside a platter of barbecued seafood, such as prawns, squid and fish kebabs.

TASTY PARTNERS

What are the best flavourings and herbs to use with tomato?

Tomatoes respond well to liberal seasoning with white or black pepper or, in sandwiches and salads, to peppery leaves such as cress and watercress. You can add extra depth to cooked tomatoes with a splash of dry sherry or a dash or Tabasco, or some aniseed, cumin, fennel or paprika.

Tomatoes are commonly served with garlic and basil, but take well to a wide range of other herbs. Fresh mint and parsley are used in the following recipe for Fattoush, an Arabic puréed salad that is a relative of the famous Spanish cold

Freshly cooked pasta of your choice zings with summer flavours when topped with a tasty home-made Napoletana Sauce and some shavings of Parmesan.

soup, gazpacho. Fattoush can make a good starter or a light lunch, or top it with a hard or soft-boiled egg to make a more substantial dish. It can be prepared an hour or two in advance, and served either chilled or at room temperature.

Fattoush

SERVES: 4 as a starter
PREPARATION TIME: 15 minutes
COOKING TIME: none

---

250 g firm, vine-ripened tomatoes, skinned and roughly chopped
4 spring onions, roughly chopped
1 small green pepper, deseeded and roughly chopped
½ cucumber, roughly chopped
1 clove garlic, peeled and chopped
3 tablespoons chopped fresh parsley
1 tablespoon finely shredded mint
Juice of ½ lemon
3 tablespoons olive oil
Salt and black pepper
1 pita bread
To garnish: black olives and roughly torn parsley and mint leaves
To serve: lemon slices and hot pita bread

---

1 Put all the ingredients except the salt, pepper and pita bread into a food processor and process them to a chunky purée. Season to taste.
2 Lightly toast the pita bread, break it up into a shallow bowl and spread the purée on top. The mixture can be served immediately, but can also be chilled for an hour or two.
3 Just before serving, stir the salad gently and garnish with the black olives, parsley and mint leaves. Serve with lemon slices and hot pita bread.

DRYING TOMATOES

Can I dry my own tomatoes?

Tomatoes can be dried in a low oven overnight, but this can never match the flavours that develop in the natural sun-drying process. If you have an abundant crop of Roma (egg-shaped or plum-shaped) tomatoes, dry them successfully according to the following recipes. (See also the step-by-step instructions on page 364.)

Juicy tomatoes and softened pita bread are the base of Arabic Fattoush, a fresh, chunky purée of salad vegetables which brings a touch of sunshine to the table.

Oven-dried tomatoes in oil

MAKES: 3 x 250 ml jars
PREPARATION TIME: 45 minutes
COOKING TIME: 6 hours

---

2 kg egg tomatoes
125 ml olive oil, plus extra for greasing
6 plump cloves garlic, crushed
Freshly ground black pepper
Olive oil for storage

---

1 Preheat the oven to 100°C. Line three large baking trays with foil and brush with olive oil.
2 Wash the tomatoes in cold water and dry well. Cut them in half lengthways, through the calyx or stem end, and scoop out the seeds, using a small metal teaspoon. (The seeds can be added to Napoletana Sauce – see page 362 – or to a soup, stew or casserole.)
3 Place the tomatoes, cut side down, onto the oiled trays.
4 In a small bowl, mix the olive oil with the crushed garlic. Brush the oil mixture generously over the tomatoes, then grind black pepper generously over them.

5 Bake for 6 hours, or until very wrinkled and semi-dry.
6 Pack the tomatoes into clean sterilised jars and cover with olive oil. Cover and label the jars. Store in a cool, dry place.

Oven-dried tomatoes

PREPARATION TIME: 45 minutes
COOKING TIME: 6-8 hours fan-forced oven; 10-12 hours regular oven

---

2 kg egg tomatoes

---

1 Line the bottom of the oven with strong aluminium foil, to keep it clean. Preheat the oven to 100°C.
2 Wash tomatoes in cold water and dry well. Cut in half lengthways and scoop out the seeds (see the previous recipe).
3 Place the tomatoes, cut side down, directly onto the oven racks. Bake for 6-8 hours in a fan-forced oven, for up to 12 hours in a standard oven, or until dry.
4 Transfer to wire cooling racks and leave to cool completely.
5 Store in a covered glass or rigid plastic container in a cool, dry place.

OVEN-DRIED TOMATOES IN OIL

An over-abundance of fresh ripe tomatoes can be oven-dried quite easily at home; enhance them, if you like, with a garlic-flavoured oil.

1 Cut washed tomatoes in half lengthways, scoop out the seeds, and place tomatoes on a metal tray.

2 Brush garlic-flavoured oil generously over the tomatoes. Bake for 6 hours, or until semi-dry.

3 Pack the tomatoes into clean jars and cover with olive oil. Store the sealed jars in a cool, dry place.

Trifle

UPDATING A CLASSIC

Is there any way to make a trifle more sophisticated?

Yes, the traditional English dessert – sponge cake soaked in sherry or wine and topped with fruit or jam and custard – can be made more sophisticated by making simple changes to the basic recipe. For example, a Madeira cake, Swiss roll or chocolate cake can be used instead of the fatless sponge cake. And instead of soaking the sponge in sherry, try using a liqueur such as Cointreau or kirsch, ginger wine or even a dessert wine.

The crushed macaroons which are often used in trifles can be combined with, or even replaced by, ground almonds or hazelnuts. Use a strong-flavoured jam such as morello cherry or ginger. Instead of using a vanilla-flavoured custard, make egg custard and add a few drops of almond essence. And the cream may be flavoured with sugar and a spirit such as brandy or a liqueur such as Cointreau.

In the recipe below, chocolate sponge cake, kirsch and canned black cherries are combined to make an unusual trifle.

Black forest trifle

SERVES: 6
PREPARATION TIME: 55 minutes, plus 5–6 hours cooling, softening and setting time
COOKING TIME: 10–15 minutes

---

600 ml milk
1 vanilla pod
2 large eggs, plus 2 egg yolks
25 g (5 teaspoons) caster sugar
300 g chocolate sponge cake
50 g macaroons, crushed
30 g (¼ cup) ground almonds
425 g canned pitted black cherries
100 ml kirsch
300 ml fresh cream
To decorate: toasted almond flakes and plain chocolate curls

---

1 Put the milk in a saucepan with the vanilla pod and bring to the boil. Remove from the heat, cover and leave to infuse for 20 minutes, then strain and discard the vanilla.
2 Put the eggs, egg yolks and sugar in a bowl and beat together until well mixed. Pour on the cooled milk, mix well and strain back into a clean pan. Cook gently, stirring continuously, for about 10 minutes or until the custard thickens slightly.

Do not let it come to the boil. Pour it into a bowl and leave to cool.
3 Cut the chocolate sponge into small slices and arrange in a large serving bowl. Mix together the macaroons and ground almonds and sprinkle over the chocolate cake.
4 Pour the cherry syrup into a bowl. Mix in the kirsch and spoon over the cake. Chop the cherries roughly and put them on top, then cover and set aside for 2 hours.
5 Stir the cold custard until smooth and pour it over the cherries. Cover and chill for 2 hours.
6 Whip the cream lightly and spread or pipe it over the custard. The trifle can be served immediately, or covered and chilled overnight. When ready to serve, decorate with flaked almonds and chocolate curls.

Trout

FARMED AND WILD

What is the difference between rainbow trout, brown trout, ocean trout and salmon trout?

Rainbow trout is a fish with silvery and multicoloured skin, with a red stripe running lengthways along the sides of the male fish. The delicate white flesh is sometimes tinged pink. Normally it will feed one, although farmed trout can be larger.

Brown trout, with greenish brown spotted skin, white flesh and a stronger flavour, is the wild trout found in rivers, and also at fish farms.

Ocean trout is the same species as brown trout, but looks different as it goes out to sea and returns to rivers to spawn. Because it looks rather like a small salmon, with silvery skin and pink flesh, it is sometimes called salmon trout.

GOOD LOOKING

How can I identify a fresh trout?

As with all fish, look for firm flesh and shiny skin. The eyes should be clear and protruding, and the gills a bright red colour. And it should smell fresh and not look muddy.

Most experts agree that trout should not be washed but simply wiped with a cloth. Then remove the guts, gills and any weed from the mouth that might taste bitter.

FRESH CATCH

If I catch a trout, should it be frozen whole, or gutted first? And how do I cook it?

Gut it as soon as possible, by the waterside if you can manage it. It is a myth that keeping the guts in freshly caught fish helps to preserve them; if there is a delay before it will be frozen, it can affect the flavour. Then clean and dry the fish thoroughly before wrapping it well in freezer film. Trout can remain frozen for up to four months.

Trout can be fried, grilled or baked, but the best possible way to enjoy freshly caught fish is to cook it immediately, and as the recipe below shows, you don't need pots, pans, an oven or even cutlery.

Trout in foil

SERVES: 2
PREPARATION TIME: 5 minutes
COOKING TIME: 20–30 minutes

A few sheets of heavy-duty aluminium foil
2 fresh trout, gutted
A few fresh herbs, such as chives, dill, parsley or fennel
50 g butter, melted, mixed with 3 tablespoons chopped mixed fresh herbs, optional

1 Preheat a barbecue or light a small wood fire. When the embers have become very hot, put a fish in the middle of each sheet of foil - if the sheets are small, you may need to use two per fish instead.

2 Tuck the herbs into the cavity of each fish and wrap the parcels up, folding in the ends. Put the fish on the barbecue or directly over the ashes of the wood fire. Leave to cook for about 20–30 minutes, turning once. When the foil is starting to char, the fish will be cooked.

3 Unwrap the foil, taking care not to burn your fingers. Brush the fish with herb-flavoured melted butter if you have made some and eat out of the foil with your fingers.

VARIATION

The fish can be cooked in an oven, preheated to 200°C, for 20 minutes, but it will lack the smoky flavour.

Some cooking foil and a small fire are all you need to turn trout into a feast. A riverside setting is optional.

Turkey

TURKEYS WITH TASTE

How can I choose a turkey for Christmas with the best flavour?

Turkeys have been introduced into Australia mainly through British and Canadian breeding lines. Today they are bred to produce light-coloured, lean-fleshed birds which are all flavourful and juicy. They are not intensively reared and are allowed to mature naturally in open sheds, feeding from open feed pens. Buy fresh turkeys from good butchers or reputable poultry dealers. Frozen turkeys are available in large supermarkets.

THE RIGHT HELPING

How do I calculate how much turkey to buy?

Allow 500 g of dressed bird (that is, without its head, feet or giblets and before stuffing) on the bone per person, for a turkey that weighs up to 6 kg. With a larger bird, allow 375 g per person. Remember to add a little extra if you enjoy leftovers.

STUFFING FACTS

How can I work out how much stuffing I will need – and is it safe to stuff the body cavity?

You will need 250–300 g of stuffing for the neck cavity of a 5.5–6 kg bird. Do not stuff the body cavity as there could be a risk of salmonella poisoning (see *Stuffing*). If this amount seems inadequate, make double the quantity and cook the rest separately.

SPOILED FOR CHOICE

What stuffings besides sage and onion go well with turkey?

There are many possibilities. For something different, try one of the recipes on the right. You can even use two different stuffings with one bird, one in the neck and the other cooked separately.

Sausage and bacon stuffing

MAKES: *enough to stuff and accompany a 6 kg turkey*
PREPARATION TIME: *10 minutes*
COOKING TIME: *5 minutes*

---

250 g streaky bacon, chopped
250 g premium sausage meat
250 g (4 cups) fresh brown breadcrumbs
1 tablespoon wholegrain mustard
1 tablespoon fresh thyme
Salt and black pepper

---

1 Fry the bacon in a nonstick pan until it is brown and the fat starts to run. Drain, cool and crumble it with your fingers or chop finely.
2 Mix the sausage meat in a large bowl with the bacon, breadcrumbs, mustard, thyme, salt and pepper.
3 Cool the stuffing then use half to stuff the neck flap of the turkey (see page 367). Put the rest in a buttered dish, cover with foil and cook on the bottom of the oven for 30 minutes.

Lemon oatmeal stuffing

MAKES: *enough to stuff and accompany a 6 kg turkey*
PREPARATION TIME: *10 minutes*
COOKING TIME: *15 minutes*

---

250 g cooked chicken breast, finely chopped
Grated zest and juice of 1 lemon
185 g (3 cups) fresh breadcrumbs
60 g (½ cup) chopped hazelnuts
125 g butter
125 g (¾ cup) coarse oatmeal
3 tablespoons chopped fresh marjoram
Salt and black pepper
2 large eggs, beaten

---

1 Mix the chopped chicken with the lemon zest, juice, breadcrumbs and chopped hazelnuts.
2 Melt the butter in a saucepan and add the oatmeal. Cook, stirring until golden and add to the chicken.
3 Cool slightly and mix in the marjoram, salt, pepper and eggs.
4 Cool before stuffing the neck flap of the bird. Put the rest in a buttered dish, cover with foil and cook on the bottom of the oven for 30 minutes.

COLD TURKEY

Can I defrost a whole frozen turkey in a microwave oven?

The most important question is, will it fit in the microwave? It is seldom feasible to defrost a turkey in a microwave unless it is a very small bird, or a turkey joint. If it does fit, follow the instructions for chicken in the microwave's handbook.

COSY JOINT

Is there any way to cook a turkey for just two people?

Yes, there are many small turkey joints available. Try breast joints or roasts, as well as whole turkey legs and breast fillets. Some small turkeys are sold already stuffed or they can be cooked with one of the stuffings on the left. The smallest whole turkeys available usually weigh about 2.5 kg.

OLD AND NEW

What are the traditional dishes to serve with turkey, and is there any way to ring the changes?

Traditionalists serve turkey with bread sauce (see **Sauces**). Chipolatas wrapped in bacon are another favourite partner, as is cranberry sauce (see **Cranberries**).

Brussels sprouts, with chestnuts or other nuts, are a traditional vegetable accompaniment, but for a lighter dish, try green beans mixed with toasted almonds. You could also add a dash of colour with a purée of parsnip and pumpkin, buttered and seasoned with nutmeg.

Roast potatoes are good with roast turkey but Hasselback (fantail) potatoes are an attractive alternative. To make these, take whole, medium-sized peeled potatoes and make several fine cuts most of the way through the potatoes so that they are just held together at the bottom. Soak or rinse them in cold water, dry, then stand the potatoes in a baking dish and cook in the usual way, basting regularly with butter. They are also delicious sprinkled with grated cheese.

SECOND TIME AROUND

What can I make with any pieces of leftover cooked turkey?

Once the turkey is completely cold, cut all the meat from the carcass, wrap or put it in a covered plastic box and refrigerate. If you do not want to keep eating turkey over the Christmas holiday, put the meat in a freezer container, pour over any leftover gravy, cover and freeze. Keep it for up to three months.

There are a variety of interesting dishes you can make with leftover turkey. Most take very little cooking, which may be a relief after the Christmas holiday marathon.

Make potted turkey by whizzing it up in a food processor with half its weight in softened butter, plus some salt, pepper, nutmeg or mace, and a dash of Madeira. Spoon into a pâté dish, press it down and cover with a layer of melted butter. Chill it for a couple of hours or until it is firm, then use it as a spread or sandwich filling. It will keep for about a week in the refrigerator.

Diced turkey can be mixed with a white sauce, or a velouté sauce made with turkey stock (see **Sauces** and **Stock**), plus lightly fried mushrooms and onions and turned into a casserole. Top this with cheese and mashed potato, or pastry, and bake until brown and bubbling. You can also make a turkey fricassée (see **Casseroles**) or layer the turkey and sauce with cooked pasta, sprinkle with cheese and breadcrumbs and bake.

For turkey with a Middle Eastern flavour, finely dice the meat, mix it with cooked wild or brown rice, nuts and raisins, season with a little ground cumin and coriander and use as a filling for filo pastry.

To make a refreshing salad, marinate turkey pieces in a generous amount of virgin olive oil, a dash of balsamic vinegar, a little crushed chilli, sultanas and toasted pine nuts. Serve with salad greens.

You can cook the Traditional Roast Turkey (see page 368) confident that leftovers will be as delicious as a freshly cooked bird.

HOW TO STUFF AND TRUSS A TURKEY

Rinse the bird under the cold tap and pat dry, then pull out any fat from inside the cavity. Cut out the wishbone from the neck end to make carving easier.

1 Place the turkey breast side down, pull back the neck skin and heap the stuffing inside the pouch.

2 Pull the neck skin back over the cavity to cover the stuffing and secure it in place with a metal skewer.

3 Turn the bird breast side up and reshape the stuffing by patting it gently. Then prepare a piece of string which is long enough to encircle the whole turkey lengthways twice.

4 Push the legs down so the ends sit up very straight. Insert a trussing needle and string through the flesh of one knee, passing it right through the bird and out the opposite knee joint.

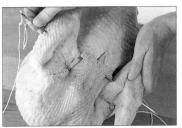

5 Turn the bird breast down and push the needle through both of the sections of one wing, through the skewered neck and then through both of the joints of the second wing.

6 Turn the bird on its side. Take hold of the end of the string where it entered the first leg joint and the end emerging from the second wing joint, pull firmly together and tie securely.

7 Turn the bird breast side up, tuck the tail into the cavity and fold the top skin over. Thread the needle right through, under the drumsticks.

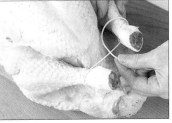

8 Loop the string around one of the drumsticks and then the other. Tie both ends of the string together and sit the turkey in a baking dish.

Succulent roast turkey with its crisp, buttered brown skin is served here with a choice of savoury stuffings, sharp cranberry sauce and rich giblet gravy.

Traditional roast turkey

SERVES: 8-10
PREPARATION TIME: 15 minutes (excluding making the stuffing and gravy)
COOKING TIME: 3-3½ hours

4-5 kg turkey
Sausage and Bacon or Lemon
  Oatmeal Stuffing (see page 366),
  or half quantities of both
125-185 g butter, softened
Salt and black pepper

1 Preheat the oven to 180°C.
2 Stuff and truss the turkey just before cooking it (see panel, page 367), using half of your preferred stuffing mixture. Put the rest into a greased ovenproof dish and cover with foil.
3 Smear the surface of the turkey with butter. Line a large baking dish with foil, bringing the edges up over the rim. Put the turkey in the centre, cover it loosely with another sheet of foil and tuck the edges inside the rim.

4 Roast for 3-3½ hours. Thirty minutes before the end of cooking, remove the top sheet of foil to allow the skin to brown and put the dish of stuffing in the oven to cook. To test if the turkey is ready, push a skewer into the deepest part of each thigh. If the juices run clear, it is cooked.
5 Allow the cooked bird to stand for 15-20 minutes as this will make carving easier (see *Carving*). In the meantime, finish making the gravy.

GRAVY EXTRAS

How do I make giblet gravy?

Always ask for a turkey with giblets as these make a rich stock for a superior gravy (see recipe, above right). Remove the liver as this would make the gravy taste bitter (if you like you can fry it then add it to the stuffing). If the turkey is frozen, look inside the cavity for the bag of giblets. Your turkey will be ruined if they and their plastic bag are cooked with the bird.

Giblet gravy

MAKES: 850 ml
PREPARATION TIME: 10 minutes
COOKING TIME: 1 hour 5 minutes

Turkey giblets, without the liver
1 bay leaf
1 onion, peeled and stuck with
  4 cloves
A few sprigs of parsley
6 peppercorns
1 teaspoon dried thyme
40 g (4 tablespoons) plain flour
4 tablespoons port

1 Put the giblets (not the liver) in a saucepan with the bay leaf, onion, parsley, peppercorns and the thyme. Cover with 1 litre of water and bring to the boil, then lower the heat and simmer for an hour. Strain and reserve the stock.
2 When the turkey is cooked and resting, pour off almost all the fat from the baking dish. Add the flour to the pan and blend it into the fat with a wooden spoon, scraping up as much sediment from the bottom of the pan as possible.
3 Cook the roux for 1-2 minutes then gradually whisk in the reserved stock and the port and simmer for 15 minutes. Taste and season. Pour the gravy into a warmed sauceboat.

Turnips

PEPPERY FLAVOUR

Is it always necessary to peel turnips, and are there other ways of cooking them besides mashed?

Turnips do not always need to be peeled or mashed. In early summer, when tiny turnips with their leaves attached are available, just wash the tender skin and boil the turnips quickly to conserve their peppery taste. Try finishing the turnips in a flavoured butter, as in the following herb-scented recipe, and serve with duck or guinea fowl, baked ham or lamb.

The pure white variety, or those with their tops flushed with pinky mauve, are an excellent choice to use in a variety of summer stews and casseroles, such as those made with lamb. Large winter turnips are yellowish white, sometimes with flashes of green. They are at their best when no larger than a tennis ball but do need to be peeled. They can be used in soups and stews.

You can cook and purée turnips with plenty of butter and pepper and combine them with potatoes or another root vegetable such as carrots. Alternatively, grate raw turnips and serve them with a dressing for winter salads, or slice large turnips, brush them with oil and grill until they are just tender.

Do not throw out the leaves of young turnips. They can be cooked in the same way as spinach and served as a vegetable in their own right, or incorporated into soup, or shredded and used as a garnish for vegetable dishes and salads.

Herb-buttered turnips

SERVES: 4
PREPARATION TIME: 5 minutes
COOKING TIME: 12–15 minutes

8-12 tiny young turnips, with leaves reserved and shredded, optional
Salt and black pepper
50 g butter
A sprig of rosemary
1 tablespoon snipped chives
1 tablespoon shredded mint
2 tablespoons chopped parsley

1 Wash the turnips gently and cut off the leaves, leaving 1 cm green stalk attached. Put the turnips in a saucepan of salted water and bring them to the boil. Cook them for about 10 minutes until they are just tender, then drain thoroughly.
2 Heat the butter with the rosemary in a wide frying pan and turn the turnips in it for 2–3 minutes until they are shiny and just begining to show patches of colour.
3 Discard the rosemary, add the salt and pepper and then scatter on the chives, mint, parsley and turnip leaves, if using. Shake the pan to coat the turnips evenly then serve them in a warmed dish

SCOTTISH STAPLE

What are bashed neeps?

Bashed neeps, which sound like turnips, are really mashed swede. The Scots call swedes turnips and the traditional bashed neeps and haggis are as essential to a Scottish Burns' night as whisky.

TVP

MEAT ALTERNATIVE

What exactly is TVP?

Textured Vegetable Protein (TVP) is made from soya beans ground into a flour after their oil has been extracted. The flour is mixed with water, then extruded to heat and expand the dough. Air is added, which helps to give a fibrous, spongy texture. TVP can be bought dried as mince in leading health food shops. When unflavoured, it tastes very bland, but is good to add other flavourings to.

Ever since TVP was introduced in the 1960s, it has been used as a meat extender by large caterers. TVP is also a common ingredient in many ready-made dishes such as vegetarian sausages and burgers. The vegetable protein is a good source of fibre, is fortified with vitamin B_{12} and is very low in fat.

To cook TVP, soak it in water or vegetable stock according to the packet instructions. Use it in well-flavoured casseroles, pies, sauces or stews. Although it is similar to tofu, TVP is more processed.

Fresh chives, mint and parsley add contrasting colour and a summery flavour to these delicious young turnips which are bathed in rosemary-scented butter.

Vanilla

PURE FLAVOUR

What is the difference between vanilla extract and essence? Is it better to use a vanilla pod?

Vanilla is the pod of a climbing orchid and widely grown in the tropics, especially Madagascar, the West Indies and Fiji. The bean pods are cured and turn black.

The extract and essence are both made by soaking vanilla pods in alcohol to leech out the flavour, but vanilla essence, which often has syrup added, is more concentrated. Look for the word 'pure' on the label and avoid artificial vanilla, which is derived from clove oil.

Vanilla pods offer the best flavour of all, for they have subtlety; vanilla essence and extract can be rather overpowering when used with a heavy hand.

POTENT SEEDS

How do I use a vanilla pod?

The strongest flavour is in the tiny seeds and the pulp surrounding them, so the pod should be split open and the seeds scraped out for adding to custards or ice creams. Infusing a vanilla pod in hot liquid is an economical way to extract the flavour, as the pod can then be rinsed, dried and used again, usually as many as two or three times.

A good way to store vanilla pods after use, particularly when they have been recycled a few times, is in a jar of caster sugar. The sugar can then absorb the flavour of the pods and they will keep almost indefinitely. Top up the sugar as you use it, for example in desserts, sprinkled over fruit such as fresh berries, or in the following recipe for a pleasantly sharp, lemon and vanilla scented sauce that is delicious served with fruit pies and steamed or baked puddings.

You can also store used vanilla pods in a bottle of brandy or dark rum. The alcohol can then be used as a flavouring agent in cooking, folded into whipped cream or simply splashed over fruit salads or ice cream. However, very fresh vanilla pods, which are moist and supple, are best kept wrapped in cellophane bags or foil; storing them in caster sugar will dry them out.

Vanilla and lemon sauce

SERVES: 4
PREPARATION TIME: 5 minutes
COOKING TIME: 10 minutes

60 g (¼ cup) vanilla sugar
1 tablespoon cornflour blended
  smoothly with 1 tablespoon water
300 ml boiling water
50 g unsalted butter, diced
Juice and finely grated zest of
  1 lemon

1 Mix the sugar and cornflour paste in a bowl. Pour the boiling water onto the mixture gradually, stirring constantly with a wooden spoon.
2 Transfer to a saucepan and heat slowly for 5 minutes, then remove from the heat. Add the diced butter gradually, stirring until each piece has melted before adding the next.
3 Stir the lemon juice and grated zest into the sauce and serve hot.

PERFECT PARTNERS

Can you tell me why chocolate is usually flavoured with vanilla?

Though the Aztecs, who first made chocolate, mixed it with many different flavourings, including chilli, it was the combination of chocolate and vanilla that appealed when these two New World ingredients arrived in Europe. Chocolate and vanilla have been almost inseparable partners ever since.

Veal

CARE FOR CALVES

How can I be sure that the veal I buy has been raised kindly?

The specific worry most people have when buying veal, or calf's meat, is that it might have been reared in very constrictive crates. Traditionally, veal calves used to be crate-reared and fed a milk-based diet in order to produce a very tender, very pale flesh. Crate-rearing is banned in Australia, New Zealand, Austria, Britain, Denmark, Germany and Sweden. However, milk-fed veal, raised humanely, is available from specialty butchers. The veal meat of Australian calves is rosier than European veal but is still very tender.

KEEP IT SIMPLE

I find that breadcrumbed veal escalopes or schnitzels are sometimes heavy. Can you give me some ideas for lighter ways to cook veal steak?

Veal escalopes taste tender and light without a coating and need only the simplest cooking methods. They should be pounded until they are about 5 mm thick, which ensures they cook quickly. If this has not been done when you buy them, place each escalope in turn between two sheets of plastic wrap and beat it with a rolling pin; as the pin touches the escalope, let it slide from the centre to the side of the escalope to stretch the meat.

To cook the escalopes, heat a little olive oil in a frying pan. When it is hot, add the escalopes, allowing each one plenty of room, and fry over a fairly high heat for about 3 minutes, turning once. Remove the escalopes and keep them warm while you deglaze the pan with a few tablespoons of white wine, lemon juice or cream.

For a change from escalopes, you could try using veal chops. Marinate them for 1–2 hours, if liked, then fry over a medium heat for 8 minutes or so, turning once. Veal chops can be partnered by more robust flavours such as eggplant, mushrooms, red or green peppers and tomatoes.

LEAN AND TENDER

Joints of veal seem too delicate to roast normally. What is the best way to cook one?

It is true that joints of veal are lean and fine-textured and, if they are not roasted carefully, tend to dry out. If you would like to serve roast veal, cook it at 160°C for 35–40 minutes per kg and baste the meat often during cooking.

Another useful way to keep a joint of veal moist is to marinate the meat first in a mixture of olive oil and lemon juice or white wine. Parsley, thyme and garlic can be added for extra flavour. The meat should be basted often with the marinade while cooking.

An easy alternative is to cook the veal joint gently in a heavy casserole dish by the moist, pot-roasting method, used in the recipe for Italian Veal Pot-roast, below. This will keep the joint tender and prevent the meat from drying out.

Italian veal pot-roast

SERVES: 6
PREPARATION TIME: 20 minutes
COOKING TIME: 3 hours

1.5 kg boned shoulder of veal, plus the bones
A bunch of herbs comprising a large sprig of rosemary, several parsley stalks and a sprig of thyme, all tied together
2–3 slices prosciutto
1 tablespoon chopped fresh sage
1½ tablespoons olive oil
1 onion, finely chopped
1 carrot, finely chopped
2 stalks celery, finely chopped
1½ tablespoons capers
3 slices lemon, free of rind and white pith
Black pepper
1 bouquet garni
300 ml medium dry white wine

1 Put the bones and the bunch of herbs into a large saucepan and cover with water. Bring to the boil, skim the scum from the surface and then simmer, uncovered, for about an hour.
2 Preheat the oven to 160°C. Place the veal on a work surface, skin side down, and cover with the ham, cutting the slices to fit and overlapping as necessary.
3 Sprinkle over the sage and some black pepper (the ham is salty so there is no need for extra salt). Roll up the shoulder and tie it securely at intervals of 5 cm.
4 Heat the oil in a frying pan, add the veal joint, brown it all over, and transfer the meat to a plate.
5 Add the onion, carrot and celery to the frying pan and fry until the vegetables are softened and lightly coloured. Mix in the capers, lemon slices and seasoning.
6 Spoon half the vegetable mixture into a heavy casserole dish. Add the bouquet garni to the casserole and place the veal on top.
7 Add the wine to the frying pan and boil for a minute or so. Pour the wine over the veal and spoon the remaining vegetables onto the veal.
8 Strain the stock from the bones and boil hard until reduced to about 350 ml. Pour the liquid around the veal, cover tightly and cook in the oven for 1 hour 40 minutes, turning the veal over about halfway through the cooking time.
9 Remove the veal, carve it into slices and arrange them on a heated serving dish. Discard the bouquet garni from the casserole. Remove the vegetables with a slotted spoon and place them on top of the veal, or, if you prefer, lift the veal slices, put the vegetables on the serving dish, and arrange the meat over them.
10 Check the sauce. If it is too thin, pour it into a frying pan and boil for a minute or so to reduce, then pour it over the veal and vegetables. If you prefer, some of the sauce can be served separately in a sauceboat.
VARIATION
You can use turkey breast instead of veal: slice open the breast to form a large piece, cover with the ham and chopped sage and roll up.

Vegetables

ORGANIC AND FRESH

I want to buy organic vegetables but they are expensive and often look quite battered. Are they OK?

Organic vegetables can seem much more expensive than conventionally grown vegetables, and, yes, they do often look sad and tired, because they tend not to sell quickly. One of the best ways to buy certified organic produce is to contact an organic cooperative and for a fixed price they will make regular home deliveries of seasonal vegetables and fruit. Alternatively, buy from a shop with a regular turnover. Because it is not sprayed with fungicides, even organically grown produce deteriorates if it is left to sit around.

COVER UP

Should I put a lid on the pot when I'm cooking vegetables?

If you are cooking vegetables with minimal liquid, it is essential to keep them tightly covered to prevent them drying out and to allow the steam to build up in the pan and cook the vegetables.

Green vegetables such as shredded cabbage or green beans can be cooked very quickly by plunging them into plenty of boiling water and leaving them uncovered so that the volatile acids which escape while they are cooking will not condense on the lid and fall back into the pan, as this can affect the flavour. This method conserves their colour, flavour and texture.

Roots and tubers such as potatoes, which are submerged in water and cooked for a longer time, are best partially covered. Covering these vegetables uses less fuel and prevents a lowering of the water level, which could leave some of them above the water. To partially cover a saucepan, set the lid askew or place a wooden spoon across the pan and balance the lid on top.

PREPARING VEGETABLES FOR STUFFING

Fresh vegetables can be used to make attractive cases for stuffings. Make sure you leave the vegetable casing thick enough so that it does not collapse during cooking.

TOMATOES

Choose large tomatoes, then cut off their tops and gently scoop out the seeds and central pulp with a teaspoon. Rub a little salt around the insides of the tomatoes and turn them over to drain for 20 minutes or so. Prepare the stuffing, then fill the tomatoes and replace the tops.

PEPPERS

Halve the peppers lengthways or across and cut away the white pith with a small sharp knife. Shake or scrape out the remaining seeds.

PUMPKIN

Cut the pumpkin in half and remove the seeds and fibre with a spoon. You can also cut out some of the flesh with a curved grapefruit knife. Leave a thick wall of pumpkin flesh if you are using the shell as a soup tureen or as a casserole dish for a stew.

CAREFUL SALTING

Is it always necessary to add salt to the cooking water when you are boiling vegetables?

Starchy vegetables and roots such as potatoes, carrots and parsnips are best cooked in salted water to allow the salt to permeate the flesh during cooking, to add flavour. For green vegetables, where the cooking time is brief, it is more efficient to add salt after cooking, and you will probably find you use less, which is a healthy option.

There is no point in salting vegetables that are to be mashed or otherwise made into a purée, since it is much easier to judge the right amount by salting the mash later.

CHOP AND FRY

What is a vegetable hash?

Hash is traditionally a dish made of leftovers in which the vegetables are fried and served hot. Bubble and squeak, made from leftover potatoes refried with cooked cabbage, is a typical hash.

Usually the mixture is stirred and turned in the frying pan to incorporate the crunchy browned bits, but vegetables can also be formed into cakes and fried until the outside is crisp and brown.

Potatoes are good used in hashes as they help to bind the vegetables together, however, other carbohydrate foods such as rice or fresh breadcrumbs, perhaps with an egg too, can be used instead.

The following recipe for hash made with freshly cooked sweet potatoes is sophisticated enough for a brunch party, served with bacon and spicy sausages or with poultry and pork. Unlike ordinary potatoes, cooked sweet potato can be quickly puréed in a food processor along with the seasonings and spices, but you must fork the cranberries into the mixture by hand to avoid breaking them up. The mixture can be prepared in advance and stored in the fridge but should be at room temperature when the cakes are shaped and fried.

Hashed sweet potato and cranberry cakes

SERVES: *4*
PREPARATION TIME: *15 minutes*
COOKING TIME: *35 minutes*

1 kg pink-skinned sweet potatoes, peeled and diced
2 teaspoons ground allspice
2 teaspoons celery salt
1 teaspoon ground coriander
Black pepper
100 g frozen cranberries, thawed
Flour for coating
Oil for shallow frying

1 Cover the sweet potatoes with water and bring to the boil. Cover and simmer for about 20 minutes, or until they are quite soft.
2 Drain the sweet potatoes, mash thoroughly and mix in the allspice, celery salt, coriander, a generous grinding of black pepper and then the cranberries.
3 Dust a work surface generously with flour, then shape the mixture into 12 cakes, turning them so that each one is well coated in flour.
4 Fry the sweet potato cakes in batches in hot oil and serve hot.

FRYING ORDER

How should I prepare vegetables for stir-frying, and in what order should I add them to the wok?

Vegetables to be stir-fried need to be cut so that as much of their surface area as possible is exposed to heat: that way they cook faster. The larger root vegetables should be cut into thin batons or sliced diagonally. Broccoli and cauliflower are best separated into small florets with the remaining thick stems sliced diagonally. Leafy vegetables should be finely shredded.

The most efficient order in which to add vegetables to the oil is: roots first, then florets, sliced pods, and beansprouts and leafy vegetables last, allowing a minute between each addition.

Add any liquid such as soy sauce with the leaf vegetables, then cover the wok to allow the vegetables to steam slightly. (See also *Wok*.)

TOP GRILLING

What is a vegetable gratin and which vegetables are suitable?

A gratin is a dish with a crusty top, usually of cheese or breadcrumbs, baked in the oven and then finished by flashing it under a very hot grill, which gives it a gleaming brown topping. Gratins make excellent winter vegetarian dishes.

Root vegetables, when combined with onions and cauliflower or broccoli florets, tomatoes, zucchini and corn kernels, make fine gratins. Extra protein can be added in the form of cheese and nuts, within the mix as well as on top.

In the gratin recipe below each vegetable is cooked separately and then combined for the final dish. Some of the preparation may be done ahead if this is more convenient. The vegetables could also be cooked sequentially in the same saucepan to save on washing up.

Gratin of vegetables and walnuts in a double cheese sauce

SERVES: 4–6
PREPARATION TIME: 20 minutes
COOKING TIME: 1 hour

400 g broccoli or cauliflower florets
500 g potatoes, peeled and thickly sliced
500 g parsnips, peeled and thickly sliced
Salt
2 medium leeks, sliced
90 g butter
40 g (4 tablespoons) plain flour
500 ml milk
2 bay leaves
125 g mild Cheddar cheese, finely grated
50 g blue vein cheese, crumbled
Black pepper
2 tablespoons coarsely chopped walnuts

1 Preheat the oven to 200°C.
2 Slice the broccoli or cauliflower florets and leave each with some of the stem attached. Slice the larger stems diagonally. Drop the florets

Walnuts add crunch and protein to this vegetable gratin, smothered in a creamy sauce of Cheddar and blue cheese. A final grilling makes the top a toasty brown.

and sliced stems into a large pan of boiling salted water and cook them until just tender, then drain.
3 Put the potatoes and parsnips separately into salted water, bring to the boil and cook for 5–7 minutes until only just tender, then drain.
4 Cook the leeks in half the butter in a saucepan until they wilt, then spread them in a large gratin dish, smearing around the sides with the butter in which they were cooked.
5 Melt the remaining butter in the saucepan, add the flour and stir constantly for 1 minute over a medium heat. Remove from the heat and add some of the milk, stirring it in a little at a time until the sauce becomes smooth.
6 Return the pan to a low heat and add the remaining milk and the bay leaves, stirring the sauce constantly until it reaches boiling point. Turn down the heat and leave to simmer, stirring occasionally, for 5 minutes.
7 Add half the Cheddar and all the blue vein cheese to the sauce and

stir until they have both melted. Season the sauce to taste, being generous with the black pepper.
8 Layer the potatoes on top of the leeks in the prepared dish, pouring a little sauce over each layer, then add the parsnips, and finish with a layer of the broccoli or cauliflower. Scatter the walnuts over the top. Pour the remaining sauce over the vegetables and then sprinkle the gratin with the remaining grated Cheddar cheese.
9 Bake for 30–40 minutes until the dish is bubbling and golden brown on top. For a super-browned top you can finish the gratin under the grill if your dish is flameproof.
VARIATIONS
Add 50–90 g chopped lean ham or drained canned tuna to the vegetables as you layer them in the gratin dish. Or, simply substitute carrots for the parsnips.

You could leave out the potatoes and parsnips, halve the quantities of milk and cheese and serve the gratin as a side dish to a meat course.

ROASTED SWEETNESS

I have only ever roasted potatoes, pumpkin, carrots and parsnips. Are there other vegetables that roast well?

Roasting fresh vegetables intensifies their sweetness and gives them a lovely caramelised finish. Sweet vegetables such as onions, peppers and tomatoes respond particularly well to the treatment. Roast vegetables need not always be served hot. The salad of roast Mediterranean vegetables (below), served with an interesting bread, makes an excellent cook-ahead starter dish for a summer or autumn dinner.

Roast vegetable salad

SERVES: 6
PREPARATION TIME: 20 minutes
COOKING TIME: about 35 minutes

About 150 ml olive oil
3 medium onions, quartered
6 shallots, peeled
6 firm egg tomatoes, quartered
3 yellow, orange or red peppers,
  deseeded and quartered
2 large eggplant
1 tablespoon red wine vinegar
2 plump cloves garlic, chopped
Flaky sea salt and black pepper
6–8 basil leaves
To serve: Italian bread rolls

1 Preheat the oven to 230°C. Pour 4–5 tablespoons of olive oil into one or two baking dishes to cover the bottom and use your hands to turn the vegetables, including the whole eggplant, in it, smoothing the oil all over them.
2 Roast all the vegetables for 20 minutes, then remove all except the eggplant and set them aside.
3 Turn the eggplant in the oil and return them to the oven for 15–20 minutes. When their skins are quite wrinkled and the flesh is soft when pierced with a skewer, remove the eggplant from the oven, allow them to cool, then cut into chunks, each with some of the skin attached.
4 Arrange the vegetables on a large platter. In a small bowl, mix the remaining oil with the vinegar and chopped garlic to make a dressing and sprinkle it over the vegetables. The salad can be served tepid or at room temperature.
5 At the last minute, grind the sea salt and pepper over the salad, and top it with torn basil leaves. Serve the salad with Italian bread rolls.

Vegetarian Diets

NO MEAT OR FISH

If I give up both meat and fish, how can I ensure that I am getting enough protein?

Since plant foods tend to contain less protein than meat, and in a form that the body finds harder to use, it is quite natural to wonder whether a vegetarian diet can meet all your nutritional needs. However, a varied vegetarian or vegan diet should supply more than enough protein, provided enough food is being eaten to meet daily energy needs.

All of the amino acids humans require can be found somewhere in the plant kingdom, but you must choose foods from all the different plant groups – grains, pulses, roots, fresh green and yellow vegetables, nuts and seeds – so that the amino acids that are present only in small amounts in one group will be supplemented by those from another. The different sources of protein do not have to be eaten together but can be consumed at different times during the day. Many traditional cuisines combined pulses with grains, such as beans on toast, hummous and pita bread, and lentil dhal with rice or naan.

HEALTHY SUBSTITUTES

I have just turned vegetarian. Can I adapt recipes that contain meat simply by replacing it with vegetarian protein substitutes?

You can. There are, for example, many soya products such as soya burgers or sausages, which are not only rich in protein and calcium but are made to look like meat, and these can be substituted in some recipes. But remember that in removing meat, poultry and fish from your diet, you are removing more than protein. Meat is also an important souce of iron, zinc and vitamin B_{12} and it is important to ensure your body gets enough of these nutrients as well.

Dried apricots, bread, fortified breakfast cereals, lentils and dark green vegetables contain iron, but the iron found in eggs, milk and plant foods is less well absorbed than the iron in meat, so you also need to eat foods rich in vitamin C (such as fruit and fruit juices, potatoes and vegetables) as this boosts the body's ability to absorb iron.

Rich plant sources of zinc are brazil nuts, peanuts, pine nuts and sesame and sunflower seeds. Vitamin B_{12} occurs naturally in foods of animal origin such as eggs, milk and dairy products, as well as mushrooms. In addition, vitamin B_{12} is now added to processed foods, including breakfast cereals, Vegemite, Marmite and bread.

YOUNG VEGETARIANS

My 12-year-old wants to become a vegetarian. How can I ensure that she gets all the nourishment her body requires?

Because of the growth spurt during adolescence, there is an increase in the nutritional needs of all young people and a well-planned vegetarian diet can meet these needs. Problems may arise, however, if the child does not follow a vegetarian

Healthy option

Dairy products are an important source of protein and calcium for vegetarians, but because many contain high levels of saturated fat, it is important not to rely on them too heavily. Choose low-fat varieties where possible instead.

diet sensibly, or if the switch to a vegetarian lifestyle is combined with erratic teenage eating habits. In addition, the high levels of fibre in a typical vegetarian diet can make it quite bulky and this may limit the amount a child can eat, resulting in reduced energy intake.

Children require less protein a day than adults, so a vegetarian diet is fine provided they eat a wide variety of foods. If a child is very young, it is best to combine cereals and pulses in a meal and include some soya products in the diet as these are high in protein.

The key is to plan the child's vegetarian diet carefully, and make sure he or she understands how to choose wisely. There is plenty of literature available and you should read through it together. Most schools now cater for students who do not eat meat or fish.

Extra care is needed if the child wants to switch to a vegan diet and cut out dairy foods. Milk and other dairy products provide most of the calcium children need, so the vegan child should eat soya products such as soya drink and tofu as well as fortified foods to provide adequate levels of calcium. Supplements may also be required to boost the child's intake of vitamins B_{12} and D.

FULL OF FIBRE

Vegetarian diets seem to include a lot more bread, pasta and rice than I am used to eating – isn't this very fattening?

Vegetarian diets do tend to be high in carbohydrate and fibre, but this is the balance that health experts are now recommending for everyone. Rather than being fattening, carbohydrate contains fewer kilojoules per gram than fat, so you can eat more high-carbohydrate foods and have a low kilojoule intake.

Carbohydrates are not as fattening as the sauces and toppings we like to eat with them. If weight gain is a particular concern, forgo butter and cream sauces and have low-fat accompaniments with your bread, pasta and baked potatoes.

Venison

RED, ROE AND FALLOW

What kind of deer does venison come from: is it wild or farmed?

The venison most widely available comes from the red deer, which is the most commonly farmed deer, followed by fallow deer. If you are buying venison from a game dealer in New Zealand you may be able to choose wild roe deer that has been shot by sportsmen.

PINK AND JUICY

Sometimes when I cook venison it is very dry. What should I do?

As there is little or no fat marbled through venison or surrounding the flesh of young venison, it must be barded during roasting or braising to keep it moist. This means covering the joint with a thin piece of pork back fat, crackling or some strips of bacon to baste it as it cooks.

Allow venison to relax in a warm place for 10 minutes before serving, even with small cuts such as steaks and chops, which should be cooked quickly and served rare to medium. Resting allows the juices to settle back into the meat and become evenly distributed so that there is a rosiness throughout.

To add extra flavour to the venison for a casserole, marinate it first in an oil and wine mixture; the liquid it then cooks in will help to keep it moist.

Healthy option

Even though venison is a red meat, it is lower in fat than chicken. Farmed venison is a good alternative to beef for people watching their fat intake. It is sold in joints, steaks, minced, and made into sausages.

GIN AND JUNIPER

I know juniper berries go well with venison, but I can't get hold of any. Is there anything else that I can use in their place?

Nothing will really replace the taste of juniper berries, but try using a couple of tablespoons of gin in the recipe instead. Gin is flavoured with juniper and will give something of the right, slightly bitter, pungent taste. In the recipe below, the meat is flavoured with redcurrants which, like juniper, have a special affinity with roast venison. Blackberries are also a good match.

Roast venison

SERVES: **6-8**
PREPARATION TIME: **5 minutes**
COOKING TIME: **1-1¾ hours**

A saddle, haunch or leg of venison
Large piece of crackling, pork back fat or 250 g streaky bacon
Black pepper and salt
1 tablespoon plain flour
600 ml game stock
2 tablespoons redcurrant jelly

1 Preheat the oven to 190°C. Weigh the venison and allow 30 minutes per kg if the joint is large and 20 minutes per kg if the joint is under 2 kg.
2 Place the crackling or back fat over the top of the meat, or place the strips of bacon, overlapping, on top of it. Season the joint with black pepper and roast for the calculated time, basting frequently. The meat should still be pink when cooked.
3 Remove the barding and allow the venison joint to rest in a warm place for 15 minutes before carving.
4 Meanwhile, pour off most of the fat from the pan, sprinkle in the flour and cook for a minute. Whisk in the stock, redcurrant jelly, and the salt and pepper. Bring to the boil and simmer for 15 minutes. Taste and season the gravy again if necessary, then strain it into a sauceboat.
5 Carve the venison thinly and, for a traditional meal, serve it with roast potatoes, red cabbage, chestnuts, gravy and redcurrant jelly.

Vinegar

MULTIPLE CHOICE

If a recipe just states vinegar, what kind should I use?

If the recipe simply states vinegar, look at the other ingredients in the dish before making your selection.

- BALSAMIC VINEGAR has a sweet-sour taste good with meat, salads or sprinkled on fresh strawberries.
- CIDER VINEGAR has a mild, slightly sweet flavour and can be used in fruit pickles and pork dishes.
- MALT VINEGAR, which is made from malted barley, is too strong to flavour salads but tastes good when served with fish and chips or used to make chutneys and pickles.
- SHERRY VINEGAR has a rich flavour that works well in meat casseroles, tomato soups such as gazpacho, and dressings for green salads.
- WHITE WINE VINEGAR is the best choice for mayonnaise and classic butter sauces. Both white and red wine vinegars are indispensable for salad dressings and marinades.
- FRUIT-FLAVOURED VINEGARS, such as the recipe below which contains summer berries, can be used on their own in fruit salads or mixed with oil to make a vinaigrette to serve with chicken, salad or vegetables such as asparagus.

The attractive colour and sweet flavour of this fruit vinegar is easily created by macerating bright summer berries in cider or white wine vinegar for two weeks.

Summer fruit vinegar

MAKES: *about 750 ml*
PREPARATION TIME: *15 minutes, plus 1–2 weeks infusing*
COOKING TIME: *10 minutes*

---

500 g fresh berries, such as raspberries, redcurrants and blackcurrants
600 ml cider vinegar or white wine vinegar
250 g (1 cup) caster sugar, or more

---

1 Pick over the berries then lightly crush them in a large bowl with the back of a wooden spoon to release some of their juices.
2 Pack the fruit into a sterilised jar (see *Chutney*), then add the vinegar.

3 Seal the jar and shake well. Keep in a cool, dark place for 1–2 weeks, shaking the jar occasionally.
4 Strain the fruit-flavoured vinegar through muslin, or a paper coffee filter, into a small saucepan and add about 250 g (1 cup) of the sugar (more if you like) for each 600 ml of fruit vinegar. Simmer the vinegar for 10 minutes, then leave until cold.
5 Decant the flavoured vinegar into a sterilised bottle and seal it with a plastic or plastic-coated cork or a glass stopper (do not use a metal stopper as the vinegar will corrode it). The vinegar is now ready to use.
VARIATIONS
Use grapes or plums in place of the red summer fruits.

ENDLESS VARIATIONS

Can I make herb-flavoured vinegars at home?

Vinegars flavoured with herbs are easy to make at home and will add piquancy to casseroles, dressings, marinades, sauces and soups.

Choose a cider, sherry or wine vinegar, and marry it with either one herb or several. When combining flavours, consider the strength of each: tarragon, for example, might well be overpowered by chillies but can be enhanced with a few green peppercorns or some garlic.

The herbs must be fresh and picked before they flower. Leave them to macerate for two weeks then remove from the vinegar: they will deteriorate if left too long. Herb-flavoured vinegars can be stored for up to a year, providing they are kept in a cool, dark place. This will help to preserve the flavour and prevent fermentation.

The following recipe can be used with fried meat, sprinkled over roast vegetables or added to a salad of bacon or chicken livers.

Chilli sherry vinegar

MAKES: *about 375 ml*
PREPARATION TIME: *5-10 minutes, plus 2 weeks infusing*
COOKING TIME: *none*

1 fresh green chilli, blanched and chopped
1 fresh red chilli, blanched and chopped
½ teaspoon mixed peppercorns
375 ml sherry vinegar

1 Put the chillies and peppercorns inside a sterilised jar. Pour in the vinegar. Seal the jar and shake well. Keep in a cool, dark place for two weeks, shaking the jar occasionally.
2 Strain the chilli-flavoured vinegar through muslin or a paper coffee filter into a sterilised bottle. Seal at once with a vinegarproof top.

Vine Leaves

LEAFY WRAPPING

How do I prepare vine leaves?

Vine leaves that are preserved in brine need only be rinsed in cold water before being used. They are available from Greek and Middle Eastern food shops as well as some delicatessens and supermarkets.

If you have fresh vine leaves, cut the stems off close to each leaf, pack the leaves into a pan, pour boiling water over them and bring to the boil. Drain immediately into a colander and run them under the cold tap. This makes them pliable enough to wrap up a filling such as the savoury mixture used in the following recipe.

Bring a touch of the Mediterranean to your meal table with these rolls made of burghul, currants, pine nuts and spices wrapped in tender vine leaves.

Burghul-stuffed vine leaves

MAKES: *16 parcels*
PREPARATION TIME: *30 minutes plus 30 minutes soaking*
COOKING TIME: *30-40 minutes*

FOR THE FILLING
125 g (¾ cup) burghul
30 g butter
1 medium onion, finely chopped
2 cloves garlic, crushed
1 teaspoon each ground coriander, cumin and cinnamon
30 g (2 tablespoons) currants
25 g (2 tablespoons) pine nuts, toasted
Salt and black pepper
1 tablespoon each freshly chopped coriander and mint

The vine leaves are wrapped around a spicy burghul mixture.

FOR THE ROLLS
16 large vine leaves in brine or prepared fresh leaves
300 ml vegetable stock

1 Place the burghul in a bowl and cover with plenty of cold water. Soak for 30 minutes, then strain.
2 Preheat the oven to 190°C.
3 Heat the butter in a frying pan and cook the onion and garlic with the ground spices for 5 minutes. Add the strained burghul and fry for 1 minute. Remove the pan from the heat and add the currants, pine nuts, salt, black pepper and chopped coriander and mint.
4 Drain the brine from the vine leaves, then rinse well and pat dry.
5 Place 1 tablespoon of burghul mixture in the centre of each leaf and roll it up, folding in the sides to form neat rolls. If you like, secure each one with a toothpick.
6 Place the stuffed rolls in a small shallow baking dish to fit closely together. Pour over the stock, cover with foil and bake for 30-40 minutes until all the liquid has been absorbed. Remove from the oven, allow to cool slightly and serve the stuffed vine leaves warm with Greek-style yoghurt or a fresh tomato sauce.

Watercress

GREEN GLORIOUS GREEN

How can I keep watercress bright green even when it is in soup?

It's simple – by not overcooking it. The following recipe is for one of the most useful all-purpose soups because it is elegant enough for a dinner party but quick to prepare for a hungry family. It does not have to be served hot and does not require stock. The watercress is chopped and added to the warm potato soup base and therefore retains all of its brilliant colour and fresh taste.

Watercress soup

SERVES: *4-6*
PREPARATION TIME: *10 minutes*
COOKING TIME: *15-20 minutes (plus several hours cooling and chilling time to serve cold)*

750 g floury potatoes, peeled
250 g small, well-flavoured waxy
  potatoes such as Fir, washed
  but not peeled
Salt and black pepper
2 cloves garlic
3 spring onions, finely chopped
150 g watercress, chopped
To garnish: 2 sun-dried tomatoes,
  chopped (optional) and
  4 tablespoons virgin olive oil

1 Slice the floury potatoes into evenly sized pieces slightly smaller than the waxy ones. In separate saucepans, bring the potatoes to the boil with 600 ml water in each pan. Add 1 teaspoon salt and the garlic to the floury potatoes. Cover and cook at a simmer.

2 When the waxy potatoes are just soft, drain their cooking liquid into the pan with the floury potatoes and set the waxy ones aside. When the floury potatoes are soft, mash them smoothly into the cooking liquid.

3 When the waxy potatoes are cool enough to handle, peel and chop them into fine dice and return them to the soup with the spring onions and watercress. Stir, taste and season with salt and pepper.

4 To serve, cool and chill the soup, or reheat it to just below boiling point. Serve the soup garnished with a scattering of chopped sun-dried tomatoes and a zigzag of olive oil.

Red sun-dried tomatoes contrast with bright green chopped watercress in this favourite soup, updated by a swirl of olive oil.

RICH SOURCE OF IRON

Is watercress really rich in iron?

It is. With 2.2 mg of iron per 100 g, raw watercress certainly makes it into the top league of healthy iron-rich vegetables. Only raw parsley, mint and lentils have more iron, and spinach has less.

Watercress is only really at its best when the leaves are absolutely fresh and vivid dark green, so avoid any with traces of yellowing. To keep watercress fresh, store it with the leaves submerged in a bowl of cold water – easier if you buy it in a bunch, not loose.

DO NOT OVERCOOK

Can you cook watercress?

Yes, but only briefly. Watercress is often wilted into hot sauces and soups, to which it adds its lively green bite. Wilting occurs in an instant when watercress comes into contact with hot liquid. It does not need any more cooking than this.

Watercress is especially useful for combining with spinach or in potato-thickened soups, which are equally good served hot or chilled (see recipe, left). Chopped watercress stirred into hot butter and seasoned with salt, pepper and lemon juice makes a simple sauce for fish and looks equally beautiful with the white flesh of sea fish or the coral pink of salmon and trout. The sharpness of chopped watercress is also very welcome when stirred into purées of winter root vegetables, particularly swede. And it is excellent in soufflés, such as those flavoured with cheese.

STRONGER FLAVOUR

Is watercress the same as the cress often used for sandwiches?

No, several different plants with a peppery taste are called cress. The larger dark green leaves of watercress have a stronger flavour and are good for sandwiches but the tiny garden or pepper cress, sometimes combined with hot mustard seedlings, is more often used.

STRIKING COLOURS

I usually serve watercress in a bowl on its own. Can you suggest a more exciting way to use it?

Watercress and other ingredients with bite make good combinations; try walnuts, onions and strong cheeses, particularly blue vein cheese. In the following salad recipe the dark green watercress makes a vibrant contrast against the scarlet of the watermelon and the salty white feta cheese.

Watercress, watermelon and feta cheese salad

SERVES: 4-6
PREPARATION TIME: 10 minutes
COOKING TIME: none

1 kg watermelon
Black pepper
4 tablespoons olive oil
1 tablespoon lemon juice
75 g watercress, washed and trimmed
150 g feta cheese, roughly chopped

1 Cut the watermelon into four or five slices, then cut the flesh from the rind and slice it into fairly thin pieces, removing as many seeds as you can and reserving any juice. Spread the watermelon slices on a flat serving dish, pour over the juice and season liberally with coarsely ground black pepper.
2 Beat the oil and the lemon juice together until they are creamy. Set aside 3 tablespoons of the mixture.
3 Lightly toss the watercress in the dressing until the leaves are shiny. Scatter the dressed watercress over the watermelon and top with the cheese. Grind on some more black pepper then trickle the reserved dressing over the finished salad.
VARIATIONS
For a winter salad, layer watercress on top of thinly sliced oranges and garnish with very thin rings of raw red onion and a few black olives. Dust the salad with coarse sea salt if the olives are not too salty. Or, make this salad with other types of ripe melon in season, such as rockmelon or honeydew melon.

Wheat

HEART OF WHEAT

I hear that wheatgerm is very good for you. How can I use it?

Wheatgerm is the heart of a grain of wheat with all the nutrients of the grain intact. It is available natural or toasted, which gives it an even nuttier flavour. Its main use in the kitchen is as a breakfast cereal, adding a crunchy bite to muesli or sprinkled over fresh fruit and yoghurt. It can also be mixed into crumble toppings, or sprinkled over bread dough.

HEAVY GOODNESS

Wholemeal breads tend to be heavy and wholemeal pastries are often stodgy. Why is this?

Wholemeal breads and pastries are made using 100 per cent wholemeal wheat flour, which is milled from the whole grain including the outer husks. This means that it contains more nutrients than the processed, dehusked white flours, but it also means that wholemeal flour needs to absorb more liquid than white flour to soften the ground husk. This often results in doughs or pastries that are heavier, though they are wholesome and nutritious with a good flavour. To avoid this heaviness, your recipe needs to be adjusted accordingly.

Wholemeal pastry is best used as a base for flan cases rather than a top crust, for it does not have the light, short or flaky texture of white flour pastry. To compensate for this, roll wholemeal pastry thinner than pastry made with white flour, and always prebake or bake blind if making a base or pastry case.

For lighter breads and pastries you can use half wholemeal and half white flour. This results in a less heavy-textured bread, like the one on page 380, which has added crunch from wheat berries, which are whole husked grains of wheat also called wheat kernels.

Wholemeal loaf with wheat berries

MAKES: *2 small loaves*
PREPARATION TIME: *1½ hours, plus overnight soaking*
COOKING TIME: *1 hour 20 minutes*

---

30 g (2 tablespoons) wheat berries, soaked overnight in cold water
15 g fresh yeast, or 2 teaspoons dried yeast plus 1 teaspoon sugar, or 2 x 10 g sachets instant rapid-rise yeast
300 ml lukewarm water
375 g (3 cups) wholemeal flour
185 g (1½ cups) strong white flour, plus extra for dusting
2 teaspoons salt
Oil for greasing

---

1 Drain the soaked berries and rinse them well. Put them in a saucepan and cover with plenty of cold water. Bring to the boil, cover and simmer for 40–50 minutes until the berries are tender. Drain and immediately refresh under cold water. Dry them thoroughly in a clean tea towel.

Rinsing the hot, softened wheat berries in a sieve under cold running water immediately stops the cooking process.

2 Dissolve the fresh or dried yeast in half the water with the sugar, or add rapid-rise yeast directly to the flour. Combine the two flours and salt in a large bowl, make a well in the middle and work in the yeast mixture and the remaining warm water to form a soft dough.
3 Turn out and knead on a lightly floured surface for 8–10 minutes until the dough is very smooth and elastic, then knead in the wheat berries. Transfer to a lightly oiled bowl, cover with plastic wrap and set aside in a warm place for about 45 minutes or until doubled in size.

4 Preheat the oven to 230°C. Grease two 500 g loaf tins with the oil.
5 Punch down the dough, knead it again briefly and divide it in half. Shape each half and put into the prepared tins. Loosely cover the tins with plastic wrap and leave to rise until the dough almost reaches the tops of the tins, about 20 minutes.
6 Remove the plastic wrap and bake the loaves for 15 minutes.
7 Lower the oven to 200°C and bake for 10 minutes more or until risen and golden. Take one of the loaves out of the tin and tap the base gently with your hand: it should sound hollow. If not, put it back in the tin and return to the oven for a few more minutes. Then cool the loaves on a wire rack.

Wine

SAFE COOLING TIME

How long is it safe to leave white or sparkling wine in the freezer?

Not much longer than the 45 minutes it takes to chill it, without damaging the taste of the wine. Set a timer or you may very well end up with an exploded bottle (liquid expands as it freezes).

White wines taste fresher at lower temperatures, and in the case of sparkling wines, chilling eases opening, prevents flying corks and reduces the chance of the wine frothing over. It is better to err on the cooler side when chilling white and sparkling wine, because once it is in the glass and held in the hand, it will warm up fairly rapidly.

WARMING RED

Is there a quick way to warm red wine to the temperature it needs to be for drinking?

Not all red wine needs to be at the temperature of a modern room, which is considerably warmer than the ambient temperature of rooms before the arrival of household heating. In any case, warming is only really suitable for the more tannic and full-bodied red wines. The majority of wines for everyday drinking may be served cooler. And a light, fruity red wine may be served slightly chilled

Wine served cooler than you like it needs only to be poured into the glass and the bowl cupped in your hands for a minute or two to warm the contents a few degrees.

WAKE UP THE PALATE

Can I serve wine as an apéritif?

Apéritifs set the palate tingling, and this is best achieved by a cool glass of something bubbly. It need not be Champagne but could be one of the many sparkling wines.

There are a number of softer, more exotically fruity sparkling wines produced today in Australia. These make delicious apéritifs when mixed with fresh fruit juices such as mango, orange or peach, or with liqueurs such as Cointreau and crème de cassis.

For those who prefer still wine, look for whites with a light fruitiness and fresh acidity. It is unwise to serve a heavily oaked wine as an apéritif. Choose instead one of the newer crisp wines made in a light, fresh style from grapes such as slightly spicy pinot or aromatic gewürztraminer or muscat.

Fine rieslings make good apéritifs thanks to their fruitiness, fresh acidity and moderate sweetness.

Vermouth and similar herby fortified wines are somewhat out of fashion, but a glass of tangy Fino or dry sherry can whet the appetite and also go surprisingly well with first courses such as seafood or soup. For some elegant winter predinner warming, choose the drier versions of the darker, nuttier Amontillado and Oloroso sherries, which are a real treat.

NEW TRADITION

What does it mean when a label says 'méthode traditionelle'?

This is one of the new terms being used to describe the best method of making sparkling wine, in which the wine undergoes a secondary fermentation in the bottle to create the bubbles.

Until 1994 the term 'méthode champenoise' was widely used for this process, but this can now only be applied to Champagne. Good value alternatives to Champagne are labelled 'traditional method', 'classic method' and 'fermented in this bottle'.

SILVER STOPPER

Is it true that a silver teaspoon in the neck of an open champagne bottle will keep it from going flat?

There is no evidence to support this idea. Instead use a stopper specially designed for sparkling wine. They are widely available, are inexpensive and also make good presents for champagne lovers.

DO NOT RUN OUT

How much wine should I allow per person for a buffet lunch? And how much for a dinner party?

It is more relaxing to know that you have catered for all your guests to drink as much as they want than to run out of wine. But that need not mean that you waste money or your wine. Some retailers operate a sale or return policy on unopened bottles, and any unfinished open wine bottles can be restoppered and drunk within a couple of days.

In these health-conscious days, fewer glasses of wine will be consumed at a buffet luncheon than 20 years ago, but you should allow two to four glasses per person (a 750 ml bottle will fill five to six good-sized glasses). The nature of the menu generally served at a buffet lunch means that far more white wine will be consumed than red; work on the ratio of 2:1. Lower to mid range priced wines served for parties do not need to breathe, so they can be opened as required.

Dinner party wine quantities are easier to predict as wines may be selected to match the courses. Allow a total of four glasses (red or white) for each guest.

ENTERTAINING WINES

I never know what wines to serve at a dinner party. Can you give me some easy rules of thumb?

There are some basic precepts: first, begin with the lighter styles of wine and move onto those with more body. This usually means a light white or red with the starter and a heavier white or red (possibly one that has been oak-aged) to accompany the main course. Dry wines should be drunk before sweet, so stay with drier wines with the cheese and before the dessert, unless you intend to open a bottle of port with the cheese, in which case it should follow the dessert. But many people prefer cheese after the dessert even when they are not going to drink port with it.

A final dessert course can be accompanied by a dessert wine, such as a botrytis-affected riesling or semillon. Always aim for a wine that is sweeter than the dessert, otherwise the wine will appear thin and tart. This may appear an extravagance, but many sweet wines are available in half bottles. Many late harvest muscats and rieslings are rich enough to be dessert wines.

SHOP ASSISTANCE

The selection of wines on sale is bewildering. Where do I start?

First decide on your budget and ask the advice of a wine merchant, telling him or her the occasion for which you want the wine and the food that you will be eating with it. Many merchants have an extensive knowledge of wine. Alternatively, read the labels and any shelf-edge ticketing: retailers devote a lot of time putting helpful information across to the wine consumer.

The wine columns of newspapers and magazines are also a good source of suggestions, so read and experiment. When you find a wine you enjoy, make a note of it. It is all too easy to forget the name on your next visit to the bottle shop. A wine's character is derived mainly

HOW TO OPEN A BOTTLE OF CHAMPAGNE

All sparkling wines are under a great deal of pressure in the bottle, so when opening them you should do it correctly and with great care.

1 Start by chilling the bottle. This not only makes the wine more refreshing but also eases opening and prevents it from frothing over.

The most elegant method is to immerse the bottle in a silver bucket of ice and water for 20 minutes or so. Alternatively, chill it for 45 minutes, but no longer, in the freezer or for up to 2 hours in the refrigerator.

2 Remove the foil at the mouth of the bottle. Untwist and loosen the attachment of the wire muzzle and slip the muzzle off, all the time covering the end of the cork with your thumb to guard against the possibility of it suddenly flying out.

3 Hold the bottle securely at an angle, pointing it away from yourself and others, and from any fragile objects nearby. Grip the cork firmly, hold it still and then twist the bottle. Ease out the cork, allowing a controlled release of pressure.

Do not fight a sudden release of the pressure. As long as you have a firm grip of the cork, the bottle can be opened safely. By holding the bottle at an angle, with a dry cloth for a better grip, any frothing over should be limited. If it froths, dip a finger down the neck of the bottle and the bubbles will subside.

UNDERSTANDING A WINE LABEL

While traditional European wines are labelled after the region they come from, Australian wines are generally known by the grape variety they are made from.

1 The producer's name.
2 The year in which the wine was made.
3 The grape variety used.
4 The region where the grapes were grown and the wine was made.
5 The company that bottled the wine.
6 The country of origin.
7 The quantity of wine in the bottle.
8 The alcoholic strength, shown as a percentage of the total contents.
9 Additives in the wine.
10 Number of standard drinks in the bottle.
11 Further information about the wine, including show awards, and the winemaker's suggestions.

or country of production, the name and address of the bottler or producer, as well as the volume of wine in the bottle and its alcoholic content (see panel, left). Non-mandatory information may be given to help the consumer choose and this could include awards won, or the method of production – for example, if the wine has been fermented in the barrel, or aged in oak barrels to give a certain flavour.

WINE AND FISH

People say that you can't drink red wine with fish. Is this true?

It depends on both the fish and the wine. Few people would consider a full-bodied shiraz the ideal partner for a delicate dish of flounder or whiting. In fact, for most of us the tannin in the red wine reacts with the fish on the palate to create a metallic taste. But some lighter style red wines, such as those made from pinot noir grapes, are lower in tannin and these are a much more pleasing match for fish.

In broad terms, it is safest to stick to the old maxim of red wines with red meats and white wines with white meat and fish, but pay careful attention to the weight and intensity of the flavours of the food to be served, as well as to the levels of acidity and sweetness in the sauces. Big flavoured fish dishes need hearty, robust white wines. Those with a high level of acidity or any degree of sweetness, need a wine with a slightly sweet edge, if the wine is not to appear thin and weak in contrast.

DEEP BREATHING

Is it really necessary to open wine and let it breathe?

Not all wines need time to breathe: older red wines will deteriorate rapidly once they are exposed to the air, while prolonged exposure to air causes all wine to decline.

But allowing the wine to breathe can help to release the bouquet and taste of the wine in readiness for drinking: young tannic reds will

from the grape variety or varieties from which it is made. Australian winemakers have made choosing wine easier for the consumer by labelling wines according to grape variety, such as chardonnay, shiraz, cabernet sauvignon and so on. This practice has now been adopted in some of the other traditional winemaking countries. If you discover that you like the taste of a Hunter

wine made with the verdhello grape you will probably also enjoy a Western Australian verdhello.

WHAT IS ON THE LABEL

What do wine labels mean?

The labels on the front, and sometimes the back, of a bottle give authenticity and provide information, such as the region become softer and fruitier if they are given some aeration.

Wine begins to breathe as soon as you pull the cork, although this has only a little effect because the surface area of wine exposed to the air is so small. The best method of aerating the wine is to pour it from the bottle into a decanter.

But most soft red wines require little time to breathe. And it is not usually necessary to allow white wines to breathe because their bouquet opens out quite quickly once the wine has been poured into the glass.

VEGETARIAN PARTNERS

Are there any wines that go well with vegetarian meals?

In partnering wine with vegetarian food, try to match the strength and taste of the wine to the flavour of the dish, paying attention to the sweetness and acidity. Many vegetables, such as carrots, have a degree of sweetness, and could be matched with slightly off-dry styles such as chenin blanc. Tomatoes have a high level of acidity and so could take a cool-climate white such as a riesling.

For meals with a Mediterranean flavour, softer red wines such as Chianti, or a local cabernet merlot blend, are appropriate. A rich gewürztraminer or deep-flavoured shiraz go well with spicy food.

SORTING OUT STORAGE

How should I store my wines if I don't have a cellar?

The two greatest enemies of wine are heat and light. The ideal temperature range for a cellar is 10–15°C with no wild fluctuations. The best option is usually a dark cupboard under stairs, or a south-facing wall with a cover over the wine to keep out the light. Bottles with corks should be stored horizontally to keep corks moist. Dry corks shrink and let air in and wine out, both detrimental to the wine.

If you have invested seriously in wines, you should rent cellar space.

SAFE KEEPING

It goes against my nature to waste anything, but I am uncertain about leftover wine. How long will a bottle keep once it has been opened?

Mature wines decline rapidly once their corks have been drawn and it is best to drink and enjoy them immediately. But with most leftover wine, there is no harm in just replacing the cork as long as at least half the wine remains – any less and there will be too much air in the bottle, which will spoil the flavour. The more air in the bottle, the faster the wine will deteriorate.

Keep the recorked bottle in the refrigerator: heavy red wines will keep for three or four days; lighter reds and white wine will keep for one or two days, but they should be removed from the refrigerator an hour before you drink what is left.

There are also gadgets on the market that can extend the life of an opened bottle up to a week. Some work by sucking out the air and creating a partial vacuum in the bottle. Wine preserved by any method (including just replacing the cork in the bottle) is perfectly acceptable for use in cooking. However, if the wine smells like vinegar, throw it away. If you would not want to drink it, then you should not cook with it either.

FINE COOKING WINE

How much does the quality of wine matter when I cook with it?

The quality of the wine used in cooking matters more in dishes such as fruit salad, where the wine is not heated, than in dishes that require reducing or simmering. But do not be tempted to use any wine that is faulty or has any off-flavours as cooking will not eradicate them.

When wine is used in cooking, the alcohol evaporates as the wine is heated but the flavour intensifies, so choose enjoyable wines for cooking. In most cases you will need a wine that is fairly robust but not too expensive.

USING SHERRY AND PORT

Can I use our half-empty bottles of fortified wines such as sherry and port in cooking?

Sherry and port can be used to pep up casseroles, gravies, sauces and soups, and to marinate meats and fish. Sherry is a good substitute for rice wine in Asian cooking, and you can add it to fruit cakes, custards and sweet sauces. Port can replace the water when making a syrup to poach fresh fruit.

THE BEST CHOICES

How can I tell which sort of wine is best to use in recipes?

You will get a better result if you match the wine to the ingredients in the dish – this is particularly true when combining red wines and delicately flavoured foods such as fish or poultry. To avoid a coarse flavour, choose lighter red wines that are not too oaky in character. For coq au vin a red wine such as a cabernet sauvignon is preferable to a shiraz. Choose a pinot for red wine sauces to serve with salmon.

Be selective, too, when matching fish with white wines. Delicate fish such as sole and trout need white wines with lower acidity, such as a chardonnay.

When you are cooking with fortified wines such as port and sherry, do not reduce the wines early during cooking because the taste will be too concentrated. Instead, add the wine at the end of cooking, heating it just enough to burn off the alcohol; you will use less and the flavour will not be too strong.

In the case of enclosed dishes such as pies, the alcohol should be evaporated while making the filling – do not expect that it will burn off while the dish is in the oven – or the aromas will be overpowering when the pastry is cut open.

If you are using gelatine, for example to make a sauternes jelly, heat the wine to burn off the alcohol before you add the gelatine to the liquid as alcohol will reduce the gelatine's setting power.

For the Cheese Fondue (below) choose a dry white wine such as a sauvignon blanc.

Cheese fondue

SERVES: 6-8
PREPARATION TIME: 30 minutes
COOKING TIME: 20 minutes

2 cloves garlic, halved
500 ml dry white wine
Freshly grated nutmeg
Black pepper
200 g each Cheddar, Emmental and Gruyère cheese, coarsely grated
1 tablespoon cornflour
3 tablespoons extra wine or water
3 tablespoons kirsch, optional
To serve: 2 French loaves, cut into 2.5 cm cubes

1 Rub the garlic around the inside of the cooking dish then place inside. Pour in the wine and heat until it is warm but not hot. Discard the garlic, then season the wine to taste with nutmeg and black pepper.
2 Add the cheese to the pan and stir over a medium heat until it melts. Increase the heat and stir until the mixture begins to bubble slightly.
3 Mix the cornflour with the extra wine or water then stir it into the cheese mixture and keep stirring until it is smooth, well blended and bubbling, but still has a thin milky layer of liquid on the top. Stir in the kirsch.
4 Place the fondue dish over a spirit or candle burner and serve at the table with the bread. To eat fondue, each diner spears a cube of bread (or a boiled potato) onto their fork then dips it into the fondue dish to coat it with the thick, hot mixture.

Wok

QUALITY COUNTS

Is one kind of wok better than another? Do different types of hotplates require different woks?

Cast-iron woks are generally the best as they conduct heat more evenly and quickly than any other material, but they do need more careful treatment and seasoning with oil and salt (see *Frying*).

Traditional woks are round-bottomed and need to sit properly over the heat without wobbling. As most gas rings are set with metal prongs, these provide a steadier base than electric rings set flush with the surface. But you can now buy slightly flat-bottomed woks that can be used on any stove, and also round metal wok-stands that hold woks steady above the rings of both gas and electric hotplates.

MASTERING THE ACTION

Is there a knack to using a wok?

Yes, what is most important is the stirring action: you should use your wrist to scoop, flip and push the food continuously. A wok ladle has a curved end that is designed to get right to the bottom of the wok so that it is easy to flip the food over when stir-frying. Whether you use a wok ladle or a wooden spatula, every bit of food in the wok must be moved about constantly, over the entire surface of the wok. Most foods need no more than 5 minutes cooking, less with intense heat.

Using a wok ladle to stir-fry makes it easier to scoop and move the food continuously – an essential technique.

STIR-FRY SAUCES

Stir-fried vegetables sometimes need a sauce to flavour them. Can I make one myself?

Yes, very easily. The basic sauce for stir-frying is simply a blend of seasonings: salt or soy sauce, pepper and a little sesame oil. You can also add oyster sauce, sherry, Chinese wine or any of the Chinese bottled sauces such as black or yellow bean, and a selection of fresh flavouring ingredients such as galangal, ginger, lemon grass and fish sauce, as in the recipe below for stir-fried vegetables. Soy and fish sauces are used in Asian cooking instead of salt so if you use them, do not add any extra salt.

Mushroom, snow pea and baby corn stir-fry

SERVES: 4
PREPARATION TIME: 10 minutes
COOKING TIME: 8 minutes

6 large mushrooms, sliced
24 large snow peas, topped and tailed
12 baby corn cobs, left whole or sliced in two if large
2 tablespoons vegetable oil
1 clove garlic, crushed
1 tablespoon sesame oil
1 tablespoon fish sauce
100 ml water
2 teaspoons cornflour, blended smoothly with 1 tablespoon water
2 tablespoons sherry or Chinese rice wine

1 Bring a small pot of water to the boil and blanch the mushrooms, snow peas and corn cobs separately for a minute each. Drain and rinse them under the cold tap.
2 Heat the vegetable oil in the wok and fry the garlic for about a minute until it is brown. Add the blanched vegetables and stir-fry for a minute.
3 Add the sesame oil, the fish sauce and the water and stir vigorously as the liquid comes to the boil.
4 Add the cornflour mixture and the sherry or wine to the wok and continue stirring for a minute. When the sauce has thickened, transfer the vegetables to a plate and serve.

KEEPING COLOURS FRESH

Is there a way to stir-fry fresh green vegetables without them losing colour?

Yes, you can stop green vegetables from turning a dingy colour by first blanching green vegetables in boiling water for a few seconds and

A protective covering of green cabbage leaves keeps these wok-steamed salmon steaks beautifully moist and tender.

then running them under a cold tap. This will retain the green and as the vegetables have been slightly cooked, it will also speed up the stir-frying time, which is another excellent way to keep green vegetables fresh and bright in colour.

NEVER BURNING

All my stir-fry recipes call for very hot oil. How do I stop the oil burning in a wok when I need to cook at a high temperature?

As soon as the oil begins to smoke, the prepared food should be put in and stirred rapidly.

A wok is designed to cope with high temperatures. You'll find that nothing will burn if your stir-frying action is so vigorous and continuous that no morsel of food comes in contact with the hot wok base and the hot oil for more than a few seconds at a time.

VERSATILE WOK

Can I use my wok for anything other than stir-frying?

The wok is an extremely versatile cooking utensil. It can be used for braising, boiling and steaming as well as for stir-frying.

With a domed lid , it can be used to braise a whole chicken, duck, or a large joint of meat.

The wok is also especially effective for steaming. Put a pair of bamboo chopsticks across the bottom of the wok. Put the food in a deep plate and rest the plate on top of the chopsticks. Add water up to a level just above the chopsticks. Cover with a lid that fits over the wok without pressing down on the food to allow the steam to circulate and cook the food gently. In the recipe for Steamed Salmon Steaks on the right, cabbage leaves cover the fish to prevent it drying out.

Steamed salmon steaks

SERVES: *2*
PREPARATION TIME: *8 minutes*
COOKING TIME: *20-25 minutes*

---

2 salmon steaks, 200 g each
1 tablespoon finely shredded ginger
1 tablespoon light soy sauce
1 tablespoon sesame oil
½ teaspoon black pepper
1 tomato, quartered
2 large cabbage leaves

---

1 Place the salmon steaks well apart on a deep plate. Top with the ginger, soy sauce, sesame oil and the pepper and place the tomatoes on the side.
2 Loosely cover the salmon and its topping with the cabbage leaves.
3 Place a set of chopsticks in the wok then place the plate on top. Add water to the wok to a level no higher than the base of the plate; cover and steam over a high heat for 20-25 minutes, or until cooked.

Yoghurt

ALIVE AND ACTIVE

What does 'live' yoghurt mean?

With the exception of long-life yoghurt, all yoghurts contain active but friendly bacteria and are therefore 'live'. Yoghurt is a cultured product, produced by fermenting milk with bacteria. Several kinds of bacteria can be used, but two of the most common are *Lactobacillus bulgaricus* and *Streptococcus thermophilus*.

To make yoghurt, the milk is first heated to destroy any unwanted micro-organisms, then a yoghurt starter containing the chosen bacteria is added to set and sour the milk. This produces a refreshing, slightly acidic flavour. The bacteria remain active even while the yoghurt is refrigerated, so the level of acidity gradually increases. This limits the storage life of yoghurt, which will eventually come to taste unpleasantly tart.

DIFFERENT CULTURE

What are bio yoghurts? Is it possible to make them at home, and are they more nutritious than ordinary yoghurts?

Bio or BA yoghurt is made with different live cultures, called *bifidus* and *acidophilus*. It is often claimed that these particular bacteria aid digestion by supplementing the body's natural flora. When these bacteria are used as the starter for your own yoghurt they will reproduce and make bio yoghurt. Bio yoghurt is not as sharp as ordinary yoghurt, and has a milder, creamier flavour. All yoghurts are easier to digest than plain milk, because of the action of the bacteria, and they are a good source of calcium and phosphorus, which are essential for strong teeth and bones. Yoghurt is also said to be good for maintaining the general health of the skin and the digestive system, and yoghurts that have soluble fibre added to them may help to lower the level of cholesterol in the blood.

EASY ECONOMY

I spend a lot of money at the supermarket on fresh yoghurt; can I make my own?

It is easy and economical to make yoghurt at home. The exact flavour and texture will depend on the type of yoghurt used as the starter, the fat content of the milk (the higher the fat content, the thicker the yoghurt) and the time the yoghurt takes to thicken.

Practically any kind of milk can be used to make yoghurt: whole, reduced-fat, pasteurised, sterilised, UHT, dried or evaporated. But fresh commercial yoghurt must be used as the starter for each new batch. Homemade yoghurt should not be used as there is no way of knowing if it may have become contaminated with micro-organisms that would interfere with the setting of the new batch.

YOGHURT MAKERS

Do I need any special equipment to make yoghurt at home?

Yoghurt can be made in a vacuum flask or an electric yoghurt maker. The latter maintains a constant temperature providing ideal conditions for making yoghurt, and the finished product tends to be more consistent in texture. A yoghurt thermometer, to test the temperature of the milk as it is heated, is also useful.

But as the recipe above right shows, it is easy to make delicious, economical yoghurt at home using only an ordinary vacuum flask.

Homemade natural yoghurt

MAKES: 600 ml
PREPARATION TIME: 5 minutes, plus 24 hours standing time and 6 hours chilling time
COOKING TIME: 5 minutes

---

600 ml milk
1 tablespoon natural yoghurt

---

1 Pour boiling water into a vacuum flask to sterilise and warm it.
2 Blend 2 tablespoons of the milk with the yoghurt and set it aside.
3 Pour the remaining milk into a saucepan and heat it until it is just about to boil. Remove the saucepan from the heat and set it aside until the milk has cooled to 45°C. Alternatively, to test it without using a yoghurt thermometer, the milk is ready for the next step when you can hold your finger in it comfortably while you count up to ten.
4 When the milk is ready, stir in the blended yoghurt starter and whisk them together lightly.
5 Empty the water out of the flask, pour in the milk mixture, seal and leave to stand for 24 hours in a warm place such as an airing cupboard. Do not be tempted to move the flask during this period of incubation as the yoghurt will separate and be inedible if it is disturbed.
6 Pour the yoghurt into a bowl and whisk until smooth. Cover and chill for at least 6 hours until thickened.
VARIATION
If you are using sterilised, UHT, dried or evaporated milk instead of whole milk, simply heat the milk to 45°C and then stir in the fresh starter before proceeding as above.

FREEZE IT FOR LATER

Can I freeze yoghurt?

Full-fat yoghurts generally freeze better than lower-fat ones, although they will separate when thawed. All yoghurt should be defrosted slowly and given a good whisk before being used. Plain yoghurt can be kept frozen for up to two months. Yoghurt with added fruit, honey or flavouring freezes slightly better than the plain variety, and can be kept frozen for up to three months in the sealed carton it came in. Homemade flavoured yoghurt should be frozen in sturdy plastic containers with tightly fitting lids.

STAND IN FOR CREAM

If a recipe calls for cream, could I use yoghurt instead?

Yes, yoghurt can be used instead of fresh cream in many dessert recipes, such as cheesecakes, fools, ice cream, mousses and cold soufflés. The flavour of the finished dessert will be sharper when made with yoghurt rather than cream, but it will be just as satisfying.

Yoghurt is also an excellent substitute for sour cream in savoury dips, marinades and salad dressings. And in the Middle East it is strained overnight through a sieve lined with muslin to produce a soft yoghurt cheese, called *labne*. This is served plain, or flavoured with herbs such as thyme.

There are many types of yoghurt available, ranging from those with a very low fat content to creamy and thick Greek-style yoghurts, which can contain up to 7.5 per cent butterfat. But even the thickest yoghurt contains less fat and kilojoules than fresh cream, so it makes for healthier dishes.

YOGHURT BRULEE

Can you suggest a yoghurt dessert that isn't too complicated?

Rich, full-fat yoghurt makes a delicious dessert simply mixed with a strongly flavoured honey or topped with sliced or puréed fruit. Or try this quick yoghurt brûlée: put some fresh fruit, such as stoned cherries, or raspberries, in the base of individual ramekins. Cover with thick Greek-style yoghurt and sprinkle a thin layer of soft brown or demerara sugar all over the top. Put the ramekins under a preheated hot grill until the sugar starts to bubble, then chill for 2–3 hours until the topping sets hard.

KEEP IT STABLE

Is there any danger of yoghurt curdling if I add it to a hot dish?

Yoghurt may safely be added to hot dishes such as casseroles, curries, sauces, soups and stews, provided it is done off the heat, at the end of the cooking time, just before serving, and as long as the mixture is not brought to the boil again after the yoghurt has been added.

But yoghurt will curdle when it is boiled, unless it has been stabilised (see below). Yoghurt must also be stabilised if it is to be added to a dish which is going to be reheated to boiling point, or if it is going to be used to marinate food, such as chicken or lamb, where some of the marinade will remain on the meat during cooking.

To stabilise yoghurt, blend 1 tablespoon each of cornflour and water and stir this mixture into 600 ml of yoghurt. Bring the mixture to just under boiling point, simmer gently for 10 minutes and then use in the recipe.

Even though Greek-style yoghurt has a higher fat content than ordinary yoghurt, it will nevertheless curdle when boiled so it, too, needs to be stabilised if it is going to be heated, as in the recipe for Mixed Vegetable Curry (above right). Stabilising the yoghurt is a precaution rather than a necessity here, as it is all too easy to overcook the yoghurt and make it curdle. This will not affect the flavour but the curry will not look as smooth and attractive as it should. With the yoghurt stabilised, the curry can be made ahead of time and reheated.

Mixed vegetable curry

SERVES: 4–6
PREPARATION TIME: 20 minutes
COOKING TIME: 50-55 minutes

1 tablespoon olive or sunflower oil
1 onion, sliced
1 fresh green chilli, deseeded and
    finely chopped
2 cloves garlic, crushed
1 teaspoon each ground cumin,
    ground coriander, and chilli
    powder (hot or medium)
1 parsnip, diced
250 g carrots, sliced
1 sweet potato, diced
250 g button mushrooms, wiped
    and halved
250 g cauliflower florets
20 g (2 tablespoons) plain flour
50 g (⅓ cup) sultanas
250 g chopped tomatoes
150 ml vegetable stock
150 ml dry white wine
Salt and black pepper
1 teaspoon cornflour
150 ml natural yoghurt
100 g frozen peas
1 teaspoon garam masala
To garnish: fresh coriander leaves

1 Heat the oil in a large saucepan, add the onion, chilli and garlic and stir-fry for 3 minutes. Add the spices, stir and cook for a further 3 minutes.
2 Mix in the parsnip, carrots, sweet potato, mushrooms and cauliflower, and cook gently for 3 minutes more. Sprinkle the flour on, stir it in well, and cook for a further 3 minutes.
3 Add the sultanas, tomatoes, stock and wine and season generously. Stir gently but thoroughly. Bring the dish to the boil, cover and simmer gently, stirring occasionally, for 25 minutes until the vegetables are just cooked.
4 Meanwhile, blend the cornflour with 1 tablespoon water and stir it into the yoghurt. Heat the mixture in a saucepan until almost boiling, then simmer for 10 minutes.
5 When the vegetables are only just cooked, add the frozen peas and cook for a further 5 minutes. Finally, stir in the stabilised yoghurt and garam masala and heat through.
6 Serve the curry garnished with sprigs of fresh coriander leaves.

Zabaglione

NO WAITING

Can zabaglione be made ahead of time and kept for a while?

No. The sweet confection called zabaglione should be made at the last minute. If it is left to stand for more than 5–10 minutes, it will start to separate. It will also separate if it is cooked for too long, or if the mixture gets too hot while it is being whisked. Once made, the zabaglione should immediately be poured into stemmed glasses or dessert dishes, and served while it is still warm and frothy.

Zabaglione

SERVES: 4
PREPARATION TIME: 5 minutes
COOKING TIME: 10-15 minutes

4 large egg yolks
60 g (¼ cup) caster sugar
75 ml Marsala
To garnish: toasted flaked almonds

1 Put the egg yolks into a mixing bowl, add the sugar and whisk them together quite briskly for a minute. Gradually mix in the Marsala, whisking a little more gently.
2 Put the bowl on top of a pan of gently simmering water. Whisk the mixture briskly for 10-15 minutes until it becomes thick and creamy and stands in soft peaks.
3 Immediately pour it into serving glasses, or dishes, and decorate with the flaked almonds. Serve the warm zabaglione immediately, with or without sponge fingers or delicate biscuits on the dish underneath it.

A warm frothy mixture of Marsala, egg yolks and sugar makes a last-minute dessert. Top zabaglione with flaked almonds and serve it with almond biscuits.

SWEET FROTHY SABAYON

What is sabayon? Is it just another name for zabaglione?

Yes, it is the French corruption of the word zabaglione. Both are made by whisking egg yolks and sugar with alcohol (usually white wine in the case of sabayon, but sometimes sherry or Madeira), but they are served in different ways. Whereas zabaglione is served as a warm dessert, sabayon is usually cooled as soon as it is frothy by plunging the pan into cold water while continuing to whisk it and then used as a dessert sauce. Whipped cream or flavourings such as vanilla and citrus peel are sometimes added.

Zest

ZESTY FLAVOUR

What is zest and how do I use it?

Zest is the outermost part of the rind of oranges, lemons, limes and other citrus fruit. This part of the rind is full of tiny capsules containing a very highly flavoured volatile oil, and it is this oil that gives an intense flavour to many savoury dishes, sauces, cakes, desserts and preserves such as the Honeyed Lemon Curd (right).

For the purest flavour, the zest must be removed from the fruit without even the smallest trace of the bitter white pith underneath it. The easiest way to do this is to use a zester or a stainless-steel potato peeler, or you can rub it carefully against the finest cutter on a grater.

Fruit that has been waxed should be washed first, very gently with a soft brush and in warm, not hot, water. Scrubbing the fruit hard can damage the skin which will then release the oil, and it will be washed away with the water.

Honeyed lemon curd

MAKES: about 750 g
PREPARATION TIME: 20 minutes
COOKING TIME: 25 minutes

Finely grated rind and juice of
*   4 large juicy lemons, preferably*
*   unwaxed, gently washed and*
*   wiped dry*
4 large eggs, lightly beaten
100 g unsalted butter, diced
250 g (1 cup) caster sugar
2 tablespoons thick honey

---

1 Put all the ingredients into a double or heavy-bottomed saucepan. Stir continuously with a wooden spoon over a medium heat until the sugar has dissolved, then continue cooking for a further 25 minutes, stirring all the while, until the curd will coat the back of the spoon. Be careful not to let the mixture boil.
2 When the mixture has thickened, remove the saucepan immediately from the heat to stop the curd from further cooking.
3 Pour into clean, warm jars, cover with waxed discs and seal.

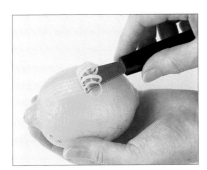

To produce fine, even strands of zest, hold the fruit firmly with one hand and pull the zester along the side.

Zucchini

EDIBLE SKIN

Is it necessary to peel zucchini?

The skin of young zucchini is thin and need not be removed for most purposes, but the dark green skin of older zucchini can be bitter and should be removed.

One garnishing treatment calls for just some of the skin to be discarded: using a potato peeler, shave the vegetable thinly lengthways to produce very thin slices. Throw away the first slice and the last, which consist mostly of green skin, and drop the remaining, green-edged slices into a pan of boiling water. Drain and refresh them under the cold tap as soon as the water returns to the boil.

YOUNG AND FRESH

I have read recommendations to salt zucchini slices before cooking. Is it necessary and why?

Salt draws out water from moist vegetables, a process known as disgorging. Left to grow, zucchinis would become marrows, and therefore be very wet indeed, but picked young they are merely juicy.

The best zucchini are those up to 10 cm long, which do not need disgorging. There is no point in salting zucchini if you are then going to cook them using a moist method such as steaming, poaching, braising or stir-frying.

Rather than salting larger zucchini, you can help to reduce the moisture content by choosing a dry cooking method.

TASTY WAYS

I usually lightly fry slices of zucchini. Is there any other way to cook them?

Zucchini lend themselves to several different cooking methods. You can split them in half lengthways and grill them; cut them in long diagonal slices and cook on an

oiled, ridged pan; or halve them lengthways, scoop out the seeds, then stuff with a vegetable, meat or grain filling and bake.

A classic Italian cooking method is to batter and fry them. Top and tail the zucchini and cut lengthways into batons; dust with flour then dip them into a simple batter made from plain flour and water. Drop in batches into oil heated to 190°C and deep-fry until crisp and golden, about 3–5 minutes. Drain on kitchen paper towels and serve immediately, with grilled fish or as part of the collection of battered fried fish called *fritto misto*.

Zucchini are also essential in the classic French recipe, Ratatouille. The following version is light, healthy and tasty.

Ratatouille

SERVES: 4 as a starter or
accompaniment
PREPARATION TIME: 20 minutes
COOKING TIME: 25–30 minutes

---

2 tablespoons olive oil
2 onions, chopped
1 plump clove garlic, crushed
1 green capsicum, seeded and sliced
1 small eggplant, cut into 2 cm
*   cubes*
4 zucchini, sliced
500 g tomatoes, coarsely chopped
Salt and black pepper

---

1 Heat the oil in a large heavy-based frying pan over a medium heat. Add the onion and garlic and cook for 5 minutes, or until soft, stirring occasionally with a wooden spoon.
2 Stir in the capsicum, eggplant and zucchini, cover and simmer for 10 minutes.
3 Add the tomatoes, stir well and bring to the boil. Reduce the heat to medium-low; simmer, covered, for 10 minutes, or until the vegetables are tender. Add salt and pepper.
4 Serve the ratatouille hot as an accompaniment to roast or grilled lamb, or transfer to a bowl and leave to cool, then chill, covered, in the refrigerator. Serve as a starter with warm French bread or as part of an antipasto platter.

Glossary

ACIDULATE To add lemon juice or vinegar to cooking or soaking water to prevent certain vegetables and fruit from discolouring.

AMUSE BOUCHE/GUEULE French term meaning 'mouth amuser', this is a miniature appetiser designed to titillate the palate before dinner.

ANTIPASTO The Italian hors d'oeuvres; it can be a single item but is usually a plate of six to eight different foods.

BAKE BLIND To bake an empty pastry case with the base weighted down with greaseproof paper and dried beans or rice to prevent the case rising during cooking.

BALLOTINE A leg of chicken, or a whole small bird, boned and stuffed before cooking.

BASTE To spoon liquid or melted fat over food during cooking to prevent it drying out and add extra flavour.

BEIGNETS Fritters; beignets soufflés are made from choux pastry and deep-fried.

BLANQUETTE A white stew, usually of veal or chicken, made without frying the meat first and thickened with an egg yolk and cream liaison.

BLINI A thin pancake made with buckwheat flour, using yeast as a raising agent.

BRINE A strong solution of salt and water that is used for pickling or preserving.

CEVICHE Fish or shellfish marinated in lime juice until the fish is 'cooked' by the action of the acid, and served with a sharp dressing.

CHANTILLY CREAM Fresh cream whipped until it holds its shape, with icing sugar and vanilla essence folded in to taste. It is often piped over desserts and cakes.

CHARLOTTE A dessert made in a mould lined with slices of buttered bread, filled with fruit and cooked.

CHASSEUR A dish or a sauce that is made with white wine, mushrooms, shallots, tomatoes and tarragon.

CHINE To remove the backbone from a rib roast or rack of meat before cooking, to make carving easier.

COCOTTE/RAMEKIN A small fireproof dish in which individual portions of food are both cooked and served.

CONFIT A dish of duck or goose cooked in its fat, packed into jars and covered with more fat to preserve it.

CONSOMME A clarified soup, usually made with meat.

COULIS A sauce made from vegetable or fruit purée.

CREOLE French-influenced tropical cuisine, also found in Louisiana in the United States of America, flavoured with chilli, peppers and tomatoes.

DEGLAZE/DEGLACER To dissolve the brown sediment left on the bottom of a pan after roasting or frying by adding liquid and stirring.

DEVILLED Food seasoned with a spicy sauce, usually pepper, chilli and mustard.

DISGORGE/DEGORGE To extract bitter juices from vegetables by salting, soaking or washing.

DRAWING (*of poultry*) To pull out the entrails, leaving a clean carcass.

DROPPING CONSISTENCY Term used to describe the correct consistency of a cake mixture before baking: it should drop off the spoon with gentle persuasion.

EGG WASH Beaten egg, sometimes mixed with a little water, brushed over pastry and bread before cooking, to give a shiny golden finish.

EMULSION A smooth, stable mixture of oil or melted fat and egg yolks, plus vinegar or citrus juice, such as hollandaise or mayonnaise.

FLORENTINE A savoury dish that contains spinach and Mornay sauce, usually with eggs or fish.

FLUMMERY A dessert made from eggs and milk, rather like blancmange, flavoured with ground almonds.

FOLD IN To incorporate a light airy mixture, such as whisked egg whites, into a heavier one by using a gentle cut and lifting motion.

FRANGIPANE A filling for pastry tartlets or flans made with butter, eggs and ground almonds and flavoured with almond essence, kirsch or orange flower water.

FRAPPE Iced, or set in a bed of crushed ice.

FRITTATA A substantial flat omelette which includes a variety of vegetables and cheese, eaten hot or cold.

GALANTINE A type of terrine, usually made with poultry, which is cooked and set in its own jelly, served cold.

GANACHE Chocolate and cream mixed together over heat to form a very rich filling used in truffles, or for coating or filling cakes.

INFUSE To extract flavour through immersion and soaking in hot water.

JULIENNE Vegetables, or citrus rind, that have been cut into very fine strips.

KNOCK DOWN/KNOCK BACK To punch or knead risen dough to push out bubbles that may have formed unevenly shaped holes.

LIAISON The ingredients for thickening and enriching a sauce, soup or stew, such as egg yolk, cream or blood.

MACEDOINE Small, diced mixed vegetables, usually including root vegetables.

MACERATE To soak food, usually fruit, in a syrup or liquid such as alcohol, to allow the flavours to mix.

MIREPOIX A bed of roughly diced vegetables, usually carrot, celery and onion, used in stocks and braising.

MOUSSELINE A raw meat or fish purée mixed with cream, used as a stuffing or to make quenelles or cooked in small moulds and served warm with a sauce.

REDUCE/REDUCTION To thicken and concentrate the flavour of gravy, sauces, soups and stocks by boiling.

RICE PAPER A lightweight, edible paper made from the pith of a tropical tree, used as a base for macaroons and other sweetmeats.

RUB IN To use the fingertips to combine fat with flour and other dry ingredients until the mixture looks like fine breadcrumbs.

SALMIS Game birds or duck that are first lightly roasted or browned in fat, then jointed and stewed in a wine sauce.

SCALD To heat milk until on the point of boiling.

SCORE To cut through the skin of joints, particularly pork, before cooking to make carving easier.

SEAR/SEAL To brown meat rapidly all over in fat, to give it flavour and colour.

SLAKE To dissolve thickening agents, such as cornflour, in a little cold liquid before they are added to the hot liquid which is to be thickened.

SOUSE To marinate and cook strips of oily fish in a pickling mixture containing vinegar, spices and flavourings.

SPATCHCOCK A poussin or small chicken split open by removing the backbone, then cleaned, flattened and grilled.

STEEP To soak a food for several hours, so it absorbs flavour from the solution (as in marinating), releases the flavours present in food, or reduces the salt content.

SWEAT To gently stew food, usually vegetables, in butter, oil or a little stock until very soft but not coloured.

WELL A hollow or dip made in a pile of flour into which other ingredients are placed prior to mixing.

$\mathscr{I}$NDEX

Bold numbers indicate headlist entries
and *bold italic text* indicates recipe entries.

Cheese 75-80

ACKNOWLEDGMENTS

The publishers would like to thank the following individuals and organisations for their assistance in the preparation of this book:

Australian Dairy Corporation (Bianca Stafrace), Glen Iris, Vic; Biological Farmers of Australia, Qld; Bush Tucker Supply Australia (Vic Cherikoff), Gladesville, NSW; Caroline Kelly, Consultant Nutritionist & Dietitian, Grafton, NSW; CSIRO Division of Food Science & Technology, North Ryde, NSW; Edgecliff Health Foods, Edgecliff, NSW; FLORAfoods (Bill Shrapnel, Consultant Nutritionist), Marrickville, NSW; Game Farm Pty Ltd (Michael Windebank), Galston, NSW; Herbie's Spices (Ian Hemphill), Rozelle, NSW; National Association for Sustainable Agriculture Australia Ltd, ACT; National Health & Medical Research Council, Australia; National Meat Association, Sydney, NSW; Organic Action (Jenny Bennett), Sydney, NSW; Organic Retailers & Growers Association of Australia; Pepe's Game Farm, Windsor, NSW; Penny's Butchers. Mosman, NSW; Pure Beef Company, Kangaroo Valley, NSW; Queensland Fruit and Vegetable Growers (Abigail Ulgiati), Qld; Steggles Turkeys, Newcastle, NSW; Stephen Affleck, Primary Producer, Wallendbeen, NSW; Sydney Fish Market Pty Limited (Maria Papadopoulos), NSW; Sydney Market Authority (Sue Dodd), Flemington, NSW; Tyrrell's Wines (Peter Russell), Pokolbin, NSW.

PICTURE CREDITS

The photographs in this book are the copyright of Reader's Digest and the photographer for each is listed below.

KARL ADAMSON
Step-by-step photography, except 53, 157, 185, 197, 213, 283, 337, 364, 372.

GUS FILGATE
Backgrounds, 1-9, 12, 15, 17, 19, 20, 23, 30, 31, 36, 45, 47, 49, 50, 52, 62-63, 72, 76, 77, 78, 81, 99, 104, 107, 112, 115, 118, 126, 131, 134, 146, 156-7, 160, 166, 174-5, 177, 181, 183, 193, 194, 197, 199, 202-3, 204, 216, 218, 222-3, 224, 227, 229, 231, 232, 234, 241, 243, 244, 246, 250-1, 253, 256, 259, 261, 264, 265, 270, 273, 279, 289, 297, 298, 301, 303, 304-5, 313, 320, 323, 325, 327, 330, 332, 344, 347, 349, 350, 352, 354, 356, 360, 363, 369, 373, 376, 388.

JOHN HOLLINGSHEAD
25, 53, 74, 76, 77, 78, 97, 106, 138, 144. 157, 167, 185, 197, 213, 250, 254, 268, 271, 274, 283, 284, 306, 317, 319, 321, 337, 338, 362, 364, 365, 372, 377.

VERNON MORGAN
7, 10, 27, 33, 34, 39, 51, 56, 59, 61, 64, 66, 71, 86, 87, 90, 92, 101, 111, 116, 123, 128, 141, 143, 154, 158, 164, 171, 172, 189, 192, 207, 209, 215, 221, 236, 237, 247, 276, 281, 282, 285, 286, 290, 293, 309, 314, 328, 335, 340, 357, 368, 378, 385.